LOYAL TILL DEATH

A Diary of the 13th New York Artillery

Guy Breshears

HERITAGE BOOKS
2012

HERITAGE BOOKS
AN IMPRINT OF HERITAGE BOOKS, INC.

Books, CDs, and more—Worldwide

For our listing of thousands of titles see our website
at
www.HeritageBooks.com

Published 2012 by
HERITAGE BOOKS, INC.
Publishing Division
100 Railroad Ave. #104
Westminster, Maryland 21157

Copyright © 2003 Guy Breshears

Other Heritage Books by the author:
Loyal till Death: A Diary of the 13th New York Artillery
Major Granville Haller: Dismissed with Malice
To Seize Their Lands: Manifest Destiny in Washington State

All rights reserved. No part of this book may be reproduced or transmitted in any form or by any means, electronic or mechanical, including photocopying, recording or by any information storage and retrieval system without written permission from the author, except for the inclusion of brief quotations in a review.

International Standard Book Numbers
Paperbound: 978-0-7884-2326-0
Clothbound: 978-0-7884-9497-0

TABLE OF CONTENTS

FOREWORD v
PREFACE vii
INTRODUCTION ix
OCTOBER 1861-APRIL 1862
    A war deadly to officers 1
MAY 1862-SEPTEMBER 1862
    Treu bis in den Tod 47
OCTOBER 1862-APRIL 1863
    A disagreeable state of betweenity 107
MAY 1863-JUNE 1863
    Stop; face about; do not retreat any farther! 141
JULY 1863-SEPTEMBER 1863
    You pays your money and you takes your choice 181
OCTOBER 1863-JANUARY 1864
    I have the honor to report 253
FEBRUARY 1864-AUGUST 1864
    Our beloved and gallant Captain Wheeler 301
SEPTEMBER 1864-JULY 1865
    The Veteran Soldiers of the Battery 345
APPENDIX A   Historical Sketch 427
APPENDIX B   Commands that the Battery was attached to 433
APPENDIX C   Battery Service 435
APPENDIX D   Battery Officers 437
APPENDIX E   Inscription of the New York State Monument at Orchard Knob, Chickamauga and Chattanooga National Military Park 439
APPENDIX F   Inscription and Dedication of Battery Monument, Gettysburg, PA 441
APPENDIX G   Eulogy of Capt. William Wheeler 445
NOTES 461
BIBLIOGRAPHY 465
INDEX 467

Foreword

Some of the most beautifully crafted letters by any soldier in the Civil War were written by William Wheeler, a Union artillery captain in a New York regiment. And yet until the publication of this volume, these letters were available only in a privately published collection printed in 1875 under the title: *In Memoriam: The Letters of William Wheeler*. Few libraries have that volume, and many of the best historians of the Civil War have never seen the letters or even heard of Wheeler. I learned about them myself only because one of those rare volumes came to me through the estate of my great grandmother, Julia Davenport Wheeler Strong, a sister of Captain Wheeler.

A few years ago, I told the story of Wheeler as a chapter in my survey of American history called *American Realities*. In an essay on the Civil War, I paired William Wheeler with a southern artillery officer, Charles Colcock Jones, Jr., whose letters appear in one of the best known anthologies of southern letters, *The Children of Pride*, edited by Robert Manson Myers. Arguably Wheeler's story and letters are easily as appealing and informative as those of Jones.

The editor of the present Wheeler volume, Guy Breshears, was a student of mine in a class where I used this essay on the Civil War. He became fascinated by Wheeler's story and began a years-long pilgrimage of research and travel into documents and battlefields pertaining to Wheeler's history, decorated his jacket with the emblem of Wheeler's artillery company and included Wheeler quotations on his Christmas cards. His fascination with this remarkable man led to a natural question: why not republish William Wheeler's letters, making them more accessible to readers today? The answer was this edition of the letters, complete with a substantial glossary of explanatory notes.

Thanks to this publication, William Wheeler's observations on camp life and battle experience are for the first time available in a modern edition. As examples of Wheeler's vivid accounts of daily life: he describes traveling through the mountainous parts of Virginia where the soldiers "went fishing, blackberrying, and cherry-picking, and where at times it seemed more like a charming summer picnic 'long drawn out' than anything else." Wheeler describes a train journey on the Baltimore & Ohio Railroad, through the "mysterious lights and shadows of a perfect moonlight autumn night," and on across Indiana where the citizens cheered the soldiers at each stop and ladies gave them cake, cold meats, doughnuts, handkerchiefs, towels, and soap.

William Wheeler fought in many of the great engagements of the Civil War, including Gettysburg, where his artillery company was located at Cemetery Hill (as he called it) at the heart of the battlefield. Wheeler and his men were on the receiving end when Confederate General Robert E. Lee unleashed the greatest artillery barrage ever known in America. "The air," said Wheeler, "was literally alive with flying projectiles." Cemetery Hill was hit with a hailstorm of shot, ranging from six-pound missiles the size of cricket balls to Whitworth rifled shot so huge they gave "rise to the story of the rebs firing railroad iron." An infantry-man's leg, blown off by a direct hit, whirled "through the air like a stone, until it came against a caisson with a loud whack."

Wheeler wrote evocative accounts of army life; he also wrote revealing descriptions of his own feelings about the war. He admitted his excitement at being a participant at Gettysburg. Shortly after the battle he wrote home: "Somehow or other, I felt a joyous exaltation, a perfect indifference to circumstances, through the whole of that three days' fight, and have seldom enjoyed three days more in my life." He also wrote again and again about his commitment to the Union cause: "The war," he told his mother, "has become the religion of very many of our lives, and those of us who think, and who did not enter the service for gain of military distinction, have come more and more to identify this cause for which we are fighting, with all of good and religion in our previous lives."

These are a few of the literary and historical treasures contained in the letters of William Wheeler. Thanks to the fine work of Guy Breshears, his words finally have a chance to reach the wider audience they deserve.

J. William T. Youngs
Professor of History
Eastern Washington University

Preface

When nations go to war their armies generate a large quantity of papers including orders, reports, memos and personal letters to and from home. After the war is finished these papers are put away and collect dust until viewed again by someone who is interested in those papers.

The American Civil War is no exception. The 13th New York Independent Light Artillery Battery was mustered in service on October 15, 1861 and mustered out on July 28, 1865. Between these dates it fought in several well-known campaigns and lesser-know battles. Members of the unit fought and died during this time and their deeds were recorded.

At the end of the war this unit, and most of its papers, vanished into the annals of history and were forgotten by a grateful nation until now. This is a record of citizens, with little or no military experience, who evolved into professional soldiers that rose to the challenges of everyday hardship. While many survived the ordeal others did not.

The idea of this book started many years ago while I was still a university student. It was here that I was first "introduced" to Capt. William Wheeler and a curiosity grew on who this man was and what was the unit he commanded. As those who have done any type of research know it is time consuming and often frustrating. Because of my curiosity I've collected numerous files, from various sources, on some of the battery officers and other military personnel.

This work is an organized collection of many of the files that I have obtained. It is organized similar to a "unit diary" and could be considered what the battery would have written if it could.

While editing this book I have left most of the material the way it was written. Because of the variety of spellings of names and places I have standardized many of them in order that the reader be less confused on who and what is being written about. However, because of the various styles of handwritings it was a challenge to try and figure out what was being written about. If I have made any errors I apologize in advance for it.

When maps are mentioned as being included in some reports I have chosen not to include them.

Also, when the Wheeler letters were first published initials, and not full names, were used. Where the identity of the person being written about is known the name is used; where the name has not been discovered then the initial is still retained.

I would like to thank the staffs at the Chickamauga and Chattanooga National Military Park, National Archives and Records Administration, New York State Archives, Kennesaw Mountain Historical Association and the United States Army Military History Institute for their invaluable assistance for this project. I would also like to thank Dr. J. William T. Youngs for introducing me to Capt. Wheeler, giving me encouragement and guidance for this project and the writing of the foreword for this work. I would also like to thank John Clavin for his assistance.

This project is dedicated to the soldiers of the United States Army and the volunteers who fell defending the Union between 1861-1865. If there be any glory in war, let it rest on men like these.

Finally, to my Mother to whom I have often caused great sorrow. May I also be loyal till death.

INTRODUCTION

Union light artillery batteries were typically supplied with six guns of the same type (either the 12-pound smoothbore Napoleon or the 10-pound wrought-iron rifle) and generally commanded by a captain. Two guns, directed by a lieutenant comprised a section. Each gun was manned by a crew of seven and was pulled by a six-horse team which also carried its limber which contained 50 rounds of mixed ammunition. Each battery had its gun's caisson pulled by another six-horse team which carried another 150 rounds of ammunition, a spare wheel and other equipment.

Light artillery units were used for direct field support of infantry units in battle and in many cases fought hand-to-hand when their positions were being threatened. This is different from heavy artillery units that were generally raised for the defense of vital areas and saw very little, if any, combat.

Ideally each battery contained 144 officers and men and each artillery regiment consisted of twelve batteries. However, there were many light batteries raised that operated independently outside of any regimental organization and were often known by the name of their commander.

Further, Union doctrine stated that there should be 2-3 artillery pieces per 1000 troops and concentrated in divisional groups. This meant that there were 4-6 artillery batteries per 12,000 infantry. This grouping of batteries proved effective when massed fire was needed because they could be deployed as one unit.

October 1861-April 1862
A war deadly to officers

October 21, 1861
Letter of William Wheeler
Camp Observation, MD

Dear Mother

For the first time, for more than a week, has it been practicable for me to give you any account of my doings; but I suppose that John[1] has told you how I was put on duty, immediately upon my return from recruiting on the North River, and kept so almost without cessation until Thursday when we left the city; in fact I hardly had three hours' sleep any night for a week, and several nights have been entirely sleepless. It was extremely comforting to me to have John with me during those last two days, when I could not go home to see you, and was too much worried to write. I was sworn in on Tuesday, as second lieutenant, the Major[2] going as captain with the understanding that when the Second Battery was raised I should be raised a peg. The First Lieutenant[3] become so elated at being sworn in that he got drink, and has not been heard of since, and as the Major is not very well posted on the English work of command, I have had the command of the men entirely, and have had an immense amount of work and responsibility thrown upon me.

On Thursday afternoon, at about 3 PM, we got everything in readiness, and went up to the quarters, and ordered the men to fall in. They utterly refused to do so till they had received a part of their month's pay, which had been promised them. After some talk and expostulation, I go them marched out of quarters, and on the Eighth Avenue cars, which took us to Barclay St. Then we march to Pier No 2, and took the Perth Amboy boat. We reached the secesh village of Baltimoreabout 8 ½ AM. I stood on the platform and managed the brake nearly all the way.

At Baltimore the Union Defense Committee gave us a good breakfast; then we had a dreary ride to Washington, occupying eight hours in going forty miles. At Washington we put our soldier in barracks, and there we were visited by the Sanitary Commissioners, who took several of our sick men up to their home, where they were so well cared for that we took away sic with us the next morning.

After breakfast we marched out to Georgetown, where we embarked on a canal boat, on the canal beside the Potomac. We voyaged on that rapid vehicle, and anchored for the night about two miles from Washington. We started again Sunday morning, and soon came in sight of the secession pickets on the opposite side; however they did not pepper us, as that matter of picket shooting has been discontinued by mutual consent. About 3 PM we reached Edwards' Ferry, where we disembarked, and found a very warlike state of affairs. Our men had two batteries in position, and behind the rise of the hill were some 1500 or 2000 infantry and cavalry. We marched off to Poolesville, a distance of about four miles, and then found that General Baker's camp was five miles further off. We stumbled up there in the dark, and at last saw a vast array of lights, marking our destination. They seemed to cover every hillside, and to be without number. Soon we were among them, and cordially received by General Baker. Luckily we did not have to sleep in the tents that were put up for us, for the head wagoner was a German, and invited the men to bunk in, in his covered wagons, which were filled with straw. The Major and I occupied the tent of the quartermaster of the Brigade, but we were badly off for blankets, and I spent a night of sleepless on account of the cold...... Our men have been hard at work today, hewing wood and drawing water, fetching rations and fixing tents, and building kitchens. I have had it all to superintend. We are miserably fitted out in all things

October 23, 1861
Letter of William Wheeler
Camp Observation, MD

Dear Coz
Somewhat contrary to my own individual expectations, I did get off from New York the same week that I left H P, but fortunately did not go on Tuesday, since then I should have been in a melancholy state of unpreparedness, and fit only to be an officer of a rag-tag and bobtail cadets. I was mustered into the US service on Tuesday afternoon, when we departed, about ninety strong, by way of Amboy, Elizabeth, Harrisburg, and Baltimore to Washington which we reached after a tedious journey of twenty-six hours. The hills were covered with camps, but as we did not pass to the southward, we saw nothing of the great army of the lower Potomac, which is under the supervision of General McClellan in person... We are encamped on a

elevated breezy situation, so breezy in fact, that at this present moment I am expecting, every instant, that my tent will comedown on my head, an close to us are encamped four regiments of the Brigade, viz.: Baxter's Philadelphia Zouaves, Owen's Irish Phila. Regiment, Morehead's Twenty-eighth Pennsylvania, and the First California Regiment[4], or rather the remains of it, as it first battalion was almost entirely cut to pieces in the bloody and disastrous fight at Conrad's Ferry the day before yesterday. Of course you must have read an account of it in the newspapers, but you can form no idea of the disheartened feeling which such a piece of criminal mismanagement infuses into soldiers. It is pretty well understood that the troops were thrown across the river with full knowledge that they could not be easily withdrawn, and with the probability that they would be attacked by the enemy in force. The result is that our Brigade has lost about 350 men, killed, drowned, wounded, and missing, being of the First Battalion of the First California, our crack regiment; the Fifteenth Massachusetts has also suffered dreadfully, and the Twentieth Massachusetts and the New York Tammany Regiment[5] have been badly cut cup. Lastly, but not least, we have lost General Baker, and almost everyone of our best officers who were in action, is either killed or wounded. At Edwards' Ferry I saw General Banks, who had come down with a large part of his Division, and was busily engaged in throwing troops across the river. I very much fear that the Tragedy of Conrad's Ferry may be repeated on a larger scale. I can assure you, my dear Coz, that we feel right in the midst of things, and I am disgusted that the want of our horses and guns prevents us from taking an active part. This is an entirely different thing from Seventh Regiment soldiering; it is actual, bloody war, and this fact is impressed upon me very strongly by meeting officers one day in courteous society, and seeing them on the next, mutilated or dead. This emphatically a war deadly to officers, and I have fully made up my mind never to see any of you again. Major Sturmfels went away today to Washington and I am left in command of the company, so I feel in quite a responsible position, as I am determined to keep everything right and straight until his return......We have plenty of secessionists all around us, and we are obliged to keep a sharp lookout, as I am convinced that all of them are a set of rascals, and that they keep their co-rebels in Virginia constantly informed of our movements. Many of them in this vicinity belonged to a cavalry troop, which was raised to assist the South, and although some of them have been disarmed and have taken the oath of allegiance, yet I am sure they would rise and cut our throats, if they saw the enemy cross the Potomac in force. In fact, while I have been writing these lines, an order has come to me from Colonel Owen, commanding the Brigade, to permit no person in citizen's clothes to pass the lines; this is no more that what our Company has been doing before, as Major Sturmfels has European ideas of strictness and regularity in these matters. I expect, if I live, to pass a tedious and painful winter; already it is getting too cold to sleep much at night, and unless we take some large city and winter there, I fear that there will be a great deal of suffering. Our men as yet have no overcoats, and their blankets are of a very poor character, and insufficient to keep off the winter's cold. I shall think of you often, and of I, and all New York and New Haven friends, and of music and study and society, and shall hope that I shall not be forgotten here in camp.

October 30, 1861
Letter of William Wheeler
Camp Observation, MD

Everything is quiet in this neighborhood now. Occasionally we hear firing or cannonading from our pickets, but this shoot across the river does not amount to much. Our own camp lies in full view of the enemy of the other side, and we can see just where their encampments are, in the hollow the hill, but they keep very shady in the day-time. They might shell up if they had any long-range guns in position, but I imagine that they are hardly well enough off in good ammunition to be able to indulge in that kind of target-shooting. I wish we had our guns. If the enemy, who is said in heavy force at Leesburg, should attempt to cross the river, and there should be a general engagement, there would be nothing for us but to retire to the rear with the camp followers…… Major Sturmfels has been absent from the company now for a week, and during that time I have reigned supreme in our little encampment, and have communicated directly with Colonel Owen, the commander of the Brigade, as if I were colonel of a regiment. I am sorry that the state of my foot does not permit me to drill my company as dismounted cannoneers. I have been found lying on my bed most of the time studying. I got hold of Monday's Herald yesterday, and found in it a comparatively correct account of the conflict of Ball's Bluff, only it places the numbers engaged, and the loss, rather too high. I was informed by the brigade surgeon that only 1200 were engaged in all, and of that number all but

500 had already reported themselves; so that number will cover the total loss....The weather for the last few days has been really delicious, perfect October time, and the sunsets over the Virginia hills are golden curtains, let down I long waves of blue and purple, and I only wish that I were more free from bodily ailment, and could enjoy more the peaceful Indian Summer. When evening comes on, our little company street resounds with songs. Last night we had a regular German concert, many of our men being old campaigners in Faderland, and very beautiful are some of the soldiers songs they sing, noble too in sentiment.......My oven works to a charm, the draught is perfect; in token of excellence of my fire, I have written the whole of this page by its light. My only fear is that my chimney (made of beef barrels) may catch fire some cold night, as this is not an uncommon catastrophe.......I should like a few sheets of blank music paper; I want to copy out the bugle calls for my bugler.

November 5, 1861
Special Orders No. 2, Sturmfels' Light Artillery
Camp Observation, MD

I   Non-commissioned officers in charge of police parties shall with their police parties attend at morning and evening drill.

II   The old guard, when relieved, by the new guard is excused from morning drill of that day but shall without any excuse attend at the afternoon drill. The company is required to be ready to fall in at the sound of the bugle.

III   On and after tomorrow, Nov 6th, any non-commissioned officer or private, who absents himself from drill or any general roll call, will be tried by court martial and punished accordingly. There will be two calls sounded on the bugle for each of the three general roll calls, which are, Reveille, Retreat and Tattoo; the first call sounded in each case will be a signal to get ready to fall into ranks; the second, which is the last, signifies fall in.

IV   There will be two calls sounded for guard mounting; the first call is sounded 15 minutes before guard mounting, the guard shall then be ready to fall in for inspection.

By order
Wm Wheeler
1st Lieut Comdg Company

November 8, 1861
Letter of William Wheeler
Camp Observation, MD

Captain Sturmfels has been absent from us two weeks and a half, during which time we have heard nothing from him, but supposed that he was doing for us all that was necessary to equip us for the field, and now it appears that he has not even taken the preliminary stop of reporting himself to the head of his department, and that we are not recognized as existing in the service at all, and that our men will not get their pay when the paymaster comes, in spite of all the pains taken by the orderly and myself to have the must and payrolls properly made out, and sent to the Department at Washington. Besides this, our requisition for overcoats has not responded to, and yesterday, at the instance of General Burns, I made an entirely new one, on my own responsibility, which I think will bring the articles, and nothing was ever more needed. I am surprised that we have not more men on the sick list than we have. When half of them are in the hospital, and a few frozen to death, perhaps we may get what we want. Then, too, the brigade quartermaster has been changed, so that it is hard to draw supplies, for either officers or men, and we have to scratch hard for our grub. In spite of my ankle, which is still sore and lame, so that I cannot wear a boot, I have to run about all day, now to the General, and then to the Commissary, to see that we do not get cheated, now to settle some dispute among the men. I think it is not impossible that I may go down to Washington today or tomorrow, to report to General Barry in person, and see what can be done for us. I myself feel full of courage and hope, and shall take the company into my own hands, if the General thinks fit, and use my own influence to get it into the field. I only wish that my foot would heal. The doctor says that it is improving nicely, and if I must go to Washington he will send me to Poolesville in an ambulance, and from there I can go by stage to Washington. What a terrible gale of wind, and rain storm, we had last Saturday. I wish we could hear something about the Great Expedition. I have prayed fervently for its success, and have lain awake on these windy nights thinking about it. Robert Edwards' regiment, the Forty-eighth New York[6], is with it; this adds to my interest. I wish I was with him.

November 11, 1861
Letter of William Wheeler
Camp Observation, MD

    Thanks for your promptness in answering my last letter. Yours was the first received after reaching this camp, and I was saved a disappointment when the mail came in, the night of that stormy Saturday....... It is a showery, drizzly afternoon, and the men and I equally rejoice at it, for they get off drilling, and I am at liberty to write this letter, and you may be sure that I gladly embrace all such opportunities, when I have them, for when we get on the march there will be no time to sit quietly down and place ourselves *en rapport with* dear friends, but a hasty, hurried scratch must be sufficient to satisfy those at home of the safety and health of the absent one. I am sorry that you got the idea, from my last letter, that I was in poor spirits; true I then had poor accommodations and food, slept cold at night, and the responsibility of taking care of the company weighed upon me somewhat, yet I have never allowed myself to be depressed; the thought of being once more armed for the cause, and having a chance this time to strike a blow, makes me very happy and elastic; the picture I gave you was one of *physical*, not *mental* condition. Now, however, I am very much more comfortable in my way of living; I have had an oven built in my tent, of large stones, with a flue running out for some distance behind the tent, covered with stones and plastered with clay; the chimney is made of two beef barrels, placed one on top of the other; the draught is generally very good, except when the wind blows from the east, and early in the morning my boy comes I, just after reveille, and lights up a good fire, so that when I rise, I find the edge taken off from the morning frost considerably. These stoves, of this simple construction, are all the rage among the officers in this camps here, and they are a grand institution; only some of them are unable to get beef barrels, and build their chimneys of sugar barrels, which are liable to catch fire, and cause a great deal of disturbance and fun in being extinguished; the Philadelphia Fire Zouaves, the nearest regiment to us, recall their former days, and run "with the machine" to put out the officers' chimneys. *Grub*, too, has manifestly improved; we have a man who waits on our mess who is a great forager, and scours the country round for provisions, wherewith to vary the daily bill of fare, of government salt horse and hard biscuit. Not unsuccessful in his scouring either, as that excellent leg of mutton which we had for dinner yesterday, and that loud-clucking hen in the next tent might testify. A rumor, too, has been blown hitherward, of sundry turkeys in a farmyard not very remote, and I think it highly probable that we shall celebrate the New York Thanksgiving day, by fleshing our teeth in a secesh gobbler. Now, that we have learned the ropes, we live as well as anybody in the camp. It is now more than three weeks since we came here, and Major Sturmfels has been absent nearly all that time, and our pieces and horses have not yet been sent to us. I have ruled the Company in righteousness in the meantime, have seen to it that the Quartermaster and Commissary did not cheat the men, have maintained their rights, and made known their needs to General Burns, the new General of the Brigade, and, I have mustered the Company for pay, and sent the appropriate muster and pay rolls to the Department at Washington this last was a great labor, and a sort of job entirely new to me, but after about three days' solid work I made it out, and now the men will get their pay, I hope very soon. We expect the Major back in about a week, and I hoe he will bring our full equipments with him, so that we may be in condition to march across the river with this Division, if it goes. I hope that we *shall* winter in Virginia. It is very cold here, and they say that the snow lies four feet deep on the hills. I am full of anxiety about the Great Expedition: my friend Robert Edwards is with it as a lieutenant in the Forty-eighth New York. I suppose that by this time you have full accounts of the landings, etc. Our newspapers are few and far between out here. We have pretty lively times in the evenings; the Germans of my company get together and sing very sweetly, and I try to join with them. I send you a copy of one of their songs, called "Morgenroth;" it is simple but very sweet, I think, and shows a reflection and elevation of sentiment, to be found only among the Germans…..We are no longer "General Baker's Brigade," but the "First Brigade Corps of Observation, Camp Observation, Md."

November 19, 1861
Letter of William Wheeler
Camp Observation, MD

You will be anxious to know about my health, after what I wrote in my last. Well, the first dose of restoring physic was that batch of letters on Sunday; they quite set me up. On Monday my trouble, which seems intermittent in its nature, came on again, and after being out for an hour or so, attending to some business at the adjutant general's office, I was obliged to go to bed with a very bad headache. The doctor came in and said that my system required to be stimulated, and prescribed quinine and whiskey. But the real cordial came in another shape. About dark, on of the men came in, and said a gentleman was inquiring for me. Upon asking his name Mr W was brought in. I jumped out of bed, ran out doors in my stocking feet, and there was Cousin M and Mr W in their carriage. They quickly transferred themselves to my tent, and also a champagne basket full of various goodies; in fact, a little magazine of provender, which will make our larder rejoice till that box from home arrives. The horses were taken from the carriage, and put in a rustic stable, which my men had built of straw and branches; we got up a good fire in the oven, and at supper time a table, completely set out for us, was brought into my tent, and I had an opportunity of showing my guest that we did not starve in camp. We sat and talked for a while, and then escorted Cousin M to Mrs Fisher's, where she succeeded in getting very comfortable quarters for the night. Mr W spent the night with me in my tent. He took breakfast with me, Cousin M with General Burns and the brigade surgeon. Then they started for home, having given me a great deal of pleasure by the visit. How kind it was for them to come so far. I hope Cousin M will not send you an exaggerated account of my condition, so as to make you anxious. Mr W is a good Union man, and up to the times. It must be a thorn in the flesh of these secesh Marylanders, to have a gentleman among them who takes the "Tribune" regularly, and who advocates the making of Maryland a free state.

    The news from the South is most cheering, and I think that every one will rejoice that South Carolina should receive the just reward of her iniquities, and that, too, when she thought that she had removed the noise of war and tumult far from her borders. I hope that you will all have a good time on Thanksgiving Day this year. I shall think of you as eating turkey together, and shall try to put myself *en rapport* with you in that respect, if such a "bird of loudest lay" can be had.

November 28, 1861
Letter of William Wheeler
Camp Observation, MD

    I received a very substantial epistle last night, in the form of the long expected box. Everything arrived in good order, except in one instance. Please to give my thanks to every one for the torrent of good things poured upon me. I had hoped by Thanksgiving Day to have announced myself as quite recovered, but it goes very slowly, and there are steps backwards as well as forward. We had a rousing turkey for dinner to-day, but I had to content myself chiefly with looking at him, while the others made play at his gigantic proportions.

We are still in utter ignorance of what we shall do, but are prepared to stay here for some time. General McClellan may turn out to be timid and temporizing. Will not the use of the Naval Expedition be thrown away, if a simultaneous advance is not soon made?

December 8, 1861
Leave of absence request to Capt. George A. Hicks, Assistant Adjutant General, Corps of Observation
no location given

>Sir
>
>I have the honor to apply to these headquarters for a leave of absence for forty-eight hours, with permission to procure an extension of the same as the headquarters of the Army of the Potomac to transact business for company.
>And am sir you very obt Sevt
>Wm Wheeler
>Lieut Comdg Light Artillery

Extract from Special Order No. 142, Corps of Observation
Poolesville, MD

>III   Leave of absence for forty-eight hours with permission to apply at HQ for an extension is granted to Lieut Wm Wheeler, Sturmfels Light Artillery, at the expiration of which he will rejoin his company.
>By order of Brig Gen Stone

December 9, 1861
Letter of William Wheeler
Camp Observation, MD

>Dearest Mother
>
>The visit of Uncle R and John was most kind and cheering, and brought me up quite a peg. For two or three days after they left I

improved, and then began to settle down again. I feel well enough, general, but am liable to fall into fits of brown study, lassitude, in fact. I received, on Saturday last. A telegraphic dispatch from Sturmfels, ordering me to meet him in Washington, I suppose to make an effort to fix things straight. I hope to get a pass this afternoon, and to start early to-morrow morning.

December 11, 1861
Report of Dr. L. H. Holden
Washington, DC

    I certify that Lieut William Wheeler of the Light Artillery, 3d Brig, Corps of Observation has reported sick to me. I find that he is suffering from diarrhea a debility consequence on remittent fever and that in my opinion he is unfit for duty.
    L H Holden
    Surgeon, Albany

Letter of William Wheeler
Washington, DC

    I reached here last night, after a day of unmitigated torture. I walked over to Poolesville early in the morning, to take the stage, and was forced to ride to Adamstown in a fearful springless wagon, which jounce me almost to pieces, then by rail to the Relay House, so to Washington, which I reached more like a dead many than anything else. I succeeded, through the courtesy of an officer, in getting a room in the Ebbitt House. When I went into the breakfast room I was so light-headed that I should have fallen, had I not heard a voice exclaim, "Why, Mr Wheeler!" I looked round and saw Mrs R. She too me in the doctor's carriage to the hospital, where her son is sick. The doctor examined me, and insisted on writing me a certificate of disability from duty on account of weakness, and sent me down to General Williams's office. My pass to be extended to ten days.

December 18, 1861
Report of Dr. Archibald Douglas, Surgeon, 10th Connecticut Regiment
Annapolis, MD

Lieut William Wheeler of Sturmfels Light Artillery, Co A, 3rd Brigade, Corps of Observation having applied for a certificate on which to ground an application for extension of leave of absence. I do hereby certify that I have carefully examined this officer and find that he has had a severe attack of remittent fever disabling him from duty since 17th Nov 61 and he is still suffering under its effects; and in consequence thereof, he is, in my opinion unfit for duty. I further declare my belief that he will not be able to resume his duties in a less period than six weeks from date, and also that a change of climate is desirable.

Archibald T Douglas, Surgeon
10th Conn Regt

December 19, 1861
Leave of absence extension request to Gen Seth Williams, Assistant Adjutant General, Army of the Potomac
Annapolis, MD

Sir
I have the honor to apply for an extension of my leave of absence, for the purpose of recovering my health. I have already been absent on that account seven days by permission by Gen Williams. I wish an extension of six weeks.
I am your very obt servt
Wm Wheeler
Lieut in Sturmfels' Light Artillery, Co A
3rd Brigade, Corps of Observation

December 27, 1861
Letter of William Wheeler
Annapolis, MD

My Dear Mother
I write you to say that I am daily improving in my health and strength, and coming up rapidly, under the combined influence of careful treatment and phosphates. Anything is better than the

despondent indifference in which I was a camp. The only thing that worries me is, that I have not yet got my new leave of absence, and my old one expired several days since, so that I have been a sort of deserter. A furlough was written for me, by an old army surgeon, but it was drawn so incorrectly as to be of no use, and was sent back. I then got a proper certificate from Dr Douglas, of the Tenth Connecticut. This went to Colonel H, but he has gone to New York, so that my application has lain unattended to, and I am thinking of going directly back to camp without waiting for the leave. We had a pleasant Christmas here. R was longed and sighed for.

December 31, 1861
Letter of William Wheeler
Annapolis, MD

I suppose you have been kept informed about me by letters from uncle and aunt, but I will recapitulate a little. I spent the afternoon of December 11 in Mrs R's room. She made me lie down on the sofa, and tucked me up warm. In the evening, the Misses W sent their man in with a tray covered with nice things, first-rate tea and toast, which went right to the spot. I made a call on them later in the evening, and saw Mrs H and Miss J The latter I had never met, but Mrs H I has seen long ago when I was in college. At 3 PM I took the train for the junction, and reached here about eight o'clock. I have improved very rapidly ever since I came here. If my leave does not come, I shall have to go back to Camp Observation, as soon as I am fit to travel. If I get right strong and well, I shall report myself for duty when my leaves runs out; but, in the present disorganized state of our Battery, it does no harm to the public service for me to be absent. If we were ready for active operations, it would be a different thing, and it would be something to be absent a day longer than I could help

January 1, 1862
Leave of absence extension request to Gen. Seth Williams,
Assistant Adjutant General, Army of the Potomac
Annapolis, MD

Sir
I have the honor to apply for an extension of my leave of absence for forty days from the 22nd day of December 1861, being

thirty days from this day, January 1st 1862 for the purpose of recovering my health.
    I have been absent on this account ten days prior to the 22nd day of December 1861 by permission of Gen S Williams
        I am your very obt servt
        Wm Wheeler
        Lieut in Sturmfels' Light Artillery
        3rd Brigade, Corps of Observation

Letter of Dr. J. H. Thompson, Brigade Surgeon, 3rd Brigade, Corps of Observation
Annapolis, MD

    Lieut Wm Wheeler of Sturmfels Light Artillery, Third Brigade, Corps of Observation having applied for a certificate on which to ground an application for an extended leave of absence. I do hereby certify that I have carefully examined this officer and find that he is suffering from debility being the sequence of Remittent Fever and in consequence thereof he is in my opinion, unfit for duty. I further declare my belief that he will not be able to resume his duties in a less period than 30 days.
    J H Thompson MD
    Brigade Surgeon USA

January 16, 1862
Special Order No. 3
Camp Duncan, DC

I   The following named non-commissioned officers of this Battery are hereby reduced to the rank of a private solder.
Sergt John A Rush
  "   James Clarke
  "   Peter Duffy
II   The following privates are appointed to the rank of non-commissioned officers. They will be obeyed and respected accordingly.

Corpl Joseph Bohn to Sergt	Pvte James When	Corpl
" Michael McMahon "	William H Garrett	"
" Thielman Moritz "	John B Walker	"

Pvte Albert Miller   Corpl   Adam Greenfield "
E Sturmfels
Capt Comdg

January 17, 1862
Memo of Brig. Gen. William Barry, Chief of Artillery, Army of the Potomac
no location given

    I respectfully refer this commendation, through Hd Qts, Army of Potomac to Adjt Genls Office, US Army.

    Lt Wheeler, the officer mentioned herein, is very feeble and delicate; he had been absent from his duties nearly all the time: he is now absent. I respect, fully recommend that he be mustered out of the service.

    William F Barry
    Brig Gen
    Chief of Arty

Reply to memo of Brig. Gen. Barry
no location given

    Respectfully return to Gen Barry to ascertain the address of Lt Wheeler.
    By command of Maj Gen McClellan

Report to Brig. Gen. William Barry, Chief of Artillery, Army of the Potomac
no location given

    General,
    I respectfully submit to you a report against Lieut W Wheeler and Lieut J Early.

    Lieut W Wheeler has been absent from his company without leave from the proper authority since the 9th day of January 1862 and has not as yet joined his company.

    Lieut James Early has been a Lieut attached to the company. He has been discharged from the service. He has also received his pay. He drew clothing from the company amounting to $46.84 which amount he has failed to pay.

    General, I await your decision in the matter.

I am General very respectfully
Emil Sturmfels
Capt Commdg

January 18, 1862
Memo of Brig. Gen. William Barry, Chief of Artillery, Army of the Potomac
no location given

Respectfully returned- I do not know where Lt Wheeler is. He left his company two or three weeks ago on a leave of absence granted at Asst Adjt Genls Office (Army of Potomac) which leave was not approved, nor even presented to his Captain or to me- I am given to understand by his Capt. that this is the second leave of absence of this sort which Lt W has had- He is now absent "without leave"

William F Barry
Brig Genl
Chief of Art

January 24, 1862
Letter of William Wheeler
Washington, DC

Dear Mother
I have finally found rest for the sole of my foot, to a sufficient extent to take pen in hand and to tell you how I am situated. I left New York at 7 AM on Tuesday, and after the usual tedious ride, with the pleasures of a chilly storm superadded, I reached Annapolis and received a warm welcome from the friends there. I made a short call on Lieutenant W, who has just returned, and had resigned some time before reaching Annapolis. I really could not help feeling sorry for him, but still I hope the government will give him his due, by sending him to Fort Warren, and not permit him to go South and assist them in organizing that branch which they so much need- a Navy. I came on here on Wednesday afternoon, and, at an early hour, started for our camp. Some time before I reached it, I could see a long line of evergreens, worked into rustic sheds, and through them flamed out numerous red blankets, showing that at least one essential requisite for a battery has been obtained, and upon coming into camp I found that we had about one hundred and ten horses, and that we were to

fetch the guns the next day. I suppose that by this evening we shall have four pieces at camp. As the tents were all full, and as I was not quite ready to do full duty, Captain Sturmfels gave me permission to go into Washingtonfor quarters.

We have orders to cross the river, and to join General Blenker's Division, so that very possibly we may be away by Monday. I see that Alfred Rockwell has turned up a Captain of the First Connecticut Battery.

January 26, 1862
Letter of William Wheeler
Camp Duncan, DC

Dear M

Sunday has brought with it a sufficient degree of leisure and quiet to permit me to sit peacefully down and tell you how I am, and how I found matters in the Company after my absence from it...... On Wednesday I came to Washington, and found the Company where it was two weeks ago, and that it had received an increase of members, but that entirely on four legs,--we have now one hundred and eight horses, nearly our entire quota, and shall go to the arsenal tomorrow to fetch our guns,--they are said to be iron six-pounders, of Prussian make, warranted to burst, I suppose , at the fifth discharge. Although our Captain is absent, I am not in command, for a German lieutenant is promoted over me, and, as I am not ready to resign, I must e'en submit with a good grace. Besides, this lieutenant is said to be an accomplished artillery officer, and I don't want to push myself above those who are really my superiors. But, what is most unpleasant to me of all, is, that I have to live with these men, to eat their onions and drink their lager, and very rarely to hear a word of musical English from American lips, as I am almost the sole specimen of a Yankee in the Company. There are plenty of Irish, it is true, and their "rich brogue." And a river of talk well supplied with dam(n)s, can be heard at any time in the camp. Now do not think that I make a unnecessary fuss about these things, for a soldier's life had in it enough of hardship and trouble, without adding the mental agony of continual uncongeniality and disagreement of modes and habits of life. I do not "bat one jot of heart or hope," and I am far more determined, now, to see this war out, than I was when I first entered the service.

January 28, 1862
Letter of William Wheeler
Camp Duncan, DC

    The noises and rows, which always accompany pay-day, have subsided to a sufficient extent to permit me to take off my sabre and pistol, with I have been prowling through the company street, "a terror to evil-doers," and although I have had a very busy and fatiguing day, and it is now half-past eleven, yet I fell much more like having a good talk with you than like going to bed. How curious the moods of letter-writing are! They are not the same as with that faculty of conversation which enables one to express himself in easy and yet correct words. Conversation is more readily carried on' for the presence of the friend stimulates and excites, while the *imagination* must assist the letter-writer, to call up the absent face, and to hear the well-know voice in reply, and the laugh, often shared together at a stray flash of humor. I think that if people would give way to their imaginations more, when in a kindly vein, their "winged words" would be more beautiful and would nestle more warmly on the hearts of absent friends. I frequently feel like saying to my correspondents,-- "Be more frivolous, describe little things more carefully, and don't touch upon great things,--if you must, do so superficially and say no more than every one else and the newspaper say."

    We, in the field, will bear the hardships of the camp, and you, at home, will bear the anxiety for us, and will give us your prayers; only let the war last until the question has been thoroughly decided, even if it cost the lives of all now in the field, and let our institutions be founded upon a basis of real stability, which no selfish oligarchy can shake at their pleasure.

    I think that already some gleams of light are apparent in the South. May the Dayspring soon visit us, and may it really be a Dayspring from on high. Since I have been here, I have not had a single sensation of homesickness, nor any of regret. My lot is cast in with this matter and I will see it out. Courageous and patriotic words from dear and loved friends like yourself *ma chère*, go right to the soldier's heart, and give it warmth and strength to beat with full pulses in the storm.

    But upon my word, I supposed that I was going to be frivolous myself this time, and lo, I have entered into a didactic oration on the first page; please excuse me, and don't take any of it to yourself, but write me just as frivolous a letter as possible, in revenge for my harangue......I had to sleep in the same room with a monster from Illinois, of the chestnut-worm species (slightly roasted) of mankind; I suppose there are plenty more of the same sort there, but, though they may be very decent people, they are loathsome to look at. He was a peaceably disposed monster, and beyond the little singularity of going to bed in full dress (I am not so sure about the boots), behaved quite creditably. I took him for a hog contractor, but he may have been a member of Congress....I was quartered in the city until Saturday, when Captain Sturmfels went to New York; since then I have occupied his tent, and have done fully duty. When I arrived, I found the company supplied with one and eight horses, nearly their full complement; and I now begin to see how intricate and extensive a matter the charge of a battery of artillery is, when the mere cleaning, feeding, watering, and physicking of the horses is so much an affair.....We were all paid to-day, and I rode to Washington with my pockets full of money-letters, to send by Adams' Express for the men. I am willing to take a good deal of trouble in order to do this; since it both relieves the families at home, and also removes the men from temptation. I called upon Miss W and Mrs H, dirty boots and all; but as they are "doing" the soldier life, they said, the gloried my muddy boots.

February 1, 1862
Letter of William Wheeler
Camp Duncan, DC

Dearest Mother
As I understand that there is very general distress among the people at the North, and as my soldiers are pretty generally sending their money home, I follow their good example, and send you--- by Adams' Express, hoping that it may help to keep the wolf from the door....The thought of doing something for you, who have done so much for me, dear mother, almost makes me wish that you were indeed dependent on my exertions, and that I could show you, by faithful labor and self-denial, that I am not ungrateful. This money I send home because I am afraid that I may lose it here. I feel a redoubled interest in the service now that we have our guns, horses, battery, wagon forge, and everything complete, and, as I conduct the simpler maneuvers, the more difficult ones begin to become plain to me, and I have a good hope that my daily exercise and drill will constantly explain the study of tactics which I pursued quite

industriously in that hillside of Camp of Observation. Of course I do not expect ever to be a really good artillery officer, in the proper sense of the word, but still I may be able to do something in the service, and accomplish more than if I were merely a lieutenant of infantry. Yesterday I went down to the arsenal with the caissons for some ammunition, and as I had hardly any officers with me, I felt quite a weight of responsibility upon me. I was continually apprehensive lest one of them might fall into some unfathomable mud-hole, from which our young, untrained horses would never be able to pull it up. Then, at the railroad crossing, I was again very nervous, for on the day when we brought the pieces, the cars came along close to us, and the horses of one carriage got tied up in a hard knot. But no such accident happened to me, and I brought my charge back all right. This getting on horseback seems to put new life into me; and although I have no horse of my own, I can get along with one of the company horses until the government receives some animals more worthy to be straddled by officers than those now in their stables. Last Thursday was pay-day, and we had a terrible time with the men for two days after. I won't dilate upon the disagreeable subject, but only say that I almost lost my faith in human nature, so many of the best and most reliable men probed wholly bad and unreliable under the influence of drink. I am sorry to be obliged to inform you that our living here is very bad. The mess at Camp Observation was luxury compared with it. There is no system; each picks what he can find, and then sits "silently apart gorging himself in gloom,"—I would not say gorging, for that presupposes an amount of food not easily attainable. Captain Sturmfels is anxious to get across the river to Virginia, so that we may be settled and have things decent and comfortable....As soon as I get comfortably quartered I shall be quite content.

February 4, 1862
Battery Orders No. 4
Camp Duncan, DC

I   Privates Charles Hempen and Charles Link are hereby appointed sergeant in the 13th NY Battery from Feb 1, 1863. They will be obeyed and respected accordingly.
II   Privates Henry Miller, James Clarke, John O'Connor, Christian Gutbrad, Henry Tintenfass & Thomas Regan are hereby appointed corporal in the 13th New York Battery, from Feb 1, 1862. They are to be obeyed and respected accordingly.

Emil Sturmfels
Capt Comdg Battery

February 7, 1862
Letter of William Wheeler
Camp Duncan, DC

Dear Friend
It is a long time since I have written to you,--not, I think, since I sent you the last heft of my "Electra,"—and I feel ashamed of myself for my long silence; but yet I must plead the shadows of an excuse. Your scholarly, quiet, and decorous life seems so far removed from the dirty and commonplace existence of us here in camp, that hardly more than a faint echo will reach your ear when I speak, and you cannot be expected to take much interest in my stories of drill and guard duty and muddy misery, when in any newspaper you can read accounts far more thrilling and exciting about soldier life. People in general are, I imagine, pretty well disgusted with the subject of the war, and we have to content ourselves with exciting an interest for us in the family circle and no farther. But I feel a very warm interest in what you are doing and studying, old fellow, even in that absorbing Sanskrit, although I am hardly prepared just now to undertake the translation of the Vedas or Hitopadeça (isn't that the cove's name?) with you, after the manner of Electra. I can't quite give up the old classical boys even now; I have a Leipzig "Horace" on my table, and find an occasional ode right jolly reading for odd snatches of time....My fellow officers get letters from their wives, and read me extracts abut their little boys, and their naïve inquiries after "father," and then, when their faces soften and their eyes glisten, I know that my life is very barren and incomplete, and that I have a great mystery to learn and as yet no one to teach it me....Come with me to our camp, three quarters of a mile east of the Capitol, and let me introduce you to our officers. Captain Sturmfels, the getter-up of the Battery, with whom I tent, is a very queer specimen of humanity; jolly, hasty, practical, unreliable, philosophic, childish, and, worst of all, addicted to rising at abominably early hours, and punching me in the ribs until I follow his example. At any rate, an educated officer, and one who seems to enjoy a pretty good reputation for experience among other German officers. (You observe that this paper looks a little greasy; probably the captain has been using it to enfold a Schweine-bifstek, as I constantly find that favorite dish of his in all

parts of the tent.) Next, Lieutenant Molitor. An officer from the General Staff of Würtemberg, well-posted in military matters, but so thoroughly attached to European tactics as to be quite unfit to manage American troops; he is likewise conceited enough to shipwreck the best man that ever lived. Then, Lieutenant Carl von Linden (I only give his first name, as his intermediate names are legion, and would occupy too large a part of my letter), a hohe Herrschaft, and husband of the Gräfinn somebody, and feels it all over, as is seen at first glance. He drinks vast lager, rides pretty well, as he was a cavalry officer before, knows no English, because he is too lazy to learn, consequently is of very little use to us, and is in all respects "ein echter Schwab." Then, Lieutenant Singer, a watchmaker from New York, about forty years old, and of rough, harsh appearance, but a real good, kind-hearted fellow, entirely reliable and unpretending, and one who stands up to his work like a man; the stables are especially under his care, and it makes me laugh to hear him rush out of bed at night whenever any disturbances arise there.....But then, we have floods of German grub: Schweins-bifstek, Sauerkraut, Brat und Leber-wurst, Zwiebel und Knoblauch, Urisokohl, and all these washed down with plentiful potations of Lager-Bier, Rheinwein, and Schnapps. Add to this that the cooking is all done in our tent, and you "square the awful product" immediately; the consequence is that a strange confusion of goods takes place, and, though I do not, like poor Tom, have "ratsbane in my porridge and halters in my pew," yet I often see a string of Wurst laid on my portfolio, and poor "Horace" has a bunch of Knoblauch on his cover spite of his protest—

"Parentis olim si impia mann
Senite guttur fregerit,
Edit cicutis allium nocentius."

I think that before long I shall myself become a good German plain cook, and will be able, when I come home, to turn you out abominations of all kinds, gentle reminders of the Hotel Bellevue. This morning three of us started off before sunrise for a ride and trot-practice. On our way home we visited the market at Washington, and I was deputed to do the marketing. We then dashed up Pennsylvania Avenue, I with two fat chickens, slung one on each side of my saddlebow, like JohnGilpin's bottles, "to keep the balance true." Alas! My fate was as sad as his, for suddenly the connecting link between the birds broke, and they plumped down deep into the mud, whence they were extracted by a small boy whom I hired to dive for them. (Fine chance for a parody on "Wer wagt es, Rittersmann oder Knapp, zu tauchen in diesen Schlund!") You would revel in the constant opportunities for speaking German which are afforded here. I go right in and talk, utterly regardless of mistakes in German, as I had to do yesterday with an awkward squad of gunners in the "school of the piece," as the technical terms are different and often peculiar; but I go fearlessly ahead. Our pieces are 6-pounders 3-inch rifled guns, beauties for maneuvering, as they are quite light, and I think that they will turn out well in action. I already feel and affection for them, and they be to me as a sweetheart, yea, as many sweethearts. We have had marching orders for some time to cross the river and join General Blenker's Division, but the weather has been miserable, and we may not go for two weeks.

February 23, 1862
Letter of William Wheeler
Hunters Chapel, VA

Sunday is a day of work as well as any other, but we do not drill or undertake any lengthy job likely to take all day. This morning I was hard at work for four hours unloading ammunition and packing it in our caissons. This was decidedly a work of necessity, for the stuff had come up from the arsenal three or four days ago, and ever since then it had been too wet to venture to unpack it. To-day the weather was very fine, so we took advantage of it to get our precious ammunition stowed away, and I was handling the canister, shells, and case-shot, instead of going to church. I intend to take my horse next Sunday and ride over to General Franklin's Division to see Jo J and go to church with him. He is about three miles and a half from here, in the Alexandria district. The sight of a single friendly face would be a great treat to me here, but I have to make duty take the place of friendship, culture, and most other desirable things. I am now decidedly the laboring oar of the concern, for domestic ties impair the efficiency of two of our officers, for the wife of Lieutenant von Linden is at Washington, and he goes there as often and stays as long as he possibly can. The other afternoon who should appear in camp but Madame Sturmfels with three fat, flourishing images of the illustrious captain. He quartered them in a house near by our encampment, put himself on the sick list, and has gone up there to stay with them, and left me to have command of the battery. This keeps me very busy, but then I can manage matters according to my own ideas of what is right, and the responsibility is honorable and exciting. On Washington's Birthday our Battery went out for inspection and review; but that is a long story. I feel still the same delightful state of uncertainty about my daily food; but who cares much for such trivial things when every newspaper brings such delightful, reviving news of the success of our arms in every quarter. I think I could have lived for a week on the news of Fort Donelson alone. How you New Haven folks must rejoice in the success and glory of Captain Foote, who, it seems to me, stands out more prominently than any other commander, as distinguished for his gallant conduct and cool bravery......Still, the great battle will yet take place in Virginia, ad we shall be ready to be in it, for our men are ambitious and quite enthusiastic. Having guns and horses to take care, and duties of both interest and difficulty to perform, seems to have transformed some of them from drunken wretches to eager, careful workers. I never could have stood the monotony of infantry service.

February 25, 1862
Battery Orders No. 4(a)
Hunters Chapel, VA

Corporal Sebastian Losh is hereby reduced to the ranks for drunken and disorderly conduct upon the 23rd Feby 1862
Private Thomas Regan is hereby promoted corporal vice Losh reduced. He will be obeyed & respected accordingly.
By order of
Emil Sturmfels Capt
Comdg Battery

February 28, 1862
Letter of William Wheeler
Hunters Chapel, VA

  Your right kindly and "frivolous" letter, dated February 1st, was duly received by me at Camp Duncan, although directed to General Blenker's Division, for, as you very sensibly suggest, the movements of so celebrated an officer as myself are to well known for my letter ever to go astray, and General McClellan was, at that time, in the habit of daily calling on the Washington Postmaster, and saying to him, "Lieutenant Wheeler is still at Camp Duncan;" so that it was through this considerate behavior on the part of the Commander-in-Chief that I was spared the agony of having your letter delayed. I was much amused with the whole epistle, and thought it a right jolly production for an unhappy being with headache, toothache, bad cold, etc. you can't be too frivolous in a letter. One laughs at some comical idea warms the heart of the reader towards the sender more than a page full of endearments, and you say in your heart, "He must indeed love me if writing to me inspires him with such gladness and lightness of heart." The necessary labors, accompanying the receipt of our guns and ammunition, and the preparations for moving out to this camp, kept me so busy in Washington, that I got no chance to write you, and since we have been in Dixie my time has been still more fully occupied in the arranging of our new camp, and with drills, etc. And now, I am going out on picket to-morrow morning with my section, I cannot refrain from writing you a few lines (perhaps the last I may write), to let you know that I am well and think of you, as I may not have facilities to write again soon.

    We broke up at Camp Duncan on the 12th of February, and marched down to Washington, through Pennsylvania Avenue, across the Long Bridge into Virginia, and then through much mud to this camp, where the Teutonic element has its head-quarters, and revel in endless streams of lager, infinite plantations of sauerkraut, and strings of small but seductive sausages. We selected our camp on a very fine piece of elevated ground, the dryest in the neighborhood, near to the main road, and with good springs of water handy. And now after two weeks of steady hard work; after building a brush stable, also a kitchen, fixing up all the tents nicely and comfortably with board floors, and getting generally settled down,--lo and behold, the order comes that the whole Division must hold themselves in readiness to march at two hours' notice; and so, all our toil will be for naught. I start for the extreme outposts to-morrow morning with my section (the first, containing the first and second pieces), which is the best in the Battery, and I think it very likely that the rest will follow soon; so that you see we are likely to get a pop at your friends the seceshers after all. My whole heart and soul have been wrapped up in my battery, especially since we came out here. I have drilled the whole six pieces at once, and find that it is the only way in which thoroughly to secure the fruits of my study. We turn out on Washington's Birthday for inspection and review by General Blenker. There were three batteries of light artillery, sixteen pieces in all, and we fired a salute of a hundred guns. Although our horses had had very little drill, I succeeded in conducting them and the men through several quite difficult maneuvers, and was very much relieved when I saw the horses stand the firing without running away and tearing everything to pieces.

The thing that gives me plenty of spirit and enthusiasm is that I am extremely well mounted. My horses is a beautiful dark day, with a sort of metallic reflection in his skin, has a jolly little head, and is, in a points, nicely and strongly put together. I call him "Barry," after the Chief of Artillery, and pet him enormously. He will follow me like a dog, eats sugar out of my hand, and rubs his head on my shoulder when I caress him. You shall ride him too, one of these days, if you will be a good girl, and not *secesh* too much.

March 9, 1862
Letter of William Wheeler
Hunters Chapel, VA

Dearest Mother

My letters to and from home are my only means of communication with the outer world. I am always in camp and have not been to Washington once since we have been out here. When my isolation is interrupted by letters from the dear friends, I feel repaid for all discomforts, and prepare myself to endure all that is endurable, and in my case there unendurable has not been reached yet. I think that there must be something in the free and out of door life that hardens and strengthens me to bear what inharmonious and incompatible in my mental and social existence.....If there is anything like a general engagement, they will need all the guns they can get, and I think that our greenhorns can drive, load, and fire well enough to take part. My heart is full of anxiety when I think of that final struggle, not on my own account, that may come when we go to the field, but for the almost indescribable greatness of the interests at stake. A born coward ought to fight will for this once, as such another opportunity will never come up in the world's history, to inspire courage and noble daring... Where do you suppose this letter is being written? Has it any peculiar smell, like Michael's boots, for example? For I am writing it in the stable, sitting on a camp-stool, in the nice clean stall with my horse, General Barry; in fact it is the pleasantest place in the camp; for such occupation my tent is too warm, this lovely spring day, but here, with the sweet branches of pine and hemlock trees on every side, protecting me from the wind, and with the clear blue sky all overhead, I can write my letter, and yet not lose all the calm and happy influences of God's light and air. The General is very inquisitive, and has several times, smelled and bit at my paper; he is a regular nibbler, and the other day walked behind me and ate up half of a Herald, which I had under my arm. He is now quite lame, his foot is adorned with a fine bran poultice, which I hope will bring him all right in a day or two. I sympathize with him in his trouble, and pay him several visits every day, with a little sugar or salt to tickle his equine palate with.

March 15, 1862
Letter of William Wheeler
Hunters Chapel, VA

Dear Aunt Elizabeth
Perhaps my next will contain something more interesting than dull descriptions of camp life in this great lazy army of the Potomac.

A move is to be made very soon; troops from all parts are concentrating in this neighborhood, and even the brigade to which we are attached in Maryland, General Burns's, has just marched in and gone to Bailey's Cross Roads. The whole Division received special notice, on last Saturday, that three days' preparation would be allowed to get into perfect marching order. I think that the forward move would have been make to-day if the weather had continued good... The winds play the very mischief with us, in our somewhat exposed situation. A violent southwester, a week or so ago, proved fatal to most of the tents in our encampment; at first one Sibley tent broke from its moorings and collapsed, then another and another, then the tent of the orderly sergeant went by the board, and the fields around were whitened with official documents of every description. Then the captain's rose and made a graceful pirouette on one pole, and subsided on the ground. I expect every minute to see my tent follow its example, and, for the whole day, my tent mate and I took turns in sitting on the fly, to break the force of the hurricane. I did not sleep a wink, and the tent rocked like a boat on the waves; but morning found us all right.

In summer this be a lovely place for an encampment; beautiful ranges of hills, crowed by forts bristling with cannon and abatis, and between them fine level spots for drill and parade, with excellent streams of water all around. The name of the camp is taken from a homely red wooden building erected by a farmer of the name of Hunter, and used as a place of worship; it has been degraded from its former high use, to serve as a magazine for quartermaster's and commissary's stores. This Division is called the German Division, and the officers at head-quarters have to do business in a polyglot fashion. I greatly outraged the assistant adjutant general by refusing to recognize a German order which was sent to me, when I was in command.

Every moment is precious to us now, as we shall have to go into the fight with the others, and it would be desirable for us to be able to do a little more execution among the enemy than our own men. I am endeavoring to interest the men in the subject, as much as possible, and to call out their latent enthusiasm. They take hold very much better than I could have dared to expect, and there is considerable emulation among the different pieces, to see which shall be best drilled and best maneuvered. I rode over to General Franklin's Division to see J J, and fund that he had been ill at home for some weeks with a bad fever. On my way back I inquired for Fort Richardson, and found that it was within a gun-shot of our encampment, and that I had been three weeks so near to the Fourth Connecticut, and to my friend T T who is the adjutant of it. The regiment is a wonder of neatness, and was pronounced by General McClellan's committee of inspection to be the finest regiment in the volunteer service. How splendidly Commodore Foote has born himself. He and Lyon are, to my mind, the heroes of the war so far. Connecticut has no reason to be ashamed of her sons.

I am in excellent health and spirits, and am growing fat, in spite of hard fare and poor accommodations.

March 16, 1862
Battery Orders No. 5
Fairfax Court House, VA

Sergeant Michael McMahon
Corporal John O'Connor
Having been adjudged by sentence of Battalion Court Martial to be reduced to the ranks, they do hereby cease to be non-commissioned officers of this Battery.
Wm Wheeler
1st Lt Comdg Battery

March 17, 1862
Battery Orders No. 6
Fairfax Court House, VA

I   Corporal Henry Miller is hereby promoted sergeant of this battery vice McMahon reduced to the ranks; he will be obeyed and respected accordingly.

II   Private John Ouh is hereby appointed guidon of this battery, vice Miller promoted.

Wm Wheeler
1st Lt Comdg Battery

March 19, 1862
Letter of William Wheeler
Fairfax Court House, VA

    I have at last a moment of leisure at my command, and my trunk has just come up from camp, so that I have an opportunity to drop you a line,--a baker's dozen of artillery officers are sitting in the room. Our head-quarters were formerly the parlor of a very decent house, and there is a perpetual clatter of tongues disputing, about horses, points of discipline, and other military matters, while now and then a beer glass comes down empty in a very emphatic manner. But I have found it necessary to make myself very often deaf and callous to these things, otherwise my life would be very hard to bear. My last letter to John was written from our last camp, Taylor's Cross Roads, and just before I got it finished, a hurried order came to march; I thrust it into my pocket and rushed off to make preparations, Captain Sturmfels being absent. In less than an hour we were off on the road to Fairfax, and a heavy rain, which seemed to follow us on our marches like a tutelary genius, poured pitilessly down. The road was at first pretty good, but became ever worse as the Division advanced, and at last the mud got so deep as to give us much trouble. My section went through everything without a halt, but two or three of the other carriages were not so fortunate, and I had to halt the column and send back teams to pull them out of the mud. In consequence we were a long time on the road, and when we reached this place, I was thoroughly soaked as if I had been dipped in a pond. Then we had to find quarters for men and horses, especially the latter, and this was no easy matter, as the cavalry had come in before us, and horses' heads peeped out of school-room windows, and the ferrule gave way to the cowhide. Many of the inhabitants had fled, and their houses were generally taken possession of for officers' quarters; in smaller houses were some families remaining, and some of the old campaigners in our Company managed to billet themselves there in very comfortable quarters, and about sixty of our men took up their abode in the Courthouse where "Old JohnBrown" was tried and condemned, and immediately constituted a court, and proceeded to reenact the scenes of November, 1859.

We expected to have to march off the next day to some point in advance, but the plans seem to have been changed.....The soldiers have behaved very well; to be sure the fences have suffered somewhat, when firewood was not elsewhere to be had, and a stray pig or fowl may have mysteriously come to an untimely end; but no houses have been burned, and the inhabitants and their property have been treated much better than rebels deserve. We have not been idle since coming here. We have had two or three very good drills, both in section, battery, and battalion, and yesterday we took part in a grand review of General Sumner's Corps d'Armée. At least 40,000 men must have been there, and they were drawn up in two lines of battle, and a reserve. We were in the second line of battle, and I had the honor of commanding the Battery. General Sumner is a rather elderly man, with a shrewd and pleasant face, a squeaky voice, and gray hair. He was enthusiastically cheered as he passed along the lines. It is on occasions of this kind that I feel the want of my jolly little horse, which is still at Hunters Chapel. The animal I now ride is excellent for mud work, and very sure footed, but unfit for a show occasion.

I think of you very often in my mental and moral loneliness, and try to make old family and home memories supply the place of present good influences.

March 29, 1862
Letter of William Wheeler
Fairfax Court House, VA

When I wrote to you last, I was not at all in the mood for it, and simply intended to throw you off a few lines as a bulletin of my condition and prospects, and with the expectation of soon having an opportunity to write you again, when I could really commune with you in spirit, as many times before, but have been so busy and active with preparations, marches, bivouacs, and drills, that the favorable moment could not be seized. And I had promised myself the luxury of a talk with you this very rainy morning, when Captain Schirmer, commanding the light artillery, ordered a court martial, and detailed me as judge advocate of it: so my pen had to deal with melancholy facts of drunkenness, insubordination, and disobedience, rather than serve as interpreter of kind thoughts and wishes from me to you.

But while I was deep in charges and specifications, and the piles of paper around me were growing decidedly Alpine in their character, one of the officers came in and handed me three letters. I glanced at the beloved crow-tracks on the outside, and broke one open, when the president began to look impatient, and the member next to be said in German, "put up your love-letters, and attend to business." So I thrust them into my breast-pocket, but that one glance was enough to show me that they were far more worthy to be called "love-letters" than those which usually bear that name; for one was from Aunt Elizabeth, one from L R P, and one from yourself.....After having convicted three or four unfortunates of various military offenses, and sentenced them to such pleasant little amusements as "Guard duty four times a week," "Hard labor for a month," "Reduction to the ranks," and "Loss of pay," I set myself down to a greedy devourment of my letters, all of which were most kinds, and made me ask myself what right a poor devil of a soldier had to have such good friends, and that they should continue to take such a tender interest in him. Letters like these pierce the thick rhinoceros hide of insensibility which the soldier must wrap himself. So, this morning I was reckless enough, and thought of nothing but blood and wounds and fried secessionists for breakfast; but now, I can't help feeling "low" and soft, with glimpses of a home-life somewhere, and a strong touch of nostalgia under the ribs; and when I go down stairs to bed (we go down to bed here, and up-stairs to work), I know that I shall not have spunk enough to kick out the fellows, who, I feel sure, are lying with their dirty boots on my mattress.

We came into this pleasant village, through which the tide of retreat and advance has so often ebbed and flowed, a week ago, having marched here from Taylor's Cross Roads in a tremendous rain-storm. The place was full of soldiers, and men and horses were quartered in the court-house, in churches, private houses, and wherever they could make a lodgment, but only the deserted houses were taken possession of. In cases of where the inhabitants had a sense to remain in their dwellings, no soldiers were forced upon them against their consent. We artillery officers, some fifteen in number, have a very respectable house to ourselves. It belonged to a man named Jackson, who is said to be a near relation of the man that shot Ellsworth. (N B That Jackson must have a large family connection—at least five hundred Jacksons have turned up in this war who were said to be his relations.) It was not at all disagreeable to get a roof over our heads once more, after bivouacking for a week. Sleeping in the open air is not unpleasant, when you have the blue sky and stars overhead, although, the ground may be hard and damp, and the wind cold ad stiffening,--*that* one can stand, but when it rains and soaks you through, and you have no dry clothes to put on, but must act on the principle of "Every many to his own clothes-horse," ugh! Then the fun ceases to be perceptible, even with my very excellent field-glass.... You ask me what I think of General McClellan and the "Tribune" attacks. I must say that I have lately given up thinking as an occupation, but whatever ideas I may have of the conduct of the General in a military point of view, as a soldier, I have nothing to do but to hold my tongue and do my duty. At the same time you know my opinions on the subject of slavery, and that this matter will never finally settled until the root of the matter is cut up. Too much blood and treasure have been expended by the North, to permit a mere temporary soldering up of the affairs,--to break out again worse than before.

March 27, 1862
Letter of William Wheeler
Manassas, VA

For nearly three weeks I have been moving from one bivouac to another, except during the time that we were at Fairfax Court House, and then there was such a bustle and constant excitement, that letter-writing was quite out of the question. Perhaps it would be better for me to give you a little account of our marchings and counter-marchings, as it will enable you better to follow me. On Monday, March 10, we moved out of Camp Hunters Chapel, and went as far as Annandale; then by a very bad road to Taylor's Farm, where we were encamped for three days. Up to that day, we had very fine weather, and the two nights which R spent in camp with mere were just adapted to an amateur bivouacker, but the next day set in dark and misty, and at night we had a hard rain which knocked away all traces of romance about sleeping out of doors. At eleven AM a very sudden order came to march, and we were soon on our way to Fairfax Court House in as heavy a rain-storm as I want to see, unless through a window-pane, and the roads being very bad, halts were numerous, and we had to sit still on our horses and take it. Still we were much better off than the infantry, or *doughboys* as they are called in army parlance, and one of my men told me that he saw a foot-soldier lying stark dead in the woods from cold and exposure. At Fairfax Court House we stayed for a week, had drills and inspections when the weather permitted, and were reviewed once by General Sumner, who now commands this Corps d'Armée of the Army of the Potomac. It consists of three Divisions, Richardson's, Sedgwick's, and Blenker's, and counts from thirty to forty thousand men. I commanded our Battery at the review, and had the honor of answering some questions put by the General. On Monday last, we were at a battalion drill, we received orders to march, and were off in little more than a half an hour; had a splendid night march to Centreville over a first-rate road. We had a very cold bivouac; in the morning I examined the fortifications, and saw the famous wooden guns, painted black, which you must have read about in the papers. The earthworks are not very formidable in their character, but on account of their position, at the head of a long slope, something like a garden-law, which furnishes very little protection to besiegers advancing, it would be hard to take it in from without very great loss. Early the next morning we again took up our line of march, and after some hard pulling through the mud we came to Bull Run. It was much larger, I should think, than it was last summer,--quite a respectable creek, about three feet deep at the point where we crossed it (Blackburn's Ford, I think), and not more than fifty or sixty yards wide. I sat on my horse in the middle of the stream, the water reaching just above my fee, and directed, and managed until the whole of the Battery had crossed over, and as I sat there, my mind would revert to that day in July last, when our troops crossed it in flight, and to that dreadful Monday when the news reached us at the North, ad we thought that all was lost to the Republic. Then as we advanced further, the beautiful blue mountains beyond Manassas showed their head, in some places covered with snow, and soon we struck upon the railroad which was so serviceable to the rebels in the campaign of last autumn. And so we emerged upon the plateau of Manassas, a find bit of almost level ground, with woods on two sides, and mountains beyond; an admirable place for a camp, and with the secessionists had improved its advantages very decidedly, but building camps of log-huts, in spots sheltered from wind and storm. These huts are shingled, and plastered with mud, and must have been far more comfortable than the tents in which we spent the winter. We encamped on the further end of the plateau, and then, yesterday morning, the Division moved off toward Manassas Gap and Winchester, to effect a junction with General Banks. Our Battery and the Sixty-fourth New York[7] were left behind to guard this place, an arrangement which did not please me greatly, until I was assured by Captain Schirmer[8], who commands the Battalion, that there would be no fighting, and that our horses would be much more able to do severe duty, if they could get a day's rest and plenty of forage; so I was pacified, and moved up and took possession of some of those nice secesh huts to await further orders; if there should be a battle, we shall have to go right forward, and if a retreat, we will have to cover it. I am sorry that I asked of you so great an undertaking as I fear the getting up of that flag must be.....Even if we never carry it into battle, I shall feel most deeply grateful to you for the kindly and tender interest that induced you to make it, and shall look upon it as a proof of the love you bear towards me, and also towards the cause which is so mutually precious to us all.....I have not yet heard it positively stated that Blenker had been removed from his command. At any rate, I saw him yesterday at the head of his staff, moving with his Division. I would give a good deal to have Sigel for our commander, as then we should have plenty of hard work and tough knocks, with the clear assurance of victory at the end; but Sigel, if he should take any command here, would have a Corps d'Armée and not merely a Division.

March 30, 1862
Letter of William Wheeler
Manassas, VA

My Dear Sister Theodosia

I have received your very nice and kind letter the other day, just after our arrival at this place, and with it the *carte-de-visite*, which looked at me so truthful and natural. I was a first almost startled, and could hardly realize that it was not my little sister herself, who, in some mysterious manner had pasted herself on a card. I am now sitting in a quite comfortable shanty, one of those which the "Secesh" built last winter to accommodate their troops. They are quite substantial, built of logs, and plastered with mud; the roof is made of shingles, and keeps the rain out, except when it rains very hard.....We have pretty hard times to get anything to eat, as most of the supplies have gone further on. After drinking sugarless coffee for a few days, we have no coffee at all, and no water fit to drink. Of course, under such circumstances, the hen-roost and barnyards of the rebel folks have to suffer considerably. I have now in my cap the feather of a guinea-hen, from one not a thousand miles away. Of her untimely end I will say nothing, except that she was extremely tough, and that I shall abstain from guinea-hen in future.

April 2, 1862
Battery Orders No. 7
Manassas, VA

Private Edward Baldwin
"   Charles Keane
are hereby appointed corporals in this battery. They will be obeyed and respected accordingly.
Wm Wheeler
1st Lieut Comdg Battery

April 4, 1862
Battery Orders No. 8
Manassas, VA

I   Sergeant Thielman Moritz 13 NY Batty is hereby reduced to the ranks for drunkenness on duty.
II   Corporal William H Garrett 13 NY Battery is hereby promoted sergeant, vice Moritz reduced. He will be obeyed & respected accordingly.
Wm Wheeler
1st Lt Comdg Battery

April 9, 1862
Letter of William Wheeler
Washington, DC

You will be somewhat surprised at the heading of this letter, but a little wind of business has blown me here, and I take advantage of a little leisure time after breakfast, before assaulting the departments, to answer your very jolly and refreshing letter, which I received at Warrenton Junction, just as I was coming away. It was just the kind of letter that I like to get,--a picture of home and New Haven matters, with a good close of peppering thrown in. General observations and reflections in a letter between intimate friends are generally "nichts nutz," unless made in a way that illustrates the character of the person making them. It is the neat little touches thrown skillfully in, that make the home picture glow with life, and make the heart of the absent member beat warmly as he looks at it,-- the one is like the bland, unmeaning allegorical pictures of the French school; the latter like the homely but delightful interiors of Teniers and Dow. I had some hint of the dissipation in which N H was indulging from Timothy Dwight, who also spoke of you as "pars fui" thereof, but I had no idea of the extent to which you had been engaged in it till I heard it from yourself....to let you know a little about myself. I spent nine days altogether in the shanties of Manassas, and lived in plenty and prosperity, drawing the necessaries of life from Uncle Sam on the one hand, and on the other foraging for double rations of corn and hay, and occasionally picking up stray horses, oxen, sheep, pigs, and poultry of every kind. My horse-stealing experience was neither very pleasant nor successful. I got tow old "clams" from a deserted farm-house, which got played out on the very first march, and two good horses from the sheriff of Prince William's County, whom I had heard to be a vile secesh, but who turned out to be one of those Union men who are now getting to be so plenty in the South, and I had to fork over the animals or run the risk of a row with General Sumner, although I needed them extremely to move my battery. You may be sure that I felt much as Robin Hood did when the sheriff of Nottinghamshire got the head start of him, and made up my mind not to meddle with sheriffs in future. On Thursday last our rest was broken up by the arrival of a troop of the mounted rifles, to cover us on our march to Warrenton, and the next day General Sumner came through and ordered us to depart immediately. So I set off with my detachment, being the largest one I had had command of, with half the cavalry in front, the other half behind our wagons, and two at my own back as *garde d'honneur*. We started late in the day, and marched to the Jersey settlement near Bristow, where we encamped for the night on the farm of Major Snow, a Northern man. We took supper and breakfast with him very pleasantly, and did not despoil him, except for a few oats for our horses, and a king-bold for one of our wagons. The officers slept on the floor of his very handsome parlor, and I napped it gorgeously on the rug before the fire (*more antiquo*). It rained in the night, and in the morning the roads were very bad, and we had a journey of extreme difficulty and fatigue. We had to cut roads, ford streams, and dig out the wheels of our carriages with shovels from the putty-like mud. I was constantly in the saddle for some fourteen hours. At last we reached Warrenton Junction, the camp of the Division, and the men lay down in the mud perfectly fagged out. I had to lead the way myself in order to start out a wood-chopping party, and, after cutting down a good size oak, I too was not sorry to succumb. Early the next morning the Division had orders to march; but Captain Sturmfels said our horses were not fit to go, so I sent only one section with Lieutenant Singer, and was ordered myself to Washington to get some new horses. I started off immediately, had two days of rough travel in this horrible snow-storm, and got here last night. I fear that I shall not have much luck, but intend to try everything to get them, as it is miserable to be so close to the enemy and yet constantly impeded by the want of the means of moving.

I enclose a couple of secesh shin-plasters for John. The S C is rather interesting.

April 12, 1862
Letter of William Wheeler
Washington, DC

Your very kind letter reached me safely at Manassas, having ridden the stormy waves of Bull Run, and then having been carried all the way out to Warrenton Junction, where the rest of the Division was lying, and brought back again to me. From these experiences it suffered nothing, except perhaps a slight stiffening from getting wet and being dried again, and a faint odor of "Limburger," from being so long on the person of the Division PM. Unfortunately I have it not with me, and so must answer it from recollection, and not *punctuatim et seriatim.*

Your account of your work shows me that you have not at all taken my advice in regard to secluding yourself, but have grown worse, if anything, rather than better. Far be it from me to say that your time is ill-spent in making yourself a thorough scholar, and in going to the sources of language for a firm foundation; but is it not a species of refined selfishness for you to give yourself wholly to this self-accomplishment? and do you not forget that, whether as a teacher or a preacher, your work is to be done, and your influence put forth in the living, breathing Now, and that if your fairest life is in the Past, you cannot know and appreciate the Present as you should? These scholarly pursuits are the most beautiful in the world, if they are kept subordinate to the great aims of duty and daily labor, and made co-workers in attaining some great and noble end; but when made an *end in themselves*, their life is gone, and the more the mind gains of knowledge, so much the more does the soul lose of freshness and working power. Look at the scholarship of Dante, of Milton; deep grand, and beautiful as it was, how it was transfigured by the heavenly light of religion and patriotism, till the student was quite forgotten. But this is certainly a queer sermon for a rough soldier to be preaching to a scholar, and forgive me for speaking out. The life I lead myself is just the opposite. Everything is intensely practical, just what lies before our feet, and in the immediate horizon; to keep the men and horses alive and healthy; to drill and march them well; to manage provision and forage carefully; to be always ready for anything that may occur; to have everything about the guns and equipments in perfect order; and for us officers to ride long, eat hearty, watch well, sleep sound,--this is our life, and a most sensual and beastly life too, if it were not for a few sparks of duty and love of country, that keep the heart aglow in the wildest night-storm, sustain the body through fatigue and privations, and eve make our rough campaigning "bright, with something of an angel light." Since we came into the field I have been so well in body, and so glad in spirit, that I have felt almost exultant, and my feelings have been just those of the cove in the "Two Voices," who "sang the joyful pæan clear," etc, q.v......In my present life, and especially in our Division, there is very little to help serious thoughts. Sunday passes unobserved and often unknown, and there is not a single soul in the whole came with whom I can walk, talk, or sing in sympathy on that day.

April 19, 1862
Report of Lt. Col. Timothy M. Bryan, Jr., 12th Massachusetts Infantry
Warren Junction, VA

Sir: In compliance with Special Orders, No 37, issued from brigade headquarters, I have made a reconnaissance to the North Fork of the Rappahannock River, and have the honor to submit the following as my report:

My command consisted of seven companies Twelfth Massachusetts Volunteers, Major Burbank commanding; five companies Ninth New York State Militia [Eighty-third Infantry], Lieutenant-Colonel Atterbury commanding; five companies Twelfth Indiana Volunteers, Lieutenant-Colonel Humphrey commanding; four companies Rhode Island Cavalry, Captain Gould commanding; two sections Matthews' battery, Lieutenant Godbold commanding; one section Thompson's battery, Lieutenant Brockway commanding; one section Sturmfels' battery, Lieutenant Molitor commanding, making a total of about 1,500 infantry, 160 cavalry, three sections of artillery with the new ordnance gun, and one section artillery with Parrott 10-pounder guns.

I had issued orders for the command to form in the rear of the camp of the Twelfth Massachusetts Regiment at 10 o'clock, but by some misunderstanding in the change of detail for the cavalry they were not reported present till 12.30 AM Another half hour was occupied in detailing the advance and rear guard and flankers and getting the command under way, so that it was 1 o'clock before the rear left. Not having any map of the country or guide, I requested Lieutenant Tucker, of the Maine Cavalry, to accompany me, he having traveled the road once before. I put him at the head of the advance guard, and to his services we are indebted for our early arrival at our destination.

The roads are terrible for artillery, the caissons frequently cutting in hub-deep, so that our march was necessarily impeded much more than we could have wished.

We arrived at a cross-road near our scene of action about 7 AM, and Lieutenant Tucker thinking they led to fords on our flanks, I dispatched a company of cavalry, about 40 men, down each to reconnoiter and warn me of any attempt to intercept our rear. The road on the left Lieutenant Wyman reports as leading directly to the ford below the bridge, as laid down on the map, about one-eighth of a mile below. Lieutenant Wyman received information from an officer and 2 men across the river as to the direction of the ford in the river, who also told him it was fordable horseback. When they found the Lieutenant was not inclined to cross they called him to halt and fired upon him, but without effect. The lieutenant on the road to the right, having gone down some 2 miles and not seeing the river ahead, returned nearer the main column to guard the right flank. I then went forward with Lieutenants Godbold and Tucker to select a position for our guns. I found at once that the enemy were strongly fortified. The banks on the opposite shore overlook those on this side some 20 feet at least. Earthworks could be seen in front and on both our flanks on all the prominent hills, and troops could be seen employed building others. These works were laid out with consummate skill, each one in rear commanded and strongly defended by its faces or flanks those in front, and they were so arranged that an enfilading fire could be brought on an enemy opposite in every available position he could occupy. The master-hand of General G W Smith was plainly seen in their construction. I soon discovered that there was little choice of position, there being only two hills that were at all tenable should the enemy have many guns. These I occupied, as the enclosed sketch will show, viz:

The hill on the left by two sections, under Lieutenant Godbold, and one section Parrotts, Lieutenant Barry, their support being the Twelfth Massachusetts Volunteers, Major Burbank.

The hill on the right, distant about three-fourths of a mile, directly north-northeast, was occupied by a section under Lieutenant Brockway, the support being the Twelfth Indiana, Lieutenant-Colonel Humphrey. The section under Lieutenant Molitor and the Ninth New York Militia, Lieutenant-Colonel Atterbury commanding, I left as a reserve. The cavalry I placed on the flanks and in the woods in the rear.

Having thus disposed of my force, I had the pieces run by hand to the crests of the hills, and as the last echo of the rebel band at guard mounting died away I gave them as a chorus the right piece of Lieutenant Godbold. This was a splendid shot. The shell struck nearly the center of the large fort opposite, and bursting, scattered the men on all sides, doubtless killing some. This work was being completed, and the parapet was covered with men at work. The next shot went a little to the right, and the next also. This giving them some encouragement, they returned, and opened fire with two brass 6-pounder smooth-bores, their shot and shell falling short about 30 yards. The fifth shot from Lieutenant Barry's battery blew up the magazine in that work and silenced their guns. When the magazine exploded dark objects were thrown upward, probably men, but I could not say whether they were troops or the logs of which the magazine doubtless was built. This silenced that work.

Lieutenant Barry had thrown a shell through some tents and many in the parapet, tearing it terribly, so that this work was pretty well used up, when suddenly two masked batteries enfiladed us. I made a slight change in our position and replied. These I found were also smooth-bore 6-pounders. We returned their fire briskly for some moments, when I saw two sections of a battery galloping rapidly to our right. I sent word to Lieutenant Brockway, who fired two shells at them, one killing 3 men and a horse. These were seen to fall, the distance being not over 1,500 yards on a level plain. They, however, moved on, getting in the woods, and went I could not ascertain whither, though I sent three good scouts to follow them.

Lieutenant Brockway then threw a few shot and shell at a house, said to be headquarters, and near which were some Sibley tents. By the side of one of these tents a trooper dismounted and came forward to reconnoiter. The first shell struck him down and sent his horse flying across the field. The soldier (or officer) struck did not move during the engagement, and laid there when we left, so I presume he was killed. Several shells struck around the earthwork in front and numerous horses ran from the woods in the rear. One round shot went entirely through the house, but not a gun was fired by the enemy from this point.

Two masked batteries, however, opened on Lieutenant Brockway, one a 24 or 32 pounder, which enfiladed the line of skirmishers of the Twelfth Indiana and also the battery. The first ricocheted from the crest of the hill, and making two bounds, passed immediately over Lieutenant-Colonel Humphrey, who, being on foot, fell flat, and I thought him killed. This shot passed down the rear of the whole line of the Twelfth Indiana, between them and their reserves, and several others of the same sort did the same thing, but they never moved an inch till I ordered the battery to take another position and try the earthworks on their extreme left. Hardly had they taken position and opened fire when a masked battery in front, and not over 1,000 yards distant, replied. The brush in front of this being knocked down by their fire, Lieutenant Brockway directed one of his pieces upon it with such effect that at the second fire one of the enemy's guns was knocked over and the horses of the battery seen galloping away over the fields. They fired but one more shot, and were silenced. The heavy gun still kept up its fire on the extreme left of us, and I, having shot and shell brought me from all the batteries, concluded to bring in Lieutenant Brockway and Colonel Humphrey, not knowing where the sections that had passed to our right had gone. I called them in nearer the main body to cover its flank, and started with 3 dragoons to the river's bank to ascertain, if possible, their effective force. I had not proceeded far when a battery within short range opened upon me. I therefore dismounted and crawled to the top of a hill near some low cedars. There I distinctly saw three different regiments under arms in front of their tents back of the woods, two of which had batteries, or sections of batteries, on their right. One of these regiments had tents.

In the woods were tents sufficient for three more regiments: though many of these were wedge-tents, and I might have been deceived. The fiver was very precipitous on both sides, the less so on that of the enemy, our banks being about 70 feet high. A regiment of cavalry in line was also visible. The river was, I should think, 75 or 80 yards wide. The force of the enemy I estimated at between 5,000 and 7,000 infantry, at least one regiment of cavalry, three full batteries of 6-pounder smoothbores, and two siege guns, 24-pounders. They used no rifled guns whatever.

Finding no place for my infantry to open an effective fire, even with their rifles, without great exposure from grape and canister, and knowing it was not your wish to risk a general engagement with a force greatly superior to our own and well entrenched, or even a skirmish which might be disastrous to us, I rode back and ordered the entire force back out of range, as I saw them taking a gun, drawn by eight horses, in the masked battery between the woods and their large works which we had silenced.

I had hardly moved my command when they opened there with a 24-pounder shell, but badly out of range and in our rear. They fired four or five times and ceased. I then rode to the right to examine the bridge, and had but just arrived where I proposed to reconnoiter when a masked battery with grape and canister opened so near me I could distinctly see the men working their pieces, the shot flying entirely too close to be pleasant. I changed my position, but only to find a section of light battery drive up, and unlimbering sent a round shot within 10 feet of me, splashing mud over both myself and horse. I therefore saw but little.

The bridge I could not see, as it was hidden by the bluff. Lieutenant Wyman informed me there is but one pier standing, and that somewhat damaged; that the abutments are not entire, and that the place where the second pier should be is vacant, which is between the opposite bank and the first pier. He thinks the building of the bridge would be difficult, and I agree with him, as the river is wide, and just above is a dam, which gives the stream quite a current at present. A large amount of timber was collected near the ford, though in what state of entirety I cannot say. The railroad is entire from the bridge on our side back 4 miles. From this point the rails have either been carried off by the Confederates for their own use or buried in some neighboring fields. The sleepers for about a mile are cut in two, and from there toward Warrenton Junction are removed and burned.

The houses on our road with two exceptions were entirely deserted, one of these, belonging to an officer, Lieutenant Gordon, rebel army, containing a white family, who were taking care of it for him. Hearing they were giving information to the enemy as to our scouts before, I arrested the father and son, a lad of seventeen years, and put a guard over the woman till I returned.

The other is a house of Mrs Broom. On our approach an Irishman and young Mr Broom mounted and galloped down toward the river. I sent two cavalry after them across the fields, who soon returned with both. These I kept till I received your orders to release them. The town of Rappahannock, a village of twelve or fifteen houses, is deserted.

The land hereabout is not cultivated, with the exception of two or three fields of thinly-growing wheat. Forage for man or beast is not to be had. I saw but four cows and one two-year-old colt during the trip; not a fowl of any kind at any house. Small streams of very muddy water are numerous, and some of the fields appear to have had clover in them in years gone by. The soil is clayey, and becomes a stiff paste in wet weather. The country is well wooded, generally oak, with some clumps of pines, gently undulating to the river, where it rises abruptly 60 or 70 feet on the bank.

We met no pickets or scouts of the enemy during the entire march, and returned to camp without suffering any loss whatever of men or horses. The position occupied by the enemy I should think difficult to drive them from in front. By making a march so as to throw the men in rifle pits before daylight, and thus cover them from grape and canister on this bank from the other, would force them to cross and attack or drive them back while we did so, as their works are within good rifle range.

This was your expressed wish to me, but unfortunately the cavalry reported too late for me to reach the point designated till 7 AM I should have then remained quiet until next day, throwing up works during the night, but I did not know the surrounding country. Besides, I was anxious to engage them, lest they might send re-enforcements toward Fredericksburg, which you desired us to prevent, if possible, and which I think was accomplished.

To attack on the flanks with a considerable force, particularly above on their left flank, having a good guide who knows the fords well, I should think would be successful, as they evidently feared an attack in that quarter, and therefore sent the two sections of a battery referred to in that direction. Their work seemed all open in the rear.

In conclusion, allow me to express to you my heartfelt thanks for your kindness in placing me in command of the picked men of your command, and I believe the Second Brigade (General J J Abercrombie commanding) is universally admitted to be the finest body of men in the service, and notwithstanding their fatiguing march, without any sleep at night, they, both officers and men, were ready to undergo any future amount of hardship, and all seemed anxious to acquit themselves as heroes. I would especially mention the fine gunnery of Lieutenants Godbold, Brockway, and Barry. I never saw finer practice by older officers in the US Army. Captain Gould and Lieutenant Wyman, Rhode Island cavalry, rendered much valuable assistance on the march, the former by the precision with which he conducted the advance and rear guards and flankers, and the latter as scout, bringing in much useful information from dangerous points. To Lieutenant Tucker, Maine cavalry, is due our safe-conduct to our point of destination.

The officers and men, without exception, displayed exceeding coolness while under a sharp fire of shot and shell for nearly two hours without firing a gun, which is considered the most trying position in which infantry can be placed.

I am, sir, very respectfully, your obedient servant
T M Bryan, Jr
Lieut Col Twelfth Mass Vols Comdg Reconnaissance

April 29, 1862
Letter of William Wheeler
Alexandria, VA

I came to Washington for the purpose of getting some new horses, and after I had them all picked out, and was ready to march with them to Warrenton Junction, Captain Sturmfels took it into his head that it would be very dangerous for us to march over the mountains to join the Division, and that it would be better for the

Battery to come by rail and go by way of Harper's Ferry,--an idea involving much expense to the Government. But as he insisted upon it, I had to leave the horses and go out again by rail. When I reached Warrenton Junction I found that one section of the Battery had been sent out, with other troops, on an important reconnaissance, to the Rappahannock, about ten miles off. At the same time, pretty steady firing was heard in that direction, and soon a message was sent, asking for reenforcements. A company of Maine Cavalry started off immediately, and I accompanied them. We rode and rode, and at last were almost in the enemy's claws, when an orderly overtook us, and told us that the reconnoitering party had accomplished its object and had retired. The force we had engaged consisted, in all, of about sixteen hundred infantry, two hundred cavalry, and eight pieces of artillery. They regularly surprised the enemy as he was mounting guard, silenced two of his forts, and blew up his magazines, but the force we had was too small to permit of their crossing the river and capturing the forts, so they withdrew in good order, with very little loss. On Sunday, April 20, we broke camp, put our pieces and caissons on the cars, having left Lieutenant Molitor with the cannoneers in charge of them. I took the drivers and their horses and march to Alexandria by the road. We had two days of incessant rain, and several broad and swift creeks to swim, but we made a rapid march, and got to Alexandria Tuesday afternoon, where we found everything all right, except battery wagon and forge, which were to come on the next train, but which had been kept back by the destruction of Bull Run bridge by the freshet. This kept us in Washington several days; at last they have arrived here, and I have come over with horses to bring them to Washington; tomorrow we are go on to Cumberland and so to Romney.

May 1862-September 1862
Treu bis in den Tod

<u>May 15, 1862</u>
Letter of William Wheeler
Franklin, VA

Dear Mother
The reason why I did not write while at Washington the second time was that I was in a state of chronic disgust at the way in which Battery affairs were going on. I was the only officer who was willing to duty at the barracks where our men were quartered, and was constantly there during the day-time. We had got some new horses, and as we had no proper stables, they were continually running away, and causing endless trouble and anxiety. The mere were very hard to keep in check, and would get off into the city and get drunk and neglect their duty, and then I used to get the credit of all the damage they did, and all the rows they kicked up...At last we got orders to go to Harper's Ferry. After twenty hours of very disagreeable traveling, we reached Sandy Hook, east of Harper's Ferry, and there learned that the bridge had broken down, and we had no safe means of getting across. So we were obliged to go to work and unload our horses, which had been standing, closely packed in the cars, for a day and night, and the poor things showed evident marks of biting, rubbing, and other hard treatment. We waited at Sandy Hook two days for the bridge to be completed. It is a lovely situation, on the Potomac, surrounded by high and abrupt hills. One of these I climbed, and found on the top of the Observatory which Colonel Geary[9] had built, to watch the enemy from. The view is as fine a panorama as could well be imagined. On the one side the long, pleasant valley of the Potomac, lying between ranges of high rolling land; on the other the abrupt bluffs, through which the river forced its way in some period long gone by, leaving the cloven promontories standing out, like the two halves of a broken stone, fitting into each other. Off to the west lay a beautiful stretch of level farm land, sleeping in the warm sun of a May Sabbath, the grain fields just beginning to wear a lovely green, which made a

fine contrast with the deep verdure of the pine and oak forests, which clothed the uplands. The same afternoon we received orders to prepare to march, so we packed our horses into the cars, and put all the men on board, in order that we might be able to start off as soon as the bridge was finished. We had to spend the night in the cars, after all. Passing over the bridge was no joke, as a train of coal cars which had passed just before us had caused it to sink two feet, and our train consisted of more than forty cars, very heavily loaded. Very few remained in the cars while crossing, but I thought it hardly fit for a soldier to bother himself about such things, so I confided in the loyalty and good management of the B & O RR, and rode peacefully over. We got to Martinsburg in the evening; but it was too late to see much of this outpost of secesh. Early the next morning we reached our place of destination, New Creek, which is now the principal depot of supplies for the Army of Western Virginia. There we unloaded the cars, and got everything trim. *We*, means Lieutenant Dieckmann, now in command of this Battery, and myself. He has been in command about five weeks. He does his duty right up to the handle, and it is a pleasure to work with and under such a man. I do not feel at all disturbed at having him put over me, as I certainly have not experience enough to fit me properly for a Captain of Light Artillery, and used often to be worried in my mind as to what I should do in doubtful circumstances. From New Creek we marched to Burlington, remained there a day, and joined the First Brigade of our Division, under General Stahl. The next morning we marched out of Burlington, for Petersburg, twenty-nine miles distant; after making fifteen miles the Brigade went into camp for the night, when just as we were getting supper ready, an order came on from General Fremont to hurry on all the available cavalry and artillery to Petersburg, by forced marches, so we had to harness up again and go forward, fully expecting to see the enemy by break of day. In this we were disappointed, and went into Petersburg right peacefully, about two AM. There we found General Fremont and a few troops. Our absent section of tow guns, which marched from Warrenton Junction early in April, came in with more Artillery. They had endured all the privations and dangers of that very rough march. I went down the road to meet them, and rode up with the section past General Fremont, who stood on an eminence receiving the troops. As soon as we had passed, I was accosted most heartily by my friend S from New

York, who is on General Fremont's staff. I dined with him that day, and met Colonel Albert, Chief of Staff, Fazougi, who made the great charge on Springfield with the body guard, and others who names are inseparably connected with the "Hundred Days in Missouri." Early the next day the whole concern broke up at Petersburg, and marched, post haste, in this direction to support Schenck and Milroy, who were opposing, with seven thousand men, a force of sixteen thousand under Jackson. We made about half the distance the first day, and the next were rejoicing in the prospect of a fight, as our Brigade was in the advance; but, after advancing a few miles, we learned that our generals had repelled the enemy, and retreated successfully, awaiting our arrival to drive the enemy back again. You must pardon the uncircumstantial and somewhat careless character of my letters, but my fingers have got more accustomed to the bridle rein than to the pen, and my life is so unsettled that I hardly a chance to collect my ideas before it is hurly-burly, march off again, and perhaps not another opportunity to sit quietly down for a week.

May 17, 1862
Battery Orders No. 14
Franklin, VA

In accordance with Special Orders No 9, from headquarters Mountain Department, the resignation of Captain Emil Sturmfels[10] 13 New York Batty and that of Second Lieut Carl von Linden 13 New York Batty having been accepted and they having been honorably discharged the service of the United States, they do cease to hold command as officers of this Battery from May 15, 1862
By order,
Dieckmann 1st Lieut[11]
Comdg Battery

May 23, 1862
Letter of William Wheeler
Franklin, VA

    All right, the flag has arrived in perfect safety, and my heart is full of warmest gratitude to you, for the kind interest you take in me and my men, and the noble sympathy with us in our work and suffering for the cause. You will not regret one toilsome hour spent over that beautiful work; indeed, not one stitch can be looked upon as taken in vain, when you think that it has filled rough commonplace soldiers with a sort of patriotic inspiration, and now they feel a sort of a *chivalry* when they think of their flag and the fair stranger who love their aim so well as to send it to them. The motto is exactly what I would have chosen if I had been wise to think of it, "Loyal till Death:" may we ever be so, upholding the truest and noblest of laws, our Constitution, and yet not merely with modern obedience and good citizenship, but with true old-fashioned *loyalty*. And for our German boys the motto speaks with a friendly voice, and not that of an utter stranger, "Treu bis in den Tod," is the same motto, only slightly veiled by the change in language. When I first saw the flag, my heart smote me for having imposed upon you a work so toilsome, elaborate, and costly, and had you been almost any one else I should have been sure that it had been executed with some hard feelings towards me, but I know well the true and faithful love you bear our cause, and that when you go into a thing you do it with a whole heart.

  The presentation should have taken place that very evening, but we were disappointed about getting some "Lager" or other liquid in which to drink healths to you and the banner, so I had it nicely fixed on the staff of the guide-flag, and it marched at our head to this place closely veiled, and so the company have not see it yet, for, on account of almost incessant rains and other *contretemps*, it has been impossible to find a day proper for such a *festa*. But it shall be presented very soon with appropriate ceremonies, and then you shall hear both from me, and the jolly little standard-bearer, whom I have mentally selected for the honor. I hope that Mr T will in reality carry out his promise of getting us a staff from Mount Vernon, as that would make the whole matter very complete.....

  I opine that the day of retreating in this region has for us gone by. A depot will be established here for forage and provisions, and forts are being built to protect them; we shall then press on to Stauton, repair the railroad, and from that point ever on and on. At present we are tied hand and foot by our want of food for ourselves and our horses; we are seventy miles from the nearest depot, and everything must be brought by teams, and cross swollen rivers. You will be shocked to hear that , for four days, some of the infantry regiments had not even hard bread, and some of the men were so hungry that they paid two dollars for an ordinary loaf of bread. This very day, while writing this, I have seen a crowd buying large ginger cakes at a dollar a piece. Our Battery has been better off than most other corps, but unless provisions come to-day, I expect that we shall all go hungry to bed. Our Division has had it pretty hard ever since we marched out, having been without tents for two months and a half, and we feel pretty well posted as far as *exposure* goes, but this starving is another phase of soldier life to which we must also accustom ourselves. For myself, I am in pretty good health, and fortunately have not much appetite, so I don't mind much. We lie in the very heart of the mountains, and our marches are often through right pictureques country; the chief drawback is that it rains almost every day, and when it does not rain, it is very hot, and then we have a thunder-storm in the afternoon.

General Fremont's head-quarters are quite near us; I have several acquaintances on his staff, and have received much politeness from them......You must tell L that this letter is for her, too, and that my thanks are equally hers for her interest and assistance. The work seems to go on nobly both in Virginia and further south; I had hardly hoped last fall that we should make such rapid progress. Just a year ago I was in camp at Washington[12], but it was queer soldiering compared with this. Now we have the genuine article, all but the fighting, and God grant that we may have that too one of these days...

May 25, 1862
Letter of William Wheeler
Franklin, VA

Dear John
I saw in the "Tribune," yesterday, a speech by Parson Brownlow in which he speaks of the miserable condition of the Union men in East Tennessee, and the confidence that he felt in speedy succor from Fremont's Corps. I fear that he trusts in a broken reed, for, at present, that army corps (not so very strong either) has it hands full enough with Jackson's force, and it is in a somewhat desperate condition, being unable to go either back or forward, and standing a fair chance of starving if they continue to lie here. There is no depot of provisions here, and in fact none within seventy miles, and there are plenty of bushwhackers between here and New Creek to cut off our trains. All the infantry regiments, until yesterday, were without bread or crackers, coffee or sugar, for four days, and many of the poor fellows came over to us and begged for a piece of cracker to satisfy their hunger. We were better off, and by careful management succeeded in holding out until yesterday afternoon when the train

arrived, with thirty barrels of crackers for 15,000 men! Even that was attacked on the road by guerillas, and three or four of the covering party shot. Our poor horses far worse; they have not had a proper feed for twelve days, and not four rations of grain in all that time. They manage to keep themselves alive by nibbling a little grass, but that gives no strength. We send out wagons every day into the surrounding country, but the country is so poor, as a grain raising district, that they come back with the poorest mockery of a few ears of corn. I am afraid that our men do not confine themselves to the legitimate object for which they are sent out, for various articles make their appearance which not even the largest stretching could bring under the head of forage. My own quarters became adorned the other day with a set of blue cups, plates, and saucers; a large milk pan and coffee mill turned up yesterday, and I strongly suspect that the very comfortable bench on which I write, was once the ornament of some Methodist or Presbyterian house of worship. Sitting on this bench is the nearest approach I have made to going to church for some months. M W's banner reached me in safety! I have not presented it because no beer has been attainable. The banner is really exquisite, the richest and elaborate one I ever saw: on one side a wreath of oak and laurel, with crossed cannon and U S inside; on the other, a magnificent eagle, with a scroll and Excelsior on it in his mouth; underneath the motto in German characters, "Loyal till Death," above the number 13. The Generals of the Division have seen it, and pronounced it superb. I am afraid it was a very borous and expensive undertaking, but the effort is fully appreciated.

June 12, 1862
Letter of William Wheeler
Mount Jackson, VA

Dearest Mother
After the passage of about ten days I write you from the same place from which I wrote John, but you must not think that this interval of time has been spent in rest here. On the contrary, we have made forced marches in the direction of Stanton, have fought a battle, and have made a rapid retreat, and reached this place at about noon to-day, a thoroughly used up set both of men and horses. However, I managed to snatch a little sleep this afternoon, and feel quite away this evening, so I eagerly seize this opportunity to let you hear from me, not knowing what the morrow may bring forth, nor how suddenly

we may have to march again........Be sure that I shall take good care of my health, and shall not expose my life except when duty demands it, and if I fall in the performance of that duty, you will know that is so pleased the Director of all events, and will not sorrow unduly at my dying in the noblest way, and for the highest and best cause. You will wish to know something about our recent movements. About eight days ago the pontoon bridge over the Shenandoah at that point was finished, and our army moved across and marched rapidly after Jackson, who was still but a short distant in advance of us. If we could have saved the bridge and if the rains had not raised the river too high to prevent our immediately rebuilding it, we should have caught this prince of bushwhackers, together with the train and prisoners which he took from Banks. But the elements seemed completely against us, and we lost him by about a day. The second day's march brought us to Harrisonburg. Here we shod our horses, and go everything in readiness for the approaching fight. On Saturday night our cavalry made an attack on the Rebs, but were met by a much larger force than they had expected, and were driven back with loss. On Sunday we marched out in full force to beat up his quarters; the women gazed at us, as we marched through the town, their eyes streaming with tears, for it was their own husbands and sons and brothers that we were to meet in mortal combat. By 10 AM the heavy thunder of the cannon showed that the work had commenced, and that our advance was engaged, and soon the rolling fire of musketry told us that it had come to closer quarters. General Schenck's Ohio Brigade had the extreme right wing; then came General Milroy's Virginia, then our First Brigade, the Second, on the left wing; this was our position in the afternoon. Our right wing pushed their left wing back; in the centre the fire was very hot, and Blenker's own regiment, the Eighth New York, suffered dreadfully, being exposed to a galling fire from a whole brigade under cover, while they stood out in a wheat field; still they maintained their ground gallantly and were well supported by Schirmer's Battery, which did great execution. On the left the Third Brigade was just going to charge the enemy, and were aching for the encounter, when they were withdrawn and we were ordered up at double quick to support them. We had got into a piece of meadow among the woods, and were abut to clear the woods and turn the enemy's flank, when our Brigade was also withdrawn, not having fired a shot. Our Battery had no orders to retire, so we stood still while the infantry drew to the rear. For a little while we were in great peril,--we were between the fire of one of our own batteries and the enemy's infantry,--still our men were very cool and collected, and only wanted a chance to do something. Towards night the firing ceased, and we encamped on the border of the battle-field, our Battery covering the left wing from the top of a high hill. The enemy sloped during the darkness, and in the morning was "non est inventus," so we, who were in the extreme advance, lost the chance of distinguishing ourselves. It was a pretty equal fight. Our loss in killed and wounded must have been six hundred. That of the enemy could not have been less than one thousand, as our artillery cut some of his regiments up badly. Had our two brigades, which hardly fired a shot, been allowed to go into the fight, the results would have been probably been far different, and our victory would have been thorough and complete. Still it cannot be denied that this Jackson is a man of decided genius, and that very few in our army are fit to compete with him. Thus on Tuesday he fought our army and prevented our further advance, in the night he crossed the bridge, which he burned after him to prevent us from following, and, having received reënforcements under Longstreet, beat back Shields who was advancing on the other side of the river. On Tuesday his combined forces returned against us, now treble our number, and we were forced to retreat. Our Brigade was the rear-guard, and I had the honor to cover the extreme rear with my section. The road was about the worst I ever saw. When I had got about six miles I found several of our heavy caissons almost hopelessly bemired; the captain told me to send my section on, and gave me the pleasant task of fetching on those caissons. It was an awful job, as you may imagine. As the horses had had no feed for two days, they were very weak; but I persevered, and march through Harrisonburg at three in the morning, with everything safe and sound. A rest until 8 AM, and then we marched again, luckily on a good road, or our poor horses would have fallen dead; here we hope for rest and feed and food and reënforcements: it is also said that General Sigel is to take command of the Corps. If he does, I feel the most perfect confidence that we shall end this doubtful campaign with brilliant victories. I will not harrow up your sensibilities by speaking of the horrors of the battlefield. It was bad enough to have seen them without repeating. I had an opportunity, during a halt, of tending a whole barnfull of our wound soldiers, some of them with three bullets in them; one poor fellow pierced by seven, and yet not seriously injured. They all agreed in the statement that they had been very kindly treated by most of the enemy among whom they fell,--a few acting barbarously, but the most with tender and delicate humanity. This makes me feel more kindly to our erring brothers than before. Would that we could join hands and be friends once more. I am in excellent health, but have not known what it was to be dry. At night I have flung myself down by the nearest fire without blankets and have slept sweetly, regardless of deep mud or pouring rain. I love you all as much as eve, if I am a shabby, muddy soldier worn our with hard work, and unable, from sheer fatigue, to write you an interesting or satisfactory letter.

June 14, 1862
Battery Orders No. 15
Mount Jackson, VA

Private Peter Duffy is hereby promoted sergeant of this batter vice Garrett reduced. He will be obeyed & respected accordingly.
Julius Dieckmann
Capt Comdg Battery

June 15, 1862
Letter of William Wheeler
Mount Jackson, VA

As usual, my first thought on reading your letter, and the pleasant accounts of social life and family life which it contained, was, How strange all this is! And can it be possible that I shall ever again be civilized, and take my place again among old friends and dear relations, who have never had this primitive nomadic life to live. But in one point I can sympathize with you thoroughly, and that is in love for outdoor life, and for the fresh, young, bride-like earth, dressed in the robe of this loveliest of seasons. I find great difficulty sometimes in realizing that anything is awry or at war here in this beautiful valley where all is so green and fair and bright. For many days we had almost incessant rain, and life on the march was not highly agreeable, especially as at night we had to lie down in mud or water. But now the rainy season seems to have come to an end, and the summer has fairly set in, with wild flowers in the woods, and fragrant clover in the fields, and beautiful starry skies at night, and fee with the German poet, "How art thou still so fair, thou wide, wide world!" A nomadic, gypsy sort of life it is, even the luxury of a tent being only allowed when we camp for several days, as at the present time.

I should have greatly enjoyed being with you at the Easter festival, to see the flowers and hear the anthem, and join with all my heart in the service of the day. I spent Easter Sunday at Catlett's Station in a pouring rain, putting the Battery on the cars, to be taken to Washington, and on Pentecost Sunday we were fighting all day at Cross Keys. In fact Sunday is very seldom a day of rest with us, and it often comes and goes without our being aware of it. When peace comes again, I shall appreciate Sunday more than ever.

June 23, 1862
Battery Orders No. 17
Strasburg, VA

I   Orderly Sergt Thomas H Fennessy is hereby appointed acting 2nd Lt in this Battery, vice Lieut Albert Molitor detailed to Gen Sigel's staff.
II   Sergeant Joseph Bohn is hereby appointed acting 1st Sgt in this Battery vice Fennessy, acting Lieut.
III   Corporal Henry Tintenfass is hereby appointed acting Sergt in this Battery vice Bohn, acting 1st Sgt.
They will be obeyed & respected accordingly
Julius Dieckmann Capt
Comdg 13 NY Batty

Letter of William Wheeler
Strasburg, VA

My Dear Auntie
If I could succeed in looking upon this whole campaign as a sort of summer excursion or jaunt, nothing could be more pleasant and enjoyable. I have seen some of the finest scenery in the country, and that in sunshine and storm, at midnight and at sunrise, have live always in the open air and in perfect health, spite of privations and exposure to rain and dew; have had the additional spice of a little danger occasionally, and the sensation of a bold, free life, and yet there has always been something which came in to spoil my enjoyment; it may have been the rough and reckless men we have under us, but more than this was the feeling that we were invaders, laying waste a fair and blooming country, and that our opponents were men fighting to save their firesides and their homesteads. It is by no means agreeable to deprive farmers of their grain and hay, and to

carry off favorite horses amid the tears and supplications of the women folk; and you can yourself imagine how hard it was when we came back from Cross Keys, to see in Harrisonburg and New Market the women dressed in black and weeping as if their hearts would break. I cannot help mentally transferring the whole trouble to the Northern country, and thinking how I should feel if the "Louisiana Tigers," or some such notorious corps, should have a chance to march through Connecticut. Indeed I am sometimes in danger of forgetting the real reason and object of the war, because my mind is constantly occupied with the superficial losses and miseries which are daily before my eyes, but which "endure but for a moment," and which, when we succeed, will bring for us "a more exceeding weight of glory," in a preserved Constitution and established laws. Just at present our prospects are not as good as they were, and unless the North responds promptly to the President's call for more troops, it is not unlikely that the Union men now in Virginia may be crushed and driven back by mere weight of numbers. The size of our army has been greatly overrated,--all the men in hospitals, in garrison, and in camps in the Northern states having been counted to swell the number, while the Southern force has been correspondingly underrated....This is a superb region as far as scenery goes. Right above us is a ridge crowned by a natural fortress, with towers and bastions as complete as can be, undoubtedly one of the highest points in Virginia. On every side there roll off beautiful deep valleys, full of orchards, and farmhouses, and fields of grain; and on the higher slopes are countless blackberry pastures, just like those in which my soul use to delight among the Catskills. Children seem to be the greatest wealth of this region; the soil is not first-rate and farming has scanty products, but children of all ages, from the little lisping toddler to the dark-eyed boy of sixteen, not quite old enough "to go with Jackson." If animosities are transmitted to the next generation we shall have a good crop of rebels in this region...I think of you all at home a great deal, especially just this week, Commencement, when the old college friends are coming together at New Haven, and another class goes away from its classic home.

June 25, 1862
Battery Orders No. 18
 Cedar Creek, VA

The following non-commissioned officers are hereby appointed in this Battery.

Corporal James Clark as Sergeant
Private　Alexander Ballmann as Corporal
"　　　　William H Garrett　　"　"
"　　　　Theodore Guerts　　"　"
"　　　　William W Mabies　"　"
"　　　　Thielman Moritz　　"　"
"　　　　Frederick A Nort　　"　"
"　　　　Francis F Roache　　"　"
They will be obeyed and respected accordingly
Julies Dieckmann Capt
Comdg 13 NY Battery

**Leave of absence request to Gen. Adolph Von Steinwehr, 2nd Brigade, 2nd Division, 11th Army Corps
Cedar Creek, VA**

Sir
I have the honor to make application for a leave of absence for the recovery of my health, the state of which renders me unfit for duty as well appear by the annexed certificate of Dr T Millspangh, Surgeon 13 NY Battery. I would respectfully ask for a leave of absence for thirty days.
　　Respectfully
　　Julius Dieckmann
　　Capt 13 NY Battery

**June 26, 1862
Letter of Dr. T. Millspangh, Surgeon, 13th New York Artillery
Cedar Creek, VA**

Capt. Julius Dieckmann of the 13th NY Battery having applied for a certificate on which to ground an application for leave of absence. I do hereby certify that I have carefully examined this officer and find that he is suffering from the last 5 weeks from Rheumatism and that in consequence thereof he is, in my opinion, unfit for duty. I further declare my belief that he will not be able to resume his duties in a less period than thirty days.
　　T Millspangh
　　Surgeon 13th NY Battery

July 19, 1862
Battery Orders No. 19
Shencks Farm, VA

I   Sergeant John Reinhard is hereby reduced to the ranks for disobedience of orders and disrespectful conduct.
II   Corporal Thielman Moritz is hereby promoted sergeant of this Battery vice Reinhard reduced. He will be obeyed & respected accordingly.
Wm Wheeler
1st Lt Comdg Batty

July 22, 1862
Report of Col. William Lloyd, 2nd Brigade, 2nd Division, 1st Army Corps
Luray, VA

General: In obedience to your order of the 20th I proceeded yesterday with the troops assigned to my command for the purpose, and took possession of and now occupy Luray, with the Seventy-third Pennsylvania, five companies of the Sixty-eighth Pennsylvania [New York] Infantry, and one section of Dieckmann's battery, all under command of Lieutenant-Colonel Muhleck, of the Seventy-third; the Sixth Ohio and mountain howitzers, under command of Major Stedman, and the Fourth New York Mounted Rifles, Lieutenant-Colonel Nazer. We are now encamped on the high ground immediately south of Luray. Captain Abell, Sixth Ohio Cavalry, is acting as provost-marshal, and with his company as provost guard occupy the court-house, and the house lately vacated by the rebel citizen Bost is used as a hospital, under charge of Surgeon Finch, Sixth Ohio Cavalry.

I directed a reconnaissance to be made this morning at 5 o'clock to Columbia Bridge, under command of Lieutenant-Colonel Muhleck, with six companies Seventy-third Infantry and four companies Sixth Ohio Cavalry, Captain Barber, and the section of artillery. They reached the ford without meeting the enemy. Captain Barber crossed with the cavalry, and scoured the woods and roads for 2 miles south of the ford. No appearance of the enemy was found, and no indications that any scouts, patrols, or other parties of the enemy have crossed the ford for ten days.

I directed a reconnaissance at the same hour this morning to the White House Ford, under command of Lieutenant-Colonel Nazer, Fourth New York Mounted Rifles, with four companies Sixty-eighth Infantry and four companies Fourth New York and the two howitzers. They arrived at the ford about 9 o'clock. Some rebel cavalry, not more than 7 appeared across the river shortly after the party reached the ford within rifle range. We learned that 15 rebel cavalry had crossed the ford yesterday morning and recrossed about 9 o'clock; that about 40 cavalry crossed the night of the 20th and recrossed about 2 the next morning. We know that this party rode through the town of Luray and back the same night, shouting for Jeff Davis, but committing no other indiscretion. I accompanied the party under Lieutenant-Colonel Muhleck about 4 miles, when, with my adjutant, Captain Richart, and a small escort of cavalry, I proceeded to White House Ford, reaching the river a mile above the ford, and reaching the ford shortly after the arrival there of the party under Lieutenant-Colonel Nazer. A few shots were exchanged with the rebel cavalry, but a shot or two from the howitzers started their party back toward the gap. This ford is 4 miles from Luray, on the turnpike leading to New Market, and about 6 miles from the gap, which overlooks the valley west of the Peaked and Massanutten Mountains. Columbia Bridge Ford (the bridge being destroyed) is about 8 miles from Luray. Both these fords are at present passable for troops of any class.

From these expeditions and the most reliable information I could obtain I am satisfied that no rebel force of any description at present occupies this valley. The rebel cavalry that have visited Luray and sometimes annoyed the Sixth Cavalry are portions of some four or five companies that make Harrisonburg their rendezvous, and from time to time send to New Market and thence into this valley one or two companies to observe our movements.

With as little delay as possible I will direct a suitable expedition into the gap to observe the valley from New Market to Mount Jackson. I will also send patrols southward daily, which will enable me, I hope, to give you the earliest possible intelligence of any appearance of the enemy in this direction.

Very respectfully, your obedient servant,
W R Lloyd
Colonel, Commanding Second Brigade

July 29, 1862
Letter of William Wheeler
Sperryville, VA

As we are lying quiet here, enjoying both rest and fine weather, I cannot resist the temptation of answering your last most kind letter, as I do know how soon the orderly may come dashing up with orders for us to be ready to march in two hours. The last installment of letters was a very pleasant one to me, only my pleasure was considerably diminished by the news that John was also coming out to fight, and that in the Infantry[13]. The fatigues, exposures, and dangers of that branch of service are so great that I am very anxious lest he should find himself unable to bear them, and what would you all do at home if anything should happen to him? I think that when you all have only tow boys, and no one else to lean upon, the most self-sacrificing patriotism could not call upon you to let us both go. I have spoken more at length in my letter to him, but I suppose that he has too decidedly put his hand to the plough to think of turning back....the North must hurry up and send down those three hundred thousand new recruits, or else the rebels may succeed in making a dash at our broken and reduced columns, forcing their way through and perhaps seriously menacing Washington and Baltimore.....If our armies in Virginia are defeated, the apathetic people of the North may have the satisfaction of seeing reckless Southerners in their streets, and the farmers in rich New York may see their grain taken to feed the cavalry of Ashby and Hampton. I should greatly dislike to hear of their camping on the green at New Haven, and eating down the elms to make their fires.....Strange to say the premonition I expresses on the first page has come true. An order came a few minutes ago for us to be ready to march at 6 AM to-morrow morning, with one days' rations, probably to support our advance posts, which have been attacked and driven back. It is nearly midnight, but there is a stir of men dressing rations, and a light at the fires where they are cooking them. I must close this letter in order to take a little sleep, before the toils of to-morrow. Think of me as healthy and hearty, and as loving you with all my heart.

August 4, 1862
Battery Orders No. 20
Sperryville, VA

Private John Reinhard is herby appointed sergeant of the 4th Detachment 13 New York Battery vice Clark reduced. He will be obeyed and respected accordingly.
Julius Dieckmann Capt
Comdg 13 NY Battery

August 17, 1862
Letter of William Wheeler
camp near Rapidan River, Culpepper Co., VA

Dear Grandfather
Just now we are having a quite unexpected rest. I had supposed that, after our long sojourn at Thornton's Gap and Sperryville, we would go right on when once started, and not stop until we should be absolutely compelled to do so, but there seems recently to have been a change in the war policy, and McClellan is retiring from Richmond, apparently to concentrate upon us here, as Burnside has already done...... I suppose that you have already seen full accounts in the papers of the battle of Slaughter Mountain, as it is called, and properly so, for it was a slaughter of General Banks' troops, and nothing else. We were stirred up at Sperryville with orders to march forthwith, and at 6 PM we were in readiness, but did not get off before 10 PM. We marched all night and all the next day, through excessive heat and dust. As we approached Culpepper Court House, we heard very heavy cannonading and musketry fire, but did not push on to the battlefield, because it was already too late to do any good, and the troops were excessively fatigued. The next day we arrived, early in the morning, at the field, having marched again in the night, and found that General Banks had substantially maintained his position, but that his troops had suffered dreadfully from a contest with such overwhelming numbers as had been poured upon them. Had they retreated to Culpepper Court House, they would have met the advance brigades of our Corps, and the enemy, if he had dared to follow, would have been thoroughly whipped. The loss of life that occurred in so shot a time is almost unparalleled in the history of war, and it must have been one of the hottest engagements of the campaign. I see that the Fifth Connecticut suffered severely, and that

my friend Edward Blake, Major in that regiment, was wounded and taken prisoner. I wish that we had been pushed more rapidly forward, in spite of heat and fatigue, and then should have doubtless have succeeded in sparing many valuable lives to the country. Sunday, the day after the battle, was excessively hot, and very little was done beyond scouting and skirmishing. Monday was devoted to bringing off the wounded and burying the dead, hostilities having been suspended for that purpose. Our men and the rebels mingle freely together on the battlefield, and conversed; many found old friends and school fellows, and even relatives, in the opposing forces. The piles of dead men and horses, in all possible forms of mutilation, made a horrible sight, and it was not until late in the evening that the dead soldiers were all interred. I think that General Pope's official account is quite fair and impartial, and that the rebels lost the most, though not perhaps very much. We lay near the battlefield, and then marched a few miles to this place, a couple of miles from the Rapidan River, in the midst of a beautiful country, which rolls and undulates like the waves of the sea, and is finely wooded with superb oak forest... I am much disturbed by John's move in the recruiting line. I do not think that the most ardent patriotism could demand more than one from our family, and when both are gone who will look after mother and the girls, to say nothing of you and Aunt Elizabeth? It is a thing that may easily happen, that neither of us will ever come back. I think that very few of the army now in the field will ever see their homes again; the new conscripts will win the glory of finishing the war, and will carry home our banners in triumph. But the work must and will go on in spite of all temporary considerations and family ties, and the sooner the good people of the North come to see and acknowledge this, the better...... I sometimes find myself indulging in most unpatriotic wishes that I was under the dear old elms once more, if only for a little space. I am only pretty well; but I take the best care of myself that I can, and hope soon to be better.

Letter of William Wheeler
camp near Rapidan River, Culpepper Co., VA

Your letter was such a nice, kind, jolly one, that it put me immediately into the writing vein; and besides my opportunities for writing are so few and so widely separated just at present, and the chances of continued life and ability to talk to you are so uncertain, that I have adopted the principle of writing whenever I feel like it, without regard for retributive justice. And especially should I dislike to go down to Hades with your letter unanswered on my hands; my ghostly form would continually revisiting "the glimpses of the moon," and vainly endeavoring, with a phantom hand, to indite a shadowy epistle to one, still most substantially in the flesh. All that you told me about New Haven, the Commencement festivities, the boating party; etc., was intensely interesting to me, in spite of the frightful aggravation I experienced inwardly at being unable to be there with you and help you.

Oh, for an oar in my hands once more, a crowd of the old sort following my stroke, and a few ladies, also of the old-fashioned sort, to make a good solid boat-load worth the pulling of *Atlanta*, *Thuli*, and *Una* men? Just one pull with such surroundings to South end, a lazy day spent in pleasant talk, and watching the long sun-lit ripple rolling in from the Sound; a moon-lit row back to the dear old city, with plenty of songs, and the next day you may put me, like Uriah the Hittite, in the forefront of the battle, and let me take my chance.

You interested me very deeply with what you said abut what you had seen and heard in the hospitals. I shall be curious to hear from you from you some of those stories,--write them down, if you think there is any danger of you forgetting them. And, my dear child, I felt so very grateful to you for the interest you felt in our poor, wounded boys; it is the cup of cold water to the disciples and supporters of our great cause, and it shall by no means lose its rewards.

I have some queer times foraging in this part of the country. The soldiers interpret General Pope's order "to subsist on the country they pass through," in the most liberal manner, and I have had the pleasure of knocking several such extensive raids on the head, and driving off these self-made "quartermasters" and "commissaries of subsistence." At one house, I interfered in favor of a sheep, some bee-hives, and the potato-patch, and was rewarded by being invited into the house, where I met the prettiest girl I have seen in Virginia,--a real stunner, with light brown hair and perfect features, and an arm like the Venus of the capitol. I grieve to say that I was quite enthralled by this she-rebel, and the next night, being out foraging for hay, I stayed to supper, and come home so late that I found a party just saddling to go out and rescue me from the bush-whackers. The captain gave me three days on guard, but I think that it was worth it on the whole. Then, to cap the climax, being sent down to Culpepper after stores, I stopped there yesterday morning on my way back and took breakfast.

If we have occasion to retreat, I shall manage to get wounded near that house, and have "sweet Maud Muller" (I don't know her real name), to take care of me. Joking apart, I have nothing in the present to interest me, and nothing in the future to hope for, except an honorable ending for myself, and the full success of the cause. My immediate surroundings and associations are very, very hard to endure, but I shall hold on, praying at least for health, if not happiness.

I picked up a letter on the battle field the other day, from a young married lady in Georgia to her two brothers in the army, and it might have been from you, so pleasant and naïve was the style. She chatted about her little baby, and how it resembled its young uncles, etc., and my heart smote me when I thought that perhaps their life-blood had soaked the very ground where I stood.

September 4, 1862
Battery Orders No. 21
D'Anglais, VA

Private Edward Trafford, Private John A Rush are hereby appointed corporals in this Battery for good conduct in the Battle of Aug 29 & 30 1862 at Bull Run.
Julius Dieckmann Capt
Comdg 13 NY Battery

September 5, 1862
Letter of William Wheeler
near Chain Bridge, VA

Dearest Mother
I take the first opportunity offering itself to give you intelligence of my entire safety and welfare, if it be only a few lines. I was in the hottest of the fight all day Friday, and all the afternoon of Saturday, and exposed myself considerably to keep our boys up to the scratch, but got nothing except a slight scrape on the top of the head from a piece of shell, and a bruise on the cheek from a canister ball; both of these little wounds are almost quite well, and almost without medical assistance, and I sincerely recognize the protecting hand of God in my preservation. The Battery highly praised by General Sigel. As soon as I get the chance I will write again. This must suffice for the present.

Very much love to all.

September 9, 1862
Report of Dr. J.Y. Cantwell, Surgeon, 82nd Ohio Regiment
Mary Hall's Farm, VA

1st Lt Albert Molitor, detailed to Maj General F Sigel's staff, having applied for a certificate on which to ground an application for leave of absence, I do hereby certify that I have carefully examined this officer, and find that he is suffering from prungo and chronic diarrhea. And that, in consequence thereof, he is in my opinion unfit for duty. I further declare my belief that he will not be able to resume his duties in a less period than fifteen days.

Leave of absence request to Maj. Gen. Franz Sigel, commanding 1st Corps, Army of Virginia
Mary Hall's Farm, VA

General
Respectfully referring to the within testimony of Surg Cantwell I request you will grant a leave of absence for fifteen days to Washington to the undersigned.
Very respectfully
Yours most obedient Servt
Albert Molitor
1st Lt. detailed to the staff of the 1st Corps d' Armee

September 10, 1862
Letter of William Wheeler
camp near Fort Ethan Allen, VA

Dearest Mother
Your welcome letter has just come to hand, giving me assurance that you had got my hastily-penned note, and were relieved from all immediate and harassing anxiety on my account. I did the best I could communicate with you, but on account of our being so constantly on the move, officers always in the saddle, and horses in the harness, it was impossible to call the next five minutes our own; so I could only send you a pair of words. I think you can hardly fail to be interested in my experiences for the last three weeks. My last letter to N H was written to Annie[14] from the banks of the Rapidan, and in

that I remember I spoke of the speedy advance of our forces in the direction of Gordonsville; how ignorant I was of the state of affairs was proved by the fact that the very next morning we had orders to be ready to march to the rear in an hour, and before the sun went down our long, slow-moving trains were drawing off in the direction of Culpepper Court House. Our Corps, which had the post of honor in the rear, drew out into the road, and lay there all that night, and a good part of the next day, waiting until the enormous trains and the Corps in front of us should have reached the positions assigned to them. We passed through the foul region of Slaughter Mountain, with great offense to the eye and nose; the men had all been buried, but the pile of slaughtered horses still showed where batteries had stood in the hottest fire. We passed through Culpepper that afternoon, and, by dint of steady marching, came to the Rappahannock in the night. Here we took up position to cover the passage of the river, and stood to our guns until about noon the next day, when we, too, passed over, and the bridge was burned behind us. Thence on from Jeffersonville to White Sulphur Springs,--the Saratoga of the South; but the place of the summer loungers in the streets was filled with soldiers, and the sick men lay in the great hotels which had, two years before, been so full of "dance and delight." Here we hoped for a day's rest, so much needed by both men and horses , but we were allowed only one good sleep, and then off again, after breakfast, to the Rappahannock, along whose banks a fierce, long-range artillery duel was to be kept up for about a week. The first day our four rifled guns came into action, my six-pounders being kept in reserve as too short range. One of our gunners made a splendid shot that day, at over a mile, and dismounted a secesh gun, but this feat was ascribed in the papers to Captain Schirmer's Battery, as have a dozen things that our Battery had done. The only loss that our artillery sustained that day was Captain Buell[15], commanding the reserve artillery, and just the man we could worst afford to lose. A shell passed through his horse, wounding him in both legs, and then the horse fell on him, and caused internal injuries, of which he died that same evening. He was really a charming fellow, quiet, gentle, yet firm and active; his whole Battery loved him to devotion, and I enjoyed his society greatly, ever since we came under his command at Sperryville For the next two days we had plenty of marching, but little fighting. The next day we were separated from the reserve artillery, and sent to General Milroy's, and ever since we have been connected with this king of the bush-whackers. We had not had occasion to complain that we have been neglected, in getting our full ration of fighting. In fact, before we had been with him two hours he had the rifled guns in full operation on a hill, while I crept forward with my two pieces towards a hill well in the advance. We were well covered by our own pieces until we reached the brow of the hill, and came into battery in an apple orchard; we drove the enemy's cavalry out of the woods, but could not do much to the enemy's battery, which was too long range for us, and their balls and shells tipped the trees about us in a lively manner. The chief of artillery saw that we did not reach them, and ordered us down the hill again; pretty soon Sigel came along and saw my section standing idle, and inquired the reason; upon hearing that Captain Schirmer had sent me back, he said, "Take your section up on the hill again and fire away;" so up I went to a part of the hill more directly in front of the enemy's batteries. Instead of stopping on the summit, I had my guns run down the easy slope towards the enemy, by hand, and thus advanced until I was several hundred yards in front of our lines, and had brought the hostile batteries completely within my range; then we went to work, and, by keeping sharp look-out, succeeded in shutting up every gun which the Rebs planted in front of us. Once they ran a gun well up before a bank and masked it, so that it fired three times before I could exactly find it; when I did, I laid my guns right for the muzzle, and it assumed a dignified silence. By afternoon our Brigade moved further on, and we had no more work of importance till the evening before Friday's battle. Then we shelled the woods where the enemy lay, just at nightfall, and the shells with their burning fuses made a beautiful firework. That night each cannoneer slept at his post by the gun, and we all snoozed soundly, for we knew that we should have plenty to do the next day, and having seen Jackson's handiwork at Manassas, were right anxious to go on and catch the Valley Fox, whom we had been so long hunting. Alas, it turned out too much like the story of the man who caught the Tartar. Up early, placed our Battery in a commanding position, and engaged a hostile battery for an hour or tow, until we drove them away, and then advanced to their position. (N B This credited in the newspaper to Schirmer's Battery.) Beyond was a high ridge, on which the enemy had many batteries planted, and a large part of his force concentrated to attack this. Milroy now advanced with his Brigade, and our Battery alone, being only supported by long range fire from batteries on the ridge we had left. He entered a piece of open ground, behind the woods which sheltered him from the batteries on the hill, and throwing skirmishers and a regiment into the woods on the right, tried to carry the railroad embankment in his front. The Battery was not placed in position, but just stood close behind the infantry in column, utterly useless, and itself in danger. After a sharp fight in the woods, our men had to retire, when suddenly a couple of rebel brigades came swarming over the railroad embankment, and our Brigade had to beat a hasty retreat. We did not move until the enemy were pretty near, and then we went back through the opening, the bullets flying in great abundance. Just as my second piece had passed the opening, a shot brought down one of the pole horses, and stopped us short; my first thought was, "The piece is lost;" my next, "It shall be sold dear," and I sprang down, and with the assistance of one man, unlimbered it. I seized the rammer, and we had one shot fired before the other officers know that we were in danger. The other cannoneers came up, but I held on to the rammer, and did Number One in pretty lively style. The other pieces came into battery on a hill behind us, and opened fire; then the batteries above us began to operate at short range, and between shells, canister, and musketry fire, we had it hot enough. But we soon drove the infantry back to the embankment, and gave our infantry a chance to halt and reform. A reserve horse had been brought up with harness, and was hitched in under the hottest fire, when all was ready, I had the piece limbered up, and followed the rest of the Battery to the opening in the fence. Just at the opening, the reserve horse was shot two or three times, and had to cut him out of the harness and carry the branch myself for some distance. While acting as Number One, I was struck on the cheek by a canister shot and thought I was hurt, but it swelled two days and then passed off. A splinter of shell struck me on the head, cutting three little holes, and burying itself next to the bone. This grew very sore, and the doctor, after taking out a piece of my felt hat, which was driven in also, tried to extract the metal, but could not do it. However, I have poulticed it, and it has healed up entirely. (This exploit of ours, which saved the Brigade, is attributed in the newspaper to Hampton's Pittsburgh Battery[16]. I don't care a cent for newspaper praise, but it comes hard for the men to have others steal their well-earned laurels.) In the afternoon we were sent to an important position until our ammunition was exhausted. The fire was really infernal, and we lost several men killed or badly wounded, and many horses. I was astonished to find that the idea of danger was so little present with me, even in the hottest of fire: but I suppose that it was because I kept myself occupied and worked hard at my duty. A shell struck the piece I was working, and ploughed a great furrow down it; but I hardly noticed it at the time. In fact, I think that the extreme front is the safest as well as the most honorable place. I have seen many a man knocked over by these bounding shots, when he thought he was all safe in the rear. We are hoping soon to get into Washington to refit, as we have lost many horses, and want some of our guns mended. In *our* General (Sigel) we have the most entire confidence, and his corps will follow him anywhere. I suppose you have heard from John about our meeting at the end of the Long Bridge. It was truly a delight, and a joy inexpressible to me, after these many months, during which I have seen no friendly face, grasped no friendly hand. I felt proud of the old fellow, looking so neat in his fatigue uniform, and doing his duty in so prompt and business-like manner. He seems to have a find company. What a startling contrast they would make, if ranged alongside of my poor travel-worn, battle-weary raga-muffins. I need rest greatly, and to recruit my health. I would rather stand by my post, and trust to time and rest to heal me, than to go into hospital. I am afraid this egotistical letter may have wearied you.

September 12, 1862
Report of Brig. Gen. Robert Milroy, Independent Brigade, 1st Corps
near Fort Ethan Allen, VA

Sir: I have the honor to submit the following report of the movements of my command since the departure from Woodville, Va., on August 8, 1862:

From the evening of the 13th to the 18th remained in camp on the banks of Crooked Creek. Nothing of importance occurred during the interval excepting the capture, on the 16th, of a lieutenant and 3 privates of the Second Virginia while on picket by a party of rebel cavalry. At 4 PM of the 18th received orders to prepare to fall back as far as Sulphur Springs, the enemy being reported as advancing in great force from Richmond. I soon had my brigade in readiness, and remained under arms until 4 AM, when orders were received to move with my brigade in the rear, General Pope's command having required all night to withdraw.

On the 19th we marched all day, passing through Culpeper, and en-camping at midnight about 4 miles north of that place, on the Sulphur Springs road.

On the 20th at daylight resumed march toward Sulphur Springs, reaching there at 5 PM without any signs of the enemy in our rear.

Started on the morning of the 21st, with brigade in advance of corps, in the direction of Rappahannock Station, to re-enforce Banks and McDowell, who had thus far prevented the enemy from crossing the river at that point, and found a heavy artillery engagement going on. We arrived about noon, and were ordered to rest near General Pope's headquarters until a position in the field could be assigned me. About 2 PM I was ordered to advance toward the river and take position on the right of King's division. After advancing about a half mile my brigade was divided, yourself, general, taking two regiments along the road, myself moving with the other two through the fields, a small squad of rebel cavalry, who had been watching our movements from the edge of the woods in front of us, fleeing at our approach.

Upon arriving at the edge of the woods I halted my column and allowed the sharpshooters and skirmishers some five minutes in advance. I then started my two regiments, crossed the woods, about a quarter of a mile in width, and halted, finding ourselves on the right of the line of skirmishers then engaged, established by General Patrick, of King's division. Remaining here some two hours, the enemy making no demonstration, I fell back to the fields in the rear of the woods to rest for the night. In the mean while you, general, had placed my infantry and battery in position near the road on my right. Thus disposed of, we rested until the following morning.

On the morning of the 22d I was early ordered to take the advance in the direction of Freeman's Ford, about 1 ½ miles in front and to the right of us, where the enemy had massed the night previous, and were then holding the ford. When within a quarter of a mile of the ford, in order to reconnoiter and select position, I hurried forward, accompanied by my cavalry, being screened in my approach by a long belt of pines bordering on the river. Arriving at the edge of the pines I halted my cavalry, and, accompanied by my staff, crossed the road and ascended an eminence commanding the ford. Scarcely three minutes had elapsed when the enemy opened upon me from two batteries with grape and shell. I immediately hurried my cavalry across the road to a safe position, and ordered my battery, under Captain Johnson, forward on the double-quick. Too much praise cannot be awarded the captain for the promptness and skill exhibited in bringing his battery into position. In less than five minutes after receipt of the order he had his pieces in action amid a perfect shower of shot, shell, and canister from three of the rebel batteries, and in ten minutes after had silenced their heaviest battery. He continued engaging the enemy for about two hours, compelling them to constantly change the position of their guns, when, his ammunition having given out, I asked for another battery. Captain DeBeck's battery[17], of McLean's brigade, was sent me, he in turn being relieved by Captain Buell, of the reserve artillery, in about two hours. The enemy ceased firing about 3 o'clock PM

My infantry, which at the commencement of the action I had placed under cover of the woods on either flank of the battery, had suffered but little---some 2 killed and 12 or 13 wounded by canister and shell.

About 3 PM, wishing to ascertain the cause of the enemy's silence, I determined to cross the river, and accordingly sent for my cavalry, numbering about 150 effective men. I then crossed the ford, sending a company of sharpshooters across and deploying them, ordering their advance up the hill occupied in the morning by the enemy's batteries, myself with my cavalry in the mean while going around by the road. Arriving at the summit of the hill, I discovered the greater part of the enemy's wagon train, accompanied by their rear guard, moving up the river in the direction of Sulphur Springs. Their cavalry, upon discovering us, gave the alarm, hurrying off their teams and stragglers in the greatest confusion. I posted a platoon of cavalry as vedettes, at the same time throwing forward 20 of my sharpshooters, who commenced skirmishing with their rear guard. Being merely reconnoitering, and not having sufficient force to pursue their trains, I ordered my two remaining companies of cavalry into line, under protection of the hill.

The remainder of the company of sharpshooters I deployed as skirmishers, ordering them to feel their way into the woods on my left. They had scarcely entered the woods when they met the enemy's skirmishers, and from their number and the length of their line I inferred that they had a large force to back them. Shortly after they opened a heavy fire to my left and rear beyond the woods I had thrown my skirmishers in, which I afterward learned was the attack of the enemy upon Bohlen's brigade, which had crossed the river below me. It now being sundown, and not being allowed to bring any force across, I returned, my brigade resting for the night without changing position.

At 7 AM 23d received orders to move in the direction of Sulphur Springs, my brigade bringing up the rear of the corps. When a short distance *en route* I was directed to take a road on my left, a rougher but shorter route to the Springs, the main body of the corps having continued on the main road. Upon coming into the main road again I found myself in advance of the corps. When within a mile of the bridge across Great Run I found our cavalry in line of battle behind the woods. Upon inquiring the cause, I was informed that the enemy were in force at and across the run and had fired on them. Upon this information I passed them with my brigade, and finding the rebel guns in position across the creek, I placed my battery in a commanding position on this side and commenced shelling them, at the same time throwing my infantry into the woods, who soon found and opened a brisk fire into the rebel infantry in front of them on our side of the creek, my men being exposed from the commencement to a cross-fire of grape and canister from a masked battery across the creek. But notwithstanding all these odds we soon forced them across the creek and to retire for protection behind their guns. The enemy having torn up the bridge, and it now being dark, I encamped my brigade for the night a short distance back from the banks of the creek.

Next morning, 24th, a strong pioneer party having been put to work on the bridge to repair for our artillery to cross, I crossed my infantry upon the sleepers, not waiting for my cavalry or artillery. I deployed a strong skirmishing party and was soon on the track of the enemy, who had fallen back during the night to their main body, which had crossed the river by the bridge at Sulphur Springs, my skirmishers advancing as far as the Springs. As soon as my infantry appeared on the heights commanding the bridge across Hedgeman's River the enemy, who were in position, opened fire from the opposite shore. I sent back for my battery and returned their fire. The other batteries of the corps soon coming up a general artillery engagement ensued, which resulted in our driving their gunners away, leaving their pieces very temptingly displayed. Wishing to take advantage of this unexpected opportunity in securing their guns, I had just crossed the bridge, with one of my regiments (the Fifth Virginia[18]) following close behind, and when nearly in reach of the prize found myself in a hornet's nest. As if by magic the woods and hills became alive with the enemy; the deserted batteries were suddenly manned, and a semicircle of guns nearly a mile around us commenced pouring a steady stream of shell and canister upon the bridge. I called to my regiment, which was then crossing, to retire, which it did in very good order and rapid style. Our batteries immediately responded to their fire, thus drawing their attention away from us. In a moment the air was perfectly alive with shot and shell, and I took advantage of their elevation to join my command.

At this juncture I received orders to take the advance of the corps in the direction of Waterloo Bridge, 6 miles above Warrenton Springs. I got my brigade in motion and arrived at the bridge about 5 PM I placed Dieckmann's battery in position on a commanding eminence on the left of the road and near the bridge, immediately opening fire upon a rebel battery across the river, at the same time throwing my skirmishers down near the bridge and along the bank, where they were soon engaging the rebel skirmishers. Thus matters stood when darkness partially put an end to the firing, but the enemy opened on us furiously several times during the night with small-arms, which was promptly replied to.

On the morning of the 25th the batteries on both sides opened again, and continued through the day without serious loss to us. About 3 PM I received orders to burn the bridge at once at all hazards, and to this end brought forward my four regiments of infantry to engage the enemy's infantry, concealed in the woods near the bridge on the opposite bank. By keeping up a steady artillery and infantry fire I succeeded in covering a party firing the bridge, which, being of heavy oak, burned but slowly, and it was not till dark that the bridge was entirely consumed. We then received orders to march to Warrenton, my brigade to bring up the rear of the corps. We left about 9 PM and arrived at Warrenton next morning at daylight. Here we remained in camp until the morning of the 27th, when we received orders to take the advance in the direction of Gainesville.

My cavalry, upon arriving at Broad Run, within 4 miles of Gainesville, found the bridge on fire, and the rebel cavalry with one piece of artillery drawn up on the opposite side. Major Krepps, commanding my cavalry detachment, immediately ordered a charge, and after two successive charges succeeded in putting them to flight. By this time my infantry had arrived, and I set the Pioneer Corps to work repairing the bridge, which was executed with such promptness that in fifteen minutes after we were enabled to cross our artillery. Meanwhile I had pushed ahead with my cavalry and infantry in the direction of Gainesville. When within 2 miles of Gainesville I sent a platoon of cavalry with a regiment of infantry and a section of my battery to hold the road leading to Hay Market Station. With the rest of the brigade I continued on the main road, and upon approaching Gainesville found we had intercepted Longstreet from joining Jackson, Ewell, and Hill, who had just passed up the railroad toward Manassas Junction.

At Gainesville we took some 200 prisoners, stragglers from Jackson's army. I here received orders to halt my brigade for the night.

Next morning, 28th, took the advance toward Manassas Junction, arriving within a mile of the Junction at noon. I halted to await further orders. I accordingly turned my infantry aside into the shade of the woods, and sent my artillery ahead as far as the Junction, there being no water for them nearer. Upon visiting the railroad station at the Junction I found an immense amount of Government stores in cars, which were yet burning, having been set on fire by the rebels the night previous, after having helped themselves to all they could carry off. At 3 PM I received orders to join the balance of the corps, then marching in the direction of New Market. I accordingly moved across the country and soon overtook them. After marching about an hour skirmishing commenced in front. I was ordered to go forward and take position on Schenck's left, and pressed forward through the woods and underbrush in the direction of the rebel firing, which seemed to recede as I advanced. It finally grew dark, but I pushed forward in the direction of the firing, which had gradually grown into the thunder of a desperate battle. It becoming so dark, and the nature of the ground not admitting of my battery being pushed forward, I left it in charge of two companies of infantry, and started forward with my four regiments in the direction of the heavy firing, which suddenly ceased with great shouting, indicating, as we judged, a victory by the rebels. It being now 9 o'clock, and the darkness rendering the recognition of friend or foe impossible, I withdrew to my battery, which was on a line with the front of the corps, then fully a mile in my rear, resting my brigade here for the night.

On the following morning (the 29th), at daylight, I was ordered to proceed in search of the rebels, and had not proceeded more than 500 yards when we were greeted by a few straggling shots from the woods in front. We were now at the creek, and I had just sent forward my skirmishers, when I received orders to halt and let the men have breakfast. While they were cooking, myself, accompanied by General Schenck, rode up to the top of an eminence, some 500 yards to the front, to reconnoiter. We had no sooner reached the top than we were greeted by a shower of musket balls from the woods on our right. I immediately ordered up my battery and gave the bushwhackers a few shot and shell, which soon cleared the woods. Soon after I discovered the enemy in great force about three-quarters of a mile in front of us, upon our right of the pike leading from Gainesville to Alexandria. I brought up my two batteries and opened upon them, causing them to fall back. I then moved forward my brigade, with skirmishers deployed, and continued to advance my regiments, the enemy falling back.

General Schenck's division was off to my left and that of General Schurz to my right. After passing a piece of woods I turned to the right, where the rebels had a battery that gave us a great deal of trouble. I brought forward one of my batteries to reply to it, and soon after heard a tremendous fire of small-arms, and knew that General Schurz was hotly engaged to my right in an extensive forest. I sent two of my regiments, the Eighty-second Ohio, Colonel Cantwell, and the Fifth Virginia, Colonel Zeigler, to General Schurz' assistance. They were to attack the enemy's right flank, and I held my other two regiments in reserve for a time. The two regiments sent to Schurz were soon hotly engaged, the enemy being behind a railroad embankment, which afforded them an excellent breastwork.

The railroad had to be approached from the cleared ground on our side through a strip of thick timber from 100 to 500 yards in width. I had intended, with the two regiments held in reserve (the Second and Third Virginia Regiments), to charge the rebel battery, which was but a short distance from us over the top of a hill to our left, but while making my arrangements to do this I observed that my two regiments engaged were being driven back out of the woods by the terrible fire of the rebels.

I then saw the brave Colonels Cantwell and Zeigler struggling to rally their broken regiments on the rear of the forest out of which they had been driven, and sent two of my aides to assist them and assure them of immediate support. They soon rallied their men and charged again and again up to the railroad, but were

driven back each time with great loss. I then sent the Second
Virginia to their support, directing it to approach the railroad at the
point on the left of my other regiments, where the woods ended,
but they were met by such a destructive fire from a large rebel
force that they were soon thrown into confusion and fell back in
disorder. The enemy now came on in overwhelming numbers.
General Carl Schurz had been obliged to retire with his two
brigades an hour before, and then the whole rebel force was turned
against my brigade, and my brave lads were dashed back before
the storm of bullets like chaff before the tempest. I then ordered
my reserve battery into position a short distance in the rear, and
when five guns had got into position one of the wheel horses was
shot dead, but I ordered it to unlimber where they were, and the
six guns mowed the rebels with grape and canister with fine effect.
My reserve regiment, the Third Virginia, now opened with telling
effect. Colonel Cantwell, of the Eighty-second Ohio, was shot
through the brain and instantly killed while trying to rally his
regiment during the thickest of the fight.

While the storm was raging the fiercest General Stahel came to
me and reported that he had been sent by General Schenck to
support me, and inquired where he should place his brigade. I told
him on my left, and help support my battery. He then returned to
his brigade, and soon after being attacked from another quarter I
did not again see him during the day. I was then left wholly
unsupported, except by a portion of a Pennsylvania regiment,
which I found on the field, and stood by me bravely during the
next hour or two. I then rallied my reserved regiment and broken
fragments in the woods near my battery and sent out a strong party
of skirmishers to keep the enemy at bay while another party went
forward without arms to get off as many of our dead and wounded
as possible. I maintained my ground, skirmishing, and
occasionally firing by battalion, during the greater part of the
afternoon.

Toward evening General Grover came up with his New
England brigade. I saw him forming a line to attack the rebel
stronghold in the same place I had been all day, and advised him
to form line more to the left, and charge bayonets on arriving at
the railroad track, which his brigade executed with such telling
effect as to drive the rebels in clouds before their bayonets.
Meanwhile I had gathered the remnant of my brigade, ready to
take advantage of any opportunity to assist him I soon discovered

a large number of rebels fleeing before the left flank of Grover's brigade. They passed over an open space some 500 yards in width in front of my reserved regiment, which I ordered to fire on them, which they did, accelerating their speed and discomfiture so much that I ordered a charge. My regiment immediately dashed out of the woods we were in down across the meadows in front of us after the retreating foe, but before their arriving at the other side of the meadow the retreating column received a heavy support from the railroad below them, and soon rallying, came surging back, driving before their immense columns Grover's brigade and my handful of men.

An hour before the charge I had sent one of my aides back after a fresh battery--the ammunition of both my batteries having given out--which arriving as our boys were being driven back I immediately ordered them into position and commenced pouring a steady fire of grape and canister into the advancing columns of the enemy. The first discharge discomposed them a little, but the immense surging mass behind pressed them on us. I held on until they were within 100 yards of us, and having but a handful of men to support the battery, ordered it to retire, which was executed with the loss of one gun. I then rallied the shattered remnant of my brigade, which had been rallied by my aides and its officers, and encamped some three-quarters of a mile to the rear.

The next morning, 30th, I brought my brigade into the position assigned them, and remained in reserve until about 4 PM, when I threw it across the road to stop the retreating masses which had been driven back from the front. I soon received an order to move my brigade off to the left on double-quick, the enemy having massed their troops during the day in order to turn our left flank. I formed line of battle along the road, my left resting near the edge of the woods in which the battle was raging. Soon our troops came rushing, panic-stricken, out of the woods, leaving my brigade to face the enemy, who followed the retreating masses to the edge of the woods. The road in which my brigade was formed was worn and washed from 3 to 5 feet deep, affording a splendid cover for my men. My boys opened fire on them at short range, driving the rebels back to a respectful distance. But the enemy, being constantly re-enforced from the masses in their rear, came on again and again, pouring in advance a perfect hurricane of balls, which had but little effect on my men, who were so well protected in their road intrenchment. But the steady fire of my brigade, together with that of a splendid brass battery on higher ground in my rear, which I ordered to fire rapidly with canister over the heads of my men, had a most withering effect upon the rebels, whose columns melted away and fast recoiled from repeated efforts to advance upon my road breastwork from the woods. But the fire of the enemy, which had effected my men so little, told with destructive results on the exposed battery in their rear, and it required a watchful effort to hold them to their effective work. My horse was shot in the head by a musket-ball while in the midst of the battery cheering on the men. I got another, and soon after observing the troops on my left giving way in confusion before the rebel fire, I hastened to assist in rallying them, and while engaged in this the battery took advantage of my absence and withdrew.

I had sent one of my aides shortly before to the rear for fresh troops to support this part of our line, where the persistent efforts of the rebels showed they had determined to break through. A fine regiment of regulars was sent, which was formed in the rear of my brigade, near the position the battery had occupied. The rebels came around the forest in columns to our right and front, but the splendid firing of the regulars, with that of my brigade, thinned their ranks so rapidly, that they were thrown back in confusion upon every attempt made. About this time, when the battle raged thickest, Lieutenant Esté and Lieutenant Niles, of General Schenck's staff, reported to me for duty, informing me that General Schenck had been seriously wounded and his command thrown back from the field. Most thankfully was their valuable assistance accepted, and most gallantly and efficiently did they assist me on that most ensanguined field until 8 o'clock at night in bringing up regiments, brigades, and batteries, cheering them on to action, and in rallying them when driven back before the furious fire of the enemy.

Shortly after sunset my own brigade had entirely exhausted their ammunition, and it being considered unsafe to bring forward the ammunition wagons, where the enemy's shells were constantly flying and exploding, and the enemy having entirely ceased their efforts to break through this part of the line and had thrown the weight of their attack still farther to my left, I ordered my brigade back some one-half of a mile to replenish their ammunition boxes and there await further orders. I remained on the field with Lieutenants Esté and Niles, my own having been sent to see to my regiments. The enemy continued their attacks upon our left until long after dark, which it required the most determined and energetic efforts to repel At one time, not receiving assistance from the rear, as I had a right to expect after having sent for it, and our struggling battalions being nearly overcome by the weight and persistence of the enemy's attack, I flew back about one-half mile to where I understood General McDowell was with a large portion of his corps. I found him and appealed to him in the most urgent manner to send a brigade forward at once to save the day or all would be lost. He answered coldly, in substance, that it was not his business to help everybody, and he was not going to help General Sigel. I told him I was not fighting with General Sigel's corps; that my brigade had got out of ammunition some time before and gone to the rear, and that I had been fighting with a half dozen different brigades, and that I had not inquired where or to what particular corps they belonged. He inquired of one of his aides if General ----- was fighting over there on the left; he answered he thought he was. McDowell replied that he would send him help, for he was a good fellow. He then gave the order for a brigade to start, which was all I desired. I dashed in front of them, waved my sword, and cheered them forward. They raised the cheer and came on at double-quick. I soon led them to where they were most needed, and the gallant manner in which they entered the fight and the rapidity of their fire soon turned the tide of battle. But this gallant brigade, like many others which had preceded it, found the enemy too strong as they advanced into the forest, and was forced back by the tremendous fire that met them. But one of General Burnside's veteran brigades, coming up soon after dark with a battery, again dashed back the tide of armed treason, and sent such a tempest of shot, shell, and leaden death into the dark forest after the rebels that they did not again renew the attack.

Perhaps some mighty cheering which I got our boys to send up about that time induced the rebels to believe that we had received such re-enforcements as to make any further meddling with our lines a rather unhealthy business. Feeling certain that the rebels had been completely checked and defeated in their attempts to flank us and drive us from the field, and that we could now securely hold it until morning, by which time we could rally our scattered forces and bring up sufficient fresh troops to enable us to gain a complete victory on the morrow--I felt certain that the rebels had put forth their mightiest efforts, and were greatly cut up and crippled--I therefore determined to look up my little brigade and bring it forward into position, when we would be ready in the morning to renew the contest, and renew the great, glorious drama of the war. I left the field about 8 o'clock PM in possession of our gallant boys, and with Lieutenants Esté and Niles started back in the darkness, and was greatly surprised, upon coming to where I expected to find my brigade, with thousands of other troops, to find none. I kept on half a mile farther in painful, bewildering doubt and uncertainty, when I found you, general, and first learned from you, with agonizing surprise, that our whole army had been ordered to retreat back across Bull Run to Centreville.

Comment is unnecessary. I felt that all the blood, treasure: and labor of our Government and people for the last year had been thrown away by that unfortunate order, and that most probably the death-knell of our glorious Government had been sounded by it. The highest praise I can award to the officers and soldiers of my brigade, in all the hard service and fighting through which we have passed, is that they have bravely, cheerfully, patiently, and nobly performed their duty. Colonels Cantwell, of the Eighty-second Ohio, and Zeigler, of the Fifth Virginia, deserve particular mention for their coolness and bravery in the long and desperate fight of the 29th with the rebels at the railroad. In the death of Colonel Cantwell the country, as well as his family, have sustained an irreparable loss. No braver man or truer patriot ever lived. He constantly studied the best interests of his soldiers and of the country, and his men loved, obeyed, and respected him as a father. Truly the loss of such an officer in these trying times is a great calamity.

I avail myself of this opportunity to return my thanks to the members of my staff, Captains Baird, Flesher, and McDonald, and Lieutenants Cravens and Hopper, for their promptness, bravery, and efficiency in the transmission and execution of orders. Captain Baird, unfortunately, in attempting to return to me on the field on the evening of the 30th, after dark, in company with one of my orderlies, Corporal Wilson, Company C, First Virginia Cavalry, took a wrong path, which led into the enemy's lines, and they were both captured and are still prisoners. My brigade surgeon, too, Maj Daniel Meeker, is always at his post, whether in field of danger, camp, or hospital. His superior science, skill, and patient industry have proved the greatest blessing to our sick and wounded soldiers.

Lists of my killed, wounded, and missing have been sent

you.

    I have the honor to be, very respectfully, your obedient servant,
        R H Milroy
        Brig Gen, Comdg Indepdt Brig, First Corps, Army of VA

September 13, 1862
Report of Capt. Michael Wiedrich, Battery I, 1st New York Light Artillery Fort DeKalb, VA

    Major: In accordance to general orders of this date I transmit you the following report:
    On arriving, on the 22d of August, near Freeman's Ford, I was ordered by General Schurz to advance with my battery. After advancing about a quarter of a mile Captain Schirmer, chief of artillery, ordered me to relieve Captain De Beck's battery, which had been in action for some time. On nearing the place I was met by Major-General Sigel, who ordered me to place two 10-pounder Parrott guns in a new position on a hill in some woods near the river. After posting those pieces Major-General Sigel ordered me to take my other two Parrott guns to the right of Captain De Beck's battery, which I did, and left my two howitzers in reserve. The fire of the enemy was very hot where the two sections of my battery were posted. Here we had 5 killed and wounded, as follows: Killed, Private Florida Enoch; wounded, Sergt. Jacob Bock, in the breast and foot; Sergt Christian Stock, in the arm; Corpl John Blau, in the breast; and Private George Himmel, in the face. We also had 2 horses killed and 10 others rendered unfit for further service, which had to be shot. There was also at the same time one of our limber boxes set on fire and exploded, but did no other damage.
    August 24 we were engaged at near White Sulphur Springs, also at Waterloo Bridge. At the latter place Private George Lother was wounded. We were also engaged at the latter place August 25, but sustained no loss. We were also engaged in the battles at Ball Run, August 29 and 30. Went in action on the 29th at about 10 o'clock AM, when we were ordered forward by Captain Schirmer, chief of artillery. After advancing a short distance we were met by Major-General Sigel, who ordered me to take a position on the right of the road, to support the infantry in case they should be driven back. After remaining in this position

about half an hour Major-General Sigel came to me and ordered me ahead with the four Parrott guns to support Captain Dilger's battery, which order was executed as promptly as possible by taking a position on which the enemy had the range with one of his batteries, but in about fifteen minutes after we opened fire on it and it was silenced. We kept our position until about 3 o'clock in the afternoon, when our ammunition gave out and we were obliged to retire to get a new supply. After getting the ammunition we started again to take our former position, but finding that Captain Dieckmann was there with his battery I returned to where I had left my two howitzers in the forenoon. Soon after coming into action there Lieutenant Schen-kelberger had his leg shattered by a shell; also Private William Moller, the arm; both of which had to be amputated.

    After using up the remainder of our ammunition I retired with my battery to near Major-General Sigel's headquarters, where I remained during the night. On this day we had one piece dismounted and on another the axle shot through, but I am happy to say that we brought all of the pieces out of the reach of the enemy.

    August 30, after receiving a new supply of ammunition, I was ordered, with mine and Captain Buell's battery, to report to General Schenck, who ordered me to report with four Parrott guns to Colonel McLean, and keep my howitzers and Captain Buell's 6-pounder brass guns in reserve. We remained in a position in front of his brigade on a low hill with the 10-pounder Parrotts until about 4 o'clock PM, when at this time Colonel McLean sent me an order to follow his brigade to take a position on a hill to the left of the road. After coming into action in a position selected by General Schenck, Major-General McDowell called me to him and wanted to know what I was going to do, and forbade me to open fire for fear of injuring our own men, of which there was one battery about 500 yards in front to our right and some infantry a short distance in advance of that battery to our left. One of the enemy's batteries was directly in our front, behind some woods. When, a few minutes afterward, the aforesaid infantry was repulsed by the enemy, Major-General McDowell took his infantry and artillery from our left and moved in front of my battery toward the right flank, leaving our left, as it looked to me, uncovered. When, soon after he was gone, the enemy's infantry advanced out of some woods directly in front, where Major-

General McDowell stood, and attacked my battery, Colonel McLean came to our support with his brigade. The fire on both sides was very sharp, and the overwhelming numbers of the enemy forced us, after a hard contest, to fall back on another hill in our rear, where we came in position again and remained till nearly dark, and after exhausting our ammunition we fell back toward Centreville, where we arrived next morning.

Very respectfully, your obedient servant
M Wiedrich Captain
Comdg Battery I, First Regiment NY Artillery

September 14, 1862
Letter of William Wheeler
camp near Fort Ethan Allen, VA

Dear Coz

It is extremely aggravating to me to think that I shall not be able to be present at your wedding, but if I am there, it must be either as a cripple or an invalid, for my battery is *my* plighted bride, "until death do us part," or until peace do see us once more an united land. To tell the truth, I have not the slightest idea that I shall ever see any of you again, and I endeavor always to banish from my mind the pleasant picture of a reunion with the family at New Haven, for when I dwell on it too much, it makes a feeling of regret sometimes arise, and that always interferes with duty; no, I prefer to accept the belief that I *must* fall, and if I *should* survive, it would be so far a pleasant disappointment. The days are looking very dark know, our arms are meeting reverses in every direction, and it requires no prophet to announce that many toilsome marches must be made, and many more battles fought, and thousands of brave men yet fall, before this quarrel shall be settled on the permanent and righteous footing that we seek.

I will not trouble you with any account of how we marched down to the Rapidan, and then how we marched back again; how we shot at the rebels across the narrow Rappahannock, like boys fighting across a handkerchief, and how the artillery of our Corps held the many fords of that river against the overwhelming numbers of the enemy; then how we marched in post haste to Manassas, when we found that the wily Jackson had got in Pope's rear, and was threatening his communications; how our Corps bore the brunt of the battle all day Friday, and covered the repulsed left wing on Saturday night, and were ready to renew the fight the next morning, had we not been ordered away; how we marched back, full of wrath at leaving a field that we had twice won, and were still able to hold, and took our gloomy march to Centreville, Fairfax, Vienna, and at last came under the shelter of the forts on Georgetown Heights, where we now are; all this is not pleasant to repeat, but as an offset, I can assure you, that it was all down without haste or panic, and that "Battery No. 13" stood gallantly by its flag, served its guns under the hottest fire, with coolness and skill, and finally, in spite of loss of men and horses, brought them all off the field, not without words of praise and commendation from our idolized Sigel. We had it the toughest on Friday afternoon, when we were sent by General Sigel to hold a hill from which several of our batteries had already been driven; here three rebel batteries of excellent guns, and finely served, rained shot and shell upon us; a section of a regular battery by our side was silenced and compelled to retire, and then the whole fire was concentrated upon us. I can assure you that I had no idea of ever coming alive out of that *inferno*.

John's regiment is in Washington learning to drill and discipline; last week he was on guard at the Long Bridge with his company. I knew that he was there, and determined to see if he would know me after our long separation, so I pulled my hat down over my eyes, rode up and give him my pass, as if I would go over the bridge. He looked at it, said it was all right, and was just about to pass me, when he gave one look at me, and then sprang forward like a mad creature. It was a happy meeting, and we spent the afternoon together. His regiment makes a fine appearance, and I think that he will become a first-class officer. May he be spared to the end!

September 15, 1862
Battery Orders No. 22
camp near Fort De Kalb, VA

I   Quartermaster Sgt James C Carlisle is hereby appointed action 2nd Lt 13 NY Battery vice Lieut Albert Molitor, Detailed to Gen Sigel's staff

II   Sergeant Charles Hempen is hereby appointed Acting QM Segt vice Carlisle promoted.

Julius Dieckmann Capt

Comdg 13 NY Battery

September 16, 1862
Report of Maj. Gen. Franz Sigel, First Army Corps, Army of Virginia
near Fort De Kalb, VA

Colonel: I have the honor to submit the following reports:
1.--OPERATIONS PREVIOUS TO THE BATTLES OF THE 29TH AND 30TH AUGUST.

After the battle of Cedar Mountain, the retreat of the First Corps from the Rapidan behind the Rappahannock, and the several engagements of that corps near Rappahannock Station, Freeman's Ford, and Sulphur Springs, we advanced to Waterloo Bridge on the same day we had taken possession of Sulphur Springs--on the 24th August. The brigade of General Milroy occupied a position on the north side of the bridge, extending his line of sharpshooters along the shore of the river. The main body of the corps was encamped between the bridge and Sulphur Springs and behind it the corps of Major-General Banks and General Reno's division. The enemy had advanced from Rappahannock Station along the south side of the river in a line parallel with the route taken by our troops, and was trying to cross at the above-named ford (Freeman's) and the bridges at Sulphur Springs and Waterloo. On the night of the 24th of August his camp-fires extended from Waterloo Bridge to Jefferson Village, a distance of 4 or 5 miles, his main force, of about 30,000 men, occupying the latter point.

Early on the morning of the 25th a sharp skirmish commenced at the (Waterloo) bridge, which was reported to me by General Pope to have been destroyed by General Buford, but which was found on our arrival in good order and strongly defended by the enemy. While we were taking position on the north side the enemy began to break up his camp at Jefferson and to mass his troops on the south side of the bridge. By noon twenty-eight regiments of infantry, six batteries, and several regiments of cavalry of the enemy had arrived and taken their position. I had the night before given notice of the enemy's strength and movements to Major-General Pope, and now again informed him of the position of affairs, as the disposition he had made of our forces was evidently based on the supposition that the enemy would force the passage of the river between Bealeton and Waterloo Bridge. In the mean time I had been directed to march to Fayetteville and form part of the center of the army, to be arrayed in a line extending from Waterloo Bridge to Bealeton Station.

In accordance with this order General Milroy should have been relieved in the morning by a brigade of General McDowell. Another brigade of the Third Corps (McDowell's) had to march to Sulphur Springs. In the forenoon of the same day General Roberts, of Major-General Pope's staff, delivered to me a verbal order to hold my position at Waterloo Bridge under all circumstances and to meet the enemy if he should try to force the passage of the river, and that General McDowell would be on my right, with the cavalry brigade of General Buford, and General Banks on my left.

Soon afterward I received intelligence that a large force of the enemy's cavalry had crossed on my right and was moving toward Orleans, and that another force had crossed on my left, at Sulphur Springs, and taken possession of that place. I immediately ordered General Beardsley, with the Ninth New York Cavalry and four mountain howitzers, to Sulphur Springs, to shell the enemy out of the place, which he did. The rest of my cavalry, consisting of three companies of the First Virginia and two of the First Maryland, I ordered toward Orleans, for the purpose of protecting my right flank. Meanwhile cannonading was kept up near the bridge, and from all indications I supposed that the enemy would avail himself of the opportunity to make a combined attack against my position. I therefore sent to the left to find Generals Banks and Reno, and to the right to look after General McDowell's troops, especially the cavalry brigade, and was not a little astonished to learn that Generals Banks and Reno were, by orders of General Pope, on their march to Bealeton,and that no troops could be found on my right except the cavalry brigade of General Buford, which was encamped 4 miles behind us on the Warrenton road. To confuse matters still more I received a dispatch from General McDowell, one section of it directed to Major-General Banks, asking for news from his corps, and the other directed to myself, informing me that I would join my pontoon train at Fayetteville. I sent this dispatch to General Banks, and requested him to furnish me with what information he could, so that, in the absence of instructions, I might be enabled to direct my movements properly. I also sent to Generals Pope and McDowell, at Warrenton, for an explanation and for orders, but General Pope had left for Warrenton Junction, and General McDowell did not furnish me with any instructions.

It was now nearly sunset, and my situation exceedingly critical Threatened on my right and left flank; an army of 30,000 menacing my front and separated from me only by a shallow river, fordable at many points for infantry as well as cavalry and artillery; no supporting force within 8 or 10 miles---I supposed that it was not really the intention of the commanding general to leave me in this position. I was corroborated in my opinion by the answer of General Banks, who advised me to march to Fayetteville, and by the fragmentary paper saying that I would find my pontoon train at that point. Considering all this I resolved to march to Fayetteville at night, and made my preparations accordingly, although I did not believe in the correctness of the whole plan.

Just at the moment when my troops were about to move one of my officers returned with an order of General Pope, directing me to march to Warrenton and to encamp there. I put my troops in motion in compliance with this order and cautiously withdrew from Waterloo Bridge, as I had not a single company of cavalry to cover my retreat. Before withdrawing, however, I ordered the destruction of the bridge, which was accomplished, under the direction of General Milroy, after much exertion and some loss of life.

At 2 o'clock next morning (August 26), as I was entering Warrenton with my rear guard, I received another order from General Pope, through General McDowell, directing me to "force the passage of the Waterloo Bridge at daylight." As this was a matter of impossibility, the troops having marched the whole night on a very inconvenient road, I reported to Major-General Pope this fact, and received orders to stay at Warrenton.

During the day I ascertained that the enemy was marching by Thoroughfare Gap to Manassas, and on the following night that his main army was encamped at White Plains, the advance guard east of Thoroughfare Gap and the rear at Orleans. This news was brought in by all the scouts sent out by me, with some cavalry, to Sperryville, Salem, and Gainesville, and was immediately communicated by telegraph to Major-General Pope. It was also reported to me that the enemy was moving during the night (Tuesday); that Jackson would be in Manassas next day

(Wednesday), and that Longstreet had not yet joined him, but was 2 miles from Salem at noon on Wednesday, the 27th.

In view of these facts I proposed to General McDowell, to whose command the First Corps had been attached since its arrival at Waterloo Bridge, to concentrate our forces at Gainesville, and thereby separate Longstreet's troops from those of Jackson, taking the enemy at Manassas in the rear, and by forcing him to evacuate Manassas effect a junction with the army of General McClellan. This movement was executed.

On the morning of the 27th the First Corps left Warrenton for Buckland Bridge, on the road to Gainesville, with directions to take possession of the bridge, and thereby open the road to Gainesville. The brigade of Brigadier-General Milroy advanced rapidly toward the bridge, and drove the enemy, who was stationed there with some cavalry and artillery, back toward Gainesville, while the pioneers repaired the bridge, which had been set on fire and partially destroyed by the enemy. In a short time the whole of General Milroy's brigade had passed the river and pressed forward against Gainesville, making on their way about 150 prisoners. I now ordered General Schurz to pass the river and follow General Milroy and to take position behind him. The division of General Schenck also crossed the river, and the infantry brigade of General Steinwehr remained in reserve at the bridge. Such was the position of the First Corps on the evening of the 27th.

During the night General McDowell's corps arrived at Buckland Mills, and I received orders at 3 o'clock in the morning to march to Manassas and to take a position, with my right resting on the railroad leading from Warrenton Junction to Manassas Junction; so, at least, I understood the order.

On this march our cavalry, sent out to the left in the direction of Groveton, was shelled by the enemy, about 1½ miles distant from the road on which we marched; and, besides this, an artillery engagement, began between the corps of General McDowell and the enemy. I immediately halted, ordered the whole corps to counter-march, and formed in order of battle on the heights parallel with the Centreville-Gainesville road. The enemy's infantry and cavalry pickets were about 300 yards from our line, and our skirmishers had already advanced against them, when, on a report made to General McDowell, I received orders to march forthwith to Manassas Junction. I reluctantly obeyed this order,

marched off from the right, and was within 2 ½ miles from
Manassas, when our cavalry reported that Manassas was
evacuated by the enemy, and that General Kearny was in
possession of that point. As I was sure that the enemy must be
somewhere between Centreville and Gainesville, I asked
permission to march to New Market, whereupon I was directed to
march to Centreville. This order was in execution, and the troops
prepared to cross the fords of Bull Run, when our advance met the
enemy on the road leading from New Market to Groveton and
Sudley's Ford, this side of Bull Run. About the same time I
received a report from General Pope that the enemy was
concentrating at Centerville. Supposing that this was correct, I
directed the brigades of General Milroy and Colonel McLean to
advance against the enemy this side of Bull Run, on the road to
Sudley Springs, and left General Stahel's brigade and General
Schurz's division near the fords, the latter division facing toward
Centreville.

As soon, however, as I had ascertained that Centreville was
evacuated by the enemy I followed with these troops to assist
Brigadier-General Milroy and Colonel McLean, who, under the
direction of Brigadier-General Schenck, were briskly engaged
with the left of the enemy's forces, whose right had engaged a
brigade of the Third Corps. Our artillery advanced steadily until
the darkness of night interrupted their movements. They encamped
for the night near Mrs Henry's farm, one regiment taking position
on the Centreville-Gainesville turnpike, the main force fronting
toward Sudley Springs and Groveton.

2.--BATTLE OF GROVETON, NEAR BULL RUN, ON
FRIDAY, AUGUST 29, 1862.

On Thursday night, August 28, when the First Corps was
encamped on the heights south of Young's Branch, near Bull Run,
I received orders to "attack the enemy vigorously" the next
morning. I accordingly made the necessary preparations at night
and formed in order of battle at daybreak, having ascertained that
the enemy was in considerable force beyond Young's Branch, in
sight of the hills we occupied. His left wing rested on Catharpin
Creek, front toward Centreville; with his center he occupied a long
stretch of woods parallel with the Sudley Springs-New Market
road, and his right was posted on the hills on both sides of the
Centreville-Gainesville road. I therefore directed General Schurz

to deploy his division on the right of the Gainesville road, and by a change of direction to the left to come into position parallel with the Sudley Springs road. General Milroy, with his brigade and one battery, was directed to form the center, and to take possession of an elevation in front of the so-called "stone house," at the junction of the Gainesville and Sudley Springs roads. General Schenck, with his division, forming our left, was ordered to advance quickly to an adjoining range of hills, and to plant his batteries on these hills at an excellent range from the enemy's position.

In this order our whole line advanced from point to point, taking advantage of the ground before us, until our whole line was involved in a most vehement artillery and infantry contest. In the course of about four hours, from 6.30 to 10.30 o'clock in the morning, our whole infantry force and nearly all our batteries were engaged with the enemy, Generals Milroy and Schurz advancing 1 mile and General Schenck 2 miles from their original positions.

At this time (10.30 o'clock) the enemy threw forward large masses of infantry against our right, but was resisted firmly and driven back three times by the troops of Generals Milroy and Schurz. To assist these troops, so hard pressed by overpowering numbers, exhausted by fatigue, and weakened by losses, I ordered one battery of reserve to take position on their left, and posted two pieces of artillery, under Lieutenant Blume, of Schirmer's battery, supported by the Forty-first New York Volunteer Infantry, beyond their line, and opposite the right flank of the enemy, who was advancing in the woods. These pieces opened fire with canister most effectively, and checked the enemy's advance on that point. I now directed General Schenck to draw his lines nearer to us, and to attack the enemy's right flank and rear by a change of front to the right, thereby assisting our troops in the center. This movement could not be executed by General Schenck with his whole division, as he became briskly engaged with the enemy, who tried to turn our extreme left.

At this critical moment, when the enemy had almost outflanked us on both wings, and was preparing a new attack against our center, Major-General Kearny arrived on the field of battle, and deployed by the Sudley Springs road on our right, while General Reno's troops came to our support by the Gainesville turnpike. With the consent of General Reno I directed two regiments and one battery, under Brigadier-General Stevens, to take position on the right of General Schenck--the battery on an eminence in front and center of our line, where it did excellent work during the rest of the day, and where it relieved Captain Dilger's battery, which had held this position the whole morning. Three regiments were posted between General Milroy and General Schenck, and two others, with two mountain howitzers, were sent to the assistance of General Schurz. Scarcely were these troops in position when the contest began with renewed vigor and vehemence, the enemy attacking furiously along our whole line, from the extreme right to the extreme left. The infantry brigade of General Steinwehr, commanded by Colonel Koltes, was then sent forward to the assistance of Generals Schenck and Schurz, and one regiment was detailed for the protection of a battery posted in reserve near our center. The troops of Brigadier-General Reynolds had meanwhile (12 o'clock) taken position on our left. In order to defend our right I sent a letter to General Kearny, saying that Longstreet was not able to bring his troops in line of battle that day, and requesting him (Kearny) to change his front to the left, and to advance, if possible, against the enemy's left flank. To assist him in this movement I ordered two long-range rifled guns to report to him, as his own battery had remained in reserve behind his lines.

At 2 o'clock in the afternoon General Hooker's troops arrived on the field of battle, and were immediately ordered forward by their noble commander to participate in the battle. One brigade, under Colonel Carr, received orders, by my request, to relieve the regiments of General Schurz' division, which had maintained their ground against repeated attacks, but were now worn-out and nearly without ammunition. Other regiments were sent forward to relieve Brigadier-General Milroy, whose brigade had valiantly disputed the ground against greatly superior numbers for eight hours.

To check the enemy if he should attempt to advance, or for the purpose of preparing and supporting an attack from our side, I placed four batteries of different commands on a range of hills on our center and behind the woods, which had been the most hotly contested part of the battle-field during the day.

I had previously received a letter from Major-General Pope, saying that Fitz John Porter's corps and Brigadier-General King's division, numbering 20,000 men, would come in on our left. I did, therefore, not think it prudent to give the enemy time to make new arrangements, and ordered all the batteries to continue their fire, and to direct it principally against the enemy's position in the woods before our front. Some of our troops placed in front were retiring from the woods, but as the enemy, held in check by the artillery in the center, did not venture to follow, and as at this moment new regiments of General Hooker's command arrived and were ordered forward, we maintained our position, which Generals Milroy and Schurz had occupied in the morning.

During two hours, from 4 to 6 PM, strong cannonading and musketry continued on our center and right, where General Kearny made a successful effort against the extreme left of the enemy's lines.

At 6.15 o'clock Brigadier-General King's division, of Major-General McDowell's corps, arrived behind our front, and advanced on the Gainesville turnpike. I do not know the real result of this movement, but from the weakness of the enemy's cannonade and the gradually decreasing musketry in the direction of General Kearny's attack I received the impression that the enemy's resistance was broken and that victory was on our side; and so it was. We had won the field of battle, and our army rested near the dead and wounded who had so gloriously defended the good cause of this country.

3.--BATTLE OF THE 30TH OF AUGUST

On Saturday, the 30th of August, I was informed by Major-General Pope that it was his intention to "break the enemy's left," and that I, with the First Corps, should hold the center, Major-General Reno should take position on my right, and General Reynolds on my left.

The First Corps took position behind Groveton, on the right of the Gainesville turnpike. My request to have two batteries in reserve behind the center for certain emergencies--one of General Reno's and one of General Reynolds' division--was not complied with, although all my batteries were more or less worked down, several pieces unserviceable and short of ammunition, and many horses killed or disabled.

Having taken position as ordered the corps of Major-General Porter passed between the enemy and our lines and was forming in line of battle on the open field before the First Corps and that of General Reno, masking thereby our whole front. Not understanding the object of this movement, and being requested by one of the staff officers of General Porter to give my opinion in regard to the ground before us, I immediately rode over to the general (Porter) and suggested that, in accordance with the general plan, his troops should pass more to the right, join those of General Kearny on our extreme right, and direct his attack against the enemy's left flank and rear. I also informed him that there were too many troops massed in the center, and that General Reno and myself would take care of the woods in his front. Whilst this was going on I received repeated reports that the enemy was shifting his troops from the Gainesville turnpike to his right. I therefore ordered the Fourth New York Cavalry, under Lieutenant-Colonel Nazer, to advance in that direction between New Market and Groveton, passing behind our left, and to scout the country as far as they could go. I also sent one regiment of General Schenck's division to' the left of our position, as an outpost, to observe the enemy's movements. After the lapse of about an hour I received notice that the cavalry pickets had found the enemy, and that the latter was moving against our left. I sent the messenger that brought this intelligence to General Pope's headquarters. Shortly afterward I received an order by Colonel Ruggles, chief of staff of General Pope, to occupy the "Bald-headed Hill" on my left with one brigade, which I did immediately. Meanwhile General Porter's troops, who had not changed their position, advanced into the woods where we had lost a thousand men the day before. About this time on our left, where General Reynolds was posted, the musketry and cannonading began to increase. The troops of General Porter had wholly disappeared in the woods, which led me to believe that the enemy had left his position in front, and that it was the intention of General Pope to advance the First Corps on the Gainesville turnpike. Suddenly heavy discharges began in front, the corps of General Porter having met the enemy, who was advantageously posted behind a well-adapted breastwork--the old Manassas Gap Railroad track. At the same time the enemy opened with shell and solid shot against our center and left wing. Our batteries replied promptly and spiritedly, and from the general appearance of the battle it was evident that we had the whole army of the enemy before us.

    It was now about 5 PM, when, awaiting the further development of the battle, I received a dispatch through General McDowell, and written by General Porter, expressing his doubt as to the final result of his attack, and requesting General McDowell to "push Sigel forward." Although I had not received positive orders from General Pope, I immediately made the necessary preparations either to assist General Porter or to resist an attack of the enemy should he repel General Porter and advance against my own position in the center, by directing General Stahel to deploy his brigade in front and General Schurz to form his regiments in a line of reserve. During the execution of these movements General Porter's troops came out of the woods in pretty good order, bringing a great number of wounded with them. In answer to my question why they were retiring after so short a time, they said that "they were out of ammunition." Expecting that the enemy would follow up this retrograde movement of a whole corps with a strong force, I kept my troops well together to meet such an event.

Thus we stood when, suddenly, incessant volleys of musketry betrayed the enemy in great force on our left, and showed clearly his real plan of attack. To assist Colonel McLean's brigade on our left I directed General Milroy to join his brigade with that of Colonel McLean. In executing this order, however, General Milroy directed his brigade more to the rear and left than was intended by me, so that by this disposition an interval of several hundred paces was left between these two brigades, by which the enemy penetrated, attacking Colonel McLean's troops in the rear, and compelling them to change their front to the left. They thereby partially evacuated the position they had occupied on the hill. It was at this moment that General Schenck was severely wounded at the head of his troops, whom he had repeatedly led forward against the overwhelming masses of the enemy.

When this was the condition of affairs on our left, General Reynolds, who at the beginning of the battle had deployed his troops in front and to the left of Colonel McLean's brigade, changed his position, and withdrew his battery from a hill to the left of the Gainesville turnpike, near Groveton. The enemy immediately took possession of the hill, posted a battery there, and spread his infantry out over the high and wooded ground before Colonel McLean's brigade and on the flank and almost in rear of our center. To dislodge the enemy from his new-gained position I ordered forward three regiments of infantry, under Colonel Koltes, who, under a terrible artillery and infantry fire, boldly advanced against the hills, but could not regain the lost ground.

In this attack I have to regret the loss of the intrepid Colonel Koltes, who was killed while executing the movement ordered.

His brigade, though nearly decimated, succeeded in protecting our center and preventing the turning of our flank.

It was now evident that to avoid the destruction of our troops from the sweep of the enemy's batteries, and as the main attack was now on our left, I ordered General Schurz to withdraw his division from the low ground, under cover of our artillery, and take position on the hills near the stone house, one brigade to face toward the left. The brigade of General Stahel followed this movement, and formed in line of battle on our right. Immediately in front of this position, on a hill to the right (north) of the stone house, I placed a battery of the Fourth Regulars, which I had met on the turnpike. This battery behaved nobly, and maintained its position until the last hour. Captain Dilger's battery occupied a more advanced position near Groveton, Captain Dieckmann's was on our left, and Captain Schirmer's on our right, with General Stahel's brigade.

General Milroy, with his brigade, and the assistance of several additional regiments which he had brought forward, succeeded in repulsing the enemy on the left. In this gallant exploit his horse was shot under him. We maintained our second position until night had closed in upon us, when General Pope ordered a general retreat.

Following the troops of Generals Porter and McDowell, my corps crossed Young's Branch, where it remained for two hours, until the commands of Generals McDowell, Reno, and Kearny had crossed Bull Run by the ford near the stone bridge, and the whole train had passed over the bridge. It was now between 9 and 10 PM I then marched to the turnpike, crossed the bridge over Bull Run, and took position on the left and right of the bridge, throwing my pickets out on the other (south) side of the creek toward the battlefield. Soon afterward an officer of General McDowell's staff directed me to fall back, as the enemy was threatening the line of retreat. It was now after midnight, when I ordered my command to continue its march toward Centreville, first destroying the bridge across Bull Run. Our rear guard was composed of part of General Schurz' division, two pieces of Captain Dilger's battery, and a detachment of Colonel Kane's Bucktail Rifles, which had come up with several guns collected on their march of retreat.

I reached Centreville at daybreak on the 31st of August, my command encamping in front of and occupying the intrenchments of that place.

Our losses during the two days' battle in killed, wounded, and missing, according to the official lists sent in, are 92 officers and 1,891 noncommissioned officers and privates.

To be just to the officers and soldiers under my command I must say that they performed their duties during the different movements and engagements of the whole campaign with the greatest promptness, energy, and fortitude. Commanders of divisions and brigades, of regiments and batteries, and the commanders of our small cavalry force, have assisted me under all circumstances cheerfully and to the utmost of their ability, and so have the commanders of the two batteries of Major-General Banks' corps (Captain Roemer's[19] and Captain Hampton's), under Major Keefer, attached to me since our arrival at Freeman's Ford. It also affords me pleasure to mention the faithful services of the members of my staff and of such officers as were detailed to me for special duty. To them, as well as to the officers and members of my escort, the pioneer companies, and to my scouts, I hereby express my high regard and warmest gratitude.

I have the honor to be, very respectfully, your obedient servant,

F Sigel,

Major-General, Commanding Corps

Report of Capt. Hurbert Dilger, Battery I, 1st Ohio Light Artillery camp near Minor's Hill, VA

General: Respecting the part my battery took in the late conflicts of the 29th and 30th of August, 1862, I have the honor to report the following:

On Friday, the 29th of August, the battery was ordered, under the protection of Colonel Koltes' brigade, to the support of General Schenck's division, upon the left flank of the First Corps. I advanced to the left of the road and took position upon the outermost elevation in our front, just opposite a large battery of the enemy, which, mounting about ten guns, was posted upon the hill inclosing the valley. After two hours' incessant firing the enemy's guns were silenced for a while--in consequence, no doubt, of the successive explosion of two of their caissons. During this pause, which was improved to prepare the battery for the continuance of the contest for the important position, opportunity was also afforded me to support the infantry on our right, that had been compelled to fall back across the railroad track, with two pieces of artillery posted on the right of my battery. The enemy's battery, however, was not long in making its appearance again. I engaged it until Wiedrich's battery and two pieces of Dieckmann's battery were sent by my request, through order of General Sigel, to my assistance, and after I had exhausted all my ammunition, of which there was not an over-supply, to my relief. By this time the fire of the enemy slackened its concentration upon this position.

The loss I sustained during this engagement, which lasted four hours, was 22 horses, and 4 men slightly wounded. The damage to the guns was slight so that they could be repaired in the evening.

On the morning of Saturday, the 30th of August, the battery was assigned to Colonel Krzyzanowski's brigade. While the division was advancing I took position on the left of the battery that was posted on the summit of the hill fronting the enemy's battery which I engaged yesterday. Being apprised by you, general, of the danger that was threatening our center, I took the only two guns that had not been brought into position, on account of the want of room, with me, and engaged with them the battery that was in the act of flanking us from the corner of the woods. Having remained stationary for about half an hour, I perceived one of our infantry regiments, being in full range of the enemy's guns, falling back upon the battery. I tried to bring this regiment to a stand and to make it advance again, but the bursting of the enemy's shells in the midst of them, having a demoralizing effect, rendered my efforts unavailing. Ten minutes afterward two columns of the enemy's infantry appeared in our front, which, notwithstanding the steady firing upon them by our artillery, advanced with sharpshooters in their front toward the battery, compelling me to leave this position. Falling back about 100 yards, I again brought my pieces to bear upon them until they withdrew. During my withdrawal, which was executed in a gallop, the enemy poured two volleys into me, but totally without effect.

As soon as the enemy's infantry had retired beyond the reach of my shells I again engaged the battery until one of my guns became dismounted by the demolition of an axle. As by this time all the batteries that were near me had withdrawn I thought it my duty to do the same. At sunset, having secured the dismounted piece below the caisson in the manner prescribed, I arrived upon the hill in the rear from whence General Sigel directed the retreat, which I was ordered to assist in covering with two pieces of my battery. From this moment nothing more transpired that is worth alluding to.

All this day the principal movements and maneuvers of the battery (I) had been directed independent of other commands. In spite of the severe cross-fire of cannon and musketry it was subjected to on this day we sustained no loss at all, either in men or horses, with the exception of the dismounting of one of my guns. Officers, non-commissioned officers, and cannoneers fought with the utmost bravery and to my entire satisfaction.

I have the honor to be, general, your most obedient servant,
H Dilger
Captain, Comdg Battery I, First Ohio Volunteer Artillery,

September 19, 1862
Letter of William Wheeler
camp near Fort De Kalb, VA

Dear Grandfather
Your very kind letter reached me a few days ago in the first regular camp we occupied after the battle, and it was very welcome to me, both as showing the kindly interest you cherish in me and my welfare, and also because it informed me that you were freed from anxiety on my account. I have written to mother, giving an account of our retreat from the Rapidan and also of the battle on Friday, in which we largely participated....I was as thoroughly used up on Friday night as I ever recollect being in my life, for I had some hard work all day, as a cannoneer, and then the cessation from the excitement of battle caused a sudden reaction which produced both mental and physical fatigue. However, I managed to sleep pretty well, on ground which we had won from the enemy in the morning, and at break of day proceeded to hunt up the ammunition train and to replenish our exhausted boxes. Then we marched out of camp, and proceeded to the Stone Hospital, of which you will have seen frequent mention made in the newspapers. Here we lay in reserve, waiting for the moment when the eye of our sagacious leader, General Sigel, should see where to push us forward with most effect in line of battle. Past us filed the long lines of the corps of McClellan's army, comparatively fresh after a rest of a few days, and who had not been engaged on the previous day. Some of the regiments, as for example the Brooklyn

Fourteenth, the New York Fifth, (Duryea Zouaves), looked quite full, but the bran new uniforms, and fresh unburned faces showed that the ranks wasted by battle and disease, had been to a great degree filled up with recruits, men as yet untried. I saw quite a number of friends among these regiments, among them Col Wm Wainwright, formerly Major of the Twenty-ninth New York, with which we were long brigaded. By the Hospital we lay, listening to the roar of the cannon and the sharp rattle of the musketry, and watching the course of the battle, which began with greatest intensity on the right of the centre, and gradually worked round towards the left wing, where the rebels got some batteries in position, and thus established a cross fire on our troops. Just about this time, when our troops in the centre were falling back, and the hills and fields to the rear were covered with stragglers and attendants on the wounded, our Brigade, General Milroy's, was ordered to the left wing, and we went joyfully onward, hoping to do our share to redeem the battle, which seemed in danger of being lost. At the same time, a fresh body of troops had gone up to the centre, and I there saw a bayonet charge made, by at least a whole brigade, which I shall never forget. Steadily the long line march on, the banners rising and falling as they passed over the undulating ridges, but still going steadily forward, under a murderous fire from both infantry and artillery. The enemy fall back, and take refuge in a wood, where they are reinforced and make a stand,--still our men pass on, and it seems as if they opposing lines were within touching distance. At last our line staggers under the infernal fire bearing upon it; the wounded are seen first brought to the rear, and finally our men retire a short distance, and resign a part of the ground they had so gallantly won. Now our Brigade marches up on the left, and plunges into the woods to clear them; our Battery takes up a position on the open ground, and proceeds to shell the woods, over the heads of our own men. As we advance nearer to the woods, we improve our range, the fire becomes hotter, and the rebel sharp-shooters creep up as close as they can, and pick off our cannoneers. The noise of fighting is in the wood comes closer, and it become evident that they enemy are driving our men back, so I take one six-pounder and go, through a shower of bullets, to take part of the woods where our men are just emerging, closely followed up. We come into position, wait until our own men are well out of the way and they gray jackets are already beginning to swarm out, when we let go a few rounds of canister at one hundred yards' distance, and back they go again in a great hurry. We then retire with the retiring infantry, but only about fifty yards, and then again unlimber and fire, until a fresh regiment comes up and enters the woods. I then rejoin the Battery and we take position on a hill and wait for orders; no orders come, and night comes on, and all is quiet, except occasionally a few volleys from the extreme left, which General Reno is holding, and nothing whatever is seen of panic or disturbance on the battlefield, which we now hold…..At last an aid from General Sigel comes up and orders us to Centreville, and we proceed thither in perfect order. Of the panic we saw little or nothing, as it occurred mostly in the rear among stragglers, teamsters, and ambulance drivers. Why we retreated I cannot say, but I feel sure that we would not have do so if Sigel had been in Pope's place. Of what has since happened you know more that I. I have been miserable in health since the battle, caused by cold and exposure; but cannot take time to rest, as one officer is wounded and one is on detached service. We are now being repaired and refitted….I have seen John and his regiment; they are quartered near Washington's Monument. He makes a fine looking officer, and bears himself well among his men. You must miss him greatly in New Haven. May he never know the hardships and perils which I have gone through the past summer. I can hardly venture to hope that we shall both ever be reunited with you at home. For myself, I thirst for active service, and am miserable when lying in camp, as at present.

September 20, 1862
Memo of Charles Walter
Central Guard House, Washington DC

Arrest Lieut Molitor for stealing a US horse.

To the Commander of the Central Guard House
Charles Walter

September 28, 1862
Letter of William Wheeler
Centreville, VA

Dearest Mother
Your letter, dated September 23, reached me late last night at Fairfax, to which place I had made a night march from Fort Ethan Allen, where I had been detached on picket for a week.....I am, in truth, a very unsightly object to look upon; I wear the same jacket and the same vest that I did when we marched out of camp last February, and they bear spots acquired in half the counties of Virginia; still I cannot cast them away without a feeling of regret, thinking oh how many a cold night march they have kept me warm, how often soaked by the May showers and dryed again, how often brushed up to make a martial appearance when passing triumphantly through secesh towns, and how often carelessly rolled together to make a pillow for my bed on the ground before the bivouac fire; indeed, so many of my best thoughts and most ardent labors are associated with those weather-beaten garments and faded epaulets, that I cannot believe they look so badly as my friends say; and yesterday I went quite coolly in them to drive with General Abercrombie, and after dinner did the agreeable to a couple of fair damsels visiting Fort Ethan Allen. My week on picket was every way a pleasant one, except that I was sick part of the time, having got badly chilled in one of those cold nights, as I had no tent and had to sleep under a tarpaulin....Then one of my Corporals, a nice young Englishman, took his blankets and fixed up my shanty to keep the cold out, and built me a good bed, so that I managed to keep warm and did not get any worse; still, I lay in bed for three days in much pain, and my bones all felt very sore. Joseph S and young A from the class of '63, both on General Abercrombie's staff, were unremitting in their attentions, brought me doctors, and books to read, and looked after the material wants of my men, and were in general so kind that I felt quite sorry yesterday afternoon when the order came for me to rejoin the Battery at Fairfax; and General Abercrombie, too, didn't want to

let me go away from his command, but was obliged to, as General Heintzelman countersigned General Sigel's order to that effect. We packed up and got off about dark, and a pretty tough march of some fourteen miles brought us to the Court House by midnight it was hard pull for me, as I could not sit my horse, got chilled again, and did not sleep when I ensconced myself within my tent; and worst of all, the Battery was ordered to Centreville early the next morning. But I have succeeded in getting there more comfortably than I had expected, and shall like quiet and take all possible care of myself, as I have no idea of becoming useless for the Fall Campaign. I thirst for active service, and hope that we shall soon get a chance to take part in a decisive battle in favor of the Union cause; the mere thought of Bull Run (and the battlefield lies even now stretched out before my eyes as I write), Harper's Ferry, Mumfordsville, makes me sick; why, Colonel D' Utassy[20] with the Garibaldi Guard, from our old Division, could have held the fort alone for twenty-four hours, and been rescued. The rebels are welcome to my somewhat attenuated length of five feet ten, but now with any vitality in it. I have read General Milroy's report, and it is in many respects true, but still a picture of the General's excited state of mind, and it is evident that he hardly knew half the time what he was about. A braver man never lived; he seems to drink in excitement and intoxication from the sound of the bullets, and to be perfectly happy when in the very tempest of battle, but he knows nothing about the object of artillery or the way to use it, and I am heartily glad that we are to have nothing more to do with him. General Sigel's report is soon to appear, and then I hope that our Battery will be spoken of more scientifically and judiciously. I see that I have been unusually egotistical in this letter, but do not believe, dearest mother, that my thoughts are not with you on this calm, beautiful Sabbath afternoon; I feel quiet and very happy, and picture you to myself as you go down to church among the falling elm leaves, and sit in your pew with John and Theodisa[21], but no raven head of hair at the end; I pray ever most fervently that I may be allowed to meet the dangers of battle alone, and that he may be spared them. You cannot well lose us both.....To me this contest and cause are the same that the quest of the Holy Grail was to Sir Galahad.

> "To me is given
> Such hope, I know not fear."

September 30, 1862
Letter of William Wheeler
Centreville, VA

    I feel a little inclined to grumble because you confined yourself to one small sheet, and passed over many topics of interest with a bare mention which aggravated me very much, just as with a child to whom one is showing pictures in a book and passes over the prettiest with a turn of the leaf. But you must do better next time, and expand more on those little matters which constitute the filling-in touches of life; if necessary, have a pigeon-hole in your desk, labeled, "Wheelerisch Memoranda," and lay in these hints from day to day for future letters....I will not weary you by expanding on the subject of the battle of Bull Run, as it has already been set forth at full length in the newspapers....What surprised me greatly was the so very faint an idea of danger was in my mind at the very hottest of the fight; I was so thoroughly occupied with working my piece to the best advantage, that I hardly noticed the bullets whistling and shells exploding around, and even some of the most revolting sights of bloodshed and death seemed to me very natural under the peculiar circumstances. I have also observed the truth of Horace's assertion,--

        "Mors et fugacem persequitur virum,
        Nec parcit imbellis juventæ
        Poplitibus timidoque tergo,"

For nothing was more usual than for a shell to strike in the Battery, cut a furrow alongside my foot, and then making a high ricochet in the air, come down several hundred feet to the rear, and cut some cowardly skedaddler right in two, a fate which he would have probably have escaped if he had stood up to his work. Well, our men retired, but, I am convinced, wholly without sufficient cause; indeed, I believe that if Sigel had not had positive orders he would have held the field all night, which in fact he did not do until late in the evening. And for our Corps and our Battery, I have the consoling consciousness that we did our duty fully, and obeyed the order to withdraw with the greatest reluctance. There is a radical defect in the formation of our Army; its regiments, brigades, division and corps, especially the latter, are too small to be thoroughly serviceable and manageable, and there are too many officers of high rank, each possessing a sort of half-cut independence; these corps are not much larger than divisions eight months ago, the divisions have sunk to brigades, and many brigades cannot show a full regiment of fighting men. Now what could Sigel do with his handful of men, perhaps twelve thousand in all? What he *did* do is pretty generally known; what he *might* have done if he had a full corps of twenty-five thousand to thirty thousand men is aggravating to think of. And now newspapers are inquiring "What is Sigel doing?" What can be expected of him, with a small corps that suffered far more than any other in the late fight (and yet did not lose a gun or a flag), with his best brigade (Milroy's) detached and sent to Western Virginia? He has now some five thousand men, a superb command with which to fall upon the enemy's read and cut him off, as seems to be demanded by many! How can the government expect to succeed while they ignore the men who mean *fight*, and give everything to softly warriors like McClellan, who are afraid to hit the enemy too hard? But the chief cause of the present deadness in affairs is the neglect of the Governors of States to forward their quotas; six hundred thousand men look very big on paper, but so long as they are not raised they do us very little good in practice. New York State alone owes yet forty thousand men, and the day of drafting will be delayed until the time for autumn fighting is past, until the roads here become again unfathomable, and the secesh call out their last resources, and gather strength for the next year's struggle; so we are always a month or two behind, and the enthusiasm and spirit of our troops evaporates, under this system of timidity and delay. A section of our Battery has just returned from an expedition with the cavalry, in the direction of Warrenton, and report that the cavalry captured there, and in the neighborhood, some sixteen hundred secesh; how true this is I cannot tell. I should have commanded the section on the expedition myself, if I had been well enough to stand the march, for as senior Lieutenant I have always the right demand the privilege of being detailed, and in customary for me to do that sort of work with my section from the left wing. But I am now very much better than I have been.

October 1862-April 1863
A disagreeable state of betweenity

October 9, 1862
Letter of William Wheeler
Centreville, VA

My Dearest Mother

I answer your most welcome letter with expedition, in order to quiet any anxiety on my account, and also to reassure you as to the probability of my being engaged in any actual fighting when you are assisting at M W's wedding. I was very miserable when I first came here, my complaint having been greatly aggravated by long continuance and want of rest and care. By lying quiet in my tent, and almost magical effect of the pills which you sent, I soon began to improve, and now am as well as ever, and have an appetite like a wolf whenever I do a little extra work. We were paid off on the 1st, and the Captain went off on the 2d, which was pretty hard on me, as I was thus left to stem the tide of drunkenness and quarrelling almost entirely alone. However, the boys behaved much better than could have been expected, when they had been four months without pay, sent home a great deal to their families, and paid off their debts exemplarily. There was of course noise, and fighting, and trouble, but less than ever before on pay-day.

On Sunday I started off with a picked party and a loaded wagon, to turn in a lot of old horses and useless harness to the Quartermaster in Washington. It was extremely doubtful whether we should succeed in getting all of the old creatures over the twenty-five miles, but by starting on Sunday afternoon, and going that night to Falls Church, resting there and going on the next morning, we arrived at Washington Corral with our full freight of condemned horse-flesh.

I was in the city a day and a half, ordered a neat uniform, and had a *carte-de-visite* taken of my head and shoulders, which I think will be good. Then I came out by the Long Bridge and found Company G, Fifteenth Connecticut Volunteers, on guard on the Virginia side. Lieutenants Goodrich and French[22] were there, but the Captain was in camp, so I rode on to Camp Chase, and found the respected fraternal about a mile from where we lay last winter, things, to stay to tea. I saw a nice dress parade, enjoyed an excellent cup of the home English Breakfast, and then we talked together till it was quite late, and he got for me the countersign, and then I had a splendid ride under the full autumn moon, and through the soft airs of Indian summer, back to Centreville, which I reached at 1 AM

John was looking very well indeed, and seems to enter into the spirit of his work admirably, especially in his longing for active service, which does not seem any great probability of his getting in the Fifteenth CV. Nor am I sorry for this. I am a much greater coward about him than myself, as I have seen how numerous the causalities among the officers of an infantry regiment are, especially among those that expose and distinguish themselves. I am very much afraid that we shall lose our General of the Eleventh Army Corps. It is stated positively that he has tendered his resignation, and as the Government does not seem prepared to give him satisfaction they can hardly avoid accepting it.

Letter of William Wheeler
Centreville, VA

I can assure you that the regrets which I had experienced before at being unable to be with you in "the dreadful hour," were deepened and made more poignant by the array of attractions you present to call me thither, and by the warm-hearted steadiness with which you insist that I *must* be there. So pleasant a child of hope it is too hard to stifle with one inexorable word, "impossible;" and yet that word must be written; and, to show you wherein that impossibility consists, I inclose a copy of "General Orders No 28," from the head-quarters of our Corps, and what our General sees fit to order, that, I must obey without grumbling or discontent. Or, perhaps, we could represent the affair as "urgent official business;" but then the rub would be to state it in the application in such a way as to make it *seem* so to the powers that be. I think that the only resort left will be for you to make a direct application to the President, and support it by all the influence of our *powerful and illustrious family*. Surely, if you and L and R should unite in making up a Round Robin to the Executive, I am sure that the stony-hearted Abe would relent at the sight of so much beauty and worth in tears, and he would immediately dispatch the Fifteenth

Connecticut Volunteers to bring me leave of absence for ten days, with, however, this important condition, that I should not fail to bring him (ye said Abraham) a hunk of the cake.

No, there is no help of it; and I will not further aggravate myself my thinking of my own misfortune in losing so pleasant a family reunion. I will rather think of you and your happiness, ----- 's[23] resignation under affliction, of the talks gotten up by our mothers and aunts and uncles, of the harmless fun perpetrated by the "young fry,"—in all of these, except of course the last, I shall be with you in spirit, and you can imagine my old jacket and shoulder-straps as lending variety to the toilettes of the guests actually present....This golden Indian summer time is just the season for marching and fighting, and I chafe at our present inaction. Why don't they send up on troops enough to move with, or, if we have troops enough already, why don't we "pitch in?" There are mysteries about the conduct of this war that puzzle and almost disgust me, but I manage to keep my faith in "something" alive, although I can hardly say what that "something" is. At present it is mostly confined to the sturdy determination of the people of the North to bring the war to a just and honorable termination.

The 15th October is an anniversary for me too, as on that day I was mustered into service, and shall then have been a United States soldier just one year. May the first anniversary of your wedding day see the country reposing in perfect peace.

October 11, 1862
Battery Orders No. 23
Centreville, VA

I Private James McGowan of this Battery for drunken and disorderly conduct upon guard and for violently assaulting the corporal of the guard upon the night of October 9th 1862 is adjudged the following punishment.
1st To be deprived of 10 (ten) dollars of his monthly pay for one month
2nd To be put on guard every alternate day for twenty days
3rd To apologize to Corporal Baldwin in the presence of the Battery for his violent and abusive conduct

II   Private Carl [name not readable] of this Battery for remaining absent from camp longer than his leave of absence permitted is adjudged the following punishment
To be put on guard every alternate day for ten days
Julius Dieckmann Capt
Comdg 13 NY Battery

October 25, 1862
Battery Orders No. 24
Fairfax Courthouse, VA

Private George Weis of this Battery for drunkenness on guard is adjudged the following punishment
To be put on guard every alternate day for 10 days
Julius Dieckmann Capt
Comdg 13 NY Battery

October 30, 1862
Letter of William Wheeler
Fairfax Courthouse, VA

    I thought of you all a great deal on the 15th, and took pleasure in calling up the familiar faces of every one present at the family assemblage at Springwood. On that same day I was starting out with my section on a reconnaissance to Chantilly with the cavalry. I was so weak, that I could hardly sit in my saddle, and my toes trembled in the stirrups, but I had already missed two expeditions (being on my back in bed) and thought that the excitement might do me good.
    We went out on the road towards Aldie and Middleburg, came into battery on a commanding hill, and the cavalry went ahead to scour the country. We remained there that afternoon, watching the skirts of the distant woods for any traces of rebel cavalry, and then bivouacked under the open sky by our fires. The night was cold and frosty, and I could hardly say that I was fairly asleep all night; but it did me a great deal of good, and when the next day w were relieved, and went into camp, I felt fifty per cent better. The same evening Captain Johnson's Battery[24] arrived at Centreville to relieve us, and the next morning we bade adieu cheerfully to the exposed and dusty wind hills of that region, and marched to Fairfax Court House, where we are now encamped on the northeast side of the town, in a well sheltered spot on the edge of a wood, and on exactly the same place

where the Battery stood when being reviewed by General Sumner last March. This doesn't look as if we had made much progress since then, and we have slipped down three stairs for tow we have got up. But I have great faith in the army which is now coming into the field, and also in the firm determination of the people and the President, to treat the war as a serious matter. The rebels have been serious ever since last spring, and we see the results....For myself, I am not satisfied at sitting down now, and allowing these golden days to slip away unimproved...I am as comfortably fixed as if we were to stay here for months. I have a nice army cot, which folds up, a writing table, a neat little stove, with a first-rate brick chimney on the outside, (put up by a mason in my section from bricks brought from a ruined house near by), and good boards over a good part of my tent floor. I made my calculation that if we stayed ten days, I should get the worth of my money, and if longer it would be so much gain. When we made winter quarters I intend to make myself thoroughly comfortable if it be any way possible. The two Divisions of our Corps went a few days ago, and indulged a sham battle, skirmishers thrown forward, battalions deployed, artillery placed in position, and pushed forward from height to height, and bayonet charges made by full regimental line. We maneuvered with Steinwehr's Division, which is mostly composed of new regiments. The fresh troops did remarkably, especially the Twenty-sixth Wisconsin and Thirty-third Massachusetts[25].

November 6, 1862
Letter of William Wheeler
Gainesville, VA

Your last most welcome letter reached me the day after I wrote to you, and must have passed mine on the way. I can hardly undertake to respond to you in a worthy manner, for it is late at night, and my toes are very cold, besides, we are to march to-morrow morning, and if I expect to rise betimes I must see that I turn in before long. The dreams of winter quarters at Fairfax, in which many of the men indulged, were all dissipated on the first of the month by an order to march early on the morning of the next day: which order pleased me hugely, and I set to work and put the ammunition of the whole Battery in general, and of my section in particular, in tip-top order. The next morning, at the appointed hour, we were all packed up, and horses hitched in, but could not move, as the road was occupied by

General Heintzelman's corps, on its way to Centreville. By noon we got off, and reached this place. Our road lay exactly across that part of the battlefield where we had struggled so hard on Friday the 29th, and, strange to say, we stopped at noon on the very hill on which our Battery had stood for two hours in the afternoon in the most infernal fire. This gave us an opportunity to examine the locality with some care. On the back slope of the hill were some ten or fifteen graves of our men, among them that of young Hutchinson of my section, whose poor mother I had the pleasure of consoling with a letter, giving an account of his gallant bearing, and his glorious but almost painless death....Many of our poor horses were lying on the slope, shriveled to skin and bone, and the meadow beyond was sown broadcast with missiles of every pattern and caliber. I then rode over to the valley where M came so near leading us in to our destruction, and I saw my two pole horses, one on the hillock where we first unlimbered and fired, the other by the opening of the fence leading into the road, where I played his part for a number of dangerous rods. The space near the railroad embankment, where M's men had been driven back, and where the rebels had in turn been forced back by our canister, was covered with graves poorly dug, and scantily covering the miserable forms within. I was very much depressed by the whole sight, but not shaken in my old resolution to see the end of the matter, or be like these poor men. Some of our men, who were on the hill occupied by the rebel batteries which annoyed us so, state that horses fairly covered the hillside, showing the enemy had not passed unscathed through that Gehenna of balls.

In the afternoon we came through to this place, which is a small village of a few houses on the slopes of the Bull Run Ridge. The Manassas Gap Railroad is completed to this place and beyond. The locomotive has a friendly and civilized appearance, and our boys always cheer it. General Sigel arrived here in person to-day, and to-morrow we are to advance, probably to Warrenton, and no one knows what may happen.

I am very well indeed, don't mind sleeping out of doors these cold nights, but prefer a bed in a warm tent decidedly. I am fully prepared to stand a fair share of hardship for the next month.

November 15, 1862
Battery Orders No. 25
Aldie, VA

I   Sergeant Joseph Bohn is hereby appointed Orderly Sergeant 13 NY Battery vice Fennessy discharged.
II   Corporal William Garrett is hereby appointed sergeant of 4th Detachment, vice Bohn promoted.
They will be obeyed & respected accordingly
Julius Dieckmann Capt
Comdg 13 NY Battery

November 21, 1862
Letter of resignation request to Maj. Gen. Franz Sigel, commanding Reserve Corps, Army of Potomac
Washington, DC

General
    The undersigned most respectfully begs leave to tender unconditionally and immediately his resignation as 1st Lieutenant of the 13th Battery NYSV. The reason that prompted him to take this step is to be found in the malicious dealings of his captain, Cpt. Julius Dieckmann towards him as officially proven by General Orders No 38, wherein is said: "And the Court did therefore honorably acquit the accused, First Lieut Albert Molitor, 13th Battery NYV Art, and find that the prosecution seems to have been prompted by malice."
Very respectfully
Your most obdt servt
Albert Molitor
1st Lt 13th Battery NYSV
Detailed to the staff of the Eleventh Corps

November 25, 1862
Memo to Capt. Louis Schirmer, Chief of Artillery, 11th Army Corps
no location given
    Within application for resignation [for Lt Molitor] respectfully recommended, and leave of absence granted until said resignation be accepted.
        Julius Dieckmann, Capt
        Comdg 13 NY Batty

Letter of William Wheeler
Chantilly, VA

Dear Aunt Elizabeth

Our Corps has, by the new arrangements and division of the Army of the Potomac into four parts, come into the Reserve, and thus we are lying present in a disagreeable state of "betweenity," neither having the comfort of winter quarters nor the compensating excitement of active operations in the field. I am hoping that Jackson, who is said to be still at Bunker Hill and Charlestown, may make a dash in this direction, in the hope of getting to Washington in the read of the main army, now down on the Rappahannock. But I think that would be a little too hardy for the Shenandoah Valley Fox.

I do not wish to triumph over the fallen, but I must say that I consider the removal of McClellan as just and necessary. He has been tried, and found wanting in those qualities of swiftness, energy, and ready talent which are absolutely needful in a leader who would successfully combat the genius of Lee, the dash of Stuart, the daring rapidity of Jackson. Whatever else we may say of the rebels, we must also confess that they have managed to pick out their best men, and have put them at the head of their army. The material of the bulk of their army is certainly inferior to the mass of ours, and our artillery is much the best, while we allow only a slight superiority to their cavalry. But material is nothing so long as it is not rightly moulded and put to use. With the prospect of victory when advancing and impunity when retreating, the dirty, half naked, ill-fed white trash of the Southern army will march twenty miles a day, and fight days on empty stomachs; and, with the enthusiasm inspired by such leaders, our boys would do and suffer as much and more. I have had an opportunity to see it proved, that officers who are willing to expose themselves, and lead their men intelligently, will never lack support. The material of our Battery, for example, is by no means first-rate, and they do for the most part answer to the description of "hirelings;" but I doubt if there are many places so hot that they would not follow their officers into with cheerfulness. In fact, so all-important are the virtues of courage and firmness out here, that one has a tendency to forget that any other virtues are worth more practicing; but I have succeeded in keeping alive one more, Faith,-faith in the soundness of the Northern hearts, and in the honesty of the President; faith in the approval of the Ruler above, and in the consequent success of our cause. In regard to religious matters, I have thought a times that I have grown entirely callous; but when I have heard a piece of hymn music, or read a few tender lines of admonition from mother, or ridden out in the pleasant autumn afternoon among the woods and thought; or listened to our colored servants singing some old camp-meeting tune, in a minor and melancholy key, by their fires at night, I have felt that it was not so. I suppose that Thanksgiving Day will be the day after to-morrow in New Haven, and I deeply regret, as ever, that I cannot be home upon that day. It is the festival above all others which I have always been accustomed to spend at home, and now I am again absent. I know that you will remember John and myself when you sit around that family table, and you may be sure that we will be thinking of you. I have cause for gratitude that this year I am in excellent health, awhile on last Thanksgiving Day I was so sick that I had merely to look at the gigantic turkey, but could not touch it. I have already projected a foraging expedition to-morrow, to procure a gobbler to be sacrificed to St. Thanksgiving, and it will go hard with any secesh farmer who refuses to hand him over for a reasonable compensation in greenbacks. We have been going into geese pretty extensively lately, as our cook gets them up on a most palatable manner. The other day I rode several miles with two live ganders slung one on each side of my saddle like holsters....I have a first-rate darkey, rejoicing in the name of Glenmore. He has been with me nearly for months, and has kept my horses in first-rate condition. He is a ludicrous object, having a nose like the pyramid of Cheops, and orifices in it like the secondary craters of Vesuvius. He is a great favorite with most of the men, who call him Chocolate, and he has the jolliest and most infectious laugh you ever heard. I feel quite attached to him, and should be very sorry to lose him.

November 29, 1862
Memo of Capt. Louis Schirmer, Chief of Artillery, 11th Army Corps
no location given

      Respectfully returning with the opinion that Lieut Molitor has no good reason for tendering his resignation. That the military law will protect him against any malice from Captain J Dieckmann. I therefore disapprove his resignation and recommend that he be ordered back immediately to his Battery for duty.

December 8, 1862
Memo of Maj. T. A. Meysenburg, Assistant Adjutant General,
11th Army Corps
Fairfax Court House, VA

Accepted for the interest of the services. Order for honorable discharge given [to Lt Molitor]

December 9, 1862
Letter of William Wheeler
Chantilly, VA

Dearest Mother

Your letter dated, December 2, was duly received, and gladdened my heart in the midst of this bleak wintry weather like a breath of spring, and I take advantage of this pleasant sunny morning, when it is possible for me to inhabit my tent, to answer you. In the first place, that turkey, with the fixings, etc., for which the collective mouths was to be the Phoenix, or pattern bird, of our cook-house, towards which all future poultry was to strive, and whose virtues should be emulated by geese and chickens yet unhatched, this noble animal, I say, with all his seductive surroundings, is by this time very unpleasant both to look at and to taste of, and indeed it would be too much to expect of him that he should remain more than two weeks on the way, and yet preserve his original sweetness; in other words, the box has not yet arrived. But although I could not eat turkey, I thought of you all day long, as in church, but in a pew which had tow vacant seats; then the Thanksgiving dinner, at which I *know* that John and I were missed; and still more in the pleasant, quiet evening, when you sat together and talked. I think that never before in my life had I personally so many reasons for being thankful; a year ago this day I was setting out for Washington, doubtful whether I should ever reach it, and with my whole system thoroughly on the verge of dissolution; for my recovery, I have, next to God, to thank Uncle R and Aunt H; then I am very thankful for having been able to see you and my other friends once more, and to strengthen my heart with assurance of your love and sympathy; then brought through the hardships and exposures of the march and the camp, and the dangers of the battlefield, I find myself now in perfect health, and with a frame to some extent inured to bear everything that may occur in an ordinary campaign. If I were not deeply thankful, I should be indeed ungrateful. The cause of the country, it is true, has experienced no such improvement in the last year, but still we hope every for a happy and righteous ending, in spite of the mutterings and threats of some members of the Democratic party at the North, and the unfriendly attitude of France.

About what I said on the subject of being awakened to religious thoughts by passing circumstances. I think that you must have received a very incorrect idea, and one which I would not wish you to entertain. The state of the case is this: as a general rule, the chaplains here in the field either wholly neglect their duty, or else so perform it, that they might far better have remained in their tents, and others are talkers who are utterly without any conceptions beyond their pay and their position; now, I have been brought up to consider religion and its exercises and meditations as something serious and awful, and since I have thought at all, I have thought that in this matter a man must be sincere and honest above all things, so if I pray, I cannot avoid placing my whole being in a position of the greatest humility before Him to whom the prayer is offered, and at the same time the greatest earnestness and eagerness in demanding help. But an attendance at church which is merely habitual, a reading of the Bible which is merely mechanical, and a way of praying regularly, but with the mouth alone, these things blunt the religious sense, and satisfy a man's soul with what is really nothing. For these reasons I will not attend the ministrations of chaplains which do not edify me; but whatever I *do* say on this subject you can thoroughly believe.

I have heard nothing from John directly for a month and a half, and feel very much worried by hearing that he is ill. I have written to him since we came here, but have received no answer. If he gets will over his troubles, and gets nicely toughened up, it will have been a great advantage to him. I should have gone in to see him, but my duty here has been quite constant, and it would have been hard to get away.

The weather has been very trying most of the time since we came here. About seven ago we had a furious wind storm, that lasted three days and nights, and ended in snow, which fell to depth of eight inches. It was utterly impossible to keep warm in my tent, and the only way was to lie and take it. It was especially hard upon our poor horses, which seemed to lose in two days all that they had gained by three weeks' good feed and car. Yesterday my section went to work and built a nice evergreen stable, big enough to hold our horses (thirty-three), and more too; my little mare Jenny has the warmest corner of it, and it is entirely protected from the wind. In former years, about this time or a little later, I have also worked in evergreens; but then it was to deck churches, or to fix and trim Christmas trees for the young ones. I think that our present work for our poor, irrational dumb beasts is just as pleasant, and as must a labor of love as the other. And now, just as we have the job completed, comes an order to be ready to march at a moment's notice. You can imagine that those who have built log huts, and got themselves nicely fixed, are not very amiable at the prospect of moving. I feel very glad of it, and hope that we may yet do something before the roads become impassable. I should greatly enjoy a few days at home this winter, but it doesn't look much like it just now, and the orders are very strict that no one receives a leave of absence on doctor's certificates, unless it is absolutely necessary for the preservation of life or health; and I am glad to say that I am not a candidate for any such certification. Captain Dieckmann is encouraging a nascent rheumatism, which he thinks will bring him home at Christmas as it did last July; but I unfortunately have no pet malady which appears so conveniently. If a month or so later we take up winter quarters, the matter will doubtless be different, and in that hope I live, for I so long earnestly after you and the girls.

    I received a charming letter from Uncle W the other day; so long as the folks at home write such patriotic, hopeful, cheering letters, they may be sure that their representatives in the field will fight well. The violets in your letter were delicious, and the whole of it was as fragrant and sweet to the smell outwardly as to the hear within.

December 17, 1862
Battery Orders No. 26
camp near Falmouth, VA

I 2nd Lieut Frank Singer of 13th NY Battery is hereby appointed 1st Lieut of this Battery, vice 1st Lieut Albert Molitor 13 NY Battery honorably dismissed the service by Special Orders No 123, Headquarters 11th Corps. He will be obeyed & respected accordingly.
II   Quartermaster Sgt James C. Carlisle is hereby appointed 2nd Lt of 13 NY Battery vice F Singer promoted. He will be obeyed & respected accordingly.
III   Sergeant Charles Hempen 13 NY Battery is hereby appointed QM Segt 13 NY Battery vice Carlisle promoted. He will be obeyed & respected accordingly.

Julius Dieckmann Capt
Comdg 13 NY Battery

December 20, 1862
Letter of William Wheeler
Stafford Courthouse, VA

Your last kind letter, dated December 15, came to hand this morning, and filled me with thankfulness, in hearing that you were all well at home, and also relieved me to some extent from the excessive anxiety I have felt about John for the last fortnight. I have not heard from him directly now for nearly two months. I was afraid that he might be so rash and unwise to march with his regiment, to scenes of hardship and exposure which he was totally unfit to encounter; so you can imagine how glad I felt to hear that he was still at Washington, and was contemplating a further trip to Annapolis, which we can now call the "Convalescent Hospital" for our family, as well as the army in general. Judging from my own experience, I think that he could hardly be in a better place than there, with Aunt H to nurse him, Uncle R to judiciously supervise and starve him, and A to amuse and couster him up as soon as he came down-stairs. Still it must have been extremely trying for him to have to lie still while his regiment marched off to active service, though I do not really know where the Fifteenth Connecticut went to, or what battle they were engaged in[26]. As for our Corps, we have had a rough time of it indeed. We marched from Chantilly by the way of Fairfax CH and Fairfax House; come to the Occoquan River. Up to this point our main trouble was the slippery condition of the roads, on which our horses were frequently falling, with great danger both to man and beast. But this was decidedly a minor evil, compared with what came later. A succession of warm days thawed the frozen ground, and for five or six hard marches we struggled over hills and lakes of mud, and through ravines of putty-like soil, such as can be see in perfection only in Eastern Virginia. At the passage of the Occoquan we found some fine forts, one above the other, like a terrace, which if defended would have been very costly to take; but they were deserted, and there were no signs of their having been recently occupied. On Sunday we were at Dumfries, near Quantico Creek, and then we had three days of the toughest sort of work to reach the high ground on the left bank of the Rappahannock, near Falmouth. There we learned that the attach had been made without us, and had failed, and as there was a danger that the enemy might throw himself on our line of communications, and cut off Burnside's supplies, we were moved back to this important place, to guard the railroad, and our whole Corps is now assembled here. In some respects the march was more trying than that of last May and June from Franklin to Harrisonburg. It is true we did not have the night marches or the thunder showers, but then we had mud *ad infinitum*, eight days' marching without rest, scarcity of provisions, winter nights, and the depressing thought that we could not march as fast as the infantry through the mud, and that we must sometimes call upon them to help us to extricate our bemired wagons. Several times was I indebted for a lift to the stout hands of the Fairfield County boys of the Seventeenth Connecticut Volunteers, Colonel Noble[27], who were for several days in the same brigade with us. What was worst of all was, that when we to Falmouth, we came the day after the fair, and had not fight at all, and had to take our caissons back as full as we brought them. Still it was very acceptable to get a rest here. Bivouacking in the middle of December is no fun, and we should have suffered most severely if the weather had not been unusually mild. At Dumfries, the team wagons were left behind without my knowing it, and so I came off without any blankets, except one on my saddle, and I had to make fatigue and a good fire supply the place of them. In fact, one night I was so used up that I slept in my jacket, without blanket or fire, and felt no ill effects. One night, however, I caught it,--it was the night before we marched to Falmouth. When we lay down around the fire, the stars were shining brightly, and all was serene. Towards morning I woke up and found the rain dashing in torrents in my face,--a cold, driving winter rain,--still I was too tired to seek shelter, even if there was any to be found, and went to sleep again. Unluckily I lay in a too level place, and when I awoke in the morning I was the "Gentleman of the Lake," and soaked to the skin all down my back. To add to this, by noon it cleared off bright and cold, and the piercing winds made me shiver in my wet clothes. I hardly thought I should get to camp. However, I arrived there safe, and slept dry that night, and by the next evening got the chill out of my bones. But you must not be at all disturbed on my account, when I tell you these things; fatigue and exercise are potent antidotes to cold and exposure. I am twice as buoyant, and hopeful, and happy, on a hard march, as when vegetating in camp. One goes through almost as much on a hunting tramp or a skating party, and who would complain of a little extra privation with our motives before us? I hope you do not feel discouraged at Burnside's partial failure. I continue full of hope till all is gone. This letter must be your Christmas box from me; very, very Happy Christmas and Happy New Year to you, dearest mother.

December 24, 1862
Letter of William Wheeler
Stafford Courthouse, VA

It is Christmas Eve, when "Peace on earth and good will toward men" is the text, and although nothing is said of good will toward *women*, yet I suppose that they are included, and so will pardon your long silence to-me-ward, and will do my best to spend this evening with you in thought and spirit, at least, if not in person, as in very happy years in the past.

Nothing among us here indicates the time. The country is too poor to furnish us with a turkey to diversify our pork and crackers, even if we had the money to purchase one, as we are even without a glass of wine for toasts, as several of our sutlers have been captured on the road. I determined, however, to do the best in my power, so I went out into the woods, and got a most beautiful little *holly-tree*, with splendid leaves and full of berries, which we planted at the foot of the flagstaff. There are a pair of symbols for you! Above, the emblem of equality, free thought, free speech, justice to all men; below, the emblem of respect for what is old and reverend, the ornament of this great festival of faith and religion. No freedom can be dangerous that is so rooted and grounded.

And while I am speaking of this, I would further say, that there are very many now fighting in this army, who have apparently lost sight of all early training, and have given up all religious habits, and who seem to think of nothing but their military duties; that is, you see, at first, only *the flag*, but if you could search deep down you would find the holly tree there too.

It is beginning to rain, which is a very improper proceeding for weather on Christmas Eve. I am officer of the day, and when I make my midnight round by the sable, I shall have a fine chance to verify the Catholic legend that at midnight, on Christmas, all "beasts of the stall" go on their knees. I have seen plenty of horses do this in the day-time and irrespective of church festivals.

I need not tell you that we had a tough time of it, marching down here, as the newspaper all speak, "ad nauseam," of the mud and other hindrances. The roughest part of it all was to hear Burnside's cannon when we had only reached Dumfries, and were, still, two long days' march from the scene of the conflict. It was also vile in the extreme to reach Falmouth, after seven days' incessant marching, and then to have to turn round and march straight back again. This being on the outskirts of battles, hearing the guns, and meeting the ambulances filled with wounded. I have had enough of, and I long for the excitement of another good hot artillery fire, like that on Friday afternoon at Bull Run. I almost long (I am almost ashamed to confess it) for my quietus; not that I despair of our success ultimately, or have any doubts of its completeness, but why should I live when so many better men are falling. Then, too, my anxiety for the cause, and my restiveness under my uncongenial surroundings, would forever quiet. A real good, honorable death might perhaps give some brightness to a dull and useless life. Do you think that I am too sad and gloomy? But what else can you expect of a man who is about to wash down with cold water a Christmas dinner of bean-soup and crackers?

December 26, 1862
Battery Orders No. 27
Stafford Courthouse, VA

I   Corporal Edward Baldwin 13 NY Battery is hereby appointed Sergt vice Duffy relieved of his position.
II   Corporal Christian Gutbrad 13 NY Battery is hereby appointed Sergt vice Hempen promoted.
III   Private James Lynch 13 NY Battery is hereby appointed Corporal.
These non-commissioned officers will be obeyed & respected accordingly.
Julius Dieckmann Capt
Comdg 13 NY Battery

December 29, 1862
Letter of William Wheeler
Stafford Courthouse, VA

Dearest Mother
Your letter dated, December 24 came safely to hand with the inclosed draft, which I was glad to dispose of to our sutler for something less... It is very lucky for me that he did not attempt to follow us to our march from Fairfax out here, as he would probably

have been captured at Dumfries with the rest, and my things would have shared his fate, and fallen into the hands of the rebel cavalry. A new way of sending things is by mail. I know one regiment in our Corps which receives three pairs of boots at least by every other mail, and some of the regiments with Burnside had their Christmas turkeys sent on in this way. If you could send me one it would be a regular treat on our mess-table, where we have the unvarying round of crackers for supper. Bread is not to be obtained anywhere, as the sutlers find that it pays better not to bring out anything but whiskey and tobacco....Christmas Day passed off very drearily; the day before I went out and got a little holly-tree, which I planted at the foot of the flag-staff, where it looked very pretty, and quite lighted up the places.

I had a pleasant call from young H of the class of 1859, and Captain Wm Lusk[28] of the Seventy-ninth New York, "the Highlanders," who have been in almost every hard fight since the first Bull Run, except the Peninsular battles, a rough experience for such a slight, delicate boy, but in spite of it he looked well, and bright, and hopeful. When John comes back from camp I intend to make a day of it down in Burnside's army, and to refresh myself with a sight of the cheerful, undesponding spirit which prevails there, in spite of all their reverses.

December 30, 1862
Letter of William Wheeler
Chantilly, VA

And even now you must not allow yourself to fall into the error of supposing that I have anything particular to say: I only palm off my worthless goods on you, in the hope that you will think rather of the writer than of the written, and send me back a letter telling of yourself, of New Haven and my family, of mutual friends, and their sayings and doings, and dispatches from that dear old student world from which I am now sometime an unwilling exile. You can really form no idea of the peculiar feelings I have towards that college time, and everything connected to it; classmates, friends in other classes, our lady friends of the period. "Hornet's Nest," and even such actual and living realities as my mother and the rest of the family, our house, the elm trees, all partake of a certain vague and shadowy beauty and excellence; it is my "Lost Bower." It is true the loafer within me says, "Recall that vanished time, dwell again in that Bower," but the worker says, "No, you have much more real duty to perform than that;" and so, although I cannot boast of much energy or success in action, I have yet a little too much of the earnest man in me to settle down into scholarly idleness. Still I love to hear about the old times, and the old friends, and you cannot interest me more than when you tell me all the New Haven gossip, what mischief Timothy Dwight is about, and the last joke indulged in by B....Of our late movements I have but little to say, except that between November 2 and November 19 we made a circumbendibus from Fairfax Court House, through Centreville, Painesville, and Aldie, round to this place, which is only six miles from "the point or place of beginning." At Aldie we had a superb place for winter quarters; our pieces in fine position, plenty of food, forage, and game in the neighborhood, and pretty girls sown broadcast over the land, whose charms were rendered still more piquant by their attitude of fierce by harmless defiance. In fact we had arranged ourselves nicely for a long stay; had plundered the church and schoolhouse of their stores and even carried off the superb gilt candelabra with a marble bottom, from the pulpit, as likewise the preacher's chair; my Captain (who along was the sacrilegious perpetrator) remarking pithily about this last article, that it was a real benevolence to the poor people to remove it, since the parson would not preach so long if he had to stand up all the time; or at any rate, as I suggested, he would have to effect "a change of base" à la McClellan. As if to punish us for our evil deeds, Burnside did change his base, and Sigel's Corps having been put in the reserve, he moved his head-quarters to Fairfax Court House, and we moved to Chantilly. Why they put Sigel in the reserve I can't imagine, unless it were that they were afraid of a dash in the read from Jackson, and considered our Flying Dutchman the only man fit to look after him. I don't know what our Corps amounts to now, as we have a large number of new regiments which are perfectly untried, and which don't promise much; but the old crowd, which fought at the Rappahannock and Bull run, were as compact and serviceable a little body of men as you could find in the army. Even here, we accomplish more than the Grand Army before Fredericksburg. You will undoubtedly have read in the papers about General Stahl's[29] reconnaissance to Berryville and its results; it was a most successful affair, and our men behaved excellently, using their sabres only, and gave the enemy "tüchtige Hiebe." The prisoners were not a bad looking lot, and kept their pluck up finely, considering the circumstances; the Pennsylvania colts, stolen by Stuart and now recaptured, made a truly beautiful show.

The brigade we are now attached to, the first of the First Division, commanded by Colonel von Gilson of the DeKalb Regiment[30], and a first-rate soldier to boot, is much more jolly and sociable than any we have before been connected with; and every few nights we, the artillery officers, get a solemn order to "report ourselves at such or such a regiment, where there is Bier; cheese and bread will also be furnished; gentlemen will bring with their own cigars, or pipes empty." The Forty-fifth New York is the jolliest, and has moreover a stunning Sing-Verein, which is a delight to hear. Still, the German, when he gets jolly, is somewhat beastly, and you hear far more coarseness than *any* crowd of young Americans; I infinitely prefer the quiet supper with a chosen crowd, as we have had them together, and then a sensible chat over the apples and Madeira until the small hours. My Captain is a regular character; he is about forty-five years old, is as gray as a badger, and has a queer, thin profile; he has a way of putting himself in a passion, which would be terrifying to the uninitiated, but which has come to serve me only with amusement. He cannot speak English at all, and is not disposed to learn it, so we have to communicate entirely in German, and this has been of very great service to me, as he speaks very correctly, I might almost say classically, and often corrects me when I make a mistake. But, whatever his faults and failings may be, he has one virtue which outweighs them all: he is truthful and reliable, and is one of those men who believe in keeping a promise, even when lightly made, at every risk. You can imagine that with such a man I have no trouble getting along with.

January 13, 1863
Report of Dr. [name not readable], Surgeon, 45th New York Regiment
Stafford Court House, VA

First Lieutenant Frank Singer, 13th NY Battery Capt. Dieckmann having applied for a certificate on which to ground an application for resignation. I do hereby certify, that I have carefully examined this officer, and find that he is suffering on Rheumatisms caused from a blow of a horse received at Centerville. I further declare my belief that he will not be able to resume his duties again.

January 14, 1863
Letter of resignation request to Capt. Julius Dieckmann, 13th New York Artillery
Stafford Court House, VA

    Sir

    I have the honor to state, that I now hold a commission as First Lieutenant of the 13th New York Battery since December 15th 1862.

    That by the blow of a horse which I received in the abdomen while one duty October 8th 62 at Centerville VA, and in consequence of which I was under medical treatment all the time since I feel constantly a heavy pain in my body, which disables me to hold any longer the high responsibilities of my present commission and therefore beg leave to tender my resignation accompanied by a medical certificate requesting a honorable discharge from the Military service of the United States.

    Most respectfully
    Your obedient servant
    Frank Singer
    Fist Lieutn 13th NY Battery

January 15, 1863
Letter of William Wheeler
Stafford Courthouse, VA

    I have been very much troubled to hear of your ill-health, so long continued and so severe, and have often wished that I could give you one of my own superabundance, for I have most of the time been so healthy as to get extremely restless and uncomfortable when lying in camp, and felt never better than when marching all day and sleeping soundly in a mudhole. I had to go through a toughening process at first, it is true, and John is undergoing the same now; but after it is over, it seems as if some steel had been imparted to the constitution. I hope most earnestly that you may become so restored as to be able to work once more with all vigor on your chosen way; but if it should not be so, you must not give overmuch at this enforced inactivity, remembering, that "God does not need either man's work, or his own gifts"; and that "they also serve who only stand and wait"; this last thought has comforted me more than once when I have heard the noise of battle at the front, and we were standing in impatient idleness in the reserve. My dear boy, in every battle in life there must be a reserve, and he who directs these battle will know when to bring it into action.

I have traveled the upper half of Virginia pretty thoroughly since last spring; under Fremont, we starved in Franklin, marched down the Shenandoah Valley, fought at Cross Keys, and came back to Winchester; then, under Sigel, we explored the Suray Valley, crossed the Blue Ridge again, went via Culpepper and Cedar Mountain to the Rapidan; then, under Pope (Sigel being still our corps commander), we made a good retreat across the Rappahannock, fought a week up and down its banks, then two days' hard work at Bull Run, where our Corps did and suffered pretty much all that was done and suffered, except the skedaddling; and since then we have been moving about Fairfax, Aldie, Chantilly, etc., until we came down here to support Burnside, and, fortunately, arrived too late to be victimized at that slaughter by Fredericksburg. Such is a hasty outline of my movements; a large part of the time has been spent among the mountains of the Allegheny and Blue Ridge, healthy, free, and glorious, where we foraged, and went fishing, blackberrying, and cherry-picking, and where at times it seemed more like a charming summer picnic "long drawn out" than anything else; that want that I have experienced most has been of that which your wife places as second in her list of 'temporal blessings,' viz., friends; and for months I have gone without meeting a single person with home I could talk about anything more deeply interesting than duty and the probability of our catching Jackson. Indeed, at times, I have become very much depress by this want of intercourse and sympathy, and nothing but the outdoor life, spent in the saddle, and the healthy excitement of the march and the bivouac, has saved me from being very miserable. It is when we are lying quiet in camp for some weeks that a man gets to feel how hard this life is to bear; no books, no friends to exchange thoughts with, no flowers, no gentle woman's society, no music except when the Brigade Band gives us the "SSB," or when some poor boy is laid in the stranger earth of Virginia to the solemn cords of Pleyel's Hymn. And this last consolation we all have, that if our soldier-life is very hard, it is also very short, and our death is honorable, and we ask of the passer-by, not like Archytas the "pulvis ter injectus," but rather three simple words of praise and kindness.

I enjoy the artillery service very much; it is the only arm in which intelligence is needed in every rank, and an officer of artillery has really a fine wide field for study. I have in my own section fine young sergeants and corporals, whom it is a pleasure to bring forward and perfect in the elements of our branch, and who fully answer the description which Victor Hugo gives of the sergeant of artillery, in the fifth volume of his "Les Misérables": "Of fair complexion, with a very mild face, and the intelligent air peculiar to that predestined and formidable arm." I regret very much that I did not get with our Battery the chance which that "Captain Wheeler did at West Point, to distinguish himself, although, even when all is done, a corps gets no praise unless it has a newspaper correspondent in tow, who is stuffed and flattered and deceived. At Bull Run no less than three splendid feats achieved by our Battery were ascribed to others by newspapers, while the dry details of General Milroy's report did us justice; but the romance is always ready by more than the history.

January 16, 1863
Extract of Special Orders No. 5, Headquarters, Grand Reserve Division
Stafford Court House

     5   The following named officers having tendered their resignation are honorably discharged from the military service of the United States:
     Lieut Frank Singer, 13 NY Baty
     By order of Maj Genl Sigel

January 18, 1863
Letter of William Wheeler
no location given

     Yesterday we received positive orders to stand ready to march this morning at break of day, and had made all our preparations to do so; but last night the order was countermanded, and so we have a quiet Sabbath after all....The idea of marching and having something to do put me in good spirits, and I have strong hopes that this time we shall accomplish something. What we want is a good fair contest of army against army, followed by a decisive victory. If we obtain this, I don't care much whether I live to see the results of it or not. The day for any individual to distinguish himself by single acts of daring has gone by, and the utmost devotion and bravery are now merely a part of every man's daily duty. It is now no compliment to say "brave officer," "brave soldier," but it is a disgrace to have anything else said. You will not, of course, think of sending anything edible to me by mail, especially as we are about to march. The fact is, we lived too well at Chantilly, and when we came here on hard tack we felt the change, though I am now quite reconciled to it.

January 22, 1863
Battery Orders No. 28
  camp at Acquia Creek

I   First Lieut Frank Singer having tendered his resignation and the same having been accepted, he has been honorably discharged the service of the United States, by Sp. Ord No 6, HQ Grand Res. Div. January 16, 1863.
II   Second Lieut Henry Bundy is hereby promoted to First Lieut vice Singer discharged.
III Orderly Sergeant Joseph Bohn is hereby appointed Second Lieut vice Bundy promoted.
IV   Sergeant Theilman Moritz is hereby appointed Orderly Sergeant vice Bohn promoted.
V   Private Ernest Volmer is hereby appointed Sergeant of 1st Detachment, vice Moritz promoted.
The appointments and promotions herein announced shall date respectively from the 16th of January 1863, and the officers and non-commissioned officers therein named shall be obeyed & respected accordingly.
Julius Dieckmann Capt
Comdg 13 NY Battery

January, 1863
Extract from "Records of Events" on the several returns for January, 1863, Center Grand Division, Army of the Potomac, commanded by Maj. Gen. George Meade
  no location given

ELEVENTH ARMY CORPS, COMMANDED BY BRIG GEN N C M'LEAN
FIRST DIVISION
    January 20, the First Division marched from Stafford Court-House; three regiments of the First Brigade and two sections of the Thirteenth Independent New York Battery to Acquia Landing; and two regiments, with one section of same

battery, to Potomac Creek Bridge; the Second Brigade to Belle Plain Landing.

February 3, 1863
Battery Orders No. 29
Brooke's Station, VA

The Commander of the Battery calls the attention of the company to the following orders
I   There shall be roll call three times each day in the Battery, as follows, at Reveille (7AM), at Noon, and at Retreat (5PM).
II   Immediately after each roll call, feed call
III   At nine o'clock in the morning, and at four in the afternoon, water call. At water call, each sergeant shall take charge of his detachment, the horses without saddles, and all shall proceed to water together under the command of the officer of the day.
IV   Each driver shall have his horse properly groomed by the time water call sounds in the morning.
V   No man shall leave camp or take his horse out of camp without permission from the commanding officer. Those disobeying these orders shall be punished according to Military Regulations.
Julius Dieckmann
Capt Comdg 13 NY Battery

February 22, 1863
Letter of William Wheeler
Brooke's Station, VA

    The era extending from the second of February (date of your last letter), to February (date above), is a very much smaller one than that from December 3 (date of *my* last letter), to February 2, and this would perhaps be, to a right mind, convincing of the fact that you did not yet deserve to hear from me; but when I reflect what an unpleasant state of affairs it would bring about if we should all get what we deserve, I think it better not to introduce this principal, and prefer to go it after the G R, and write promptly to others as I would have others write promptly to me. It is true, I doubt very much if I shall receive my reward directly from you, but the grand principle of compensation *must* be obeyed, and doubtless the recompense will be manifested in an extra and unexpected epistle from my cousin A, or perhaps another pleasant little reminder from the Philadelphia doves, who are not only "harmless," but Ys....I was not a little interested in your account of the Philological Society, and your paper on the Prometheus question. I should greatly enjoy looking in upon one of your meetings, and sitting in reverence at the feet of some of those distinguished philologs while they enlightened the world on "Anaphora and Chiasmus," or similar important topics. The truth is, I have not the patience nor the industry to pursue these inquiries into the dryer recesses of language; I prefer to take the results of others' labor, as furnished in grammars, etc., and then to read the classics for the thoughts they contain, as a part of the general treasure of Thought contained in books, whether ancient or modern. That careful industry by means of which a student so thoroughly elaborates a language as to make the ring of its words and the turning of its verses as familiar to him as his own tongue, that capacity of becoming a Greek with Sophocles, and a Roman with Horace, is given, it seems to me, to a very chosen few, and can hardly be sought as an object by any but the professional student. You and I may become excellent German scholars, but Goethe's "Der Fischer" will never sound to us as perfect as to German ears, and however enthusiastic we may be for Dante's "il tremolar della marina," and the anariumon gelasma, which are sweet to us because half translated into the universal language of similar sound which is shared alike by all, still is not like English to our ears, not like Shakespeare's "Full fathom five thy father lies," of Byron's "Tremulous silver of Euphrates' wave." But your essay on the subordinate part played by Zeus in the "Prometheus" was something higher than mere scholarship, and I should like very much to see the whole paper, rather than the few hints of it which you gave me. Did it occur to you to look at Shelley's "Prometheus Unbound," in connection with your work, or do you despise the moderns entirely? I think it is his finest work, and well worth studying for the exquisite melody of many passages; he seems to adopt to the view which you combat, and makes Jove hear all the odium of having inflicted an unjust punishment upon the suffering Reformer (for Prometheus is certainly the original of that species, the first Protestant), and also to get the worst in arguments with him, and to be blackguarded unmercifully, while behind all rises a dim shape called "Demogrogon," who is evidently the chief and bottle-washer, and who indulges in certain prophecies of Delphic obscurity and generalizes worse than the "Declaration of Independence" according to Choate. It seems to me that the question narrows itself down to this: injustice had been done to Prometheus, if not by the mere fact of punishment, then certainly by the manner of it, and the unseemly taunts with which it was accompanied. Now we can look upon Zeus, either as a form of the Supreme Being, or as an executor and prime minister of the orders of Fate; that he is not the former, appears everywhere in Æschylus, and it would certainly be impiety to impute injustice to the Supreme Being. That he is the later, appears to me in "Prometheus" just as much as anywhere else, and his subjection to some higher power is shown by his terror about the mysterious marriage which he was to contract, and which was to be his ruin. All this he would have know and prevented if he had not been a deity "zweiter classe." The whole, in fact, illustrates the "Responsibility of Prime Ministers," leaving no trace of wrong upon the character of the mysterious king upon the throne behind....With regard to the state of the country, I think it is not by any means so unfavorable as many of our friends at home seem to suppose; we have made great advance in our opinions upon my subjects, such as drafting, arming of the Negroes, etc., and I hope to see the campaign carried on in the spring with a vigorous policy and to a successful issue. The army will obey every properly issued and communicated order from head-quarters; so long as the President and the Secretary of War are all right, Congress may blow, legislatures may resolve, and knots of rebel sympathizers may make a show of resistance, but it will amount to nothing; if violent resistance be made to the enforcement of the draft, we can easily spare a couple of veteran regiments who would enjoy nothing more than to drag out concealed rebels and stay-at-homes, and make them bear their share of the burden. In fact, I should have no objections myself to be sent to New York with my section; there is a fine position for artillery on Broadway below Canal street, commanding the streets as high as Eleventh, and the balls would ricochet splendidly on the hard pavement. No; the army may as a mass have dime ideas of principles and rights, but they *do* know that they have been working and fighting in this cause, and they do not propose to give up and own themselves thrashed, just because their friends at the North are unwilling to make some slight sacrifices also. I believe in the North's being made to *feel* the war, which she has not yet done as a nation, and to really offer up something t wing this great, almost infinite good. Among the articles in the stupid Atlantic Monthly of this month, is one entitled, "The Law of Costs," which has some good ideas, though uncouthly and obscurely worked up. The more we undertake to do this matter cheaply, the longer it will remain to be done. The guns are even now echoing from hill to hill, and across the fields of snow, as the batteries are firing salutes in honor of Washington's birthday. I hope that the next anniversary will see this question nearer a happy solution.

February 28, 1863
Battery Orders No. 30
Brooke's Station, VA

I   Sergeant Henry Miller is hereby appointed Orderly Sergeant vice Moritz discharged from Feb 18, 1863.
II   Corporal James When is hereby appointed Sergeant from Feb 18, 1863, vice Miller promoted.
III   Privates William Suckendick, John O'Connor, Charles Bonner, Theodore Guerts, Joseph Dalton are hereby appointed Corporals in this Battery. These non-commissioned officers will be obeyed & respected accordingly.
Julius Dieckmann Capt
Comdg 13 NY Batty

March 1, 1863
Battery Orders No. 31
Brooke's Station, VA

In accordance with Gen Order No 2 from HQ 1st Division 11th Corps, the following order is communicated to this Battery
I   The men are reminded of the proper salute to be made to officers, whether belonging to this Battery or strangers and of the proper demeanor to be observed when conversing with officers. Non-commissioned officers will see that their Detachments are instructed in the proper mode of saluting, both with & without arms.
II   At Reveille & Retreat roll calls, and in general, at all roll calls, the men will fall in with jackets, a dark blue blouses, properly buttoned. At Reveille & Retreat, the first call will be sounded at least 10 minutes before the assembly; this gives opportunity for proper preparation.
Julius Dieckmann Capt
Comdg 13 NY Battery

March 3, 1863
Battery Orders No. 32
Brooke's Station, VA

Private John Fridrichs of 13th NY Battery having failed to return at the proper time, when absent on furlough, and now having been absent without leave for 5 days viz from Feb 23 to Feb 28 is hereby adjudged to forfeit to the United States one months pay, subject to the approval of the Chief of Artillery
Julius Dieckmann Capt
Comdg 13 NY Battery

March 14, 1863
Letter of William Wheeler
Brooke's Station, VA

Dearest Mother
 I had hoped to be in New Haven by this time to-day, and to have spent one Sunday with you at home, after my fourteen months' absence. My application for a leave has not yet been heard from. I think it not unlikely that the pleasant weather of the last two or three days has suggested ideas of marching, and that in consequence, no more furloughs will be granted. Perhaps this is for the best, after all. If I should go home, the parting would be most painful, the crust of insensibility and of absorption in my duty would be cast off,--I should be like a soft-shell crab, who had cast his shell prematurely, and had come out of his retreat tender and shivering among his hard-shell companions.
 I thought that I had been constant enough in duty to deserve so much consideration, and had looked upon my furlough as sure to come in a day or two.... You must not look upon me as if I were only a first lieutenant of infantry, for our service is so interesting, and at the same time so valuable, that I would not exchange places with a field officer of infantry. Perhaps I may get my battery one of these days; if I should not, you must not think that I am by any means thrown away. I came by accident into this Company, and have done my duty for eighteen months without much cessation, and if promotion should come to me I would accept it, but I would not seek it.
 [The leave of absence having been sent, he was at home for a few days.]

March 18, 1863
Battery Orders No. 33
camp near Brooke's Station, VA

Privates William Earl and Jacob Falk of 13th NY Battery, having failed to return at the proper time twice when absent of furlough and having been absent without leave respectively as follows: Private William Earl for 2 days, viz from the 8th to the 10th of March; and Private Jacob Falk for 3 days, viz from the 8th to the 11th of March. Each is hereby adjudged to forfeit to the United States one months pay subject to the approval of the Chief of Artillery.
It is further ordered that whereas Privates Wilmot and Geiger of this battery were on yesterday absent from camp with their horses without leave and in disobedience of battery orders, they the said Wilmot and Geiger are hereby adjudged to undergo 3 extra guards each.
Julius Dieckmann
Capt Comdg 13 NY Battery

March 22, 1863
Battery Orders No. 34
camp near Brooke's Station, VA

The Chief of Artillery conceiving that battery order no 33 whereby one months pay each is ordered to be deducted from the pay of Privates Earl and Falk of this battery for having exceeded their furloughs would operate as a punishment inflicted on their families rather then on them individually; it is therefore ordered that battery order no 33 be revoked and said Privates William Earl and Jacob Falk are hereby ordered to stand guard once in every 3 days during a period of 2 months.
By approval of Capt L Schmier Chief of Art
Julius Dieckmann
Capt Commanding 13th NY Battery

March 30, 1863
Letter of William Wheeler
Brooke's Station, VA

    I am once more back again in camp, settled down to my old work, and am able to look back on my hurried visit home; although everything passed so rapidly as to make the whole seem like a dream, hardly more vivid than many dreams of home which I have had in camp and bivouac, yet there was an inexpressible satisfaction in meeting you all face to face once more, before entering upon the distractions and occupations of the spring campaign.

[After a few days spent in New York, he went to Annapolis for a day, and then on to Washington.]

I left the Ebbitt House in Washington on Thursday, for the 8 AM boat. By 3 PM I was at Brooks' Station, the Captain having come to the cars to meet me, while in the background stood Glenmore with the horses, and I felt that I was once more in the traces, and must buckle down to work. The next morning an accident happened which might have resulted seriously, if it had occurred in the night time, and as it was, it came near destroying all our worldly goods. Shortly after breakfast, as I was talking with the Captain, I heard a great shouting and yelling, by our quarters, and looking round I saw the tent occupied by Lieutenant Carlisle and myself in a blaze. In a moment, a half a dozen men were cutting at the tent ropes, pulling up the pegs, and tearing away the tents, to get the burning mass away from our beds, and trunks, and clothes; in this we succeeded entirely, but I burned the fingers of my left hand considerably. We immediately set to work to get a new house over our heads; men were sent off to cut trees, and horses drag them, and by night a stately edifice of logs had arisen, and by spreading a fly on top, we made a shelter for our goods from the rain, which was beginning to fall. The next day the house had it chinks stopped with chips, and plastered with mud, a mason from my section took the contract for building the chimney, which, with a foundation of stone, and a continuation of brink, would shame that of many a farmer's house in Virginia. A nice frame door of canvas stretched on boards was made. We moved into our new residence last night, and found it far more roomy and airy than the had been; roof twice as high, and a nice, open fire-place, which gives out far more heat than the old stove had done, so that we do not repine at all at the conflagration. I shall not be sorry to get on the move soon. Our present camping ground was excellent for winter, but it is too low and marshy for spring, and will be unhealthy before long. Since I began to write this letter, I have been called off to look after one of my corporals, who had been taken suddenly ill. I brought him to the Division hospital, where the doctor told me it was congestive fever, and kept him there.

April 11, 1863
Letter of William Wheeler
Brooke's Station, VA

    Here we are still lying, lapped in inactivity, waiting for fine weather and roads practicable for artillery-carriages and team wagons, and in the meantime fretting our very hearts out with *ennui* and spring restlessness, which can find no outlet nor object upon which to exert itself. But I know that you will be kind and considerate enough to make allowances for the stupefying influences of idleness and winter quarters, and will not refuse to accept a commonplace letter, made up out of nothing, just as you would one setting forth the "moving accidents" of march and bivouac, and picket and foraging, and "hairbreadth scapes in the imminent deadly breach." The actors now are languid officers wearing new uniforms, drinking wine and making visits; lazy men with decent jackets, clean button, and washed faces; horses fat, guns polished, carriages painted, harness cleaned; the epoch of reviews, inspections, ladies in camp, soft bread, commissary whiskey, and furloughs to New York. I wave a bit of paper containing the magic works, "March-orders," and presto! change. You see, on a spring evening, our Battery coming into camp, after a long day's march, and I can imagine that you ask, "Are those dirty creatures on horseback the same with those fine officers whom we saw last winter? Are those wild and ragged animals those well-clad soldiers? And what made them exchange their horses for these meagre brutes?" You then see, further, how, after a most scanty meal, both on the part of men and beasts, they all lie down on the bare ground, and sleep most soundly, perhaps in mud and rain, until the bugle blows the reveille at sunrise, and then again to the road; or perhaps they "take position," and have a fight. And yet, strange as it may seem, the latter kind of life, with all its privations, is infinitely superior to the former, comfortable as it may be; for one who has youth and health, and an animating principal of action within, it is full of zest and interest, and I do not know when I have felt a more joyous elevation of spirits, than when riding through Virginia oak woods, on some lovely summer morning, a good horse under me, the music of birds above, and below, the creaking of caissons, and the ringing of "jingling bridle-reins," and the inspiring prospect of a conflict with an enemy a few miles ahead.

    My first day in camp was celebrated by the burning down of my tent, from which I had great difficulty in rescuing my clothes and books. Some of my friends hinted that I had got my house when I was at New York, and had then set it on fire to get the insurance, but, probable as this hypothesis might seem, I am myself inclined to think it became ignited from a spark falling upon the canvas, which was already dry as tinder. However, I did not repine at my loss, but set the men of my section to work, house-building, immediately.

So now we have a shanty, put up in two days, far more comfortable than a tent, and have so far had two weeks enjoyment of it; next winter I intend to put up such a house as soon as we go into winter-quarters. Perhaps you think that I am mistaken in saying "next winter," as if I had not doubt of our still being in the field; I reply that I can hardly hope for such decided successes, before that time, as to permit of a reduction of the army, and my maxim is to be provided for the worst, and above all things *not to under-estimate our enemies*. It will take all the men we can brig into the field, and all the energy those men possess, to make a decided impression on the rebels this year; I believe in not being elevated or thrown off our guard by success, and not unduly depressed by the want of it, but to keep steadily on at our work, until it is finished. And even then it will be better to be joyful, than boastful or triumphant; this war will be bring *one* advantage at least, if it cures us of these disgusting qualities.

President Lincoln reviewed our Corps yesterday, and I, for one, did not feel ashamed of our old Eleventh Corps, and I doubt if the President has seen, in the whole Army of the Potomac, a hardier or more soldierly looking set of men. He rode past on a splendid black horse, followed by his two little boys, on ponies, and then cam an enormous and splendid cortege of at least two hundred officers.

The weather, after great changefulness, many an unseasonable snow and rain storm, has at last apparently settled down fine, the roads are rapidly drying up, and we may look for marching orders shortly now. The air is delightfully soft and mild, and the grass is sprouting. I send you a little sprig of trailing arbutus from near our camp; it does not grow here in the same profusion as in Western Virginia, where I used to pluck it in long streamers, and twist it round my hat.

April 17, 1863
Affidavit of Capt. Julius Dieckmann, 13th NY Artillery
Brooke's Station, VA

I, Julius Dieckmann, being duly sworn do depose and say that I have been duly commissioned as Captain of the 13th New York Battery, from the 15th day of May 1862, a vacancy existing at that time for the said position and I having been only appointed thereto, and that I have done duty as Captain in the said Battery from the 15th day of May to the present time.

Also that I have made every attempt in my power to be mustered into the service of the United States as a Captain, but without success.

  Julius Dieckmann
  Capt Comdg 13th NY Battery

Affidavit of Lt. Col. Louis Schirmer, Chief of Artillery, 11th Army Corps
Brooke's Station, VA

I, Louis Schirmer Lieut Col, Chief of Artillery, 11th Corps being duly sworn do depose and say that Julius Dieckmann was duly commissioned as Captain of the 13th New York Battery from the 15th day of May 1862, and that he has done duty as Captain in the said Battery from the said 15th May 1862 to the present time.

Also that he has made every attempt in his power to be mustered into the service of the United States as Captain but without success.

  L Schirmer, Lieut Col
  Chief of Artillery
  11th Corps

Affidavit of Lt William Wheeler, 13th New York Artillery
Brooke's Station, VA

I William Wheeler, being duly sworn, do depose and say, that I have been duly commissioned as First Lieutenant in the 13th New York Battery from the 15th day of October 1861, a vacancy existing for the said position at that time, and I having been duly appointed thereto; ad that I have done duty as First Lieutenant in the said battery for the said 15th day of October 1861 to the present time. Also that I

have made every attempt in my power to be mustered into the service of the United States as First Lieutenant but without success.
Wm Wheeler

Affidavit of Capt. Julius Dieckmann, 13th New York Artillery Brooke's Station, VA

I Julius Dieckmann, being duly sworn, do depose and say, that I am Captain of the 13th New York Battery, that William Wheeler has his commission as First Lieutenant from the 15th of October 1861, that he has to the best of my knowledge & belief done duty as First Lieutenant from that date.

Also that he has made every attempt in his power to be mustered into the service of the United States as First Lieutenant, but without success.
Julius Dieckmann
Capt, Comdg 13th NY Battery

May 1863-June 1863
Stop; face about; do not retreat any farther!

May 4, 1863
Report of Lieut. Col. Adolph von Hartung, 74th Pennsylvania Infantry
  no location given

General: Herewith I have the honor to send to you a report concerning that part of the battle of Chancellor's farm in which the Seventy-fourth was engaged, May 2.

Before beginning the fight, the regiment was formed in line of battle facing the Plank road from Fredericksburg to Orange Court-House, Different regiments of the First Division of the Eleventh Corps were in the same manner posted on our right and the Sixty-first Ohio[31] on our left.

At about 5.30 PM the regiments on our right were suddenly attacked in very great force by the enemy, and his attack was directed on our right flank and back. The regiment on our right broke through the ranks of the Seventy-fourth Regiment in such a manner that the regiment got at once thrown in such disorder that a restoring of order was an utter impossibility. The first we ever knew of the enemy was that our men, while sitting on their knapsacks and ready to spring to their arms, were shot from the rear and flank. A surprise in broad daylight, a case not yet heard of in the history of any war, was so complete that the men had not even time to take their arms before they were thrown in the wildest confusion. The different regiments on our right were in a few minutes all mixed up with the Seventy-fourth. The enemy pressed heavily. Some guns of Dieckmann's battery in front, without firing a single shot, broke through the whole mixed crowd, and the regiment could, under such circumstances, do nothing else but retreat through the woods.

Preserving as much order as possible, I led the regiment back behind a rifle-pit near the old headquarters of Major-General Howard. About 50 paces in front of this rifle-pit, right near the road, I found Major-General Howard, who was crying, "Stop; face about; do not retreat any farther!" This was well said, but impossible to be done. The troops were entirely mixed up, the panic was great, the enemy pressed heavily, the rifle-pits in the rear was already glittering with bayonets, and occasional shots from behind were showing the greatness of the danger of trying to rally the troops in front of the pit. To obey the order of Major-General Howard at this moment and at this place would have been certain useless destruction to every man of my regiment. The rifle-pit alone and nowhere else was the right place for rallying the troops. There the greatest order was soon restored, and the regiment awaited calmly the approach of the enemy. Different regiments were on our right and left. On our right I remember the One hundred and nineteenth and Sixty-eighth New York Regiments[32], all well rallied again. We were soon furiously attacked, but the enemy was handsomely checked and driven back. The men stuck to their colors and fought bravely, but renewed attacks of superior forces and flank movements of the enemy made all the troops on our left fall back. Our artillery, too, retreated, and broke through the rifle-pits and through our ranks. The troops on our right, too, withdrew, and the Seventy-fourth Regiment, nearly left alone, could not keep up the defense any longer, and consequently retreated. A part of the men, as it does always happen, got separated from the main part of the regiment and retreated on their own hook.

    The main part of the regiment retreated in the greatest order up to a point near Major-General Hooker's headquarters, where the whole Eleventh Corps was rallied again. The whole regiment was soon rallied again, some few stragglers excepted, who joined during the night and next morning.

    At roll-call, held at about 10 PM, 60 men were missing; of these 3 officers and 16 men are positively either killed or wounded, the rest taken prisoners or missing.

    I have the honor to take this opportunity to mention to you the names of the following sergeants of this regiment detailed for color guard, who, in a moment of the greatest danger, behaved most nobly and bravely, and to whom the whole regiment is indebted for not losing its flag: Sergeant [George] Ekert, color-bearer; Sergeant [Henry] Bender, Company A; Sergeant [George] Nissel, Company D: Sergeant [Joseph] Frey, Company G, and Sergt W Kruger, Company B.

    I am, general, your most obedient servant,
    A Von Hartung
    Lieut Col, Comdg 74th Regiment Pennsylvania Volunteers

May 9, 1863
Report of Maj. Allen Brady, 17th Connecticut Infantry
camp near Brooke's Station, VA

General: In compliance with instructions, received from division headquarters this morning, I have the honor to make the following statement of the part taken by the Seventeenth Connecticut Volunteers in the engagement of May 2:

The regiment, under command of Col William H Noble, was placed in position to support Dieckmann's battery. The right wing, commanded by Colonel Noble and Lieutenant-Colonel Walter, was posted in the garden (in rear of the house occupied as headquarters by Generals Devens and McLean), along the garden fence, extending the whole length of the front, and partially covering the two sides, thus forming portions of a square.

The left wing, under the direct command of Maj A G Brady, was in line of battle along the Culpeper road, and on the right flank of Dieckmann's battery, continuous with the general line of battle of the brigade, though separated from the next regiment on our right by a space somewhat greater than that occupied by the right wing before its advance, of about 75 yards into the garden.

During the day we had two companies out on picket, one from each wing. These were driven in about 5 PM, rapidly pursued by the enemy.

Our right wing could not fire upon the enemy while our pickets were retreating, but as soon as the rebel line was unmasked by the pickets we poured several severe volleys into their ranks, until, being overpowered by the rapid advance of the enemy in overwhelming numbers, we were compelled to retreat, in obedience to command and in good order.

The left wing was exposed to a cross and enfilading fire, which caused the major commanding to order the men to lie down. They remained firmly at their posts, exposed to a galling fire, until after the battery which we were supporting had retreated without firing a gun.

I must here state that not a man belonging to the battery stood at his post when the attack commenced, neither did they undertake to fire a gun. After the battery had retreated, and as our left wing could not see the enemy, but was exposed to the most galling fire, I gave the order, and marched them out by the left flank, in good order.

Soon after the colonel had retreated with the right wing, which was posted in the garden, he was wounded. The lieutenant-colonel (Charles Walter) is supposed to have been killed in the garden. This left the command of the regiment with the major, which he assumed at once, and rallied the men behind the rifle-pits near General Howard's headquarters, and remained there until driven out at the point of the bayonet and superior force. The regiment again made a stand at the rifle-pit on the right of the road, and remained until driven out, and again retreated toward General Hooker's headquarters, and again made a stand in the woods under the battery, and compelled soldiers from other regiments to rally with us. Here we remained until ordered to change our position to the hill in rear of the batteries and near General Hooker's headquarters.

We entered the fight with 3 field and 5 commissioned staff officers, 27 line officers, and 482 enlisted men.

The following is a list of the casualties of the regiment:

Officers and men Killed		Wounded	Missing	Total
Officers		4	6	10
Enlisted men	1	31	78	110
Total	1	35	84	120

I have the honor to be, general, very respectfully, your obedient servant,
 Allen G Brady
  Major, Commanding Seventeenth Connecticut Volunteers

May 12, 1863
Report of Maj. Gen. Carl Schurz, 3rd Division, 11th Army Corps camp near Stafford Court House, VA

General: About the part taken by the division under my command in the operations of the Army of the Potomac from April 27 to May 6, I beg leave to report as follows:

I deem it unnecessary to speak of the marches we executed previous to our arrival on the battlefield of May 2, as my division marched along with the corps without any separate action. I will only say that all orders were executed by officers and men with promptness and alacrity, and that the men marched better, were in higher spirits, and endured the fatigues and hardships of the march by night and day more cheerfully than ever before. I have never known my command to be in a more excellent condition.

The division arrived at the junction of the Orange Court-House Plank road and the old turnpike in the afternoon of April 30. I was ordered to go into camp, facing west, on the open ground near Hawkins' farm. The disposition I made of my forces is shown on Diagram No. 1.

In this position the division remained until noon, May 1, when we received marching orders, which, to the disappointment of the troops, were countermanded immediately afterward. I then was ordered to take a position facing south, connecting with the First Division, under General Devens, on my right, and the Second Division, under General Steinwehr, on my left. I placed General Schimmelfennig's brigade on my right, connecting on his right with General McLean's brigade, of the First Division, and ordered Colonel Krzyzanowski to occupy my left, to connect on his left with Colonel Buschbeck's brigade, of the Second Division. The dispositions I made are shown in detail on Diagram No 2; in addition to which I have to observe that the two regiments forming my extreme right were ordered by me to be placed in column on the open field immediately on the left of General McLean's brigade, so as to give them liberty of movement, but that they were drawn back behind the fence and deployed in line of battle on the old Turnpike road, as I understand, by special directions from headquarters. Behind my Second Brigade, Colonel Krzyzanowski, I placed a strong reserve, so as to be able to assist Colonel Buschbeck, whose line was at the time very thin. The Eighty-second Ohio I kept farther back, as a general reserve. My pickets were at a suitable distance in front, south of the Plank road, connecting with those of General Devens on the right and General Steinwehr on the left. Captain Dilger's battery was placed at the junction of the two roads, commanding the Plank road, the valley below, and the woods beyond.

The firing we heard all along the line of the army during the day seemed to indicate that the enemy was feeling our front in its whole length. Toward evening the enemy began to throw shells from two pieces placed on an open space in the woods opposite General Devens' left, but doing no injury. This fire was not replied to by our artillery.

General Schimmelfennig received the order to send forward one regiment to capture or drive away those pieces. A short but lively skirmish ensued, in which some of our men were wounded, and the officers commanding the expedition returned with the report that the pieces had already been withdrawn. A subsequent reconnaissance proved this to be true. A negro was brought in from a farm near the place where the guns had stood, and reported that he had seen some rebel troops moving westward; but the information he gave us was very indefinite.

Meanwhile my chief of staff, Major [Ernest F] Hoffmann, was ordered by you to superintend the construction rifle-pits along our whole front, facing south. Pioneers and fatigue parties worked all night, and at daybreak the rifle-pits were nearly completed. General Schimmelfennig obstructed the wood road in his front, south of the Plank road, with abatis. The night passed off quietly, the troops of my division remaining in the position above indicated.

Early in the morning of May 2, General Hooker passed along the whole line, and was received by officers and men with great demonstrations of enthusiasm.

As the general disposition made of the rest of the corps had great influence upon the part taken by my division in the action of the evening, I beg leave to say a few words about the distribution of the forces of the First and Second Divisions in connection with mine. The extreme right was occupied by General Devens' (First) brigade, under Colonel von Gilsa, consisting of the Forty-first, Forty-fifth, and Fifty-fourth New York, and the One hundred and fifty-third Pennsylvania[33]. Part of this brigade (two regiments) was formed at an angle with the old turnpike, fronting nearly west. On the road itself one section of Captain Dieckmann's battery was placed behind an abatis. Colonel von Gilsa's left connected with General McLean's brigade, consisting of the Twenty-fifth, Fifty-fifth, Seventy-fifth, and One hundred and seventh Ohio, and the Seventeenth Connecticut Volunteers. This brigade was formed in line of battle on the old Turnpike road, with one regiment in second line and one detached as a reserve for Colonel von Gilsa. Four pieces of Captain Dieckmann's battery were pieced near General McLean's left, on open and high ground.

Immediately east of Talley's farm, where General Devens had his headquarters, General McLean's left connected with my right, consisting of the Seventy-fourth Pennsylvania and the Sixty-first Ohio, of General Schimmelfennig's brigade, deployed in line of battle on the road, having an embankment in their front and the thickest kind of pine undergrowth immediately in their rear; on their left the Sixty-eighth New York, of the same brigade, also in line of battle; the sharpshooters of the brigade in the little piece of woods between the two roads east of the open field flanking the line; the Eighty-second Illinois and the One hundred and fifty-seventh New York behind General Schimmelfennig's left, in second line, connecting with General Schimmelfennig's left; the One hundred and nineteenth New York, of my Second Brigade, occupying the southern border of the little piece of woods above mentioned; then Dilger's battery; the Fifty-eighth New York in the church grove; behind the interval the Seventy-fifth Pennsylvania, and farther to the left the Twenty-sixth Wisconsin[34], in second line, and the Eighty-second Ohio still farther back, as above stated. On the left of Captain Dilger's battery commenced Colonel Buschbeck's brigade, part of which was deployed in the rifle-pits; Captain Wiedrich's battery, from which two pieces had been detached to General Barlow's brigade, stood near Colonel Buschbeck's right on high ground. On the left of Colonel Buschbeck, General Barlow's brigade, with one section of Captain Wiedrich's battery. Farther to the left, troops of other corps. A rifle-pit was constructed, running north and south, on the west of the eminence east of Dowdall's Tavern. The Reserve Artillery, which arrived in the course of the day, was placed on that eminence.

    This position was, in my humble opinion, a good one to move from if the army had followed up the offensive, which, no doubt, had originally been contemplated. As a defensive position it presented a front only moderately strong to resist a parallel attack coming from the south. I say moderately strong, as the line, especially on our right, was very thin, and we had no general reserve. But if this position was intended to protect the right and rear of the army, a look at the map will show that it lacked some of the most essential requisites. Our right wing stood completely in the air, with nothing to lean upon, not even a strong *echelon*, and with no reliable cavalry to make reconnaissances, and that, too, in a forest thick enough not to permit any view to the front, flank, or rear, but not thick enough to prevent the approach of the enemy's troops. Our rear was at the mercy of the enemy, who was at perfect liberty to walk right around us through the large gap between von Gilsa's right and the cavalry force which was stationed at Ely's Ford, and which, at all events, had no considerable power of resistance. If it was really the intention that we should act on the defensive and cover the right and rear of the whole army, our right ought to have been drawn back toward the Rapidan, to rest on that river, at or near the mouth of Hunting Run, the corps abandoning so much of the Plank road as to enable it to establish a solid line. As we were actually situated, an attack from the west and northwest could not be resisted for any length of time without a complete change of front on our part. To such a change, especially if it was to be made in haste, the formation of our forces was exceedingly unfavorable.

It was almost impossible to maneuver some of our regiments under fire of the enemy, hemmed in as they were on the old turnpike by embankments and rifle-pits in front and thick woods in the rear, drawn out in long, deployed lines, giving just room enough for the stacks of arms and a narrow passage; and this old Turnpike road was at the same time the only line of communication we had between the different parts of our front. Such was the position occupied by the Eleventh Corps on May 2.

In the course of the forenoon I was informed that large columns of the enemy could be seen from General Devens' headquarters, moving from east to west on a road running nearly parallel with the Plank road, on a ridge at a distance of about 2 miles or over. I observed them plainly as they moved on. I rode back to your headquarters, and on the way ordered Captain Dilger to look for good artillery positions on the field fronting west, as the troops would, in all probability, have to execute a change of front.

The matter was largely discussed at your headquarters, and I entertained and expressed in our informal conversations the opinion that we should form upon the open ground we then occupied, with our front at right angles with the Plank road, lining the church grove and the border of the woods east of the open plain with infantry, placing strong *echelons* behind both wings, and distributing the artillery along the front on ground most favorable for its action, especially on the eminence on the right and left of Dowdall's Tavern. In this position, sweeping the open plains before us with our artillery and musketry, and checking the enemy with occasional offensive returns, we might have been able to maintain ourselves even against superior forces at least long enough to give General Hooker time to take measures according to the exigencies of the moment. Soon afterward we were informed that two divisions of General Sickles' corps were to attack in flank and rear the column of the enemy which we had seen marching, and you were requested to detach one of your brigades for their support. This weakened the force you might have used as a general reserve very materially.

In the absence of orders, but becoming more and more convinced that the enemy's attack would come from the west and fall upon our right and rear, I took it upon my own responsibility to detach two regiments from the second line of my Second Brigade, and to place them in a good position on the right and left of the Ely's Ford road, west of Hawkins' farm, so as to check the enemy if he should attack our extreme right and penetrate through the woods at that point. This was subsequently approved by you. The regiments I selected were the Seventy-fifth Pennsylvania and the Twenty-sixth Wisconsin. The Seventy-fifth Pennsylvania[35] had to relieve the pickets of the Second Brigade, and was replaced by the Fifty-eighth New York. The Eighty-second Ohio[36] I placed at some distance behind the left of the Fifty-eighth New York. The disposition of my troops was then as shown on Diagram No 3, and, no orders reaching me, it remained so until the battle commenced. With these exceptions, no change was made in the position occupied by the corps.

Brigadier-General Schimmelfennig, commanding my First Brigade, made several reconnaissances in his front and that of General Devens, especially on the Plank road and through the wooded country south of it; but these reconnaissances, made with infantry, were necessarily confined to a limited compass, and brought no other fact to light but that the enemy's skirmishers were found at a distance of 1½ to 2 miles in considerable number.

Meanwhile we heard General Sickles' artillery, but the firing did not continue long, so that it seemed as if the attack on the flank and rear of that column of the enemy which we had seen marching toward our right had been checked or given up.

It was between 3 and 4 PM when the section of artillery attached to Colonel von Gilsa's brigade gave two discharges, followed by a short musketry fire. We hastened to the front, and received the report that only a few rebel cavalrymen had shown themselves on the old turnpike, and that the artillery had fired without orders. All became quiet again. I ordered General

Schimmelfennig to push another reconnaissance up the Plank road. The instructions he received from headquarters were to the effect that he should avoid everything that might bring on an engagement. The reconnoitering party returned after some time with the report that they had heard the yells and shouts of a large number of men behind the enemy's line of skirmishers. The cavalry, which had been attached to your command but a few days before, and whose business it was to clear up our front and flank, repeatedly reported that at some distance from our pickets they had been fired upon, and that then, of course, they could go no farther. Immediately before the enemy rushed upon us, a reconnoitering party of that cavalry went into the woods in front of the Twenty-sixth Wisconsin; returned after about ten minutes, and informed the officers of the Twenty-sixth Wisconsin that it was all right, and then went quietly to rest behind Hawkins' farm.

It was nearly 6 o'clock when we suddenly heard a sharp artillery and musketry fire on our extreme right. I at once ordered all regiments within my reach to change front. The One hundred and nineteenth New York I took out of its position in the woods, facing south, and formed it near the junction of the Plank road and the old turnpike, facing west. The Sixty-eighth New York received the order to occupy the western edge of the same piece of woods, the southern border of which had been occupied by the One hundred and nineteenth. On the right of the One hundred and nineteenth formed the One hundred and fifty seventh New York, then the Eighty-second Illinois, and farther to the right the Eighty-second Ohio, the latter receiving from me the order to cover the left of the Fifty-eighth New York, to fire one volley if the enemy should break through the woods in front, and then to make a bayonet charge. The Fifty-eighth New York and the Twenty-sixth Wisconsin, on the extreme right, remained as they were, under the immediate command of Colonel Krzyzanowski. Captain Dilger, commanding my battery, drew his pieces back to the high ground, near Wiedrich's battery, and opened upon the columns of the enemy as soon as they showed themselves on the old turnpike.

To change the front of the regiments deployed in line on the old Turnpike road was extremely difficult. In the first place, they were hemmed in between a variety of obstacles in front and dense pine brush in their rear. Then the officers had hardly had time to give a command when almost the whole of General McLean's brigade, mixed up with a number of Colonel von

Gilsa's men, came rushing down the road from General Devens' headquarters in wild confusion, and, worse than that, the battery of the First Division broke in upon my right at a full run. This confused mass of guns, caissons, horses, and men broke lengthwise through the ranks of my regiments deployed in line on the road. While this was going on, several men of the Seventy-fourth Pennsylvania, which formed my extreme right, were shot from behind, the enemy having already penetrated into the woods immediately in the rear of our original position. It was evident that under such circumstances it was an utter impossibility to establish a front at that point. The whole line deployed on the old turnpike, facing south, was rolled up and swept away in a moment. If the regiments had remained as they were at first formed, in column on the open field, it would have been easy to give them a correct front by a simple wheeling, and the turmoil on the road would not have disturbed them. As it was, the Seventy-fourth Pennsylvania and the Sixty-first Ohio Regiments, which I had counted among the best I had, and which had never been guilty of any discreditable conduct, could do nothing but endeavor to rally behind the second line.

This second line, as above described, had changed front, and was formed behind a rise of ground between the church grove and the woods, from which the enemy was expected, but every evolution was attended with the greatest difficulty, as the scattered men of the First Division were continually breaking through our ranks.

In my extreme right, where the Twenty-sixth Wisconsin and the Fifty-eighth New York stood, things wore a similar aspect. A short time after the attack had commenced, a large number of men of the First Brigade, First Division, came running back through the woods, the enemy following closely on their heels. Captain [Frederick] Braun, commanding the Fifty-eighth New York, fell from his horse, mortally wounded, immediately after having deployed his regiment. The enemy was, however, received at that point with great firmness. The Fifty-eighth New York, a very small regiment, exposed to a flanking fire from the left, where the enemy broke through, and severely pressed in front, was pushed back after a struggle of several minutes. The Twenty-sixth Wisconsin, flanked on both sides and exposed to a terrible fire in front, maintained the unequal contest for a considerable time. This young regiment, alone and unsupported, firmly held the ground where I had placed it for about twenty-minutes; nor did it fall back until I ordered it to do so.

There is hardly an officer in the Twenty-sixth Wisconsin who has not at least received a bullet through his clothes. Had it not been for the praiseworthy firmness of these men the enemy would have obtained possession of the woods opposite without resistance, taken the north and south rifle-pit from the rear, and appeared on the Plank road between Dowdall's Tavern and Chancellorsville before the artillery could have been withdrawn. The order to fall back to the border of the woods behind was given to Colonel Krzyzanowski in consequence of the following circumstances:

The tide of fugitives had hardly subsided a little on our left, when the enemy's columns, preceded by a thick cloud of skirmishers, presented themselves on and to the right and left of the old turnpike. My regiments had hardly had time to change their position and to wheel into the new front, under what difficulties I have above stated. They had just formed behind the little rise of ground in front of the church grove when the enemy's columns issued from the woods.

The enemy's front of attack, as we saw it, extended considerably beyond our extreme right. His regiments were formed apparently in column by division, the skirmishers throwing themselves into the intervals whenever their advance was checked. The enemy was formed at least three, perhaps four, lines of columns deep, the intervals between lines being very short, the whole presenting a heavy, solid mass.

It was observed by Captain Dilger that several regiments marched from Talley's farm by the right flank down to the Plank road and the low ground south of it, so as to envelop our left. The Seventy-fifth Pennsylvania, which was on picket, was thus taken in the rear, and in its dispersed condition found itself, of course, obliged to fall back, its line of skirmishers, which was facing south, being driven in from the flank or captured. The regiment lost a number of men killed and wounded and a good many prisoners, among the latter Lieutenant-Colonel Matzdorff.

As the enemy emerged from the woods, the regiments of my second line stopped him with a well-directed and rapid fire. Colonel Peissner, of the One hundred and nineteenth New York, a gentleman of the highest order of character and ability, and an officer of great merit, was one of the first to fall, pierced by two bullets.

The enemy was gaining rapidly on the left of the One hundred and nineteenth, which was then exposed to a very severe enfilading fire. The line fell back step by step to the neighborhood of the church grove, facing about and firing as it yielded. Meanwhile the batteries of Captains Dilger and Wiedrich had kept up a rapid fire, first with spherical case, upon the enemy's columns as they descended from Talley's farm, and then with grape and canister. In and on both sides of the church grove the regiments halted, to make another stand.

Colonel Hecker, of the Eighty-second Illinois, fell, wounded, from his horse while holding the colors of his regiment in his hands and giving the order to charge bayonets. Major Rolshausen, of the same regiment, who then assumed command, was wounded immediately afterward.

The Eighty-second Ohio was directed to draw farther to the right, and to occupy the projecting angle of the woods on the right and rear of the church grove; but, while executing this order, one of your aides directed him to occupy the right of the north and south rifle-pit, where the regiment established itself.

About that time one of Colonel Krzyzanowski's aides came to me, asking for re-enforcements, as the Twenty-sixth Wisconsin, being nearly enveloped on all sides, could no longer maintain its position. Having no re-enforcements to send, I gave the order to fall back to the border of the woods east of the open ground. The Twenty-sixth Wisconsin then marched in retreat in good order, facing about and firing as often as possible.

Meanwhile the enemy, after having forced back the One hundred and nineteenth New York by his enfilading fire, gained rapidly on the left of Captain Dilger's battery. This battery and that of Captain Wiedrich remained in position until the very last moment. Captain Dilger limbered up only when the enemy's infantry was already between his pieces. His horse was shot under him, as well as the two wheel horses and one lead horse of one of his guns. After an ineffectual effort to drag this piece along with the dead horses still hanging in the harness, he had to abandon it to the enemy. The conduct of this brilliant officer was, on this as on all former occasions, exemplary.

The enemy was now pouring in great force upon our right and left, and the position in and near the church grove could no longer be held. The two regiments still remaining there gave several discharges, and then fell back in good order. Arriving near the north and south rifle-pit, General Schimmelfennig ordered the Eighty-second Illinois to charge into the projecting corner of the woods on the right, the border of which was already in possession of the enemy. The One hundred and fifty-seventh was directed to fall back along the Plank road, so as to clear the front of the rifle-pit, which seemed to be well filled with men, and to take position on the border of the woods behind. The Twenty-sixth Wisconsin had, in the meantime, been very severely pressed on the extreme right, and there the regiment lost somewhat its compactness, the woods being very thick and the wing companies becoming detached. It was at that moment when I rejoined you behind the rifle pit, which was manned in the center by some of Colonel Buschbeck's regiments; on the left by several companies of the Seventy-fourth Pennsylvania, Sixty-first Ohio, and One hundred and nineteenth New York, and on the extreme right by the Eighty-second Ohio. Several pieces of the Reserve Artillery were still firing.

  Behind the rifle-pit there was a confused mass of men belonging to all divisions, whom we made every possible effort to rally and reorganize, a thing extremely difficult under the fire of the enemy. I succeeded once in gathering a numerous crowd, and, placing myself at its head, led it forward with a hurrah. It followed me some distance, but was again dispersed by the enemy's fire. One of my staff officers was wounded on that occasion. I tried the same experiment two or three times, but always with the same result.

  The enemy advancing on our right and left with rapidity, the artillery ceased firing, and soon the rifle-pit was given up. The Eighty-second Ohio maintained itself very bravely there until the whole of the rifle-pit was abandoned. The loss of that regiment on this spot was very heavy. It was then after 7 PM.

  The retreat now became general, and the confusion increased as the troops marched through the woods. The One hundred fifty-seventh New York, still in good order, stopped several times, firing and charging upon the pursuing enemy.

  Captain Dilger had sent his battery toward Chancellorsville, keeping one piece with him, which he brought several times into action with very good success during the retreat of the corps. The Twenty-sixth Wisconsin, Eighty-second Ohio,

One hundred and fifty-seventh New York, and the Eighty-second Illinois halted on the right of a line occupied by what was supposed to be General Berry's division. There they remained until about 8.30 PM, when they retreated farther, to an open space north of Chancellorsville.

After 9 o'clock, the order reached them to march to the rallying place of the Eleventh Corps, west of the Chancellor house. I rallied large fragments of several regiments partly behind the abatis in the woods, partly a little farther back, near the creek west of the Chancellor house. It was about 9 o'clock when I marched with them to the general rendezvous. The corps was reorganized before 11 o'clock.

Early on the morning of May 3, I was ordered to relieve General Humphreys' division, on the extreme left of the army, near Scott's Mills. Nothing happened in my front except a little skirmishing.

At about 11 PM I was relieved by the Twelfth Corps, and then took position behind the First Division, which was deployed in the rifle-pits, our right resting on the Second Corps.

In the course of the 4th, my division took a more concentrated position, five regiments being deployed in the rifle-pits and five in column, in the second line, on the extreme right of the corps. Nothing but light skirmishing in our front. So my division remained on the 5th.

Early on the morning of the 6th, we recrossed the Rappahannock at United States Ford, together with the rest of the army. On the evening of the same day, I reached my old encampment, near Stafford Court-House.

The losses suffered by my division in the action of May 2 were very severe in proportion to my whole effective force. I had 15 officers killed, 23 wounded, and 15 missing, and 102 men killed, 365 wounded, and 441 missing; total, 953. Of those reported as missing, a good many have already been found wounded in the hospitals, and it is probable that a large proportion of them were left killed or wounded on the battle-field. My whole loss amounted to about 23 per cent.

In closing this report, I beg leave to make one additional remark. The Eleventh Corps, and, by error or malice, especially the Third Division, has been held up to the whole country as a band of cowards. My division has been made responsible for the defeat of the Eleventh Corps, and the Eleventh Corps for the failure of the campaign. Preposterous as this is, yet we have been overwhelmed by the army and the press with abuse and insult beyond measure. We have borne as much as human nature can endure. I am far from saying that on May 2 everybody did his duty to the best of his power. But one thing I will say, because I know it: these men are no cowards. I have seen most of them fight before this, and they fought as bravely as any. I am also far from saying that it would have been quite impossible to do better in the position the corps occupied on May 2; but I have seen with my own eyes troops who now affect to look down upon the Eleventh Corps with sovereign contempt behave much worse under circumstances far less trying.

Being charged with such an enormous responsibility as the failure of a campaign involves, it would seem to me that every commander in this corps has a right to a fair investigation of his conduct and of the circumstances surrounding him and his command on that occasion. I would, therefore, most respectfully and most urgently ask for permission to publish this report. Every statement contained therein is strictly truthful, to the best of my information. If I have erred in any particular, my errors can easily be corrected. But if what I say is true, I deem it due to myself and those who serve under me that the country should know it.

I am, general, most respectfully, your obedient servant,
C Schurz
Major-General, Comdg Third Division, Eleventh Army Corps

May 13, 1863
Report of Maj. Gen. Oliver Howard, 11th Army Corps camp near Brooke's Station, VA

General: I have the honor to submit the following report of the operations of this corps during the recent movement:

First day, Monday.—The corps left this camp at 5.30 AM, April 27, and marched toward Kelly's Ford, via Hartwood Church. We made 14 miles, and encamped about 1 mile beyond Hartwood. The troops were in position by 4 PM. My main wagon train was parked near the road that leads from the Ridge road to Banks' Ford.

Second day, Tuesday.—The head of the column left camp promptly at 4 AM, and the entire corps was in camp near Kelly's

Ford at 4 PM, having marched 14 miles. At 2 PM on the same day, I visited the commanding general at Morrisville, where I received specific instructions and intimations of his general plan. At 6 PM the pontoon bridge was commenced, under charge of Captain Comstock, of the Engineers. The bridge-layers were mostly by detail from my command, and were new at the work. Some 400 men of Colonel Buschbeck's brigade crossed in boats. The enemy's picket, after a single shot, fell back. At 10 PM the bridge was completed and the crossing commenced. A regiment of cavalry (the Seventeenth Pennsylvania, Colonel Kellogg) reported to me, and was crossed, following the infantry advance guard. The colonel was ordered to send scouts and patrols up the different roads and to picket our front. Owing to the darkness of the night and the ignorance of the guides, it was nearly daylight before the troops were all in position.

Third day, Wednesday.—The Twelfth Corps, General Slocum, took the advance on the march toward Germanna Bridge. The Eleventh Corps followed. The Twelfth had some skirmishing in front, and the Eleventh had its rear of column shelled by a couple of light pieces, supported by cavalry. The Seventeenth Pennsylvania Cavalry was ordered to cover the rear and protect the train against this annoyance, which it failed to do; but a portion of Stoneman's cavalry came up and relieved our right flank. This corps commenced crossing the Rapidan at 11 PM, and by 4 AM was in camp, except the rear guard and train.

Fourth day, Thursday.—The corps followed the Twelfth, leaving camp at 7 AM, and encamped near Dowdall's Tavern at 4 PM As soon as the head of my column reached this point, I went to Chancellorsville and received my orders from General Slocum. He told me I was to cover the right, posting my command near Hunting Creek. General Slocum gave me to understand that he would take care of the entire front from Chancellorsville to my position; but afterward one of his division commanders sent me word that I would have to take about three-fourths of a mile of the front, so as to connect with General Slocum's right, as ordered. This I did, and located my command with reference to an attack from the front in a direction perpendicular to the Plank road; also from the right along the Plank and old Turnpike roads. My right rested in the vicinity of the point marked "mill" on the map; but no mill was in existence. I sent a force of two companies to the point where the Ely's Ford road crosses Hunting Creek. At this point

General Pleasonton had a force of cavalry and some artillery. My corps was distributed as follows: The First Division occupied the right; the First Brigade, Colonel von Gilsa, deployed two regiments and two companies of another nearly at a right angle with the old range Court-House turnpike, and to the north of it the rest of the First Division, extending along this turnpike, deployed, with two regiments in reserve, and the Third Division, General Schurz, prolonged this line eastward, facing south-southeast. He had three regiments of General Schimmelfennig's brigade deployed and two regiments in reserve. He had also two regiments of Colonel Krzyzanowski's brigade in the front line and two regiments in reserve. On the proper front, General Steinwehr, commanding Second Division, had two regiments deployed and two in reserve—all of Colonel Buschbeck's brigade.

On the morning of May 2, General Birney had relieved a portion of General Steinwehr's division from the front line, viz, General Barlow's brigade. This I placed in position for a general reserve of the corps. The artillery was disposed as follows: Two pieces near General Devens' (First Division) right, enfilading old turnpike; the rest of Dieckmann's battery on the left of General Devens, Covering approaches along the Plank road. Four guns of Wiedrich's battery were placed near Steinwehr's right, and two guns near his left, covering approaches from the front. Dilger's battery was posted near the intersection of the turnpike and the Plank road. Three batteries were in reserve, and so placed as to be used on any of the approaches. Our front was covered with rifle-pits and abatis.

On Friday, May 1, at 12 m, I received the order to march along the Plank road toward Fredericksburg, and take position 1 mile in rear of the Twelfth Corps. We had hardly left camp before the order was countermanded, and we resumed the old position.

Early Saturday morning, General Hooker visited my corps and rode along my front lines. At one point a regiment was not deployed and at another a gap in the woods was not filled. The correction was immediately made and the position strengthened. The front was covered by a good line of skirmishers.

I should have stated that, just at evening of May 1, the enemy made a reconnaissance on our front with a small force of artillery and infantry. General Schimmelfennig moved out with a battalion and drove him back.

During Saturday, the 2d, the same general made frequent reconnaissance's. Infantry scouts and cavalry patrols were constantly pushed out on every road. The unvarying report was, "The enemy is crossing the Plank road and moving toward Culpeper."

At 4 PM I was directed to send a brigade to the support of General Sickles. I immediately took General Barlow's brigade by a short route to General Sickles' right, some 2½ miles from the Plank road to the front.

At about 6 PM I was at my headquarters, at Dowdall's Tavern, when the attack commenced. I sent my chief of staff to the front when firing was heard. General Schurz, who was with me, left at once to take command of his line. It was not three minutes before I followed. When I reached General Schurz's command, I saw that the enemy had enveloped my right, and that the First Division was giving way. I first tried to change the front of the deployed regiments. I next directed the artillery where to go; then formed a line by deploying some of the reserve regiments near the church. By this time the whole front on the north of the Plank road had given way. Colonel Buschbeck's brigade was faced about, and, lying on the other side of the rifle-pit embankment, held on with praiseworthy firmness. A part of General Schimmelfennig's and a part of General Krzyzanowski's brigades moved gradually back to the north of the Plank road and kept up their fire. At the center and near the Plank road there was a blind panic and great confusion. By the assistance of my staff and some other officers, one of whom was Colonel Dickinson, of General Hooker's staff, the rout was considerably checked, and all the artillery, except eight pieces, withdrawn. Some of the artillery was well served, and told effectively on the advancing enemy. Captain Dilger kept up a continuous fire until we reached General Betty's[37] position.

Now as to the causes of this disaster to my corps:

1 Though constantly threatened and apprised of the moving of the enemy, yet the woods was so dense that he was able to mass a large force, whose exact whereabouts neither patrols, reconnaissances, nor scouts ascertained. He succeeded in forming a column opposite to and outflanking my right.

2 By the panic produced by the enemy's reverse fire, regiments and artillery were thrown suddenly upon those in position.

3 The absence of General Barlow's brigade, which I had

previously located in reserve and *en echelon* with Colonel von Gilsa's, so as to cover his right flank. This was the only general reserve I had. My corps was very soon reorganized near Chancellorsville, and relieved General Meade's corps, on the left of the general line. Here it remained until Wednesday morning, when it resumed its position, as ordered, at the old camp.

The division and brigade commanders showed the greatest attention to duty and a hearty co-operation with me at all times.

By a reference to the tabular statement, it will be seen that a large proportion of the regimental commanders engaged were killed, wounded, or taken prisoners. Captain [Francis A] Dessauer, of my staff, was killed while fearlessly at work rallying the men. The aggregate of killed, wounded, and missing is 2,508.

I feel confident that this command will yet honor itself and the noble cause we sustain, and I ask for it another opportunity for demonstrating its true spirit.

Very respectfully, your obedient servant,
O O Howard,
Major-General

May 14, 1863
Letter of William Wheeler
Brooke's Station, VA

Dearest Mother

Since we came back to this camp, I have been very much occupied with reports, inventories, and other matter which are necessarily attendant upon a great battle, and so I just dispatched you a line on the 6th. I have felt very much depressed in spirits, and hardly equal to having a good talk, even with you. But I have to-day received your letter, dated May 5, and I feel impelled to let you know all about it at once, that you and the friends at home, who are the only ones whose opinion I care much for, may not be led by newspaper stories or prejudiced reports, to do injustice to our Corps, whose misdeed are now in every one's mouth, and upon whom is cast the entire weight of blame, that belongs in higher quarters.

I do not know that I can do better than tell you about the whole affair from the beginning of the march on, as you may take an interest in what is already beginning to be historic. The first "eight days rations," which we draw in the expectation of making our attempt, about the middle of April, were quietly consumed in camp, as a series of violent storms swelled the streams, and made moving impracticable, but on Sunday, April 26, we received a renewal of the same order, which was speedily complied with, and soon after came the order of march, which was to begin at 5 ½ o'clock the next morning. At about midnight who should turn up but our Paymaster, and as the rolls were all singed, he made a quick job of it, and paid the Battery off in just thirteen minutes; this added to the excitement of breaking up winter-quarters, drove away sleep from the camp, and the hum of conversation and laughter was heard until the bugle blew reveille, and we prepared to bid farewell to our pleasant winter-quarters, little thinking that in ten days more we should be re-occupying them again, broken but not beaten. Everything was packed up, six days forage was fastened on the pieces and caissons, and on the off horses, shelter-tents were distributed among the men, while our comfortable wall tents and stately Sibleys were left standing, for the benefit of the Hospital Division, a branch of service destined in a few days to surpass all others in importance. Our march was a first rather slow, as the Second and Third Divisions, which lay more towards the front, had first to get their unwieldy lengths in motion. Everything not absolutely necessary had been curtailed; one ambulance accompanied each brigade, abut not a team-wagon was to be seen in the whole line of march, the trains being all in the rear, and arranged in the order in which they were likely to be used, viz: ammunition, ambulances, supplies. Every man had eight days rations and sixty rounds of ammunition, and thus provided, we could afford to have our teams in the rear and to move on in light marching rig.

The first day we reached Hartwood church, a distance of about fifteen miles; but even this march, though not a long one, tried the infantry very much, as they were soft from the long idleness of winter-quarters, and their haversack and cartridge-boxes were unusually heavy.

At different points on the road we were joined by the Twelfth Corps, General Slocum, and the Fifth Corps, General Meade, which fell in behind us. The next day we reached Kelly's Ford early in the afternoon, and went into camp, preserving the utmost silence, all orders being given by word of mouth without drum-beat or bugle signal, and the men were not permitted to show themselves on the bank. The value of these precautions was

shown by the fact that we took the enemy entirely by surprise; a
detachment from Steinwehr's Division crossed the river, drove the
enemy out of the rifle pits, and occupied the opposite shore, and
then, with great dispatch and success, the engineers laid down the
pontoons, and, under cover of night, our whole Corps passed the
river and gained the heights about half a mile back. This was a
pretty hard job for the artillery, as they sent us no guide to take us
through the level swamp laying between the rive and the hill; and
we floundered about in mud and mire until nearly daybreak; two
hours sleep, on a plank taken from a fence, and a wash in a dirty
pool, quite refreshed me, and by six o'clock we stood in readiness
to renew our march, now upon the south side of the
Rappahannock. The Twelfth Corps crossed at daybreak, and filed
piles us, taking the advance, and the Fifth Corps followed us in the
rear. We march steadily on, the roads were good and we were in
high spirits, and everything looked well. Before long we struck
upon the Fredericksburg plank-road, and when approaching the
ford over the Rapidan, at Germania Mills, the artillery of our
Corps was ordered to pass through the infantry of the Twelfth
Corps at double-quick, so as to take position and drive away any
hostile artillery that might dispute the passage. While trotting over
this road, which was a good deal worn and full of ruts, we had a
chapter of disagreeable accidents; a caisson, in the first section,
broke in the middle from a sudden jolt, and tow men sitting on the
rear box were thrown violently to the ground and seriously
injured, one having his ribs broken and his hip out. Almost at the
same time a man was jolted off from a caisson, in the second
section, and the wheel passed over his leg, cracking the bone. I
had ordered my drivers not to go quite so rapidly and had no
trouble. Our arrival at Germania Mills, on the Rapidan, was so
sudden that a body of rebel infantry and cavalry had scant time to
get across the river and escape, while a company of pioneers and
engineers, who were engaged in building a large bridge over the
river, and had all the timbers ready collected and shaped for that
purpose, were made prisoners, to the number of about eighty men.
It would seem from the building of this bridge, that Lee had the
intention of making much the same movement that we were
making,--going to one of the upper fords of the Rappahannock in
order to cross and flank us, and thus we anticipated him in his own
maneuver. Our own engineers took hold of the bridge timber, and
laid down enough of the string pieces to enable the infantry to pass

over dry shod; in the meantime the artillery had to ford the river, which was no small undertaking, as the stream was deep, the current very swift, and the bottom full of large stones. A line of cavalry, standing over their girths in water, showed where we were to pass; but the violence of the current was so great, and the foots so uncertain, that I felt almost sure that some carriage would be swept away; but nothing of the kind happened, and ,as our ammunition chests were pretty water-tight, we managed to "keep our powder dry." I did not succeed in doing the same by my own person, as my horse had to swim once, which necessitated a very wet seat to me; and the Captain's horse went headforemost into a hold from which I never expected to see him emerge. There were some ludicrous incidents; one of the pack-mules, loaded on each side with a box of rifle cartridges, walked deliberately off the sting piece into the river, saying probably, with Hamlet, "Who would fardels bear," etc.; on in, a few desperate plunges freed him from his burden and he swam ashore and rushed off friskily, switching his tail as joyously as if he had not just been a four-legged caisson, the slave of an ordnance officer. When the Eleventh and Twelfth Corps were all safely over (Fifth Corps had crossed at another point) the bridge was destroyed and our guns were planted along the banks to prevent the enemy from coming up on our rear from the direction of Culpepper or Gordonsville, and disturbing our peaceful slumbers, which we enjoyed that night in a pouring rain. The next day, April 30, we continued our line of march on the Fredericksburg plank-road, passed through the small village of Wilderness, and advanced nearly to Chancellorsville, where General Hooker had his head-quarters. General Howard established his head-quarters near the intersection of the Orange Court House road, or Plank Road, with another road running about northwest; and our Division head-quarters was at a farm-house upon the last-mentioned road, about half a mile from the intersection. Close by this farm-house our Battery went into camp, and General McLean's Brigade[38] lay all around us, the Seventeenth Connecticut to our right, the Fifty-fifth, Twenty-fifth, Seventy-fifth, and One Hundred and Seventh Ohio[39] behind us, and to the left of us. The point of attack indicated to us was the front, viz., towards the Plank Road, which came converging from the southwest, and upon which, the theory seemed to by, the rebels were sure to make their attack; the idea did not seem to occur to the generals that the enemy might go a little further to the west and northwest, and attack our right wing on the flank and rear. Friday, May 1, came, and the infantry commenced entrenching themselves in the road, front as before to the Plank Road, by digging rifle pits and banking the earth up on the fence, securing it with fence rail and strong pegs. In the evening there was considerable firing to the left, with some musketry; we sent off our first section[40], with Colonel Gilsa's Brigade[41], to take position on the extreme right and protect the flank; a very good precaution against an enemy of moderate force, but not much against forty thousand men.

    The next morning we received an order from General Howard to carefully measure the distance from our Battery to a clear elevated spot in front, near the Plank Road, on which it was apprehended the rebels might endeavor to place a battery and shell our position, and we were told that "we would find it of the greatest importance to have an accurate knowledge of the distance," thus showing that still the attack was expected in front, a heavy flank not dreamed of. In the meantime Jackson was silently massing his army in front of the First Brigade, and on its flank, and yet with such perfect secrecy and skill that the miserable scouts we sent out reported three or four hundred dismounted cavalry, and nothing more. Lieutenant Bohn, thinking that dismounted cavalry were getting too numerous, threw a couple of shrapnels among them but was ordered by General Devens to stop, as he was "shooting our own men." About this time General Hooker rode down through our lines, seemed well satisfied with the state of affairs, and returned, and yet at the very moment when he cast his approving glance over the right wing, the enemy's swarms were closing in upon it, unseen but sure, and there was not a single cavalry vidette to bring us certain information of this deadly snare. Frequent intelligence was sent both to Howard's and Hooker's head-quarters announcing the heavy massing of the enemy on the right, and yet no reinforcements were sent, and no orders to retire to a more favorable position. Perhaps they thought our weak Division, of about 4,000 each, were going separately to withstand the sudden onset of ten times their number, and that in a position most unfavorable, and where the intrenchments, built against the front, were nothing but a weakness when taken in flank. Noon came, no information of an attack, and still we kept our guns trained on the clear spot in front. At 3 PM, all was still; suddenly the silence was broken by the shots of skirmishers, then sharp volleys of musketry with rapid firing of canister from the right, where Lieutenant Bohn was with his section, and almost at the same moment our Battery was enfiladed from the right by the enemy's shells with fell and burst with most fatal effect. The first shell struck two pole horses in Lieutenant Carlisle's section, then burst, and one piece cut in tow the pole of my first piece, while another went on and killed a lead horse on the second. The next two shells were almost equally destructive. We endeavored to place our pieces in the new direction, but before we could do so, the First Brigade came, forced back on McLean's, bringing Bohn's section with it, and it was impossible to fire for fear of killing our own men, who blocked up the road. So we had nothing for it, but to retire to the first hill, where we could take position and accomplish something. I limbered up my first piece with the limber of the caisson and then got both my pieces off safe, retiring quietly. I was just about to mount my horse when the attack began, and gave him to a cannoneer to hold while I unlimbered the caisson. While he was holding him a bullet hit the poor little Frank on the haunch and he broke away and ran past the Battery which was now moving on ahead, giving the Captain and the men the idea that I had been shot from his back. Well I got my piece off all right and followed on foot; as I came a couple of rods further where, through a depression in the ground, the pieces had passed from the field into the road, I found Lieutenant Carlisle with his whole section in a sorry plight, all the horses on one gun had been shot, and all but the pole horse on the other, together with two or three of the drivers, and in a fit of desperation Carlisle had ordered his men to unlimber and fire canister. But the depression was so deep that no sight could be got of the enemy who were on the plain above. I took hold of the third piece and tried to help run it up the bank, but we could not do it. I then sprang to the other gun and told Carlisle that the only possible safety was to cut the dead horses, limber up the gun and take off with the pole horse alone. It had been great folly to unlimber them, in the first place, and though he was brave as a lion the predicament rather puzzled him, as well it might. The sergeant cut out the lead and middle horses, and the corporal raised the trail to limber up the gun when a shot struck him, and he dropped the trail on my toes, at the same moment the rebs rushed over the hill and poured a volley into us at very close range, severely wounding poor Carlisle in three places. I don't see how I escaped. I suppose I owed it to the fact that I was on foot. I then made rapid tracks to catch my section; the first hill was full of artillery in position, and firing, and our Battery had found no room to take position, and so was compelled to go further back. At the Third Division breastworks I amused myself in rallying our infantry, but they could not be held.

    The vehemence, energy, and desperation with which the rebels came on was really superb, and the numbers were so overwhelming that a brigade or division line of battle made no show at all, but was immediately flanked and enveloped on both wings. The Third Division, commanded by the celebrated Republican orator Schurz, did worst of all; it vanished like the dust of the balance at the first assault, and gave no support to McLean's gallant Brigade which did its to keep back the tide of gray back, but in vain, and Steinwehr's First Brigade was too weak to stand up against the refluent wave of Schurz's runaways. I don't tell you anything now from hearsay, but what I saw with my own eyes, for as I knew that my section was not in position on this hill, and was in safety on this road, I felt some curiosity to see how the thing went and so I took it pretty easy, keeping as near the enemy's front and our rear as I conveniently could.

    All at once I heard my name called, and saw at my side Major Fineauff[42] of the One Hundred and Fifty-third Pennsylvania Regiment, of whom you have heard me speak as my fellow student at Berlin, one of my few friends out here on the field. He has been on General Devens' staff, and was wounded in the leg, or rather lamed and severely contused. I lugged him alone for some distance, resisting his frequent requests to me to lay him down and leave him. I gave him a drink of whiskey which gave him life, and at last had the satisfaction of leaving him with a party of his own regiment who brought him safely off. Arrived at the foot of the hill leading to the plateau on which General Hooker's head-quarters stood, *i.e.*, the village of Chancellorsville, I found the Twelfth Corps hastening to our relief, and across the crest of the hill a large number of batteries, mostly brass twelve pounders, medium range, placed in position, while most of the rifled long guns had been sent further to the rear. I spent some time in searching for our Battery, but without success, and then went back to the hill and served as cannoneer in Dilger's Battery[43] of our Corps, during the whole of the fierce attack of the rebels that ensued. It was queer that the officer in whose section I served, had within a fortnight been a trembling candidate before a board of examination of which I had been secretary, and where I had put him through with all sorts of questions. At the foot of the hill was a wood, which was held partly by the rebs, and partly by the Twelfth Corps; the enemy made several attempts to drive our men out, and the steady roll of musketry was really appalling. Once they succeeded, but then the batteries on the hill opening drove them back with great loss, and our men retook their position. The next (Sunday) morning I found my section in the right, in the new line, with the First Corps, General Reynolds. The rest of the Battery was at the United States Ford, to which place most of the long range artillery was sent, as being of little use in such close hand to hand bush fighting. Here I was ordered to report to General Reynolds with two guns of Schirmer's Battery[44] and my own section. General Reynolds sent me to General Wadsworth, who commanded one of his Divisions, and he placed me in a fine position, above his Division, who were splendidly intrenched, and I got the regiment which covered me to throw up a breastwork before my gun, high enough to cover the bodies of the gunners. While reporting to General Wadsworth I had the pleasure of meeting young Carrington of the Class of 1859, who was on his staff. There were ten pieces of us all together on this hill, and I longed for an attack, as we had capital infantry with us, and could have repulsed almost anything. But nothing did turn up then, and towards evening I was ordered down to the United States Ford, where we lay for a day and a half, and then, on the 5th, crossed the river in a dense fog, and marched back to our old camp, arriving here in a rain and hail storm which was the most extensive one I ever saw. The hailstones being in some instances, actually larger than hen's eggs, and knocking men off their horses. So, here we are, after an absence of eight days, in the old camp again, having lost two guns, three caissons, twenty-five horses, one officer, and thirteen men, having not had the smallest chance to accomplish anything valuable. In fact there was far too much artillery in that fight, and too many rifled guns which were of no use at all. If a battery was not very well supported by infantry, it might be taken in one desperate rush, as there was no good opportunity to retire. With regard to the conduct of the Eleventh Corps, I have heard some say that they would not fight because they did not have Sigel; this is absurd, and yet allowance must be made for the great influence on the men, produced by their losing the man on whom they leaned unreservedly, and whom they would follow to the death, and getting in his place a person unknown, peculiarly uncongenial to the German mind, and considered by them as a parson in uniform. But any Corps so scattered, and strung along an extended line, could not have failed to be overwhelmed by the force brought so suddenly against it; and a most steadfast bearing to the enemy would have brought with it annihilation, without staying their progress; would have doubled the lists of killed and wounded without having been of benefit. I know that the regiments of our Battery, viz., McLean's Brigade, fought as well as men can fight, and only fell back when further fighting was madness. The fact lies in this nutshell. General Hooker allowed General Howard to scatter his corps along too great a line, and then allowed the Corps thus scattered to be flanked, and now it seems to be the fashion to throw the blame of this mismanagement upon the conduct of the Corps, which seems to me most unjust. Well! Enough of this vindication; if any of my friends ask what I have say about the "flight," "panic," etc., of the Eleventh Corps, you can show them this. Both of my horses were hit, but neither severely. Jenny got a spent ball right on the side of her nose, but the wound is now entirely healed. Frank got a ball on his haunch, but the wound was improving finely, when, what should he do the other night but commit suicide, by hanging himself in his halter; in the morning he was quite dead. He was a beauty and a fine trotter. I felt miserably about it. My poor darkey boy took it so much to heart, that, after burying him with many tears, he could not bear to stay any longer about the place and decamped, which was even more painful to me than losing the horse, as I had taken much interest in him as was really fond of him. We were afraid that we might lose Lieutenant Carlisle; he was shot in the arm, the leg, and the side. What troubled him the most was the loss of his section, and when he became delirious he was crying cannoneers to do this and that and not to desert the gun. He is better now and has been sent off to Washington with a fair prospect of recovery. Most of our wounded are doing well except the Corporal who was shot at my side; he will probably lose his leg. As to the whole affair I do not feel discouraged. I am sure that the enemy received greater loss than he inflicted, and that he cannot stand many such blows, while we on the contrary seem, like Antæus, to gather strength from our falls. The death of Stonewall Jackson is a great misfortune to the rebels, but I do not feel like exulting over the grave of such a brave, wise, and energetic antagonist—"peace be to his ashes." You must make this long letter do for sometime now, as I have a great deal of writing to do.

May 19, 1863
Letter of William Wheeler
Brooke's Station, VA

My Dear Friend
Although I have several debts to pay that are older than yours, and you stand by no means near the top of my list, yet your last letter dated April 23, but which I did not receive until about May 9, came to me so pleasantly upon my return to this camp, breathing so much quiet, and peace, and happiness, after my hard marching, and bloody fighting, that I feel peculiarly impelled to send you a few words in reply; and these words shall be, if you please, not at all about the war and the late battle, but mere chat and friendly talk. If you would like to hear about our march to Kelly's Ford, our passage of the Rappahannock, and then of the Rapidan, the battle of Chancellorsville on Saturday—with an explanation of how the misfortune of our Corps occurred,-- I would rather have you ask my mother to read you that part of my last letter to her, than write it all over again myself. Suffice it to say, that I stayed with another officer's section in the face of the enemy, and tried to help it get off until I was the only many on the spot unhurt, two corporals being shot down at my side, and the officer receiving three bullets; I probably escaped by being on foot, and did not think it my duty to stay behind to rally the infantry, that not being a branch of my business. I hate to brag, or to talk about what I did, but it becomes necessary sometimes, when the corps to which one belongs is charged by the newspapers with having indulged in a universal panic and flight. I only know that if I had one of the reports for those sheets in my tent for a brief half hour alone, one of us two would have a badly punched head. But enough of this.

Your letter treating of music, and pictures, and children, was to me indeed "humanizing," and I could not help asking myself how it was that my nature had not become more brutalized of my life of "murder and rapine," as the "Richmond Enquirer" would call it, but on the contrary, become as sensitive as ever upon your mention of those tender and beautiful objects; I think that when a certain love from them has become a part of a man's nature, the absence of them, and the want of a cultivation of the corresponding tastes, does not really diminish this love, but rather, other ruder tastes are etched away by the influence of time and use, leaving these in bolder relief. I don't know whether this be correct metaphysics, but it is true as far as I am concerned. What you tell me of this book of "Mendelssohn's Letters," interested me much, and if you really can part with the book, without hope of ever seeing it again, I should be much obliged to you for sending it to me. By my hand lies a very jolly book entitled "Reisehumoresken; auf einer Wanderung durch die Schweiz und Oberitalien," which has to us here a peculiar interest from its being an only memento of a very gallant officer, Captain von Mensel, of General McLean's staff, with whom I had a pleasant talk half an hour before the sudden attack, in which he disappeared mysteriously, just like Ed. Blake at Cedar Mountain, and we cannot learn whether he was buried promiscuously on the field, or whether he perished in that burning hospital. These genial little books of travel are to me very delightful, and it requires very little imagination for one to place himself in an Italian vettura, or on the bow of one of those ridiculous little "Dämpfers," on a Swiss lake, and to listen to the homely humor of the German, the gabble of English girls, and the ignorant impudence of their companions.

I sometime like to take a retrospect of the years that are just past, and never more than just as this time, and in this month; in 1857, I was a week out of New York on the *Australia*; in 1858, I had just left you and The Form, at Athens, and had gone to Naples; in 1859, I was gnashing my teeth over a certain ---[45]; in 1860, I was being admitted to the bar; in 1861, I was supporting a starving officer's mess at Franklin, Virginia, among the mountains, with the fruits of my angle. And, after this "roaming with a hungry heart," I also share Ulysses' determination, "to strive, to seek, to find, and not to yield;" every defeat of ours puts the end farther off, but makes our work more sure and thorough, and the final peace more deep and noble; the longer we work upon the laying of our foundation stones, the more pains we take with the selection of our site and the nature of the ground we build on, the more beautiful and lasting will be our edifice, which we can then entrust to the religion of coming centuries to complete, and it will shine from its rocky base to the pilgrims of the future, as the Parthenon did to us five years ago, beautiful, golden, when we sailed up to the Piræus. And yet home, friends, genial society, books, music, all these are so delightful, that I do not dare to think of them much; the only way is to keep the nose steadily down on the grindstone of duty, and then you don't bother about anything else. I like to hear from you very much, for you have such a straight-forward way of going at things that I feel perfect confidence in all your utterances, and take them all as gospel, feeling at times almost willing to "lay my sweet hand in yours, and trust you."

What comes hard for me to stand just now, is going to the hospitals; I am not exactly right well, and the sight of so much suffering among gallant boys who never wavered on the field, is often too much for me; and yet I try to go, for our poor fellows feel pleased with their officers come in often and inquire about them. The other day I went to see a corporal of our Battery, one of the two shot down at my side; he was on the field and in the enemy's hands several days before being sent over, and his wounds had been neglected. He was a very fine-looking young Irishman, with a good organization and deep susceptibility to both pain and pleasure; one of his wounds had affected the nerves, and the pain came in great wrenches and spasms that made him gnash his teeth and beat his feet on the bed in agony. I became so sick that I could hardly get to the door. The other corporal, who was hit within half a foot from me, received a bad shot in the foot, and came so exhausted to the hospital, that the doctor would not take his leg off; to-day they have given him up, as mortification has set in. When I see these things, I am perfectly astounded at the capacity of delicate ladies, like Miss S W and my Cousin Anna, to go through the scenes with composure, appreciated before the greatness of the service and the sacrifice. But still these acts of devotion and self-sacrifice are not without their stimulus and reward, too; I have never seen anything that went more to my heart than this; after I had sat down by the bed of a poor mangled hero from the ranks, had spoken to him words of praise for his conduct, sympathy for his pain, and offered to do what I could for him, to see his eyes watch me as I left the tent, and to hear his grateful "Thank you for your kindness, Lieutenant." I intend to try to overcome the prejudices of my sensitive Wheeler nose, and to do something more in this way....Think of me as in pretty good health, and remembering you with constant affection.

May 21, 1863
Letter of William Wheeler
Brooke's Station, VA

The immediate toils of battle are over; the wounded are either agonizing and dying with the painful and mortifying wounds in the field hospitals, or where their hits were slight, are hopping around on sticks and crutches, and looking eagerly forward to the time when they shall be sufficiently restored to exchange the half-rations of the hospital for the full fare of the camp; and the uninjured, having fairly rested themselves from fatigue and excitement, are beginning to feel ennui and fatigue much more severely than from the hardest march, and to wish that Hooker would hurry up again and make another "reconnaissance in force" across the Rappahannock, but this time with fuller results. I hope that you have not allowed yourself to be so prejudiced by the newspapers, against our Corps, the Eleventh, as not to be willing to hear a word of explanation. One very great disadvantage under which we labored was, that shortly before the march, our well-trusted Sigel was replaced in the command of the Corps by General Howard, a stranger, and one in whom we had no confidence; and still further, our Division commander, McLean, who was greatly beloved by his troops, was superseded by Devens, also an utter stranger, and one who brought with him mostly a new and inexperienced staff. The disposition of the Corps in the line of battle at Chancellorsville was also very faulty, it being stretched out over a long line, a mile away from the Twelfth Corps, and connected with it only a few pickets. Then there was no cavalry to scout on the flank, and the consequence was, that while we were expecting patiently an attack from the front, the wily Jackson had massed his forces on our right, and even thrown part of them into our rear, thus completely enveloping our Division, and exposing the men, some of whom were raw troops, to a fire on three sides at once. The enemy's attack was in great force and most fierce, his men advancing steadily at a rapid walk, loading and firing as they came, and our First Brigade narrowly escaped being taken prisoners *en masse*. There was no "coign of vantage," no advantageous position, at which to make a stand, as the breastworks and rifle pits had all be constructed with reference to an attack from the front, and consequently were enfiladed by an attack from the right. In fact, we had no chance; and the men who, at Bull Run, under Sigel, kept the heights of Groveton for a long summer's day, against the desperate assaults of Longstreet's whole army, finally driving him back, and who came the next day to rescue of the fugitive and demoralized army of the Peninsula, would not rally under a general whose arrangements had proved so futile and deceptive, and to rally under whom would have been to meet repeated defeat and disgrace, without profit. I am sorry to say, that General Howard, on his first coming to the Corps, made himself conspicuous by his zeal in promoting religious observances, and in showing his respect for the Sabbath, to say nothing of a somewhat ostentatious display of personal piety, and now his religious character has to bear the burden of his military errors, and it is said pretty generally, and that with justice, that he obeyed only the last half of the command, "Watch and pray." Don't suppose now, that I look at this in a flippant way at all; I think that no characters are more admirable than those of men like Havelock, Hedley, Vicars, or our own Commodore Foote, who, being once soldiers, did their duty and their work as such with all their might, and yet were none the less thoughtful, earnest, and pious men. But with regard to our own General, I feel very much as Cromwell did about that cavalry officer who began to pray aloud in his saddle just as the Ironsides were about to charge at Marston Moor. I hope that he will be removed from command before we go into fight again, for hardly a man in the Corps has the slightest confidence in his ability or capacity, and if he is to lead us, the greatest disasters may be expected....In this fearfully hot weather which we are having just now, I often sigh for the mountains of Western Virginia, in which we were campaigning a year ago, and at time my thoughts go still further back, to the deck of the old *Australia*, six years ago; do you remember, at about this date we had got well free from the storms and head-winds of the Gulf Stream, and were making good time before a fine southwest wind, and after the hot day was over, doubly enjoying the cool evening walk on deck, and many a homesick talk about the friends who had been for a fortnight under the western horizon. That summer and autumn which we spent together, and during which we learned to know and love each other better than before, has always had to my mind and memory a peculiarly rosy and pleasant hue, and I look forward to no greater pleasure than that of sitting down with you at some future day, and, armed with our respective diaries as books of reference and suggestion, wandering through the Louvre once more, visiting Belgium and the Rhine, and clambering over Switzerland with our Alpenstocks. This has all been brought very freshly before my mind by a jolly little German book which I have been reading, called "Reisehumoresken," a vacation ramble through Upper Italy and Switzerland. The author, who was formerly correspondent of the "Cologne Gazette," is a keener observer of peculiarities and eccentricities in his fellow-travellers, than of the marvel of nature, or rather,, he seems to restrain the expression of his enthusiasm on this latter point, leaving it to be inferred more from hints than from glowing descriptions, but still, what he says about the Monte Rosa region, which occupies almost half of a volume, made me feel more regretful than ever that we did not diverge from the Rhone Valley when at Leuk, and take in this superb mountain. If I recollect right, we had a battle royal on the subject, but it was finally decided to abide by the original plan, unchangeable as the laws of the Medes, which we had laid down with remorseless pencil on Keller's map, in the fourth story of Meurice's. It is rather aggravating to think of those delightful days, out here where there is no genial society, nothing to read, and where we vibrate from the stagnation and ennui of camp, to the absorbing care and fatigue of the march, and the excitement of the battle; in this too

"A sorrow's crown of sorrow is remembering happier things."

For this reason I was glad that my furlough did not allow me to remain longer at home, and thus get used to comfort and to find the presence of friends a necessity. As it was, my visit was so fleeting and short, that it seemed just as unreal as some visits home which I have made in my sleep and from which I have been summarily recalled by the sound of the reveille bugle. I am in for steady work now until we go again into winter-quarters, that is, if my life be spared so long, and if I do not before that time receive some disabling wound. I am, of course, not insensible of the very great disadvantage, to a professional man, of losing several years at the very commencement of his careers, of breaking away from his books and papers to the rough and demoralizing life of a soldier, and you may be sure that I would not do it if I did not consider myself called to it by the voice of most sacred and imperative duty. It astonishes me that any young man in the north, who has his health and is bound by no family ties, can fail to feel the same. It is a great work which will be done, and then how shameful for a man to have to tell his children in after years, "I looked on, while others braved the dangers and wrought the deliverance." And yet, at the same time, I show my own weakness and inconsistency, by my anxiety about my brother, John who is with General Peck at Suffolk[46], and whom I would give my life to see safely home again; I don't believe my mother worries as much about him as I do.

May 25, 1863
Resignation request to Maj. Gen. Oliver Howard, 11th Army Corps
Brooke's Station, VA

    Sir
    I have the honor to tender herewith my resignation as Captain of the 13th Independent Battery, New York State Vols, the leave to be unconditional and immediate for the following reasons:
    1st I was originally mustered in for only two years and had no expectations nor intention of serving for a longer time.
    2nd Very urgent family circumstances demand my immediate presence in Brooklyn NY.
    3rd My Battery, consisting at present of only four guns, is amply supplied with officers.
    The above is respectfully submitted
    Julius Dieckmann
    Comdg 13 New York Battery

May 26, 1863
Extract from Special Orders No. 97, 11th Corps
no location given, Virginia

    6   The following named officers having tendered their resignations are honorably discharged the military service of the United States.
    Capt J Dieckmann, 13th NY Baty[47]
    By order of Maj Genl Howard

May 27, 1863
Battery Orders No. 35
Brooke's Station, VA

The resignation of Captain Julius Dieckmann, 13th New York Battery having been accepted, and he having been honorably discharged the service of the United States by Special Order No 97, Headquarters Eleventh Corps, Army of the Potomac, May 26, 1863, I hereby assume the command of this Battery from May 26, 1863
Wm Wheeler
1st Lieut Comdg Batty

Battery Orders No. 36
Brooke's Station, VA
I   Orderly Sergeant Henry Miller will take command of the Left Section 13th NY Battery until further orders
II   Sergeant Edward Baldwin will do duty as Orderly Sergeant until further orders
III   Sergeant James When will take command of the Sixth Detachment 13th NY Battery until further notice
They will be obeyed & respected accordingly
IV   Private John Lewens is hereby appointed Corporal of the 13th NY Battery to rank from March 1st 1863. He will be obeyed and respected accordingly
Wm Wheeler
1st Lieut Comdg Battery

May 31, 1863
Letter of William Wheeler
Brooke's Station, VA

    There have been important changes in the Battery since I last wrote you. Captain Dieckmann has sent his resignation and General Howard, the next day, sent for me to report to him personally. I did so, and he received me very kindly, asked me how long I had served with the Battery, whether I had ever commanded it, whether I could drill it, etc., and how we did in the late battle, and then dismissed me, apparently well enough satisfied, for the Captain's resignation was returned the same evening approved—accompanied by a pass to Washington—and the next morning my nomination as Captain, by the Chief of Artillery, went on to Governor Seymour at Albany, so that, unless something unusual happens, I shall before long receive my commission, and shall then have the Battery in which I have so long served, for my very own. You will believe me when I say, that while I feel very glad at the prospect of receiving this promotion, this feeling is decidedly overbalanced by the hope of making the Battery more useful and efficient, more capable of doing something for the general cause. And this I believe I can do. The captain of a battery has a very independent position, and it lies with him almost entirely whether his battery is a good and serviceable one or not.

Please tell John when you write that it is not impossible that, in a few days, he will not have to lower his rank by writing to me as Lieutenant any more.

June 9, 1863
Affidavit of William Wheeler, 13th New York Artillery
Brooke's Station, VA

William Wheeler being duly sworn deposes and says that he is the senior 1st Lt and commanding officer of the 13th Battery NY Artillery that Henry Bundy has been regularly appointed a 1st Lieut in said battery by the Governor of New York to fill a vacancy occasioned by the resignation of 1st Lt F Singer on the 16th day of Jan 1863. That to his certain knowledge Henry Bundy has done duty as a 1st Lieutenant in said battery under this appointment since the 16th day of Jan 1863 and that said Henry Bundy has made all proper efforts to be mustered in as a 1st Lieut of said battery since the 16th day of Jan 1863 but without success until the present time. The said Wm Wheeler further swears that Henry Bundy was last mustered for pay as a 1st Lt on the 30th day of April 1863.
Wm Wheeler 1st Lieut
Comdg 13 NY Battery

Affidavit of Henry Bundy, 13ᵗʰ New York Artillery
Brooke's Station, VA

Henry Bundy being duly sworn deposes and says that on the 15ᵗʰ day of May 1862 he was appointed a 2d Lt in the 13ᵗʰ Battery NY Artillery by the Governor of the State of New York to fill vacancy occasioned by the resignation of Lt. Von Linden on the 15ᵗʰ day of May 1862. That he has done duty as a 2d Lieutenant under this appointment since the 15ᵗʰ day of May 1862. That since said 15ᵗʰ day of May 1862 he as made all proper efforts to be mustered in as a 2d Lieut of the 13ᵗʰ Battery NYA but without success before the present time. The said Henry Bundy further swears that he was last mustered for pay as a 1ˢᵗ Lieutenant on the 30ᵗʰ day of April 1863.
Henry Bundy 1ˢᵗ Lieut
13ᵗʰ NY Battery

Affidavit of Henry Bundy, 13ᵗʰ New York Artillery
Brooke's Station, VA

Henry Bundy being duly sworn deposes and says that on the 16ᵗʰ day of January 1863 he was appointed a 1ˢᵗ Lieut in the 13ᵗʰ Battery NY Artillery by the Governor of the State of New York to fill vacancy occasioned by the resignation of Lt. F Singer on the 16ᵗʰ day of Jan 1863. That he has done duty as a 1ˢᵗ Lieutenant under this appointment since the 16ᵗʰ day of Jan 1863. That since said 16ᵗʰ day of Jan1863 he as made all proper efforts to be mustered in as a 1ˢᵗ Lieutenant of the said battery but without success before the present time. The said Henry Bundy further swears that he was last mustered for pay as a 1ˢᵗ Lieutenant on the 30ᵗʰ day of April 1863.
Henry Bundy 1ˢᵗ Lieut
13ᵗʰ NY Battery

June 12, 1863
Battery Orders No. 37
Brooke's Station, VA

I   Sergt E. Baldwin will take charge of the right section 13ᵗʰ New York Battery until further orders; he will be obeyed & respected accordingly

II   Sergeant Henry Tintenfass will do duty as Orderly Sergeant until further orders. He will be obeyed & respected accordingly

Wm Wheeler 1ˢᵗ Lieut

June 22, 1863
Battery Orders No. 38
camp on Goose Creek, VA

The lieutenant commanding takes pleasure in congratulation the Battery upon the improved appearance made by it at the inspection of yesterday, and especially the drivers upon their horses, which received great praise from the Chief of Artillery. It is only by taking great pains, by observance of orders and preservation of good discipline, that we can make the Battery what it ought to be and do our duty to the general service. One thing remains and that is to never forget that we are soldiers both in dress and bearing and manners both towards equals and superiors in rank to show a pride in the uniform we wear.
Wm Wheeler 1ˢᵗ Lieut
Comdg 13 NY Battery

June 23, 1863
Battery Orders No. 39
Camp on Goose Creek, VA

The lieutenant commanding observes that many of the non-commissioned officers of this Battery are deficient in many of the elementary principles of Artillery drill and are equally negligent of the condition of their detachment. This will be corrected in the following manner:
Examinations of non-commissioned officers will be held once in 2 weeks or at larger intervals, if circumstances make it necessary. The examinations will be upon the following points:
1 Nomenclature of the piece, limber and caisson
2 Explanation of the principals of pointing and ranging
3 Explanation of the different kinds of ammunition and the modes of preparing them for action
4 Explanation of the principles of rifled cannons and their advantages
5 Actual drill of non-commissioned officers as a detachment
6 Actual drill of detachments by each non-commissioned officer both in marking, in manual of the piece and mechanical maneuvers

7 Explanation (by sergeants) of all ordinary maneuvers with the Battery hitched up
If any non-commissioned officer shall fail to pay satisfactorily of 3 successive examinations his name will be reported to the Chief of Artillery for the reduction to the ranks and his place will be filled by some person who has shown himself proficient in these matters.
Wm Wheeler 1st Lieut
Comdg 13 NY Battery

July 1863-September 1863
You pay your money and you takes your choice

July 9, 1863
Letter of William Wheeler
Boonesborough, MD

    I eagerly take the first breathing moment to drop you a single line, to let you know that after all our fatiguing marches and hard fighting I am still preserved for more service, and am also in excellent health. We had had unparalleled hard work, marches daily of twenty to thirty miles, and are all pretty well worn out. I won't attempt just now to tell you anything about the battle of Gettysburg, except to say that my Battery was hotly in action on all three days of the fight, and did very good service. We were most of the time on Cemetery Hill. On the 1st, when poor Reynolds pushed us all forward so rashly, we were in the extreme advance, and I had one piece shot all to pieces, and when we feel back I was obliged to leave it, but on the 5th, when we took possession of the battle-field, I went out and got it tinkered it up and brought it off. Besides this I picked up an abandoned twelve-pounder gun, belonging to the Third Corps, and thus came out of the affair with five guns, while I went in with only four. Since the battle we have been marching day and night,--last night's was about the first sleep I have had for a week. Worse yet, it has rained incessantly, and I have hardly known what it was to be dry. The battle was a splendid success; all talk about it being a drawn battle is absurd; prisoners were taken by the thousand and the rebel loss was fearful.

    But I have no time to write more; my pieces are in the advance, in position, and we look for work.

    I write sitting on a cracker-box on a caisson.

July 10, 1863
Congratulatory order of Maj. Gen. Oliver Howard, 11th Army Corps
Boonesborough, MD

    The general again thanks his command for what has been done during the last month. You have now met the enemy, and feel conscious that you have done your duty.

    On the 1st day of July, with the First Corps and Buford's division of cavalry, you held double your numbers in check from

12 m. until night, and thus opened the way for the victory that followed.

On the 2d, you held an important position during the cannonade, and repulsed the enemy, when already within your batteries and breaking through your lines.

On the 3d, the same post was strongly held under the severest cannonade of the war. Our batteries, aided by our infantry, contributed a full share to the repulse of the enemy's last attempt to drive the army from its position.

The Eleventh Corps, as a corps, has done well—well in marching, well in fighting; the Sacrifices it has made shall not be forgotten. In the retrospect, your general feels satisfied. Now, we must make one more effort. Let there be no wavering, no doubt. Our cause is right and our success sure.

    O O Howard
      Major-General, Commanding

July 11, 1863
Battery Orders No. 40
 camp near Boonesborough, MD

I   Corporal Francis F Roache of this Battery is hereby reduced to the ranks for cowardly behavior in the late battle at Gettysburg on the 1st of July.

II   Private Schaedler is hereby appointed Lance Corporal, until a vacancy shall open; he will be obeyed and respected accordingly.

III   The lieutenant commanding thanks the men of the Battery for their patience and gallant conduct under the danger and hardships of the late marches and battles, and hopes that they will continue to hold up high the name they have won.

Wm Wheeler 1st Lieut
Comdg 13 NY Battery

July 13, 1863
Battery Orders No. 41
Funkstown, MD

I   Quartermaster Sergt Charles Hempe is hereby ordered to report back to the Battery for duty; he will deliver the seams & other Battery property to Sergeant Baldwin.

II   Sergeant Edward Baldwin is hereby appointed Quartermaster Sergeant of the 13th New York Battery; he will enter immediately upon his duties & will be obeyed & respected accordingly.
Wm Wheeler 1st Lieut
Comdg 13 NY Battery

July 24, 1863
Battery Orders No. 42
New Baltimore, PA

I   1st Lieutenant Charles L Hunten 134th Regiment NYV is hereby announced as detailed for duty in the 13th NY Battery by orders from headquarters 11 Corps. He will be obeyed and respected accordingly.
II   Acting Orderly Sergeant Henry Tintenfass will take charge of the right section until further orders.
III   Sergeant William H Garrett will take charge of the left section until further orders.
IV   Sergeant Ernest Volmer will do duty as Orderly Sergeant until further orders.
V   Corporal John O'Connor will take charge of the 1st detachment until further orders.
VI Corporal Gustavus Dietr will take charge of the 4th detachment until further orders.
These non-commissioned officers will be obeyed and respected accordingly.
Wm Wheeler 1st Lieut
Comdg 13 NY Battery

July 26, 1863
Letter of William Wheeler
Warrenton Junction, VA

Dear Grandfather and Aunt
You at home will I think begin to wonder where I am, and why I have not written home before, but if you had know how hard we have been at work and how constantly we have been marching, your wonder would change into surprise and thankfulness that I have not been used up entirely and that I am still able to do duty. As I am indebted to you both for letters, I take this opportunity to write you a double-barreled one, not knowing when I may have access to pen and

ink and enough of quiet leisure to compose my ideas. From Boonesborough I dropped a line to mother, informing her of my safety up to that point, but was not able to give her any account of our doings and sufferings during the days of the battle of Gettysburg. I will know give you some description of those scenes from my point of view. After we had been quiet refreshed by our halt in the pleasant camp on Goose Creek, and had, most luckily for us, got our horses into condition again, we marched, on June 15, to Edwards' Ferry, and the next morning crossed the river on our pontoons, and marched up through Poolesville and pat our old Camp Observation, where I had had my first real experience of a soldier's life. The streets of Poolesville were full of people, almost all of them wearing the real old secesh scowl, and I did not see a single United States flag displayed. The artillery took a road for itself that day, in order not to be encumbered by the infantry, and we made a march of almost thirty miles to reach Jefferson City, where we camped in long wet grass, exposed to a heavy rain storm. The next morning my Battery marched with one brigade to Burkettsville, which lies at the front of South Mountain, and was the scene of the battle of that name in last September, at which the heroic General Reno lost his life. Here we lived on the fat of the land, which is always one of the perquisites and advantages of going off with an independent force. The army had neither eaten out of the country, nor raised the prices extravagantly, consequently spring chicken, fresh bread, mile, and butter were the order of the day. This pleasant state of affairs lasted only a day and we had to rejoin the Eleventh at Middletown, from which we marched, the same afternoon, for Frederick City. Both at Middletown, and along the road, were numerous instances of enthusiastic and outspoken patriotism, which went right to our hearts, and mad us feel full of fight; here a party of young girls and children stood and waved handkerchiefs and tiny flags; there a hotel or public building displayed a good expanse of red, white, and blue bunting; there a good old lady stood at her door with her servants, and dispensed cups of cold water to every thirsty soldier, while the gray-haired husband stood by her side, he eyes half full with patriotic and sympathizing tears, and "Good luck to you boys, God bless you." Our whole march in the fertile and beautiful county of Frederick was delightful; indeed its prosperity and richness, the "peace on earth and good will toward men" that reigned there, seemed to us all to be a type of out bountiful and happy Union, while the devastated crops, the deserted homesteads, the bitter and hostile faces of Virginia which we had just left behind, represented, not less truthfully, the hideous and destructive nature of Secession, and well as its results. The spirits of the whole army was superb. When we passed through the towns flags were displayed, music struck up, cheers rang along the column of march and when camp was made, after a toilsome march, signing was heard from the quarters of the weary, footsore soldiers.

We passed through Frederick after nightfall, and did not see the place; the next day we marched to Emmitsburg and rested there, preparatory to the approaching conflict. Early on the 1st of July we started for Gettysburg, about eleven miles distant. I was ordered to report with my Battery to General Steinwehr's Division, and thus got ahead of the other batteries which were in reserve with the First Division. We were marching along, thinking of anything but an approaching fight, when suddenly one of General Howard's aides came galloping up and ordered me forward at double quick. The roads were very stony, and my wheels were in very bad condition, but ahead I went; the gun-carriages rattling and bouncing in the air; feed, rations, kettles and everything else breaking lose from the caissons, the cannoneers running with all their might to keep up, for the road was so very rough, that I was afraid to have them mount, for fear of the repetition of the accident which befell us while trotting to Chancellorsville. For at least four miles the race continued, and I brought my whole Battery safely into position on the right of Gettysburg, but luckily did not have to fire immediately; my breathless cannoneers made their appearance one by one, and soon each detachment was full. On the left, and in front of the town, there was brisk fighting going on. Reynolds (who was in command of our Corps and his own, the First) had pushed his men forward through the town, and was most rashly trying to drive a much superior enemy from the opposite heights. After passing through the town, we came into a hollow, consisting of farms, orchards, and ploughed land, completely commanded both by the Gettysburg heights and by those in the hands of the enemy, and it seemed to be fated that whoever ventured into that hollow was sure to be defeated. We tried it the first day, and Johnny Rebs the second and third days. Captain Dilger's Battery of our Corps was in front of the town, hammering away at a secesh battery on the heights; but, as he had only smooth bores, he was no match for his opponent and was getting cut up badly, so I was ordered forward to help him. I limbered up and went through the town at a trot, the ladies waving their handkerchiefs, and giving us *all* possible cheer and encouragement. I came into battery on Dilger's right, and soon showed the enemy that they had three-inch rifled battery to contend with, and they had to shut up entirely. At about the same time the First Corps, which was on our left, succeeded in driving the enemy along the slop of the hill, and we scared them well as they ran. At this moment everything looked auspicious, and Captain Dilger told me that he would move his Battery, under cover of mine, about five hundred yards further forward, in order to give his guns better play, and then that I should follow him and support him. This he did, and as soon as he got into position a dreadful fire was opened upon him, and I had the chief benefit of this as I moved after him; all the shots fired too high for him fell into my Battery; one struck a drive of a gun and swept him and his two horses right away; strange to say, while both horses were killed, the driver only lost a leg! As we came near the place where we were to take position, we came suddenly on a very substantial fence which the men could not tear down, and we had to wait, under a very heavy fire, until axes could be brought from the caissons and a hold hewed through the fence. While waiting here, I saw an infantry man's leg taken off by a shot, and whirled like a stone through the air, until it came against a caisson with a loud whack. When we got into position we were again too much for the opposing battery, and were getting along finely, when suddenly, on our right, there issues from the base of the hill two great gray clouds, which moved steadily forward towards the infantry of our Corps[48]. At the same time the advance of the First Corps along the face of the hill was checked, and they were driven back. A fierce infantry fight began on our right, our men held a small wood, near the poor house, with determination, and I turned once section of my Battery to the right and fired canister into the columns of the rebels, taking aim at their red battle-flags, which we knew only too well after the fight at Chancellorsville. This lasted for awhile, but the enemy had massed their infantry too heavily for us, and after losing tremendously our men had to withdraw. We held our position until the rebs had got almost in our rear, when we withdrew with our batteries to another position on the road, where we fired a few more canisters and then retired into the town. While crossing the fields, one of my guns was dismounted by a shot, and, after making the greatest efforts to get it off, I was obliged to leave it on the ground; but on the 5th of July, when we took possession of the entire field of battle, I went down with my blacksmith, mended the carriage, and brought the gun off in triumph. We did not get into the town a minute too soon, as the enemy were there almost as soon as we were, and shot some of our men in the street. We passed through the town and took position on Cemetery Hill, which is a high bluff above the town, at the termination of its principal street. There was a lively musketry fight in the lower part of town, which ended in the enemy's getting possession of several cross streets below, while our men held on to the upper part; and during the whole of the next tow days there was a constant skirmishing from doors and window. From the tops of some of the houses the rebs managed to get an aim at Cemetery Hill and picked off many a man from the batteries there. The sun went down on the 1st July, leaving us where we were in the morning; that is, having gained the Gettysburg heights and having been repulsed in an attempt to gain the other heights; while General Reynolds had fallen victim to his own rash attempt, and both Corps had been very seriously cut up. During the night our much needed reinforcements came up; the Second and Third Corps on our left and the Twelfth on our right, and we took a good night's rest, preparatory to the next day's work. The next morning there was brisk skirmishing all along the front, but only desultory shots from the artillery. At about two o'clock in the afternoon the artillery of the Second Corps became hotly engaged on the left, and our boys all stood on tiptoe to watch the contest. Just then General Howard rode up and said, "Never mind the left, boys; look out for your own front"; and sure enough, a few minutes afterward, we saw puffs of smoke,--which we knew well enough arose from the hills opposite to us,--then boom of the guns and the bursting of the shells among us. They soon got an answer from us; we had nine three-inch rifled guns[49] in a row there, from Hall's Second Maine Battery, Wiedrick's Battery, and mine. Besides these, there were the brass guns of Dilger's Ohio Battery, and "G" of the Fourth Regulars[50], although they were more service at close quarters. We did not fire very rapidly, but every shot was aimed with deliberations and judgment, as my corporals were cool and skillful. The result was that in half an hour the enemy's fire slackened, as they had to move their batteries to get out of our fire. Soon they opened again, more fiercely than ever; but we quickly got their new rang, and punished them severely. They placed one battery of very long range on our right flank, and completely enfiladed us; luckily for us they did not get the range for some time. A twenty-pounder Parrott battery was brought up from the Reserve, and this kept them quiet. By 4 ½ PM my ammunition was exhausted, and Major Osborn, our new Chief of Artillery, relieved my Battery with another, and sent mine back to replenish; at the same time he asked me to remain with him and assist him in his very arduous duties, as he had charge of all the batteries on Cemetery Hill, and his regular adjutant was completely used up. This exactly suited me, as my blood was up, and I did not like the idea of going back with my Battery. Until nightfall I was hardly out of fire once, and I was raised to the highest pitch of excitement; the dangers was so great and so constant that, at last, it took away the sense of danger. I placed several batteries on the hill, under the Major's orders, and at length I went back to the Artillery Reserve to bring up a supply of ammunition. While proceeding down the Taneytown road I was a witness of the tremendous attack upon the Third Corps, and of their breaking and fleeing, after a fierce conflict. As this Corps held our extreme left wing at that time, my first thought was that all was lost, and that the enemy would push through to the Baltimore Pike and cut off three Corps at the front; but I had underrated General Meade's capacity of husbanding his reserves and massing his forces. Hardly had the broken fragments of the Third Corps crossed the pike when the firing was renewed in the woods, and on the crest of the hill, where the whole Fifth Corps had been thrown in to reinforce the left wing, and a few minutes later, as if to make assurance doubly sure, I met the First Division of the Twelfth Corps right to the left wing; and in case this should not prove enough, I saw a little further back, among the woods, the dark masses of the Sixth Corps, the strongest corps in the army, waiting to be moved to any point. However, the dose administered by the Fifth Corps proved sufficient. Our line of battle was almost in the shape of a horseshoe, with the reserves on the inside, and these had to march only a short distance in order to reinforce any point threatened. I went back to the Major, and hardly had I got there when the enemy made a most desperate attack upon our extreme right, where a portion of the Twelfth Corps was intrenched. This fight continued a good part of the night, and was renewed at daylight; but the point having been well reinforced, the enemy was repulsed with terrible loss. Late at night, I went down the Baltimore road, to the camp of the Artillery Reserve, to see that my Battery was put in shape for the work early the next morning. Our Chief of Artillery, and all of us who commanded batteries, felt a little pride in keeping Cemetery Hill manned by Eleventh Corps Batteries as constantly as possible, although there were thirty batteries which had not fired a shot. I had a great hunt for ammunition, and even then did not find what I wanted, or what suited my guns; but I managed to get about fifty rounds apiece, (I should have had two hundred), and went back to the hill again. As on the previous day, it was brisk skirmishing along the front, some hard fighting in the town, and desultory artillery firing; but about 1 PM Lee's one hundred pieces (I believe that he had more in position), opened all at once, and, as far as noise went, it was the most terrible cannonade, that I ever witnessed, and the air was literally alive with flying projectiles, from the six-pound solid shot, which looks like a cricket ball, to the long Whitworth rifled shot, which has probably give rise the story of the rebs firing railroad iron. My pieces stood in a peculiarly bad place, as they were at the foot of the hill, practice was not as good as it used to be, and the situation was not as deadly and dangerous as on Friday afternoon at Bull Run, or on Sunday morning at Chancellorsville. In this place I lost some horses but no men. The fire was still at its height, when a request came from General Hunt, Chief of Artillery, to Major Osborn to send him a battery for General Webb of the Second Corps, who feared an infantry attack. The Major handed me the order and off I went to the hill where the Second Corps was, just above General Meade's head-quarters, and reported to General Hancock, who showed me the position I was to take. As I came up and unlimbered on this crest, the rebels were within four hundred yards and were making a charge across our front upon a battery which stood at my right. Luckily for us, they did not see us until we got into position, and had poured a couple of rounds of canister over the heads of our own infantry, who were lying behind a stone fence in front of us. Then they turned their attention somewhat to us and a battery of theirs opened very fiercely upon us, and made things very hot; but we paid no attention to their battery, and just kept canister going into them. Once a double round of canister struck close to their flag, and I saw a dozen of them drop, and the whole column wavered and halted; but the standard-bearer waved his flag and they moved on again, but in a weary and spiritless manner. Just at this moment what should the infantry in front of us do but get up and leave! The Battery seemed lost, but I got hold of some of them, then told them not to let the Eleventh Corps boys laugh at them, and in this way, first a squad, and then the whole regiment, was rallied and got back to the fence again, and about every reb who came up on to that hill was either killed, wounded, or captured. We then went back to our Corps and soon the fighting for the night was over. I went over a part of the battle-field that night, and did what I could to make the wounded comfortable; but very soon this seemed a hopeless undertaking; our wounded were removed in ambulances as fast as possible, but the rebel wounded, who were almost all of them in our hands, received extremely little attention, and lay scattered over the field in groups of twenty, fifty, or even a hundred, trying to help each other a little. Our men could not help it; most of them were too much worn out to raise a hand, and the regular Ambulance Corps could not begin to attend to our own wounded boys. I was glad to do a little something for them, even if it were only to turn them on their side, and give them a glass of water. Utterly as I detest a living active rebel, as soon as he becomes wounded and a prisoner I don't perceive any difference in my feeling towards him and towards one of our own wounded heroes. I suppose this is very heterodox, but I can't help it. I found a Colonel of a Mississippi Regiment shot through the breast, a man of stately bearing, and a soldier of his regiment told me that he was Judge of the Supreme Court of that State. Now here was a man, evidently one of the real old original Secesh; but I forgot that, took him into a barn, made him a straw bed, fixed a pillow for him, got him a cup of coffee, and ignored the fact that he gave me no word of thanks or farewell when I left him. The scenes of the battle-field were very right, and I will not trouble you with any description of them; I will only mention a rencontre which I had with General Meade on Friday afternoon. I was with my Battery at the foot of the hill, waiting for orders and expecting to be called upon to be relieve one of our Corps batteries, when an elderly Major General with spectacles, looking a good deal like a Yale Professor, rode up and asked me if I had a full supply of ammunition. I told him that I had as full as supply as I could get on the field, having been to the ammunition train with an order from Major Osborn, but without success: whereupon he got excited and said, "You must have ammunition; the country can't wait for Major Osborn or any other man; go immediately to the Artillery Reserve and order General Tyler[51] to send up a wagon load." Now I might have told him that there was not a round of three-inch ammunition left with the Artillery Reserve, as I had been there myself shortly before; but something in his face warned me against answering back; so I put spurs to my horse, and got round the corner of wood, where I stayed until he had left the premises and then came back, to learn it was General Meade himself. And so the battle closed. We had repulsed the enemy at every point, with very great loss, had taken an immense number of prisoners (I saw several thousand with my own eyes, besides the wounded ones), and had remained in possession of the field, to say nothing of pursuing the enemy from the 5th until this day. I am sure that the importance and decisiveness of the victory cannot well be overrated. I have no time to tell you of our forced march back to Emmitsburg, Middletown, Boonesborough, and Hagerstown. The enemy's crossing under our noses, at Williamsport and Falling Waters, was a masterly maneuver, but I do not think that Meade is at all to blame for it. Our marches since then have been severe, and the men are getting sick with bilious fever on all sides. Thus far I have borne up splendidly and have not been off duty for an hour. I hope and pray that I may continue as well. Major Osborn has forwarded a new demand for my commission to Governor Seymour, and accompanied the request with expression of approbations, both towards me and the Battery, which have made me feel very proud. I have enjoyed the Major's society greatly. He is a gentleman and a soldier, a most energetic and gallant mane, and he contributed greatly, by the management of his artillery, in resorting their lost prestige so brilliantly to the Eleventh Corps. I am now entirely without officers. I have applied for a commission for Henry Miller, my Orderly Sergeant. I hope in a month or two to get everything fixed up in good shape and to get two more guns....The time may vary a few months, a few years, or even a few decades, but the job will be settled and that all right too. I am, in this matter, like St. Paul's Charity, ready to bear, believe, hope, and endure all things for the cause, knowing that if we do so, we also, like Charity, shall never fail. This has been a most egotistical letter, but I know you want to hear about me, and not about the army in general or anybody else.

July 28, 1863
Leave of absence request to Maj. Thomas Osborn, Artillery Brigade, 11th Army Corps
Warrenton Junction, VA

Major
I have the honor to request that leave of absence be granted me to go to Washington DC for the purpose of having some checks cashed to pay men employed in the service of the Quartermasters Dept of the Artillery & Artillery Ammunition train of the 11th Corps. They have not been paid for the past 5 months & need money & it is impossible to have the checks cashed here. I have besides other business connected with the Quartermasters Dept to attend to in Washington.
Most Respectfully
Your obdt Sert
Henry Bundy 1st Lieut

AAQM Army 11th Corps

July 29, 1863
Report of Maj. Thomas Osborn, Artillery Brigade, 11th Army Corps
no location given

   Sir: I have the honor to report, concerning the part borne by this command in the battle of Gettysburg on the 1st, 2d, and 3d instant, that on the morning of the 1st instant I- moved from Emmitsburg toward Gettysburg with the artillery of the corps, consisting of five batteries, and marched in the following order: Captain Dilger in advance with the Third Division, Lieutenant Wheeler with the First Division and in the center, the three remaining batteries following closely in rear of the center division.
   I herewith enumerate the batteries of the command: Battery G, Fourth US Artillery, commanded by Lieut B Wilkeson, six light 12-pounders; Battery I, First Ohio Artillery, commanded by Capt H Dilger, six light 12-pounders; Battery K, First Ohio Artillery, commanded by Capt L Heckman, four light 12-pounders; Battery I, First New York Artillery, commanded by Capt M Wiedrich, six 3-inch, and Thirteenth New York Independent Battery, commanded by First Lieut W Wheeler, four 3-inch guns. Total, 96 guns.
   After moving 5 or 6 miles, I received notice from Major-General Howard that the First Corps was already engaged with the enemy at Gettysburg, and that I should move the artillery to the front as rapidly as possible.
   A little after 10 AM the first battery (Dilger's) reached the town, and was ordered by General Schurz to the front of and 300 yards beyond the town, where he took position, and at once became engaged with a rebel battery about 1,000 yards in its front. This battery was soon supported by another, when Captain Dilger was compelled to stand the fire from both until the arrival of Wheeler's battery half an hour later, when I ordered Lieutenant Wheeler to report to Captain Dilger. The result of this artillery duel was one piece of Wheeler's battery dismounted and five pieces of the enemy's, which they left upon the ground; besides, they lost comparatively heavier than we in horses and *materiel*.
   During the short struggle both batteries changed position several times, and did so with excellent results and in the best

possible manner, Captain Dilger using much judgment in the selection of his several positions. They did not leave their immediate locality until the corps was ordered by the commanding general to fall back to Cemetery Hill.

About 11 AM Lieutenant Wilkeson reached the field, and was ordered to report to General Barlow, commanding the First Division, which was engaged about three-fourths of a mile from the town and on the left of the York pike. The battery was assigned position by General Barlow, and when I reached the ground I found it unfortunately near the enemy's line of infantry, with which they were engaged, as well as two of his batteries, the concentrated fire of which no battery could withstand. Almost at the first fire, Lieutenant Wilkeson was mortally wounded, and carried from the field by 4 of his men. The command of the battery now devolved upon Lieutenant Bancroft. By changing position several times, the battery maintained its relative position until the division fell back to the town, when it retired to Cemetery Hill. During this engagement the battery was separated into sections or half batteries, and its struggle to maintain itself was very severe and persistent.

Captain Heckman was not ordered in until the corps had begun to fall back. He was then put into position, with a view of holding the enemy in check until the corps had time to retire through the town to the hill beyond, and though he worked his battery to the best of his ability, the enemy crowded upon it, and was within his battery before he attempted to retire. He was compelled to leave one gun in the hands of the enemy. I think no censure can be attached to this battery for the loss of the gun. The battery was so severely disabled otherwise that I was compelled to send it to the rear, thus losing the benefit of it during the fight of the second and third days.

Captain Wiedrich was assigned, on his arrival upon the field, to a position on the hill immediately in front of the cemetery entrance and overlooking the town. He was engaged several times during the day with the enemy's artillery at long range. He maintained the same position during the three days' fighting, but on this PM Colonel Wainwright, chief of artillery First Corps, took command of his battery, with the artillery on that side of the Baltimore pike. The artillery of the corps ceased firing for the day, when the corps fell back to Cemetery Hill.

I would remark here that during the PM of the 1st and the AM of the 2d, I furnished Colonel Wainwright, chief of artillery First Corps., with ammunition from the Eleventh Corps train, the train of the First Corps not being within reach. This of necessity caused considerable annoyance later in the engagement, on account of the difficulty in procuring a supply of ammunition sufficient to cover the great expenditure we were compelled to make through the engagement.

On the morning of the 2d, I applied to General Hunt, chief of artillery Army of the Potomac, for a greater amount of artillery than we then had, as our position was finely adapted to its use, and I did not consider that we had sufficient to assist our small infantry force in holding the position if the enemy should attack us in heavy force. The following batteries were ordered to report to me: Battery H, First U.S. Artillery, Lieutenant Eakin, six light 12-pounders; Fifth New York Independent Battery, Captain Taft, six 20-pounder Parrotts; Battery O, First West Virginia Artillery, Captain Hill, four 10-pounder Parrotts; Battery H, First Ohio Artillery, Captain Huntington, six 3-inch rifles; Second Maine Battery, Captain Hall, four 3-inch rifles; First New Hampshire Battery, Captain [Edgell] six 3-inch rifles. Total, 32.

Heckman's battery having been sent to the rear and one gun of Wheeler's battery dismounted, gave us on the morning of the 2d a total of fifty-two guns.

In the morning, before General Slocum had occupied his position, and while he was doing so, I placed three batteries on the right of the Baltimore road, commanding the ravine between the two prominent hills on our right; yet, as General Slocum withstood every assault on his lines without assistance, later in the day I withdrew these batteries to the hill. As soon as the enemy developed the position he would probably occupy with his batteries, I placed mine in position commanding them. By the assignment on the hill, Dilger had the right, resting next the Baltimore road and parallel with the Emmitsburg road; on his left, and in order, were Bancroft, Eakin, Wheeler, Hill, and Hall, commanding the enemy's batteries to the right of the town; and across the Baltimore road I placed Taft in rear of and perpendicular to Bancroft; also Huntington in rear of and perpendicular to Wheeler, but farther in the rear of Wheeler than Taft was of Bancroft, so that Taft's battery would not obstruct his line of fire.

By this assignment of artillery, I commanded with a reputable number of guns every point on which the enemy could place artillery commanding Cemetery Hill. I also occupied every point of the hill available for artillery, and during the engagement every gun, at different times, was used with good effect, and the fire of no one gun interfered with the fire of another. A sharp curve in the side of the hill also afforded good and convenient protection for the caissons. Most of the day the firing of the enemy's artillery was irregular, they scarcely opening more than one battery at a time, and when they did so we readily silenced them.

On our entire front the enemy held a fine crest for the protection of artillery, at a distance of 1,000 to 1,400 yards from us; but at the time the heavy attack was made on the extreme left of our line, the firing was very severe, and especially upon the hill. They engaged the greater portion of our whole line, and from both the right and left of the town much of the fire was concentrated on our position, but we soon gained a decided advantage over them, and long before the infantry struggle on the left was decided, we had silenced most of their guns.

In this artillery fire, Lieutenant Eakin was wounded in the hip, and carried from the field.

Between 7 and 8 o'clock in the evening, a rebel brigade charged from the town upon the hill and upon Captain Wiedrich's battery. The charge was very impetuous, and the infantry at first gave way, and the battery was held for a moment by the enemy, when the cannoneers rallied with the infantry, and, seizing upon any weapons they could reach, threw themselves upon the enemy, and assisted to drive them back. All was done that could be, both before and after the repulse of the enemy, by the use of canister upon their ranks.

Colonel Wainwright speaks in highly complimentary terms of both officers and men for their gallant conduct on this occasion. Although the command was much exhausted by the two days' work, most of the night was passed in replenishing the batteries with ammunition and making repairs.

On the morning of the 3d, we were in position the same as on the 2d, but little was done during the AM by our corps. Occasionally a rebel battery would open upon the cemetery, evidently with a view to obtain the exact elevation and time to make their fire effective in the PM's work on our position. At each attempt we silenced them, with but little loss to ourselves.

About 2 PM they opened along our whole front with an unbroken line of artillery, and also heavily on our right flank, apparently using every description of missiles and field artillery. The crest which the enemy occupied varied from 1,000 to 1,900 yards distance, and afforded an excellent protection. I judge that the guns of not less than one-half mile of this front were concentrated on our position, besides several batteries on our right, which enfiladed our position, excepting Captains Taft's and Huntington's batteries.

Our artillery endured this fire with surprising coolness and determination. No battery even showed a disposition to retire, and several times during the cannonading we silenced several of their batteries, but at a moment's cessation on our part, they would reopen upon us. The fire was extremely galling, and by comparing the rapidity with which the shells fell among and passed by our guns with the rapidity with which our guns replied, the number of guns playing on the hill was very much greater than the number in position there; probably double.

Our guns were worked with great coolness, energy, and judgment, but as no satisfactory results were obtained, I ordered all our guns to cease firing, and the men to lie down to await developments. At the same time the artillery of our entire front ceased firing, and a few moments later the infantry of the enemy broke over the crest from where their artillery had been playing, and made their grand charge across the plain upon our lines. The left of the charging column rested on a line perpendicular to our front, then stretching away to the right beyond our view, thus offering an excellent front for our artillery fire. We used, according to distance, all descriptions of projectiles. The whole force of our artillery was brought to bear upon this column, and the havoc produced upon their ranks was truly surprising.

The enemy's advance was most splendid, and for a considerable distance the only hinderance offered it was by the artillery, which broke their lines fearfully, as every moment showed that their advance under this concentrated artillery fire was most difficult; and though they made desperate efforts to advance in good order, were unable to do so, and I am convinced that the fire from the hill was one of the main auxiliaries in breaking the force of this grand charge. But while the enemy was advancing, and after having been repulsed, I insisted that the artillery fire should be turned intensely upon the infantry, and no notice whatever was to be taken of their artillery.

I am not able to speak of any one or more batteries as deserving especial notice over another. Every battery did its whole duty; the officers proved themselves brave and efficient, and the men on the battle-field were most willing, brave, and gallant; in fact, the only fault I could mention was too great willingness to use ammunition at small squads of men and on unimportant objects, yet this was not carried to excess.

The artillery of the reserve proved all that could be expected or even asked of it; without their assistance I do not conceive how I could have maintained the position we held. I feel most thankful for their assistance, and the very willing and cordial manner in which it was rendered.

I would also speak of Lieut George W Freeman, acting assistant adjutant-general of the command, for the great assistance he was to me and to the whole command during the engagement.

I am unable to give any definite estimate of the amount of ammunition expended during the engagement. After we had exhausted the supply with the batteries, I replenished from our train. Colonel Wainwright, on the PM of the 1st, also replenished from our train, and, after this source was exhausted, I drew from the reserve train of the army.

The casualties of this command are as follows.
Our loss in pieces and horses is as follows:

Horses killed.
Battery G, Fourth U.S. Artillery   31
Battery I, First Ohio Artillery (one piece disabled)   28
Battery K, First Ohio Artillery (one piece lost)   9
Battery I, First New York Artillery (one piece dismounted)   18
Thirteenth New York Independent Battery (one piece dismounted)   12
Total   98

I am, respectfully, your obedient servant,
T W Osborn
Major, Commanding Artillery, Eleventh Corps

Report of Lt. William Wheeler, 13th New York Artillery
Warrenton Junction, VA

Sir: I have the honor herewith to transmit a detailed report of the part taken by the Thirteenth New York Battery in the battle of July 1, 2, and 3, at Gettysburg, Pa.

On July 1, I marched from Emmitsburg with the Second Division (General Steinwehr), but, when within about 5 miles of Gettysburg, I was ordered to move forward at double-quick, which I did, proceeding at a rapid trot, and losing a large amount of forage from the roughness of the road.

Upon arriving at Gettysburg, I took position, by your order, on the right of the town, but soon received orders to move through the town to the front, and to support Captain Dilger's battery. In passing through the town, the rear body of two of my caissons broke down. One of these was subsequently recovered, but the other was too badly shattered to be repaired. I took up my position on Captain Dilger's right, and as soon as my guns had got the range of the hostile battery, they responded to it with good effect. Under their cover, Captain Dilger moved several hundred yards forward into a wheat-field. As soon as he commenced firing, I limbered up and followed, again taking position on his right. A very heavy fire was opened on us here both in front and upon the right flank, but we continued to hold the position.

The enemy then massed his infantry and threw them upon the troops on our right, who fell back after some severe fighting. I changed the direction of my right section, and fired into the advancing column of the enemy with canister, but did not succeed in checking them. I did not leave this position until the enemy was almost in rear of my battery. I then moved back to a point on the road near the town, and held this until the enemy were again nearly behind me, and the infantry supports had withdrawn.

While moving across the field to this point, a shot struck the axle of one of my pieces and broke it, dismounting the piece. I slung the piece under the limber with the prolonge, and carried it for some distance until the prolonge broke, when I was obliged to abandon the gun, but recovered it on the 5th, and it is now in serviceable condition. I then moved through the town, and was assigned by you a position on Cemetery Hill, being on the left wing of the batteries of the corps.

On the morning of July 2, my battery threw a few shells at the rebel train, &c., without eliciting a response.

At about 2 PM the rebel batteries opened along our front and on our right flank. My battery replied to them with good effect, and the guns directly in my front were several times silenced and compelled to change their position.

At about 5.30 PM my ammunition became exhausted (as I had lost 200 rounds in the caissons that broke down), and you sent another battery to relieve me. I took my battery to the Artillery Reserve train, and filled up with percussion and canister, which was the only 3-inch ammunition on hand.

During the morning of July 3, I lay in reserve behind Cemetery Hill. During the heavy cannonade from 1 to 3 PM, I lost some horses, but fortunately no men.

At about 4 PM I received an order from you to go to assist the Second Corps, upon which a very heavy attack was being made. I immediately reported to General Hancock, who showed me my position. Upon coming into battery, I found the enemy not more than 400 yards off, marching in heavy column by a flank to attack Pet-tit's battery, which was on my right and somewhat in advance of me. This gave me a fine opportunity to enfilade their column with canister, which threw them into great disorder, and brought them to a halt three times. The charge was finally repulsed, and most of the enemy taken prisoners. I then returned to the corps at Cemetery Hill.

My loss consisted of 4 men severely wounded, 6 slightly wounded, and 3 missing; 12 horses killed.

My men behaved with courage and spirit, and are anxious for another opportunity to try their 3-inch guns.

I beg leave to mention by name Orderly Sergt Henry Miller and Corporals [Edward] Trafford, [John] O'Connor, and [John A] Rusk, as distinguished for coolness and skill.

Eight hundred and fifty rounds of ammunition were expended.

The above is respectfully submitted.

Wm Wheeler

First Lieutenant, Comdg Thirteenth New York Battery

Report of Capt. Hubert Dilger, Battery I, 1st Ohio Light Artillery
no location given

Major: In regard to the part my battery took in the engagement July 1, 2, and 3, near Gettysburg, Pa., I have the honor to report:

The battery arrived at Gettysburg at about 10 AM July 1, attached to the division of Maj Gen C Schurz, commanded by Brig Gen A Schimmelfennig, who ordered me to take a position between the Taneytown and Baltimore road, wherever I might find it necessary, to which order I complied by putting one section, Lieutenant [Clark] Scripture commanding, on the highest point of the field. A four-gun battery of the enemy immediately opened fire at about 1,400 yards on this section, and compelled me very soon to bring my whole battery into action. During this heavy artillery duel, the enemy had been re-enforced to eight pieces, of which two advanced [To within] 800 or 1,000 yards, but I finally succeeded in silencing them, with a loss of five carriages, which they had to leave on the ground, after several efforts to bring them to the rear with new horses.

Short time afterward, a rifled battery commenced to play on me, and you brought, at my request, Lieutenant Wheeler's battery to my support, and gave me the honor of taking charge of both batteries. I instantly advanced Lieutenant Weidman's section about 600 yards on our right, on the Baltimore and Harrisburg road, and returned from there the other four pieces of my battery on the left, under protection of Lieutenant Wheeler's fire, about 400 yards.

In advancing, a ditch (5 feet wide and 4 feet deep, crossing the field in our front) had to be filled up, so as to form at least a passage for a column by pieces, which was executed under a very heavy fire. Lieutenant Wheeler followed as soon as my pieces were in position, and we remained here until the enemy's infantry commenced to mass on our right flank 100 yards, supported by about four batteries, which concentrated their fire on us, one of them enfilading our line completely, causing great damage to men and horses, and disabling one piece of mine and one of Wheeler's battery.

Our final retreat was executed in the same manner as the advance, and our infantry falling back toward the town, which could only be reached on one road, I sent all the pieces back excepting one section of each battery, commanding with them the entrance of the town as long as possible. The two rifled guns had to retire first, because I would not expose them too much at this short range, at which they commenced to become useless.

Our infantry having reached the town, I left my position, and was relieved on the Market road by two pieces of Battery G, Fourth US Artillery.

The main road was completely blockaded by artillery, infantry, and ambulances, and I took the first road to the left, marched around the town, and rejoined my command on Cemetery Hill, having lost on this day 14 men, 24 horses, and 1 piece disabled.

During the whole engagement, three of my caissons were always employed to carry ammunition, and as slowly as I directed the fire, we were twice nearly out of ammunition.

In regard to the ammunition. I must say that I was completely dissatisfied with the results observed of the fuses for 12-pounder shells and spherical case, on the explosion of which, by the most careful preparation, you cannot depend. The shell fuses, again, were remarkably less reliable than those for spherical case. The fuses for 3-inch ammunition caused a great many explosions in our right before the mouth of the guns, and it becomes very dangerous for another battery to advance in the fire of his batteries, which kind of advancing of smooth-bore batteries is of very great importance on the battlefield, and should be done without danger. I would, therefore, most respectfully recommend the use of percussion shells only.

The other three days, major, I had the honor to stay under your immediate command, and cannot report any fact of special importance, excepting the loss of 2 men and 4 horses more.

The behavior of officers and men of my battery was excellent. Also, I am very much obliged to Lieutenant Wheeler for his kind and gallant assistance on the first day.

I have the honor, major, to sign, your obedient,
H Dilger
Captain, Commanding Battery I, First Ohio Artillery

August 1, 1863
Report of Brig. Gen. Charles Devens, Jr., 1st Division, 11th Army Corps
Boston, MA

Colonel: My report of the proceedings of the First Division, Eleventh Army Corps, in the operations connected with the battle of Chancellorsville has been necessarily delayed by the fact that I was wounded in the battle of May 2, and that I have not been able to obtain as yet the reports of the subordinate commanders, with the exception of that of the commanding officer of the First Brigade, and partially that of the commanding officer of the Second Brigade. No report has been received by me from any commanding officer of a regiment, and I am, therefore, obliged to make this as a preliminary report, the defects of which will be supplied hereafter in case anything in the reports of those officers (when I see them) should require notice.

The division crossed the Rappahannock River at 1 am on the morning of April 29, and the same day marched to the Rapidan, which it crossed the same night at Germanna Ford.

On April 30, the division moved to a point on the Turnpike road from Fredericksburg to Gordonsville, running through Chancellorsville, near where another road (sometimes called Brock's road) intersects it. Both these roads were carefully reconnoitered by the major-general commanding the corps, accompanied by myself to a distance of from 4 to 6 miles out from the position taken by the division, and pickets placed upon them, extending on Brock's road about 3 miles out. After this reconnaissance, the line of the Second Brigade was formed along the Turnpike road, facing south toward the Plank road, which intersected the Turnpike road about three-fourths of a mile to our left, the right resting on a woods. Beyond, but in the edge of the same woods, half a mile farther to the right, the First Brigade, under Colonel von Gilsa, was formed at right angles, facing to the west, connection between the two being kept by half a regiment. All the regiments of the division were thus in line, with the exception of those used in picketing and two which were used, by order of the major-general commanding the corps, as a reserve in another part of the line. The division remained in this position during this day and until the night of May 1, when, by orders of the major-general commanding, communicated through Major [Charles H] Howard, the brigade of Colonel von Gilsa was drawn in, so that it connected by the left with the Second Brigade. Two of his regiments formed in a prolongation of the line of the Second Brigade, and the remainder formed across from the Turnpike road to the Brock road, facing westerly, as before. A section of a battery was planted upon the road facing west, and supported by the infantry of the First Brigade.

During the night of the 1st, rifle-pits were constructed along the front of the Second Brigade, under the direction of Major [Ernest F] Hoffmann, chief engineer of the Eleventh Army Corps. A picket line was thrown out at a distance of from half a mile to a mile, and stretching well around, covering our right flank, the pickets on Brock's road still remaining in position. The two regiments taken from my division on the previous day having been returned to me, I had now in reserve the Seventy-fifth and Twenty-fifth Ohio.

During the forenoon of May 2, the line was visited and the dispositions for defense carefully inspected by the major-general commanding the army, accompanied by the major-general commanding the Eleventh Corps. Some slight alterations suggested by General Howard were immediately adopted.

About 11 AM a large moving column, in which could plainly be distinguished infantry, artillery, cavalry, and wagons, was seen moving rapidly from a point to the left of our position toward our right, with the evident intention of either passing around our right or of retreating. Of this fact the major-general commanding the corps was immediately apprised by me, but he had already become aware of it.

Shortly after, skirmishing took place along the line of my Second Brigade, caused by some rebel cavalry, indicating the vicinity of the enemy's pickets. Soon after, 2 men, who stated that they had been sent out from another portion of the line as scouts, were brought in by my pickets, reporting that the enemy were moving in great force upon our right flank. They were immediately sent by me to corps headquarters, under charge of a trusty sergeant, with orders that after reporting to General Howard they should at once proceed to the headquarters of the major-general commanding the army.

Several reconnaissances, made by a small body of cavalry placed at my disposition, discovered early in the afternoon bodies of the enemy's cavalry moving upon our right. One of these portions, under the command of Lieutenant [Henry T] Davis, of my staff, was fired upon, and the fact immediately reported by him to the major-general commanding the corps. Colonel von Gilsa's skirmishers were, between 3 and 4 o'clock in the afternoon, attacked by the skirmishers of the enemy, with the evident intention of feeling our position. After this, Colonel von Gilsa's skirmishers were pushed farther to the front, and the major-general commanding the corps again rode down the line. After his return, a company of cavalry was sent me for the purpose of making further examination of the woods, which examination, though not thoroughly made, was still sufficient to show that the enemy's cavalry were deployed along the front of my First Brigade, accompanied by some pieces of horse artillery. I directed the captain commanding the cavalry to return and report at corps headquarters.

At about 6.30 PM the enemy were reported as advancing in great force upon our right flank. This report was immediately telegraphed to headquarters, and I proceeded at once, under a heavy fire of shell, with my staff from my headquarters, at the left of the line, to the position of Colonel von Gilsa. The enemy were moving down in line embracing the right and left of the Turnpike road, with the intention of attacking at the same time our front and rear.

Desirous of protecting as much as possible the line of Colonel von Gilsa, I ordered the Seventy-fifth Ohio, under Colonel Reily, to support him on the right. The Twenty-fifth Ohio, the only other regiment of my reserve, was at once ordered to deploy in rear of the line of Colonel von Gilsa for its support, facing to the west.

As it has been suggested that the First Division was to some extent surprised, I deem it my duty to say that in riding down the entire line I found no officers or men out of their assigned positions, but all prepared to meet the attack. The line of skirmishers along the front of both brigades behaved with great resolution, keeping the enemy back as long as they could be expected to resist so fierce an attack by so overwhelming a force; in fact, they emerged from the woods at the right of the Second Brigade at the same time with the attacking force. From the great extent of the enemy's line, as soon as it came in contact with ours, we were completely outflanked on the right, and the fire began to be felt in the rear of the Second Brigade, while the skirmishers of the enemy were finding their way to the rear of and firing on the First Brigade, commanded by Colonel von Gilsa. I had at this time a full view of that portion of the enemy's line which was deployed upon the right or southern side of the road, and, later, of that which appeared on the left or northern side. The formation of the enemy, as well as could be seen in the smoke and confusion of the battle (and I think I distinguished it accurately), was that of a line of regiments in double column, closed in mass, or at half distance, numbering from 25,000 to 30,000 men.

In the position the division was to receive such attack in so large force, no other division being at the time engaged or able to support it, the line of General Schurz being a prolongation of my left, it was rapidly forced back after the main body of the enemy finally engaged it. A change of front at this time by the Second Brigade would have been impracticable under so severe a fire, and, even were it otherwise, I should have considered it unwise, as pivoting upon either flank would have separated the two brigades or else cut me off from General Schurz on my left, and in nowise have saved me from being outflanked by the enemy.

Notwithstanding the necessary confusion in which the division was forced to relinquish its first position (no order to retreat having been given), I think that a second line might have been formed within the lines of General Schurz had his division been able to maintain its position. The retreat of my own, however, must undoubtedly have added to the difficulties encountered by the command of that officer.

The Seventeenth Connecticut, under command of Major Brady—its colonel having been wounded and lieutenant-colonel killed—was, in fact, rallied and reformed in that position. A battery of artillery, under Captain Dieckmann, formed a portion of my command. Of this one section, as before stated (posted on the Turnpike road, under command of Colonel von Gilsa), did good service until obliged to retire or be abandoned to the enemy. The other four pieces were stationed at the left of the division. When forced back with my own retreating troops, I did not find them in position. No report has been received by me from the officer commanding.

Another attempt was made to rally the men in the rifle-pits running north and south, at the extreme left of General von Steinwehr's position, and with partial success. As we were forced from this point, which was the last occupied by portions of the Eleventh Corps, I was compelled to quit the field, having received a severe and painful wound in the commencement of the action, against the effects of which I had been struggling for more than an hour.

The command of the division now devolving upon General McLean, he reported to me that the division was not entirely reformed until a late hour in the evening, near General Hooker's headquarters at Chancellorsville. While it is a matter of great regret that the division could not maintain the position assigned to it, it would be unjust to attribute its defeat to misbehavior or causeless panic.

Of about 4,000 men reported that day for duty, the names of at least 1,600 have been forwarded to corps headquarters as killed, wounded, and missing; and, although of the latter a considerable portion are probably prisoners, that fact itself shows that they did not basely yield their position, but were enveloped by the masses of the enemy while endeavoring to maintain it. The field officers did their duty faithfully, and a majority of the commanders of the regiments are included in the lists of killed, wounded, and missing. I especially commend Colonel von Gilsa for his resolute exertions, to which I was a witness during all stages of the action.

I am under especial obligations to the adjutant-general of the division, Captain [Oscar] Minor; to the inspector-general, Major [John F] Frueauff, and to my aide, Lieutenant Davis, First Massachusetts Cavalry, for gallantry and fidelity, also to Captain von Meusel, from the staff of General McLean, temporarily serving with me.

I am, colonel, very respectfully, your obedient servant,
Chas Devens, Jr
Brigadier-General

August 4, 1863
Letter of William Wheeler
Catlett's Station, VA

If we rest here for some weeks, as there is talk of our doing, I hope to get track of Sunday again, and at least to have some music. There is a good piano and melodeon at Mr Catlett's, where General Howard has his head-quarters, and I have been introduced to Mrs Catlett, a lady of intelligence and refinement, I shall go up there pretty soon and try to beat up a crowd to sing, out of the General's staff.

I spent a pleasant Sunday, about two weeks ago near Waterford, just after we crossed the Potomac. The artillery made a very early march and got into camp by 11 AM. Somehow, I got into a farm-house, close by my quarters, which was a fine old homestead, belonging to an old gentleman named Pierpoint, and he had a pleasant wife and three pretty daughters. There I spent pretty much the whole of the day, tried to get the girls to sing with me out of the "Carmina Sacra," had a good dinner, and successfully resisted all efforts of both General Steinwehr and Schurz, to get me out of the house. I never saw such perfect idyllic simplicity as prevailed in the family. They belonged to the Society

of Friends[52], and one of the girls who had been as far as
Alexandria, and had once seen dancing, was looked upon with
wonder by the rest. The youngest, however, who was a little
mischief, after T U style, declared loudly that if *she* got the chance
she would dance, *too*; she didn't believe it was so very wicked. I
did not bother my head abut the trouble in New York; I only
wished that they would send me with my Battery to the city for a
couple of weeks, to enforce the draft. I would much rather fire
canister into those drunken Irish rowdies, than into the secesh
brethren, who, although deluded, are worth all the Paddies that
ever had a brogue....I try to do my duty fully, and then look to
results, not heeding if the material is used up on the process. My
own life I reckon no dearer than the rest, if I can win the end. You
see, dearest mother, this war has become the religion of very many
of our lives, and those of us who think, and who did not enter the
service for gain or military distinction, have come more and more
to identify this cause for which we are fighting, with all of good
and religion in our previous lives, and so it must be if we are to
win the victory. We must have an impulse, made of patriotic fire
and a deeper feeling, which takes its rise in the thinking soul. If we
have this, then we can bear our standards and our military pride
high up, for they will have a foundation. I am and have been in
good health, almost without intermission, even when so many
were falling sick about me, but I think that the putrid swamp
would have done for me, too, as well as for the others. Did you
hear whether Robert Edwards came safe out of that attack on Fort
Wagner[53]? I saw that his regiment was badly cut up.

August 9, 1863
Letter of William Wheeler
Catlett's Station, VA

Indeed, when I allow myself to think of the quiet delights
of home,--the libraries, music, the refining and humanizing
influence of dear friends—glorious Sabbath evenings like this, not
spent in seeing horses groomed, or in repacking ammunition, but
in singing "Tallis," and "Solitude," and "Bemerton" and with you,
and mother, and the girls, and Aunt Elizabeth, with my hand
clasped in somebody's, I can assure you that a half feeling of
regret, and a whole feeling of longing, comes over me, so that it
requires a really painful effort to repress it, and to reach forward to

those things that are before, even if I do not forget those things that are behind. Sunday evening is my regular time for this sort of Lot's-wife longings and lookings back, partly because the vacant time allows them, and the day suggests them, and partly because of the duties of the next day will cure any undue homesickness. Now we are to have a big drill to-morrow morning at 5 AM, and I rely upon that to do away with the evil effects of my this evening imagining myself sitting by mother, and listening to you singing "When gathering clouds."

You will be shocked at hearing I indulged in another of our favorite menagerie "loads" in the heart of the battle at Gettysburg. It was on the first day, when General Reynolds pushed us through the town, and made and offensive (more to us than to the enemy) attack upon a superior force in a superior position. My Battery and another were in the extreme advance, and were fighting hotly with some rebel batteries, when the rebel massed their forces, threw out three heavy columns, and very soon drove our infantry back, and enveloped the batteries in a dangerous manner. I did not wait for this state of affair, but immediately left the rebel batteries the whole talk, and began to try to break up the rebel columns with canister. The captain of the other battery, Captain Dilger, would not believe that they were not our own men at first, although their blood-red battle-flags were plain enough in sight, and at last he asked me, "Wheeler, which *are* the rebels and which are our men?" Whereupon I retorted upon him with the same answer as that which the snowman so triumphantly crushed the "little boy." "You pays your money and you takes your choice." Somehow or other I felt a joyous exaltation, a perfect indifference to circumstances, through the whole of that three days' fighting, and have seldom enjoyed three days more in my life.

When I was in Maryland, I did not cease to admire the beauty of the county of Frederick. I really think that there is hardly a piece of ground in the country, equal to that rolling land just east of the slopes of South Mountain. The fields so undulating and yet so fertile, with charming buildings nestled out of the way in so many hollows, the stretches of golden wheat, bending under the blessing of sunlight, and the soft, delicious, purple-blue of the mountains, ever near at hand, which seemed, like many plain, generous people in daily life, to say, "We are not very high above you, and don't pretend to anything great, but we watch over you constantly, and we send down pure perennial streams of water to cheer and bless your fields and meadows."

August 29, 1863
Affidavit of Capt. William Wheeler, 13th New York Artillery
Catlett's Station, VA

William Wheeler being duly sworn deposes and says that hew is the captain and commanding officer of the 13th Independent Battery, N York Vol Artillery. That he has been regularly appointed a Captain in said battery by the Governor of New York to fill a vacancy occasioned by the resignation of Capt. Dieckmann on the 26th day of May 1863.

That he has done duty as a captain in said battery under this appointment since the 26th day of May 1863 and that he has made all proper efforts to be mustered in as a Captain of said battery since the 12th day of August 1863 but without success until the present time.

The said Wm Wheeler further swears that he was last mustered for pay as a 1st Lieut on the 30th day of June 1863.

Wm Wheeler Capt
Comdg 13 NY Battery

August 31, 1863
Report of Maj. Gen. Oliver Howard, 11th Army Corps
no location given

General: On the evening of June 30, the First Corps, with the exception of one brigade and the supply train at Emmitsburg, was located in the vicinity of Marsh Run, on the direct road from Emmitsburg to Gettysburg, and nearly midway between those towns. The Eleventh Corps was at Emmitsburg.

Just at sunset I received a request from General Reynolds, commanding First Corps, to meet him at his headquarters. He then showed me the order from your headquarters placing him in command of the First, Eleventh, and Third Corps; also the circulars of the commanding general dated June 30, together with a confidential communication. The purport of these papers was that a general engagement was imminent, the issues involved immense, and all commanders urged to extraordinary exertions. General Reynolds and I consulted together, comparing notes and information, until a late hour. I then returned to Emmitsburg. A circular from your headquarters, of June 30, required corps commanders to hold their commands in readiness to move at a moment's notice.

At 3.30 AM July 1, orders were received from your headquarters to move the Eleventh Corps to within supporting distance of the First Corps, which was to move to Gettysburg. I immediately sent an aide-de-camp to General Reynolds to receive his orders.

At 8 AM orders were received from him directing the corps to march to Gettysburg. The column was at once set in motion, my First Division, General Barlow commanding, following the First Corps by the direct route; my Third, General Schurz, and my Second, General Steinwehr, in the order named, taking the route by Horner's Mill. One battery accompanied the First Division; the remainder of the artillery (four batteries), under command of Major Osborn, accompanied the other two divisions. The distance by the direct route was between 10 and 11 miles, and by the other about 13. As soon as the corps was set in motion, I pushed on with my staff by the direct road, and when within 2 miles of Gettysburg received word from General Reynolds, pointing out the place where I was to encamp; but on approaching the town, heavy artillery firing was heard. For some little time I endeavored, by sending in different directions, to find General Reynolds, in order to report to him in person.

In the meantime I went to the top of a high building in Gettysburg, facing westward. I saw firing beyond Seminary Ridge and not far from the seminary. Toward the right, masses of cavalry were drawn up in order, to the east of the ridge and to the northeast of the town. A portion of the First Corps, of General Wadsworth's command, was between me and the seminary, taking position near the railroad. Another division of this corps was moving by the flank with considerable rapidity, along the ridge and in a northeasterly direction. I had studied the position a few moments, when a report reached me that General Reynolds was wounded. At first I hoped his wound might be slight, and that he would continue to command; but in a short time I was undeceived. His aide-de-camp, Major [William] Riddle, brought the sad tidings of his death. This was about 11.30 AM Prior to this the general had sent me orders to move up at double-quick, for he was severely engaged.

On hearing of the death of General Reynolds, I assumed command of the left wing, instructing General Schurz to take command of the Eleventh Corps. After an examination of the general features of the country, I came to the conclusion that the only tenable position for my limited force was the ridge to the southeast of Gettysburg, now so well known as Cemetery Ridge. The highest point at the cemetery commanded every eminence within easy range. The slopes toward the west and south were gradual, and could be completely swept by artillery. To the north, the ridge was broken by a ravine running transversely.

I at once established my headquarters near the cemetery, and on the highest point north of the Baltimore pike. Here General Schurz joined me before 12 m, when I instructed him to make the following dispositions of the Eleventh Corps. Learning from General Doubleday, commanding the First Corps, that his right was hard pressed, and receiving continued assurance that his left was safe and pushing the enemy back, I ordered the First and Third Divisions of the Eleventh Corps to seize and hold a prominent height on the right of the Cashtown road and on the prolongation of Seminary Ridge, each division to have a battery of artillery, the other three batteries, supported by General Steinwehr's division (Second), to be put in position near me on Cemetery Hill.

About 12.30 [PM] General Buford sent me word that the enemy was massing between the York and Harrisburg roads, to the north of Gettysburg, some 3 or 4 miles from the town. Quite a large number of prisoners had already been taken by the First Corps. They reported that we were engaging Hill's corps, or a portion of it, and that an aide of General Longstreet had arrived, stating that he would be up with one division in a short time. About this time the head of column of the Eleventh Corps entered and passed through the town, moving forward rapidly toward the position ordered.

The news of Ewell's advance from the direction of York was confirmed by reports from General Schurz, General Buford, and Major [Charles H] Howard, my aide-de-camp, who had been sent in that direction to reconnoiter. I therefore ordered General Schurz to halt his command, to prevent his right flank being turned, but to push forward a thick line of skirmishers, to seize the point first indicated, as a relief and support to the First Corps.

Meanwhile word was sent to General Sickles, commanding Third Corps, and General Slocum, commanding Twelfth, informing them of the situation of affairs, with a request that General Sickles forward my dispatch to General Meade. General Sickles was at that time, about 1 PM, near Emmitsburg, and General Slocum reported to be near Two Taverns, distant between 4 and 5 miles from Gettysburg.

At 2 PM a report of the state of things as then existing was sent to General Meade directly. About this time I left my chief of staff to execute orders, and went to the First Corps. I found General Doubleday about a quarter of a mile beyond the seminary. His Third Division was drawn up to his front and left, facing toward the northwest, making a large angle with the ridge. The artillery of this division was engaging the enemy at this time. His First Division (Wadsworth's) was located a little to the right of the railroad, and his Second Division (Robinson's) on Wadsworth's right. The First Corps, in this position, made a right angle with the Eleventh Corps, the vertex being near the Mummasburg road. The cavalry of General Buford was located mainly upon the flanks. After inspecting the position of the First Corps, and examining the topography of that part of the field, I returned to my former position at the cemetery.

About this time (2.45 PM) the enemy showed himself in force in front of the Eleventh Corps. His batteries could be distinctly seen on a prominent slope between the Mummasburg and the Harrisburg roads.

From this point he opened fire upon the Eleventh Corps, and also more or less enfilading Robinson's division, of the First Corps. The batteries attached to the First and Third Divisions, Eleventh Corps, immediately replied, and with evident effect One battery of the enemy, a little more than a mile north from the cemetery, near the Harrisburg road, could be distinctly seen, and as I had a battery of 3-inch rifled guns, under Wiedrich, near my position, I directed him to fire, provided he could reach the enemy. He did so, but his shells for the most part fell short. Soon after, complaint came that they reached no farther than our own cavalry; however, I never heard that any of our own men were killed or wounded by this fire. The reason of this irregularity was the poor quality of the ammunition there used. Subsequently these guns did most excellent service.

I now sent again to General Slocum, stating that my right flank was attacked, and asking him if he was moving up, and stating that I was in danger of being turned and driven back. Before this, my aide-de-camp, Captain [Edward P] Pearson, had been sent to General Sickles, requesting him to move up to Gettysburg as rapidly as possible. Owing to difficulty in finding General Sickles headquarters, this message was not delivered until 3.30 PM

At 3.20 PM the enemy renewed his attack upon the First Corps, hotly pressing the First and Second Divisions. Earnest requests were made upon me for re-enforcements, and General Schurz, who was engaged with a force of the enemy much larger than his own, asked for a brigade to be placed *en echelon* on his right. I had then only two small brigades in reserve, and had already located three regiments from these in the edge of the town and to the north, and I felt sure that I must hold the point where I was as an ultimate resort. Therefore I at first replied that I could not spare any troops, but did afterward permit General Steinwehr to push out Colonel Coster's brigade beyond the town, to cover the retreat. General Buford was requested to support the center, near the right of the First Corps, as well as he could with his cavalry. A third battery was sent to the front, and put in position near the Third Division, Eleventh Corps.

At 3.45 [PM] Generals Doubleday and Wadsworth besought me for re-enforcements. I directed General Schurz, if he could spare one regiment or more, to send it to re-enforce General Wadsworth, and several times sent urgent requests to General Slocum to come to my assistance. To every application for re-enforcements, I replied, "Hold out, if possible, awhile longer, for I am expecting General Slocum every moment." At this time General Doubleday's left was turned, and troops of the enemy appeared far outflanking him, and the enemy were also extending beyond my right flank.

About 4 PM I sent word to General Doubleday that, if he could not hold out longer, he must fall back, fighting, to Cemetery Hill and on the left of the Baltimore pike; also a request to General Buford to make a show of force opposite the enemy's right, which he immediately did. I now dispatched Major Howard, my aide-de-camp, to General Slocum, to inform him of the state of affairs, requesting him to send one of his divisions to the left, the other to the right, of Gettysburg, and that he would come in person to Cemetery Hill. He met the general on the Baltimore pike, about a mile from Gettysburg, who replied that he had already ordered a division to the right, and that he would send another to cover the left, as requested, but that he did not wish to come up in person to the front and take the responsibility of that fight. Injustice to General Slocum, I desire to say that he afterward expressed the opinion that it was against the wish of the commanding general to bring on a general engagement at that point.

At 4.10 PM, finding that I could hold out no longer, and that the troops were already giving way, I sent a positive order to the commanders of the First and Eleventh Corps to fall back gradually, disputing every inch of ground, and to form near my position, the Eleventh Corps on the right and the First Corps on the left of the Baltimore pike. General Steinwehr's division, of the Eleventh Corps, and the batteries which he was supporting, were so disposed as to check the enemy attempting to come through the town, or to approach upon the right or left of Gettysburg. The movement ordered was executed, though with considerable confusion, on account of the First and Eleventh Corps coming together in the town.

At 4.30 PM the columns reached Cemetery Hill, the enemy pressing hard. He made a single attempt to turn our right, ascending the slope northeast of Gettysburg, but his line was instantly broken by Wiedrich's battery, in position on the heights.

General Hancock came to me about this time, and said General Meade had sent him on hearing the state of affairs; that he had given him his instructions while under the impression that he was my senior. We agreed at once that that was no time for talking, and that General Hancock should further arrange the troops, and place the batteries upon the left of the Baltimore pike, while I should take the right of the same. In a very short time we put the troops in position, as I had previously directed, excepting that General Wadsworth's division was sent to occupy a height to the right and rear of our position. In passing through the town we lost many prisoners, but the enemy, perceiving the strength of our position on the heights, made no further attempts to renew the engagement that evening.

About 7 PM Generals Slocum and Sickles arrived at the cemetery.

A formal order was at the same time put into my hands, placing General Hancock in command of the left wing. But General Slocum being present, and senior, I turned the command over to him, and resumed the direct command of the Eleventh Corps; whereupon General Hancock repaired to the headquarters of General Meade.

The eventful day was over. The First and Eleventh Corps, numbering less than 18,000 men, nobly aided by Buford's division of cavalry, had engaged and held in check nearly double their numbers from 10 in the morning until 7 in the evening. They gave way, it is true, after hard fighting, yet they secured and held the remarkable position which, under the able generalship of the commander of this army, contributed to the grand results of July 2 and 3.

This day's battle cost us many valuable lives. Major-General Reynolds, a noble commander and long a personal friend, fell early in the action. Lieut B Wilkeson, a young officer of exceeding promise, was mortally wounded while in command of Battery G, Fourth US Artillery. Brigadier-Generals Barlow and Paul were severely wounded. For mention of other distinguished officers killed or wounded, I would refer to reports of corps, division, and brigade commanders.

Major Osborn, commanding artillery of Eleventh Corps, reports that his artillery dismounted five of the enemy's guns, which were left on the field. He lost one of his own, which had been dismounted in the action.

I am conscious of an inability to do justice to the operations of the First Corps, never having received a single report from it. Doubtless the general commanding it gives directly and in full sufficient data to enable the commanding general to appreciate its noble behavior as well as its terrible sacrifices.

On the morning of July 2, about 3 AM, the commanding general, who had previously arrived, met me at the cemetery gate, questioned me about the preceding day, and rode with me over the position then held by our troops. I expressed my opinion strongly in favor of the position. The general replied that he was glad to hear me speak thus, for it was too late to leave it. The Eleventh Corps was disposed with its center near the Baltimore pike—the First Division, General Ames, on the right; Third Division, General Schurz, in the center, and the Second Division, General Steinwehr, on the left. The batteries of the First and Eleventh Corps were united, being put in position with regard to the kind of gun. Colonel Wainwright, chief of artillery First Corps, took charge of all batteries to the right of the pike; Major Osborn, of the

Eleventh, all batteries in the cemetery grounds to the left of the pike.

Very little occurred while the other corps were coming into position until about 4 PM Just before this, orders had been issued to the division commanders to make ready for battle, as the enemy were reported advancing on our left. Now the enemy opened from some dozen batteries to our right and front, bringing a concentrated fire upon our position. The batteries of Wainwright and Osborn replied with great spirit. Artillery projectiles often struck among the men, but in no case did a regiment break, though suffering considerably.

About 6.30 PM I sent word to General Meade that the enemy's batteries on our extreme right had been silenced or withdrawn. After the cannonading had ceased, and the enemy s infantry attack upon the left had been repulsed, another attack, said to be by Rodes' division, commenced between 7 and 8 PM, beginning between Generals Slocum and Wadsworth, and extending along the front of Ames to the town of Gettysburg. A brigade of General Schurz's division was ordered to support General Ames. Another brigade of General Schurz pushed to the support of General Wadsworth, upon his right. Afterward General Greene, of the Twelfth Corps, came and thanked me for the good service done by this brigade. Lieutenant-Colonel [August] Otto, of General Schurz's staff, present with it, was highly commended. The attack was so sudden and violent that the infantry in front of Ames was giving way. In fact, at one moment the enemy had got within the batteries. A request for assistance had already gone to headquarters, so that promptly a brigade of the Second Corps, under Colonel Carroll, moved to Ames' right, deployed, and went into position just in time to check the enemy's advance. At Wiedrich's battery, General Ames, by extraordinary exertions, arrested a panic, and the men with sponge-staffs and bayonets forced the enemy back. At this time he received support from General Schurz. Effective assistance was also rendered at this time by a portion of General Steinwehr's command at points where the enemy was breaking through. This furious onset was met and withstood at every point, and lasted less than an hour.

At 9.30 PM the old position was resumed by the regiments of my corps, Colonel Carroll remaining between Ames and Wadsworth. Lest another attack should be made, Ames' position was further strengthened by the One hundred and sixth

Pennsylvania Regiment, from the Second Corps. At the moment my left was weakened, as also at other times during the engagements, General Newton was ready with re-enforcements from the First Corps.

July 3, at 5 AM, heavy infantry firing commenced on the right. It continued with more or less severity until after 10 AM Neither the artillery nor infantry of the Eleventh Corps were much engaged. Occasionally an attempt was made by the enemy to put batteries in position, and some shots were fired. He always received a prompt reply from our batteries, and failed to receive any advantage.

At about 1 PM a terrific cannonade opened upon us from the west, northwest, north, and northeast, hurling into the cemetery grounds missiles of every description. Shells burst in the air, in the ground to the right and left, killing horses, exploding caissons, overturning tombstones, and smashing fences. There was no place of safety. In one regiment 27 were killed and wounded by one shell, and yet the regiments of this corps did not move excepting when ordered.

At 2.30 PM we ceased our artillery fire. Soon after, the enemy's artillery also ceased, when a line of his infantry appeared, emerging from the woods upon Seminary Ridge, his left nearly opposite our front, and the line extending far to the left. Our batteries again opened fire, using shells at first. The gaps made by them seemed to have no effect in checking the onward progress of the enemy. Still his line advanced steadily, gaining ground gradually toward his right. When near our line of skirmishers, the batteries opened upon them with grape and canister from the hill. The infantry also commenced firing. The enemy's lines were broken, and the plain in our front was covered with fugitives running in every direction. Colonel Smith's brigade[54], of General Steinwehr's division, was pushed to the left and front, to the support of the First Corps, moving forward. At this time great numbers of prisoners were taken, in which this portion of the Second Division bore a part.

This was the last attack made by the enemy at the battle of Gettysburg. During the night he withdrew his entire force to and beyond Seminary Ridge.

Were I to accord praise to individuals, I would hardly know where to begin or where to end. I noticed Generals Schurz, Steinwehr, Schimmelfennig, and Ames; Colonels Orland Smith,

Coster, Krzyzanowski, and von Gilsa, commanding brigades; also Major Osborn, commanding the artillery, and his battery commanders, and commend them for bravery, faithfulness, and efficiency in the discharge of duty.

I was highly gratified at the conduct and effectiveness of the artillery under Major Osborn. His report shows that he had three batteries at least sent to him from the Artillery Reserve besides his own. No officer could work harder or do better than he did during the battle.

I have mentioned General Barlow, who was so severely wounded the first day. General Schurz commends him highly for coolness and bravery on the field.

My inspector-general, acting chief of staff, my adjutant-general, my quartermaster, my chief commissary, and my aides, all were as brave and efficient as they could possibly be.

We all mourn the death of one specially beloved, Capt J J Griffiths, aide-de-camp, who lived through the battle, but was mortally wounded during the reconnaissance of the Sunday following.

Every staff officer, in fact every officer and soldier who remained with his command, was almost constantly exposed to death or wounds during those three memorable days. My gratitude is so much due to them all that it seems almost invidious to particularize.

I wish to testify in this report to the hearty co-operation and generous support that I received from my associate corps commanders.

The grand results of the battle of Gettysburg are destined to bestow deserved and lasting honor upon the general commanding, and with him every true officer and brave man will claim a share; and yet no candid mind can review those scenes of horror, and doubt, and ultimate joy without feeling constrained to acknowledge the Divine hand which controlled and directed the storm.

    Respectfully,
    O O Howard
    Major-General

September 5, 1863
Letter of William Wheeler
Catlett's Station, VA

    I am beginning to emerge in some degree from the state of torpor and indifference in which I have been lying from nearly a month past, and to feel some interest in what surrounds me. I don't know what has been the matter with me. I have been fully able to do my duty, have drilled my Battery everyday to their hearts' content, have sat on court martials, boards of examination and survey, and have felt lively enough as long as I had any excitement, but when this had passed by I was all down again,-- my appetite was (and is) most capricious, and, above all, a feeling of unconquerable lassitude, which I could only shake off when some matter of great importance came along....You will be able to form some idea of my state of apathy, when I tell you the news of Robert Edwards death, which reached me first through your letter, failed to move me as I should have expected. I know that I felt it most deeply, but I could not shed a single tear. I could only feel a desire to avenge him, and think that such a noble, glorious death was well suited to his gallant, enthusiastic nature, and a fit close to his generous, self-sacrificing life. I cannot help looking at it as a soldier; we have death so constantly before our eyes that it loses it terrors, and the question with us is not so much whether we shall die or not, but how we shall die and among what surroundings. And the highest, most desirable type of death for the infantry officer, is that met on the enemy's ramparts, with the colors in his hand. It is true, a life of devotion and usefulness is suddenly closed, the hearts of friends are torn with anguish, because they will never see his flashing eye and active form again, and because that home will always be desolate; but was not the event ordered by a higher power, and who said, "I will take this beautiful soul to me *now* in its bloom of youth, and he shall be spared the evil days to come." And if in this struggle death is to come to me, may it come as it did to Young Crosby[55], "among my guns in battery," and successfully resisting a hostile attack, dying of a mortal stroke,--

    "What time the foemen's ranks are broke."

Dear John, from whom I received a most affectionate and cheering letter yesterday, warmed my heart by speaking of Robert in such a kind, appreciative way. He expressed what I wanted to express, only my heart was too full, and my frame of mind too gloomy, for me to find the proper utterance. My daily prayer now is, that it may not happen to my brother. I really believe that I am must less unselfish and patriotic than you are, for I think more of his safety than of the service he is doing for the country, and wish it were possible that he could be safe home again. I know, dear mother, that you will not be wearied by this expression of my affection for him, as it is only a proof of my love for you, for that you know is the greatest of all. John seems in splendid trim and spirits, and to be enjoying his staff life very much. I am glad that he has a place where he can keep himself clean and comfortable, and have decent associates. For myself, and I have seen considerable of all arms of the service, I prefer my own position to any other. I like to have the command of me, and to say, like the centurion, "Go! and he goeth;" and then as Captain of a Battery, I am independent and as comfortable as a Brigadier. We were reviewed by General Howard the other day, and he praised my horses very highly. We did not get a chance to drill before him, which was a disappointment to me, as it is pretty generally acknowledge that my men are the best in the Corps at the manual of the piece. I have made several small raids out into the country around here, and have got acquainted with several families in the neighborhood of Greenwich. Last Sunday, Lieutenant Mickle (who is a noble, Christian fellow) and I went out to old Rev Mr Balch's, a Presbyterian clergyman, and spent the evening. The family consists of the old gentleman and his wife, his son, and two daughters, all grown, and are of the real old-fashioned Presbyterian sort, keeping Sunday like the C's. The old gentleman is a graduate of Princeton College and Seminary, and talks about the churches in Cedar Street, and Wall Street, and Drs. Romeyn and Mason, in a way that would interest you very much. He seems to be a sort of chronicle of the last fifty years, and says things that are really quite striking and interesting, such as, "I was present in the Senate when Josiah Quincy began the whole matter, and spoke the first word of secession." From this you can perceive that he is a rebel of the most virulent type, and his two daughters are just as bad. But after the political discussion had waged for some time, we opened the piano, and we had some of the old hymns after the old style, "Ariel," "Greenland's Icy Mountain," "Italian hymn," etc., which did me good, and then we stayed with them to evening worship. He expects to preach to-morrow, and Lieutenant Mickle and I are going to lend a had at singing, and to stay to dinner. It is strange that opinions and sentiments about the war can be so violent one moment, and the next, all the disputants have their heads close together about one hymn book, or are kneeling at one family altar. Religion is the only thing that can lend any humanizing influence to this war. These good people are instant in good words, and, after giving a soldier a good dinner, they will put some nice, simple little book into his hand, which, for sheer politeness, he will not be able to refuse. Just at this moment one of the men is singing some hymn about the "Lion and the Lamb," to a rough, sailor melody.

September 6, 1863
Battery Orders No. 43
Catlett's Station, VA

Private William Boe is hereby appointed Corporal in the 13th NY Battery for good conduct at the Battle of Gettysburg from July 1, 1863 vice Roache reduced.
He will be obeyed & respected accordingly.
Wm Wheeler Capt
Comdg 13 NY Battery

Battery Orders No. 44
Catlett's Station, VA

The Commander has observed with pain that quite a number of the Company are ignorant of the elementary principles of reading and writing, and that a still larger number read poorly and write still worse. He desires to give all those whose education on these points have been neglected, an opportunity to make at least a beginning. No non-commissioned officer should fail to read & write well and as every private should look forward to promotion it is his duty to qualify himself for the post in this respect. Bright intelligent young men ought to be ashamed to have their letters home written by comrades and their names signed to the pay-roll by the officers.
On this account, there will be school-house held every day or as often as the circumstances of the campaign will admit and Corporal John

Lewens is hereby relieved from guard duty and will take charge of the class in writing which will assemble tomorrow afternoon at 2 o'clock. I wish it to be understood that these attendance is not compulsory but I hope that no man will be ashamed to come forward & make advantage of it. The class of reading will be commenced as soon as the books can be procured from Washington & due notice will be given.
Wm Wheeler Capt
Comdg 13 NY Battery

September 9, 1863
Report of Maj. Gen. Oliver Howard, 11th Army Corps
no location given

General: On the morning of June 28, my corps was located in the Middletown Valley, Md., two divisions near Middletown and one holding Boonsborough Gap.

About 2 PM an order was received to march to Frederick. Head of column left Middletown at 3 PM, and arrived in camp north of Frederick, near Wormer's Mill, at 8 PM The entire corps, including train, was in camp by midnight.

At 11.30 PM the order came relieving General Hooker, and assigning General Meade to the command of the army; also the order of march for the following day. The First and Eleventh Corps were to march to Emmitsburg; the Eleventh to leave the turnpike to its left, marching by Creagerstown. The day was rainy, the roads heavy, and the march wearisome, yet the troops were in camp at Emmitsburg by 7 PM, having made about 20 miles.

At 8.30 AM June 30, an order was received from headquarters to take position on the north side of Emmitsburg. The enemy was reported advancing on Gettysburg from Chambersburg. The First Corps, General Reynolds commanding, was moved to a position half way between Emmitsburg and Gettysburg, on Marsh Run. In case of attack, the Eleventh Corps was directed to support the First Corps. Subsequent orders, however, directed the First Corps to fall back to Emmitsburg in case of attack. General Buford's division of cavalry was already near Gettysburg. From this time until July 5 following, the ground is covered by my report of the battle of Gettysburg.

At 4 AM July 5, the enemy were reported moving to the rear in full retreat. Reconnaissances discovered the enemy's rear guard about 2 miles to the west of Gettysburg. This was immediately reported to General Meade.

During the 4th and 5th, about 500 prisoners were taken by the corps from the enemy's wounded and stragglers.

On the evening of the 5th, at 5.30 PM, General Meade's order to march to Middletown, by the way of Emmitsburg, Utica, and High Knob, in two days, was received. The corps encamped near Rocky [Rock] Creek that night. The Fifth and Eleventh Corps were combined for the march, under my direction. The Fifth Corps encamped upon the same creek. At this halt, an order was received from your headquarters not to proceed with the march until further orders.

The next day, July 6, the order for march was received, my corps being ordered to Emmitsburg. At 7 PM the order was received to execute the former order of march to Middletown.

The head of column left camp at 3.30 AM July 7, and about 8 PM the head of the column reached Middletown, Md. Owing to the difficulty in crossing the mountains, and the fact that the artillery horses were nearly broken down by previous fatigue, only one division (General Schurz's) succeeded in reaching Middletown; the First and Second Divisions and artillery remained near High Knob. The Fifth Corps encamped between Utica and High Knob.

The next day, July 8, the march was completed before 11 AM The road over the mountain near High Knob was steep, narrow, and very rocky, so that it was with the greatest difficulty that the artillery and trains were brought over. On this account the Fifth Corps was conducted by another route, crossing the mountains a little farther south.

At 1 PM an order was received to march at once to Boonsborough Gap. The Third Division had executed the march at 5 PM, when General Buford, who was engaging the enemy, sent me word that he was hard pressed, and asked for re-enforcements of infantry. The Third Division (General Schurz's) was immediately sent forward through the town of Boonsborough, while the First and Second Divisions and artillery were placed in position to the left of the pike, on the western slope of the mountain, co-operating with the First Corps, located on the right of the pike.

At 7 PM the Third Division took position on the Hagerstown pike northwest of Boonsborough and 1 mile beyond. As soon as the enemy saw our infantry approach, he retired toward Hagerstown.

During July 9, the First and Eleventh Corps remained in position, excepting that the Sixth Corps, passing through the Gap, took position near Boonsborough, relieving my Third Division. During this day every exertion was made to supply shoes and clothing that were needed.

On the morning of July 10, the Sixth and First Corps were pushed on to Beaver Creek and my corps to Boonsborough. I had hardly arrived in camp when the order to report to General Sedgwick at Beaver Creek was received. The corps renewed the march, and took position about 4.30 PM on the right of the Sixth Corps, near the Hagerstown and Smoketown road, 2 ½ miles from Funkstown. Occasional artillery firing was heard toward Funkstown.

July 11, the First, Eleventh, and Sixth Corps, under General Sedgwick, remained in position.

At 4 AM July 12, my First Division, under General Ames, marched to Hagerstown, to support Kilpatrick's cavalry. This force succeeded in entering Hagerstown, capturing some 100 prisoners.

At 11 AM the remainder of the corps marched to Funkstown; passed through the town; crossed the Antietam Creek, and took position on the right of the First Corps, about a mile south of Hagerstown.

At 7 PM the three corps, Sixth, First, and Eleventh, were marched to the left, in order to make connection with the rest of the army, already in position on the west bank of the Antietam. The Eleventh Corps still occupied the right of the line near Funkstown.

During the night, some covers for the artillery and rifle-pits were constructed. The general commanding called together his corps commanders during this evening, and counseled with them with regard to the enemy's position, strength, and intention, and asked their opinion with regard to making an attack upon the enemy, as affairs then stood. The decision was not to attack then, or until further information should be obtained.

July 13, one brigade was sent to Hagerstown as an outpost, and a support to the cavalry in case of necessity. I spent the day in personal reconnaissances, so as to obtain as accurate knowledge as possible of the enemy's works, a portion of which were in view from the church steeples in Hagerstown. I sent General Schimmelfennig with one regiment of infantry to reconnoiter the enemy's left. Before this regiment had passed Hagerstown, General Kilpatrick started to accomplish the same purpose, his cavalry being supported by a regiment of Pennsylvania militia, whereupon General Schimmelfennig joined the reconnaissance.

As soon as the cavalry skirmishers had approached the enemy's lines, he opened a brisk fire from infantry or dismounted cavalry. One or two pieces of artillery also fired at random from a battery near the Williamsport road. After this reconnaissance, and all the information I could collect, I was impressed with a belief that the enemy would retreat without giving us battle, and it was with a hope of being able to make a lodgment on the enemy's left that I then asked permission to make a reconnaissance at 3 AM of the next day (the 14th). Subsequently, the commanding general's order for several simultaneous reconnaissances at 7 AM reached me. I also received word, in answer to my request, that orders had already been sent out, which would probably effect the purpose I proposed.

On the morning of the 14th, a report was received from Hagerstown that the enemy had evacuated his position in that vicinity. At 11.20 AM orders were received from General Sedgwick to march to Williamsport, via Hagerstown. The enemy had completely crossed before my corps arrived. The inhabitants reported that he crossed on a bridge at Falling Waters, on flat-boats at Williamsport, and at a deep ford a little distance above that place; that many men and horses were drowned in fording the Potomac; that the bridge, boats, and all had been built at Williamsport and floated down to Falling Waters. The corps encamped near Leister's Mill, on Conococheague Creek, 1 mile from Williamsport.

At 1 AM July 15, the order of march for the next day to Berlin reached Middletown at 6 PM My train moved to Jefferson.

We took up the march at 5 AM of the 10th, and proceeded, via Jefferson, to Berlin. We went into camp near that place. Here orders were received and issued, directing the troops to replenish stores and prepare for an active campaign.

On the 17th, we remained in position.

On the 18th, orders having been received to follow the First Corps across the pontoon bridge at Berlin, observation was made as to the time when the First Corps should have crossed, when further orders were received to follow Buford's division of cavalry. My train and artillery began the crossing at 6 PM, and encamped near Lovettsville, Va. The infantry began the march at 4 AM of the 19th, and the entire corps encamped about 4 PM near Warner's farm, on the Waterford and Hamilton road.

On the 20th, the corps marched under orders to Mountville, via Mount Gilead, making about 16 miles. During this march the enemy's guerrillas and bushwhackers annoyed us considerably, capturing a few stragglers.

During the 21st, the corps remained stationary, sending out scouting parties in different directions, one of which from General Schurz met a detachment of Mosby's guerrillas, and, after a little skirmish, recaptured those taken the day before.

On the 22d, a forage train, having started before its guard was ready, lost nine wagons, eight of which were retaken, but without the animals.

On the morning of the 23d, orders were received at 3.40 AM to march to New Baltimore. Head of column left camp within an hour from the receipt of the order. The weather was very warm and sultry. Head of column arrived at New Baltimore about 6 PM

On the 24th, the corps remained in camp, opening communication with the First Corps at Warrenton and receiving supplies from White Plains. Information received this day from general headquarters that but one division of the enemy was found at Front Royal; the rest of his force reported to have gone toward Culpeper and Gordonsville.

On the 25th, the march was made from New Baltimore to Warrenton Junction, in the vicinity of which the corps has been ever since, excepting Gordon's division (i.e., First Division of this corps), detached and sent to Alexandria for embarkation August 6.

General Gordon joined the corps at Berlin. Ten regiments, each about 500 strong, four of them being nine-months' troops, joined the cords as follows: Three at or near Funkstown with General Tyndale; the rest at Berlin or *en route* thither. One of these had but two days to serve, and left the corps near Hagerstown, viz, One hundred and sixty-ninth Pennsylvania.

During the entire campaign I received the most hearty cooperation from my division commanders, from the commander of the artillery, as also from every member of my staff.

I believe the corps successfully executed every order of the commanding general of the army. Sometimes the marches were long and tedious, but they were always performed with cheerfulness, and very little straggling can be laid to our charge.

I feel grateful to the officers and men of the corps for the part they have borne in this eventful campaign, and whatever misrepresentation or prejudice may have set against them, they nevertheless deserve the gratitude of their country.

I have the honor to be, respectfully,
O O Howard
Major-General

September 10, 1863
Affidavit of Capt. William Wheeler, 13th New York Artillery
Catlett's Station, VA

William Wheeler being duly sworn deposes and says that he is the captain and commanding officers of the 13th Indept New York Battery.

That James C Carlisle has been regularly appointed a 1st Lieutenant in said battery by the Governor of the State of New York to fill a vacancy occasioned by the promotion of Lt Wheeler on the 12 day of August 1863.

That to his certain knowledge James C Carlisle has done duty as a 1st Lieutenant in said battery under this appointment since the 12 day of August 1863 and that said James C Carlisle has made all proper efforts to be mustered in as a 1st Lieutenant of the 13th Indept New York Battery since the 12 day of August 1863 but without success until this present time.

The said Wm Wheeler further swears that James C Carlisle was last mustered for pay as a 2nd Lieutenant on the 31 day of August 1863.

Affidavit of 1st Lt. James Carlisle, 13th New York Artillery
Catlett's Station, VA

James C Carlisle being duly sworn deposes and says that on the 26 day of May 1863 he was appointed a 1st Lieutenant in the 13th New York Battery by the Governor of the State of New York to fill the vacancy occasioned by the promotion of Wm Wheeler on the 26 day of May 1863.

The he has done duty as a 1st Lieutenant under this appointment since the 12 day of August 1863. That since the 12th day of August 1863 he has made all proper efforts to be mustered in as 1st Lieutenant of the 13th New York Battery but without success before this present time.

The said James C Carlisle further swears that he was last mustered for pay as a 2nd Lieut on the 31 day of August 1863.[56]

September 25, 1863
Letter of William Wheeler
Catlett's Station, VA

I really shall have to make a formal defense of myself for visiting in the families of natives of this region, as you seem to think that I am failing in devotion and loyalty to the cause in which I am engaged. Now I think that you look at the thing in too theoretical a light, and this is owing to your distance from the scene of operations. I know you too well not to be sure that, in spite of your thorough patriotism and hatred of all that is hostile to our cause, you would yet be the first to help the wounded and destitute and ruined, even in Virginia. For myself, while I will yield to no man in the obstinacy of the fight and the endurance of the march, still, when a man is wounded or a prisoner, when a woman is lonely and distressed, they rise in my view from the position of rebels to that of our common humanity, and as men and women, I treat them with kindness, though rebels. And do not think for a moment that I sympathize with these people in any of their ideas, or that I allow them to suppose that I am anything but an extreme Emancipationist, determined on seeing the end of the secession movement and of slavery, provide it is granted to me to live so long. We talk about books and person, sing, play games, eat melons and peaches, and in the course of the evening we usually manage to treat them to the "Star Spangled Banner," and a few more of the national airs, which ought to do a secessionist's ears a great deal of good. (Strange to say, since writing the above, a circular from General Howard has come in, in which he observes that it has come to his knowledge that officers in the Corps, and especially the artillery officers, are in the habit of visiting at the houses of rebel secessionists, and recommending that it be stopped: quite an argument in your favor, but I will not back down from what I have just said.)

Lieutenant Carlisle returned about a week ago, quite well, though not very strong, but able to fill my place. When absent yesterday, my First Sergeant, Harry Miller, now promoted to a Second Lieutenancy, came back from New York to be mustered in as an officer, so that I have no longer the whole concern on my hands, and feel much less anxiety. He used to attend me at Camp Observation, and took such good care of me when I was sick there. He has passed through the successive grades of corporal, sergeant, and orderly sergeant, and after distinguishing himself in several battles, has now arrived at an officer's rank, which he well deserves. The defects of education (which he is daily overcoming, as he is thirsty to learn) are greatly overbalanced by his real manliness and stamina, his fidelity, willingness, and pluck; if I tell him to take his section into a position and keep it there till I relieve him, he will do so, if not a single man comes out alive, and that is the kind of officer I want to have under me. We had a superb review of the corps artillery here last Saturday, before General Hunt, Chief of Artillery of the Army of the Potomac; all the fine batteries were drawn up in a single line by your humble servant— as Major Osborn had charged me with the duty of forming them for review, and I can assure you that the muzzles of the guns were in a bee line from right to left. General Hunt told the Major that the artillery was as good as any in the army, and the horses were the best he had seen. He spoke with particular praise of my Battery horses. My school is in a flourishing condition; the boys built a table and desk, with forms, out of split logs, and set it up under the shade of the trees, and every day at 2 PM the schoolmaster, an old corporal whom I detailed for the purpose, fetches the spelling-books and the writing materials, and sets his classes their lessons. You would be pleased to see the eagerness with which men from twenty to forty years of age seize upon this opportunity for repairing the defects of their early education, and the progress which they all make is most encouraging. The attendance is not compulsory, but the schoolmaster has more than he can attend to. I can assure you it does me good to see that patient row, sitting at the rough table which they themselves had hewn out of the hard oaks of the forest, rough, wild boys, many of them, but every eye softened and brightened by the feeling that they were learning something higher and better than card playing or whiskey drinking. Certainly, Victor Hugo was right when he said, "that what was necessary to purify and cleanse the subterranean abysses of the lowest class, was Light;" and this purification is greater to proportion to the nature of the light admitted, the greatest is obtained when "the entrance of Thy Word giveth light."

I am hoping that very few of the men, if any, will have to call upon the officers to sign their names for them on the next pay-roll.

September 27, 1863
Report of Brig. Gen. Henry Hunt, Chief of Artillery, Army of the Potomac
no location given

General: I have the honor to submit the following report of the operations of the artillery of this army in the battle of Gettysburg, July 1, 2, and 3:

On July 1, Reynolds' (First) and Howard's (Eleventh) corps and Buford's division of cavalry, the whole under the command of Maj Gen J F Reynolds, engaged the enemy on the west and northwest of the town of Gettysburg. On the west of Gettysburg, about a third of a mile distant, there is a ridge running nearly north and south, parallel to the Emmitsburg pike. This ridge, on which the seminary is situated, is crossed by the Cashtown pike about 100 or 150 yards north of the seminary, and some 50 yards farther on it is cut by a railroad. On the west of the seminary is a grove of large trees, and the summit of the ridge and the upper part of both its slopes are more or less covered with open woods through its entire length. The ground slopes gradually to the west, and again rising, forms a second ridge, parallel to and about 500 yards distant from the Seminary Ridge. This second ridge is wider and smoother than that upon which the seminary stands, and terminates about 200 yards north of the point at which the Cashtown road crosses it. Near this point, and to the south of it, are a house and barn, with some five or six acres of orchard and wooded grounds, the rest of the ridge being cleared. It was in the skirmish near this house that General Reynolds fell, and over the country covered by the ridge that the First Corps fought. To the north and east, beyond where the Seminary Ridge terminates, the country is more flat, and this ground was occupied by the Eleventh

Corps, the front of which was in a nearly perpendicular position to that of the First Corps, and faced the north.

About 10.15 AM Hall's battery (Second Maine, six 3-inch) was ordered into action by General Reynolds on the right of the Cashtown road, on the second ridge, and some 500 yards beyond the seminary. The enemy had previously opened fire from a battery of six guns at a distance of about 1,300 yards, and directly in front of this position, on Reynolds' troops, and Hall, on coming into action, replied with effect. In the course of half an hour, a body of the enemy's infantry approached the right of Hall's battery under cover of a ravine, and opened upon him at a distance of 60 or 80 yards, killing and wounding a number of his men and horses. The right and center sections replied with canister, while the left section continued its fire on the enemy's battery. The supports now falling back, Captain Hall found it necessary to retire, which he did by sections.

Soon after, the Third Division (Rowley's), First Corps, occupied the open ground on this ridge with Cooper's battery (B, First Pennsylvania, four 3-inch), which took post in an oat-field, about 380 yards south of the Cashtown road.

The Second Division (Robinson's) occupied a road on the west slope of the Seminary Ridge, north of the railroad, and the Eleventh Corps came into position on the flat ground farther north, and in a position nearly perpendicular to that of the First Corps. Colonel Wainwright, commanding the artillery of the First Corps, sent Stewart's battery (B, Fourth United States, six 12-pounders) to report to General Robinson, and ordered Reynolds to move with his battery to the support of Calef's horse battery (A, Second United States, six 3-inch), which had been placed in position by General Wadsworth on the spot just occupied by Hall's (Second Maine, six 3-inch), and was sharply engaged with the enemy's battery in its front. Reynolds had hardly taken position when the enemy opened a severe fire from a second battery immediately on his right. The cross-fire of the enemy's two batteries caused both Calef's and Reynolds' to retire, Reynolds taking up a new position at right angles to the ridge, with his left covered by the woods, near the house and barn referred to. While executing this movement, Captain Reynolds was severely wounded in the right eye, but refused to quit the field. The enemy's battery soon after ceased its fire. At the request of General Wadsworth, Colonel Wainwright posted Wilber's section of Reynolds' battery in the orchard on the south side of the Cashtown road, where he was sheltered from the fire of the enemy's battery on his right flank by the intervening house and barn, and moved the other two sections to the south side of the wood, on the open crest.

In the meantime the Eleventh Corps had taken position, and Dilger's battery (I, First Ohio, six 12-pounders), attached to Schurz's division, soon became engaged with one of the enemy's batteries at 1,000 yards distance, which was soon re-enforced by another. Dilger maintained his position until re-enforced by Wheeler (Thirteenth New York Independent, four 3-inch), sent to his assistance by Major Osborn, commanding the artillery of the corps, when a sharp contest ensued, the result of which was one piece of Wheeler's dismounted and five of the enemy's, which Major Osborn states they left on the ground. The enemy suffered the most loss. During this action, Captain Dilger several times changed the positions of his batteries with excellent effect, selecting his ground with judgment.

About 11 AM Wilkeson's battery (G, Fourth United States, four 12-pounders) came up, and reported to General Barlow, who posted it close to the enemy's line of infantry, with which it immediately became engaged, sustaining at the same time the fire of two of his batteries.

In the commencement of this unequal contest, Lieut Bayard Wilkeson (Fourth US Artillery), commanding the battery, a young officer of great gallantry, fell, mortally wounded, and was carried from the field. Lieutenant Bancroft succeeded to the command, and by changing position and distributing his sections, in order to meet the different movements of the enemy, succeeded in maintaining himself handsomely until the division fell back to the town, when he withdrew to Cemetery Hill.

About 4 PM the troops were withdrawn to Cemetery Hill, and Schurz's division, with Heckman's (K, First Ohio, four 12-pounders) and Wiedrich's (I, First New York, six 3-inch) batteries, were posted so as to cover the movement of the corps, Wiedrich's being placed on the hill in front of the cemetery entrance. Heckman worked his guns well, and held his ground until the enemy entered his battery. He then retired with the loss of one gain, the battery being so much crippled that it was sent to the rear, and was not again called into action.

Wiedrich's battery was actively engaged, and about 4.30 PM the enemy made an attempt to turn our right, but his line was very soon broken by the fire of this battery, and the attempt failed.

The First Corps was withdrawn about the same time as the Eleventh. Colonel Wainwright, commanding the artillery of this corps, understanding the order to hold Cemetery Hill to apply to Seminary Hill, posted Cooper's battery (B, First Pennsylvania, four 3-inch) in front of the professor's house. Captain Stevens (Fifth Maine, six 12-pounders) was soon after posted by General Doubleday on Cooper's right. Soon after, the enemy emerged in two strong columns from the woods in front, about 500 yards distant, outflanked our line nearly a third of a mile, then formed in two lines of battle, and advanced directly up the crest. During this movement, Reynolds battery (L, First New York, six 3-inch) opened on the columns, but the fire of his sections was much interfered with by the movements of our own infantry in their front. Colonel Wainwright therefore moved these two sections, under Lieutenant Breck, to a strong stone wall on the seminary crest, near Stevens' position. The movement was not ordered until the enemy, outnumbering our troops 5 to 1, were within 200 yards of the battery. Lieutenant Wilber's section of the same battery soon after fell back with his supports (L, First New York, six 3-inch; Fifth Maine, six 12-pounders, and Cooper's, B, First Pennsylvania, four 3-inch) to the same position, thus concentrating sixteen guns. Stewart's battery (B, Fourth United States, six 12-pounders) was also on the same line, half of the battery between the Cashtown pike and the railroad, the other half across the railroad, in the corner of a wood. The enemy's lines continued to advance across the space between the two crests, but when the first line was within about 100 yards of the seminary, Lieutenant Davison, Fourth US Artillery, commanding the left half of Stewart's battery, placed his guns on the Cashtown pike, so as to enfilade the whole line. This movement, well sustained by the other batteries, brought the first line to a halt, but the second, supported by a column deployed from the Cashtown road, pushed on. An order was now received by Captain Stevens from General Wadsworth, directing his battery to withdraw, but Colonel Wainwright, not knowing this, and still under the mistaken impression as to the importance of holding Seminary Hill, directed all the batteries to maintain their positions.

In a few minutes, however, all our infantry were seen rapidly retreating toward the town, and the batteries were all limbered to the rear, and moved off down the Cashtown pike, maintaining a walk until the infantry had left it. By this time our retreating columns were lapped by the enemy's skirmishers, who opened a severe fire from behind a fence within 50 yards of the road. As soon as the road was clear, the batteries moved at a trot, but it was too late to save all the material. Lieutenant Wilber's last piece (L, First New York, six 3-inch) had 1 of its wheel-horses shot, and, by the time this could be disengaged, 3 others were shot and Lieutenant Wilbur's own horse killed. It was impossible to move the piece off, and it was lost. No blame apparently can be attached to the officers of this or of Heck-man's battery (K, First Ohio, four 12-pounders) for the loss of the two guns in the retiring of the two corps. It was the necessary result of the obstinate resistance made to the enemy, so as to cover the withdrawal of their respective corps. Three of the caisson bodies of Stewart's battery were broken down, 1 of his caissons exploded, 2 of his guns had been disabled by the breaking of their pointing rings, and 3 of Hall's guns dismounted.

    The losses of the batteries of the First Corps in these operations were heavy; 83 officers and men killed and wounded, including 6 officers wounded (Capt G T Stevens and Lieut C O Hunt, Fifth Maine, severely; Capt G H Reynolds, L, First New York, severely; Lieut J Stewart, Fourth Artillery, slightly; Lieut J Davison, Fourth Artillery, severely; Lieut W C Miller, B, First Pennsylvania, slightly), and about 80 horses, a large proportion of the latter between the Seminary Ridge and the town, the enemy having at that time a fire upon them from both flanks and the rear, and no infantry replying. The batteries passed immediately through the town, and were placed with those of the Eleventh Corps in position on Cemetery Hill, so as to command the town and the approaches from the northwest. The batteries north of the Baltimore pike in front of the cemetery gate, under the command of Colonel Wainwright, chief of artillery, First Corps, were posted as follows: Stewart's battery (B, Fourth United States, four light 12-pounders) across the road, so as to command the approaches from town; then Wiedrich's (I, First New York Artillery, four 3-inch), Cooper's (B, First Pennsylvania Artillery, four 3-inch), and Reynolds' (L, First New York Artillery, five 3-inch), in all thirteen 3-inch guns, along the north front, some of them in such a position that they could be turned to bear upon the town and the field of battle of the 1st. Stevens' battery (Fifth Maine, six 12-pounders)was posted to the right and some 50 yards in front of this line, on a knoll, from whence they could obtain an oblique fire upon the hills in front of our line, and a flanking fire at close quarters upon any attacking columns.

Each of the guns in these batteries had a small earthwork thrown up in its front, to afford a partial shelter from the fire of the enemy's sharpshooters. Osborn's batteries (Bancroft's, G, Fourth U.S. Artillery, six 12-pounders; Dilger's, I, First Ohio, six 12-pounders; Wheeler's, Thirteenth New York, three 3-inch), of the Eleventh Corps, with the exception of Wiedrich's, transferred to Colonel Wainright, Heckman's, crippled and sent to the rear, and one gun of Wheeler's dismounted, were placed in the cemetery grounds, to the north of the Baltimore road.

On the night of July 1, the commanding general left Taneytown, and reached Gettysburg about 2 AM of the 2d. Soon after his arrival, he directed me to see to the position of the artillery, and make such arrangements respecting it as were necessary. I examined the positions at Cemetery Hill, so far as the darkness would permit, and then accompanied the general and Major-General Howard in an inspection of the west front of the field, occupied by the Second and Third Corps. Cemetery Hill commanded the positions which could be occupied by the enemy to the north and northwest. Toward the south the line occupied the crest of a gentle elevation, which, concealing everything immediately behind it from the observation of the enemy, commanded the ground to the west, which sloped down gradually for a few hundred yards, and then rising, formed another crest, varying from half to three-quarters of a mile distant. The summit of this crest was wooded, and toward the south bent eastwardly and crossed the Emmitsburg road, forming a very favorable position for the enemy's artillery, and affording concealment to his movements in that direction. About half or three-quarters of a mile south of the cemetery our own crest and the ground in front of it were broken by groves of trees, and still farther on by rough and rocky ground. At a distance of about 2 miles from Cemetery Hill, a high, rocky, and broken peak formed the natural termination of our lines. The broken character of the ground in front of the southern half of our line was unfavorable to the use of artillery. From the cemetery, as a center, the right of our line extended toward the east, and lay on the north of the Baltimore pike. The ground is hilly, heavily wooded, and intersected with ravines and small water-courses, very unfavorable to the use of artillery. The First and Eleventh Corps were stationed on and near Cemetery Hill. The Second Corps (Hancock's) stretched along the crest on the left of the Cemetery Hill, with the Third Corps (Sickles') on its left. To the right of the cemetery lay a portion of the First Corps (Newton's), and beyond it the Twelfth (Slocum's).

At or near daylight, Major-General Slocum reported to the commanding general that there was a gap between the left of his line and the right of the First Corps, which he feared would be taken advantage of by the enemy, as he apprehended an immediate attack. The general commanding then gave me directions to make the necessary arrangements to meet the emergency. I considered this, in connection with the order previously given me, as a recognition, for the present, at least, of the position I had held at Antietam and Fredericksburg, as commander of the artillery of the army, and proceeded to make the necessary dispositions and to give all directions I considered necessary during the rest of the battle. In order to cover the gap between the First and Second Corps, the batteries of the Twelfth Corps (Muhlenberg's, F, Fourth United States, six 12-pounders; Kinzie's, K, Fifth United States, four 12-pounders; Winegar's, M, First New York, four 10-pounders, and Knapp's, E, Pennsylvania, six 10-pounders) were placed so as to command the outlet from that interval toward the Baltimore pike, and such of the batteries on Cemetery Hill as commanded the ground and its approaches from the side of the enemy were also placed in position. The interval between the lines was too Broken and too heavily wooded to permit the artillery to Be placed on the immediate line of battle. These positions were held by the batteries until the infantry line was completed and well strengthened, when the artillery was arranged for any attack the enemy could make.

The batteries at the cemetery, under command of Colonel Wainwright, remained as already described, and Major Osborn, chief of artillery of the Eleventh Corps, was directed to take command on the south of the road. I re-enforced him with half of Hall's battery (Second Maine, three 3-inch) from the First Corps, the other hair being disabled, and five batteries (Eakin's, H, First United States, six 12-pounders; Taft's, Fifth New York, six 20-pounders; Hill's, C, First West Virginia, four 10-pounders;

Huntington's, H, First Ohio, six 3-inch, and Edgell's, First New Hampshire, six 3-inch) from the Artillery Reserve, thus placing at his disposal, including the three batteries (Bancroft's, G, Fourth United States, six 12-pounders; Dilger's, I, First Ohio, six 12-pounders, and Wheeler's, Thirteenth New York, three 3-inch) of his own corps remaining to him, six 20-pounder Parrotts, twenty-two light rifles, and eighteen light 12-pounders. These were stationed as follows: On the right, resting next the Baltimore road and facing the Emmitsburg, Dilger; on his left, Bancroft; then, in the order named, Eakin, Wheeler, Hill, and Hall. These eighteen light 12-pounders and ten light rifles commanded the enemy's positions to the right of the town. In rear of Bancroft and perpendicular to him were Taft's six 20-pounder Parrotts; on Taft's right and rear were Huntington's 3-inch guns; these batteries facing the north. This arrangement, in connection with that of Wainwright, Brought all the positions within range of the cemetery that the enemy could occupy with artillery under a commanding fire. The batteries were all brought into requisition at different periods of the battle.

July 2, during the morning, several moving columns of the enemy, passing toward our right, were shelled, and compelled to make detours, or seek the cover of ravines to make their movements.

At about 3.30 PM the enemy established a battery of ten guns (four 20-pounders and six 10-pounder Parrotts) in a wheat-field to the north and a little to the east of the Cemetery Hill, and distant some 1,200 or 1,300 yards, and opened a remarkably accurate fire upon our batteries. We soon gained a decided advantage over them, and at the end of an hour or more compelled them to withdraw, drawing off two of their pieces by hand. Twenty-eight horses were afterward found on the knoll. The enemy suffered severely, and, although we were successful, we had cause to regret that our 4½-inch guns had been left at Westminster, as the position offered great advantages for them.

The enemy endeavored to re-establish his Battery farther to his right, but as we could in this position bring a larger number of guns to Bear than before, he was soon driven off. Cooper's battery (B, First Pennsylvania, four 3-inch), which had suffered severely in this affair, was now relieved by Ricketts', from the Artillery Reserve.

In this cannonade, Lieut C P Eakin, First US Artillery, was badly wounded and carried off the field, and Lieut P D Mason, First US Artillery, assumed command of the battery.

About the same hour, 3.30 PM, as the enemy was seriously annoying the left of the Twelfth Corps, three guns of Knapp's battery, under command of Lieutenant Geary, and Van Reed's section of K, Fifth US Artillery, were placed in an eligible position, about 200 yards from the right of the First Corps. As soon as their presence (Knapp's Pennsylvania Battery, 10-pounders, and Kinzie's, K, Fifth US Artillery, light 12-pounders) was noticed, the enemy turned his battery (eight guns) upon them, but after a spirited contest of thirty minutes, in which he had a caisson blown up, his guns were silenced. The conduct of both Lieutenants Geary and Van Reed is highly spoken of by their chiefs of artillery.

When the infantry of the Twelfth Corps crossed over to the support of the Third Corps, on the left of our line, these guns were withdrawn and rejoined their batteries.

About sunset the enemy again opened from a knoll in front of the cemetery, distant about 1,800 yards, and this was soon followed by a powerful infantry attack on the position by General Rodes' Louisiana [?] brigade. As their columns moved out of the town, they came under the fire of Stevens' battery (Fifth Maine), at 800 yards distance. Wheeling into line, they pushed up the hill. As their line became unmasked, all the guns that could be brought to bear upon them, some twenty, were opened, first with shrapnel and then with canister, with excellent effect. The center and left were beaten back, but their right worked their way up under cover of the houses, and pushed completely through Wiedrich's battery (I, First New York, six 3-inch) into Ricketts' (F and G, First Pennsylvania, six 3-inch). The cannoneers of both batteries stood well to their guns, and when no longer able to hold them, fought with handspikes, rammers, and even stones, joining the infantry in driving them out, and capturing several prisoners. This attack of Rodes was mainly repelled by the artillery alone. The loss of the enemy was reported to be large by their wounded in the affair, who afterward fell under the care of our surgeons in Gettysburg.

About 12 m a detachment of Berdan's Sharpshooters was sent into the woods near the point where the enemy's crest opposite the left of our army cuts the Emmitsburg road, and reported the enemy as moving in force toward our left flank.

About 2 PM General Sickles formed his corps in line to meet an attack from this direction, his right resting on the Emmitsburg road, in a peach orchard, in advance of the center of our left, and his line extending in a general direction toward Sugar Loaf or Round Top, a peak which terminated our line on the left. At this time I reached the ground, and found Captain Randolph, chief of artillery Third Corps, making arrangements to station his battery on the right, those on the left having already been posted as follows: Smith's battery (Fourth New York, six 10-pounders) on the extreme left and on a steep and rocky eminence in advance of Sugar Loaf, and on his right Winslow's (D, First New York, six 12-pounders), in a wheat-field, separated from Smith by a belt of woods. I accompanied Captain Randolph, first sending to General Tyler, commanding the Artillery Reserve, for two batteries, one of light 12-pounders and one of rifles, and assisted him in posting the other batteries as follows: Clark's battery (B, First New Jersey, six 10-pounders) on the line to the left of the peach orchard; Ames' (G, First New York, six 12-pounders), from the Artillery Reserve, in the orchard, both facing the south, and perpendicular to the Emmitsburg road: then along the Emmitsburg road and facing the west, Randolph's (E, First Rhode Island, six 12-pounders), and Seeley's (K, Fourth United States, six 12-pounders) batteries, Seeley's well to the right of Randolph's. While Ames and Clark were moving up, the enemy opened a brisk fire upon them from a position near the Emmitsburg road and on the opposite side of it.

By this time, about 3.30 PM, Major McGilvery came up from the Artillery Reserve with three batteries—Bigelow's (Ninth Massachusetts, four 12-pounders); Phillips' (Fifth Massachusetts, six 3-inch), and Hart's (Fifteenth New York, four 12-pounders)—which I ordered into position on the left of Clark's. As I saw that more batteries of the enemy were getting into position on the south of the Emmitsburg road and forming opposite to this line, I sent to the reserve for more rifled guns, and then, as Smith (Fourth New York, six 10-pounders) had not opened, I went to his battery to ascertain the cause. When I arrived, he had succeeded in getting his guns into position, and just opened fire. As his position commanded that of the enemy and enfiladed their line, his fire was very effective, and with that of Ames (G, First New York, six 12-pounders) and Clark (B, First New Jersey, six 10-pounders) in front, soon silenced that battery. In the meantime the enemy had established his new batteries to the north of the road, and Smith turned his guns upon them. I now moved along the line and examined the condition of the different batteries. Winslow (D, First New York, six 12-pounders) had not yet been attacked, his position facing a wood at short range that the enemy had not yet occupied. Bigelow, Phillips, and Hart were hotly engaged, and the battle soon raged along the lines.

In the meantime the additional batteries ordered from the reserve—Thompson's (C and F, Pennsylvania, six 3-inch) and Sterling's (Second Connecticut, four James and two howitzers), and Ransom's brigade, consisting of Thomas' (C, Fourth United States, six 12-pounders), Weir's (C, Fifth United States, six 12-pounders), and Turnbull's (F and K, Third United States, six 12-pounders) batteries –were brought up by General Tyler in person. Ransom's brigade was formed on the crest, above general headquarters, and soon after Turnbull's, Weir's, and Thomas' batteries were ordered forward to join Humphreys' division, taking position on the right of Seeley.

Some time after, two batteries of the Fifth Corps—Watson's (I, Fifth United States, four 3-inch) and Walcott's (C, Massachusetts Artillery, six 12-pounders)—were brought upon the ground by some staff officer of General Sickles; but for this there seemed to be no necessity, abundant provision having been made to supply all needs from the Artillery Reserve. The effect was to deprive the Fifth Corps of its batteries, without the knowledge and to the inconvenience of the commander of the corps. The batteries were exposed to heavy front and enfilading fires, and suffered terribly, but as rapidly as any were disabled they were retired and replaced by others. Watson (I, Fifth United States, four 3-inch) relieved Ames' battery (G, First New York, six 12-pounders); Thompson's (Pennsylvania, six 3-inch) took position near it, relieving Hart (Fifteenth New York, four 12-pounders). Turnbull's (F and K, Third United States, six 12-pounders) was posted near the Emmitsburg road. The officers and men performed their duties with great gallantry and success, notwithstanding the unfavorable nature of the ground, which gave the enemy all the advantages of position, driving off several of the enemy's batteries, silencing others, and doing good execution on his infantry, until about 5.30 or 6 PM, when the line was forced back, and the batteries were compelled to withdraw.

So great had been the loss in men and horses, that many of the carriages had to be withdrawn by hand and others left on the field, which, with the exception of four, were afterward brought off. Three of these belonged to Smith's battery (Fourth New York, six 10-pounders), on our extreme left. The guns were stationed on the brow of a very precipitous and rocky height, beyond a ravine in front of our line. The difficulty of getting these guns up the height had caused the delay in Smith's opening his fire. He fought them to the last moment in hopes of keeping the enemy off, and in the belief that the ground would be in our possession again before the guns could be carried off by the enemy. He got off one of the four guns he had placed on the height, but was compelled to abandon the other three. The fourth of the guns lost belonged to Thompson's battery, the horses being all killed, the men engaged in hauling off the other pieces by hand, and his infantry supports having left him. In withdrawing, many acts of gallantry were performed, the enemy in several instances being driven out from the batteries by the cannoneers and such assistance as they could procure from the infantry near them. The line reformed on the crest, which constituted our original line, and repulsed all further attacks.

    The batteries of the Second Corps were posted on the morning of the 2d by its chief of artillery, Captain Hazard, First Rhode Island Artillery, as follows, from left; to right, connecting with the batteries of the Third Corps on the left, and those on Cemetery Hill on the right: Rorty's (B, First New York, four 10-pounders), Brown's (B, First Rhode Island, six 12-pounders), Cushing's (A, Fourth United States, six 3-inch), Arnold's (A, First Rhode Island, six 3-inch), and Woodruff's (I, First United States, six 12-pounders). The enemy opened upon them several times during the morning, but were always silenced by their concentrated fire.

    When the Third Corps fell back, about 6 PM, their batteries opened a vigorous fire, and the two left batteries (Rorty's and Brown's) conformed their movements to those of the infantry. When the crest of the hill occupied by our lines was reached, it gave the batteries a commanding position; a rapid fire was opened, and the enemy gradually driven back. Brown's battery suffered so severely in men and horses that it became necessary to send two guns to the rear.

    The artillery of the Fifth Corps arrived on the field between 4 and 5 PM Hazlett's (D, Fifth United States, six 10-pounders), Walcott's (C, Massachusetts Artillery, six 12-pounders), and

Watson's (I, Fifth United States, four 3-inch) batteries, with the First Division of the corps; Gibbs' (L, First Ohio, six 12-pounders), and Barnes' (C, First New York, four 3-inch), with Second Division. I have already stated that Watson's and Walcott's were taken from their positions by order of Major-General Sickles, and noted their services. Walcott's was not engaged, but was under fire; 6 men wounded, and 6 horses killed and wounded.

  About 4.30 PM Hazlett's battery was moved to the extreme left, placed in position on Round Top, and immediately opened upon that portion of the enemy's force which attacked the First Division, and continued it until night with marked effect, as its fire enfiladed the enemy's line. Guthrie's section of Gibbs' battery was posted on the same hill on the right of Hazlett, and Walworth's section at the base of the hill, commanding the ravine in front of Round Top, the remaining section being held in reserve. These sections did excellent service, especially Guthrie's. On this afternoon, Lieut Charles E Hazlett, Fifth US Artillery, a young officer, who had gained an enviable reputation for gallantry, skill, and devotion to his country and the service, received a mortal wound, and died the same evening.

  For more detailed reports of the services of the artillery in the action on our left, I respectfully refer to the reports of General Tyler, commanding Artillery Reserve, and to the reports of the chiefs of artillery of the Second, Third, and Fifth Corps, transmitted herewith. It will be perceived that the batteries suffered severely in officers, men, and horses, losing a large proportionate number of officers—3 killed (Lieut. Charles E Hazlett, Fifth Artillery, commanding Battery B; Lieut M Livingston, Third Artillery, commanding Turn-bull's battery; Lieut C Erickson, Bigelow's battery); and 12 wounded (Capt D R Ransom, Third Artillery, commanding Regular Brigade, Artillery Reserve; Capt J Thompson, C, Pennsylvania Artillery; Capt N Irish, D, Pennsylvania Artillery; Capt Patrick Hart, Fifteenth New York Battery; Lieut T F Brown, Hazard's battery; Lieut Samuel Canby, Fourth Artillery, Cushing's battery; Lieut J K Bucklyn, First Rhode Island, Randolph's battery; Lieut F W Seeley, Fourth US Artillery, commanding Battery K; Lieut M F Watson, Fifth U.S. Artillery, commanding Battery I; Lieut J L Miller, Thompson's battery, mortally; Lieut E M Knox, Fifteenth New York Battery; Lieut E Spence, Ricketts' battery).

The night of the 2d was devoted in great part to repairing damages, replenishing the ammunition chests, and reducing and reorganizing such batteries as had lost so many men and horses as to be unable efficiently to work the full number of guns.

By daylight next morning this duty had been performed so far as possible, and, when it was found impossible to reorganize in time, the batteries were withdrawn, replaced by others from the Artillery Reserve, and finished their work during the next morning.

On the evening of July 2, a portion of Slocum's corps (the Second) [Twelfth], which formed the right of our line, was sent to re-enforce the left. During its absence, the enemy took possession of a portion of the line in the woods, and it was resolved to drive him out at daylight. Knapp's battery (E, Pennsylvania, six 10-pounders) was placed on the hill known as Slocum's headquarters, and near the Baltimore pike, and Winegar's battery (M, First New York, four 10-pounders) at a short distance east of it. These batteries overlooked and commanded the ground vacated by the corps.

At 1 AM of the 3d, Muhlenberg's (F, Fourth United States, six 12-pounders) and Kinzie's (K, Fifth United States, four 12-pounders) batteries were posted opposite the center of the line of the Twelfth Corps, so as to command the ravine formed by Rock Creek.

At 4.30 AM these batteries opened, and fired without intermission for fifteen minutes into the wood, at a range of from 600 to 800 yards. Soon after daylight, Rigby's battery (A, Maryland, six 3-inch) was also placed on the hill, and at 5.30 AM all the batteries opened, and continued firing at intervals until 10 AM, when the infantry succeeded in driving out the enemy and reoccupied their position of the day before. In this work the artillery tendered good service.

At our center, on and near Cemetery Hill, the batteries were in position very nearly the same as on the previous day. Those outside of the cemetery gate and north of the Baltimore pike, under the command of Colonel Wainwright, First New York Artillery, were, from right to left: Stevens' (Fifth Maine, six 12-pounders), Reynolds' (L, First New York, four 3-inch), Ricketts' (F, First Pennsylvania, six 3-inch)—which had relieved Cooper's (B, First Pennsylvania, four 3-inch) the night before—Wiedrich's (I, First New York, four 3-inch), and Stewart's (B, Fourth United

States, four 12-pounders). The batteries south of the pike, and under command of Major Osborn, First New York Artillery, were: Dilger's (I, First Ohio six 12-pounders), Bancroft's (G, Fourth United States, six 12-pounders), Eakin's (H, First United States, six 12-pounders), Wheeler's (Thirteenth New York, three 3-inch), Hill's (C, First West Virginia, four 10-pounders), and Taft's (Fifth New York, six 20-pounders).

On the left of the cemetery the batteries of the Second Corps were in line on the crest occupied by their corps in the following order, from right to left: Woodruff's (I, First United States, six 12-pounders), Arnold's (A, First Rhode Island, six 3-inch), Cushing's (A, Fourth United States, six 3-inch), Brown's (B, First Rhode Island, four 12-pounders), and Rorty's (B, First New York, four 10-pounders), all under command of Captain Hazard, chief of artillery.

Next on the left of the artillery of the Second Corps were stationed Thomas' battery (C, Fourth United States, six 12-pounders), and on his left Major McGilvery's command, consisting of Thompson's (C and F, Pennsylvania, five 3-inch), Phillips' (Fifth Massachusetts, six 3-inch), Harts (Fifteenth New York, four 12-pounders), Sterling's (Second Connecticut, four James and two howitzers), Rank's section (two 3-inch), Dow's (Sixth Maine, four 12-pounders), and Ames' (G, First New York, six 12-pounders), all of the Artillery Reserve, to which was added, soon after the cannonade commenced, Cooper s battery (B, First Pennsylvania, four 3-inch), of the First Corps.

On our extreme left, occupying the position of the day before, were Gibbs' (L, First Ohio, six 12-pounders) and Rittenhouse's (late Hazlett's, D, Fifth United States, six 10-pounders) batteries. Gibbs' was, however, too distant from the enemy's position for 12-pounders, and was not used during the day, although under fire. Rittenhouse was in an excellent position for the service of his rifled guns, on the top of Round Top. We had thus on the western crest line seventy-five guns, which could be aided by a few of those on Cemetery Hill. There was but little firing during the morning.

At 10 AM I made an inspection of the whole line, ascertaining that all the batteries—only those of our right serving with the Twelfth Corps being engaged at the time—were in good condition and well supplied with ammunition. As the enemy was evidently increasing his artillery force in front of our left, I gave instructions to the batteries and to the chiefs of artillery not to fire at small bodies, nor to allow their fire to be drawn without promise of adequate results; to watch the enemy closely, and when he opened to concentrate the fire of their guns on one battery at a time until it was silenced; under all circumstances to fire deliberately, and to husband their ammunition as much as possible.

I had just finished my inspection, and was with Lieutenant Rittenhouse on the top of Round Top, when the enemy opened, at about 1 PM, along his whole right, a furious cannonade on the left of our line. I estimated the number of his guns bearing on our west front at from one hundred to one hundred and twenty. I have since seen it stated by the enemy's correspondents that there were sixty guns from Longstreet's, and fifty-five from Hill's corps, making one hundred and fifteen in all. To oppose these we could not, from our restricted position, bring more than eighty to reply effectively. Our fire was well withheld until the first burst was over, excepting from the extreme right and left of our positions. It was then opened deliberately and with excellent effect. As soon as the nature of the enemy's attack was made clear, and I could form an opinion as to the number of his guns, for which my position afforded great facility, I went to the park of the Artillery Reserve, and ordered all the batteries to be ready to move at a moment's notice, and hastened to report to the commanding general, but found he had left his headquarters. I then 'proceeded along the line, to observe the effects of the cannonade and to replace such batteries as should become disabled.

About 2.30 PM, finding our ammunition running low and that it was very unsafe to bring up loads of it, a number of caissons and limbers having been exploded, I directed that the fire should be gradually stopped, which was done, and the enemy soon slackened his fire also. I then sent orders for such batteries as were necessary to replace exhausted ones, and all that were disposable were sent me.

About 3 PM, and soon after the enemy's fire had ceased, he formed a column of attack in the edge of the woods in front of the Second Corps. At this time Fitzhugh's (K, First New York, six 3-inch), Parsons' (A, First New Jersey, six 10-pounders), Weir's (C, Fifth United States, six 12-pounders), and Cowan's (First New York Independent, six 3-inch) batteries reached this point, and were put in position in front of the advancing enemy. I rode down to McGilvery's batteries, and directed them to take the enemy in flank as they approached. The enemy advanced magnificently, unshaken by the shot and shell which tore through his ranks from his front and from our left. The batteries of the Second Corps on our right, having nearly exhausted their supply of ammunition, except canister, were compelled to withhold their fire until the enemy, who approached in three lines, came within its range. When our canister fire and musketry were opened upon them, it occasioned disorder, but still they advanced gallantly until they reached the stone wall behind which our troops lay. Here ensued a desperate conflict, the enemy succeeding in passing the wall and entering our lines, causing great destruction of life, especially among the batteries. Infantry troops were, however, advanced from our right; the rear line of the enemy broke, and the others, who had fought with a gallantry that excited the admiration of our troops, found themselves cut off and compelled to surrender. As soon as their fate was evident, the enemy opened his batteries upon the masses of our troops at this point without regard to the presence of his own. Toward the close of this struggle, Rorty's (B, First New York, four 10-pounders), Arnold s (A, First Rhode Island, six 3-inch), and Cushing's (A, Fourth United States, six 3-inch) batteries, which had lost heavily in men and horses, were withdrawn, and as soon as the affair was over their places were filled with fresh ones.

  Soon the necessary measures had been taken to restore this portion of the line to an efficient condition. It required but a few minutes, as the batteries, as fast as withdrawn from any point, were sent to the Artillery Reserve, replenished with ammunition, reorganized, returned to the rear of the lines, and there awaited assignment. I then went to the left, to see that proper measures had been taken there for the same object. On my way, I saw that the enemy was forming a second column of attack to his right of the point where the first was formed, and in front of the position of the First Corps (Newton's). I gave instructions to the artillery, under command of Major McGilvery, to be ready to meet the first movements of the enemy in front, and, returning to the position of the Second Corps, directed the batteries there, mostly belonging to the Artillery Reserve, to take the enemy in flank as he advanced. When the enemy moved, these orders were well executed, and before he reached our line he was brought to a stand. The appearance of a body of our infantry moving down in front of our lines from the direction of the Second Corps caused the enemy to move off by his right flank, under cover of the woods and undergrowth, and, a few minutes after, the column had broken up, and in the utmost confusion the men of which it was composed fled across the ground over which they had just before advanced, and took refuge behind their batteries. The attacks on the part of the enemy were not well managed. Their artillery fire was too much dispersed, and failed to produce the intended effect. It was, however, so severe and so well sustained that it put to the test, and fully proved, the discipline and excellence of our troops. The two assaults, had they been simultaneous, would have divided our artillery fire. As it was, each attack was met by a heavy front and flank fire of our artillery, the batteries which met the enemy directly in front in one assault taking him in flank in the other.

    The losses of the artillery on this day, and especially in the assault on the Second Corps, were very large. The loss in officers was 3 killed, 2 mortally and 9 severely wounded. Killed: Capt J M Rorty, B, First New York; Lieut A H Cushing, Fourth United States; Lieut G A Woodruff, First United States (mortally wounded); Lieut J S Milne, First Rhode Island; Lieut A H Whitaker, Ninth Massachusetts (wounded severely); Capt J Bigelow, Ninth Massachusetts; Lieut A S Sheldon, B, First New York; Lieut H H Baldwin, Fifth United States; Lieut J McGilvray, Fourth United States; Lieut R C Hazlett, Fourth Pennsylvania Battery; Lieut J Stephenson, Fourth Pennsylvania Battery; Lieut H D Scott, Battery E, Massachusetts; Lieut W P Wright, First New York Battery; Lieut W H Johnson, First New York Battery. Captain Rorty, who had taken command of his battery but three days before, fell, fighting, at his guns. Lieutenants Cushing and Woodruff belonged to a class of young officers who, although of the lowest commissioned rank, have gained distinguished army reputation. The destruction of *materiel* was large. The enemy's cannonade, in which he must have almost exhausted his ammunition, was well sustained, and cost us a great many horses and the explosion of an unusually large number of caissons and limbers. The whole slope behind our crest, although concealed from the enemy, was swept by his shot, and offered no protection to horses or carriages. The enemy's superiority in the number of guns was fully matched by the superior accuracy of ours, and a personal inspection of the line he occupied, made on the 5th, enables me to state with certainty that his losses in *materiel* in this artillery combat were equal to ours, while the marks of the shot in the trees on both crests bear conclusive evidence of the superiority of our practice.

This struggle closed the battle, and the night of the 3d, like the previous one, was devoted to repairs and reorganization. A large number of batteries had been so reduced in men and horses that many guns and carriages, after completing the outfit of those which remained with the army, were sent to the rear and turned in to the ordnance department.

Our losses in the three days' operations, as reported, were as follows:

Casualties, July 1, 2 and 3.

Organizations	Number of guns	Killed Officers	Men	Wounded Officers	Men	Missing	Horses
In the corps	212	5	57	18	361	52	565
Artillery Reserve	108	2	41	15	171	15	316
Total	320	7	98	33	532	67	881

Of these 320 guns, 142 were light 12-pounders, 106 3-inch guns, 6 20-pounders, 60 10-pounder Parrott guns, and a battery of 4 James rifles and 2 12-pounder howitzers, which joined the army on the march to Gettysburg. This table excludes the Horse Artillery, 44 3-inch guns, serving with the cavalry. It will be seen that the Artillery Reserve, every gun of which was brought into requisition, bore, as in all the campaigns of the Army of the Potomac, its full share, and more, of the losses.

The expenditure of ammunition in the three days amounted to 32,781 rounds, averaging over 100 rounds per gun. Many rounds were lost in the caissons and limbers by explosions and otherwise. The supply carried with the army being 270 rounds per gun, left sufficient to fill the ammunition chests and enable the army to fight another battle. There was for a short time during the battle a fear that the ammunition would give out. This fear was caused by the large and unreasonable demands made by corps commanders who had left their own trains or a portion of them behind, contrary to the orders of the commanding general. In this emergency, the train of the Artillery Reserve, as on so many other occasions, supplied all demands, and proved its great usefulness to the army.

For a more particular account of the operations of the artillery and of their relations to those of the other arms of service,

I respectfully refer to the report of the commander of the Artillery Reserve, and to those of the chiefs of artillery of the army corps, transmitted herewith, to which reports I also refer for the names of those who distinguished themselves by their conduct and courage.

I have to acknowledge my indebtedness to these officers: Brig Gen R O Tyler, commanding Artillery Reserve; Col C S Wainwright, First New York Artillery, First Corps; Capt J G Hazard, First Rhode Island Artillery, Second Corps; Capt G E Randolph, First Rhode Island Artillery, Third Corps; Capt A P Martin, Third Massachusetts Battery, Fifth Corps; Col C H Tompkins, First Rhode Island Artillery, Sixth Corps; Maj T W Osborn, First New York Artillery, Eleventh Corps; Lieut E D Muhlenberg, Fourth U.S. Artillery, Twelfth Corps, for their zealous co-operation in all the administrative labors that devolved upon me, and for the efficiency with which they discharged their duties in the field.

My staff Lieut Col E R Warner, First New York Artillery, inspector of artillery; Capt J N Craig, assistant adjutant-general, and Lieut C E Bissell, aide-de-camp—performed the duties devolving upon them with intelligence and gallantry.

Upon Lieutenant-Colonel Warner fell much of the labor required in the reorganization of batteries withdrawn from the field and in replacing them. These duties and others which devolved upon him were discharged with his accustomed energy and thoroughness. Lieutenant Bissell was my only aide, and was, therefore, busily employed. He was much exposed, his duties keeping him more or less under fire at every point at which attacks were made.

In my report of the battle of Chancellorsville, I took occasion to call attention to the great evils arising from the want of field officers for the artillery. The operations of this campaign, and especially the battle of Gettysburg, afford further proofs, if such were necessary, of the mistaken policy of depriving so important an arm of the officers necessary for managing it. In this campaign, for the command of 67 batteries (372 guns), with over 8,000 men and 7,000 horses, and all the *materiel*, and large ammunition trains, I had one general officer commanding the reserve, and but four field officers (Brig Gen R O Tyler, U.S. Volunteers, commanding Artillery Reserve; Lieut Col F McGilvery, First Maine Artillery, commanding brigade Artillery Reserve; Col C H Tompkins, First Rhode Island Artillery, Sixth Corps; Col C S

Wainwright, First New York Artillery, First Corps; Maj T W Osborn, First New York Artillery, Eleventh Corps; Capt J M Robertson, Second US Artillery, commanding First Brigade Horse Artillery; Capt J C Tidball, Second US Artillery, commanding Second Brigade Horse Artillery).

In the seven corps, the artillery of two were commanded by colonels, of one by a major, of three by captains, and of one by a lieutenant, taken from their batteries for the purpose. The two brigades of horse artillery attached to the cavalry were commanded by captains, and there was one field officer in the reserve. The most of these commands in any other army would have been considered proper ones for a general officer. In no army would the command of the artillery of a corps be considered of less importance, to say the least, than that of a brigade of infantry. In none of our corps ought the artillery commander to have been of less rank than a colonel, and in all there should have been a proper proportion of field officers, with the necessary staffs. The defects of our organization were made palpable at Gettysburg, not only on the field, but in the necessary and important duties of reorganizing the batteries, repairing damages, and getting the artillery in condition to renew the battle, or take the road in efficient condition on the morning after a conflict.

I respectfully and urgently call the attention of the commanding general, and through him of the War Department, to this subject.

Not only does the service suffer, necessarily, from the great deficiency of officers of rank, but a policy which closes the door of promotion to battery officers, and places them and the arm itself under a ban, and degrades them in comparison with other arms of service, induces discontent, and has caused many of our best officers to seek positions, wherever they can find them, which will remove them from this branch of the service. We have lost many such officers, and unless something is done to cure the evil we will lose more.

The reports of the horse artillery were rendered to the cavalry officers under whose orders they served, and I have not yet received all of them. As their operations were detached from those of the main body of the army, and do not naturally connect with them, I reserve them as the subject of a separate report.

Very respectfully, your obedient servant,
Henry J Hunt

Brigadier-General and Chief of Artillery, Commanding

October 1863-January 1864
I have the honor to report

October 8, 1863
Letter of William Wheeler
Nashville, TN

My Dearest Mother

I suppose that you have gleaned from the papers some information about the flitting of the Eleventh and Twelfth Corps from the Army of the Potomac. Nothing could have been more sudden than our departure from Catlett's Station, or more at variance with the arrangements which were being made there. Orders have been given to the Corps to take a strong position on Cedar Run, to cover the railroad, and several strong forts were ordered to be built, defending the post, in a large semicircle, from the Cedar Run bridge through General Howard's head-quarters round to the station. These forts were to be constructed with care and elaboration, and were to bear the names of Eleventh Corps heroes who fell at Chancellorsville and Gettysburg. The construction of Fort Dessauer[57], which covered the railroad bridge and was the most important point of all, was intrusted, said the order, to the Thirteenth New York Battery, and the Twenty-seventh Pennsylvania Regiment, under supervision of Captain Wheeler. I had got my digging parties hard at work, and the bastions and platforms for my guns had already begun to rise, when suddenly we were ordered to suspend operation, lay in rations for a month, and have everything packed up, and the same evening saw my guns put on the cars, and my horses marching off towards Alexandria. We made a very stiff march, leaving Catlett's Station at midnight, and arriving at Alexandria at three o'clock the next day,--a distance of forty-five miles. The guns of all the batteries were sent on immediately, over the Baltimore and Ohio railroad, and each battery commander followed with his horses, as fast as he could get them loaded into the horse-cars. I will not weary you with a detailed account of our most fatiguing journey. Suffice it to say that both men and animals were most distressed and pulled down by it than by the severest forced march. I enjoyed the scenery of the Baltimore and Ohio railroad exceedingly, and rode on top of the cars all the way, while crossing the mountains.

We passed through the superb region from Piedmont to Grafton in the splendor of a delicious autumn, which showed all the gorgeous coloring of the infinite stretches, and under the mysterious lights and shadows of a perfect moonlight autumn night. The few inhabitants seemed intensely Union, and confident of being able to guard the mountain passes leading to Wheeling with very little aid from Government. At Benwood we struck the Ohio river and crossed to Bellaire. Here another shipment was necessary, and a day of misery was spent in accomplishing it. My horses went out in the first train, together with those of Captain Dilger, whom I found a pleasant companion. We passed through Zanesville and Columbus, Ohio, and at daybreak found ourselves at Richmond, Indiana. Here began a perfect ovation. The good Quakers, by whom the town is mostly settled, took our poor hungry boys into their houses and gave them breakfast, and many a kind word of cheer. At every town in Indiana, great crowds of ladies came to the cars, with baskets of bread and cake and pie, cold meats and chickens, sourkrout for the Dutchmen, and doughnuts for the Yankees, and pressed it upon the men, without distinction of rank, in the most charming manner. Our reception at Centreville and Cambridge City beat everything in this line. Besides the articles mentioned above, the ladies gave us clean handkerchiefs and towels and pieces of soap, most welcome gifts to men who eyes were half blinded, and whose faces and hands were grimy, with the dust of a week's railroad journey. I am sure that they will not fight the worse, for having seen how dear the cause is to the best and most beautiful in the land. At Indianapolis we reshipped again for Jeffersonville, where we crossed the Ohio again to Louisville, Kentucky. I was delighted with Louisville, which is certainly one of the finest cities in the country, and indulged in a glorious bath, etc., which will always be fresh in my memory; and at the St Charles Restaurant I built up the inner man with some first class grub. Once more we put our poor nags in the cars, and came on to this place, where we seem at present to be at a dead-lock, as our namesake, General Wheeler, the rebel, has been burning the bridges on the road to Chattanooga, like a naughty man, and we can obtain no transportation by rail. Very possibly we shall have to take a bare-back ride over the mountains to Rosecranz, as our guns, harness, saddled, and baggage have gone on before us, and are probably, by this time, with the Army of the Cumberland. My baggage now, consists of my sabre and overcoat, and I don't know whether I shall ever see the rest of my traps again. Nashville is a dirty, disagreeable place. I am now staying at the Continental, as I want to rest.

October 20, 1863
Letter of William Wheeler
Stevenson, AL

I send you another bulletin to report progress, since I wrote you at Nashville. I do not pretend, in these short notes, to give you any clear idea of what I have been doing and seeing on this tedious and yet hurried march, but try merely to let you know that I had got thus far, and that my health was yet preserved. Perhaps I may get an opportunity to write more at length, when the long winter days come, and I have more comfortable quarters, and my own writing materials. Well, we had a week's rest at Nashville, where we were waiting for the quartermasters to get their trains fixed up; and a miserable week it was. The hotel afforded no decent accommodation, although charging enormous prices; the city was filthy, and the specimens which we saw of the men and officers of the Army of the Cumberland did not make me feel very proud of our new associations. The expedition, consisting of about four hundred team wagons, one battery of artillery, all the artillery horses of the Corps, the officers' horses, a regiment of infantry of the Twelfth Corps, and a larger number of stragglers, were to leave Nashville on Saturday morning, and Major Osborn wanted me to take charge of the artillery, and go as second in command of the train; but I declined, both on account of feeling so unwell, and also because I did not wish to go before two senior captains, and suggested that Captain Dilger should have the command, which suggestion the major followed. However, as an attack of the train was expected from Wheeler's Cavalry, I did not like to leave the expedition, and told the Major that I would go along and give any aid I could in case of such an attack. The train was not read to start on Saturday, because many of the teams were to be composed of green, unbroken mules, running loose in the corral, and it took a long time to get them caught, harnessed, and hitched in, and even then an immense amount of persuasion had to be applied before they could be got to move on. It was a most ludicrous sight, and numbers of people rode out from Nashville expressly to see it. The "Norway rabbits" would stand straight up, and paw furiously, and jump over wagon poles and chuck their darkey drivers in the most alarming manner, and then, as if by agreement, would all lift up their voices in a most pitiful hee-haw. On Monday morning most of the teams were in marching order, and we started off on the Franklin Pike, I having charge of the rear-guard. We marched fifteen miles to Lavergne through pitiless rain, halting for hours to get refractory mules subdued and to repair broken wagons and harness, and come into park in a mudhole after nightfall. The officers in the advance had been discreet enough to hut up good quarters on their arrival, and I found Colonel Long, the commander, and the artillery officers comfortably ensconced in the parlor of a very fine house, making themselves agreeable to the ladies of the house, and listening to superb singing of the daughter, Miss Ellen Harris, who gave Union songs, and secesh airs, darkey melodies and opera morceaux with equal facility. I went into the bedroom where there was a fine blazing fire, and dried myself a little, and then joined the party in the other room, where I spent a very pleasant evening. Miss Harris, was a very handsome girl with magnificent eyes and decidedly the quickest and sharpest young lady I ever saw in my life; a little too much like a flash of lightning. I slept that night before the fire in the spare-room, and felt much better, in the morning, than when I left Nashville, as then I felt hardly fit to mount my horses. Rough marching and field work bring me one to health quicker than any medicine. We marched that day to Murfreesborough, passing over the bloody battle-field of Stone River, fought on the last day of 1862. The trees were filled with bullets sometimes as high as sixty feet, and the trunks in some cases were bored through with shells. We saw a monument of stone, partly finished, which is being raised over the dead of General Hazen's Brigade, who are all buried in one sad inclosure. The fortifications of Murfreesborough are the finest field-works that I have seen anywhere. Here, as elsewhere, we reap the fruits of the engineering labors of the rebels. This place is guarded by some of the Twelfth Massachusetts. We went to bed thoroughly wet, and it rained all that night and all the next day, upon which we had a most fatiguing march to Shelbyville. I was half dead when we got there, and was glad to rush out of the rain into the nearest home where there was a light; it proved to have been deserted by its owner, and was occupied by some refugees. We halted at Shelbyville to await the arrival of the train; it is a pretty thrifty looking place and known as the "Yankee town," two-thirds of the inhabitants being Unionists. In the afternoon, having dried ourselves and brushed off the Tennessee mud, Lieutenant Mickle and I went out to study the natives. We first went and bought a turkey, and left him to be roasted; then we got up a pretext for calling at the home of Mr. Bob Matthews, the head secesh in the place, whose three daughters were keeping house alone, the old man having thought it better to leave for Southern parts. You see we were pretty well posted on the Virginia rebs, and wanted to know if the Tennessee variety resembled it. We had a very pleasant call, and then went to Mr Cowan's for our turkey. Mr Cowan took us into his parlor, before a delightful fire in an open grate, and had some of the most agreeable conversation that I have had since I left home. Mr Cowan is a canny Scotch Irishman, and thoroughly understands the whole question of the war, and is a strong Union man in his judgment, but does not believe in ruining himself by any premature demonstrations. He suffered enough the other day, when Wheeler's Cavalry entered the town and carried off about all the goods from his store, besides plundering the town. It was a premature union meeting that drew down the rebel vengeance on that place. We stayed to supper, and Mrs Cowan, a pleasant motherly lady, the very counterpart of Mrs I W, gave us some excellent tea and muffins, which went just to the right spot. The next day was more propitious and we marched to Tullahoma moving the wagon train behind us, and thus being able to advance with greater speed. That evening at Tullahoma was most superb, like the most perfect weather of our Indian summer. The next day we marched through Deckerd, over Elk River to Cowan, at the foot of the Cumberland mountains. The rain set in again, continued all night, and in the morning we were half soaked before we began the ascent of that most rough and rugged mountains.

    It was worse than the Alleghenies or the Blue Ridge, as the road consisted merely of slabs of smooth rock, sometimes standing on end, and deep gullies between them. I hardly expected that we could get over at all, but we had all the batteries at the summit before noon, and by two PM were at Tantallon Station, at the base of the principal ridge. There we found the pickets of our own Corps, and felt somewhat at home.

    We left the Battery, Captain Wiedrich's, at Tantallon, to be brought on by its own horses, and pushed on twenty-five miles further, to his place. We reached it after dark; in the morning we discovered that Lieutenant Miller, with my four guns, and the cannoneers, were in the fort, and we made all speed to join them, leaving the others to go on to Bridgeport. I was very glad to get my men all together again, and to find that every one was well. I expect to march to Bridgeport with my guns to-morrow. I myself am greatly in need of rest, and when I got here yesterday it seemed if I had a heavy weight on my brain and could not keep still, sitting or lying. I am better to-day, and hope to escape any serious illness, if I can only get this cold out of my bones.

November 4, 1863
Battery Orders No. 45
Lookout Valley, TN

The commanding officer observes that the men of this command are very remiss in showing proper respect to their superiors and neglect the military salute; the following rules will be observed in regard to this matter:
1   Every enlisted man upon meeting or passing an officer whether of his own command or a stranger will salute him by respectively raising his hand edge to the front of the visor of his cap. If sitting down he will rise when an officer approaches and salute removing the pipe or cigar from his mouth if he is using one.
2   No enlisted man will speak to an officer or make a report to him except standing respectfully before him in the position of a soldier and first saluting
3   Every private when speaking to a non-commissioned officer on duty shall address him by his military title and never by his name alone.
It is the duty of non-commissioned officers to report any violation of any of these rules especially the last such violation will be punished by hours of extra guard duty, loss of pay and by more severe means if necessary.
It is no disgrace for a solider whether he be officer or a enlisted man to show proper respect and to pay due deference to his military superior and it is hoped that the men of this Battery will show themselves to be good soldiers in this particular.
Wm Wheeler Capt
Comdg 13 NY Battery

Battery Orders No. 46
Lookout Valley, TN

Sergeant Charles Hempe is hereby reduced to the ranks from Sept 1, 1863 for attempted desertion.
Corporal John O'Connor is hereby promoted Sergeant in this Battery from Sept 1, 1862 vice Hempe reduced; he will be obeyed and respected accordingly.
Wm Wheeler Capt
Comdg 13 NY Battery

Affidavit of Capt William Wheeler, 13th New York Artillery
Chattanooga, TN

William Wheeler being duly sworn depose and says that from the 12th August 1863 until the 29th of August 1863 he made all proper efforts to be mustered in as Captain of the 13th Independent Battery, New York Artillery without success until the 29th August 1863.

The said William Wheeler further swears that he was the commanding officer of the 13th Independent Battery, New York Artillery from 12th August 1863 until the 29th August 1863.
Wm Wheeler Capt
Comdg 13 NY Battery

November 8, 1863
Letter of William Wheeler
Lookout Valley, TN

My Dearest Mother
This is Sunday, and yet you would hardly call it a day of quiet or leisure. I have to-day commenced building two forts, on two separate hills, using for that purpose all my cannoneers and fifty infantry men, not being able to escape by the plea that it was Sunday, which I artfully put in. so that, with fort building, working hard on our horses to keep them in condition, and being in readiness to get up and move house at a moment's notice, you may imagine my thoughts are not in that serene and unruffled state that I would have them for a Sunday talk with my dear mother....The service here is not like that in Virginia, and here the war has few, very few, of the softening features which it there possesses. The country is exhausted beyond conception, and so defective are the means of transportation that the army has to

struggle with the citizen for his mouthful of corn. The people of this region are, many of them, on the very border of starvation, and swarms are fleeing from it to the happier North, their children in their hand or following in a mournful train behind, their few household effects in a broken wagon, drawn by a miserable horse, and upon their faces a strong, fixed looked of despair, which it makes me sick to think of. And indeed I do not allow myself to reflect upon the necessary and collateral accompaniments of this war, as it would make me too miserable. Thanks to this expedition of General Hooker, the whole army is not moderately well provisioned, and yesterday our men got whole rations for the first time since we came here, having had half and even quarter rations before. Bragg's army must be in a deplorable condition; deserters are coming into our lines continually, by squads, and even by companies, who declare that they could not stand it any longer, with no blankets to cover them and with nothing but a small ration of parched corn to eat. They also say that if it were not supposed by most of their troops that they would be forced into our ranks if they should come over, the army could not be held together. The nights lately have been intensely cold, so that under several blankets my feet have been like ice. If we suffer this with out complete clothing and camp equipage, what must be the state of the thinly-clad rebels. Speaking of clothing, you must have laughed at my ill-luck with regard to my baggage, and my apparelless condition. I am not at all uncomfortable, as I have an excellent pair of artillery pants, a government shirt, socks, boots, and drawers, but my appearance is not stylish. I shall fight against ennui this winter and shall look to my friends to help me, both by writing me long letters and sending me anything readable. My Catlett's-station school under the oak is suspended for the present, as my cannoneers are all fort building, and my drivers are out foraging for their horses nearly every day; but if we make any permanent winter-quarters I shall try to get a log school-house built and set it running again, if I can raise the necessary stationery.

November 12, 1863
Letter of William Wheeler
Lookout Valley, TN

Here the infantry throw up rifle-pits and build corduroy roads, while the artillery have to construct their own forts as well as defend them, and besides this go foraging for their horses outside the pickets, at the imminent risk of being tickled by the guerrillas' rifles; and all these duties have been performed, until a day or two ago, on quarter and half rations. You will laugh when I tell you that, one day, your poor cousin, whose appetite is famous for its power of renewing itself three times daily was obliged to satisfy said appetite by make his faithful steed divide his scanty dinner with is master, and by dining sumptuously off a handful of "maize au naturel."

Don't think that I am at all bothered by these little inconveniences. I am in good health, lively spirits,--am eager for something to do, and ready for anything that may turn up; and, if you could be transported here by magic for an hour or so, I don't think that you would consider me particularly "mouldy." The fact is, that longer I am engaged in this war, and the more I see of the South, and the more I learn of the plans, views, and principals of our adversaries, the more am I contented with my own course in joining the army; and now I do as a matter of the most positive duty, what I undertook, partly from a spirit of restlessness and love of action.

I have felt the deepest pity for the miserable condition of the poor whites of the South, and I think that, at the hands of the so-called chivalry, a heavier reckoning will be demanded for these people, than for their black bondsmen. That, in the aggregate, the condition of the Negro has been improved, and his moral and intellectual faculties developed, by his connection with the white man, cannot, I think be denied. But what has the dominant class done for the poor white in their midst? They have closed the doors of industry upon him, their own brother, thus keeping him poor; they have refused him education, thus keeping him ignorant; and they have encouraged him in all the vices that spring from idleness, thus ruining body, mind, and soul,-- and all this, in order to keep him as a tool for their political and, now, for their military purposes. They have been fatally successful on this point, and have so thoroughly committed their fellows, by the actual facts of war and invasion, that, in very many cases, the poor whites, alive as they now are to the game that has been played with the, have yet had their combativeness aroused, and like all men are ashamed to back out or own up whipped. Here, at the foot of Lookout Mountain, our pickets converse daily with those of the enemy, and sad stories are related of privation and suffering in their ranks. These bear their fruits in the numerous squads of deserters which come into our lines, at the rate of over a hundred a day. No army could stand such bleeding at that very long. I met a band of about forty to-day, headed by an officer, and asked them where they were going. "Home," they replied;

"this is our last march in the army." And others said, "If our whole Brigade only knew that you would neither imprison us, nor conscript us into your army, they could not be held together a week." Just think of a half a pint of corn-meal per day, and nothing else, not even fresh meat,--and a thin cotton jacket and pants, without overcoat or blanket to keep off the cold of these frosty nights! Human nature cannot endure these things, unless sustained by the conviction of performing a sacred duty, or being actuated by noble principles; and these they have not, to sustain or actuate them. It is the dread of being shot or hung that is the cohesive power of the Southern army. Only to-night, I heard a sad story, from a young man, of how his brother attempted to make a Union speck in the midst of his regiment, and succeeded, by dint of great spunk and a drawn revolver, in doing so, but was afterwards hung for it....My cry this winter will be for "something to read," and if you have any nice book that you don't want any more, just mail it out here to me, "among the gloomy hills of darkness" referred to in the Monthly Concert Hymn.

November 19, 1863
Letter of William Wheeler
Lookout Valley, TN

My intentions were most certainly virtuous with regard to your first letter (written from Long Branch during that mystic period in which you were a year younger than myself, but I grieve to say, displaying very little of that old-fashioned reverence once paid to superior age), but in this instance old Dr Young's "Procrastination," usually the thief of time, descended to petty larceny, and gouged you out a letter. Suffice it to say, that in the midst of our gay and festive times at Catlett's Station, the place we had chosen after the toils of battle to repose our wearied virtue, while we were eating and drinking, building forts, and entering into boarded tents to dwell, and warming our hands at cunningly-devised fireplaces, suddenly the order arrived to pull up stakes and depart, and when we got time to breath again we were under the shadow of Lookout Mountain, with plenty of rations and sutler's goods dealt out to us daily, provided we could make an eatable dish out of 20-pound Parrot shell, or could substitute Whitworth's shrapnel for canned pineapples. And by the first mail that came to our hands in this place, I received another letter from you, dated New Haven, September 26, which had, indeed, as you said, wandered after me, but with better success than you had feared....It is so pleasant, after a long time to which I have hardly had an inducement to think, a time spent in giving orders and laying down rules of discipline, in caring for bodily comfort and speculating on military events, in cracking small jokes and discussing horses and generals, to meet such a one as yourself, though only on paper, and to pass with him at once into that other world, so beloved by me, of thought, and truth, and principle, and remembered happiness, which is all summed up in the words, "Yale," "New Haven."

"Soul-like were those days of yore
Let us walk in soul once more;"

and, indeed, you will think that I have got paper enough for a pretty long walk, but there is absolutely no other to be had, and I rummaged Chattanooga yesterday, for this very *Zweck*, and was unable to raise a single sheet of the orthodox rectangular equilateral style....I should undoubtedly have been doing my duty to my country if I had come out as a private in this Battery instead of lieutenant, and to-day I could do my duty up to the handle as a cannoneer; but when I can fill the place of captain, and get a chance to go, I will do so; and if to-morrow I should receive the offer of any higher promotion, and thought that I could do the business of the place, I would not hesitate to accept it. "The tools to them that can use them;" given a certain amount of brains, industry, zeal, and right principle, to make it of the most use to the world and the right cause....I shall greatly envy you in your reading of "Œdipus Rex." I could never read it, but went rapidly through the "Œdipus at Colonus," which I thought a story fully equal in pathos to King Lear, and in some parts not dissimilarly managed....For practical wrestling and pushing in the every-day world, both of thought and of action, Yale gives a good training as any college; but what inkling has a young Yale graduate of the beautiful world of literature, unless perchance he has neglected his studies and lived in one of the libraries during his course....By the way, speaking of labor and study, there is a rather disagreeable article in the October "Atlantic," called "Life with-out Principle," some sentences in which I believe that I wrote myself, though I don't recollect ever publishing them. Especially the following: "I foresee that if my wants should be much increased, the labor required to supply them would become a drudgery. If I should sell both my forenoons and afternoons to society, as most appear to do, I am sure that, for me, there would be nothing left worth living for." I am already speculating what occupation will give me, when I return home, after supporting me simply on the food-and-shelter plan, the most time free to be employed as I wish, whether for self-improvement or that of others. But I am rather anticipation a subject which I might better discuss six months hence, when I shall have turned it over more.

You ask me for more minute experiences of my life as a soldier; these are hard to give, for very few of them are anything more than commonplace, and even the incidents of battle do not touch much more than the physical nature. The near approach of a battle can never be know with certainty; we are sometimes precipitated into an action which a few hours before we had not expected; and again, sometimes when we are cocked and primed, and have screwed our courage to the fighting point, we are balked of our little muss; this last produces a sensation similar to that of going up one stair too many in the dark, and is altogether disgusting. We are marching quietly on, when suddenly we hear a cannonade a few miles off; this makes us all feel uneasy, as we would prefer to be either in the midst of the affair or else entirely absent. Then we get an order to pass the infantry in front and get to the field as quickly as possible; the rapid movement creates a certain physical excitement, which must be good for charging infantry, but is not the thing for artillery. At Gettysburg, when I trotted through the town with my Battery, to the front, saluted on all sides by ladies' smiles and good wishes, waving handkerchiefs and banners, I felt highly elated and excited, but this mostly passed away when we got to work. Every man, however brave, must feel unpleasantly when the shells begin to fall into the Battery before it is unlimbered, but as soon as the guns are "in battery," and the work has begun, this unpleasant sensation passes away, although more or less excitement is still felt, chiefly physical, I think, and which arises partly from the sense of bodily danger and continual escape from it, and partly from the necessity of keeping all the senses on the *qui vive* to prevent the enemy from taking an advantage, by bringing out an enfilading battery, or by pushing forward suddenly a column of infantry to make a charge; I have felt greater *mental* excitement at he crisis of a game of chess played with an equal opponent. I speak this of an artillery fight on the level and in the open, subject to infantry and cavalry charges, as well as to the fire of hostile batteries; an artillery duel, from commanding and secure positions, is a different and much less exciting thing. An old soldier gets to be indifferent to danger so long as it does not affect him, but still he cannot help rejoicing continually that so many shots pass him by. As regards sleeping on the night before battle, I don't think that the prospect of an Armageddon on the morrow, would keep me awake; it is not like a duel, you know, where a man centralizes and absorbs every feeling in himself, but here every man knows that it is his duty, and that he *must* do it, and the stronger his body is the better he can do that duty, and so he "puts in a big ration of sleep." On the night before July 2d, at Gettysburg, Major Osborn, our Chief of Artillery, slept under my blanket with me, between two of my guns in battery on the crest of Cemetery Hill, and I don't think that either of us could accuse the other of either snoring or kicking.

So, you want me to violate the articles of war by pitching into my military superiors, do you? Well, I don't care if I do a little, seeing it's you. I rather like General Meade; he fought the battle of Gettysburg superbly, and I think that he did all that he could in pursuit of Lee to Williamsport. Just think, in spite of all his losses, Lee was fully equal to us in numbers; his excellent position at Gettysburg enabled him to get a day's start of us on his retreat, and thus to reach Williamsport first, where again his position was such as to prevent a successful reconnaissance, and it was impossible for Meade to know that the whole Rebel Army was not lying behind those rifle pits. It would have been the height of rashness for him to have attacked an army of equal strength in a strong position, and thereby to have lost all the advantages of the success at Gettysburg. I think that his course was just such a one as Washington would have pursued; subsequent events have showed, and will show still more plainly, his capacity as a General. There was undoubtedly an immense amount of mismanagement about the battle of Chickamauga; the men fought well, but were not well handled. I can't exactly find out how much Rosecrans was to blame, and don't like to think that he was to blame at all; McCook did certainly show great want of conduct, and had no control over his troops. General Thomas won a reputation at that battle by mere good luck, as his corps was heavily reinforced by forces from others, and no great generalship was required to drive Longstreet back, only some stubborn fighting; he is not considered of very heavy calibre. Granger is highly thought of and is a terror to the secesh. General Hooker is a splendid soldier, and is enthusiastically admired by his small force from the Army of the Potomac; there is a superabundant vitality about him which affects all who come near him, and makes one almost believe in some subtle magnetic or electric influence. On the march, he is continually among the troops, has always a friendly nod for the men and a kind word for the officers, and is to be seen at the toughest spots with advice and encouragement. He has such a find physique, that it is a right pleasant event in a day's experience, to pass his head-quarters, and see him standing in front of his tent by the fire with his hands behind his back, he regular position. Grant I have seen to or three times, but not near enough to get any idea of his character from his phiz; he is said to be restless, full of energy and excitability, a steam-engine in pantaloons; he is in every respect boss of this Western shanty, *de jure* as well as *de facto*. Of General Howard, our Corps Commander, I don't care about speaking, except to say that he is a good and brave man, and a gentleman, but more adapted to the church than to the army.

    Since writing most of the above, a day has passed, and it is now the evening of the 20th, and my Battery is under immediate marching orders, "at a moment's notice;" General Sherman troops have come in, and I think that we are going to have a row to-morrow. I am glad that I am to be at the front of it, and hope that we shall wallop them thoroughly....I have written you a long letter, my dear boy, but you won't mind if you are as fond of long letters as I am. Very much love to the Form; persuade him that this letter is to him also, and make him answer it.

November 26, 1863
Report of Col. James Barnett, 1st Division, Artillery Reserve, 11th Army Corps
Chattanooga, TN

    Captain   I have the honor to report in regard to the positions taken by the batteries under my command, as follows:
    On the night of the 23d instant, by direction of Brigadier-General Brannan, chief of artillery, I placed in positions indicated by him the following batteries: Company C, First Ohio, Captain Gary; Cogswell's (Illinois) battery, of General Sherman's command; Company H, First Illinois, Lieutenant De Gress, of General Sherman's command; Company I, First Illinois, Lieutenant Burton, General Sherman's command; Twelfth Wisconsin Battery, Captain Zickerick; Company F, First Illinois, Captain Cheney; Company B, First Illinois, Captain Rumsey; Twenty-sixth Pennsylvania Battery, Lieutenant McDowell; Thirteenth New York Battery, Captain Wheeler; Company B, First Ohio, Lieutenant Baldwin. The batteries were moved into their several positions at 1 o'clock on the morning of the 24th, and were located as follows before day:

The locality of the pontoon bridge proposed to be laid below the mouth of Chickamauga Creek was covered by the following batteries: The Fifth Wisconsin Battery, Captain Gardner, of General Davis' division (six Napoleon guns), was placed in an epaulement, about 200 yards above the proposed crossing on the bottom land near the river bank. Company C, First Ohio, Captain Gary, six Napoleons, was posted on the bottom about 150 yards below the crossing. Cogswell's battery (four James rifles) occupied ground about 100 yards to the right of Company C, First Ohio. These guns were so placed as to perfectly cover the bridge and sweep the low ground on the opposite side of the river.

The first position below the bridge, which is a semicircular knob of an elevation of about 250 feet above the river, admirably calculated for a large field of fire, embracing the bridge crossing and all the low ground in front and well toward the right, was furnished with the following batteries: Company I, First Illinois, Lieutenant Burton, four James rifles; Company H, First Illinois, Lieutenant De Gress, four 20-pounder Parrott; Twelfth Wisconsin Battery, Captain Zickerick, four 10-pounder Parrott.

The next position was a wooded knob, somewhat higher than the last, and having a fire to the left and front, perfectly covering the ground to the left and front, and intended to repel any attack in the direction of the tunnel, and was armed by the following batteries: Company F, First Illinois, Captain Cheney, four James rifles; Company B, First Illinois, Captain Rumsey, one howitzer and five 6-pounder smooth-bore guns.

The next position to the right of the last overlooked more to the right toward Fort Wood, having also a good fire to break up any masses moving between the river and Mission Ridge, with less elevation than the other points, but perfectly protected from the fire of the enemy. On this ridge were placed the following batteries: Twenty-sixth Pennsylvania, Lieutenant McDowell, four James rifles; Thirteenth New York, Captain Wheeler, six 3-inch guns; Company B, First Ohio, Lieutenant Baldwin, six James rifles.

Before light on the morning of the 24th, the troops at the bridge were across to the number of two brigades, and at light the laying of the bridge was commenced, and completed beautifully and successfully without firing a shot. Before noon, General Sherman's troops having passed well over and taken up their position, but few shots were fired in the direction of his front, which were thrown by the 20-pounder Parrott battery, in the direction of the tunnel, with good effect. Upon General Howard moving up on the opposite side of the river, some twenty shots were fired by the lower battery down the river to break up anything in his front, by Twenty-sixth Pennsylvania Battery, Company B, First Ohio, and Thirteenth New York, the shells carrying well over our troops and exploding handsomely at the foot of Mission Ridge.

On the 25th, the advance of General Sherman, with the batteries which he had crossed over, rendered any firing from our front unnecessary, and, with the exception of two or three shots fired by Captain Cheney upon a rebel advance in the direction of the tunnel, no firing was done.

Total number of rounds of ammunition expended, about 100; no casualties.

I have to express my acknowledgments for valuable services rendered me in posting the batteries of the command, to Colonel Taylor, chief of artillery for General Sherman; also to Maj C S Cotter, commanding First Brigade, First Division, Reserve Artillery, and to Lieutenants Sturges and Sliney, who acted as my aides.

I am, captain, very respectfully,
James Barnett
Colonel, Commanding

December 5, 1863
Report of Brig. Gen. John Brannan, Chief of Artillery, Army of the Cumberland
no location given

General I have the honor to submit, for the information of the major-general commanding the department, the following report of the operations of the artillery in my charge during the recent battle of Chattanooga, November 23, 24, and 25:

With considerable difficulty, owing to the deficiency in transportation, I succeeded in getting sixteen pieces of heavy ordnance into position on the line of works, in addition to the two 30-pounder Parrott already in Fort Wood, by the 22d November--four 4 1/2-inch Rodman guns, with the two 30-pounder Parrott being in Fort Wood, on the extreme left; four 20-pounder Parrott in Fort Cheatham, and four 4 1/2-inch Rodman guns in Battery Rousseau, on the center, and four 20-pounder Parrott in Fort Sheridan, on the right.

These forts occupied prominent positions on the line, the guns commanding the rebel intrenchments at the foot of Missionary Ridge and Lookout Mountain, and sweeping the level ground in their front.

In addition to the heavy guns on the line of intrenchments, by the night of the 23d I had two 20-pounder Parrott on Moccasin Point, a point on the north side of the river, commanding the approach to Lookout Mountain and its most northern extremity. These guns, with the Tenth Indiana Battery and the Eighteenth Ohio Battery[58], under Capt W A Naylor, Tenth Indiana Battery, subsequently did good service during Hooker's assault on Lookout Mountain, rendering it impracticable for the rebels to concentrate on the north side of the mountain to resist his attack.

The Tenth Indiana and Eighteenth Ohio Batteries had previously been stationed on this point for some weeks, and had succeeded in cutting off, in a great measure, the enemy's communication with Lookout Mountain by the northern route.

I had also seven field batteries on the line, viz: C and M, First Regiment Illinois Light Artillery; M, First Regiment Ohio Artillery; F and G, First Ohio Volunteer Artillery; Sixth Ohio and Seventh Indiana Batteries[59], so arranged at the defensible points as to insure a safe retreat should the attacking line be repulsed.

On the night of the 23d, I had the following batteries placed in position on the north side of the river at four several points, to cover the crossing of General Sherman's command and prevent a force moving to oppose him until he had taken up position and established communication with our left: Company C, First Regiment Ohio Volunteer Artillery, Captain Gary; Company B, First Regiment Ohio Volunteer Artillery, Lieutenant Baldwin; Company B, First Regiment Illinois Volunteer Artillery, Captain Rumsey; Company F, First Regiment Illinois Volunteer Artillery, Captain Cheney; Company H, First Regiment Illinois Volunteer Artillery, Lieutenant De Gress; Company I, First Regiment Illinois Volunteer Artillery, Lieutenant Burton; Twenty-sixth Pennsylvania Battery, Lieutenant McDowell; Thirteenth New York Battery, Captain Wheeler; Twelfth Wisconsin Battery, Captain Zickerick; Cogswell's (Illinois) battery, Captain Cogswell. These batteries were under the direction of Col. James Barnett, First Regiment Ohio Volunteer Artillery, commanding First Division, Artillery Reserve, and Colonel Taylor, chief of artillery of General Sherman's command, and from their commanding positions were well calculated to effect the purpose for which they were intended.

Everything could have been in position by the morning of the 20th, but the contemplated attack having been postponed, it was unnecessary to make a final disposition of the guns until the night of the 22d.

At about 12 m on the 23d instant. I opened with the heavy guns from all points on the line on the rebel positions at the foot of Missionary Ridge and the east side of Lookout Mountain with some effect, in many instances driving the enemy from their camps and line of works. At 3 PM on the following day, I ordered a section of 10-pounder Parrott to be placed at the tannery commanding the valley road and Chattanooga Creek, where it subsequently did good service.

About 1 PM on the 23d, the infantry advanced, under cover of the guns, and carried the rebel rifle-pits, situated about 1½ miles to our front. Such batteries as could be mounted were immediately thrown out on Orchard Knoll, Brush Knob, and such other elevations as the country afforded.

With the assistance of General Sherman, who furnished me with horses for three batteries (the battery horses of the Department of the Cumberland having either died, or become so emaciated from starvation as to render but few of them fit for service), I had succeeded in mounting seven batteries; four, however, were only brought into action. These did excellent service during the attack of the 25th instant, as, being in easy range of the rebel intrenchments, they did considerable execution and aided materially in forcing the enemy to abandon those works.

On the 24th, Sherman crossed the river and formed a junction with Howard near Citico Creek, the batteries on the north side of the river effectually preventing any masses of troops intercepting them. It was, however, found too hazardous to endeavor to enfilade the rebel line from these batteries as was at first proposed, our troops: being in such close proximity.

During the 24th and the morning of the 25th, the guns of Forts Wood and Cheatham opened on all bodies of troops observed to be concentrating or moving on Missionary Ridge, distance 2 ½ miles; sometimes with good effect.

At about 3.30 PM on the 25th instant, the line made the advance that ultimately resulted in carrying the enemy's position. The guns from the intrenchments continued to play on the rebel line at the foot of the ridge until the proximity of our troops rendered such fire dangerous, when they turned their attention to the crest of Missionary Ridge, and made some excellent practice on the rebel troops moving on that position.

This engagement has proved beyond doubt the utter worthlessness of the projectile known as the Rodman projectile, furnished the Rod-man 4 1/2-inch guns, and unless other and better projectiles be obtained I consider that these guns will be little better than useless.

There is a radical defect in the fuses of the shells furnished this department, which I believe to originate in the inequality of their composition, rendering the explosion of the shell at the calculated time very uncertain. I have also remarked that the partitions in the fuses are very thin and liable to burst, thus causing the explosion of the shell in a shorter period than the time for which the fuse was cut. In fact, the entire practice with shell was very unsatisfactory, the shell either exploding too soon or not at all.

The following guns, carriages, caissons, limbers, ammunition, &c., were captured from the rebels during the engagement of the 24th and 25th and subsequent pursuit of the enemy:

By General Davis' division, at Chickamauga Station	24-pounder guns	2
By General Geary's division, on Lookout Mountain	field pieces.	2
By General Osterhaus' division, on Missionary Ridge	do	1
By General Wood's division, on Missionary Ridge	do	12
By General Sheridan's division, on Missionary Ridge	do	6
By General Johnson's division, at Graysville	do	4
By General Baird's division, on Missionary Ridge	do	1
Claimed by Generals Baird and Wood	do	6
Claimed by Generals Wood and Sheridan	do	6
Total		40

Carriages for light 12-pounder guns	19
Carriages for 10-pounder Parrott	4
Carriages for 6-pounder guns	8
Carriage for 3-inch gun	1
Carriages for 6-pounder James, 3.80-inch bore	3
Carriages for 12-pounder howitzers	3
Total	38

Caissons for light 12-pounder guns	17
Caissons for 10-pounder Parrott	3
Caissons for 12-pounder howitzers	3
Caissons for 6-pounder guns	3

Caisson for 3-inch gun	1
Caissons for 3.80-inch James rifle	2
Total	29

Limbers for light 12-pounder guns	13
Limbers for 10-pounder Parrott	4
Limbers for 6-pounder guns	7
Limber for 3-inch gun	1
Total	25

A good many parts of harness were also captured, but no complete sets.

	Rounds
Ammunition for 12-pounder guns	805
Ammunition for 12-pounder howitzers	283
Ammunition for 6-pounder guns	332
Ammunition for 10-pounder Parrott	216
Ammunition for 3-inch guns	57
Ammunition for 3.80-inch James rifle	151
Total	1,844

This is all that has come in up to the present time.

I am indebted to Maj J Mendenhall, assistant chief of artillery, for valuable assistance previous to and during the three days' battles. Captain Stokes, Chicago Board of Trade Battery, acting as additional aide-de-camp, had charge of the batteries on the right of the line of intrenchments, which were served under his direction with skill and effect. Capt Louis J Lambert, assistant adjutant-general, and Lieut T V Webb, aide-de-camp, of my staff, performed their duties with promptitude and to my satisfaction.

I am, general, very respectfully, your obedient servant,
J M Brannan
Brig Gen, and Chief of Arty, Dept. of the Cumberland

December 27, 1863
Battery Orders No. 47
Bridgeport, AL

I   The Captain commanding congratulates the men upon their excellent conduct upon the late march and the patience with which they endured both cold and hunger and fatigue, and the readiness which they showed when any duty was to be done. I can only say that I am proud to have such soldiers under me.

II   The winter quarters will be built as quickly as possible and as much as possible in a uniform style. I hope that this Battery will not allow their quarters to fall behind those of other Batteries in niceness and appearance.
III   The Sergeants will tent and mess together by themselves; a person will be detailed to cook for the non-commissioned officers' mess.
Wm Wheeler Capt
Comdg 13 NY Batty

December 28, 1863
Report of Maj. Gen. Oliver Howard, 11th Army Corps
Lookout Valley, TN

Captain: I have the honor to report upon the operations of this corps during the battle of Chattanooga, and during the march that followed, until its return to this camp.

In accordance with instructions received through your headquarters, the infantry, with three batteries, left this point at 1 PM. November 22, ultimo. The remaining two batteries, Wiedrich's (Battery I, First New York) and Heckman's (K, First Ohio), were left behind and established under General Hooker's directions. They participated to some extent in the glorious work of getting possession of Lookout Mountain. My original instructions contemplated placing the Eleventh Corps in reserve on the peninsula between the bridges of Brown's Ferry and Chattanooga, in order to act with General Thomas at Chattanooga or with General Sherman, as the exigencies of the battle should determine. Subsequent instructions from your headquarters, dated November 22, directed me to cross the pontoon bridge at Brown's Ferry at 2 PM of that day, and move thence to Chattanooga direct. This change, as I understand, was based on the report of the chief engineer of the department that it was practicable to re-enforce Sherman along the south bank of the Tennessee without trusting to the treacherous pontoons. The north bank of the river is high, and intermediate between the Chattanooga bridge and the point 3 miles above, selected for Sherman's crossing, is a prominent knoll in the river bank, which overlooks the broad interval on the other shore spread out between the heights of Chattanooga and Mission Ridge. The ridge springs from this interval land between the Chickamauga and the Tennessee and stretches off for miles in a southwesterly direction, leaving the Chickamauga on the left. I sent a battery (Wheeler's, Thirteenth New York) to the knoll described. He commanded all the low ground as far as his guns would reach, and, in conjunction with Fort Wood, situated on the south bank and near to Chattanooga, prevented any large force from occupying such points as might separate Sherman from the main body. My remaining force, about 6,000 strong, moved over the bridge into Chattanooga and took post to the right of Fort Wood. The rebel signal officer's report from Lookout, read by one of our officers, was that a large force, apparently a corps, had passed into Chattanooga. This, taken in connection with the fact that General Sherman's troops had been and were still passing along Lookout Valley, now in plain view and now hidden by hills, makes it probable that Bragg took my force for a part of Sherman's, and therefore was in doubt as to the principal point of attack, if, indeed, he believed yet that any attack at all was intended. Bad roads, and, perhaps, other unforeseen hindrances, delayed the march of the troops that were to operate on our left, so that Sunday night, November 22, the general movement intended for the morrow was postponed. I received the order direct from General Thomas, and also through your headquarters. My command remained during the night as posted.

Monday, November 23, deserters reported that the enemy intended to retreat, and some deserted camps visible from Fort Wood gave rise to the rumor that the retreat had begun. During the morning a reconnaissance was ordered, General Granger's corps being selected to make the movement and mine held in readiness for support.

At 1 PM, General Granger deployed to the east and south of Fort Wood, facing toward Mission Ridge. The enemy on the ridge and on the few high intermediate points were gazing on the magnificent display, and apparently without thinking that so fine a parade without any attempt at concealment was a demonstration against them.

As soon as formed, the lines moved briskly forward, driving in the enemy's outposts and taking Orchard Knob, a small hill little more than half way to the ridge, and 1 mile south from the Tennessee.

The enemy had here a small epaulement for two guns and rifle-pits. During this operation I had, by General Thomas' directions, sent a battery (Company G, Fourth Regulars) to the next height, Brush Hill, southeast of Fort Wood, nearly opposite the center of Granger's line. Afterward, during the battle this battery was moved forward to Sheridan's front line on Granger's right, having been replaced by Dilger's (Company I, First Ohio). Lieutenant Merkle, commanding the regular battery, was highly complimented for good firing.

General Grant determined to hold Orchard Knob. A creek, the Citico, having two small branches, bends around in the low ground, its general direction northwest, and flows into the Tennessee half a mile north of Fort Wood. The western branch passes near Orchard Knob.

I was directed to move up to this creek, covering the approaches to Granger's left. The land near the creek was for the most part covered with woods. Major-General Schurz with his division of infantry was ordered to take the right of this line, and General Steinwehr with his division the left. The two divisions were deployed with great promptitude. The skirmishers were more or less engaged as they advanced along the entire line, and quite briskly in Steinwehr's division. The latter had 3 killed and about 20 wounded, mainly in the Thirty-third New Jersey, here for the first time engaged, and with credit; General Schurz, 1 killed and 12 wounded.

The enemy was forced back beyond the creek, and the line occupied as directed. This ended the engagement of the first day of the battle. The troops threw up slight breastworks during the night and next morning.

From the map it will be noticed that the Atlanta railroad, passing south of Fort Wood, runs northeast nearly parallel with the river. The East Tennessee railroad, passing north of Fort Wood, crosses the other before entering the tunnel through Mission Ridge. My line cut both these roads, and its left rested just across the Citico on the river.

At 9 AM of the 24th, General Steinwehr, by my direction, moved the Seventy-third Ohio Regiment across the Citico near its mouth, which, deploying nearly at right angles to the general line, handsomely cleared our immediate front as far as the East Tennessee railroad. As there was difficulty in recrossing the creek, the regiment was halted in this position and served as a cover to a movement that shortly took place.

General Sherman had now effected a crossing of the Tennessee just below the mouth of South Chickamauga. I was directed to open communication with him by a brigade. General Steinwehr detailed Colonel Buschbeck's, which I accompanied in person, with a small escort of cavalry. Some skirmishing occurred on our right, and thinking we might meet resistance from that quarter, I had Krzyzanowski's brigade, of General Schurz' division, brought forward as a support. Very little opposition being made, the junction with Sherman was effected just as he was placing the last boat of the bridge.

Already two of his divisions had been thrown over in boats, and had covered their bridge by a line of breastworks. From this place to the north end of Mission Ridge, the distance is a mile and a half, the ground mostly low and undulating. The general pointed out the hill he should first attempt to secure. He requested me to allow Colonel Buschbeck's brigade to remain and skirmish on his right, while he advanced toward the ridge. The brigade was ordered to remain. I then returned to my corps by the route we had come. Believing Colonel Krzyzanowski could take care of his brigade, situated as he was under the cover of Wheeler's guns from the opposite shore, I concluded to leave him on the northeast side of the Citico to keep open the communication along the river with Buschbeck's brigade.

During this march, and while returning, heavy cannonading was heard in the direction of Lookout Mountain, and at 5.20 PM we were cheered with the news that General Hooker had carried the heights and secured the eastern slope of the mountain.

Dilger's (Ohio) battery had been sent to the Chattanooga Creek and fired effectively, preventing a movement of the enemy between Hooker and Palmer, and covering the building of a pontoon bridge across the creek.

Early in the morning of the 25th, I issued orders to my divisions, in accordance with General Thomas' instructions, to conform to the movements of General Sherman; as he moved forward along the ridge, I was to advance and complete my connection with him. In order to effect this, after hearing that he had reached the tunnel of the East Tennessee railroad, I directed General Steinwehr to push forward his left till it rested on this railroad, which he accomplished with very little opposition. During the whole morning, from daylight, the enemy were seen marching along the crest of Mission Ridge toward General Sherman's position.

At 9.45 AM an order was received by me to march toward General Sherman, looking out well for my right flank. An aide from General Grant urged me to hasten, as General Sherman needed re-enforcements.

At 10.45 AM my head of column arrived at the pontoon bridge, where I halted and massed my troops, starting to report in person to General Sherman. He sent me the order through Lieutenant-Colonel Meysenburg, of my staff, and afterward repeated it to me, to take post on his left, closing a space that had just been left vacant by troops that had been pushed farther to the right in support of the main attack along the ridge.

The corps was placed as directed, its left resting on Chickamauga Creek, near Boyce s Station, and its front well covered by a good line of skirmishers. The right rested high up the ridge, on a work constructed and occupied by a part of General Blair's corps. Here, again, my troops covered themselves with breastworks. The report that General Sherman had reached the tunnel was premature.

Instead of finding a continuous ridge of land, as one would suppose, looking from Chattanooga, that portion of Mission Ridge north of the East Tennessee railroad is broken into transverse ridges, with deep ravines between them. The enemy's troops had possession of the first ridge or hill north of the tunnel, on my arrival, and a fierce contest was going on between them and the attacking party for its possession.

Colonel Buschbeck's brigade, or rather a part of it, as General Steinwehr had detained two of his regiments with him, was bearing a part in this action. Having been assigned to General Ewing, this brigade went into action with that of Colonel Loomis, of Ewing's division. The conduct of the Twenty-seventh Pennsylvania, under Lieutenant-Colonel McAloon, was most highly complimented.

The main attack was along the crest of the ridge, and Colonel Loomis was trying to support it by a movement from the front. McAloon actually led his regiment up that steep acclivity, 500 or 600 feet high, under a terrific fire of grape and musketry, and stayed there till he was mortally wounded. Lieutenant-Colonel Taft behaved with equal intrepidity with the Seventy-third Pennsylvania, till he was killed. His troops drove the enemy from some buildings and held them. Subsequently, after his death, some of his company commanders culpably allowed themselves and many of their men to be taken by the enemy. It is alleged in excuse for them that they exhausted their ammunition; that Colonel Loomis left their flank exposed, and their position was turned.

General Sherman did not succeed in dislodging the enemy, but these vigorous assaults served to accumulate against us a heavy force, and thus weakened other portions of the enemy's line. It is due to the true-hearted men who nobly sacrificed their lives at this point, or who are now suffering with painful wounds, that their names and their regiments should not be overlooked. They contributed all they could to the grand result.

News arrived in the evening that General Thomas had carried Mission Ridge by direct assault, that General Hooker had moved to Rossville and got upon the enemy's left flank, and that the enemy were in full retreat.

The enemy left our front during the night. The battle of Chattanooga was over, and it was a success. The news flew like wildfire, and the Chickamauga hills echoed with our soldiers' victorious cheer.

By direction of General Sherman, about 5 AM of the 26th, the corps crossed the Chickamauga, near its mouth, by a pontoon bridge, already there, and proceeded toward Chickamauga Station, ascending the creek. At 7 AM we overtook Davis' division that had crossed in the night. The fog was so dense that you could not discern a horse at 100 yards.

General Davis reported to me on my arrival, as the senior officer. I desired him to keep the lead, and make his own dispositions. We pushed forward carefully till the fog cleared away, being delayed somewhat by reports that the enemy were moving in force toward our left.

We reached Chickamauga Station at 12 m, Davis' advance skirmishing with the enemy. Two siege guns, about 1,000 bushels of corn, 10 pontoons, and considerable flour were captured here. Large quantities of flour and corn were burning when we arrived. General Sherman joined us at this point, and the pursuit was continued.

Just before dark Davis' advance came upon the enemy's rear guard posted on the farther edge of a small opening in a forest, some 3 miles this side of Graysville. Two brigades were deployed, and soon succeeded in dislodging and driving this force. In the meantime, I had brought up my command and posted von

Steinwehr's division on Davis' right, and massed Schurz' division in reserve. We encamped at this point.

November 27, march resumed at 6 AM At Graysville I met Generals Palmer and Sherman, and learned that General Hooker's column was already on the way to Ringgold. I was directed to move on the north side of the Chickamauga, and if possible reach the railroad between Dalton and Cleveland. I found that the best practicable route on that side of the creek led through Parker's Gap, so that I marched thither. After passing the gap I detached two brigades, one from General von Steinwehr, or rather, from Colonel Buschbeck (General von Steinwehr, owing to sickness, having left us at Graysville), and another (Hecker's) from General Schurz. These brigades, and a section of Dilger's battery, under command of Col Orland Smith, marched on to the railroad.

My aide-de-camp, Maj C H Howard, with a squad of cavalry, accompanied the expedition. The remainder of Schurz' division (Tyndale's and Krzyzanowski's brigades) were moved forward 2 miles, the better to support Colonel Smith, if required.

Colonel Smith's orders were to proceed to Red Clay, destroy as much as he could of the railroad, and, if possible, return the same night. This work was done, and well done. A rebel officer, having dispatches from Kelly's cavalry division at Cleveland to Bragg, and a few other prisoners were captured. Some 3 miles of railroad track were torn up, the sleepers burned, and the rails bent by the fire; 3 cars and the depot building were destroyed. The brigades then returned to Parker's Gap, reporting to their commands between 12 and 1 at night. They had made a continuous march of 27 miles, besides this extra work at the railroad.

This operation prevented, for the present, the possibility of Longstreet joining Bragg by railroad, and it equally prevented the passage of any re-enforcements from Bragg to Longstreet.

The pursuit of the enemy had now ended. We had in possession about a hundred prisoners gathered on the march. The next morning the order was issued that the corps should rest one day, and afterward return to Chattanooga. That afternoon General Sherman made known to me that General Grant had instructed him to move to the Hiwassee to operate against Longstreet. He wanted his entire column, and issued orders to me accordingly, designating the route I should take. The rest of the day and night was, therefore, spent in preparation.

Wagons belonging to the different brigades were on the road, many of them stuck in the mud, all the way from Parker's Gap to the mouth of the Chickamauga. As the command was short of rations the wagons had to be brought up before the next morning. By extraordinary exertions this was done, and three days' rations distributed.

One battery and all of the wagons, except the ammunition, were sent back to Chattanooga.

November 29, the corps marched from Parker's Gap to Cleveland, 20 miles. A company of 60 rebel cavalry in Cleveland and its immediate vicinity escaped toward Dalton as we approached. The rebel provost-marshal, Captain Henly, was captured.

November 30, the corps marched to Charleston, on the Hiwassee. On learning of our approach a company of rebel cavalry, about 300 infantry, and several wagons left toward Athens. We found the pontoon bridge broken, swung around, and many of the boats stove and others rapidly floating down stream, the railroad bridge partially destroyed, the stringers having been sawed off, and two of the trestles thrown down. A detachment of rebels on the opposite bank were trying to destroy three cars loaded with stores, whereupon Wheeler, with a section of his battery, opened fire and drove them off. From these cars we subsequently obtained some two days' rations of flour and seven or eight days' of salt, and a quantity of spikes, which came in play in repairing the bridge. Several boats were rescued by Col Orland Smith, by which he crossed a regiment immediately. During the rest of the day and the following night the railroad bridge was repaired, planked over, and rendered passable for artillery and wagons..

December 1, the crossing commenced at 5 AM We arrived at Athens by 4 PM, and encamped about 2 miles beyond; march for the day, 14 miles. Here we heard the report that Longstreet had attacked Burnside at Knoxville and been repulsed on Sunday, November 29.

December 2, the corps left camp at 5.30 AM, for Philadelphia and Loudon. About 3 miles this side of Sweet Water the advance came upon a detachment of the enemy's cavalry. As soon as the infantry skirmishers approached within musket range the cavalry would leave. We kept them in sight till we arrived at Sweet Water, at which place we were directed by Major-General

Sherman to make a halt in order to allow Colonel Long with his cavalry to pass us. This small brigade of cavalry was instructed to move forward and make a dash into Loudon with a view to save the enemy's pontoon bridge and stores at that point. I was directed to follow Colonel Long and give him support in case he needed it. We marched to within about 3 miles of Loudon, having made that day 23 miles, when it became dark. The roads were too bad, and the command too weary to proceed farther that night. A section of Wheeler's battery was sent forward to Colonel Long at his request.

December 3, we broke camp at 4 AM and marched for Loudon. Colonel Long's cavalry was about 2 miles from town. His advance picket not nearer than 1 mile. On his approach the evening before, the enemy had opened upon him with artillery, so that he deemed it prudent not to make the dash. On entering the town, we found that the rebel General Vaughn's command, consisting of a small brigade of infantry, artillery, and a detachment of cavalry had evacuated, having destroyed from 60 to 75 cars containing supplies of commissary stores, clothing, and ammunition, 3 locomotives, and, finally, their pontoon bridge. The railroad bridge at Loudon, previously burned, had not been rebuilt. The stone piers were standing. The main channel of the Tennessee is between the Loudon shore and the first pier. We found this channel completely filled with the rubbish of locomotives, cars and their contents, which had been set on fire before being run into the river.

Notwithstanding this wholesale destruction of property, there was distributed among the inhabitants and stored in warehouses a sufficient quantity of rebel provisions to feed my command for three days; this after leaving sufficient for the rebel wounded, captured in hospital at Loudon, about 75 in number. These were a part of Longstreet's wounded from his unsuccessful assault at Knoxville on the Sunday previous.

There were two redoubts upon the heights on the west side of Loudon, one of which was located upon a position of natural strength, and made to face southward: the other was nearer the river and facing toward it. One of my batteries was located in the latter, and on the appearance of some squads of rebel cavalry upon the opposite bank, opened fire. Considerable artillery firing was allowed in accordance with instructions, in the hope that the guns might be heard by General Burnside at Knoxville, and he thus be made aware of the approach of re-enforcements.

Off against the redoubts the river makes a sudden bend, forming a peninsula. The road leading to the rebel pontoon bridge passes across this peninsula, making the bridge about three-fourths of a mile from town by land and 6 by water.

One incident occurred at Loudon which made a strong impression upon my mind. Along the entire route from Parker's Gap to Loudon we were cheered by the most lively demonstrations of loyalty on the part of inhabitants. Therefore we never lacked for information as to roads, bridges, fords, location of the enemy, &c.

But here a man, who had been a major in the rebel service and resigned, came to me and without laying any claim to loyalty, stated that he had drifted with the current, but since our recent victory was satisfied that Tennessee would resume her place in the Union. He gave me information so accurate that I was able to sketch the works at Knoxville and the enemy's position. He also gave me the enemy's strength, with the names of the officers commanding at different points, all of which proved to be substantially correct.

The next day Colonel Hecker, commanding Third Brigade, Third Division, sent a regiment across the Tennessee, which skirmished with the enemy's cavalry and took possession of four rifled guns, which General Vaughn had been compelled to abandon. They also captured a rebel flag.

I must not omit to mention about thirty rebel wagons that the enemy had partially destroyed by cutting the spokes of the wheels. In anticipation of crossing the Little Tennessee at Davis' Ford, I set a detachment at work to repair these wagons sufficiently to enable their transportation to the ford, 6 miles, and to construct from them a bridge suitable for infantry.

I found that there were not enough wagons to stretch across the river, a distance of upwards of 750 feet, and therefore made movable trestles to complete the bridge. It had been hitherto understood that my command was to march to Morganton, to cross a bridge in process of construction by General Blair, my corps to cross in rear of General Blair. Finding that this would not only occasion a loss of time, but greatly increase the distance to be marched by my command, I obtained permission from General Sherman to make the bridge, as indicated, at Davis' Ford. The captured wagons were loaded with plank from the depot, and by 6 PM the bridge was commenced.

Colonel Boughton with his regiment, One hundred and forty-third New York Volunteers, cheerfully undertook the work. Other plank were procured from neighboring barns, the loyal people not only cheerfully consenting, but lending a helping hand in the work. While at Loudon we heard of a raid in our rear upon Charleston by rebel cavalry. Nothing reliable from Burnside yet. My corps marched at 1 am, and reached Davis' Ford in time to begin the crossing at daylight. The bridge, thrown obliquely across, more than 1,000 feet long, was completed in season, two-thirds or more made of wagons with connecting planks, the remainder of light trestle work. The horses, artillery, and wagons crossed simultaneously by the ford.

While at Loudon, an order was received from Major-General Sherman, announcing that his army would be commanded as follows: The right wing, General F P Blair; center, Maj Gen Gordon Granger; left wing, by myself, and that the different commanders would act independently and on the offensive, marching to the support of each other at the sound of the guns. My corps reached Louisville, Tenn, by dark, having made above 20 miles.

At Unitia, we learned that a courier, passing that morning with dispatches from General Burnside, said that Longstreet was beginning his retreat. This was the first positive information of the fact received by me.

At Louisville I saw a boy just from Knoxville, who said Longstreet was in full retreat. This boy, son of a loyal citizen, had carried through to General Burnside dispatches which his father, then with Colonel Byrd at Kingston, had succeeded with the help of a sister in forwarding from the latter place. The sister traveled some 18 miles, through a country occupied by the enemy, and crossed the Tennessee in the night. We learned that Longstreet's retreat commenced the day before, and that there had been some rebel cavalry hovering about Louisville until the day of our arrival. My command was allowed to rest the following day.

Sunday, December 6, in person I visited Knoxville, where I met Major-General Sherman, and received instructions to commence the return march on the morrow. It was decided that General Granger's corps should remain as re-enforcement to General Burnside, in accordance with the first plan and order of Major-General Grant, which had designated General Granger's command to move to the relief of Knoxville. Besides the fact that my corps was, to a large extent, without tents, one or two brigades without blankets, and nearly all either suffering from bad shoes or entirely destitute of shoes, having turned directly from the pursuit of Bragg, without going back for anything, these considerations made it advisable that we return as soon as possible to our camps, now that the pressing necessity was over. On the march back the commissaries generally preceded the corps, and seizing the mills notified the inhabitants to bring in wheat and corn, which they purchased and ground in readiness for distribution on the arrival of their respective brigades. The mills were kept running night and day. The salt captured at Charleston on the way up lasted till our return to the same place. By means of this we were able to make use of the cattle and sheep of the country, which were sufficient for our purpose. The region of our march also abounded in sorghum or home-made molasses, which was purchased in quantity and issued to the troops. This was found a suitable substitute for sugar. For coffee, wheat in the grain was issued.

No complaint of want of food came to my ears.

The loyal inhabitants were no less demonstrative on our return than on our march up. One lamentable fact came under my observation: the habit of depredations upon the property of citizens prevailing among certain portions of our army, too little checked by officers. Instances of great outrage came to my knowledge, and of suffering on account of such misconduct by the troops, even among people of undoubted loyalty.

While called upon through necessity to impress supplies, I ordered proper receipts in all cases to be given, and restrained theft by the severest sanctions.

We returned, by comparatively easy marches, recrossing the bridge of wagons at Davis' Ford.

At Athens a halt was made, by direction of General Sherman, except that one brigade, Colonel Hecker's, was sent forward to Charleston to repair the bridge and hold it.

The cavalry guard, on hearing of the approach of the enemy, had abandoned the Charleston Bridge and fled. It was, however, only partially destroyed by the enemy, so that Colonel Hecker repaired it again in a couple of days.

General Sherman had located Davis' division abreast of Hecker's, farther up the river at Columbus, thus threatening to move down the old Federal road past Bragg's right, while the rest of his force was in the vicinity of Tellico Plains, for the purpose of supporting Colonel Long's cavalry, which had gone in pursuit of one of Longstreet's trains, through Murphy, NC.

Supplies were expected by the river to Cotton Port, and I was directed to impress wagons, and have the stores brought to Athens, with a view to a concentration at that point, but by mistake no supplies were landed there.

As soon as Colonel Long returned, the march was continued to Chattanooga. At Cleveland my troops were cheered by the arrival of a day's rations of hard bread and coffee, which I had arranged to have meet me at that place.

My corps, followed by Davis' division, passed through McDaniel's Gap.

The road was execrable, a third of the men without proper clothing, very many barefooted, and now a heavy rain added to the discomforts and difficulties of the march. Yet our devoted soldiers toiled on without complaint.

We arrived at our old camp in Lookout Valley, December 17.

The corps had endured the extreme fatigue of a three days' battle, engaged in the pursuit for two days, effectively destroyed the railroad communication between Longstreet and Bragg, and then turned northward, and made a march of 120 miles, to the relief of Burnside, and then immediately returned to its old camp; and when we consider that this was accomplished under such unfavorable circumstances as wretched roads, no transportation, few blankets and tents, with rivers to cross without bridge trains, and supplies to be collected from the country, why may we not speak of our soldiers, with pride, as equal to any in the world?

I wish to commend my division and brigade commanders for the energy and constancy they manifested during this campaign. More than I can express is due to the untiring efforts of the different members of my staff. Lieutenant-Colonel Asmussen, assistant inspector-general, evinced his usual activity and ability. Lieutenant-Colonel Meysenburg, assistant adjutant-general; Maj C H Howard, aide-de-camp, Captain Stinson, aide-de-camp, and Captain Pearson (Seventeenth Infantry), commissary of musters, were, as heretofore, fearless in action, and ever ready on the march to do everything required of them without flagging. Major Hoffmann, my engineer, gave me great assistance. The medical director, Surg D G Brinton, US Volunteers, aided by Surg Robert Hubbard, medical inspector, and Captain Rowe, chief of ambulances, relieved me from all care regarding the sick.

Captain Scofield, assistant provost-marshal, and Lieutenants Gilbreth, Palmer, and Wickham, deserve mention for their cheerfulness and alacrity in duty by day and night.

My chief of scouts and road engineer, E H Kirlin, rendered valuable service. Lieutenant-Colonel Long, Seventy-third Ohio, in the different towns through which we passed, acting as provost-marshal, was untiring in his exertions to preserve order.

Herewith you will find a nominal list of the killed and wounded in this corps at the battle of Chattanooga, and a map of the positions.

Respectfully,
O O Howard
Major-General

December 31, 1863
Battery Orders No. 48
Bridgeport, AL

Corporal Trafford is hereby appointed Sergeant in the 13th New York Battery vice H. Tintenfass promoted to rank from Sept 1, 1863. He will be obeyed and respected accordingly.
Wm Wheeler Capt
Comdg 13 NY Batty

January 1, 1864
Battery Orders No. 49
Bridgeport, AL

The larger portion of the non-commissioned officers of this Battery having been mustered out of service in order to be mustered in again as Veterans and it having been necessary for them to be mustered in as privates, the following reappointments are made:
Prvt Henry Tintenfass to be 1st Sergeant with rank from Sept 1 1863
" Edward Baldwin to be QM Sergeant with from July 13 1863
" William H Garrett to be Sergeant with rank from Nov 8 1862
" Christian Gutbrad to be Sergeant with rank from Dec 26 1862
" Ernest Volmer to be Sergeant with rank from January 22 1863
" James When to be Sergt from Febr 28 1863
" John O'Connor to be Sergt from Sept 1 1863
" Edward Trafford to be Sergt from Sept 1 1863
" Frederick A Nort to be Corp from Jan 27 1862

"   James Lynch to be Corp from Nov 1 1862
"   Deidrich Funk to be Corp from Nov 1 182
"   John Lewis to be Corp from March 1 1863
"   William Boe to be Corp from July 1 1863

Corporals John A Rush, Charles Bonner and William Suckendick not having been mustered out will retain their former ranks without any reappointment.

Private James Eskdale is hereby appointed Corporal in 13th New York Battery from January 1, 1864

Each and everyone of these non-commissioned officers will be obeyed and respected accordingly.

Privates [name not readable] and Adams appointed Artificers, Private Brown and [name not readable], Blacksmiths, Privates Roller and Weisheimer, Bugler, all to date from original appointments.

Wm Wheeler Capt
Comdg 13 NY Batty

January 5, 1864
Report of Maj. Thomas Osborn, Chief of Artillery, 11th Army Corps
Bridgeport, AL

Colonel I have the honor to report the part borne by the artillery of this command in the engagements of the 23d, 24th, and 25thNovember, near Chattanooga, and the march toward Knoxville, Tenn.

The batteries of this command are:
Second Division: I, First New York Artillery, Capt M Wiedrich; G, Fourth US Artillery, Lieut C F Merkle.
Third Division: I, First Ohio Artillery, Capt H Dilger; Thirteenth New York (Independent), Capt W Wheeler; K, First Ohio Artillery, Lieut N Sahm.

My instructions, as received from Major-General Howard, were to leave the batteries of Captain Wiedrich and Lieutenant Sahm in the valley to assist Major-General Hooker, if required, and to take a sufficient number of horses from these batteries to fully equip the remaining three batteries; to direct Captain Wheeler to report to General Brannan, chief of artillery of the Army at Chattanooga, for assignment to protect the troops of General Sherman in crossing the Tennessee River above the town. Captain Dilger and Lieutenant

Merkle were to accompany the corps to Chattanooga. These dispositions were made as directed on the 22d.

On the afternoon of the 23d, by direction of General Howard, I placed the battery of Lieutenant Merkle on a slight eminence on the left of General Sheridan's division, and reported to General Sheridan for orders. I also placed Captain Dilger on the right of the same division. This division at the time was being moved forward with the main line of battle. A few shots were fired by Lieutenant Merkle this PM

On the morning of the 24th he was moved forward, taking position with the main line of battle, and occasionally, when circumstances appeared to require, fired a few shots, generally with good effect. On the 25th, he again opened about noon, clearing the ground for an advance of the division. A little later moved forward with the advanced infantry, and from the outset of the charge by which Mission Ridge was carried he did fine work, by assisting materially to clear the enemy from their trenches and disturbing their fire greatly while our troops were climbing the hill.

The position to which Captain Dilger had been assigned unfortunately did not admit of his taking an active part, his position being such as to cover a plain over which it was feared the enemy would attempt to reach our rear.

Early in the morning, on the 24th, Captain Wheeler took position, under the immediate direction of Major Cotter, near and a little below the crossing of General Sherman. He was only required to fire about 20 rounds at long range, the enemy not massing sufficiently near his position. Colonel Barnett, of the Ohio artillery, in command of all the artillery at this position, speaks of Captain Wheeler's practice and evident good judgment.

Captain Wiedrich, in command of the batteries in the valley, engaged his batteries in the advance of General Hooker at the capture of Lookout Mountain, his own battery remaining as when the corps left the valley, on the range of hills running parallel to and between Lookout and the valley below. Lieutenant Sahm's battery he placed on the crest between his position and the creek, and by this means gained an admirable cross-fire with batteries placed on the same range to their right. In the attack on the mountain they are reported to have done good service. Generals Hooker, Butterfield, and Osterhaus have spoken of their practice as excellent.

On the 26th, Lieutenant Sahm's battery was moved to Rossville with General Hooker's column and left at that point. On the same day Captain Dilger, Captain Wheeler, and Lieutenant Merkle reported to the corps then at Chickamauga Station. On the 27th, at Graysville, Captain Wheeler and Lieutenant Merkle were ordered to report to General Hooker at Ringgold. Both batteries again reported to the corps on the 28th, at Parker's Gap, not being engaged during this absence. A gun carriage of Captain Wheeler broke down on the march, and, being unable to repair the carriage, the captain sent the gun to his camp in the valley in a wagon. Captain Dilger accompanied the corps from Graysville to Red Clay on the 27th, and on the 28th returned to Parker's Gap.

Expecting the corps to move to Lookout Valley, the general directed me to move Lieutenant Merkle's battery at the head of the column, and, by reason of a separation at this moment, I did not participate in the trip to Knoxville. Having reached the valley, I brought the three batteries to their former camp and did what I could to again fit them for service.

Captain Dilger and Captain Wheeler accompanied the corps to Knoxville. Captain Wheeler reports having used his battery upon the enemy at the crossing of Hiwassee River, and again at the Tennessee River, opposite Loudon. I have received no report of Captain Dilger of this march. On the 20th December, the batteries returned to their old camp in the valley. It is a gratification to say that during these operations not one artillery officer or man was lost or injured, and everywhere officers and men did well. The artillery practice was everywhere good. The command lost very largely in horses.

When the corps moved from its camp on the 22d the horses were greatly reduced, both by the long passage from Virginia to this place and by starvation in the valley. I could then only horse three batteries indifferently. The roads over which we marched were very bad; much of the time we could get no forage either from the depots or in the country. The horses were continually giving out from exhaustion and want of food. Captain Wheeler and Captain Dilger report that they were unable to move with the column to and from Knoxville without impressing a considerable number of horses and mules in the country. Under the circumstances I think each battery did all that could be expected of it.

I regret the artillery of the corps could not have remained with the corps and fought in the principal engagement with it. It being, as it was, distributed through the army, it could gain little or no credit of its own, as all it may have earned would naturally be claimed by and accredited to the commanding officer of the troops with which it was serving during the engagement. The losses were confined to the loss of horses and ordnance property, a considerable amount of which was rendered unfit for further service.

I am, colonel, respectfully, your obedient servant,
Thos Ward Osborn
Major and Chief of Artillery, Eleventh Corps

Letter of William Wheeler
Bridgeport, AL

From the effects of the battles at Chattanooga, and the ensuing forced march to Knoxville and back, I have hardly recovered yet, even bodily, although it is nearly a fortnight since I rolled into my bed here, after a twenty-mile gallop, quite used up.

You must not lose track of me because I am so far off; in this army we experience lack of everything which we used to have so abundantly in the Army of the Potomac; but while we sand being docked of our nice little supplies and winter comforts, we cannot stand being put on half rations of letters, and we shall get entirely uncivilized in this howling wilderness of Hoosiers, Buckeyes, Suckers, and Wolverines, unless you give us occasional glimpses of our dear Eastern home, and tell us that we are not entirely forgotten there.

My Battery has reenlisted under the Veteran Volunteer arrangement, and goes in for three years more, from the 1st of January, 1864; this movement was almost unanimous, almost every man reenlisting, and that when their feet were still bleeding and their bones still aching from the exposures and fatigues of the Knoxville march. We shall be mustered in, in a day or two, and then the Battery will probably go to New York on a thirty-day's furlough and to recruit. I shall not accompany them if I can possible help it, as I could hardly bear the journey, and my health is greatly in need of a little rest; besides, I have a perfect horror of recruiting, and all its accompaniments. So now I am in for it until 1867, unless the world comes to an end in 1865, according to ---[60]

and Dr Cummings, or some kindly shell or bullet gives me earlier relief. Don't think, from this, that I am low-spirited, or "down on my luck;" I am only half heart-broken about the state of the country now, and the state it must be in for a long time to come. The end and object of the war are most righteous and proper, and its final results will, after the lapse of years, be beneficial to all parties, and will aid the plan of Providence in teaching and elevating the nation, but all that does not shut my eyes to the terrible miseries which daily come to my notice. "Battle, murder, and sudden death," I can stand well enough; but the disruption of families, the destruction of homesteads, the closing of school-houses and churches, the starving of the people by subsisting large armies on the country, the emigration of hundreds of houseless wanderers, who, not long ago, were prosperous farmers, the disregard of all civil claims, and the treading down of the "Common Law" under the heel of "Army Regulations,--" all this must be piteously painful to any one who calls himself a citizen of the United States; and equally so to me, although I have been often compelled to commit, in the line of duty, what I should once have called great outrages.

The country around Athens, Sweetwater, and Mouse Creek was a farmer's paradise; it looked lovely even in the middle of December, with its broad corn-lands and wheat fields, sugar-cane and cotton plant, and warm, delicious sun-light over all, undisturbed by winds or storms,--like the island valley of the Avilion, "deep-meadowed, happy, fair with orchard-lawns;" the very names, Sweetwater, Mouse Creek, speak of everything plentiful and quiet and cozy. Many pleasant Union demonstrations were made along the route; in some places really superb national flags, which the ladies had wrought with their own hands, and kept hidden from rebel eyes by many a cunning device, were given to the winds, and were accompanied by waving of handkerchiefs and by hearty greeting, to which the passing of troops responded with roaring cheers. In some places the women jumped up and down with joy, and shouted "Hurrah for *our* side," which told a tale of the time when the *other* side had been uppermost, and those good people had suffered.

Sometimes this display of patriotism was prompted by mixed motives, as thus; the Battery was passing a house, at the door of which stood a woman, and on the opposite side of the road was walking a fat rooster; already a cannoneer had marked him for his own, and was *a la* David drawing a fatal *bead* on him with a "smooth pebble from the brook," when the old lady perceived the imminent danger of the bird, and determined to make a diversion in his favor; waving her hand, she exclaimed, as the swallow-tailed US guidon was just passing, "Hurrah for that dear old flag! it does my eyes good to see it again." The diversion was successful, at least as far as we were concerned, and I am sure that the carcass of that rooster did *not* adorn the camp-kettles of the Thirteenth New York Battery.

January 7, 1864
Report of Capt. William Wheeler, 13th New York Battery
Bridgeport, AL

Sir I have the honor to report the following with regard to the part taken by the Thirteenth Independent New York Battery in the battles of November 24 and 25, 1863, at Missionary Ridge, and in the arduous marches which succeeded them:

On November 22, I received 14 horses, harnessed, from Battery I, First New York, and 13 horses, without harness, from Battery K, First Ohio, and moved my battery with the corps across the first pontoon at Brown's Ferry; there I was detached from the corps and ordered by you to report to Colonel Barnett, First Ohio; this I did, and was placed by him under command of Major Cotter, First Ohio. I moved that same evening about 2 miles up the river, but did not take position.

Early on the morning of the 24th, before daybreak, I moved my battery farther up the river, and placed it in position, under Major Cotters directions, on the extreme right flank of the line of batteries covering General Sherman's crossing. This position was close to the right bank of the Tennessee River, and commanded the whole river bottom and the woods at the foot of the slope of Missionary Ridge.

At about 10 AM I fired twenty shots, by order of Major Cotter, to get the range, and also to dislodge some bodies of the enemy who were concealed there. Later in the day the troops of our corps advanced up the river bottom. I fired several shots in advance of them to drive away a line of rebel skirmishers; I ceased firing when my guns were masked by the column. During the 25th, the combat was too distant for our batteries to take any part in it.

I did not receive the order to report back to the corps until 12 m on the 26th; I then immediately crossed the Tennessee and the Chickamauga Creek, and pushed on as well as I could, the road being filled by the troops of General Sherman's corps. The next day (27th) I followed the corps as far as Graysville, where I was ordered by General Howard to march to Ringgold, which I did. On the march to Ringgold the axle of one of my guns broke, and I was obliged to abandon the carriage, as there was no forge with me; the gun I brought along, slung under the limber.

From Ringgold I marched to Parker's Gap, where I was ordered by General Howard to report to Colonel Buschbeck, commanding Second Division, Eleventh Army Corps. I continued under his command during the remainder of the march.

The roads from Parker's Gap were in very bad condition, and I had much trouble in moving my battery toward Cleveland, as my horses were extremely exhausted; I was consequently compelled to press horses from the country, giving conditional receipts for the same; and this course I was obliged to pursue more or less upon the whole march; sometimes taking mules as well as horses. I have memoranda of all animals taken and receipted for in this manner, and am prepared to account for them.

Our march lay from Cleveland to Charleston, where we crossed the Hiwassee River, thence to Athens, Sweet Water, Philadelphia, and Loudon; crossed the Little Tennessee to Unitia, and so to Louisville. Our line of march returning was the same, except that we went direct from the Little Tennessee to Philadelphia, and crossed the mountains at Cleveland instead of Parker's Gap.

At Charleston, by order of General Howard, I brought two pieces into position, and drove away a party of rebels on the other side of the Hiwassee River, who were trying to remove commissary and ordnance stores from cars left on the track. I used for the most part Hotchkiss percussion shell, which exploded extremely well. I also fired a few rounds across the Tennessee at Loudon, by order of General Howard.

I reached Lookout Valley on the 20th of December. The mules which I had pressed were all turned over to Lieutenant-Colonel Hayes, chief quartermaster, Eleventh Corps.

My losses and expenditures were as follows: Men, none; horses, 24; ammunition, 50 Schenkl percussion, 50 Hotchkiss case, 10 Hotchkiss percussion--110 rounds.

I am happy to be able to speak in high terms of the excellent behavior of my men on this forced march, and their soldierly endurance of fatigue and exposure, and sometimes of hunger.

Lieut H Miller was constantly on duty, and always did his duty' well.

The above is respectfully submitted.

I have the honor to be, your obedient servant,
Wm Wheeler
Captain, Commanding Thirteenth New York Battery

January 14, 1865
Charges and Specifications against 1st Lt. Henry Bundy, 13th New York Battery
Lookout Valley, TN

The Court met pursuant to adjournment.
Present:
Lieut Col Lloyd
Major Clauherty
Captain Higgins
Captain Jewett
Captain Schmidt
And present also the Judge Advocate
Absent:
Captain Hall

The court then proceeded to the trail of Henry Bundy, 13th New York Independent Battery and Acting Assistant Quartermaster and Acting Commissary of Subsistence of the Artillery 11th Corps Army of the Cumberland, who was called into the court and having heard the orders, convening the court read, was asked if he had any objection to any member present. To this he replied in the negative.

The court and the Judge Advocate were then duly sworn in the presence of the accused. The accused was then arraigned on the following charged and specifications.

Charge I- Drunkenness while on Duty

Specification- In this that he the said 1st Lieutenant Henry Bundy, 13th New York Independent Battery and Acting Assistant Quartermaster and Commissary of Subsistence of the Artillery, 11th Corps, Army of the Cumberland, did, while on duty, and while the said artillery 11th Corps was being loaded on board the cars at Alexandria, Virginia for shipment to the Department of the Cumberland, became so drunk as to entirely unfit him for duty.

This at Alexandria, State of Virginia on or about the 26th and 27th days of September 1863.

Charge 2nd- Neglect of Duty

Specification 1st- In this that he the said 1st Lieutenant Henry Bundy, 13th New York Independent Battery and Acting Assistant Quartermaster and Acting Commissary of Subsistence of the artillery 11th Corps did, remain away from his command, the said artillery of the 11th Corps and his commanding officer, Major Osborn Chief of Artillery of 11th Corps during the 26th and 27th days of September 1863 while the several batteries of the said artillery 11th Corps were waiting at the railroad depot in Alexandria, Virginia for cars for the transportation of the said artillery of the 11th Corps from Alexandria, Virginia to the Department of the Cumberland and did not render any assistance whatever in obtaining cars for the transportation of the said artillery or anything pertaining thereto, or in the loading of any part of the same, and he the said 1st Lieutenant Henry Bundy did neglect to proportion and turn over to the several battery commanders of the same artillery (14) fourteen car loads of forage, that he had drawn for the subsistence of the artillery animals on the route from Alexandria, Virginia to the Department of the Cumberland, making it necessary for his commanding officer, the said Major T W Osborn and other officers of the command to assume his duties in securing cars for the transportation of the command, the said artillery of the 11th Corps also proportioning and turning over to the several battery commanders (14) fourteen car loads of forage and procuring transportation for the same. He the said 1st Lieutenant Henry Bundy being absent from his command and his commanding officer and the neighborhood of the said command and did neglect to report to his commanding officer, the said Major T W Osborn or render him any assistance while he, the said Major T W Osborn was in the discharge of duties belonging to him, the said 1st Lieutenant Henry Bundy, who failed to report to or show himself to his commanding officer, the said Major T W Osborn, during the 26th and 27th days of September 1863 at which time he, the said Lieutenant Henry Bundy, appeared at the railroad depot where the said artillery was being loaded on board of the cards under the superintendence of the said Major T W Osborn, he the said Lieutenant Henry Bundy being at the time in a beastly state of intoxication.

This at Alexandria, Virginia on or about the 26th and 27th days of September 1863

Specification 2nd - In this that the said 1st Lieutenant Henry Bundy, 13th New York Independent Battery and Acting Assistant Quartermaster and Acting Commissary of Subsistence of the Artillery, 11th Army Corps did neglect his duties in connection with his command the said artillery of the 11th Corps from the time it left Alexandria, Virginia on the morning of the 28th day of September 1863 until it arrived in Nashville, Tennessee on the morning of the 7th day of October 1863 and did remain in Alexandria, Virginia until after his entire command, the said artillery of the 11th Corps, and his commanding officer, the said Major T W Osborn, had left for the Department of the Cumberland, without knowledge or consent of his commanding officer, the said Major T W Osborn, and he the said 1st Lieutenant Henry Bundy did travel alone and apart from his command and commanding officer from Alexandria, Virginia to Nashville, Tennessee on passenger trains, passing and avoiding his command, the said artillery of the 11th Corps and his commanding officer, the said Major T W Osborn, and did fail to stop at the various points, where the said artillery was reshipped, and did neglect to provide in the least respect for the wants and comfort of the men and animals of the said artillery, at the different points of reshipment on the route; and did also neglect to apply for or assist his commanding officer, the said Major T W Osborn, in securing transportation for the said artillery on the route from Alexandria, Virginia to Nashville, Tennessee and he, the said Lieutenant Henry Bundy, did neglect to contribute in the least respect to the welfare of the command, the said artillery of the 11th Corps, or assist his commanding officer, the said Major T W Osborn, in any of the various duties connected with the movement of the command, during the entire journey from Alexandria, Virginia to Nashville, Tennessee and did also fail to report or subject himself to the orders of his commanding officer, the said Major T W Osborn, and keeping him ignorant of his whereabouts from the time the said artillery left Alexandria, Virginia on the morning of the 28th day of September 1863 until the morning of the 7th day of October 1863 at which time the said 1st Lieutenant Henry Bundy was overtaken by his commanding officer, the said Major T W

Osborn, Chief of Artillery of the 11th Corps at Nashville, Tennessee, where he had been stopped by Lieutenant Colonel C H Asmussen, Chief of Staff of the 11th Corps.

All this on the route between Alexandria, Virginia and Nashville, Tennessee, on or about the time between the morning of the 28th day of September 1863 and the morning of the 7th day of October 1863

Charge 3rd - Disobedience of Orders

Specification 1st - In this that he the said 1st Lieutenant Henry Bundy, 13th New York Independent Battery and Acting Assistant Quartermaster of the Artillery of the 11th Corps, being in his camp in Lookout Valley, Tennessee, was, on the 27th day of November 1863 notified by a communication from his commanding officer, Major T W Osborn, Chief of Artillery of the 11th Corps, who with said artillery was moving to the front with the army in pursuit of the retreating enemy, that at Chickamauga Station, Tennessee, was a large amount of corn which the enemy had abandoned, said artillery being at the time in the vicinity of said Chickamauga Station, Tennessee and moving to the front. Said communication from Major T W Osborn notifying said 1st Lieutenant Henry Bundy of the existence of corn at said Chickamauga Station was accompanied by an order from the said Major T W Osborn to said 1st Lieutenant Henry Bundy requiring him to proceed at once to said station with all the available transportation of the said artillery of the 11th Corps and take possession of as much of said corn as in his, the said 1st Lieutenant Henry Bundy's, opinion the immediate necessities of the animals of the said artillery required, said order further directing him, the said 1st Lieutenant Henry Bundy, to supply the animals of said artillery at that time in an advance position at the front, with a sufficient amount of the grain thus procured at Chickamauga Station, to fill the immediate requirements of said animals, they being in an exceedingly reduced condition occasioned by the want of a proper amount of forage, said grain at Chickamauga Station being the only immediate resource for feeding the said artillery animals. The said 1st Lieutenant Henry Bundy, 13th New York Independent Battery and Acting Assistant Quartermaster of the Artillery of the 11th Corps having received said order from his commanding officer, the said Major T W Osborn, Chief of Artillery of the 11th Corps did disobey said order and did not comply therewith in the least particulars, but did remain in his camp failing to take possession of or furnish any of said grain to the animals of the said artillery as directed by his commanding officer, the said Major T W Osborn, Chief of Artillery of the 11th Corps and did fail to furnish his commanding officer with any reason whatever for the noncompliance of said order.

All this at or near Lookout Valley, Tennessee on or about the 27th day of November 1863.

Specification 2nd- In this that he the said 1st Lieutenant Henry Bundy, 13th New York Independent Battery and Acting Assistant Quartermaster and Acting Commissary of Subsistence of the Artillery of the 11th Corps having been ordered by his commanding officer, Major T W Osborn, Chief of Artillery of the 11th Corps to haul the guns and caissons of Battery "I" 1st New York Artillery with his, the said 1st Lieutenant Henry Bundy's, mules from the camp of said battery in Lookout Valley, Tennessee to Kelly's Ferry, Tennessee for the purpose of shipping said battery by boat to Bridgeport, Alabama did disobey said order and did refuse to Captain Wiedrich commanding, said Battery "I" 1st New York Artillery the use of his mules in violation of the orders of his commanding officer.

All this at the camp of the 11th Corps Army of the Cumberland in Lookout Valley, Tennessee, on or about the 15th day of December 1863.

To which charge and specification the accuse pleads as follows:

    To the specification of the first charge: Not Guilty
    To the first charge: Not Guilty
    To the first specification of the second charge: Not Guilty
    To the second specification of the second charge: Not Guilty
    To the second charge: Not Guilty
    To the first specification of the third charge: Not Guilty
    To the second specification of the third charge: Not Guilty

Before arraignment the accused had asked permission to introduce Lieut Col Allen of the 154th New York Vols[61] as his counsel in the case. The request was granted and Lieut Col Allen appeared as counsel for the accused.

January 17, 1864
Letter of William Wheeler
Bridgeport, AL

Dearest Mother

I am particular anxious to get hold of those missing letters, which much suffice to me, this year, for Christmas and New Year's gifts, with their kind wishes and salutations. John's letter was a very delightful one, and made me feel quite homesick, and a longing desire that we might have met together at New Haven during that season.

What will you say to my coming home for a while? My Battery have reenlisted in superb style, only *two* remaining out who had a chance to go into the arrangement, and the Thirteenth New York Battery has now been mustered into the service as a Veteran Volunteer Organization, "to serve for three years or during the war, unless sooner discharged, from January 1, 1864." Probably we shall start in a few days for New York, to give the men their thirty day's furlough in their State, and perhaps to recruit a little. I had not thought of continuing in service longer than next fall, and consequently did not urge the men at all to reenlist. I simply stated the conditions, the bounty, the furlough, and read the order relating to such cases, and then said I would take the names of such as desired to enroll themselves for three years more of hardship and hard-tack. But they all asked me if I was going to remain with them, and made my promise to stay a sort of condition precedent to their reenlisting, so that I felt that if the gaining of these men for the service depended upon me, I had no right to selfishly consult my own feelings, and so gave the desired promise never to leave nor forsake them, and this promise I propose to keep, unless disabled in some way. It was not without struggle that I gave up my dreams of home and friends, intellectual leisure and books, music and congenial society, all of which would be mine next October, when my time was out, and I could hang my sabre up as a relic, over my bookcase, feeling that the three years' hard work gave me a certain tile to rest awhile; but if this is not to be I may as well make up my mind to go without it, and for my personal wants and disappointments console myself with the increasing brightness of the national prospects, and the approaching probability of ultimate and entire success. We are going to give the rebs a queer stirring up down here, next spring. Knoxville and Chattanooga will both be thoroughly fortified and amply provisioned, so that we shall not have to depend upon the long line of railroad to Nashville for supplies, and will be able to make a formidable advance from either point, without endangering our communications. I think that in the next campaign the rebels will be obliged to abandon either Virginia or Georgia. If Lee concentrates his whole army against us, we are ready for him. We have been having terrible cold weather here; ten degrees below zero is not exactly comfortable in a tent. I am quite comfortable in my quarters, have a good fire-place, nice floor and good bed. I hope to be in New Haven by the middle of February, that is if you can tolerate the sight of soldiers away from their posts.

January 20, 1864
Leave of absence request to Maj. Thomas Osborn, Chief of Artillery, 11th Army Corps
Bridgeport, AL

    Major
    I have the honor to request that the enclosed application for permission to go home with my battery be forwarded to Major Genl Howard.
    Very Respectfully,
    Your obedient servant
    Henry Bundy 1st Lieut
    13th Indpt NY Battery

February 1864-August 1864
Our beloved and gallant Captain Wheeler

February 1, 1864
Battery Orders No. 50
Bridgeport, AL

In accordance with orders received from Headquarters Department of the Cumberland, this Battery will be readiness to start for New York tomorrow morning for the purpose of reporting to the Superintendent of Recruiting there, and receiving the 30 days furlough given to Veterans re-enlisting.
Every man will be dressed and uniformed as is customary on inspections with caps, knapsacks, haversacks and overcoats, the Company will be inspected before starting at 7 ½ AM precisely.
The men will remember that on the journey to New York, they are on duty and under discipline exactly as much as when on the march in the field; any act of drunkenness, noisy conduct or disobedience will be punished by leaving the offender in charge of the Provost Marshal at the nearest post and allowing him to remain their until the Battery returns from furlough.
The Commander hopes that he will not be forced to inflict so severe a punishment upon any man.
1st Sergeant Tintenfass will hand over to Corporal Bonner a list of all men who do not accompany the Battery and Corporal Bonner will attend to all rolls calls and details during the absence of the Battery.
The Battery will leave camp at 8 AM with 2 days ration and coffee in the canteens.
Wm Wheeler Capt
Comdg 13th NY Batty

March 10, 1864
Extract from the report of Maj. Gen. George Thomas,
Department of the Cumberland
Chattanooga, TN

The following regiments, &c., have reorganized as veteran volunteers since the 31st of December, 1863, viz:
Infantry: Second Minnesota, Fifty-eighth New York, Sixty-eighth New York, Forty-fifth New York, Tenth Illinois, Fifty-

ninth Illinois, Thirty-sixth Illinois, Fifty-first Illinois, Forty-fourth Illinois, Forty-second Illinois, Eighty-second Ohio, Fifty-fifth Ohio, Twenty-first Ohio, Seventeenth Ohio, Seventy-fourth Ohio, Twenty-sixth Ohio, Forty-first Ohio, Nineteenth Ohio, Thirty-first Ohio, Thirty-third Ohio, Fifty-first Ohio, Sixty-fourth Ohio, Fifteenth Ohio, Forty-ninth Ohio, Thirteenth Ohio, Seventy-first Ohio, Sixty-fifth Ohio, Fortieth Ohio, Fifth Connecticut, Thirtieth Indiana, Forty-fourth Indiana, Thirty-first Indiana, Forty-second Indiana, Twenty-second Indiana, Thirty-third Indiana, Fifty-seventh Indiana, Fifty-first Indiana, Fifty-eighth Indiana, Fortieth Indiana, Seventy-third Pennsylvania, One hundred and ninth Pennsylvania, Forty-sixth Pennsylvania, Seventy-seventh Pennsylvania, Twenty-first Kentucky, Fourth Kentucky, Eighteenth Kentucky, Twenty-third Kentucky, Third Maryland, Thirteenth Wisconsin, Thirteenth Michigan, Fifteenth Missouri, Eighth Kansas.

Mounted infantry: Seventeenth Indiana, Fourteenth Michigan Cavalry: Fourth Kentucky, Sixth Kentucky, Third Kentucky, Seventh Pennsylvania, Fifth Iowa, First Ohio, Fourth Ohio, Third Ohio.

Artillery: Fifth Wisconsin Battery; Second Illinois, H Battery; Second Illinois, I Battery; First Ohio, C Battery; First Ohio, F Battery; First Ohio, B Battery; First Ohio, G Battery; Twelfth Ohio Independent Battery; Thirteenth New York Independent Battery; First Michigan, E Battery; Thirteenth Indiana Battery.

Detachments: Second Massachusetts, 5 companies; Thirty-seventh Indiana, Company I; Thirty-seventh Indiana, 47 men; Tenth Indiana, 56 men; Twenty-seventh Indiana, 6 companies; Fifteenth Indiana, 67 men; Fifth Ohio,. 7 companies; Seventh Ohio, Company F; Twenty-fourth Ohio, Company D; Eighteenth Ohio, 62 men; Sixty-ninth Ohio, 41 men; Twenty-seventh Illinois, Company I; Twenty-seventh Illinois, 90 men; Twenty-second Illinois, 34 men; Twenty-first Illinois, Company C; Tenth Maine, Company D; First New York Artillery. Battery I, 64 men, Battery M, 64 men; First Illinois Artillery, Battery C, 40 men; Fourth U.S. Artillery, Battery F, 48 men; Fifth U.S. Artillery, Battery K, 52 men; Ninth Ohio Independent Battery, 41 men; First Michigan Engineers, 85 men; First Missouri Engineers, 84 men.

Recapitulation: Fifty-two regiments of infantry, 2 regiments of mounted infantry, 8 regiments of cavalry, 11 batteries of artillery, and 24 detachments.

I am, general, very respectfully, your obedient servant,
Geo H Thomas
Major-General, US Volunteers, Commanding

March 23, 1864
Battery Orders No. 51
Bridgeport, AL

Private John McGurrin is hereby appointed Corporal of 13th NY Battery to date from February 1, 1864. He will be obeyed and respected accordingly.
Wm Wheeler Capt
Comdg 13 NY Batty

March 24, 1864
Leave of absence request to Brig. Gen. William Whipple,
Assistant Adjutant General, Department of the Cumberland
Bridgeport, AL

I have the honor to refer the following: This battery having as an organization re-enlisted as veterans and as such received a furlough of thirty days, has now returned to duty. In the absence of the batter I received under orders taking charge of the camp and of the government property belonging to the battery. There are now present for duty four officers in all. Under these circumstances I have the honor to make application for an order granting to me a leave of absence equal to that given to the men and officers of the battery with transportation to and from the City of New York.
I have the honor to remain
Your obt sevt
James C Carlisle
1st Lt 13 NY Batty[62]

March 27, 1864
Letter of William Wheeler
Bridgeport, AL

In the midst of working and preparation, I take a few minutes to tell you of my safe arrive with my men in our Alabama home, after a pleasant journey from New York of a little more than six days. On Sunday I bade adieu to my New York friends, and Monday morning went to Park Barracks, where I found most of my delinquents, and packed them on the Fort Schuyler steamer. I went, in the afternoon, to Fort Schuyler to Williams' Bridge in a wagon. We were doomed to wait for orders till Wednesday afternoon. A small tug took us to 31st Street, ad we went to Albany by 7 PM train. On Thursday evening we were in Buffalo, Friday morning in Cleveland, and at 1 PM in Columbus. Here Lieutenant Miller and I got out to take dinner, twenty minutes being advertised for that purpose, when we had the pleasure of seeing the train go without us. So here were seven hours to be disposed of; when we had exhausted about every mode of slaughtering that most precious of earthly things, I had the good luck to stumble upon Henry Chittenden, who was most cordial, and took us both to his house, where we had supper and passed a very pleasant evening. We had a dreary night ride, and reached Cincinnati just before daybreak, where I found that trusty watch dog, the Orderly Sergeant, had got all his flock snugly gathered together in the barracks of the Sanitary Commission, and there the fourscore were snoring as if on a wager. I was right glad that my transportation to Louisville was by water. The men had only a deck passage, ad had to stow themselves among the bales of merchandise, to keep warm. Miller and I got a nice state-room, and I had a glorious nap, which was only interrupted by our arrival at Louisville on Sunday morning. An afternoon train took us on towards Nashville, which we reached Monday morning. We found the place more horrible than ever; the dirt more abundant, and the dust flying in blinding clouds. The city was full of troops, waiting for transportation to the front, but was just beginning to be depleted, as an order had come for all infantry regiments to *march* to Chattanooga. Owing to this we got shipped for Bridgeport on Tuesday afternoon; it we had had to wait for the whole of the 13,000 troops to be shipped, we might have stayed there a month. A ride of sixteen hours brought us safely to Bridgeport, with no other accident than being run into by the train behind us, and having our car pretty well smashed, though no one was hurt. We found nine inches of snow at Bridgeport, and through this we tramped from the depot to our camp; we passed over a little hill and came in sight of our old winter quarters, upon which men broke out into loud and joyful cheers. But what especially pleased me was the sight of a row of beautiful, bright, brass, light twelve-pounders, or Napoleon guns, and as I ran my eyes along and counted, lo! there were six! I can assure you that I felt very much delighted at having the Battery restored to its old footing in this respect. I was conducted to the stables, where nearly hundred splendid horses were standing. It would do your eyes good to see how splendidly I have got them matched; hardly a single pair would disgrace a private carriage. It was the pleasantest thing of all, next to getting home, this getting back. The air is delicious, the snow is all gone, to-day has been a perfect Sunday, and I have been most happy in riding with Miller across the river to call upon a Union family from the North, and having some first-rate church music together. On my return I have read in my new old Bible, and thought of you all at home. I ought to have said that I found my box all right, and it warmed my heart to see all the nice things which home love had sent. I am very busy getting rid of my old guns, and fitting up the new ones. To-morrow morning I am to move across the river, into a work at the head of the bridge over the Tennessee, where I shall probably remain until the spring movement takes place. The corps which are to be put in most actively are the Eleventh, Twelfth, Fourteenth, and a Division of the Fourth Corps. The batteries will be fitted up in superb style, and will be expected to do the lion's share of the work. I am Chief of Artillery of the Third Division. My command is over twelve guns[63]. I feel very happy at being at my work again, and am full of hope and courage, for the spring and summer campaign. I have enough to read for a good while, and hope to scare up some antagonists at chess. Have made good use of my little gun already.—have some nice messes of quails and pigeons. I will write again as soon as we are settled down in our new camp.

March 29, 1864
Battery Orders No. 52
Bridgeport, AL

There will be an examination of the non-commissioned officers of this Battery at my quarters on Saturday April 2nd at 10 AM. The following will be the subjects for examination.

I   Naming the parts of the light 12 pd gun, carriage, limber and caisson
II   Description of the ammunition of the light 12 pd gun and the mod of preparing it
III   Table of ranges of the light 12 pd gun
IV   Drilling by detail in the manual of the piece
V   Marching a detachment
Attention is called to Battery Order No 39
Wm Wheeler Capt
Comdg 13 NY Batty

NO DATE GIVEN
Extract from the itinerary of the Army of the Cumberland, Maj. Gen. George H. Thomas, U.S. Army, January 1-April 30, 1864
no location given

    March, 1864 for 11th Army Corps
    Third Division, commanded by Brig. Gen. Hector Tyndale
    During the mouth the division has been performing guard duty along the U.S. military railroad from Bridgeport to Wauhatchie, sending out continually scouting parties in a southerly direction. The Fifty-eighth and Sixty-eighth New York Veteran Volunteers, the Eighty-second Ohio Veteran Volunteers, and the Thirteenth New York Veteran Battery have returned from their furloughs. The Sixty-first Ohio Volunteers, having re-enlisted as veterans, have gone to Ohio. Battery K, First Michigan Artillery, has been detached from the division, and Battery I, of same regiment, has joined the division from Nashville.
March 24, the organization of the division was changed to two brigades by virtue of Special Orders, No 60, headquarters Eleventh Corps.

April 1, 1864
Letter of William Wheeler
Bridgeport, AL

    I will not say that I felt as glad to see camp as I did to see New York; gladness does not express it at all; it was, rather, a quiet feeling of satisfaction and contentment, a happiness in being back at work again, different in kind, but not inferior in degree, to the delight I felt in looking across the Jersey Flats, and seeing the spires of Trinity and

St John's And it was very pleasant to feel this sense of contentment at coming back to the Army, and friends at home must not look upon it as evincing any want of affection for them, or any neglect of home; a man must do with his might what his hand findeth to do, and my job, at present, is to make my Battery efficient in the time of preparation, and active in the day of action; and to do this work well, all skill and thought and enthusiasm should be employed, and so I thank God that I am willing to leave New Haven, the opera, philharmonics, etc., for the "good time coming," whenever that may be. And yet it is right pleasant, when my officers have retired to their tents, to sit before the big fire-place in my rude quarters, and think over my thirty days at home, and recall so many dear faces, and the affection and kindness shown me by every one. It is the remembrance of such acts, and the words of approval and encouragement with which they are accompanied, that spirit a man up, and keep his heart warm and strong in his rough work. And I am sure that the harder and more sincerely a man does his duty, the more closely he loves and cherishes the remembrance of his friends....No man of taste cares for vulgar fame, but the thought of having the eyes he loves best smile approval, will nerve him up to anything.

  I found upon my arrival at Bridgeport, that I was already in possession of six fine brass guns, of the kind known as light twelve-pounders, or Napoleon guns; they have been turned over by Battery F, of the Fourth United States Regulars, and are the *same guns* which Frank Crosby commanded at Chancellorsville, and by which he fell[64]. *May I never have a worse fate!*

  Every day the scores of inhabitants, chiefly women, pass the camp on their way to procure supplies from the Commissaries, and I am sure that you never saw such creatures in your life, so ragged, dirty, and woe-begone,--such spiritless faces, and drooping, slouching figures; they are hardly worthy of being classed as Caucasians, but more nearly realize the idea of some intensely inferior race, the Papuans, or Australian Indians, or the Diggers. And I do not believe that the war has reduced them to this; it is the normal condition of the "poor white trash." Nothing that I have ever heard or seen of the injustice and injury done by slavery to the black, ever made my blood boil so with indignation, as this spectacle of white men, the same flesh and blood as ourselves, offshoots, perhaps, of the same families that dispense such elegant hospitality in Virginia and South Carolina, to see these, I say, brought lower than the slave, and all by that same system of slavery that says, "we will not have the white man work," and thus denying them the power of acquiring worldly prosperity, and at the same time, causing mind and body to rust in miserable inaction. The slave who works, thus becomes the physical and mental superior of the white man who does not, and the slave-holders have little or nothing to fear from their degraded white brethren. There seems little chance of elevating these people for a generation to come; we shall have to settle this country with Northern men, and I am sure that Bridgeport, at the junction of two great railroads, on a most noble river, the centre of a region rich in coal, and iron, and saltpetre, and marble, and corn-lands, will one day be a splendid city; under the hand of Southern enterprise it had grown to a place of *four* houses!

April 2, 1864
Battery Orders No. 53
Bridgeport, AL

I   Corporal William Suckendick is hereby reduced to the ranks for ignorance of his duties and incapacity as displayed in the examination of March 31, 1864
II   Corporal Deidrich Funk is hereby appointed Guidon of the 13 NY Battery, vice Henry G Craft discharged
III   Privates Charles Krauss, Joseph Clavin and David Driscoll are hereby appointed Corporals in the 13 NY Battery from April 1, 1864
They will be obeyed and respected accordingly.
Wm Wheeler Capt
Comdg 13 NY Battery

April 14, 1864
Letter of William Wheeler
Bridgeport, AL

My Dear Mr Hadley
Your kind note, in reference to Mr Lee, whom you caused to enlist for my Battery, has been duly received, and permit me to thank you most sincerely for the interest you have taken in my command. The acquisition of a single good man is right acceptable, and the Spring is just the time when we need all our available force at the front. I think that I shall be able to make it comfortable for this new recruit, physically at least; the moral and religious advantages of a Battery are not very great, but I think that the general tone, and the sense of self-respect, are much higher than in the Infantry. He will, at

least, have an opportunity of doing and enduring in the cause. My Battery has never been in the reserve, and this spring it will probably have a prominent part to play, as it belongs to General Hooker's new Corps, the Twentieth, which will doubtless be pushed into the thickest of all the fights. If I survive the campaign, I shall hope to thank you in person for you kindness and thoughtfulness in my behalf.

April 16, 1864
Battery Orders No. 54
East Bridgeport, AL

The following order is made with regard to daily duty in this Battery.
I   Guard Duty
The Guard shall be under the charge of the Battery Officer of the Day (who is also officer of the Guard), and shall consist of one Stable Sergeant, one Corporal, and as many men, not less than ten, as circumstances may demand.
Guard mounting shall take place at 9 o'clock AM the guard falling in at the proper call. The First-Sergeant shall carefully inspect the guard and will allow no man to go on guard not uniformed, as on inspection, that is with cap, jacket buttoned, clothes brushed and boots clean. He shall [assign] the cleanest man of the guard to be orderly for the day. He shall also see that the post on the guns is provided with a properly clean sabre. The corporal of the guard is responsible for the proper behavior of his guard and that they are instructed in all challenges and salutes.
II   Stable Duty
Stable call shall be sounded twice in each day when all drivers will clean their horses under personal supervision of their sergeants, thoroughly reporting to their respective sergeants who will report to the Battery officer of the day at the pickle rope; who will always be present there; sergeants are forbidden making this report anywhere but at the picket ropes.
The Stable Sergeant shall superintend the issuing of forage shall conduct the horses to water and back in an orderly manner and shall make special reports of all horses sick or injured during his tour of duty.
III   Police Duty
The Corporal of Police shall fall in his police every morning at reveille and thoroughly police the camp. After guard mounting, the

new Corporal of Police shall report to the Battery Office of the Day for special orders.
Wm Wheeler Capt
Comdg 13 NY Batty

April 19, 1864
Extract from Special Field Orders No. 110, Department of the Cumberland
Chattanooga, TN

 XVI. The following assignment of batteries is hereby made:
To be assigned to the Twentieth Army Corps: First Division, Twentieth Army Corps—Battery M, First Regiment New York Volunteer Artillery; Battery I, First Regiment New York Volunteer Artillery. Second Division, Twentieth Army Corps—Battery E, Pennsylvania Independent Artillery; Thirteenth Independent Battery New York Volunteer Artillery. Third Division, Twentieth Army Corps—Battery C, First Regiment Ohio Volunteer Artillery; Battery L, First Regiment Michigan Volunteer Artillery. Fourth Division, Twentieth Army Corps—Ninth Ohio Battery, Twentieth Indiana Battery.
 XVI. The following changes and assignments of batteries are hereby ordered:
Battery B, First Regiment Ohio Volunteer Artillery, is assigned to duty in the garrison of Bridgeport, Ala., to report to Maj W P Edgarton, First Ohio Volunteer Artillery, commanding garrison artillery. Battery K, First Ohio Volunteer Artillery, Capt Lewis Heckman, is relieved from further duty at Bridgeport, Ala., and is assigned to duty at Stevenson, Ala., to form the permanent garrison of that post.
The Ninth Ohio Battery, Fourth Division, Twentieth Army Corps, will proceed to Bridgeport, Ala, forthwith, reporting to the chief of artillery, Twentieth Army Corps. The Second Kentucky Battery is relieved from further duty at Decherd and Elk River, and will relieve the Ninth Ohio Battery at Tullahoma, Tenn.
By command of Major-General Thomas

April 21, 1864
Letter of William Wheeler
Bridgeport, AL

Dearest Mother

We have been in a regular fever of excitement here for a couple of weeks past, about the consolidation of these two Corps,--the Eleventh and Twelfth. Lookout Valley was the Mecca to which all curious officers made their pilgrimages, and every last arrival from that classic locality had to undergo a regular cross-examination as to the latest news, how Old Jose looked, what he said, and who were to have the new Divisions. The work is at last completed, and the new organization is announced; the Generals of Division in the Twelfth Corps all retain their places, while those of the Eleventh Corps have to take a back seat. The German element is played out, and in everything except the name, the Eleventh Corps is put with the Twelfth, our Divisions and even Brigades being broken up and distributed to the various Divisions, and even in the name the Twelfth Corps will retain its identity; the number of the new Corps is the Twentieth.

It is rather hard for an officer like myself, who has been with the Corps from the very first, and has shared its hardships and dangers, its good report of second Bull Run, Gettysburg, and Mission Ridge, and its evil report of Chancellorsville, to see the identity of the Corps merged into that of a rival Corps; but orders are orders, and I consider nothing unbearable that comes from the proper authority.

The new Corps is going to be magnificently equipped, and commanded by a man who is more like old Stonewall Jackson, than any man in our army, we shall have a force of over 30,000 men in one mass, 25,000 of them for active service in the field, the remainder to guard the railroad, and if Fighting Joe does not make an impression on rebeldom, with this force, I shall be most grievously mistaken. It is a heart-stirring feeling, to belong to an army composed of such troops, so superbly equipped, and likely to have such a proud history. The Divisions of the new Corps are to be commanded as follows: First, General Williams; Second, General Geary; Third, General Rousseau; Fourth, General Butterfield; the artillery is assigned to Divisions, two batteries to each Division; my Battery and Knapp's Pennsylvania Battery[65], a splendid volunteer battery, belong to General Geary's Division, and I am the Division Chief of Artillery. I have as fine a lot of horses as you would wish to see, and the other Battery has a supply equally fine, and when a few little deficiencies of equipment shall be supplied, and the spring movement takes place, I think that the Second Division will let itself be heard from. Major Reynolds, our chief of artillery, is an excellent officer, and very particular and critical. Lieutenant Mickle is his adjutant, and I am very glad that he remains connected with the artillery; he is a most cheerful and fine spirited fellow, and it does me good to meet him. I am afraid that I have bored you somewhat with my long account of the organizing of this army, but I want you to know just what I am about, and what my surroundings are. In every social point of view, the change is one for the better. I shall now be thrown among full-blooded Americans, and those mostly of the New York or New England type. I had a very pleasant introduction to some of my new comrades the other evening: Colonel Ireland, who commands a brigade in General Geary's Division, gave a reception at his head-quarters at Stevenson, and F S, who is an intimate friend of the Colonel's, asked me to go down there with him. Then we took the evening train at Bridgeport, and jolted down to Stevenson by 7.30 PM. We were among the first arrivals, and I was very glad to have an opportunity of making the acquaintance of Mrs. Ireland. She is a very intimate friend of Captain S's wife, and his introduction was sufficient to insure me a cordial reception. The room were draped with flags of the regiments of the Brigade, and festooned with evergreen starts and loops, and ornaments of all kinds and shapes, formed from swords, bayonets, and sashes, lighted up the walls splendidly. In the hall hung the musket, knapsack, and accoutrements of a solider, taken, the Colonel said, at hap-hazard from the ranks of a regiment. The musket shone like silver, not a speck of dust was on the equipments, and the knapsack, fully packed with overcoat and blanket, was a very neat and symmetrical object. Soon the guests began to arrive; a great many elegantly-dressed officers, and a very few ladies; it would make the eyes of a city belle snap to see the number of gentlemen that pounced upon each individual lady. The jolliest of the ladies was a Mrs Wilkinson, wife of Captain Wilkinson of the One Hundred and Forty-ninth New York, bearing certain proofs in his phiz of belonging to that noble race that bled at Concord. I took Mrs. W in to supper, which, by the way, was a regular success for the field, as being substantial as well as elegant. The officers present danced with each other very gracefully, and treated me with great consideration, when they learned that I was assigned to their Division. The ladies from the country, who had been hunted up for the occasion, were a queer lot; one or two of them were said to be great heiresses, but of a different style from Northern girls whether heiresses or not. They did not know how to dance, to walk, to talk, or to appear at ease; and they seemed to look upon the fun and good hits made by the really smart officers, as very undignified; they actually behaved as if they had never seen a gentleman before in their lives. I never want to hear any one say anything in favor of Southern ladies, about their charming ways, and their graceful languor,--give me rather the poorest New England school-marm,--the force of language can no further go. S and I came home at the respectable hours of 4 ½ AM, having had a very nice time. I like him better, the more I see of him. He is just as good as he can be; I like to hear him talk about his wife and children (he has four, three boys and a girl), in whom he is completely wrapped up; it really makes me feel quite a hankering after domesticity. I only hope that this new organization may not compel him to be assigned from this Corps. Very many thanks to Mr B for his picture, and to Mr D for his, which I found in the box.

April 22, 1864
Memo to Maj. Gen. George Thomas, Department of the Cumberland
Cleveland, TN

General, I have learned that it will be necessary to reduce the number of batteries in the 20th Army Corps. If so and there is no objection thereto I would be pleased to have Wheeler's 13th N York Independent Battery assigned to this corps.
Very Respectfully,
O O Howard
Maj. Gen.

April 23, 1864
Letter to Capt. Perkins, Assistant Adjutant General, 20th Army Corps
Bridgeport, AL

Captain

I have the honor to urgently and respectfully request that the court martial before which I was cited to appear on or about the 12th day of January last to answer to charges preferred against me by Maj Osborn Chief of Artillery of the 11th AC and which was adjourned before the conclusion of my trial, on account of the absence of important witnesses, may again be reassembled at the earliest day for the prosecution and if possible the completion of its labors in my case. My reasons for the urgency of this request are:

1st The important witnesses referred to above are now present, their term of service is about expired and they will, before long be mustered out of service and return to their respective homes, in which went it will be next to impossible to procure the testimony which is material.

2nd I have suffered the disgrace of being under arrest for more than three months and I am most anxious to return to duty, if acquitted by the Court.

I have the honor to be
Your most obedient servant
Henry Bundy 1st Lieut
13th NY Ind Battery

April 28, 1864
Memo of Capt. Francis Lackner, Judge Advocate, 26th Wisconsin Regiment
no location given

Respectfully returned to Capt Speed AA Genl- The Court was appointed on Jany 8 1864 by Maj Genl C Schurz commanding III Div 11 Corps- The case of Lieut Bundy is not yet closed but after examining some witnesses the case was by consent of the General & of parties postponed for an indefinite time. The following are the members of the Court:

1. Lieut Col Lloyd   119 NY Vols
2. Maj Caluherty   141 NY Vols

3. Capt Higgins   143 NY Vols
4. Capt Hall   119 NY Vols
5. Capt Jewett   61 Ohio Vols
6. Capt Schmidt   26 Wisc Vols
7. 1st Lieut Gottlob 82 Ill Vols

May 2, 1864
Report of Maj. Gen. George Thomas, Department of the Cumberland
Chattanooga, TN

Colonel I have the honor to report the operations of my command for the month of April as follows, viz:

On the 2d instant a force of rebels, said to be 1,500 strong, made a demonstration in the direction of Cleveland and Charleston, E Tenn, approaching to within 8 miles of Cleveland, when they divided into parties; one going out in the direction of Ducktown, through the mountains, the other remaining and falling back toward Dalton on the appearance of a force of our cavalry sent out from Cleveland in command of Colonel La Grange, of the First Wisconsin. A scout, who arrived at Cleveland on the 3d, reported that the above movement on the part of the enemy was for the purpose of covering the approach of a force from Longstreet's army which was on its way to re-enforce Johnston by way of Murphy, NC This was afterward ascertained to be Martin's division of cavalry.

On the 5th the following changes were ordered in the organization of the Army of the Cumberland: The Eleventh and Twelfth Army Corps to be consolidated and known as the Twentieth Army Corps, commanded by Maj Gen Joseph Hooker; Maj Gen Gordon Granger relieved of the command of the Fourth Army Corps and Maj Gen O O Howard (formerly commanding the Eleventh Army Corps) in his stead.

Maj Gen P H Sheridan having been relieved from the command of the Second Division, Fourth Army Corps, Maj Gen John Newton was assigned to that command, and ordered to report to Major-General Howard.

On the 10th Brig Gen J W Geary, commanding Second Division, Twentieth Army Corps, stationed along the railroad from Bridgeport to Stevenson, was ordered to organize an expedition, consisting of two regiments, with ten days' rations, and embark on the steamer Chickamauga, taking one piece of artillery to protect the boat, and then proceed down the Tennessee River as far as Decatur, Ala., examining carefully the south bank of the river, and all streams emptying into it from the south side; destroying all boats of whatever kind he might find, and notifying the inhabitants that no more boats would be permitted to be used or built, except with the permission of the commanding officer. On returning, General Geary was to examine the north bank in the same manner, and destroy all boats he might find, except such as Major-General McPherson, commanding Army of the Tennessee, should need, and the boats at Decatur or Larkin's Ferry, which will be the only points at which communication across the river will be permitted, notifying the inhabitants of the same.

April 11 the cavalry command of the army was reorganized, forming four divisions, of three brigades each, averaging three regiments to a brigade.

Brigadier-General Geary returned to Bridgeport on the 15th, reporting the result of his expedition down the Tennessee to be that he proceeded as far as Triana, Ala., where he came upon the enemy in heavy force on both sides of the river; that deeming it advisable to proceed no farther, General Geary returned, having destroyed a considerable number of boats both going and coming.

Information gained from deserters and others estimate the strength of the rebel army at Dalton to be 45,000 infantry and about 12,000 cavalry. The enemy has two brigades of cavalry at Tunnel Hill, watching our movements at Ringgold and the gaps through Taylor's Ridge, and one brigade on the road leading from Dalton to Cleveland, picketing the approaches from that direction.

The Fourth Army Corps, Maj Gen O O Howard commanding, having been relieved from duty with the Army of the Ohio, was concentrated at Cleveland on the 22d, and camped at that place and vicinity. The First Division of Cavalry, Col Edward M McCook commanding, was still at that point picketing and patrolling the country.

Frequent skirmishes have taken place during the month all along our front, between our own and the enemy's cavalry. In quite a sharp little affair near Leet's farm, on the 23d, we lost 5 killed and 10 wounded, besides 1 officer and 12 men taken prisoners; the enemy having had an overwhelming force, succeeded in gaining our rear. A scout, who left Dalton on the 16th, reports that two divisions from Hardee's corps were to be sent to re-enforce Lee in Virginia; this force to be replaced by Loring's division from Mississippi. This man passed through the enemy's defenses at Buzzard Roost, and reports them very strong.

On the 29th a reconnaissance was made toward Tunnel Hill from Ringgold, composed of 300 cavalry under Kilpatrick and Van Derveer's brigade of infantry. They advanced to Within a short distance of Tunnel Hill, driving the enemy before them until they developed a largely superior force, when the expedition returned to Ringgold. About this time preparations were commenced for the proposed advance on Dalton in May. The Second Division of Cavalry, Brig Gen Kenner Garrard commanding, started from Columbia, Tenn., under instructions to report to General McPherson for further orders.

The Twentieth Army Corps, Major-General Hooker commanding, was directed to concentrate in Lookout Valley. General Rousseau's division, of that command, to garrison the block-houses and other points along the line of the Nashville and Chattanooga Railroad; the balance of the corps to be placed in marching order immediately.

The Fourteenth Corps, Maj Gen J M Palmer commanding, was to concentrate at Ringgold, Ga, as soon as possible; and the Fourth Corps was in readiness to move from Cleveland as soon as ordered. Garrard's division of cavalry being under orders to report to General McPherson for duty, McCook's division (First) was to move on Howard's left, and Kilpatrick's (Third) to operate with Palmer's corps from Ringgold.

Reliable information was received on the 30th from Atlanta (27th) that heavy re-enforcements to Johnston had been passing that point since the 20th, said to be from Mobile, estimated at 10,000. The same person reports from Rome (28th) that part of Polk's corps was there, numbering about 5,000, and still more arriving. Two trains with artillery, fourteen pieces, had arrived that day. Martin's cavalry division was also there, about 4,000 men; also, part of Polk's corps had reached Dalton the same day (28th).

A reliable scout, sent to Dalton from Chattanooga, reaching Dalton on the 25th, returned on the 30th, reporting that the whole of Hood's corps had been moved to the front from its old position in the immediate vicinity of Dalton. He went to Atlanta on the 27th, but learned nothing of importance there. At Resaca he saw the camps of Armstrong's division of cavalry, and at Rome he learned that Loring's and another division had arrived from Mississippi, thus corroborating information received from a different source.

During the month there have returned to this army from furlough, as veteran volunteers, eighteen regiments of infantry, one of cavalry, and four batteries of artillery, with an aggregate of 2,697 recruits gained while absent.

The quartermaster's department has been particularly active constructing store-houses, &c., at Chattanooga. I have the honor to inclose herewith lists of steamers and other transportation employed by the quartermaster's department on the Upper Tennessee, and of the military store-houses at Chattanooga and Bridgeport; also the monthly report of the transactions of the provost-marshal's department.

I am, very respectfully, your obedient servant,
Geo H Thomas
Major-General, US Volunteers, Commanding

May 6, 1864
Letter of William Wheeler
Pea Vine Church, GA

My Dearest Mother

My doubt and anxiety about John were brought to a painful certainty by your letter, which reached me just as we were marching from Bridgeport to the front, and filled me with very great sadness. I have always been very anxious about him, ever since he entered the service, and now perhaps almost the very worst of all is realized, a Richmond prison; I cannot bear to think of him as having fallen. It will be with the greatest and most painful anxiety that I shall hear further news from him; whether he is wounded or not, and, if a prisoner, what his prospects of keeping up health and spirits until exchanged....But I cannot give way to feelings in this matter, as I have my own duties to attend to, and the perpetual consciousness of great sorrow such as this, would entirely incapacitate me from performing them in a proper manner; so I cherish hope as much as I can, and rely upon the thought of John's energy and tact, which will enable him to alleviate some of the miseries of imprisonment, and to obtain for him release at the earliest possible day. I cannot help sympathizing with the mortification which his proud spirit must have felt, at being obliged to surrender after his almost first engagement[66], but according to all accounts, the resistance made was most honorable and gallant, and General Wessells[67] would have been to blame if he had not surrendered, when there was no more hop of receiving reënforcements. You must not allow yourself to grieve too much, my dearest mother, over this sad disaster; we cannot do our duty in these stormy times, without many risks and sacrifices, and when John and I came out into the field, we had no idea of avoiding our fair share of these dangers, and we are eternally grateful to you for your encouragement, and your sympathy in our plans and views of the right course to be pursued, so that we could go onward with everything in our favor, sense of duty, patriotism, and the cheering voice of those dearest to us. And so, no loss or sacrifice ought to be regretted, or unduly sorrowed over, when viewed in the light which Right and the splendid Future throw over the conflict. I shall not cease hoping that we shall once more meet under the family roof, and in the meantime I shall ask that strength may be given him to endure privation; and courage and cheerfulness to buoy his mind up in the dreariness of imprisonment. How can I communicate with him now? Shall I send my letter to you to be forwarded to him?

  You will wish to know what brought me down into this region; on Monday night we received orders to move early the next morning, and so, on Tuesday, May 4, we broke up our comfortable quarters, and the delights of Tennessee River fish, and marched to Shellmound. The next day, after a most pitiless march up the valley, we crossed Lookout Mountain after nightfall, very completely done up, and joined the other Brigade of our Division, formerly the First Brigade, Second Division, Eleventh Corps. From this point, the southern base of Lookout, our Division march, the next morning, through Russville, towards Ringgold, leaving that place to the left and marching towards a place called La Fayette. This morning we marched half a dozen miles further towards that place, but have now halted for a rest, and also to allow of the complete concentration of our Corps. It will form a most magnificent line,--almost as close as a line of battle, and containing nearly a hundred thousand men. If the rebs can make a stand against this force, they are smarter and stronger than I think them. I am quite delighted with my commanding officer, General Geary; he has great consideration for the Artillery, and tries to help it along as much as he can. He is very polite to me personally, and I feel quite at home in this strange Division already. The two batteries under my command, as Division Chief of Artillery, are in fine order, and I shall be much disappointed if I do not do good service with them. It is impossible to say what the enemy propose to do. For my own part, I would rather have them stand and fight it out here, as I think that we are far enough from our own supplies already. I do not allow myself to be over sanguine, in matters which are so vitally interesting to us all, and yet I should be greatly disappointed if we did not achieve some very decided success in the approaching battle. The country is hilly and undulating, and has been cultivated, but we see very few inhabitants; have not been able to forage much yet, and my fare is simple bacon, hard tack, and coffee; but the promised land can't be very far ahead, and there must be chickens there. I am very well indeed, and am getting my campaign tan on. If we have a fight here, look in the newspapers for accounts of Geary's Division, Twentieth Corps, and you will know where I have been at work. Let me know about John as soon as you get any information, and how he is to be addressed[68].

May 11, 1864
Report of Capt. William Wheeler, Chief of Artillery, 2nd Division, 20th Army Corps
Mill Creek Gap, GA

Sir: I have the honor to report the following with regard to the movements and operations of this command from the 3d of May, 1864, to the present date:

At 9 AM on May 3 the Thirteenth New York Battery broke camp at Bridgeport, Ala, and marched with the First and Third Brigades to Shellmound, Tenn. On May 4 the battery marched into Lookout Valley and crossed the road over Lookout Mountain. Two wheels were broken near Whiteside's. In the evening Captain McGill crossed Lookout Mountain with Independent Battery E, Pennsylvania Volunteers (Knapp's), and reported to me. On May 5 this command marched to Post Church; on the 6th to Pea Vine Church, and on the 7th to camp near Buzzard Roost. On the 8th the command marched to Mill Creek Gap; have two pieces of McGill's battery. Lieutenant Sloan's section was placed in position in front of Mr Hall's house, and, upon our troops becoming closely engaged with the enemy in the gap, opened a slow and careful fire in support. Subsequently I moved the other

four pieces of McGill's battery to a position on the left of the road leading into the gap, from which they afforded a steady support to our troops who were engaged, and covered them upon their retiring down the mountain. The six light 12-pounder guns of the Thirteenth New York Battery were held in reserve at the foot of the hill in readiness to check any forward movement of the enemy, and also guarding against any flank movement from the right. Late in the evening of the 8th I withdrew both batteries into camp behind Mr Hall's house. On the evening of the 9th two rifled guns and two light 12-pounders were placed in position so as to command the slope in front of the farm-house. The other guns were held to guard the road to right and left. This is the position of the command at the present date. I append a list of losses and expenditures: Independent Battery E, 377 rounds ammunition.
    The above is respectfully submitted.
    Wm Wheeler
    Captain, Chief of Arty, Second Div, 20th Army Corps

May 14, 1864
Letter of William Wheeler
near Resaca, GA

    It seems a rather queer thing to be writing from a battlefield, and during a battle, but such is really the case. Not far from where I am sitting, the hostile batteries are fiercely playing on each other, and the infantry are beginning to tackle each other quite seriously; but as our Corps is in reserve, we don't trouble ourselves unduly about what McPherson, or Logan, or Schofield, may be doing, and patiently await our turn to be called into the grand melée. The campaign has been a queer one, the object of it having been to amuse the enemy in front, and keep him at Dalton, while the bulk of the army should march along the range of hills within which Dalton lies, cross the ridge by one of the Gaps, cut the enemy from his communications, and take him in the rear. How far this plan has succeeded I am as yet unable to inform you. It should have succeeded perfectly. The three principal Gaps in this range are, first, at Buzzard's Roost, next Mill Creek Gap; some ten miles further to the south, Snake Creek Gap. Buzzard's Roost, strongly fortified, was threatened by two Divisions of our Corps, while Geary marched against Mill Creek Gap. This is a very steep mountain pass, thickly wooded on all sides, and commanded on the crest by breastworks, in which a large force was posted. The Second Brigade of the Division was formed in the first line, and the First Brigade in the second, and an attempt was made to scale the mountain and take the pass, as was done at Lookout. But though the men did their best, scrambling from rock to rock, and pulling themselves up by trees and bushes, yet as fast as they showed their heads above the rocky parapets at the crest, an unseen foe picked them off, and even those who were but slightly wounded were in great danger of breaking their necks or limbs by falling from the rocky ledges. At times, small parties would succeed in reaching the summit, only to find themselves confronted by a strong breastwork, over which peeped the rifles of a foe. It was impossible to aid our men much with the artillery. However, I placed the rifled battery under my command in position, and threw some shells into the Gap, with what effect it was impossible to discover. The fight was kept up until night fall, when our men retired down the mountain, protected by the artillery from being pursued, and camped just in front of the Gap; so that if the enemy would not let *us* over, we could be prepared to do the same by them. In this affair our Division lost about three hundred and fifty killed, wounded, and missing; but it was not labor in vain, as the attention of the enemy was thereby drawn to this Gap, and General McPherson, with the Fifteenth and Sixteenth Corps, crossed the mountain at Snake Creek Gap almost without opposition; but I believe that he failed in thoroughly cutting the railroad communications at Resaca, and thus it is to be feared that the bulk of the enemy have slipped away to Atlanta, leaving only a rear guard before us. Since I have been writing this, the infantry firing has become much more heavy, and there is reason to hop that we are to have a chance at their main army. We lay for three days at Mill Creek Gap, and it rained frightfully and changed from extreme heat to severely chilly weather, which made us all a little ill. We marched on the 11th, passed the Snake Creek Gap, closely followed by the Eleventh and Twenty-third Corps, and yesterday began a lively skirmishing with the rebels, who are evidently on the retreat,--their object being to get safely to Atlanta, and ours to cut them off, and make them fight. The result I cannot announce. I can only say that General Howard with the Fourth Corps took Dalton yesterday, and will be to-day on the enemy's rear, and that thus far everything looks well. Our hearts have been cheered by the glorious news from the Army of the Potomac; we all rejoice in their triumphs just as if we still belonged to that grand army. I only hope that we may be able to show some similar good service in the public cause. I continue in the same state of miserable uncertainty about my brother's fate. I am sure that you will let me know as soon as you hear anything. I wish that the present movements in Virginia might result in the release or escape of all our prisoners. Do not fail to write me soon, and let me know all you can learn about him and about all at home. Thus far this has not been a very sever campaign for either men or animals. I have kept my horses in pretty good condition, and my men have been well supplied with rations. Fro myself, in my capacity of Division Chief of Artillery, I held on to my ambulance for head-quarters, but fear greatly that it may be taken for general use in case of a big fight. It is very convenient as a dry and comfortable sleeping place, and I am now writing this letter from the driver's seat. Now I have written you a stupid letter, but one can't get up much on the edge of a battlefield, when in momentary expectation of being ordered in. Be sure that if we are I shall do my duty as I best know how.

May 20, 1864
Letter of William Wheeler
camp near Cassville, GA

My Dear Aunt
A day of rest at last, after so many spent in marching and fighting, enables me to answer your very kind letter, and to send assurances of my health and safety up to this date, to all the friends at home.
Your letter was a great relief, containing the information of John's comparative safely, even though he be a prisoner. Although I am not of a very sanguine temperament, yet I am very confident that his energy and tact will bring him safe through the horrors of even a Richmond prison, and that he will return again, alive and hearty. At any rate this is the view I must take; any more gloomy view of things would make me too wretched to perform my duty properly. When I wrote last to mother, we were lying in reserve, awaiting orders to move forward. In less than half an hour after that letter was mailed, our Corps began to move down towards the left, to form a junction with the Fourth Corps, under General Howard, against whom the rebels were massing heavily. I rode

with General Geary in the advance of the Division, and reached the scene of conflict just in time to witness the most fortunate arrival of our men, who turned the enemy back, just as they were about to flank General Howard. A brigade of the First Division of our Corps took the Indiana Battery out of the very clutches of the rebs, as the covering infantry of the Fourth Corps had run away from it, and it was manfully holding its ground without support. This ended the fighting of the 14th May. The batteries of the Division marched to the left in the night, a most tedious and intricate march, requiring about eight hours to make five miles, and arriving in camp at 4.30 AM after a sleepless night. The next morning, Sunday, the 15th, the real fighting commenced. The enemy were intrenched on a line running almost north and south, parallel to, and covering the railroad; the country is very hilly and thickly wooded, admirably adapted to bushwhacking, but utterly unfit for extended movements in line, or for artillery operations. The rebel defenses consisted of rifle-pit and fence-rail breastworks at all points, and on the summits of the ridge were earthworks, and quite elaborate embrasured forts. The flanks were protected against any serious demonstration by the tangled character of the country. *My role* was of course not a very important one, but I placed the whole of the Thirteenth New York Battery in the best positions I could find, their brass guns being the only ones that could be used in such a country.

    The assistance they gave did not amount to very much, but it would have been important in case our men had suffered any decided repulse.

    The day was spent in assaults upon the enemy's position, points being gained and then lost again, but ground gradually gained until about four PM when General Hooker made an attack with his whole Corps, and took several of the fortified knobs; this decided the contest, and after making a midnight onslaught, to deceive us, cover their retreat, the enemy decamped, and abandoned Resaca, moving directly south, both on the railroad and by roads running parallel to it. A similar mode of pursuit was adopted; Sherman did not give the enemy any head start, but pushed on at daybreak the next morning, moving the Fourth and Fourteenth Corps directly through Resaca, McPherson's troops west, and our Corps east of the railroad, where we made a great circuit for the purpose of flanking Calhoun, and crossed the Conesauga River, but brought up against the Coosawatchee River, as we had neither pontoon bridge nor boats. In the night of the 16th we hunted up a couple of old ferry-boats, put them end for end, planked and secured them, and crossed the whole Corps the next morning, and marched to Calhoun, which the enemy had been obliged to leave. You see that General Sherman's plan of march is to move armies in parallel lines, but have them converge and concentrate at all important points. Thus, for example, we see the other Divisions of our Corps in the morning, lose them during the day, and meet again at night. This was also the style of marching we pursued in going to Knoxville. On the 19th General Howard had quite a sharp fight with the rebs, but outfought them and pushed on. The other Corps continued to flank march, and the advance of our army is at Kingston, the junction of the branch railroad to Rome, thus cutting of that important place and compelling its abandonment. We are at Cassville, east of Kingston, in the beautifully valley of the Etowah, enjoying supremely a few hours' rest after our hard marches. The country is very lovely and well cultivated, as far as it is cleared; but immense tracts in this section are still covered with heavy timber, chiefly oak and nut-wood. The inhabitants have generally vamoosed, the male ones almost without exception, and have taken with them their two legged property, evidently looking upon that as too portable as to be left to the Yanks. Thus far the campaign has been a severe one on both men and horses, as far as fatigue and work are concerned, but supplies have come up with great regularity, and we have not been compelled to forage on the country, though I think that we shall come to that soon. Our Corps lost heavily in the battle of the 15th, the entire loss being about two thousand. What the loss of the whole army is I do not know, but should think that five thousand ought to cover it. We have taken a number of prisoners, and about twenty guns. Several of my friends were killed or wounded. Lieutenant-colonel Lloyd of the One Hundred and Nineteenth New York, was killed, and the Adjutant of the One Hundred and Thirty-fourth New York wounded in the head. While passing from one of my batteries to the other, I got by mistake into a cross-fire, and found it very hot for a few minutes, and got a smart slap on the arm from a spent ball. Still all our fighting here has been mere child's play compared with that in Virginia. If we could only get a fair chance, on a fair field, we would give you a victory to record not much inferior to those of the Army of the Potomac. I do not like to see all the work being done by others when we are ready and willing to do our share. If the work goes on through the summer as it has begun, I shall be able to leave the serviced at the expiration of my term with a clear conscience.

We are in pretty light marching order, as all wagons containing officers' baggage have been sent to Ringgold, unloaded, and sent again to the front with forage. I have seen my old friend Captain S once or twice on this march. He is now Division Quartermaster in the Fourteenth Corps. I take great interest in everything, even the smallest detail, from New Haven, and your letters are sure to entertain me.

May 22, 1864
Letter of William Wheeler
Cassville, GA

As to-day is a real "day of rest," unlike the last two Sundays, which were spent fighting, and as letter-writing is not only permitted but also encouraged by General Sherman, in a very spicy circular issued yesterday, in which he gave the press correspondents a gorgeous rap over the knuckles, and as to-morrow we resume our line of march for Atlanta, with the prospect of a very sound bellyful of hard work and hard fighting before we reach that interesting spot, I think that I will try to start with as clean a record as possible with my correspondents, and your letter dated April 27 is very noisy and clamorous in its demands to be attended to, so that after reflecting for some time whether I had better take the bantling up and spank it thoroughly or administer a soothing dose of paregorie, I have decided upon the later course. I desire, in the first place, to object to a statement of yours to the effect that you were not in my debt; if you were not, you certainly ought to be, for I spread myself on an epistle to you shortly before I left Bridgeport, and really I cannot be held responsible for the bulls of Uncle Sam's Briefträgers; you must write me whenever you feel like it and the gadfly of Sanskrit remits his exertions for a season, without revolving the question of who wrote last, or casting up our epistolary accounts to see where the balance lies, and I am sure that you will be good and kind enough to do so. I love to read your letters; you can't talk to much "shop" for me; some other people talk about marriages, and removals, and fairs, and concerts, and similar pomps and vanities of this wicked world, and seem to think I have not retained civilization enough to care for culture or scholarship; while you pay me the compliment of taking it for granted that I have not, in a couple of hard, rough years, thrown off my love for those beautiful studies. I don't care how deep you go into questions, or how dark and abstruse they may seem to me; it is like looking into the dusky alcove of a superb library; you *know* that there are treasures there, and that when your eyes become accustomed to that solemn light, you can find them. As for your proposition to get up a translation in the way you spoke of, it was most kind of you to be willing to ask me with my dim ideas of grammar and roots, to go with you in such an undertaking; but perhaps some of these days, when I shall have emerged from the nomadic state, I may take you at your word; though even in literature and æsthetics I should require a considerable amount of refreshing and posting.

Did it ever occur to you to place Shakespeare beside any one of the three great Greek dramatists? I was thinking about it only to-day, and carried out the thought to some length, although it was an unsatisfactory business without the text of any of them at hand. Has it been done already; and if so, how and by whom? I should really like at some time to put down some time to put some of my ideas on this point. I do not think that the study of Tennyson would help a man much in working up Sophocles; he is, I think, eminently unclassic, except, perhaps, in his beautiful rhythm: he might have written fine Greek lines at the University, but his ideas are not Greek. There is no modern production to be compared with the "Hermann and Dorothea" of Goethe in its classic beauty; I read it once more when I was at home, and was more charmed than ever. Tennyson is essentially a writer of the Romance school, strongly tinged and influenced by the liberal Christianity of the Broad Church; a man who has deeply studied the best models, and has profited vastly by the study; he has caught the rhythm and melody of the Greeks, but not their power. "Ulysses" is a modern picture on a ancient subject, and the superb lines in it, as well as the whole casting, are from Dante. "Morte d'Arthur" is only a translation of the old legend into sonorous verse, containing a few lines almost literal from Homer, and a passage on prayer which reminds me always of that about the Λιταί[69]. For *my* part, I should as soon look to a star to explain the source of light in the sun, as study Tennyson preparatory to pitching into Sophocles.

I propose, one of these days, when we commence that translation together, to begin also another job with you, namely, a literary course based on the classics and beginning with Dante (your nose having been previously kept on the Italian grindstone long enough to post you on the original), then Shakespeare, a little of Milton, Rabelais, Cervantes, and Sir Thomas Browne. I am also desirous of knowing something for myself of those bugbears of our youth, Voltaire, Rousseau, Diderot, and Helvetius; if I read these with you, it would do me no harm, you know.

But enough of books; you will want to know where I am at this present writing. We are about half a mile from the pretty village of Cassville, county seat of Cass County, Georgia, which is really quite charming for a Southern town, and contains several churches, a college (which has for some time been used as a hospital), and a Ladies' Seminary: this last affair was occupied up to the last moment by the fair schoolgirls, who at last fled with great precipitation, leaving many of their clothes and toilet articles prey to the Yankee invader; even sweet little notes were picked up, wherein gallant young reb officers expressed their thanks for bouquets of flowers, and "sich like." The valley of the Etowah is very beautiful, and in Northern hands would be a paradise; it seems too bad for this lovely country to be ravaged by war, but the people would not be warned, and they are reaping the fruits of their folly. Every house is either entirely deserted, or else occupied only by a few women and children; a man at home is a curiosity. Our Division Head-quarters is a fine house out of town, where I love to go and loaf, and look at the roses, and scent the honey suckles and jessamines that run all over the porch and up the trees, and make me think of that arbor at the hotel in Athens, six years ago this month. I won't bother you with any account of our fight at Resaca; we whipped the rebs well, and most of the fighting was done by our Corps, though the Batteries did not have a great deal to do. We have all been indignant at General McPherson for not cutting the enemy off as early as May 10th; he had the chance, and might have done it. If Hooker had been in his place, we might have captured the whole of Johnston's army; as it was, we only forced him to make a clean and orderly retreat, and to-morrow we start to break our heads against Atlanta or any intervening obstacles. I hope that the blows struck may be heavy and incessant; then, perhaps, we may settle all the heads of this Hydra.

May 30, 1864
Letter of William Wheeler
near Dallas, GA

I can't say exactly how the epistolary account stands between us, but am inclined to think that I am quite decidedly your debtor, and so here goes for a few words, although the first line of works, not more than two hundred yards from the enemy's position, where bullets are constantly flying within a few yards of my paper, is not exactly the best place for a quiet and thoughtful chat. But we have been lying here for four days now, and are getting accustomed to the steady whiz of the bullets, to say nothing of the occasional boom of a rebel shell, and the idea of writing you a letter under fire is rather amusing than otherwise, so I snatch a scrap of my rapidly diminishing stock of paper, borrow the finest pin in the crowd, and try to see how much I can work in on a little space. I do not need to tell you that I have been preserved safe and sound through the fight at Rocky-faced Ridge, the battle at Resaca, and the action of the 25th at this place. Suffice it to say, that they were bloody affairs for our Corps and Division; the losses of the Twentieth Corps since we left Bridgeport amounting to nearly five thousand. The action of Wednesday last was a curious one. We had left the fertile valley of the Etowah, and had entered the woody and mountainous country on the western part of the Altoona ridge, hoping to be able to anticipate the enemy in reaching one of the gaps, and to compel him to give battle in the comparatively level country before Altoona. On Wednesday morning we pushed forward from Burnt Hickory to Pumpkin Vine Creek, repaired the bridge which the pickets had half burned, and crossed our Division over, the other Divisions being on other roads. After marching a couple of miles, we met the enemy in force and attacked him fiercely, driving his force back. It was very lucky for us that we did so, as we learned from prisoners that Johnston's whole army was before us, and nothing but anxiety had prevented the whole Division from being taken or cut to pieces[70]. The other Divisions were sent for and came up at double quick, when Hooker hurled them upon the enemy with his customary impetuosity, and drove them back about a mile and a half, storming one of their best positions,--that which we are now holding; and I sincerely believe that nothing but the coming on of a most thick darkness prevented him from driving them headlong from their stronghold. Our loss was heavy; about two thousand. General Howard, General Palmer, and General Schofield arrived with their Corps the next day, ad we took up a line opposite to that of the enemy, and since then the Vicksburg tactics of fighting from trenches have been adopted.—a most tedious and vexatious way of fighting, I think, and one calculated to demoralize an army of spirit. Here we have been for four days in dirty trenches, without taking off our clothes, and started up every few hours by an attack either real or sham. Last night the rebs made a serious attempt to drive us out, and we awaked from our first sleep about 11 PM to hear a most ferocious fire from their line which had advanced to within one hundred yards of our works. My men sprang to their guns and treated them to a few doses of canister that soon drove them back, and their officers could not get them out again. Our works alone saved us from destruction. I anticipate a still rougher assault to-night, but they won't get the Thirteenth New York Battery without pretty hard work. This whole campaign is going to be a severe and deadly one, and I don't expect to come out of it all right; and it is for this very reason that I write you under these very peculiar circumstances to assure you one more of my unaltered esteem and love for you, which have not continued the same from childhood up. My dearest brother is a prisoner, and you must join me in prayers and hopes that he may have strength to bear, with patience and cheerfulness, the severe trial of personal confinement and mental inactivity. May he be restored to his home, without suffering any shock either to his health or spirits. I feel at time almost desperate when I think of the still distant termination of the war, and of the blood and treasure that must yet be expended before truth and justice shall prevail; but I think that a man is less miserable when actively engaged in the war, than when an anxious watcher and spectator at home. Perhaps the poor fellows who fell the other evening, and whose graves are at my feet as I write, are the happiest and most enviable of all. You must not think that I am downhearted; but the constant strain of lying here under fire, and witnessing the constant slaughter going on, on the skirmish line, while the air is heave and polluted with the smell of dead men and horses yet unburied, does not tend to make a man's fancy bright or his spirits high. I almost envy the lot of the men of the Army of the Potomac. They have the heavy fighting and also the greater and fairer wreaths of laurel. I am afraid that the country will ask Sherman what he has been doing all this time, while his brother in arms has been doing so much. Rumors are prevalent that our Corps is to be relieved from this trench-work, and is to be employed on a flank movement. I earnestly hope that it may be the case, as I am about used up. I hope that my next letter home may be from Atlanta, though perhaps that is a little too sanguine; only, if with our force we don't push the rebs through here, we ought to be ashamed of ourselves.

But I must close, as it is growing dark, and there is every prospect of a lively affair to-night. If this letter is duly sent, you may take it for granted that I got through all right. Now, my dearest cousin, write me soon, and at length, and give me good words which shall make my heart feel warm and strong in this distant land and rough life.

June 1, 1864
Battery Orders No. 55
near Dallas, GA

Privates Gottlieb Baumgardner, John Mahoney and Emil Schoenleber are hereby appointed Corporals in the 13th New York Battery, vice Suckendick reduced, McGurrin promoted and Bonner discharged to dates as follows: Baumgardner from April 1st 1864, John Mahoney, from April 1st, 1864 and Schoenleber from June 1st, 1864. They will be obeyed and respected. Accordingly.
For Capt William Wheeler
Henry Bundy
First Lieut Comdg Battery

June 8, 1864
Letter of William Wheeler
camp near Acworth, GA

My Dearest Mother
I think that I have not written home directly since we were at Cassville, though I sent off a sort epistle to Annie from our trenches, written under heavy fire; but this was more of the oddity of the thing, and I know that it was a very absurd letter. We have had a very hard and fatiguing fortnight of it since leaving Cassville; we started on May 23, marched through the rich and beautiful valley of the Etowah, which is worthy of being possessed and worked by free people, crossed the Etowah on pontoons, and massed our forces on its south

bank. The next day we pushed cautiously ahead, through a town called Stilesborough, where large quantities of cotton had been destroyed the day before, then began to leave the rich and fertile valley, and to enter the oak forests and barren districts of the eastern Altoona ridge, until we camped in a place bearing the euphonious name of Burnt Hickory. On Wednesday we marched through the mountains by parallel roads, towards a creek called Pumpkin Vine Creek; our Division being considerably in the advance, the other Divisions making flank demonstrations towards Dallas. At Pumpkin Vine Creek we found the bridge half burned by the rebel cavalry; but it was soon repaired, and our Division began to cross, and to pass into a ridgy wooded country, where, about two miles from the creek, we found the enemy in force, and attacked him with our first Brigade, driving his forces back quite a distance. Here very large forces of the rebels could be seen coming up, and their artillery was being planted. To our dismay, we learned from prisoners, that nearly the whole of the rebel army was in our front, both Hood and Hardee being present with their Corps. Nothing but our first brisk attack had saved us; the enemy supposed that our whole army must also be there; a determined advance on their part would have cut Geary's whole Division in pieces before it could have retreated. We made our preparations for a vigorous defense; I took my batteries back across the creek, and placed them in strong positions, to cover the crossing, and the Divisions of Williams and Butterfield, and General Howard's Corps, were ordered up on double quick. You can imagine our anxiety until they arrive; but the critical moments went by, the rebels did not improve their golden time, and as soon as General Hooker had got his three lines of battle,--General Williams' Division forming the first two lines, General Butterfield's the third, while our Division, which had been all day long skirmishing and holding the enemy in check, formed the reserve,--I followed the first line of battle with a section of my Battery, ready to place it in position as soon as a position could be found, which was too rare I that heavily wooded country. I had a fine opportunity of observing General Hooker, who rode close behind the first line, and encouraged the men immensely by his cool and easy hearing and his cheering words. Perhaps he exposes himself too much, but he get more fight out of his men than any officer I ever saw. The men went into the fight superbly; the rebels were driven steadily back, and back, until they reached a strongly fortified position that they had prepared; here they made a stand and checked our advance, and the fighting became very severe. The second line relieved the first, and the third the second; rebel batteries poured shell and canister into our ranks, and yet they pushed on. Just before dark our Division was sent in, and with two good hours for work would have carried the rebel position; but a pitchy darkness came on, and the fighting on both sides ceased almost instantaneously, and both sides began to intrench the positions in which they were resting. We had not won everything, but we had gained the crossing of Pumpkin Vine Creek, a serious obstacle, and had pushed the enemy back two miles by determined fighting, and had even gained a footing on the crest of his position. The next day was spent in strengthening the works thrown up on the night of the 25th. At daybreak on Wednesday, the 27th, the three brass batteries of the Corps were placed in position in these works.

Here we remained six days without relief, under a burning sun, constantly under fire, with the rebel works less than two hundred yards distant from us, and their sharp-shooters often stealing up to within one hundred and fifty yards, and sending their bullets into our embrasures with disagreeable sharpness and precision. Fortunately their advance works were in a hollow, and so they overshot our breastworks as a general rule; but sometimes an enterprising reb would climb a tree and get a very fair view of us, as we took our ease on the sharp stones behind our works, and then we would find it convenient to huddle up pretty close into the trenches. Night was the worst time of all; the short distance between the lines made a rush possible, at any time, from the enemy's works to ours; and then the Fourth Corps, which occupied the works to our left, had a nervous way of getting up a false alarm about three times in the course of the night, and making us tumble up to our posts, thus completely breaking our rest and depriving us of sleep. On Sunday night the rebs undertook to see if they could oust us, and came up to within fifty yards of our works in a very threatening manner; but we were wide awake, and after a hot little fight of about half an hour, they got back to their works very rapidly, and their officers could not get them out to make another assault. We must have mowed them pretty badly, as we fired twenty-four rounds of canister into them short range. Pretty business for Sunday night, was it not? We were at lat relieved in the trenched by some of the Fifteenth Corps, General Logan's, and move off to the left of the army. The exposure and wearing excitement had made us all more or less unwell. I came off better than most of the others, and a dose of opium broke up a severe attack of dysentery that had begun to come on. Since then there has been more or less fighting, mostly to our advantage. We now hold the railroad to Altoona; our next point is Marietta, then the passage of the Chattahooche River, and then onward to Atlanta. We march probably to the river to-morrow morning, and it is impossible to say when a general engagement may come on. When it does, we are confident of success, and especially that the Twentieth Corps will have plenty to do and will do it well. Our Corps has done almost all the fighting in this campaign, and has sustained a very large proportion of the losses. I think that the entire loss of our Corps since we left Bridgeport must be rather over than under five thousand. Our battles have seemed small and pigmy-like besides those in Virginia, still we are not idle and are making progress....The climate suits me as well as, or better than Virginia. In the morning and evening the air is full of the delicious perfume from the blossoms of the wild grape and the hawthorn, from thyme and other sweet grasses. The smell of these last make me think of Athens and Mount Hymettus. Think of me as well and strong, and doing the best I can, and always longing to hear from my dearest mother.

June 23, 1864
Battery Orders No. 56
 near Marietta, GA

As our beloved and gallant Captain William Wheeler[71] was killed yesterday I hereby assume command of this Battery.
Henry Bundy
1st Lieut Comdg Battery

Letter of Private Frank Lee, 13th New York Artillery near Marietta, GA

Professor Hadley
The painful intelligence I have to communicate, of Captain Wheeler's death, you will receive through other sources before this reaches you. The envelope which I send you, will observe, has his frank, which I obtained yesterday morning, there being no stamps to be procured in the Battery. When I went to him he was sitting in the ambulance writing, unconscious as I was, no doubt, of the fate that so soon awaited him. I will give the circumstances of his death as near as I am informed. At noon, yesterday, the 22d, we had orders to advance to a new position in front, the enemy having fallen back about a mile

for fear of a flank movement. Captain Wheeler, being acting Chief of Artillery for the Division, took Knapp's Pennsylvania Battery forward, while we remained where we were. Shortly after, or while they were getting the Battery in position, the enemy made two or three charges[72], evidently with a view of capturing it, as we had not breastworks. They were repulsed and driven back, however, every time, by the fire of the infantry and the artillery. It was while they were making one of these charges, as Captain Wheeler stood partly behind a tree, making observations and giving orders, that a ball from a sharp-shooter struck him in the left breast, piercing him through the heart, from the effects of which he died almost instantly…His death created a deep and solemn impression in the Battery, and a general expression of regret was manifested by all.

July 9, 1864
Obituary from the *Columbian Register*
New Haven, CT

Wheeler, William (Capt) at Culps Farm[73], GA, Chief of Art, 2nd Div, 20th Army Corps, Son of Russell of New York, June 22, Age 28

July 12, 1864
Special Orders No. 166, Department of the East
New York City, NY

Private John R Carpenter 13th New York Battery Vols enlisted Oct 1861 is hereby relieved from the charge of desertion forfeiting all pay and allowances due him to time of joining said battery in the field. He will also make good the time lost by his absence from January 1st 1862 to time of joining said battery. He will be sent to Fort Columbus for transportation to said battery now with Major General Sherman's command.
By command of Major General Dix

July 27, 1864
General Orders No. 7, Army of the Cumberland
near Atlanta, GA

In accordance with General Orders No ~Hd Qts, Dept of the Cumberland, dated July 18, 1864 the batteries of the Corps are hereby

detached from the Divisions and will constitute a separate command under the Corps Chief of Arty.
Battery commanders will report to Major J A Reynolds Chief of Artillery who will assume immediate command of the Artillery of the Corps.
By command of Maj Gen Hooker

General Orders No. 1, Artillery 20th Corps
near Atlanta, GA

I   In accordance with Genl Orders No ~ Headqts, Department of the Cumberland dated July 18th 1864 and General Orders No 7 Headqts- Twentieth Corps dated July 27, 1864 I hereby assume command of the artillery of this Corps.
II   Capt Chas Aleshire, 18th Ohio Battery is announced as Assistant to the Chief of Artillery.
III   First Lieut Wm Mickle, 134th NY Vols is announced as Actg Asst Adjt Genl of this command and will be respected and obeyed accordingly.

    J A Reynolds
    Major 1st NY Arty
    Chief of Artillery
    20th Army Corps

General Orders No. 2, Artillery 20th Corps
near Atlanta, GA

The following reports are hereby required of the batteries of this command and will be forwarded promptly at the time specified:
Daily report of casualties, daily report of expenditures of ammunition, weekly report of effective force on Sunday including the casualties of the week, tri monthly report on the 8th, 18th and 28th each month, tri monthly report of men discharged for disability, monthly return- last of each month, monthly return of casualties- last of each month.

    By order of Major Reynolds

Extract from Special Field Orders No. 205, Department of the Cumberland, near Atlanta, GA

    At his own request Maj Genl J Hooker Comdg the 20th Army Corps is relieved from duty with the Army and Department of the

Cumberland. He will repair to Washington DC and report to the Adgt Genl for orders.

Maj Genl Hooker's personal staff is also relieved from duty with the army that they may accompany the general.

The Quartermaster's Dept will furnish the necessary transportation.

Brig Genl A S Williams Comdg 1st Div 20th Corps will succeed Maj Genl Hooker in command of the Corps until an assignment to that command is made by the President of the United States.

By command of Major Genl Thomas

July 28, 1864
Battery Orders No. 57
near Atlanta, GA

The following alterations among the commissioned officers in Battery are hereby announced to the men
I   First Lieut Henry Bundy received his commission as a Captain of 13th New York Battery and continues to be in command of same.
II   Second Lieut Henry Miller has been promoted 1st Lieutenant.
III   Sergt. John McGurrin is commissioned 2nd Lieutenant in the later place.

The commanding officer hopes and wishes that those alterations will not alter at all friendly relations between officers and men of this Battery and that both parties will endeavor to keep up the good renown of the Battery.
Henry Bundy
Capt Comdg Battery

July 29, 1864
Battery Orders No. 58
near Atlanta, GA

The following non-commissioned officers are hereby promoted and appointed
I   Corporal William Boe is hereby promoted Sergeant in 13th New York Battery vice Sergeant O'Connor killed to date from July 20, 1864.
II   Corporal Charles Krauss is also appointed Sergeant vice Sergeant John McGurrin promoted to date from July 25, 1864

III   Private Charles Bundy and Issac Van Sciver are hereby appointed Corporals vice Boe promoted and vice Lynch killed to date respectively.
IV   Corpls. David Driscoll, Deidrich Funk and Joseph Clavin will act as sergeants of the III, V, VI pieces respectively until further orders.
All will be obeyed and respected accordingly.
Henry Bundy
Capt Comdg Battery

August 1, 1864
Report of Col. Charles Candy, 1st Brigade, 2nd Division, 20th Army Corps
camp near Atlanta, GA

Captain: In compliance with instructions, I have the honor to report the part taken by this brigade during that part of the campaign since my last official report of the 28th of May, 1864, dated near Dallas, Ga, to August 1, 1864. May 23, marched to south side of the Etowah River and encamped. May 24, marched to Burnt Hickory, Ga, and encamped. May 25, marched at 6 AM, this brigade in advance of division, and moved to Pumpkin Vine Creek, where the advance met the enemy's cavalry pickets. Skirmishers were thrown across the stream (the Seventh Ohio performing this duty), when we advanced about three miles, where we met the advance of the enemy in force, composed of infantry and cavalry. The brigade was formed in line of battle. The Twenty-eighth Pennsylvania Volunteers was ordered to advance as skirmishers to assist the Seventh Ohio, who were warmly engaged with the enemy, and who were making a stubborn resistance. After the Twenty-eighth Pennsylvania Volunteer skirmishers were in position the order was given to move forward cautiously and press the enemy to develop his force. The enemy's skirmishers were compelled to fall back to their main line, one and a half miles. Prisoners arriving, information was received that General Hood's entire corps was in my front. This fact was immediately reported to the general commanding division. The enemy advanced and poured a heavy and galling fire in the entire line. It fell most heavily on the Fifth Ohio Volunteers, who lost 7 killed and 51 wounded. The regiment wavered, but immediately recovered from the shock, and held its position gallantly. Great credit is due the officers and men for their steady nerve during this trying hour. In the mean time temporary protection was thrown up. We remained in this position until about 5 PM, when the other divisions (First and Third) arriving, the corps was formed in column by brigade and ordered to charge, the First Division in advance, followed by the Third, and the Third by the Second. This brigade was in rear of the division. After moving forward the enemy was found behind intrenchments with artillery. We took position within very short distance of the enemy and threw up intrenchments (the night being very dark and rainy). During this last advance the Fifth Ohio Volunteers lost its gallant commander, Col John H Patrick, who fell mortally wounded from grape-shot. When the brigade met the enemy first after crossing the creek (Pumpkin Vine), Lieut Joseph W Hitt, Sixty-sixth Ohio Volunteers, acting as aide-de-camp on my staff, was killed while carrying orders to the right of my line. Lieutenant Hitt was beloved by all. Although young in years (being but nineteen) he was a gallant and brave officer. Remained in this position until June 1, 1864, skirmishing heavily day and night. Attention is particularly called to reports of regimental commanders of operations, on the 25th of May especially.

June 1, was relieved by a division of the Fifteenth Corps, and moved to the left and bivouacked for the night in rear of Twenty-third Corps. June 2, moved forward in support of Twenty-third Corps on a road running toward Acworth, and remained in position. June 6, marched to the Acworth and Big Shanty cross-roads; went into camp, throwing up intrenchments. June 14, marched to near Pine Hill; massed in rear of Third Brigade of this division. June 15, the enemy having fallen back some distance and evacuated his position on Pine Hill, this brigade was ordered forward on a reconnaissance to ascertain where the enemy was; advanced about a mile; encountered the enemy's pickets; compelled them to fall back a short distance. The brigade was formed in line of battle to await the remainder of the division. At 5 PM the brigade was formed in two lines—Twenty-eighth Pennsylvania and Twenty-ninth Ohio Volunteers in first line, the Fifth and Sixty-sixth Ohio Volunteers in the second line; the One hundred and forty-seventh Pennsylvania Volunteers was on the right and in front of the other brigades; it was relieved at this time, but did not come up immediately. The order was received to charge the enemy's works. Their skirmishers were driven in precipitately. Their works were found to be very strong and garrisoned with infantry and artillery. Not being in sufficient force, their works could not be carried. My first line (consisting of the Twenty-eighth Pennsylvania and Twenty-ninth Ohio Volunteers) succeeded in getting within thirty yards of their works and maintained their position, the enemy being unable to dislodge them. The remainder of the brigade (Fifth and Sixty-sixth Ohio and One hundred and forty-seventh Pennsylvania Volunteers) immediately threw up breast-works under a galling fire from the enemy's sharpshooters. Many casualties occurred, but the position was maintained. During the night temporary works were thrown up and the enemy was harassed constantly from the fire of our sharpshooters, who kept the enemy from working their artillery to a considerable extent. Remained in this position until 2 AM of the morning of June 17, when it was discovered that the enemy had abandoned his works and left our immediate front. Their works were occupied by the advance regiments and skirmishers thrown rapidly forward, capturing a few of their rear guard. Information was immediately sent to the general commanding division, and everything prepared to follow the enemy. Moved forward about 10 AM 17th instant two miles and held as a reserve for the remainder of the division. June 19, the enemy had fallen back during the night about one and a half miles and taken up a new position; formed line on the left of the Third Brigade of this division and threw up intrenchments; nothing but heavy skirmishing along the line of this brigade. Relieved by a brigade of the Fourth Corps on the evening of June 20; moved to the right of Third Division, Twentieth Corps, to protect a gap between it and the First Division, Twentieth Corps. June 21, joined by the remainder of the division, left of brigade joining Third Division, Twentieth Corps, threw up intrenchments. June 22, two regiments were thrown forward to take position on a range of hills in our immediate front, on which were posted the enemy's skirmishers; drove them off, and the rest of the brigade moved forward to occupy the hill and entrench, which was done. June 27, the brigade was ordered to form as a reserve to the Second and Third Brigades to take and occupy a piece of woods immediately in our front and protect the right flank of the Fourth Corps, who were about to assault a position in its immediate front, and entrench ourselves if successful. We were successful, and remained in this position until June 29, when the division was relieved by a division of the Fourteenth Corps and moved to the right to relieve a division of the Twenty-third Corps on the right of the Powder Springs and

Marietta road, which was accomplished by daylight of the 30th of June.

July 3, it was discovered that the enemy had left our front; soon after daylight ordered to press the enemy. Skirmishing commenced with the enemy's rear guard, which lasted until about 12 m., when the enemy fell back three or four miles, where he was found entrenched and entrenching. The division was formed in line, this brigade in reserve. July 4, received orders to be ready to occupy the lines vacated by the First Division, Twentieth Corps, immediately on the left of our Second Division. July 5, the enemy it was discovered had fallen back again. This brigade, with the Second and Third, immediately followed them in the direction of Turner's Ferry, Chattahoochee River, where they were found occupying a ridge on the north side of the river above mentioned and strongly entrenched; went into camp for the night. July 6, moved about three miles to our position of the 5th instant and bivouacked for the night. July 7, moved to the right of the Third Division, Twentieth Corps; took position, right of brigade resting on Nickajack Creek and connecting with the Fifteenth Corps, left of brigade connecting with the Third Brigade of this division. Remained in this position until July 17. Broke camp and marched across the Chattahoochee River, and bivouacked for the night near Johnson's house. July 18, marched to near the forks of the Atlanta and Buck Head roads and formed line of battle on south side of Buck Head and Pace's Ferry road and parallel to it; threw up intrenchments and remained in position for the night. July 19, moved forward and crossed Peach Tree Creek; was again formed in line of battle and threw up intrenchments on right of Second Brigade of this division, my right resting on Peach Tree Creek. July 20, moved forward about half a mile to a hill in front of Third Brigade of this division, from which the enemy's skirmishers had just been driven. The brigade was formed in two lines of battle, the first line, One hundred and forty-seventh Pennsylvania, with the Fifth Ohio Volunteers on their right and well refused, to the rear to protect my flank; second line, Twenty-ninth Ohio, with the Twenty-eighth Pennsylvania on their right; the Sixty-sixth Ohio Volunteers, having a great portion of their regiment on the skirmish line, was held as a reserve. The front line received orders to throw up temporary breast-works, which was done. About 1 PM received orders from the general commanding division in person to deploy the brigade in single line and throw up a line of breast-works as protection against infantry along the ridge, and that the First Division, Twentieth Corps, would connect with my right, as they had received orders to do so immediately. These orders were carried into effect by me, but the First Division did not join my right, as was discovered afterward, nor did they afford any protection to my line, thus leaving my flank entirely unprotected. During this time I felt perfectly secure. About 3 PM the enemy made his appearance in my immediate front, and while battling with him in that direction the right flank and rear of this brigade was enveloped by the enemy in solid column, pouring their murderous fire in the rear of my line. It was so sudden and impetuous that the Sixty-sixth Ohio, Twenty-eighth Pennsylvania, and Twenty-ninth Ohio Volunteers were compelled to fall back. The Fifth Ohio and One hundred and forty-seventh Pennsylvania Volunteers held their ground nobly, their men falling rapidly, especially the Fifth Ohio, who were most exposed. Enveloped on three sides, it required desperate fighting to hold the ground, and if the artillery had not rendered the assistance it did the entire brigade would have been compelled to fall back and change front. The Second and Third Brigades coming to the rescue, we were soon enabled to breathe freer and maintain our ground, and punish the enemy for his audacity, which was done with great slaughter. Great credit is date Lieutenant Bundy, Thirteenth New York Battery, and his brave men, for maintaining the position and rendering such noble assistance with their guns, especially the two pieces on his right, which were changed to the right, and delivered with such telling effect, grape and canister that the enemy was compelled to halt and change his course. The enemy was driven back and the position was maintained. I cannot close this day's report without returning my sincere thanks to both officers and men for their gallant defense of the position, and their country may well be proud of them in sustaining their ground against such odds. Among the regimental commanders I must thank Col Ario Pardee, jr, commanding One hundred and forty-seventh Pennsylvania Volunteers, particularly, for services rendered that day and during those trying hours. Night coming on, the enemy retired, leaving many of his dead and wounded. The latter were removed under cover of the darkness by him. July 22, it was found that the enemy had fallen back from our immediate front. We moved forward to within one and a half miles of the city of Atlanta, formed line, when it was discovered that the enemy had taken up his position in his main works around that city. We advanced and formed line of battle within one mile of the enemy's works and threw up a strong line of breast-works. July 25, advanced the works about 300 yards nearer the enemy, which works the brigade now hold. The enemy is now using and firing from his main line of rifle-pits.

Great credit is due both officers and men for the cheerful manner they have performed the arduous duties, which this report covers, under an almost constant fire, either skirmishing or in line of battle, exposed to the inclemency of the weather and the almost unbearable heat of a southern climate. To the noble dead, their names will be handed down to posterity as heroes who sacrificed their lives for their country and flag, and to sustain one of the noblest Governments under the canopy of heaven. All of which is respectfully submitted.

I have the honor to be, captain, very respectfully, your obedient servant,
    Chas Candy
    Colonel Sixty-sixth Ohio Volunteers, Comdg Brigade

<u>August 30, 1864</u>
Battery Orders No. 59
Paces Ferry, GA

Private Louis Faes is hereby appointed corporal of this Battery to date from July 25th 1864 vice Charles Krauss promoted. He will be obeyed and respected accordingly.
Henry Bundy Captain
Commanding Battery

September 1864-July 1865
The Veteran Soldiers of the Battery

September 7, 1864
Report of Capt. Henry Bundy, 13th New York Artillery
Atlanta, GA

Sir: I have the honor to submit the following report of the part taken by the battery now under my command in the campaign just closed:
The battery was present at every engagement in which the corps has taken part during the campaign, though not on all occasions actually engaged. At the engagement before Rocky Face Ridge the battery was placed in position but did not open fire, as it was found that only long-range guns could there be made effective. At Resaca, on the third day of the engagement, the battery accompanied the corps in a movement against the enemy's right and took position on a hill, covering our infantry in a charge upon the enemy's works. After the charge and capture of two lines of the enemy's works, the battery was advanced to a new position somewhat farther to the right and within short range of the enemy's last line of works and there entrenched. During the night, the enemy having made a slight demonstration in our front, a few case-shot were used, and early on the following morning the enemy was found to have evacuated their works in our front. After the Second Division of the corps had crossed Pumpkin Vine Creek, moving to the westward of Allatoona and toward Dallas, having come upon the enemy in force, the battery was ordered back, under my command, over the creek, and with directions to take a position to cover the bridge over which the Second Division had passed. After having taken a favorable position for this object and entrenched, one section, under command of Lieutenant Freeman, was ordered forward to the position on the road held by the infantry of the division, and just preceding the advance of our infantry rapidly shelled the enemy's position in the woods in front. After the advance of the infantry this section followed up in rear of the second line; the remainder of the battery having been in the mean time ordered up, joined it during the progress of the engagement, but no other position having been found for the use of artillery the battery was not further engaged on that day. On the

morning of 27th [May], at daybreak, the battery was moved forward and placed in position in some works previously constructed within about 120 yards of the enemy's line, and in line with the Second Division. At 7 o'clock on the morning of that day we opened fire on the enemy in conjunction with the other batteries along our line, continuing it at regular intervals until about 11 AM In this position we remained six days, until relieved by other troops, firing occasionally each day as the enemy made attempts to strengthen their works or press our skirmish line. On the night of the 28th the enemy advanced from his works in line of battle, driving in our skirmishers and pressing toward our works, when the battery opened upon them a rapid fire of canister for a few moments and they fell back behind their works. The enemy used but little artillery against us in this position, and the few attempts made by them were always promptly replied to and their guns quickly silenced. The battery lost in this position 3 men wounded and 2 horses disabled. In the lines in front of the enemy's position at Golgotha, or Lost Mountain, two sections of the battery under my command were placed in position in the line of the Third Brigade on the afternoon of June 16, and shelled the enemy's works. In the evening of that day the enemy opened a battery upon our lines from a point some short distance to the left of the immediate front of my position, and having a position which enabled me in some degree to enfilade their battery I opened fire upon them, and after a few rounds they ceased firing, our practice having been remarkably accurate, as was seen by an inspection of the enemy's works the following morning, they having evacuated them during the night. In this position we lost 1 man, Peter Duffy, killed instantly by the enemy's sharpshooters whilst cutting an embrasure for one of my guns. He was a brave and efficient soldier.

On the 17th of June, the enemy being found again in position on the south side of Mud Creek, the battery was advanced to a position on the right of our corps in front of and within point-blank range of one of the enemy's batteries in a thickly wooded bluff, and after having constructed some slight cover for the guns by sinking them in the crest of the hill the battery opened fire on the enemy's position, which was continued rapidly for about half an hour, and although the enemy's battery had been previously very annoying to our infantry lines and also to another battery holding a position in our rear, they replied to our fire but very feebly for a few moments and soon were altogether silenced, and up to the morning of the 19th, when they evacuated their position, they fired less than a half dozen rounds. In this position the battery lost 4 men wounded. On the morning of the 19th the battery moved with the Second Division from our position at Mud Creek, and after having advanced about two miles and again finding the enemy in position, one gun, under my command, was ordered by General Geary to the right of the road, in an open field, and shelled the enemy's position. On the same evening we were moved and placed in position in our works on the left of the road, but did not use our guns; and on the evening following, being relieved from this position by the Fourth Corps, we moved with the division toward the right of our line, where we were placed in position and entrenched. On the 22d one section of the battery, under command of Lieutenant Miller, was ordered forward to a position on Kolb's farm, on the left of the First Division. From this position this section opened a rapid and effective fire upon the enemy's columns as they advanced to retake a position just occupied by the First Division. Here, while directing the fire of this section, Capt William Wheeler, then commander of the battery and chief of artillery of the Second Division, was instantly killed by one of the enemy's sharpshooters. The remainder of the battery joined this section while the enemy was being repulsed, and aided in throwing a few shells into their retreating and disordered columns. Works were thrown up here and we occupied them until the morning of the 27th. On the 27th the battery was ordered at daybreak to a position on a hill toward the left of our division line, where a large portion of the batteries of the corps were massed. At about 9 AM, as our infantry lines were about to advance in a general attack, one section, under command of Lieutenant Carlisle, was advanced to a corn-field in front of our lines, and opened fire with canister and bags of musket-balls on a position held by the enemy's skirmishers in and around a house in front of our lines, and from which our infantry skirmishers had failed to dislodge them. After one or two rounds the enemy broke and scattered to the rear, and I directed a few shells to be thrown into the woods on the left of the house, where some of the enemy's skirmishers were supposed still to remain. Our infantry skirmishers then advanced, and I was at the same moment directed by General Geary to advance my whole battery to the position at the house from which the enemy's skirmishers had been dislodged.

We had just gained this position, and found ourselves subjected to a cross-fire of artillery on both flanks and an infantry fire from the direction of our front, and which made it necessary to provide some cover for our guns before opening fire. While engaged in sinking our guns in the ridge we were ordered to retire and take position again in the corn-field from which we first opened fire. In this position we remained until dark, when we were ordered back to our former position in the works, from which we had advanced in the morning. In this engagement the battery had 2 men wounded. On the afternoon of the 30th the battery moved toward the right of our line with the Second Division, which relieved a division of the Twenty-third Corps. On the same evening I placed three pieces in position, under the charge of Lieutenants Freeman and Miller, the other three guns being in reserve.

On the morning of the 1st of July the three guns in position, simultaneously with the other batteries along our line, opened fire on the enemy's position, which was continued rapidly for about fifteen minutes, the enemy not replying. The enemy having evacuated their works on the night of the 2d, we advanced with the division on the morning of the 3d, and toward night were placed in position on a hill south of Noonday Creek, in which position we remained without firing until the morning of the 5th, when, the enemy having been discovered to have evacuated his works, the battery again advanced with the division, and toward evening was sent forward to an advanced position within range of a stockade forming a part of the enemy's line of works, but was subsequently withdrawn on the same evening without opening fire. On the following day we moved with the division still farther toward the left of our line, and on the day succeeding that were ordered into camp, where we remained until the evening of the 17th, when our corps crossed the Chattahoochee River. On the 19th, when the Second Division was brought into position on a ridge of hills overlooking Peach Tree Creek, the battery was placed in position, each section at different points most favorable for the purpose of shelling a wooded ridge on the opposite side of the creek held by the enemy, and late in the afternoon we opened a concentrated fire on this ridge, lasting about five minutes, under cover of which the infantry advanced and took it. On the morning of the 20th the battery advanced with the division across the creek, and about 2 o'clock on the afternoon of that day was placed in position with the division on a ridge about half a mile in advance of the creek. We had been but a very short time in position when the enemy was observed advancing upon the Third Division of the corps, which was posted on the left of the Second, and having an enfilading fire upon the enemy's columns as they advanced against the Third Division, I directed the battery to open upon them. Our fire against the enemy at this point was becoming very destructive, when suddenly another portion of their line appeared advancing against our immediate front and on the right flank of the battery. The fire of the battery was immediately directed against them, but the infantry supporting us gave way, and our right being quite exposed, and subject to a most destructive enfilading fire from the enemy's infantry, one section of the battery, under Lieutenant Miller, on the extreme right, had its gunners disabled in a few minutes, and was necessarily temporarily abandoned. I then directed the other two sections of the battery to change front to the right in order to prevent the enemy from removing the section which had been abandoned and to cover the now exposed flank of the division. The fire of our guns in this direction was effective and altogether successful; the enemy were repulsed, and in a few minutes more I was enabled, through the exertions of Major Reynolds, who rallied the infantry to my support and with his own hands uncoiled the prolonges of the guns, to have the other section withdrawn inside our lines. We continued to sweep the dense woods in our front with canister and case-shot until satisfied that the enemy had withdrawn, and subsequently continued to enfilade the enemy's lines as they fell back from the front of the First Division. In this engagement the battery lost 3 men killed on the field, and 8 wounded, 6 of whom belonged to the section of the battery which had been temporarily abandoned. Of these 11, 5 were non-commissioned officers, 2 of whom were killed, 1 receiving nine bullets and the other seven, and 3 wounded, all of them brave, reliable, and experienced artillerists. In this position we remained until the morning of the 22d without again using our guns. On the morning of the 22d, the enemy having evacuated their works in our front, the battery again advanced with the division, and in the afternoon of that day was placed in position in line with the Second Division behind works thrown up in front of the enemy's interior line north of the city of Atlanta. On the 26th, our line being somewhat advanced, the battery was distributed at angles of the advanced work and in front of two forts occupied by the enemy and covering the Peach Tree road and a part of our line northeast of it. We occupied this position for about one month, almost daily using our guns against the enemy's works, when we fell back on the evening of the 25th with the division to a position covering the bridge at Pace's Ferry, on the Chattahoochee River. Here the battery was placed in position and remained until the evening of the 2d of September, firing only three rounds--that on the occasion of some of the enemy's cavalry making a demonstration on our front. On the evening of the 2d, the enemy having evacuated this city, the battery advanced, under orders, with the division, and was assigned to its present position in the defenses of the city. The entire loss of the battery throughout the campaign was 1 commissioned, 3 non-commissioned officers, and 1 private killed in action, and 17 non-commissioned officers and privates wounded. Of these latter I have had official notice that 2 have since died. The entire number of horses disabled was 20.

I cannot, in concluding this report, omit to award the just tribute of praise which belongs to the officers, non-commissioned officers, and privates under my command for their conduct throughout this long and arduous campaign. I could not particularize any without being unjust to all the rest, for as a body, officers and men alike, they have ever evinced under the fatigue of the march and the dangers of the field, that unvarying fortitude, willing obedience, coolness, and heroism which becomes the true soldier.

Henry Bundy
Capt, Comdg 13th New York Independent Batty Vet Vols

September 9, 1864
Report of Maj. John Reynolds, Chief of Artillery, 20th Army Corps
Atlanta, GA

General: I have the honor to submit the following report of the part taken by the batteries of this corps during the recent campaign:

In the month of April the batteries were assigned to the divisions of the corps, and have operated principally with their respective divisions. The following was the order of assignment: First Division--Battery M, First New York Light Artillery, Captain Woodbury; Battery I, First New York Light Artillery, Captain Winegar. Second Division--Thirteenth Independent New York Battery, Captain Wheeler; Battery E, Independent Pennsylvania

Light Artillery, Captain McGill. Third Division--Battery C, First Ohio Light Artillery, Captain Gary; Battery I, First Michigan Light Artillery, Captain Smith. The entire command left Lookout Valley between the 1st and 5th of May. On the 8th instant Captain McGill's battery covered the withdrawal of General Geary's division from an unsuccessful assault at Dug Gap. At Resaca, on the 13th instant, Captain Gary's battery took position on Major-General Butterfield's line, enfilading and driving the enemy from a line of rifle-pits in General Butterfield's front. On the 15th Captain Wheeler took position on right of Twentieth Corps, to the north of Resaca, and shelled the enemy previous to the charge made by General Butterfield's division. Captains Woodbury and Winegar took position on the left, in General Williams' front, later in the day. Their batteries were well handled and did effective service in repelling charge of the enemy. On the 19th Major-General Butterfield's division, being in advance, met the enemy near Cassville. Captains Gary's and Smith's batteries were quickly placed in position by Captain Gary, division chief of artillery, and after firing a few rounds the enemy fell back out of range. The other divisions of the corps coming up, an advance was ordered, one section of Captain Gary's battery, under Lieutenant King, keeping with the advance. The enemy was found to be behind strong works around the town, a part of his troops moving through the town in column. Lieutenant King's section was quickly placed in position on the right of the seminary, and opened on this column with solid shot, creating great confusion among them. A battery behind their works now opened on Lieutenant King, to which he replied, making excellent shots until they ceased. The other sections of Captain Gary's battery were soon in position, and fired a few shots, but eliciting no reply ceased firing. The enemy fell back during the night. On examining the position the next morning held by his battery, four dead horses and several graves proved the correct range of Lieutenant Kings guns. No further engagement of the batteries took place until crossing Pumpkin Vine Creek, near New Hope Church, on the 25th instant. The enemy was here found to be in force, and by order of Major-General Sherman, Captain Wheeler fired about thirty rounds as a signal to the Army of the Tennessee of our position. An advance was ordered immediately after, Major-General Hooker directing one battery to follow closely, in order to render assistance if possible. Owing to the face of the country, a dense woods, the artillery could not be made use of in the advance. There were no positions from which a view of the enemy could be obtained. The advance was continued till dark, driving the enemy behind his works, and coming within canister-range of their batteries. At daybreak of the 27th instant three light 12-pounder batteries were placed along our lines and in accordance with orders from headquarters Military Division of the Mississippi, opened fire on enemy's lines, continuing until 9 AM Two more batteries were during the day placed in position. The lines were now very close; in some places less than 150 yards. Any demonstration on the part of either was met by a fire from the batteries. The enemy's sharpshooters were very annoying, keeping up a constant fire, particularly directed toward our guns, yet the loss among the batteries was light. Batteries remained in this position until the 1st of June, when the corps was relieved by the Fifteenth Corps and was moved to the left.

June 2, Captains Winegar and McGill fired a few rounds. On the 13th Captain McGill took position in front of Pine Mountain, throwing a few shells into the enemy's position. 15th, the enemy having fallen back, our troops advanced and took position in front of another strong line of works, occupied by the enemy. 16th, five batteries placed in position in our lines, and at 3.30 PM all opened simultaneously on the enemy's works. Two of their batteries replied, having very correct range on some of ours, though fortunately doing but little harm. They were, however, soon silenced and compelled to withdraw their guns entirely behind their works. On the 17th, the enemy having evacuated his works, we again advanced and came up with his rear guard near Mud Creek, on the Marietta and Dallas road. They opened on us with a rifle battery, but Captain Winegar soon compelled them to retire across the creek behind their works. Captain McGill took position on a hill to the left of the road and made some excellent shots at their lines. Captain Wheeler's battery was placed on a hill not exceeding 300 yards from the enemy's works, his pieces sunk behind the crest. The most exciting artillery duel of the campaign with us took place here. The enemy's works were at the edge of the woods, and though his position was somewhat concealed, yet our close proximity enabled us to judge well the location of his guns. The fire from his battery was rapid, and for a time with excellent range, and although within easy musket-range from the enemy's works, yet Captain Wheeler soon silenced them with trifling loss.

Prisoners taken next morning reported his fire very destructive to them, killing and wounding many in their battery. 19th, the enemy having again evacuated his works during the night, we advanced across Noyes' Creek. Captains Wheeler's, McGill's, and Winegar's batteries were lightly engaged, firing a few rounds each, when we came up to the enemy's position. 21st, corps moved to right and took position near Mr. Atkinson's house. Batteries were placed along the lines, but no firing. 22d, troops moved forward and occupied commanding position about one mile in front of the line held the day before, right resting near Kolb's house. Captains Gary's, Smith's, and McGill's batteries were placed on a commanding hill on General Geary's line. All had an oblique fire to the left and shelled the enemy as General Butterfield's division advanced to the position assigned him. Captains Woodbury and Winegar took position farther to the right on General Williams' line; Woodbury near his right and Winegar his left. At 2 PM Captain Wheeler was directed to place his battery to the left of General Williams' line, between him and General Geary. The enemy had massed his troops in front of General Williams, and at 4 PM charged furiously upon him. As they emerged from the woods, Captains Smith's and McGill's batteries were turned upon them, having an oblique fire of their lines. As they advanced they obtained a more raking fire, until they had nearly an enfilade of their whole lines. Captains Wheeler and Winegar had also part of the time an oblique fire, and Captain Woodbury a direct fire; but the latter battery being so much nearer, Captain Woodbury was enabled to use canister, which was terribly destructive to the enemy.

    Captain Wheeler had placed one section of his battery in the position assigned him, and was directing their fire previous to the arrival of the balance of his battery, when he was struck by a musket-ball and instantly killed. Captain Gary's battery, being on the left, could not be made use of, the enemy being beyond his range. The fire from the five batteries was terribly destructive to the enemy; their lines were completely broken and troops utterly demoralized before they came within range of the musketry. Their losses must have been very great, while ours, in numbers, small, but to the artillery the death of Captain Wheeler is a great loss. He was a splendid officer, capable, energetic, and very efficient. To the service his death is a great loss, and to the corps and his immediate command irreparable. During the assault the enemy's batteries opened on ours on the left, but no attention was paid to them until the assaulting party fell back. On the 27th four batteries were placed to shell the hill on our left, while the infantry of the Fourth and Fourteenth Corps attempted to take it by assault. Enemy's batteries opened on us, and after the unsuccessful assault, we returned their fire until they ceased.

July 2, in accordance with orders from headquarters Department of the Cumberland, batteries all opened fire on enemy's lines, continuing for one hour. 3d, enemy having again fallen back during the night, we advanced and came up with their rear guard near Marietta. Captain Smith's battery was brought up and opened on them, to which they replied with artillery. A sharp artillery duel now took place lasting half an hour, when they withdrew. No further engagements of the batteries took place until after crossing the Chattahoochee River. On the 19th instant Captain Bundy's and Lieutenant Sloan's batteries (Thirteenth New York and E, Pennsylvania Artillery) took position on the north side of Peach Tree Creek, above Howell's Mill, and shelled a wooded ridge on south side occupied by the enemy while General Geary's troops effected a crossing. 20th, Captain Bundy's and Lieutenant Sloan's batteries were placed in position on General Geary's line, about 800 yards from our crossing of Peach Tree Creek. Two sections of Captain Woodbury's and one of Captain Winegar's, had crossed the creek and were in column with General Williams division to the right of General Geary, when about 3.30 PM the enemy, having massed his forces in the woods in our front, hurled them upon us. Captain Bundy's and Lieutenant Sloan's batteries opened on them as soon as they came in sight. The guns of Captains Woodbury and Winegar across the creek were quickly placed in position, opening at once upon the enemy. Captains Gary's and Smith's batteries being still on the north side of the creek, were directed by Major-General Thomas to take position on the left of our corps on General Newton's front. The enemy first appeared on the left of Captain Bundy's and Lieutenant Sloan's front, but soon extended along their front and to their right. So impetuous was the charge that the supports on the right and covering Captain Bundy's right section gave way. These detachments remained nobly at their posts, working their guns until unable to do so from loss of men. The non-commissioned officers to these guns were both shot down, one having received nine, the other eight bullets, in addition to whom 6 of the cannoneers were wounded. The enemy following up the advantage thus gained, the two batteries at this point were exposed to a terrible flank fire, which was especially destructive to the horses, upward of 20 being shot here. Immediately after the cannoneers fell back from their guns, the balance of the battery changed front, fired to the right, and, with well-directed charges of canister, compelled the assailants to fall back. The infantry lines were afterward reformed and the position held. Captains Woodbury's and Winegar's guns in position did effective service, as also Captains Gary's and Smith's batteries. Lieutenant Sloan's battery is deserving of special mention for their conduct here; but too much credit cannot be given to the officers and men of Captain Bundy's (Thirteenth New York) battery for their behavior on this occasion. Had they given way the position would have been lost, and the result might have been a terrible disaster to us. The enemy evacuating his works in our front on the night of the 21st, our troops advanced on the morning of the 22d and took position on the north side of Atlanta, the batteries occupying suitable positions along the lines. In accordance with orders, they several times shelled the city in the vicinity of the depots, car buildings, and works, and fired upon the enemy's lines whenever opportunity offered of doing effective service, or replied to their batteries when they opened on us.

On the 27th of July Lieutenant Henchen, of Battery I, First New York Artillery, a brave and efficient young officer, was killed by a musket-ball. On the night of the 25th of August the corps moved back to the Chattahoochee River, taking positions at the railroad bridge, Turner's and Pace's Ferries, the batteries being assigned to positions in the lines.

On the 2d of September the corps occupied the city of Atlanta, and the batteries were placed in the vacated works of the enemy, which they now occupy. The conduct of the batteries in the campaign has been excellent. The officers have throughout evinced a commendable willingness and promptness in the execution of all their duties, and a desire to make their commands in every way as effective as possible. The men have performed their duties well, and everything required of the entire command has been well and faithfully done. The following is a list of guns found here abandoned by the enemy: Four 6-pounder guns, two 6-pounder guns (rifled), one 10-pounder Parrott, six 32-pounder guns, seven 32-pounder guns (rifled); total, twenty guns. There were also six caissons in good order filled with ammunition, besides several limbers and caissons partially broken and destroyed and a large quantity of ammunition, some fixed and in good condition, but which has not been all collected yet. The casualties in the batteries in the campaign are as follows:

	Killed		Wounded		
	Officers	Men	Officers	Men	Horses
1st New York Artillery, Battery M		2		8	10
1st New York Artillery, Battery I	1	3		10	12
1st Ohio Artillery, Battery C		2		9	8
1st Michigan Artillery, Battery I		1		9	19
Independent Pennsylvania Artillery, Battery E		1		6	15
13th New York Independent Battery	1	4	1	17	20
Total	2	13	1	59	84

List of ammunition expended:

	May	June	July	August	Total
Light 12-pounders:					
Canister	54	88	183		325
Shell	99	41	538	678	
Case-shot	306	504	660	409	1,879
Solid shot	411	421	599	341	1,772
Total				4,654	
3-inch:					
Canister	91		72	4	167
Fuse-shell	158	1,213	907	885	3,163
Percussion-shell	81	427	327	487	1,322
Case-shot	372	2,891	1,171	683	5,117
Solid shot			36	90	126
Total				9,895	
Aggregate				14,549	

I also send herewith reports of battery commander.
All of which is respectfully submitted.
I have the honor to be, very respectfully, your obedient servant,
    J A Reynolds
        Major 1st New York Arty, Chief of Arty, 20th Corps

September 12, 1864
Special Orders No. 6, Artillery 20th Corps,
Atlanta, GA

The following named commissioned officers is hereby detailed as Inspector of the Artillery 20th Corps and will report to Hd Qts as soon as practicable.
1st Lieut James Carlisle 13th NY Indpt Battery
    Maj Reynolds

September 14, 1864
Report of Brig. Gen. John Brannan, Chief of Artillery, Department of the Cumberland
Atlanta, GA

    General: I have the honor to transmit the reports of corps chiefs of artillery and battery commanders of the operations of the artillery arm of the service in your army during the campaign resuiting in the capture of the city of Atlanta:
    In forwarding these reports I will bear witness to the efficiency and valuable services performed by the artillery of your army during the entire campaign. Heavy losses were inflicted upon the rebels by the accuracy of our fire, the skillful and daring positions taken by our batteries, frequently on the skirmish line, within short canister range of strongly entrenched works of the enemy. That it has been most destructive, we have not only the evidence of what we ourselves witnessed, but also that of the enemy.
    The chiefs of artillery of corps have shown energy, efficiency, skill, and courage equal to any officers in the service. I call your attention to the reports of corps chiefs relative to subordinates. Capt A Sutermeister, Eleventh Indiana Battery, being attached to your headquarters under your own supervision, you are aware of the efficient and zealous manner he and his company have performed their part in the campaign, both with the 20-pounder Parrotts and 4½-inch guns. The organization of the artillery into brigades under the immediate command of the corps chiefs is, in my opinion, an improvement upon the former organization, and I recommend it be retained.
    We have lost the valuable services of several officers killed in battle during the campaign, viz: Capt Peter Simonson, Fifth

Indiana Battery; Capt S M McDowell, Company B, Independent Pennsylvania Artillery; Capt William Wheeler, Thirteenth New York Battery; First Lieut O H P Ayres, Sixth Ohio Battery; Second Lieut F Henchen, Company I, First New York Artillery.

Our loss in guns was four 3-inch Rodmans--two belonging to the Eighteenth Indiana Battery, lost on General McCook's raid, July 30, 1864; two of the Chicago Board of Trade Battery, lost on General Kilpatrick's raid, August 20, 1864.

I would here take the opportunity to mention the effective service of the batteries serving with the cavalry command--Tenth Wisconsin Battery, Capt Y V Beebe; Eighteenth Indiana Battery, First Lieut W B Rippetoe, and the Chicago Board of Trade Battery, First Lieut G I Robinson, commanding--during the entire campaign. In every instance where these batteries were engaged they did good service, and their commanding officers acted with judgment and gallantry.

Guns captured in battle: Four light 12-pounder guns by the Twentieth Army Corps at Resaca, May 15, 1864; six light 12-pounder guns, two 10-pounder Parrott guns by the Fourteenth Army Corps at Jonesborough, September 1, 1864.

Guns captured, abandoned by the enemy: Four 6-pounder iron guns at Resaca, May 16, 1864; 20 guns of different calibers at Atlanta, September 2, 1864; 10 guns of different calibers at Rome.

A consolidated report of casualties and expenditure of material and ammunition during the campaign is hereto annexed.

I am, general, very respectfully, your obedient servant,
 J M Brannan
 Brig Gen, Chief of Arty, Dept of the Cumberland

Casualties and expenditure of ammunition in the artillery of the Army of the Cumberland during the campaign ending with the capture of Atlanta.

CASUALTIES

Rank	Killed	Wounded	Prisoner	Total
Officers	5	6		11
Men	37	208	18	263
Total	42	214	18	274

AMMUNITION EXPENDED

	Rounds
3-inch	35,321
10-pounder Parrott	14,786
12-pounder light	29,643
20-pounder Parrott	5,059
4½-inch	201
24-pounder howitzer	3,368
Total	88,378

J M Brannan
Brig Gen, Chief of Arty, Dept of the Cumberland

September 15, 1864
Report of Brig. Gen. John Geary, 2nd Division, 20th Army Corps
Atlanta, GA

Colonel: In pursuance of orders, I have the honor to submit the following report of the operations of my command during the campaign just terminated by the capture of Atlanta:

The consolidation of the Eleventh and Twelfth Army Corps having been ordered, the three brigades composing the Second Division of the corps were, with the exception of the One hundred and ninth Regiment Pennsylvania Veteran Volunteers, which remained as the nucleus of a new Second Brigade, consolidated into two--the First and Third. The First Brigade consisted of the Twenty-eighth and One hundred and forty-seventh Pennsylvania Volunteers, and the Fifth, Seventh, Twenty-ninth, and Sixty-sixth Regiments of Ohio Volunteers, composing an effective force of 2,846 officers and men, commanded by Col Charles Candy. The Second Brigade was composed of the Twenty-seventh, Seventy-third, and One hundred and ninth Regiments Pennsylvania Volunteers, of the One hundred and nineteenth, One hundred and thirty-fourth, and One hundred and fifty-fourth New York Volunteers, and of the Thirty-third Regiment New Jersey Volunteers, containing an effective force of 1,762 officers and men, commanded by Col Adolph Buschbeck. With the exception of the One hundred and ninth Pennsylvania Volunteers, all the regiments comprising this brigade were formerly connected with the Eleventh Corps. The Third Brigade consisted of the Twenty-ninth and One hundred and eleventh

Regiments of Pennsylvania Volunteers, and of the Sixtieth, Seventy-eighth, One hundred and second, One hundred and thirty-seventh, and One hundred and forty-ninth New York Volunteers, containing an effective force of 2,643 officers and men, commanded by Col David Ireland. The artillery attached to the division comprised Independent Pennsylvania Battery E, commonly known as Knapp's Pennsylvania Battery, and the Thirteenth New York Battery, both commanded by Capt William Wheeler, as chief of the division artillery, which numbered 256 officers and men effective for the field. The total effective force of the division, including officers and men at the headquarters of the division, was 7,043, the aggregate of officers and men of all conditions present in the division being 7,607. At the date of the reception of marching orders, as for some time previously, the First Brigade garrisoned the post of Bridgeport, Ala., and vicinity. The Third Brigade occupied Stevenson and the railroad westward to Anderson. The Second Brigade, lying near the base of Lookout Mountain, formed part of the guard for the valley. On the 1st of May orders were received directing me to convene my division at Bridgeport, at which place Ireland's brigade joined me on the evening of the 2d. On the morning of the 2d I received a dispatch from Major-General Hooker directing me to hold my command in readiness to move, and during the day, from the same source, an order to move on the morning of the 3d toward Chattanooga Valley.

May 3, 1864, at 9 AM the First and Third Brigades set forward, and after marching until 2 PM I halted them at Shellmound in order that my wagon train might reach me without overtasking the mules, many of which had never before been harnessed. A few day's previously, under orders from Major-General Thomas, I had detached Colonel Pardee, One hundred and forty-seventh Pennsylvania Volunteers, with 400 men of the First Brigade, to take charge of and man one of the gun-boats recently built at Bridgeport for the purpose of patrolling the Tennessee River westward. The duties required of this detachment were performed, and, having taken up the pontoon bridge at Larkinsville, it was brought safely to Bridgeport, where the gun-boat was turned over to Captain Edwards, assistant quartermaster, and on the evening of the 3d Colonel Pardee joined me at Shellmound. Another detachment of my division joined me at the same place, being a party of mechanics whom I had detailed to construct, under my personal supervision, a roadway for wagons on the railroad bridge across the Tennessee at Bridgeport. May 4, the weather being sultry I marched at early dawn, and, with scarcely an incident worthy of note, passed through Whiteside's and Lookout Valley, crossed Lookout Mountain, and encamped in the Chattanooga Valley, the distance traveled being twenty-two miles. Here I was joined by Buschbeck's brigade, which had marched from Lookout Valley during the afternoon. May 5, my division, for the first time entirely united, marched via Ross' Gap under orders to proceed to Gordon's Springs, but the roads in that direction being thronged with troops, my orders were changed, and I marched to Post Oak Church, four miles from Ringgold. Near this point the division encamped. May 6, marched thence to Pea Vine Church, which was reached before noon; here the division encamped in order of battle. May 7, leaving Pea Vine Church my command crossed Taylor's Ridge; passed Gordon's Springs, near which I met General Kilpatrick and his command. In the afternoon, in accordance with orders from General Hooker, my Third Brigade was detached to support General Kilpatrick in his movement upon Villanow. With the other brigades I reached Thornton's farm, on the Rome road, shortly before dusk. Here I encamped, my line running parallel to the road, which was commanded on my right by a section of the Thirteenth New York Battery. The night passed without attack.

MILL CREEK GAP

May 8, I received orders as follows:

> March without delay to seize the gap in the Rocky Face Ridge called Babb's, and to establish yourself strongly at that point; take your two brigades and send word as soon as you are in position. Take no wagons and but few ambulances.

Having no map of the road or country, I took a citizen as guide and moved as ordered with my two brigades and two batteries of artillery at 11 AM The road taken was narrow and hilly, but was by several miles the most direct to the point designated, the distance by it being five miles. On reaching Mill Creek Valley, at the foot of Chattoogata Ridge (named in the order Rocky Face Ridge), my skirmishers came upon the enemy s cavalry pickets near Babb's house. These retreated hastily across Mill Creek, pursued by my skirmishers, and made their way to the mountain crest by the only road--that leading to Dalton. My preparations were immediately made for attacking the enemy, who were in plain sight along the crest of the mountain. The entire range here is known as Chattoogata Ridge, one of that numerous class in Northern Georgia to which Mission and Taylor's Ridges also belong. Its sides, steep, covered with forest, and corrugated with ridgy spurs and formations of rock, rise abruptly from the banks of Mill Creek, which flows along its base in a northerly direction. The banks of the creek are fringed with marshy thickets, and the creek itself is a sluggish, muddy stream with treacherous bottom. John's Mountain is a peak continuous with the ridge, but rising above the remainder of it about 200 feet, and situate south by west four miles from Dalton. The main road from La Fayette to Dalton crosses Mill Creek at Hall's Mill, thence winds up the steep ascent to an elevation of 800 feet from the valley, and there crosses over the ridge. This roadway has been cut out from the mountain side and through the palisades which crest the mountain, from which fact comes the name of Dug Gap. Along the top, facing westward for miles on either side of the pass, rise palisades of rock impossible to scale and to be passed only through a few narrow clefts filled with loose rocks and wide enough to admit five or six men abreast. This summit I closely scanned while forming for the attack. On either side of the pass and along the crest to John's Mountain, in addition to the natural strength of the position, were breast-works occupied by the enemy, but in what force could only be tested by attack. McGill's (Pennsylvania) battery, 3-inch Rodman guns, was placed in position in the field near Babb's house, from which they could reach the crest with their fire, and the Fifth and Sixty-sixth Ohio Volunteers and One hundred and forty-seventh Pennsylvania Volunteers, of my First Brigade, were left as guard to the artillery. The One hundred and ninth Pennsylvania Volunteers and Thirty-third New Jersey Volunteers, of my Second Brigade, were both absent, the former as guard to the wagon train, the latter having been on picket duty. With the rest of my command I crossed the creek in front of Babb's house at 3 PM, and advanced the One hundred and nineteenth New York Volunteers, deployed as skirmishers, up the mountain, followed by Buschbeck's brigade on the right and Candy's on the left, each disposed in two lines of battle. Knapsacks had been unslung and piled before commencing the ascent. Half way up the firing became lively. The enemy had posted skirmishers thickly across the steep face of the ridge, behind rocks, logs, and trees, and their fire was galling and destructive. Our skirmish lines, advancing rapidly, though they had to fairly clamber up the rough ascent, drove those opposed to them back with loss, and reached the foot of the palisades. Mean time my main lines pressed steadily forward under a severe musketry fire from the top of the palisades until the advanced regiments were halted to rest and form on the ground held by our skirmishers. The general line of advance had inclined at an angle toward the Dalton road and my extreme left was now across it. The atmosphere was hot and stifling, and the ascent was one of the greatest difficulty. After a halt of fifteen minutes, the palisades were charged impetuously by portions of both brigades, Buschbeck's on the right and Candy's on both sides of the road. The attack was a most gallant one, officers and men rushing through the few narrow apertures or clambering the precipice. Many of them gained the crest, but were met by a tremendous fire from a second line of works which were invisible from below, and were shot down or compelled to jump back for their lives. Here hand-to-hand encounters took place, and stones as well as bullets became elements in the combat, the enemy rolling them over the precipice, endangering our troops below. Failing to hold the crest after two separate assaults, our front line was withdrawn about 150 yards and reformed in preparation for another effort. Knowing that the enemy would hasten re-enforcements to the point attacked, I deemed it important to lose no time. One plan remained to be tried. My rifled battery (McGill's) had crossed the creek near Babb's house and taken position on a cleared knoll at the base of the ridge. By my order it now opened a steady and well-directed fire on the enemy's position. Under cover of this fire the Thirty-third New Jersey Volunteers, which had just arrived, was ordered to ascend the mountain and attempt to gain the crest, about half a mile to the right of the point of the previous attack, and at a place where the enemy did not show a strong force. In the mean time my main body was directed to keep the enemy in their front busily engaged and to support the movement promptly by again charging the crest in their front as soon as cheers from the Thirty-third New Jersey Volunteers should indicate their success on the enemy's flank. The order was promptly executed, but it was found impossible by the Thirty-third New Jersey to gain the palisades at the point aimed at on account of their high, precipitous formation, and they were obliged to oblique a little to the left. There finding a few narrow apertures they rushed through, where but two or three could climb abreast, and the first of them reaching the crest their loud cheers were re-echoed along the lines. At this signal the other regiments rushed again to the assault, and portions of the Twenty-eighth Pennsylvania Volunteers and One hundred and thirty-fourth and One hundred and fifty-fourth New York Volunteers again reached the summit, but it was impossible to hold it. So few at a time could clamber through the narrow clefts that the enemy overwhelmed them and forced them off the cliffs. During the several assaults to the right of the pass the Twenty-ninth Ohio Veteran Volunteers had fought heroically on the left of it, and having lost very heavily the Fifth and Sixty-sixth Ohio Volunteers had been brought up to its support. It was now dusk, and official information was brought me from Colonel Ireland, commanding my Third Brigade, that the movement on Snake Creek Gap was successful, and it was in full possession of the Army of the Tennessee. The object of my attack having been fully accomplished by securing the attention of the enemy while General McPherson's movement was made on Snake Creek Gap, I deemed further continuance of the action unnecessary and decided to withdraw to the foot of the mountain. Two sections of McGill's battery were brought across Mill Creek at Hall's Mill, and from a position at the foot of the ridge and on the left of the road they kept up a continuous fire on the enemy. The Fifth, Seventh, and Sixty-sixth Ohio Volunteers, which had not been seriously engaged, were so deployed as to cover the movement. Our dead and wounded were all removed to the field hospital, and my entire command was withdrawn and encamped around and near Babb's house, such disposition being made of the troops as to hold the position against attack from any direction. During the night breastworks were constructed encircling our encampment in an almost continuous line. Ireland's brigade, having marched from Snake Creek Gap, rejoined me about 10 PM The work assigned to this brigade had been successfully performed. In conjunction with General Kilpatrick's cavalry, it had marched from Gordon's Springs to Villanow, and from thence to Snake Creek Gap, which it held until General McPherson arrived there, thus covering the movements of the Army of the Tennessee in that vicinity from the observation of the enemy.

    For the particulars of this expedition I respectfully refer to the official reports of the operations of Colonel Ireland's brigade. I learned from prisoners and deserters that the troops opposed to us in this action comprised a brigade of Arkansas infantry, two regiments of Kentucky cavalry, and Cleburne's division, which was brought up as support during the pending of the battle; also, that the enemy lost in killed 69, which exceeded the number killed in my command, indicating that their casualties at least equaled mine. To Col Charles Candy, commanding First Brigade, I am indebted for his promptness and efficiency in handling his troops under a persistent and galling fire. Captain Wheeler, my chief of artillery, proved himself a master hand in this his first action under my command. I must mention with special commendation Captains Davis, Veale, and Lambert, of my staff, who exhibited more than ordinary gallantry, forming the troops, and assisting personally in the heroic assaults made to the very summit of the ridge. Lieutenant-Colonel Flynn and Major Fitzpatrick, of the Twenty-eighth Pennsylvania Volunteers; Colonel Fitch and Lieutenant-Colonel Hayes, of the Twenty-ninth Ohio Volunteers; Lieutenant-Colonel Jackson, of the One hundred and thirty-fourth, and Lieutenant-Colonel Allen, of the One hundred and fifty-fourth New York Volunteers; Lieutenant-Colonel Fourat, of the Thirty-third New Jersey Volunteers, and Major Cresson, Seventy-third Pennsylvania Volunteers, also deserve special mention. They with their regiments sustained the burden of the conflict and performed their duty in the most trying positions. Capt H C Bartlett, Thirty-third New Jersey Volunteers, an officer of great bravery and merit, was killed at the head of his company after he had reached the crest of the palisades. The loss in the Twenty-ninth Ohio Volunteers was particularly severe. Colonel Fitch and Lieutenant-Colonel Hayes, two of my best field officers, both received wounds that will probably disable them for further service in the field. The adjutant of that regiment was mortally and several of the line officers were severely wounded. Major Fitzpatrick, Twenty-eighth Pennsylvania Volunteers, a most gallant officer, was wounded by three bullets passing through both legs.

Casualties in battle of Mill Creek Gap, May 8, 1864

Command	Killed	Wounded	Missing	Aggregate
Commissioned officers	3	12		15
Enlisted men	46	245	51	32
Total	49	257	51	357

May 9, 10, and 11, the division remained encamped near the foot of the mountain, guarding the approaches to and from it for a distance of five miles. In compliance with orders from Major-General Hooker, early on the morning of the 11th I sent one regiment of my division, the Thirty-third New Jersey Volunteers, to the trace on my left, where it relieved two of Butterfield's regiments. May 12, my whole command was relieved by the cavalry division under Col Edward McCook, and I marched to and through Snake Creek Gap, encamping a short distance beyond its eastward opening. May 13, marched to a farm near Isaac King's house, two and a half miles from Resaca, and at 3.45 PM formed in columns of battalions across a narrow road leading into the main road from Dalton to Calhoun, Butterfield's division being in our immediate front, and Williams' in our front and left. At 7 PM formed line of division front, occupying Williams' position, covering the main road from Dalton to Rome, and throwing up a line of works. The First Brigade, resting its left upon the road, was deployed up the hill on the right, the Third and Second Brigades occupying the works upon the left.

BATTLE OF RESACA

May 14, at 4 PM, in accordance with orders, I moved with my First and Third Brigades, following the First Division past the rear of the army to the extreme left on the Dalton and Resaca main road, at which point the enemy, making a strong attack, had already gained some advantage. The distance marched was about four miles through fields and woods. Being delayed by the time occupied in taking position by the division preceding me, it was after dark when my command reached the position assigned it. The two brigades were placed in line on the left of Williams' division, covering the Dalton road; Ireland's brigade, being the extreme left flank of the army, was refused in line. These dispositions were completed and a connected picket-line established before midnight. The enemy (Stevenson's division) had been met in their successful onset by the advance of our corps, and driven back quickly in confusion to their main lines. We passed the night in quiet, having hastily erected breast-works of rails and logs. May 15, at 3 AM Buschbeck's brigade, which had been left behind by orders from the major-general commanding the corps, arrived and formed on Ireland's raft, and in his rear. My artillery and trains also came up during the night. At 7 AM I received orders to send a strong reconnoitering party, with a staff officer, to explore eastward toward the railroad. The Sixtieth New York Volunteers, Colonel Godard, and Seventy-eighth New York Volunteers, Lieutenant-Colonel Chatfield, were detailed for the purpose, and accompanied by Captain Forbes, inspector on my staff, performed the duty, striking the railroad near Isaac Adams' house, where they ascertained the enemy's cavalry to be posted, and also found our outposts from McCook's cavalry command. By 11 AM they had returned, and in accordance with orders by which our entire corps was directed to attack the enemy at that hour, my division moved to the right about three-fourths of a mile, and there formed column for attack. Owing to the extremely rough and hilly nature of the ground, and the small compass within which the entire corps was to operate in the first charge, the only formation by which my command could be handled to advantage was that of column by regiments. Ireland's brigade was formed in advance; next Buschbeck; last Candy's.

The position occupied by the enemy was one strongly entrenched on an irregular conglomerate of hills, with spurs running in every direction. The general direction of their main lines of intrenchments on these hills inclined northeastward toward a bend in the Connesauga River, forming a refused right flank to their army. On most of the elevations they had batteries protected by earth-works of various descriptions, and so disposed as to sweep in every direction the lines of approach. The very irregular formation of the ground gave the enemy unusual facilities for cross-firing and enfilading the ground to be passed over, and they, in posting both their artillery and infantry, availed themselves fully of these advantages. The hills, steep and rough, were thickly wooded; the narrow ravines between, generally cleared. Immediately in front of the position on which my command formed for the attack, a small road passed down a narrow ravine running from the enemy's main line to the Dalton road. Everything being in readiness the advance was ordered. Ireland's brigade crossed a ravine and a hill swept by the enemy's artillery and musketry fire, and drove the enemy impetuously from another hill, and, turning a little to the right, charged with wild, ringing cheers for the capture of a battery, which from a key position was dealing death on every side. At the same moment on Ireland's left a portion of Butterfield's division was racing with him for the same deadly prize. The advance of both commands reached the battery nearly together, the One hundred and eleventh Pennsylvania Volunteers, of Ireland's brigade, under Col George A Cobham, leading and forcing its way through the jaws of death, till they had their hands upon the guns and their colors on the earth-works, from which part of the gunners had been driven and the rest killed or captured. This work was a sunken one at the crest of the hill, and open toward its rear. Twenty yards in rear was a line of strong breast-works, from which a deadly shower of bullets poured around and into the battery, rendering it impossible for men to live there. Cobham, with that cool and accurate judgment which never forsook him, formed his line, now augmented by other portions of the brigade, within fifteen yards of the guns, where by the formation of the ground his troops Were less exposed to the terrible fire, while at the same time his own muskets covered the battery from the front. During the advance of Ireland's brigade a body of troops from another division, sweeping through the brigade, had severed it, and by my orders all of it, excepting three regiments, were posted in reserve, and Colonel Cobham was directed to take command of the three regiments, which had now silenced and held under command of their guns the battery. Three regiments of Buschbeck's brigade, which had advanced gallantly, driving the enemy from two hills on the left of Cobham, were not far from him. With these three regiments Colonel Lockman was now ordered to report to Colonel Cobham, which he did promptly. Between 3 and 4 PM I received orders from Major-General Hooker, commanding the corps, to relieve whatever of General Butterfield s division was then holding position in the front line. Half of my Second and Third Brigades were then with Cobham. From the remainder of my command the order was at once complied with, and all of General Butterfield's troops were relieved, and by the direct order of Major-General Hooker, as well as my own, Colonel Cobham was directed to make every effort to secure and bring off the battery in his front. To this end I sent him as re-enforcements the Fifth Ohio Volunteers from Candy's brigade and other regiments from the Second and Third Brigades, numbering in all ten regiments, and invested him with full command of all the troops at that isolated point. I had now sent him one half of my entire division. Our lines were now strengthened and established in readiness for further operations, General Williams' division being formed entirely on my left, and General Butterfield's division being wholly withdrawn and posted in reserve. Musketry firing was kept up during the afternoon and night, and strong works were thrown up on the hills occupied by our main lines.

In the isolated position held by Cobham it was impossible to erect even a slight barricade without receiving a terrible fire from the enemy fifty yards distant. In front of my left and Williams' right was a long, cleared field occupying two hills and a narrow ravine, and extending to a wooded hill on which was the enemy's main line. In front of my right was a field occupying along, wide ravine, extending from the right of my line to a cleared hill on which was also the enemy's main line. Through this ravine ran the road previously referred to. Across the ravine to my right were lines of intrenchments held by the Fourth Corps and facing nearly eastward at right angles to my front. In front of the center of my main line a series of timbered spurs and knobs extended half a mile toward the enemy's main lines to the detached position held by Cobham. The troops sent to his support by me were so disposed as to hold his flank as well as possible. The only route of communication with him was by way of these timbered ridges, which were swept in most places by musketry and artillery fire from the enemy's main lines. About 5 PM the enemy (Stevenson's division) debouched from the woods in front of my left and General Williams' right, and charged in column with the effort to gain possession of the ridges in our front. The attempt, if successful, would have exposed Cobham to attack from every side and have forced him to abandon his position, but the enemy's attack, though a spirited one, failed. A tremendous fire concentrated on him from the lines of my division and those of General Williams' almost destroyed his leading regiments (of Brown's rebel brigade) and sent the attacking column back in confusion to their intrenchments, after half an hour of sharp fighting. In this affair the artillery on both sides took an active part, canister and shrapnel being principally used. During the engagement Colonel Ireland was wounded by a piece of shell, and the command of his brigade devolved upon Colonel Cobham. That officer being already intrusted with the command of six regiments and the special work of securing the battery in his front, I directed Col William Rickards, commanding Twenty-ninth Pennsylvania Volunteers, to assume command of such regiments as remained in the main line. Wheeler's battery had taken position in my line behind log works constructed for the purpose. About dusk Colonel

Cobham reported to me in person and received instructions to dig through the works in front of the guns and bring them off with drag-ropes during the night. The necessary tools and ropes were sent out and the work performed with alacrity and tact by the officers and men under his immediate supervision. In the darkness of the night the men crept silently on-hands and knees to the little fort and carefully removed the logs, earth-works, and stones in front of the four guns. At midnight all was ready. The drag-ropes were attached and manned; a line of brave men lay with pieces aimed at the crest of the hill, and at one effort the guns were drawn out and taken rattling down the hill. The enemy on the alert, sprang over their breast-works and furiously attacked Cobham's line. The sharp musketry fire aroused all our troops. Those in the intrenchments to our right across the ravine, not knowing the meaning of it, evidently believed it to be an attack upon their main line, and opened a tremendous musketry fire, much of which poured into Cobham's lines from his right and rear. Word was quickly sent them and their firing was stopped. Cobham held his position, drove back the enemy, and sent the guns, four 12-pounder brass pieces, to my headquarters. This important achievement was immediately reported in writing by me to Major-General Hooker, commanding the corps, and by my order the four pieces were the next day turned over to the ordnance department of the corps.

In concluding the report of the battle of Resaca, I must award the highest praise to Col George A Cobham, One hundred and eleventh Pennsylvania Volunteers, whose distinguished bravery, persistence, and coolness of judgment contributed so much to our success. The officers and men temporarily assigned to his command entered heartily into the performance of the duty allotted them while death threatened on every side. The position taken and held, and the duty performed, including the capture of a strongly intrenched and well-defended battery, were such as required no ordinary amount of skill and heroism. Colonel Lockman and Lieutenant-Colonels Randall, Kilpatrick, Lloyd, and Fourat, with the troops under their command, rendered good service in their execution of all orders, the execution of which was intrusted to Colonel Cobham. Colonels Candy and Ireland, and Captain Wheeler, my chief of artillery, performed their important shares in the work bravely, skillfully, and efficiently. Lieut Col E F Lloyd, One hundred and nineteenth New York Volunteers, fell mortally wounded at the head of his regiment while charging the enemy's battery. In the same charge, Capt Charles Woeltge, One hundred and eleventh Pennsylvania Volunteers, lost his life, being shot while his hand was on the cannon.

Casualties in battle of Resaca, GA

Command	Killed	Wounded	Missing	Aggregate
Commissioned officers	2	5		7
Enlisted men	21	210	28	259
Total	23	215	28	266

May 16, shortly before daylight (in the morning) it was discovered that the enemy had evacuated, which was immediately communicated to General Hooker. The Sixtieth New York Volunteers was sent to reconnoiter in the direction of Resaca. With my entire command in advance of the corps, I followed closely to within a mile of Resaca, where I turned to the left, and after waiting for orders upwards of an hour at the crossing of the Newtown road, and ascertaining that the ferry at Newtown could not be crossed, I proceeded eastward to Fite's Ferry, which was reached about 9 AM Here I crossed half of my command in a ferry-boat, which was brought from the opposite shore, the other half, with the artillery, crossing a quarter of a mile below, the water at the ford being about three feet in depth. Passing through the cavalry command of General Stoneman, I pressed on to McClure's Ferry, on the Coosawattee (a beautiful stream 100 yards in width), on the southern banks of which I found the enemy's scouts. Posting a section of artillery on a prominent knoll commanding the opposite bank, to protect the passage, I crossed my infantry on two old ferry-boats, upon which I subsequently constructed a bridge, over which the artillery and wagons of my own and other divisions of the corps were crossed during the night, and on the following morning encamped about a mile south of the ferry. May 17, at 1 PM marched out the Resaca and Adairsville road, camping near the junction of the Adairsville and Calhoun road, about four miles from Calhoun. May 18, broke camp at 8.30 AM and made a forced march of about fifteen miles to the foot of Gravelly Plateau, on the Cassville road, eight miles from Kingston, where I encamped, Butterfield in my front, Williams in my rear. May 19, being ordered to send one regiment on a reconnaissance toward Kingston, and to be ready to support it with the entire division, I sent out the Fifth Ohio Volunteers, and soon after, under further orders, followed with the whole command, marching across Gravelly Plateau in a southerly direction, through unbroken forests, over deep ravines, moving my artillery with great difficulty. I connected with the Fourteenth Corps at 10.30 AM I moved until in sight of the railroad at Kingston, then moving eastward, and at 3 PM connected with Butterfield at Price's house, on the Cassville and Kingston road. Here I found Butterfield in line of battle, shelling the enemy in the woods beyond. By a reconnaissance sent out toward the railroad, I connected with Newton's division, of the Fourth Corps, and then moved forward (crossing Two-Run Creek) south of the main road to Cassville, pressing the rear guard of the retreating enemy and capturing a number of prisoners. Formed line, with the Fourth Corps on my right, Butterfield and Williams on my left. Artillery and musketry firing upon the evacuating foe continued until long after dark, when my command went into camp half a mile west of Cassville, near Pendegrast's house.

May 20, 21, and 22, remained in camp, inspected my command, and prepared in every way for the further prosecution of the campaign. On the 20th received orders to be in readiness to march on the 23d, with twenty days' rations, and to send all sick and wounded to the rear. May 23, the term of service of the Twenty-seventh Pennsylvania Volunteers (Col A Buschbeck) having expired, it returned home. By the departure of Colonel Buschbeck. Col J T Lockman, One hundred and nineteenth New York Volunteers, being senior officer present, was placed in command of the Second Brigade; marched at 6 AM, following Butterfield, and crossed the Etowah on pontoon bridge near Milam's Bridge, encamping on high ground one and a half miles south of the river, Williams on my right and Butterfield on my left. May 24, under orders from General Hooker to push the enemy across Raccoon Creek toward Allatoona, I broke camp at daylight and pushed rapidly to the creek, resting a line of skirmishers on it to hold the Alabama road. In this position, covering the movement of Williams and Butterfield toward Burnt Hickory, I remained until noon, when I was relieved by the Twenty-third Corps. I then moved to the right, through fields and woods, in two parallel columns, with skirmishers moving by the flank along the creek, which I crossed about noon, passing through a deep ravine and up the sides of a spur of the Allatoona range. Reaching the summit, I halted the column, and going in person to the creek, about 200 yards above the point where my troops had passed, found the artillery and entire transportation of the corps detained on account of the miserable condition of the road. After bridging the creek (at this point almost impassable) and cutting a road along the mountain side, up which the trains had to pass, I remained until the artillery and wagons had all crossed, and then moving on through dense woods, giving the road to the artillery and transportation, took the road to Burnt Hickory, a short distance beyond which I encamped, on the extreme right, Williams on my left.

NEW HOPE CHURCH

May 25, at 7 AM I marched with my command, taking the road to Dallas via bridge across Pumpkin Vine Creek at Owen's Mill. Williams' and Butterfield's divisions, moving, respectively, by roads on my right and left, were to cross the creek by other bridges. The point of concentration ordered was to be Dallas (see order of march for May 25, dated May 24, headquarters Department of the Cumberland). The major-general commanding corps and myself, with our staffs and escort, preceded the troops to the bridge at Owen's Mill, which we found burning, having just been fired. While engaged in extinguishing the flames and repairing the bridge we were fired upon from the hill opposite, proving that the enemy were here in our front. A portion of Major-General Hooker's cavalry escort fording the creek, deployed and advanced on the opposite side through the woods, driving before them a short distance what proved to be an outpost of twenty-five cavalrymen. My infantry soon came up, and the repairs to the bridge being finished by the pioneer corps, the entire division crossed; the Seventh Ohio Volunteers preceding, deployed as skirmishers, advanced rapidly in the direction of New Hope Church, Candy's brigade leading. Near Hawkins' house, one and a half miles from the bridge, our skirmishers became heavily engaged with those of the enemy, and almost immediately a furious charge was made upon us. Our skirmishers resisted. Candy's brigade was deployed into line on the double-quick, and after a sharp engagement the charge was repulsed. The skirmish line was now re-enforced, and extended to the length of a mile by the Twenty-eighth Pennsylvania Volunteers. The remaining four regiments of Candy's brigade were deployed in line of battle, and, supported by my other two brigades, moved forward, attacking and driving steadily for half a mile a heavy force of Hood's corps, which opposed us. From prisoners captured we learned that Hood's entire corps was in our front, and Hardee's not far off, in the direction of Dallas. My division was isolated, at least five miles from the nearest supporting troops, and had been sustaining a sharp conflict with the enemy for four hours. Close in my front was an overwhelming force. My command was, by order of the major-general commanding the corps (who was with me), halted and formed on a ridge in the woods, advantageous for defense, and a slight barricade of logs hastily thrown up. My skirmish lines were deployed to a still greater extent than before, and ordered to keep up an aggressive fire, the object being to deceive the enemy as to our weakness by a show of strength. During this halt a charge made by a brigade of the enemy in column upon that part of my skirmish line occupied by the Seventh Ohio Volunteers was handsomely repulsed. The skirmish line there formed nearly a right angle toward the enemy, who charged upon the center line, not seeing that upon their flank. When the three regiments neared the angle they were met by a sharp fire in front and a heavy enfilading fire from their left flank, and retreated in hasty disorder and with considerable loss. Orders had been sent, as soon as the enemy was found in force in my front, by the major-general commanding corps, to Generals Butterfield and Williams to march their divisions to the point whore mine was engaged. By 5 PM both had come up and massed, Williams on my right and Butterfield on my left and rear. Each division was quickly formed for attack in columns by brigades, Williams leading, Butterfield next, my division as a reserve, and the corps advanced upon the enemy. In the advance Butterfield's brigades moved toward the flanks, leaving me in support of Williams, who had been heavily engaged, driving the enemy some distance. I received orders to push forward and relieve his troops. This was between 6 and 7 PM The movement ordered for my division was made with great rapidity, through a dense woods, swept by a very heavy artillery and musketry fire. The discharges of canister and shell from the enemy were heavier than in any other battle of the campaign in which my command were engaged. The troops of General Williams' division were relieved by this movement, and Cobham's brigade and portions of Candy's brigade engaged the enemy furiously at short range, driving him again until after dark, when my command was halted close under the enemy's batteries and intrenchments near New Hope Church. The night was intensely dark, and a very severe thunder-storm, with cold, pelting rain, added to the gloom. It was, therefore, impossible to form a regular line with the troops, and all the dispositions of them we could make was by the fitful flashes of lightning. Breast-works were thrown up as fast as possible during the night, and the dead and wounded were all cared for before morning.

May 26, when dawn came I found the position held by my troops to be a ridge of considerable natural strength confronting another ridge at a distance of from 80 yards on the left to 300 yards on the right, on which were the enemy's main lines. Around us in every direction were thick woods. The road to New Hope Church passed through my lines occupied by Candy's brigade, the flank of which, on the left of the road, was not in connection with any other troops. At this point near the road my lines were closest to those opposing us, and sharpshooters from Candy's brigade were so posted as to command a battery in his front, preventing the enemy from working his guns, excepting now and then to deliver an occasional shot. Another battery in Cobham's front was similarly commanded by sharpshooters from his brigade. Strong skirmish lines were posted along our front and drove the enemy's skirmishers into their main line of intrenchments and kept them there for the most part during the succeeding days that we remained in this position. The battle of the 25th was altogether in the woods, affording no opportunity for the use of artillery on our side. In my front this day I ascertained that the enemy had seventeen pieces of artillery well intrenched in their second line of works on top of the ridge occupied by them. This line of works was very strong, with re-entering angles. From my skirmish line it could be closely reconnoitered, being distant only about 100 yards. In addition to this they occupied in strong force a line of breast-works nearer us at the foot of the ridge. To this work their skirmishers were all driven, and my skirmishers, advanced to the farthest point possible, were ordered to hold them there and to cover with their own fire, if possible, every piece of artillery posted in our front. Directions were also given when night came' for the construction of log rifle-pits of the V pattern for the protection of my skirmishers and sharpshooters, the number of casualties among them being quite large during the day. At noon troops of General Stanley's division, Fourth Corps, came up and connected on my left by a refused line, and by order of Major-

General Thomas relieved five regiments of Candy's brigade, which had held the left of the road since the evening of yesterday. My entire division was now formed on the right of the road from left to right, in the following order: Candy's brigade, Lockman's, then Coburn's, brigade, of Butterfield's division, and on his right Cobham's brigade, of my division. Two-thirds of each brigade formed the front line. The remainder was placed in reserve near the foot of the ridge. Under protection of our sharpshooters breastworks were erected during the day, and, wherever possible, the timber in front was slashed, forming an abatis. All of my artillery, twelve pieces, was placed in position along my line during the day and night. The enemy made frequent sorties, attempting to drive in my skirmishers, establish their own line, and prevent our throwing up works, but in every case they were driven back with severe loss. Their artillery was rendered almost entirely inefficient by the constant watchfulness of our sharpshooters, and our works progressed rapidly. After dusk, Cobham's brigade, being relieved by Ward's, of Butterfield's division, took the place held in line by Coburn, thus bringing my entire command into a connected line.

My losses during yesterday and today were 376 killed, wounded, and missing. A full statement of them will be found hereto appended. I have to enumerate among the dead, fallen in the battle of New Hope Church, Col John H Patrick, Fifth Ohio Volunteers, brave officer, who had served with his regiment since April, 1861, and here fell mortally wounded by a canister-shot, and Lieut Joseph W Hitt, of Colonel Candy's staff, a promising young officer. My three brigade commanders, Colonels Candy, Lockman, and Cobham, all displayed personal gallantry and performed their whole duty in the most efficient manner. The behavior of the officers and men under their command was excellent throughout. For twenty-four hours they were actively engaged with the enemy without opportunity to cook a single meal or make a cup of coffee. I sustained a personal loss in the capture of Capt L R Davis, of the Seventh Ohio Volunteers, who had served as aide-de-camp on my staff for two years and had earned a wide-spread reputation for his extreme gallantry and personal daring.

May 27, lively skirmishing all day, our sharpshooters preventing the enemy from free use of their guns (artillery). The enemy made occasional attempts to drive in our skirmishers, but were each time driven back to their intrenchments with heavy loss.

My artillery kept up a destructive fire, enfilading portions of the enemy's works. In this constant, watchful war between skirmishers, kept up night and day, here as elsewhere in similar positions during this campaign, my troops thoroughly proved their superiority over the enemy as sharpshooters, invariably driving them from their post. During the 28th, 29th, 30th, and 31st days of May our position and general daily routine of artillery practice and sharpshooting were unchanged. Small out-works for the protection of skirmishers were thrown up at every available point, thus diminishing my daily returns of casualties. From the 25th of May until the 1st of June my entire division was under fire, without an hour of relief. Owing to the proximity of the lines, and the nature of the ground, no one, whether in front or rear, could rest quietly with any assurance of safety. No opportunity being afforded for proper shelter, rest, and diet, the necessary result of this series of operations was a large increase of sickness.

Casualties in battle at New Hope Church, GA

Command	Killed	Wounded	Missing	Aggregate
Commissioned officers	3	17	1	21
Enlisted men	49	422	17	488
Total	52	439	18	509

June 1, being relieved by Harrow's division[74], of the Fifteenth Corps, I withdrew my command from the works and, forming in the Dallas road, marched to the rear of the left of Johnson's division[75], of the Fourteenth Corps, where the division encamped, with Butterfield on the right and Williams on the left. June 2, moved still farther to the left in the direction of Allatoona Church, within about two and a half miles of which I placed my command in position on a thickly wooded ridge in rear and in support of the Twenty-third Corps. During the day heavy storms of rain and hail prevailed, making the ground heavy, and swelling the creeks so as to render them almost impassable. Active artillery and musketry fire in the front, during which many shots passed through my camp, in which also several shells exploded. June 3, 4, and 5, remained in same position. On the 3d the Third Brigade was detached, and at 4 PM proceeded to the bridge on the Acworth road over Allatoona Creek, with orders to hold the bridge and the ford. It found the bridge in a shattered condition, but placed it in good order, remaining at this point during the 4th and 5th. June 6, the enemy having evacuated the works in the immediate front of the army, the division marched to the Marietta road, encamping on Hull's farm, near the junction of the roads leading to Big Shanty and to Lost Mountain, Butterfield and Williams on the right, the Fourth Corps upon the left. June 7, 8, 9, 10, 11, and 12, remained in same position, having thrown up breast-works to cover the roads approaching my front, advancing my skirmishers and feeling the enemy, who were found fortifying the ridges connecting Lost Mountain and Pine Hill. On the 7th Col P H Jones, One hundred and fifty-fourth New York Volunteers, having reported for duty, and being the senior officer, was assigned to the command of the Second Brigade. On the 10th orders were received to move on the Marietta road toward Kenesaw Station, but the Fourth and Fourteenth Corps, occupying the road with troops and trains, prevented any movement on the part of my command. On the 11th, the term of service of the Seventh Ohio Volunteers, Lieutenant-Colonel McClelland, having expired, the regiment departed for the North. During its long connection with my division, this regiment, by gallant service upon many fields, on which it lost heavily, earned for itself a reputation of which Ohio may well be proud. June 13, by direction of the major-general commanding corps, I moved at noon with my three brigades and two batteries of artillery to the right of the Marietta road, passed through the intrenched lines of Williams' division, and formed on a wooded spur projecting at right angles from his line of works. My left here connected with the right of Stanley's division, of the Fourth Corps, near Williams left. The general front of the Fourth and Twentieth Corps was southward; my troops in the new position taken faced nearly east. My right rested near one of the principal branches of Allatoona Creek, on the north bank of which were my pickets, on the other those of the enemy, between whom skirmishing was maintained. From this position to the summit of Pine Hill was about 1,200 yards in direct line of fire. The enemy, reaching from Kennesaw Mountain on the right to Lost Mountain on the left, held this summit as an advanced post in front of their center, their main line curving around in rear of it.

Pine Hill is very steep, conical in form, and by far the highest between Kennesaw and Lost Mountain. On its summit were batteries strongly entrenched, and around the hill, a short distance below the summit, were circumvallating works held in force. A signal station was also in full operation on this eminence, which commanded a view of the position and movements of our army. Now commenced the work for its reduction. During the day my front was strongly entrenched and my skirmish lines were advanced well out toward the hill. Under the supervision of Captain Wheeler, my chief of artillery, McGill's battery of 3-inch rifled guns was posted in our works, and the guns were trained upon the summit. June 14, early this morning my First and Second Brigades were brought up and massed respectively in rear of Ireland's right and left; McGill's battery opened upon the enemy's position on the summit of Pine Hill and kept up an accurate and effective firing by battery during the day, with occasional replies from the enemy. I noticed a group of rebel officers collected near some tents near the summit; calling Captain McGill's attention to it, I directed him to bring his battery to bear on the spot. The shells struck in the midst of and around the group, causing evident consternation among them and their immediate retreat. Prisoners afterward taken pointed out that as the spot where Lieutenant-General Polk was killed. June 15, it was discovered that Pine Hill had been evacuated during the night; our skirmish line facing southward was immediately pushed forward across open fields to a stream in the woods running westward from the hill, while troops from General Stanley's division, on my left, occupied the summit, and reversing the works, planted batteries there. Generals Sherman, Thomas, Hooker, Howard, Stanley, and others, myself among them, were soon assembled at that point, from which the relative positions held by the two armies were readily determined. A lively artillery engagement was then progressing several miles to our left, along the railroad in front of Kennesaw, also far to the right in the direction of Lost Mountain. At noon, in pursuance of orders from Major-General Hooker, I advanced my division (Candy's brigade leading) from our line of works in a southeasterly direction one mile, crossing two streams, until we reached a position in the woods to the right of and not far from Pine Hill. Here my command was halted and formed, each brigade in two lines--Ireland's on the right, Candy's on the left, and Jones' in the center. This advance was covered by the One hundred and forty-seventh Pennsylvania Volunteers deployed as skirmishers. The skirmish line drove in that of the enemy, and took possession of a line of works on the flank of Pine Hill which the enemy had not yet quite completed.

The ground on which my division was now placed was entirely in the woods, and formed a series of steep ridges with narrow ravines between, their general inclination being east and west, with frequent deviations by way of irregular spurs and small hills; no troops connected with me on either right or left. The One hundred and thirty-fourth New York Volunteers was immediately deployed in skirmish line to my left, and formed connection with the Fourth Corps skirmishers at the base of Pine Hill, three-quarters of a mile distant from my left flank. The One hundred and eleventh Pennsylvania Volunteers was deployed in like manner in front of Ireland and to his right, but could make no connection with any troops in that direction. While making these dispositions, I received orders from the major-general commanding the corps to push forward at once in assault upon the enemy. The orders were brought to me verbally by Lieutenant-Colonel Perkins, assistant adjutant-general and Colonel Fessenden, aide-de-camp, who added that at the same time the Fourth Corps would assault to my left and Butterfield's division to my right, 2 PM being the hour for the concerted movement. At 2.15 PM I advanced rapidly with my entire command, formed as stated above, Major-General Hooker then being present. The enemy, in heavy force, was encountered at once, and the battle became severe, lasting until after dark. All of my brigades were handled very handsomely by their commanders, preserving their formation in two lines while advancing, and fighting desperately over very rough and timbered ridges. The enemy were driven from two ridges, which they held with rifle-pits strongly occupied, and my troops charged impetuously up to the very mouths of their cannon, which were in a line of powerful works on a high ridge which forms part of the chain south of Pine Hill and connecting Kennesaw with Lost Mountain. Here the fighting was desperate. The enemy, driven with heavy loss into powerful intrenchments, on which they had bestowed a week's labor in preparation, and in which, in my front, they used eighteen pieces of artillery, fought from these works, knowing that if they were carried by us all to them was lost. In front of them the timber was slashed, and strong abatis, and also chevaux-de-frise of pointed stakes, had been formed. Their artillery, which had played steadily into my ranks, was now used with redoubled effort. My troops, charging into the abatis, in some places within fifty yards of the guns, by dark had silenced many of them. There had been no co-operating attack on either my right or my left, both of which the enemy had attempted to flank during our assault. This attempt of theirs was repulsed without checking my advance, the attack on my right being met by a regiment from the second line of Ireland's brigade changing front to the right, that on our left by a regiment from the second line of Candy's brigade changing front to the left. The One hundred and thirty-fourth New York Volunteers, under Lieutenant-Colonel Jackson, as skirmishers, also rendered most effective service, holding the ground between Candy and the Fourth Corps, and following up our movement with the right of his line.

Darkness coming on the battle diminished to heavy skirmish firing, the enemy also keeping up a brisk enfilading artillery fire upon us from their works extending beyond my left. My lines were established in the position gained close to the enemy's main works. So near were the opposing forces that it was extremely hazardous to attempt the construction of breast-works. The sound of an ax was the signal for a volley of bullets and canister from the enemy, but by cutting timber some distance in the rear, and carrying it up by the help of old logs, and the active use of the spade, a tolerable line of irregular intrenchments was thrown up in our front during the night. I ascertained that the position held by Ireland's brigade was in the opening of a wide re-entering angle of the enemy's works, thus exposing him to a severe fire of artillery and musketry from both flanks as well as from his front. His brigade, which in this position was within a very few yards of the enemy (so close indeed that the slightest word could be heard by the opposing forces), was toward morning quietly withdrawn about 150 yards to the rear, thus forming a refused line on my right flank. In his front a strong log breast-work was finished by morning. My skirmish line connected during the night with that of Butterfield's to my right. At 5 PM Williams' division had come up and massed in my rear. Colonel Robinson's brigade, of that division, reported to me for orders, and by my direction took position in line on a small spur about 150 yards in rear of the center of my line. On this spur his troops erected a temporary breast-work of logs. About the same time Knipe's brigade, of Williams' division, formed on Ireland's refused right and Ruger's brigade on Candy's refused left. Knipe's brigade was withdrawn from that position in the night after my skirmishers had connected with Butterfield's. The nature of the ground on which the battle of Pine Hill was fought prevented the use of artillery on my part.

During the night works with embrasures were constructed on the left of my line with the purpose of using them the next day. My thanks are due to Brigadier-General Williams, commanding First Division of this corps, for his courtesy in tendering me the services of Colonel Robinson's brigade; also, to Colonel Robinson for his promptness in responding to my wishes. His brigade, although not brought into action, was placed in a position in reserve, where in case of attack by the enemy it would have rendered efficient service. Colonels Candy, Jones, and Ireland deserve the highest commendation for the manner in which their respective brigades were maneuvered. Colonels Cobham and Pardee and Lieutenant-Colonel Jackson, in command of a very extended skirmish line, conducted their advance with skill and gallantry. Indeed it is difficult to select names for special mention in this battle where every officer and man acted with heroic determination. The members of my staff rendered me quick, intelligent, and unwearied service. The proportion of casualties among officers in my command was unusually great; among them Captain Veale, assistant commissary of musters, who, acting as aide-de-camp, was severely wounded through the lungs in the early part of the action. Among field officers wounded were Major Cresson, Seventy-third Pennsylvania Volunteers; Captain Gimber, commanding One hundred and ninth Pennsylvania Volunteers; Colonel Rickards, Twenty-ninth Pennsylvania Volunteers; Major Stegman, One hundred and second New York Volunteers, all of whom were in command of their respective regiments.

Casualties in battle of Pine Hill, GA

Command	Killed	Wounded	Missing	Aggregate
Commissioned officers	1	25		26
Enlisted men	81	407	5	493
Total	82	432	5	519

June 16, early this forenoon Butterfield's division connected with my right. Both of my batteries were placed in position near my right and left and opened on the enemy, enfilading portions of their works. The enemy's artillery replied as much as they could, while closely watched by our sharpshooters. The casualties during the day on the skirmish line, especially in the Second Brigade, were severe. The enemy made several ineffectual sorties upon us during the day, our close proximity being very harassing to them.

June 17, before 1 am, Major Symmes, Fifth Ohio Volunteers, division officer of the day, sent me word that the enemy had evacuated and the skirmishers under his command had entered their works. I immediately communicated this information to the major-general commanding corps, and, without awaiting his orders, occupied the evacuated works with my entire division, and advanced a line of skirmishers, under Major Symmes, a mile to the front, through woods, until they reached a road running eastward toward Kennesaw. Here were large, cleared fields, and the cavalry vedettes of the enemy were found posted in the edge of the woods beyond and in the field. My skirmishers were at this time connected with those of the Fourth Corps on their left and of Butterfield's division on their right.

MUDDY CREEK

At 10 AM my entire command advanced, Jones' and Ireland's brigades in front, formed in two lines, Candy's brigade, in reserve, following. At the same time Butterfield's division advanced on my right and Williams' on my left. On reaching the cleared field above referred to the corps halted for a few moments, while the enemy's cavalry skirmishers were driven in. I then pushed forward, in accordance with orders, through an extremely dense woods, guiding the center of the two front brigades by a road running from Hard-shell Church to the Marietta and Dallas road; general direction of the advance, southeast. The pickets sent out in the morning had been withdrawn, and my advance was now covered by the Seventy-eighth New York Volunteers, deployed as skirmishers. A body of the enemy's cavalry who were bivouacked in these thick woods were unexpectedly routed by heavy volleys from my advance lines and retreated in the utmost haste and confusion across the field near Darby's house, and by way of the Marietta road over Muddy Creek, being closely followed by my command. At Darby's place my division, emerging from the woods into a cleared country on the Marietta and Dallas road, formed connection with Cox's division, of the Twenty-third Corps, which, coming from the direction of Lost Mountain, had just reached that point. Here, filing to the left, my brigades formed in line on the low ground between the Darby house and Muddy Creek, Cox's division at the same time forming to my right with its left resting on the Marietta and Dallas road. My skirmishers, which were finely handled by Lieutenant-Colonel Chatfield,

continued their advance, crossing under a sharp artillery and
musketry fire the open fields in our front and establishing
themselves close to Muddy Creek, the opposite bank of which was
held by the enemy's pickets. In front of Darby's house is the valley
of Muddy Creek, which here extends close at the foot of the hill
opposite, on which the enemy were strongly entrenched with
several batteries bearing upon our position, which they used freely
on us. The banks of the creek were low and very swampy, with
fringing of thickets. The hills occupied by the enemy were heavily
timbered, rising abruptly from the creek, and crowned with a very
strong line of works. Their batteries posted here swept at short
range the Marietta road from Darby's house to the bridge on the
creek; also the entire position taken by my troops, which was
necessarily in the open field, exposed to the full view of the
enemy. In order to silence their batteries I directed Captain
Wheeler to advance the Thirteenth New York Battery to a bald hill
held by my skirmishers, within 400 yards of the enemy's main
line, and Ireland with his brigade to co-operate and sustain the
movement. These directions were in pursuance of instructions
received from the major-general commanding corps, who directed
me to occupy the ground to the left of the Marietta road, the
Twenty-third Corps being ordered to connect with me at that point
on my right. Meanwhile, McGill's battery had upon my first
reaching Darby's house taken position on the bare hill near the
house, and sustained a heavy artillery engagement with the enemy.
The movement ordered was made by Captain Wheeler and
Colonel Ireland with great spirit and in splendid style, the battery,
commanded by Lieutenant Bundy, charging on the run through
open fields swept by musketry and artillery fire, and reaching the
bald hill indicated before the enemy knew their purpose. Here the
horses and limbers were left at the foot of the hill, the guns drawn
up by hand and quickly sunk in the crest by the aid of my pioneer
corps. Ireland's brigade, advancing on the double-quick in concert
with the battery, instantly formed in support in rear of it and on
both flanks. Bundy's six guns, sunken 400 yards from the
embrasures opposite, opened a rapid and accurate fire by battery,
quickly silencing the enemy's guns, and enfilading their right
produced great havoc among their works and troops. The effect of
each shot that went crashing through their works was plainly
visible from our position. Two of the enemy's guns were
dismounted, two knocked end over end, and the rest silenced, their

embrasures were literally destroyed, and, as I afterward learned from a prisoner, a large number of their troops killed or wounded. Jones' brigade was now advanced and formed in line on the left of Ireland's, Candy's formed in reserve, all three brigades being in open fields, with the advanced lines close to the enemy.

During the afternoon Butterfield came up and formed on my left. Immediately after Bundy's battery had taken its advanced position McGill's was moved to a little elevation at the left of my line, from which he delivered an effective cross-fire, assisting materially to quiet the enemy in our front. Their sharpshooters, driven early in the day from the banks of the creek to their main line, posted themselves in trees and attempted during the afternoon to harass our gunners. Sharpshooters detailed from my command prevented them from producing the intended effect, and some of them were shot in their elevated hiding places. At dark my skirmishers were advanced close to the creek, where they dug pits in the soft ground for their protection. During the night the troops threw up breastworks of rails and earth. After dark commenced a series of very severe rain-storms, which lasted, with occasional short intermissions, for several days and nights. Our skirmish pits were filled with water, and the occupants suffered much from cramps. All the troops bivouacked in fields of soft, low ground, and without adequate shelter, suffering much from these rains, which were accompanied by chilly winds. Muddy Creek and its small tributaries became swollen to the size and power of torrents, and the low ground adjoining, parts of which were unavoidably occupied by my troops in line, were flooded with water. June 18, our general position unchanged during the day; sharpshooting continued, with a number of casualties on our side; both of my batteries continued to pour their destructive fire into the enemy's works. The enemy replied feebly and seldom. June 19, suspecting the enemy would evacuate his line, at 2 o'clock in the morning I pushed my skirmishers forward, who crossed the swollen creek in my front without opposition, entered the works, which they found abandoned, and moved half a mile beyond, the cavalry of the enemy's rear guard retiring. Having sent the One hundred and thirty-fourth New York Volunteers to support the skirmishers, I followed soon after in person; scouts of the enemy were visible on the hills about a mile beyond the creek. The works of the enemy gave abundant indications of the splendid execution of my artillery; many of the embrasures were shattered. The woods in front, cut and torn, showed how truly the artillery was aimed and what execution had been accomplished.

NOYES' CREEK

At 7 o'clock I advanced my whole command on the Dallas and Marietta road, having previously rebuilt the bridge over Muddy Creek, which had been carried away by the swollen current, crossed the creek, and reached Noyes' Creek, where I was detained a short time to repair the bridge crossing it. After considerable difficulty, the bridge being swept away while crossing by the furious stream, which was still swelling rapidly, I succeeded in passing my entire command. Moving on over the miserable road, I encountered the enemy's skirmishers three-quarters of a mile beyond the creek, and pressing them, found the enemy entrenched a short distance beyond. I speedily formed line, placed the Third Brigade on the right of the road, the First on the left, connecting with Williams, holding the Second in reserve; both batteries were placed in position and opened upon the enemy. My skirmish line advancing drove the enemy's sharpshooters behind their rail defenses, within short distance of their main line. Toward evening Butterfield came up and formed on my right, a small branch of Noyes' Creek intervening. Rain continued heavily during day and night, rendering the roads very bad and the creeks almost impassable. Skirmishing continued steadily throughout day and night. June 20, in the morning I relieved the Third Brigade by the Second, the Third retiring to the rear on my right. My artillery continued to play with considerable effect upon the rebel lines during the day. At dark my First and Third Brigades were relieved by a brigade of Wood's division, Fourth Corps. Leaving my Second Brigade in position on the left of Butterfield, I moved Candy and Ireland and the artillery to the right, across the creek, Candy's brigade going upon the right of the Third Division, Ireland and the artillery bivouacking in rear of Butterfield's right. June 21, the Second Brigade being relieved joined me early in the morning, when I moved out the Second and Third Brigades to the right or the First, forming a continuous line along the road, and connecting on the right with Williams' division, which had been moved on the previous evening. This position I entrenched strongly, placing all my artillery in the line. In the morning I sent out the One hundred and thirty-seventh New York Volunteers and One hundred and eleven Pennsylvania Volunteers, under command of Colonel Cobham, on a reconnaissance toward Marietta and Powder Springs road, similar reconnaissances having been sent out at the same time by the other divisions of the corps. Cobham developed a strong line of rebel skirmishers about three-quarters of a mile in front of my breast-works, where he maintained an active contest all day, crowding the rebel line back from our line upwards of a quarter of a mile. The reconnoitering parties of the First and Third Divisions were withdrawn during the night. Hoping to secure the object sought, I directed mine to remain.

KOLB'S FARM

June 22, at 3 o'clock in the morning Cobham's party drove the rebels from a high hill one mile in front of the main line of the division. Early in the morning I moved the command forward upon the hill gained by my skirmishers. I at once set to work fortifying my new position, which was upon an important and commanding ridge, completely developing to our view the disposition of the enemy. Perceiving the great importance of the place, I immediately communicated its capture to Major-General Hooker, who came in person. He directed me to hold the place at every hazard. I at once set about reversing the enemy's works and throwing up such others as were necessary to cover my whole command in single line, including the artillery. Whilst in this position the enemy opened a tremendous cannonade, which was not permitted to interrupt the prosecution of the work. From prisoners captured by my advanced posts I learned that Hood's and Hardee's corps were massed at no great distance in my front. This was also communicated to the major-general commanding corps, who without delay advanced Butterfield's division to the ridge on my left and Williams' to a corresponding ridge on my right, but separated by a deep ravine and low ground. Skirmishing, almost amounting to battle, continued during the morning, our lines gaining ground. My works were scarcely completed when, to close a gap between me and Williams, I ordered the Second Brigade to extend still farther to the right, reaching to the ravine before mentioned, posting in this new line on a small knoll the Thirteenth New York Battery, the ground in front consisting of cleared fields with gradual slope. The brigade had scarcely extended to the point designated when a furious attack burst upon Williams, driving in his pickets and engaging his main body. The pickets of the First

Division being driven in, the flank of my line was completely exposed, which the enemy attacked furiously, taking advantage of the cover afforded by the houses in the vicinity. The line maintained its position, keeping up a constant and heavy fire. The enemy contented himself with assaulting my skirmishers, not attacking my main line. At the moment of the attack my artillery opened upon the charging column of the enemy and continued with great effect during the entire fight, completely enfilading the rebel ranks and literally sweeping them down. After repeated attempts to carry Williams' works the enemy retired repulsed, their retreat harassed by the fire from my own and Williams' batteries, my position on the surrounding hills enabling me to pour a concentrated fire upon the enemy, sweeping with great effect the ravine in which they had sought refuge. Although my losses in this engagement compared with those on former occasions were small numerically, my artillery sustaining the force of the battle, I suffered severely in the death of my chief of artillery, Capt William Wheeler, of the Thirteenth New York Battery, who fell shot through the heart by one of the enemy's sharpshooters whilst gallantly fighting his battery. During the short time of his connection with my division he had shown himself a gentleman of refined education and a gallant officer. The losses of the enemy under the fearful cannonade were heavy. From the appearance of the field, and from the statements by prisoners, I estimate their losses between 2,000 and 3,000. June 23, in the afternoon I advanced the left of my skirmish line, and after a spirited contest captured 30 of the enemy's pickets. June 24, 25, and 26, remained in position. Skirmishing maintained throughout, the accuracy of the enemy's fire causing some loss daily. On the 26th I received orders to advance on the 27th to co-operate with a movement of the Fourth and Fourteenth Corps upon my left.

KENNESAW

June 27, early in the morning I massed my command in rear of the center of my line, Second Brigade in front, First next, and Third Brigade in rear. At about 7 o'clock the Second Brigade, of Williams' division, moved to the works on my left in readiness to occupy the line evacuated by my movement. At 8 o'clock I moved over my works, advancing rapidly under a well-directed fire from three of the enemy's batteries and under an effective fire from a heavy picket-line, across the cleared ground in front, through a belt of woods beyond, halting at its outer edge. So rapidly and well executed was the movement that many of the enemy were captured in their pits, and their line fell back speedily, not without severe loss. McGill's battery in position upon the hill from which my infantry had moved, maintained a steady fire upon the main rebel line beyond the woods. The Second Brigade having halted on gaining the edge of the woods, and the Fourteenth Corps now being heavily engaged on a high hill on my left, I formed line, placing the First Brigade on the left, and the Third upon the right; the Second Brigade, holding the center, was well advanced. The brigades, right and left, retired almost at right angels; this formation being necessitated by the Fourteenth Corps having been repulsed in its attack on my left and the First Division not yet having advanced upon my right. At the time of the advance of the Fourteenth Corps my skirmish line, consisting of the Fifth Ohio Volunteers, under Major Symmes, went forward on the double-quick across the open ground between the left of my main line and the right of the Fourteenth Corps, driving the enemy's skirmishers before them, and capturing a small house upon the immediate right of the hill on which the enemy was strongly entrenched, the position thus seized being one from which the enemy's left could be enfiladed with artillery. I determined to hold it, and accordingly sent forward re-enforcements with entrenching tools to throw up works; I also sent forward the Thirteenth New York Battery to open upon the enemy's works. The battery had just reached its new position and was preparing to open fire, when the lines of the Fourteenth Corps withdrew, and the enemy opened upon our artillery. To hold the position without support was impossible, and I accordingly withdrew the artillery to a knoll in rear of the left of my line, from which I opened a steady fire upon the enemy in my immediate front. The skirmishers held the position they had gained, despite every effort to dislodge them. The skirmish line being so far advanced, it became dangerous to fire from the battery on the hill I had left in the morning. I therefore moved McGill's battery forward to the knoll immediately in rear of my new line. From this point the battery renewed its fire, continuing throughout the day. My main line, now well entrenched, extended through the belt of woods to the open fields on the left, and on the right to a swampy marsh impassable for troops. About 3 o'clock a brigade of Williams' division came up on my right on the opposite side of the marsh. Skirmishing continued briskly through the day, and heavy artillery firing by the enemy. June 28 and 29, remained in same position, skirmishing lively, with artillery firing during the day. June 30, after dark was relieved by Baird's division, of the Fourteenth Corps, and moved to the right about two and a half miles, where I relieved Hascall's division, of the Twenty-third Corps, in works just beyond the Powder Springs road, my whole division in line before daylight.

Casualties in actions of Muddy Creek, Nancy's Creek, Kolb's Farm, and Kennesaw Mountain

Command	Killed	Wounded	Missing	Aggregate
Commissioned officers	2	11		13
Enlisted men	26	229	2	257
Total	28	240	2	270

July 1 and 2, there being no troops on my right other than a picket-line from Cox's division, of the Twenty-third Corps, which extended half a mile beyond the flank of my division, I strengthened and changed the direction of the line of works so as to protect well my right flank, placing one regiment on a post of observation well entrenched half a mile in advance of the main line of works.

MARIETTA

July 3, the enemy having evacuated his line in our front during the night, I moved in pursuit at daylight, pushing across a thickly wooded broken country toward Neal Dow Station, the Third Division advancing on my left along the Powder Springs road. Passing through the enemy's abandoned works, very lively skirmishing ensued with their rear guard, consisting of cavalry and infantry. Pressing on rapidly, I reached Maloney's Church, near which the enemy made a stand on the opposite side of the railroad. The enemy was behind the railroad embankment and hastily constructed works, from which he opened with musketry and artillery upon my advance. My troops now being at hand, I immediately placed a section of McGill's battery in position and opened upon them, whilst my skirmishers, charging forward, drove them from the railroad and the works. On the ground from which the rebels were driven we found the bodies of a colonel and 7 privates, besides 7 dead horses. At this point I made connection with the Fourteenth Corps upon my left. Changing direction and moving to the south about two miles, I found the enemy strongly posted on a commanding ridge. Here I formed line upon the extreme right of the corps. During the day took 170 prisoners. The night passed with the usual picket-firing. July 4, skirmishing in my front; the enemy busily engaged in strengthening their works and slashing timbers. During the day Butterfield and Williams moved to my right, and I extended my line to the left across the gap thus made to connect with Davis' division, of the Fourteenth Corps. July 5, the enemy evacuated during the previous night, and at daylight with my command I started in pursuit, passing through his works, elaborate and strong; marched south by east over a succession of rough and densely wooded ridges without regular roads, crossing Nickajack Creek near Ruff and Daniel's Mill. I then moved toward Turner's Ferry, the Fourteenth Corps still upon my left, the Army of the Tennessee upon my right, Williams and Butterfield following me. During the morning my skirmishers became slightly engaged with the enemy's cavalry, who retired before my advance. At 3 PM found the enemy occupying a strong line of works on hills skirting the north side of the Chattahoochee. Posting a strong picket-line along the Nickajack, closely fronting the enemy's works, I massed the division in the woods near the old factory road and on Dodd's farm, my right connected by pickets with the Army of the Tennessee, no connection upon my left with the Fourteenth Corps, which was across Nickajack Creek. From my camp we could plainly discern the steeples and chimneys of Atlanta. The sight of the city gave great encouragement to my men, who, seeing the prize which was to crown the campaign, looked cheerfully forward to its speedy possession. July 6, relieved at 3 PM by the First Division, Fifteenth Corps, and moved northward, following the First Division to the ridge road leading to Vining's Station, then going east encamped after dark in open woods east of Nickajack Creek. July 7, early in the morning moved two miles southward, and formed line on the right of the Third Division, connecting on the right at Nickajack Creek with First Division, Fifteenth Corps. Advanced my picket-line so that I might closely observe the enemy in their fortifications near the river. No skirmishing during the day--Ward's and Williams' divisions upon my left. July 8, remained in position taken on the previous day. During the night the enemy evacuated his position and withdrew across the river. July 9, at daylight advanced my pickets to the river-bank, about one mile distant, taking a number of prisoners and deserters. The enemy's pickets in plain view on the opposite side of the river. Country on both banks rough and wooded. The evacuated works of the enemy were very elaborate and strong, comprising breast-works, rifle-pits, bastions, stockades, abatis, chevaux-de-frise, and palisades. July 10, remained in camp, making every disposition for a few days' rest, and for the health and comfort of the troops. July 11 to 16, remained encamped. On the 12th the Fifteenth Corps moved up the river. I relieved their picket-line on our immediate right. July 17, at 5 o'clock in the evening moved to the right, following the Third Division. Reaching Pace's Ferry, crossed the Chattahoochee on pontoon bridge just before dusk, and taking the road branching to the left from the Buck Head road, marched two miles, and encamped near a white house west of Nancy's Creek. July 18, after a careful reconnaissance of the country by the Second Brigade as far east as Nancy's Creek, above the crossing of the Buck Head road, about noon, under orders from the major-general commanding corps, I advanced, following the Third Division, constructing two bridges over Nancy's Creek at Williams' saw-mill. Advancing skirmishers up the Buck Head road they became slightly engaged with the enemy's cavalry. I followed immediately with the division, and on reaching the junction of the Howell's Mill road (one mile east of Buck Head), encamped, throwing up works in my front covering the road.

PEACH TREE CREEK

July 19, at daylight (in accordance with orders from Major-General Hooker directing me to advance on the road via Howell's Mill) I moved with my whole command two miles to the hill overlooking Howell's Mill, where I found Davis' division, Fourteenth Corps, whose skirmishers were hotly engaged with those of the enemy across the creek at this point. Having communicated these facts to the major-general commanding the corps, by his direction I moved to the left past Casey's house, and massed my division in the woods on hills skirting Peach Tree Creek. My position here was about three-quarters of a mile from Howell's Mill, my skirmishers connecting with those of the Fourth Corps on my left. They were ordered to conceal themselves in the woods and bushes close to the creek, and not to disclose their location by firing. To my right the country was cleared. No connection was formed in that direction with the Fourteenth Corps, because to do so would disclose a portion of my movements to the enemy. Silence was enjoined upon the troops, and preparations were quickly and quietly made to force a crossing and seize a prominent hill opposite, which was held by the enemy with rifle-pits. Peach Tree Creek at this point was about twenty feet wide, and deep, with marshy banks and muddy bottom. The hills on both sides were steep, irregular, and heavily timbered, while along both banks was a narrow strip of cleared land, widening beyond my right and extending out into an open country to my left, in front of the right of the Fourth Corps. No bridges or roads crossed the stream in my front. Under personal supervision of Major-General Hooker, and also of myself, both batteries of the division were quickly posted on prominent points in the woods opposite the hill mentioned above, which projected nearer the creek than any other of those held by the enemy. Small epaulements of logs were constructed for the protection of the gunners, while the pioneer corps prepared stringers, logs, and rails for bridge construction. At 3 PM my twelve pieces of artillery opened on the hills opposite, and my skirmishers, which had been re-enforced to a very heavy line, poured in a furious musketry fire. Under cover of this a foot bridge was constructed by the pioneer corps, and Ireland's brigade filed across on the double-quick, formed on the other side into line, and charged and carried the hill. All was done very quickly. The enemy, completely surprised, fled, leaving 23 prisoners and their entrenching tools in our hands. My other two brigades followed immediately, formed on Ireland's right, and erected strong breast-works as a tête-de-pont for our place of crossing. My skirmish lines were advanced in the dusk until they encountered the newly established picket-line of the enemy, about a quarter of a mile in my front. During the night two other bridges were thrown across the creek in my rear, and roads to them were cut for artillery and wagons. The enemy during the afternoon opened a battery about three-quarters of a mile obliquely in front of my left flank, and fired a number of shots at the troops crossing the bridge, but without effect. July 20, early in the morning Williams' division crossed and formed on the hills to my right. About the same time Ward's crossed and formed line in the valley to my left. At 10 AM, in compliance with orders, my skirmishers moved forward, supported by Candy's brigade, Jones' brigade following Candy's. Crossing two timbered ridges in front of my breast-works, the enemy's skirmishers were driven, after a sharp engagement, from the third ridge in the woods and from a corn-field on the right of it. This position gained was a most important one, and was immediately, at 12 m., occupied by Candy's brigade in line. A few rails were piled up by the troops as a protection along their front. While Candy's brigade took position on the ridge a closely contested skirmish was going on between the enemy and the skirmishers of Ward's division, the latter attempting to gain possession of a large cleared hill directly to my left. A section of Bundy's battery was brought up, went into position on my left in the edge of the woods, and opened an enfilading fire upon the enemy opposed towards Ward's skirmishers advancing at the same time, the enemy fled. I now placed Jones' brigade in two lines in support of Candy's, brought up all my artillery and posted it on Candy's line, and had Ireland's brigade massed on the ridge behind Jones. Major-General Hooker informed me that General Williams had been directed to advance on my right and connect. The left of General Williams was then about 500 yards directly in rear of my right, which was much exposed, inclining (necessarily from the shape of the ridge) slightly toward the front. The position here, to be understood with reference to the heavy battle of July 20, needs accurate description. The ridge occupied by Candy and Jones was heavily timbered, as was the country in their rear and to their right. The surrounding country presented broken ridges, with deep ravines and thickets, while here and there were isolated hills and spurs. In front and to the right of my First Brigade the country was densely timbered for two miles. Directly in front of Candy and to his left it was cleared. The cleared space in his front was about 600 yards wide; that to his left opened out into the valley of Peach Tree Creek; about eighty yards to his left ran a swampy stream, a tributary of that creek. Beyond this stream rose the broad hill held by Ward's skirmishers, while his division lay in line on the lower slope of that hill, in Peach Tree Valley. Thus it will be seen that my main line occupied a position equally advanced with the skirmishers of both the other divisions. My skirmishers had advanced across a swampy rivulet about 300 yards in front of my main line, their left in the open field, and their right on a high, narrow, timbered hill in front of my right. Deeming that hill an important outpost, I directed Colonel Jones to send a regiment to occupy it. The Thirty-third New Jersey Volunteers was immediately sent, and I went to the hill to reconnoiter, directing another regiment from Colonel Jones' brigade to follow the Thirty-third New Jersey Volunteers. On reaching the hill I found my skirmishers on the crest and the Thirty-third New Jersey just arriving. On my way I met 3 prisoners, sent in from the skirmish line. They were quite communicative, saying that there were no large bodies of their troops within two miles. The Thirty-third New Jersey formed in line on the hill, and I directed a portion of the skirmish line to advance a short distance along the slope of the ridge to develop the intentions of the enemy, who were keeping perfectly quiet. Not a man of theirs was to be seen or heard in any direction. These skirmishers had advanced but a few rods when the enemy poured in a continuous fire upon us from our front and right, and were found to be advancing in very heavy force on all sides, being already within seventy-five yards, their heaviest attack being on my right. The Thirty-third New Jersey Volunteers, together with my- skirmish line, was quickly forced back to my main line with considerable loss. Scarcely had they rejoined the main body when the enemy, in immense force, rapidly and fiercely burst upon the right flank of Candy's and Jones' brigades and passed their flanks to their rear, at the same time charging on Candy's front, right, and rear. It was necessary to change front with a portion of my command to meet the impending danger. The One hundred and forty-seventh Pennsylvania Volunteers, holding that part of the front line in which my artillery was posted, remained to fight the enemy in that direction; the Sixtieth New York Volunteers, of Ireland's brigade, and the One hundred and nineteenth New York Volunteers and Seventy-third and One hundred and ninth Pennsylvania Volunteers, of Jones' brigade, assisted in support of the artillery--these five regiments, with the aid of my batteries, fighting on all sides and holding the hill, while with the rest of my command I quickly changed front and formed in the midst of the battle, connecting with General Williams' division. This was done by changing front to the right with all of Candy's brigade, except the One hundred and forty-seventh Pennsylvania Volunteers, and deploying Ireland's and Jones' brigades in one line, connecting Ireland's left with Candy's and Jones' right with General Williams' left. The following diagram will show the position:

All these changes were completed within an hour, during which the battle raged on every side of us with terrific fury. The five regiments with the batteries, as already mentioned, held throughout the hill occupied by them at noon. All my artillery was in position there and was served rapidly from beginning to end of the battle with great heroism, coolness, and skill. That hill was the key position of the entire battle; once gained by the enemy the day was lost. The enemy perceiving its importance, surged in immense masses against it, while the dispositions of my command were being made as before stated, but they stood as firm as a rock and mowed down column after column of that vast, struggling mass that charged them from three sides. I have never seen more heroic fighting. For three hours the fury of the battle along our entire line could not be surpassed. Then the tempest of sounds and missiles began gradually to decrease, and by dark nothing but heavy skirmishing remained. General Hood had massed the greater part of his entire army in this furious assault upon a single corps (and that one the smallest in our army), and was whipped back to the ground he had left in the morning. It is with a feeling of unusual admiration for the troops under my command that I record the history of their part in the battle of Peach Tree Creek. Attacked by overwhelming numbers from front, right flank, and rear, five regiments with the artillery held the key position while fighting terribly all the time. The rest of my command changed its front, formed a connected line, and threw themselves into the combat with such determination and valor that they overcame five times their number. This result was largely due to the fact that by changing my front in the manner described our troops delivered an effective and persistent cross-fire upon the enemy at the moment when they were flushed with the anticipation of victory, and, supposing themselves entrapped, they retreated, broken and dismayed. This battle was a very remarkable one as a test of the discipline and valor of our troops, and as the first defeat of the newly appointed commander of the rebel army it was glorious in its results. The field everywhere bore marks of the extreme severity of the contest, and recalled to my mind, in appearance, the scene of conflict where the same division fought at Gettysburg. Not a tree or bush within our entire range but bore the scars of battle. The appearance of the enemy as they charged upon our front across the cleared field was magnificent. Rarely has such a sight been presented in battle. Pouring out from the woods they advanced in immense brown and gray masses (not lines), with flags and banners, many of them new and beautiful, while their general and staff officers were in plain view, with drawn sabers flashing in the light, galloping here and there as they urged their troops on to the charge. The rebel troops also seemed to rush forward with more than customary nerve and heartiness in the attack. This grand charge was Hood's inaugural, and his army came upon us that day full of high hope, confident that the small force in their front could not withstand them, but their ardor and confidence were soon shaken. My artillery, served with the utmost rapidity, even while receiving volleys from the rear, poured out steady discharges of canister and shell, and we could see the great gaps in that compact mass of human beings as each shot tore through their ranks. Those masses of the enemy that charged upon my right and rear reached at one time within a few yards of Bundy's battery, but by the cool bravery of my officers and men were driven back. I cannot refrain from specially mentioning Major Reynolds, chief of artillery of the corps, who, with Captain Aleshire, my own chief, was present on my line and rendered distinguished services throughout the severest portion of the battle.

Col Ario Pardee, of the One hundred and forty-seventh Pennsylvania Volunteers, deserves special mention for the determination, discipline, and personal gallantry displayed in holding his position in support of the artillery under a terrible fire from his flank and rear. My loss in valuable officers was particularly severe. Capt Thomas H Elliott, assistant adjutant-general on my staff, was killed instantly in the thickest of the battle. His death was a severe loss to me personally, as well as to my division. He had served with me as assistant adjutant-general for nearly three years and was distinguished for his ability and gallantry. Col George A Cobham, One hundred and eleventh Pennsylvania Volunteers, a model gentleman and commander, fell mortally wounded. For one year previous to the organization of the Twentieth Corps, by the consolidation of the Eleventh and Twelfth, he commanded the Second Brigade of my division, and led it with great credit through the battles at Gettysburg, Wauhatchie, Lookout Mountain, Mission Ridge, and Ringgold. He participated with his regiment in all the battles and movements of our present campaign, and during the absence of Colonel Ireland commanded my Third Brigade in the battles of Resaca and New Hope Church. His loss is deeply felt and deplored throughout the division. Lieutenant-Colonel Randall, One hundred and forty-ninth

New York Volunteers, a brave and excellent officer, was killed while fighting gallantly in command of his regiment.

Casualties in the battle of Peach Tree Creek, GA

Command	Killed	Wounded	Missing	Aggregate
Commissioned officers	4	24	9	37
Enlisted men	78	205	156	439
Total	82	229	165	476

Four hundred and nine of the enemy's dead were buried by fatigue parties from my division in my front, and I had information, deemed reliable, that about 200 were carried back and buried by them from the same portion of the field. From these statements, and from the terrible punishment inflicted upon the enemy, crowded together in dense masses, I can safely estimate their losses in my front at the least at 2,500 men. July 21, early this morning my skirmishers were advanced about 400 yards, and found the enemy's pickets beyond. The day passed quietly, my details being occupied in burying my own and the enemy's dead. July 22, at 5 AM I advanced my skirmishers and found that the enemy had withdrawn. A general advance of the corps being ordered at 6 AM, I moved with my division through the woods across a very rough, broken country in the direction of Atlanta, my Second and Third Brigades moving in parallel columns, First Brigade following. After marching about one mile we crossed the fortifications evacuated by the enemy the night previous. These works were very strong, and were the outer line of the defenses of Atlanta. Turning here to the right in a few minutes I reached the broad road running from Howell s Mill to Atlanta. On this road the Fourteenth Corps and General Williams' division were advancing. With my Third and First Brigades I followed until near its junction with the Marietta road, where my skirmishers (connected on their right with those of General Williams' division) engaged the enemy's pickets, driving them into the main fortification of Atlanta. My Second Brigade, which had moved through the woods nearly a mile farther to the left, joined me at this point. The enemy opened upon us with artillery from a fort in our front on Marietta street. At 10 AM, by direction of the major-general commanding corps, I took position on a cleared ridge half a mile east of Howell's Mill road, and deployed my entire division, excepting two regiments, in front line, facing south and confronting the forts on Marietta street, about 1,000 yards distant. Ward's division connected with my left and Williams' with my right. Here within two hours my troops erected strong breast-works, and my artillery took position on commanding points in the line. My skirmishers advanced close to the enemy's fortifications, and there constructed outpost defenses. From my location here to the center of Atlanta was two miles. Sharp skirmishing and artillery dueling continued during the day and late into the night, shells from our guns being thrown far into the city. At 7 PM the enemy made a strong dash on our pickets, but were quickly driven back. My intrenchments were completed during the afternoon and abatis constructed along my front. July 23, artillery dueling and skirmishing continued. At noon the enemy made another unsuccessful attempt to drive back my pickets; continued to strengthen my intrenchments and abatis. July 24, my command was employed constructing an advanced parallel about 600 yards in front of the first line. At 9 PM, in pursuance of orders from major-general commanding department, a strong demonstration was made by Williams' division, arousing the enemy along our entire front and eliciting from them a sharp fire. My troops, keeping well under cover, suffered very few casualties. July 26, my new line of works, elaborately and strongly constructed, was finished and occupied by my troops at night. This parallel shortened the line of the corps so much that Ward's division was entirely relieved by a portion of mine, and the fortifications of the corps were occupied by the First and Second Divisions, the Third withdrawing behind our center in reserve. July 27, at 6 AM, in pursuance of orders transmitted from Major-General Sherman, I sent out from my division 200 men under command of Lieutenant-Colonel Walker, One hundred and eleventh Pennsylvania Volunteers, to make a demonstration against the enemy. This force drove in the pickets and established our outposts where those of the enemy had been. The Army of the Tennessee passed my rear all day, moving from the left to the right of the army. The order relieving, at his own request, Major-General Hooker from command of the corps was received today and caused expressions of profound regret throughout the command. Brigadier-General Williams was, by the same order, assigned to temporary command of the corps. July 28, the forenoon passed in comparative quiet, the enemy throwing occasional 64-pound shells, of the James projectile pattern, in our direction from heavy guns recently mounted in a fort near the railroad and close to Mrs. Ponder's house. About 1 PM the sounds of heavy battle came from the direction of the Army of the Tennessee, several miles distant to our right, and lasted until 3 PM, at which time the enemy opened heavily on my own lines with artillery, continuing their fire until dark, but causing very few casualties among our troops. July 29, in pursuance of orders, my pickets felt of the enemy frequently during the night, and again strongly at daylight, but discovered no signs of their giving way; considerable artillery firing from both sides along my front to-day. By orders of the brigadier-general commanding corps, I sent out the Sixtieth New York Volunteers, under Colonel Godard, in the forenoon to make a strong demonstration on the enemy's line. The duty was performed in fine style, driving in their pickets with the loss on our side of but 1 man slightly wounded. July 30 and 31, nothing of interest to record.

August 1 and 2, picket-firing throughout the day, which became heavy at night; artillery firing on both sides, sharp firing at intervals throughout. August 3, at 5 PM the pickets made a demonstration in their front, exciting a lively artillery fire from the rebel works, our artillery replying occasionally. August 4, received orders to have the whole command vigilant at its post. At 1 PM the sound of heavy fighting was heard on the extreme right, which ceased shortly after 3 PM; all remaining quiet until about 8.30 PM, when heavy artillery and musketry firing was again heard from the same direction. The firing lasted only about twenty minutes, after which fitful firing occurred along the lines. August 5, 6, 7,and 8, usual picket and artillery firing; 5 deserters came into my lines. August 9, a detail from the command was engaged in constructing six embrasures for siege artillery in the works of the One hundred and forty-ninth New York Volunteers, on my left. By order of General Sherman all the artillery opened upon the city, firing about fifty rounds per gun. The enemy responded feebly in my front, firing from but one fort. The enemy could be seen constructing bomb-proofs in their works; 3 deserters came in. August 10, the embrasures were finished and three 4 1/2-inch guns were placed in position, opening fire upon Atlanta at 4 PM, which was maintained throughout the night; 2 deserters came in. August 11 and 12, ordinary firing from pickets and artillery. August 13, by order of Major-General Sherman, all the artillery bearing upon the city was directed to open and continue a regular fire upon it during the afternoon and night. About 11 PM a large fire broke out in the center of the city; bells and cries of "fire" were plainly audible. The fire became larger and continued until daylight. August 14, artillery still playing at intervals upon the city. Deserters coming into my lines agree in representing great dissatisfaction existing in Hood's army. Shortly after dark another large fire broke out in the city, lasting about three hours. August 15 and 16, picket and artillery firing as usual. Verbal orders received to withdraw my command from the works on the night of the 18th and move quietly and quickly to Pace s Ferry, on the Chattahoochee, there to hold the bridge and guard the approaches to the railroad. August 17, received written orders suspending the proposed movement until further notice. August 18, at 4 AM the enemy opened heavily with artillery along his entire line, inflicting but little damage; batteries on our line promptly and actively replied. The cannonade lasted heavily until 7 AM August 19, at 4 AM the artillery along our entire line opened furiously upon the enemy, firing twelve rounds per gun. August 20, 21, 22, and 23, ordinary firing of pickets and artillery. August 24, the movement previously ordered, and which had been suspended on the 17th, was again ordered, and all the trains of the command crossed the Chattahoochee. August 25, at 7 AM received orders from corps headquarters directing me to withdraw during the night to Pace's Ferry, the hour of withdrawal to be designated at a later period of the day. At daylight sent one regiment and the pioneer corps from each brigade to Pace's Ferry to construct defensive works on the east side of the river. At 8 o'clock I proceeded in person to the ferry, superintended laying out *têtes-de-pont* and surveying grounds in vicinity with special reference to forming a line of works. At 4 o'clock in the afternoon, in consultation with General Williams, decided upon the details for the movements during the night--the troops to withdraw at 9 o'clock to the second ridge in rear of the works, and there await the movement of the Fourth Corps past my rear; the command to move to its position on the river as soon as the Fourth Corps had passed, Bundy's battery to accompany my division, the pickets to remain until the movement was completed, and then to follow the main body to the river. At 9 PM my troops withdrew from the works and massed at the point indicated. The Fourth Corps was to have moved at 9 PM, but from some cause unknown to me failed to do so. By midnight only two brigades of the Fourth Corps had passed my position. I decided not to await the passage of the remainder of the corps, as to do this would delay me until after daylight, and the road being clear I moved my division out (without interrupting in the slightest degree the march of the Fourth Corps) to the main road, over a new one through the woods which I had cut during the day, and moved rapidly on and reached Pace's Ferry about 4 AM on the morning of the 26th. The command was immediately posted--Third Brigade on the left, extending across the Buck Head road, covering the bridge at the ferry; the Second Brigade in the center, joining the Third; the First Brigade on the right, joining the Second, and connecting with Williams' division on the north side of Peach Tree Creek; Bundy's battery placed in the works of the Third Brigade. My pickets from the works before Atlanta joined my command at 6 AM the withdrawal from my works before the city, and the march of nine miles to the ferry, were all accomplished without the loss of a man or of any material.

Casualties in front of Atlanta from July 23 to August 25

Command	Killed	Wounded	Missing	Aggregate
Commissioned officers.	1	3		4
Enlisted men	14	108	4	126
Total	15	111	4	130

About noon the enemy's cavalry appeared in my front and slight skirmishing commenced between them and my pickets. At 3 o'clock a body of cavalry, dismounted, charged upon the picket-line, but were driven back with a loss of 8 killed (left on the field), some 25 wounded, and 3 prisoners, with no casualties in my command. Skirmishing continued throughout the afternoon. The artillery firing a few shells into the cavalry caused them to disperse rapidly. The enemy was busily engaged in feeling my lines. At 8 PM Colonel Minty, commanding a brigade in General Garrard's cavalry division, reported to me that the Seventh Pennsylvania Cavalry was left upon the opposite side of the river, with orders to patrol up the river as far as Soap Creek. During the afternoon Major-General Slocum, assigned to command of the corps, rode along my lines and was received with hearty enthusiasm by the men of his old command. August 27, during the day was very busily engaged perfecting my lines, constructing breast-works, rifle-pits, and abatis. The line to be held by my division being about two and three-fourths miles in length, required a vast amount of labor to place it in proper condition.

Two pieces of Knapp's battery were placed in position in a work thrown up on the right of the line for the purpose of defending the railroad bridge and other bridges at Montgomery's Ferry. Major-General Slocum to-day formally assumed command of the corps. August 28, 29, and 30 passed with slight skirmishing on the extreme picket-line, the troops busily engaged working on the defenses. August 31, at 6 AM, in obedience to orders from corps headquarters, I sent out a reconnoitering party of 200 men under Colonel Flynn, Twenty-eighth Pennsylvania Volunteers. Colonel Flynn, moving on the Buck Head road, found the enemy's cavalry pickets on the west side of Nancy's Creek. Moving to his left, he flanked and drove them and then crossed the creek, moving on the road to the right about a mile, where he again found the enemy posted in rail works on the farther edge of a cleared field. He exchanged a few volleys with them, but believing their numbers to be too great to be driven, and his object being to find, not to fight, the enemy, he retired, recrossed the creek, and, moving down the road, turned northward on a smaller road over which the corps had marched on the 18th of July. On again reaching the creek he found the enemy's cavalry, pickets on the west side. These he quickly drove, and again crossing the stream and moving about a mile and a half, met the enemy entrenched in a field near the junction of the road on which he was marching, this being the right of the same line he had encountered below. Having fulfilled his orders by ascertaining the position of the enemy, Colonel Flynn returned without loss.

September 1, day passed without change. September 2, in obedience to orders from corps headquarters, I sent out a reconnoitering party. The reconnaissance was commanded by Lieut Col Thomas M Walker, One hundred and eleventh Pennsylvania Volunteers, and was composed of the One hundred and eleventh Pennsylvania Volunteers, Sixtieth New York Volunteers, and details from the One hundred and second New York and Twenty-ninth Pennsylvania Volunteers, and twenty men from the Seventh Pennsylvania Cavalry. Captain Lambert, acting assistant inspector-general, and Lieutenant Schilling, of my staff, accompanied Lieutenant-Colonel Walker. The reconnaissance moved out at 6 AM on the Buck Head road. Skirmishers were thrown to the front immediately after passing the pickets, but the column advanced rapidly until after crossing Nancy's Creek and to the point at which the road branches to Buck Head. At this point the road gave indications of the recent passage of a column of cavalry. The main body was here halted, and the Sixtieth New York Volunteers sent down the Buck Head road to the junction of the Howell's Mill road. Having received intelligence of the arrival of the Sixtieth New York Volunteers at the point indicated, the column moved on, and the Sixtieth New York Volunteers was ordered to move toward Howell's Mill and there join the main body. On reaching the creek at the mill it was learned that Ferguson's rebel cavalry brigade, which had been encamped there, had moved a few hours previously toward Atlanta. The bridge over Peach Tree Creek at this place had been destroyed. Little delay, however, was experienced, the infantry crossing on a large log, the cavalry fording. The column pushed on toward the city. Lieutenant-Colonel Walker, accompanied by the cavalry, preceded his infantry and entered the outskirts of the city, where he met Colonel Coburn, commanding the reconnaissance of the Third Division, who had also preceded his troops. Discovering that, with the exception of Ferguson's brigade, there were no troops in the city, it was agreed that their commands should enter at the same time, which was done, the enemy's cavalry retiring before them. Lieutenant-Colonel Walker's command was the first to reach the City Hall, upon which the colors of the Sixtieth New York and One hundred and eleventh Pennsylvania Volunteers were immediately hoisted. To these two regiments, representing my division, belongs the immortal honor of placing upon the rebel stronghold the first Union flags, and to give the first practical announcement that the long campaign had ended in glorious victory--that the Gate City of the South was ours. Receiving the intelligence of the evacuation of the city, I immediately ordered forward the Second and Third Brigades and Bundy's battery, preceding them in person, thus leaving the entire line of works at the ferry to be held by the First Brigade, under command of Col Ario Pardee. The troops arrived during the evening and were massed on McDonough and White Hall streets. September 3, early in the morning my two brigades were placed in position in the fortifications, the Third Brigade in southwestern portion of the line from the East Point railroad to the McDonough road, the Second Brigade on the left of the McDonough road and south of the city. September 4, the First Brigade being ordered from the Chattahoochee, arrived in the city at 3 o'clock and was placed in position in the works on the right of the Third Brigade, west of the city. The Second Brigade was relieved toward evening by the Third Brigade, Third Division, and moved to the right of the McDonough road, the line of the Third Brigade having been shortened. The One hundred and eleventh Pennsylvania Volunteers was to-day detached for provost duty, and reported to Colonel Cogswell, commanding post. Orders were received from Major-General Sherman announcing the accomplishment by the army of its undertaking in the complete reduction and occupation of Atlanta, and indicating that the spring campaign was closed. The casualties in the battles and intervening marches described in the preceding report amount to an aggregate as follows:

Command	Killed	Wounded	Missing	Aggregate
Commissioned officers	16	98	10	123
Enlisted men	315	1,826	263	2,404
Total	2	1,923	273	2,527

The loss of field officers during the campaign has been unusually heavy. All the regiments save three and all the brigades changed commanders at least once during the campaign. These frequent changes have caused great difficulty in procuring the proper reports, and in consequence prevented me from submitting my report at an earlier period. In addition to these losses, I have since the close of the campaign been deprived of the services of a gallant officer and efficient brigade commander by the death from disease, on the 10th instant, of Col David Ireland, One hundred and thirty-seventh New York Volunteers, and captain in the Fifteenth US Infantry. Colonel Ireland had commanded the Third Brigade of my division for upward of ten mouths, and greatly distinguished himself by his gallantry in all the engagements in which his command has participated. In his death I lose a valued personal friend, the country one of its noblest defenders. My staff suffered severely, Captain Elliott, my assistant adjutant-general, and Captain Wheeler, chief of artillery, having been killed; Captain Veale, assistant commissary of musters, severely, and Captain Wilbur, aide-de-camp, slightly, wounded, and Captain Davis, aide-de-camp, captured. I cannot close this report without special reference to the officers composing my personal and departmental staff. To Capt William T Forbes, for a time acting assistant inspector-general, and acting assistant adjutant-general after the death of the lamented Elliott; Capt R H Wilbur, aide-de-camp, and assistant commissary of musters after the brave Captain Veale was wounded; Capt William H Lambert, aide-de-camp, and acting assistant inspector-general after the promotion of Captain Forbes, and to Capt J J Canfine and Lieutenants Sherwood and Armor, I tender my warmest and special thanks for the hearty accord and energetic support they at all times gave to every movement that seemed to be for the interest and success of our cause. To Capt Ira B Seymour, provost-marshal, Captain Schilling, topographical engineer, and Lieutenant Chapman, chief of ambulance, I return my thanks for their faithfulness and readiness to perform their respective duties, no matter what was to be done, or what risk to be encountered. Captain Parker, assistant quartermaster, Captain Gillette, commissary of subsistence, and Captain Wilson, ordnance officer, are deserving of the highest commendation for the successful manner in which their several departments were conducted. To my surgeon in chief, H E Goodman, myself and my entire command are under the deepest obligations for the manner in which, under his own personal supervision, the sick and wounded of my division have been attended.

Thus triumphantly has ended this campaign, unequaled in the present war for glorious victory over almost insurmountable difficulties, and unsurpassed in modern history. Thus has ended a campaign which shall stand forever a monument of the valor, the endurance, the patriotism of the American soldier. Four months of hard, constant labor under the hot sun of a southern summer; four months, scarce a day of which has been passed out of the sound of the crash of musketry and the roar of artillery; 200 miles traveled through a country in every mile of which nature and art seemed leagued for defense--mountains, rivers, lines of works; a campaign in which every march was a fight, in which battles follow in such quick succession are so intimately connected by a constant series of skirmishes that the whole campaign seems but one grand battle which, crowned with grander victory, attests the skill and patience of the hero who matured its plans and directed their execution.

Very respectfully, your obedient servant,
Jno W Geary
Brigadier-General, Commanding Division

September 19, 1864
Extract from Special Orders No. 85, Headquarters, 20th Army Corps
Atlanta, GA

  I 1st Lieut James C Carlisle 13th Indpt NY Batty is hereby appointed Inspector of the Artillery Brigade of this Corps and will report to Major Reynolds comdg.

October 15, 1864
Battery Orders No. 60
Atlanta, GA

Corporal Deidrich Funk is hereby promoted sergeant in this Battery to date from Sept 16th 1864 vice E Volmar deceased. He will be obeyed and respected accordingly.
Henry Bundy Captain
Commanding Battery

October 19, 1864
Battery Orders No. 61
Atlanta, GA

I Corporal Joseph Clavin is hereby reduced to the ranks for absence without leave.
II Privates Henry Lerz and John White are hereby appointed corporals in this Battery vice Corpl Funk promoted and Corpl Rush discharged to date from Sept 16th and Octb 16th respectively.
III Privates Adolph Sackmann and William Geiger will act as corporals until further notice.
They will be respected and obeyed accordingly.
Henry Bundy Captain
Commanding Battery

October 20, 1864
Battery Orders No. 62
Atlanta, GA

The officers of this Battery are hereby ordered to have their Detachments to drill at the pieces from 8 AM to 9 AM and 4 PM to 5 PM until further orders.
Henry Bundy Captain
Commanding Battery

November 25, 1864
Letter to a unnamed person
Tullahoma, TN

Sir
I have the honor to report that it is not possible for me fully to comply with order of this date as the order assigning me to this garrison has been lost or mislead and therefore do not know the no [number] or the date of it exactly. I have received the order about the 20th of October. It was from Head Qtrs Dept of the Cumberland. If I do not find said order soon I will apply to Hd Qtrs Dept of the Cumberland for a copy of said order.
Very Respectfully
Your obedient servant
Henry Bundy Captain
Comdg 13th New York Battery

November 26, 1864
Battery Orders No. 63
Tullahoma, TN

I   Corporal John Mahoney is hereby reduced to the ranks for drunkenness as displayed at this post on the 15th Nov from which date this order will take effect.
II   Private William Geiger is hereby appointed corporal in 13th New York Battery vice Joseph Clavin reduced to date from September 19, 1864.
Private Adam Palmer is also appointed corporal vice John Mahoney reduced to date from Nov 15, 1864
They will be obeyed and respected accordingly
Henry Bundy Captain
Commanding Battery

December 7, 1864
Report of Maj. Gen. Robert Milroy, 1st Sub-District, District of Middle Tennessee, Department of the Cumberland Murfreesboro, TN

General: In obedience to your orders I proceeded on the afternoon of the 4th instant to the relief of the block-house at Overall's Creek, four miles and a half north of this place, on the Nashville and Chattanooga Railroad, which was besieged by a considerable rebel force with artillery. I took with me, by your order, the Eighth Regiment Minnesota Veteran Volunteer Infantry, Sixty-first Regiment Illinois Veteran Volunteer Infantry, One hundred and seventy-fourth Regiment Ohio Volunteer Infantry[76], and a section of the Thirteenth New York Artillery, under Lieutenant McGurrin. I proceeded on the Nashville pike to Overall's Creek, where I found the Thirteenth Indiana Cavalry (Colonel Johnson), who preceded me some hours, engaged in skirmishing with the enemy's sharpshooters, who were deployed across the creek. I threw Lieutenant McGurrin, with his section of artillery, forward to the bluff of the creek, who engaged the enemy's battery in gallant style, which was posted on an eminence about 900 yards distant, on the opposite side of the creek, between the railroad and the Nashville pike. I at once deployed the Sixty-first Illinois as skirmishers, and sent up the Eighth Minnesota to the block-house at the railroad crossing, about half a mile below the pike, with orders to cross there, if practicable, and flank the rebel battery on the right. I then advanced the skirmishers across the creek, most of them crossing the bridge under a galling fire, and drove back the rebel sharpshooters. I then threw forward the One hundred and seventy-fourth Ohio Volunteer Infantry (Colonel Jones), who crossed the bridge under a sharp fire, both of artillery and small-arms, and formed in good order on the opposite bank. Being under the impression that the forces opposing me consisted of a portion of Forrest's cavalry, dismounted, I supposed that their three-gun battery operating against us could be run over and taken by Colonel Johnson with his gallant regiment, who were anxious to try the experiment. So, after the One hundred and seventy-fourth Ohio had formed on the north bank of the creek, the ground being favorable for a cavalry charge and the smoke of the battery and approaching darkness rendering my movements invisible, I directed Colonel Johnson to cross the bridge, pass through an opening in the line of the One hundred and seventy-fourth Ohio, charge the battery and take it if possible. The colonel moved forward on the enemy in the most splendid and impetuous style, but finding the battery strongly supported by infantry he turned and passed off to the right. I then moved forward the One hundred and seventy-fourth Ohio, which advanced with a terrific rolling fire upon the enemy, capturing a number of prisoners who dared not to arise from the ground to run away amid a sheet of lead. From these prisoners I learned that the force confronting me consisted of General Bate's division of infantry.

It being now quite dark, and the enemy having been driven back near eighty rods and ceased firing, and the Eighth Minnesota not having found a crossing, I withdrew the One hundred and seventy-fourth Ohio with the skirmishers of the Sixty-first Illinois to the south bank of the creek. These regiments withdrew in the most perfect order, bringing off their dead, wounded, and prisoners. The Thirteenth Indiana Cavalry also returned to the bridge and crossed to the south side of the creek in good order. The evening being cold I drew my force up in line on the south bank of the creek and kindled fires the whole length, and waited till 9 PM, when, not hearing of the enemy, I moved back to the fortress.

The Eighth Minnesota, being a veteran regiment of long and true service, would of course have done efficient service could they have found a crossing at the block-house; the Sixty-first Illinois, being also a veteran regiment and much reduced by long and hard service, well sustained their reputation as veterans. But the One hundred and seventy-fourth Ohio being a new full regiment, and for the first time under fire since its organization, I was most agreeably surprised at the promptness, steadiness, and bravery they evinced; no veterans could have behaved better in action, but this I discovered (as I have in every other instance where I have found an efficient and reliable regiment)is owing to the energy, bravery, and efficiency of its colonel.

My staff--Major Cravens, Captain Carson, Captain Wilkinson, Lieutenant Worthington, and Lieutenant Frowe--well deserve and have my thanks for the assistance rendered; also Capt J G Mohler, of the One hundred and fifteenth Regiment Ohio Veteran Infantry, who volunteered his services on the field and rendered himself very useful to me. Major Cravens and Lieutenant Worthington both had their horses shot under them. My thanks are also due Surgeon (Major) Birney, who volunteered as medical director, and rendered very valuable service in care of the wounded.

I captured 20 prisoners. My killed, wounded, and missing amount to 64--the Thirteenth Indiana Cavalry yet to hear from. I have no means of knowing the loss of the enemy, who fell back five miles that night; some 8 or 10 dead were counted on the field.

Enclosed I send copies of reports received from regimental commanders, giving names of killed, wounded, and missing.

I have the honor to be, very respectfully, your most obedient servant,
R H Milroy
Major-General of Volunteers

December 8, 1864
Report of Capt. Henry Bundy, 13th New York Artillery
Murfreesboro, TN

I have the honor to report that there were fifty-four men of my command engaged with the enemy in the battle on Wilkinson's pike, near Stone's River, on yesterday, the 7th instant. The casualties in men in my command were as follows: Conrad Feisel, private, wounded severely; Christopher Milley, private, wounded severely; Henry Greasel, private, wounded slightly; Joseph Clavin, private, wounded slightly. My command took no prisoners from the enemy, and I don't know what casualties my command inflicted upon them. I had four horses disabled.

I am, colonel, very respectfully, your obedient servant,
Henry Bundy
Captain, Commanding Thirteenth New York Battery

Report of Col. Edward Anderson, 2nd Brigade, 4th Division, 20th Army Corps
Mufreesboro, TN

I have the honor to report that the brigade under my command was ordered to march on the reconnaissance of yesterday under Maj Gen R H Milroy.

This brigade consists of the One hundred and seventy-seventh and One hundred and seventy eighth Ohio Volunteer Infantry, Twelfth Indiana Cavalry, Fourth and Fifth Tennessee Cavalry, and Thirteenth New York Independent Battery. En route for the field of action I was informed that the Thirteenth New York Battery was attached to the First Brigade, in the rear of which I was ordered to march. The Fourth and Fifth Tennessee Cavalry Regiments, commanded by Lieutenant-Colonel Clift, were ordered to report to Col G M L Johnson, Thirteenth Indiana Cavalry, commanding cavalry. Thus I had under my immediate command troops as follows, viz.: Twelfth Indiana Cavalry, Lieut Col Alfred Reed commanding, numbering 16 officers and 352 men (368); One hundred and seventy-seventh Ohio Volunteer Infantry, Col A T Wilcox commanding, numbering 18 officers and 496 men (514); One hundred and seventy-eighth Ohio Volunteer Infantry, Col J A Stafford commanding, numbering 17 officers and 427 men (444); making a total of 51 officers and 1,275 men-- 1,326 men.

At Overall's Creek, where the enemy opened an artillery fire upon us, I was ordered to form my brigade in the rear of the First Brigade, and in undertaking to do so I found the One hundred and seventy-seventh Ohio Volunteer Infantry, which was on the right of my command and now for the first time brought under fire, exposed to a terrible succession of shots from the enemy's battery. The officers of the regiment and my own staff officers joined in an endeavor to keep them in column, but knowing that the whole future of the regiment probably depended on preventing their breaking to the rear, I ordered Colonel Wilcox to have them lie down. Through all the artillery duel that ensued they remained in that position, of course so remote from the enemy, in their position as reserves, that they could do nothing but endure. I was glad, in occupying a position where I could watch the regiment, to notice that none appeared to flinch under this heavy fire and in a position more exposed than often comes to a regiment. After the battery had ceased firing I was ordered to march my brigade by the right flank till the right of the column should rest on the Wilkinson pike; there I again formed line of battle and undertook to march to the support of the First Brigade, which was engaging the enemy in the front. Owing to the extreme roughness of the ground, rocks, jagged and detached, being covered at intervals by brush and logs, I was forced to march very slowly, and for a distance by right of companies, to the front. When we had nearly approached the position I was ordered to occupy in rear of the First Brigade, and at about 200 yards distance, I was ordered to throw the One hundred and seventy-seventh Ohio Volunteer Infantry to the right, forming its line perpendicular to the line already formed, in order to prevent a flanking movement on the part of the enemy, who were evidently intending to get into our rear. This regiment threw out two companies to deploy along its front as skirmishers. Sharp firing along the line showed that the general had not been mistaken in supposing it necessary to protect the right flank. Major-General Milroy took the One hundred and seventy-eighth Ohio Volunteer Infantry, and, marching it left in front, led it to the extreme left and conducted it personally into battle. Of the action of this regiment I am unable to speak thereafter, but have no question as to its gallantry, as the almost reckless daring of the general cannot be other than infectious. The Twelfth Indiana Cavalry was pushed forward on the right of the pike over a cotton-field, where it lay under a hot musketry fire till it was ordered forward into the woods as the enemy retired. At this juncture I ordered forward the One hundred and seventy-seventh Ohio Volunteer Infantry, the firing having ceased on the right flank. I formed it in line parallel to the lines in front, and received orders to hold it there while the Twelfth Indiana Cavalry was ordered to the extreme front, though too late to participate in actual conflict there, the enemy having retired. On our return to the fortress the Twelfth Indiana Cavalry brought up the rear.

    The casualties in my command were happily few, as it was held almost entirely in reserve. I take pleasure in testifying to the bravery of these troops, nearly all brought in this engagement for the first time under the enemy's fire, and here, in a position most trying to any soldier, obliged to take the enemy's shots and unable to enjoy either the satisfaction or the excitement of returning their fire. No one, however, would be surprised that troops would stand gallantly under fire, as they could all the time see the general they loved in the fore front of battle, where the bullets were flying most thickly. These troops would follow General Milroy wherever he might lead. Where nearly every officer was brave it would be useless to attempt allusion to individual instances. My confidence in officers and men is unbounded.

    I report the following casualties in the three regiments under my immediate command and the other troops that report through me: Twelfth Indiana Cavalry, killed, 1 private; wounded, 1 officer (Captain Sherwood, Company E, severely in the leg), 10 privates. One hundred and seventy-seventh Ohio Volunteer Infantry, wounded, 4 privates. One hundred and seventy eighth

Ohio Volunteer Infantry, wounded, 2 privates. Fifth Tennessee Cavalry (Col W J Clift), wounded, 2 privates. Thirteenth New York Battery (Capt Henry Bundy), wounded, 4 privates. Total, killed, 1 private; wounded, 1 officer and 22 enlisted men.
    I have the honor to respectfully submit the foregoing.
    Very respectfully, your obedient servant,
    Edward Anderson
    Colonel, Commanding Second Brigade

Report of Col. Minor Thomas, 8th Minnesota Infantry Murfreesboro, TN

    I have the honor to make the following report of the operations of the Independent Brigade in the engagement of the 7th instant on the Wilkinson pike, near Stone's River:
    In moving round the fortress the enemy was first discovered in force about one mile left of the Wilkinson pike and two miles from the southwest corner of the fortress. Two sections of artillery, one of the Twelfth Ohio and one of the Thirteenth New York Batteries, were placed in position and engaged the enemy with spirit, and showed him to be well posted and in strong force. Having but a limited amount of artillery ammunition (fifty rounds per piece), the brigade was moved by the right flank until the Eighth Minnesota Regiment had crossed the Wilkinson pike, when it was formed in line of battle to the front, with its left resting on the pike, One hundred and eighty-first Ohio on the left of the pike, and One hundred and seventy-fourth Ohio on the left of it, the Sixty-first Illinois being deployed in front as skirmishers. An advance was immediately made of several hundred yards, when an interval appeared in the skirmish line. Two companies of the One hundred and eighty-first Ohio were thrown forward to strengthen it, and the line being corrected the brigade again advanced in double-quick time until the enemy's skirmishers were driven about one mile. This advance was made, forcing back a heavy line of skirmishers, and under a heavy fire of artillery, without much loss, until we had advanced to the center of an old cotton field, when we were confronted by the enemy in the timber beyond the field, well covered either by woods or rifle-pits. At this point the firing from both sides was furious and very destructive. After an incessant fire for ten or fifteen minutes, a charge was made by the whole line and the rifle-pits and woods cleared, the enemy leaving, probably,

100 dead and wounded, two 12-pounder Napoleon guns, and 197 prisoners in our hands. The enemy having disappeared, except a mounted force, which was driven pell-mell by our artillery (it having just returned from the fortress where it had gone to replenish its ammunition), the troops were withdrawn in as good order as if coming from an afternoon drill, and reached their quarters at 6 p.m. The fight was sharp and decisive, and the battleflags of our country floated again victoriously over the memorable field of Stone's River.

Inclosed please find reports of subordinate commanders, giving complete list of killed and wounded.

The conduct of the troops for steady, determined bravery, and rapidity of movement could not be excelled.

The enemy engaged consisted of Major-General Bate's division, with two brigades attached, and Forrest's cavalry, the whole force amounting to probably 4,500 men, with two batteries of artillery.

The Independent Brigade took into the fight 1,800 officers and men. Their total loss was 21 killed and 167 wounded.

Very respectfully, your obedient servant,

M T Thomas
Colonel Eighth Minnesota Volunteers, Commanding Brigade

December 10, 1864
Report of Maj. Gen. Robert Milroy, 1st Sub-District, District of Middle Tennessee, Department of the Cumberland
Murfreesboro, TN

General: I have the honor to report that, in obedience to your order, I proceeded on the 7th instant to make a reconnaissance and feel the enemy in the vicinity of this post. I took with me, by your direction, seven regiments of infantry and a six-gun battery, under the command of Captain Bundy, of the Thirteenth New York Artillery, and a small detachment of the Fifth Tennessee Volunteer Cavalry. The regiments consisted of the One hundred and seventy-fourth, One hundred and seventy-seventh, One hundred and seventy-eighth, and One hundred and eighty-first Ohio Volunteer Infantry, Sixty-first Illinois Volunteer Infantry, Eighth Minnesota Volunteer Infantry, and Twelfth Indiana Volunteer Cavalry (dismounted). For convenience, I divided these regiments into two brigades *(pro tempore)*, as follows:

First Brigade, Colonel Thomas, of the Eighth Minnesota, commanding, consisted of a six-gun battery, Eighth Minnesota Volunteer Infantry, Sixty-first Illinois Volunteer Infantry, One hundred and seventy-fourth and One hundred and eighty-first Ohio Volunteer Infantry, 1,973 strong. The Second Brigade consisted of the One hundred and seventy-seventh, and One hundred and seventy-eighth Ohio Volunteer Infantry, and Twelfth Indiana Volunteer Cavalry, 1,326 strong. Total strength of my infantry, artillery, and cavalry combined, 3,325. I started on the Salem pike about 10 AM, and threw out the detachment of the after passing our pickets. The rebel cavalry fell back rapidly before my advance Fifth Tennessee Cavalry in advance, who struck the rebel vedette in less than half a mile. I threw out a portion of the Sixty-first Illinois Volunteer Infantry as skirmishers, to assist the cavalry in driving them. Upon arriving at Stone's River, two miles out, a body of about 300 rebel cavalry were discovered across the river. I brought up a section of Captain Bundy's battery and shelled them a few minutes, when they retreated rapidly, and I crossed the bridge and continued my march. Upon arriving at Mr. Spence's fine residence, four miles out, I learned from his accomplished lady that there were two brigades of rebel cavalry, under Generals Jackson and Armstrong, at Salem, a mile farther out, and that Generals Forrest and Bate, with a large force of infantry, artillery, and cavalry, were north of me, on the Wilkinson pike, three miles from Fortress Rosecrans. I deemed it best to turn my attention in that direction, but before doing so I detailed a company and sent them back with a drove of sixty fine, fat hogs, belonging to Mr. Spence, that would have fallen into the hands of the rebels if left. I proceeded north till within half a mile of the Wilkinson pike. My skirmish line encountered that of the enemy, and in a few minutes afterward they opened on me with much rapidity from a six-gun battery stationed in the edge of a wood on the opposite side of a field in my front. I at once ordered forward Captain Bundy's battery, which replied in an equally spirited style. Having only taken along what artillery ammunition that could be carried in the limbers of the guns, the shell and solid shot of my supply was exhausted in about thirty minutes. Finding that the enemy would not come across the field to attack me, and not being able to ascertain his strength, and the left of his line, extending parallel with the Wilkinson pike, was as near Fortress Rosecrans as my right, I deemed it prudent not to engage them with my infantry without having the fortress in my rear, and accordingly fell back through the forest until out of sight of the enemy, and then moved by the right flank in a northeasterly direction until my lines were partly across the Wilkinson pike, where I formed them to the front in two lines of battle, Colonel Thomas' brigade forming the front line and Colonel Anderson's the second line. The Sixty-first Illinois was deployed as skirmishers in front of the first line. In this order I advanced upon the enemy, through the brush, cedars, rocks, and logs, under a heavy fire of artillery. I had sent my artillery back to the fortress for ammunition before commencing my last advance, and consequently had no artillery to reply to that of the enemy. Skirmishing with small-arms began very soon after commencing my advance, but my skirmish line advanced rapidly, bravely, and in splendid order, considering the nature of the ground, driving the rebels before them for about one mile, when coming to a cotton-field I found the enemy strongly posted in a wood on the other side behind a line of works constructed of rails and logs. The enemy's fire of small-arms here became so strong that my skirmishers withdrew to the flanks of my line of battle, opened on the enemy a terrible fire, while it still advanced in good order to the middle of the field, when the line halted and the fire from both sides was most furious and destructive for about ten minutes, when I ordered an advance, and the front line moved forward into the edge of the wood, where for a few minutes the roar and fire of musketry was like the thunder of a volcano, and the line wavered as if moving against a hurricane. Fearing that my front line would fall back, I ordered the One hundred and seventy-eighth Ohio Volunteer Infantry to move on the double-quick from the left of the front line, and the balance of the rear line to advance to support and relieve the front line; but before this could be fully executed the gallant regiments composing the first line, seeing themselves supported, advanced with a yell and darted over the enemy's works, capturing many prisoners and putting the enemy to a hasty flight. A rapid pursuit of half a mile resulted in the capturing of many more prisoners, one battle-flag, and two fine pieces of artillery (12-pounder Napoleons), with their caissons. The ammunition of some of the regiments being exhausted, I ordered them to halt and replenish from the ammunition wagon that overtook us at that point.

    While this was going on, I received your dispatch, general, admonishing me of the report of a large rebel infantry force from the north, and directing me to return to the fortress, if I could do so with safety. My artillery, which I had sent back for ammunition, arrived at this time, and a large body of the enemy's cavalry being in plain view I directed the artillery to open on them rapidly for a few minutes, when they rapidly disappeared out of sight.

I cannot speak too highly of the bravery exhibited by my troops, especially by those in the front regiments, under the gallant Colonel Thomas. Never did troops fight better for the time they were engaged. Every officer and man performed his duty with the most unflinching bravery and promptness. The conduct of the Second Brigade, under Colonel Anderson, also deserves much praise; for, though the regiments of the brigade did not take much part in the firing, yet their coolness and promptness in supporting the first line added greatly to its confidence and *morale*, and did much to discourage the enemy by the appearance of two lines of battle moving on them. I regret deeply the death of the brave men killed, and added their lives to the hundred of thousands of patriot heroes who have died for their country. Particularly among the killed do I regret the death of Major Reed, of the One hundred and seventy-fourth Ohio Volunteer Infantry, who fell while gallantry leading on his regiment to victory. The history of his services and adversities in the present war is stranger than fiction.

My total loss in killed and wounded amounts (as per enclosed reports) to 208, of whom 22 were killed. I have no means of arriving at a knowledge of the loss of the enemy, but from the number of dead and wounded observed on the field it must have been greater than mine. Among their dead on the field were observed two lieutenant colonels. We captured and brought in 197 prisoners, among whom 21 were commissioned officers. Forty-three different regiments are represented by the prisoners. The enemy were commanded by Generals Forrest and Bate, and about 5,000 strong.

I am much indebted to the gentlemen of my staff for their prompt, gallant, and efficient assistance throughout the day; and I avail myself of this opportunity to tender to the major-general commanding the District of Tennessee my most grateful acknowledgments for his kindness in affording me the two late opportunities of wiping out to some extent the foul and mortifying stigma of a most infamously unjust arrest, by which I have for near eighteen months been thrown out of the ring of active, honorable, and desirable service.

I have the honor to be, very respectfully, your most obedient servant,
R H Milroy

Major-general

December 13, 1864
Special Orders No -, 2nd Brigade, 4th Division, 20th Army Corps
Murfreesboro, TN

In accordance with the discretion of Maj Genl Milroy Asst Surgeon Booth 177th O V will report to Captain Henry Bundy 13th New York Battery for duty.
By order of
Edward Anderson
Col Commdg 2nd Brigade

December 26, 1864
Battery Orders No. 64
Murfreesboro, TN

I   Sergeant Charles Krauss and Corporal Issac Van Sciver are hereby reduced to the ranks for drunkenness on duty to take effect from this date.
II   Private John Mahoney is hereby appointed vice Issac Van Sciver reduced to date accordingly.
He will be obeyed and respected accordingly.
Henry Bundy Captain
Commanding Battery

January 1, 1865
Report to Brig. Gen. L. Thomas, Adjutant General
Savannah, GA

In accordance with Gen Order No 244 AGO current series 1864 I have the honor to report that I am on duty as AAIG of the Artillery Brig 20th Corps, Army of Georgia in obedience to Special Order No 85 Hd quarters 20th Army Corps dated Sept 19 1864.
I have the honor to remain
Your obt Sevrt
James C. Carlisle
1st Lt 13th NY Indpt Batty
AAIG Art Brig 20th Corps

January 8, 1865
Battery Orders No. 65
Tullahoma, TN

Corporal James Eskdale is hereby appointed sergeant in this Battery, vice Charles Krauss reduced to date from December 26, 1864. He will be obeyed and respected accordingly.
Henry Bundy Captain
Commanding Battery

March 1, 1865
Leave of absence request to Brig. Gen. William Whipple, Assistant Adjutant General, Department of the Cumberland
Tullahoma, TN

General,
I have the honor to apply for a leave of absence for twenty days to go to New York City to attend to private affairs. I have never had a leave of absence since I was commissioned and was only home once in nearly four years service and that was when I reenlisted as a veteran.
I have the honor to be
Very Respectfully General
Your obedient servant
John McGurrin 2nd Lieutenant
13th New York Indpt Battery

Extract from Special Orders No. 59, Headquarters, Department of the Cumberland
Nashville, TN

Leave of absence for twenty days, to date from time of leaving Department, is hereby granted to 2nd Lt Jno McGurrin 13th NY Indpt Btty
By command of Major General Thomas

March 4, 1865
Battery Orders No. 66
Tullahoma, TN

Private John Miller is hereby appointed corporal in the 13th NY Battery vice James Eskdale promoted to date from the first of March 1865. He will be obeyed and respected accordingly.
Henry Bundy Captain
Comdg Battery

March 27, 1865
Battery Orders No. 67
Tullahoma, TN

QM Sergeant Edward Baldwin is hereby appointed First Sergeant in 13th NY Battery vice Henry Tintenfass promoted to date from March 14. He will be obeyed and respected accordingly.
Henry Bundy Captain
Comdg Battery

Battery Orders No. 68
Tullahoma, TN

I   Commencing tomorrow March 28th there will be an inspection of the quarters by the Officer of the Day every morning at 8 o'clock. It is therefore made the duty of the non-commissioned officers to see that the quarters of their men as well as their own are in a proper condition by that time.
II   Every morning from now right after roll call the police will clean up in and around the camp.
Henry Bundy Captain
Comdg Battery

April 2, 1865
Report of Dr. L. W. Kennedy, Surgeon, 123rd New York Regiment
Goldsboro, NC

James C Carlise 1st Lieut 13th NY Independent Battery and AAIG Artillery Brig 20th AC having applied for a certificate on which to ground an application for leave of absence. I do hereby certify that I have carefully examined this officer and find that he is suffering from a gun shot fracture of the 7th and 8th ribs on left side of thorax received at the Battle of Chancellorsville May 2 1863 and there is now [not readable] of the bones with consequent exfoliation, also constant discharge of pus and that in consequence therefore he is in my opinion for a present unfit for active duty. I further declare my belief (as his case requires a surgical operation and consequently rest) that he will not be able to resume his duties in a less period than (60) sixty days. I further declare my belief that his course is necessary to prevent permanent disability.

Leave of absence request to Lt. Col. H. W. Perkins, Assistant Adjutant General, 20th Army Corps
Goldsboro, NC

    I have the honor to apply for a leave of absence in conformity with the accompanying medical certificate and for the time therein recommended.
    I am your obt servant
    James Carlisle

April 27, 1865
Leave of absence request to Brig. Gen. William Whipple, Assistant Adjutant General, Department of the Cumberland
Tullahoma, TN

    General
    I have the honor to apply for a leave of absence for twenty days to go to New York to attend to important business affairs which require my personal attention. I have not had a leave of absence for nearly two years.
I have the honor to be
Very respectfully, General
Your obedient servant
Henry Bundy Captain
Comdg 13th New York Battery

April 29, 1865
Battery Orders No. 69
Tullahoma, TN

I   Sergeant Wm H H Garrett is hereby appointed Quartermaster Sergeant in the 13th NY Battery vice Edward Baldwin promoted to date from March 14th 1865. He will be obeyed and respected accordingly.
II   Corporal Charles Bundy is hereby appointed sergeant in the 13th NY Battery vice Garrett promoted from March 14th 1865. He will be obeyed and respected accordingly.
III   Private Joseph Clavin is hereby appointed corporal in the 13th NY Battery vice Bundy promoted to date from March 14th 1865. He will be obeyed and respected accordingly.
IV   Corporal John White is hereby reduced to the ranks for twice neglecting his duties as corporal this order take effect from date.
V   Private Charles Hartman is hereby appointed corporal in the 13th NY Battery vice John White reduced. This order takes effect from date. He will be obeyed and respected accordingly.
By Order
Henry Bundy
Captain Comdg Battery

May 22, 1865
Battery Orders No. 70
Tullahoma, TN

I   Corporal David Driscoll is hereby appointed sergeant vice James When discharge- to date from May 1, 1865.
II   Private Henry Trebur is hereby appointed corporal vice Driscoll promoted, to day from May 1, 1865.
By order of
Henry Bundy Captain
Comdg Battery

May 28, 1865
Battery Orders No. 71
Tullahoma, TN

The Commanding Officer of the Battery again finds it necessary to call attention to the neglect of non-commissioned officers to wear their insignia of rank such neglect will not be tolerated and all non-commissioned officers who fail to wear such insignia will be reduced to the ranks forthwith.

The Veteran Soldiers of the Battery will also be required to wear their Veteran stripes they will not be allowed to go to town or have any privileges until they comply with this order.

Private Geo Graef and Wm Reichhartz are hereby placed on daily duty for the purpose of putting on the necessary badges of rank for non-commissioned officers and Veteran stripes for veterans; they will procure the material from the sutler of the command and charge remunerative prices—the men to pay them on first payday. They are detailed for daily duty until further orders.

By order of
Henry Bundy Captain
Commanding Battery

June 24, 1865
Battery Orders No. 72
Tullahoma, TN

Private Chas Bundy is hereby reinstated sergeant to date from the first day of June when reduced. He will be obeyed and respected accordingly.
By order of
Henry Bundy
Capt Comdg Battery

July 6, 1865
Special Orders No. 13, Military Division of Tennessee
Nashville, TN

I   The following volunteer batteries of light artillery now at Johnsonville, Tenn., are hereby relieved from further duty in this military division, and will proceed without delay to Saint Louis, Mo. The commanding officers will report on arrival to Maj Gen G M Dodge, commanding Department of the Missouri, for further orders. The guns, horses, and equipments of the batteries will be turned over to the depot officers of the respective departments at this place: Battery A, Second Missouri Light Artillery; Battery F, Second Missouri Light Artillery; Battery I, Second Missouri Light Artillery.

The quartermaster's department will furnish the necessary transportation.

II   The following batteries of light artillery are hereby relieved from further duty where they are now serving and will report without delay to the chief mustering and disbursing officer of the State to which the organization belongs, at the place of rendezvous hereinafter designated, to be mustered out of service in accordance with provisions of General Orders, No 105, current series, War Department. The guns, horses, and equipments of the commands will be turned over to proper officers of the respective departments at this place. The quartermaster's department will furnish the necessary transportation under provisions of General Orders, No 94, current series, War Department: Battery B, First Ohio Light Artillery (Bridgeport, Ala), Cleveland, Ohio; Ninth Ohio Battery (Bridgeport, Ala), Cleveland, Ohio; Thirteenth New York Battery (Tullahoma, Tenn), New York City.

III   The following batteries of volunteer light artillery are hereby relieved from further duty where they are now serving and will report without delay to the chief mustering and disbursing officer of the State to which the organization belongs, at the place of rendezvous hereinafter designated, to be mustered out of service in accordance with provisions of General Orders, No 105, current series, War Department. The guns, horses, and equipments of the commands will be turned over to the proper officers of the respective departments at Chattanooga, Tenn. The quartermaster's department will furnish the necessary transportation under provisions of General Orders, No 94, current series, War Department: Battery I, First Ohio Light Artillery (Dalton, Ga), Camp Dennison, Ohio; Battery M, First Illinois Light Artillery (Cleveland, Tenn), Chicago, Ill; Battery G, First Missouri Light Artillery (Lookout Mountain), Saint Louis, Mo.

By command of Major-General Thomas

APPENDIXES

APPENDIX A
Historical Sketch by 2nd Lt. Edward Baldwin

The Thirteenth New York Independent Battery, Volunteer Light Artillery, was organized in New York City. It was mustered into service October 15, 1861, and sent to Washington, DC, and thence to Camp Observation, near Ball's Bluff, VA., but on the Maryland side of the Potomac. As the battery had not at that time received its guns, it could not take part in the battle of Ball's Bluff, which occurred on the day after its arrival, except by patrolling the vicinity of the camp, and acting as sentinels during the absence of the infantry.

The battery was ordered to Washington in December, remaining in camp near that city until February, 1862, when it was ordered to Hunter's Chapel, VA., and assigned to Blenker's Division, after receiving its six three-inch steel rifled guns. From Hunter's Chapel the battery advanced on March 17th, to Centreville, and thence to Manassas Junction.

As this time one section made a night march to the Rappahannock, and hearing the reveille sounded in the enemy's camp we shelled them. They returned fire, but we suffered no loss.

The first commander of the battery, Capt. Edward Sturmfels, resigned about this time, and he was succeeded by Capt. Julius Dieckmann. In May, the battery was ordered to Washington to join a force then being organized for service in Western Virginia under command of General Fremont.

The battery proceeded via the Baltimore and Ohio Railroad to Petersburg, and thence marched over very rough mountain roads to the town of Franklin. After a stay of a few days at that place we retraced our route to Petersburg, thence across the mountains to the Shenandoah Valley, and down the Valley in pursuit of the Confederate forces commanded by Gen. "Stonewall" Jackson.

The battery took part in the battle of Cross Keys on June 8, 1862, and on the 9th, pursued the enemy to Port Republic; but as he had crossed and burned the bridge at that place further pursuit was abandoned. The battery remained in the Valley at Mount Jackson and Cedar Creek until July, when it marched to Sperryville to join the Army of Virginia under General Pope.

On August 8th, we marched to Culpeper Court House, and on the 9th, went to meet the enemy at Cedar Mountain, but found they had moved off during the night.

The battery also took part in the battle of Rappahannock Station, August 20th; Freeman's Ford, August 21st; Waterloo Bridge, August 22d, and White Sulphur Springs, August 23d

On August 29th, the command arrived at Manassas Junction, and near dark was ordered to go with all speed to aid of King's Division, which had met and engaged the enemy at Groveton. The battery galloped the entire distance, and went into action; but darkness set in and the fighting ceased.

On August 30th, at daylight, the battery, with Milroy's Brigade, advanced on the enemy at Groveton, the men moving the guns forward by hand, and firing as we advanced. The enemy was in a strong position behind an embankment, and after a desperate fight, Milroy's Brigade, finding they were greatly outnumbered, retired under cover of the battery's fire. In this action we lost 1 officer and 7 men wounded, and a number of horses shot. Although under a heavy fire the men succeeded in removing the disabled horses from the limbers and took the guns from the field. One gun carriage had its axle broken by a solid shot from the enemy, but the men dismounted the gun, slung it under the limber with the prolonge, and then took it from the field, after destroying the wheels to make them useless to the enemy. One section was disabled through the loss of men and horses and the breaking of the gun carriage.

After a short rest the four serviceable guns were ordered into action to engage a battery which vigorously shelled our troops as they moved towards the enemy's position. We engaged a six-gun battery of the enemy at long range and two guns at close range until they ceased firing near sundown. After dark our guns were withdrawn from the field. Our loss was 1 man killed and 3 dangerously wounded; also, a number of horses wounded and killed. The men were pretty much used up, having had hardly anything to eat for twenty-four hours, and had been fighting nearly all day.

On August 31st, the battery was in reserve. In the evening it marched to Centreville, and thence to a position several miles from the fortifications south of the Potomac. While there our disabled guns and horses were replaced and some men received from a howitzer battery which had been disabled. Being again in condition for service the command was ordered to Fairfax Court House. While there four men with two horses and a limber went in charge of Captain

Dahlgren, of General Sigel's staff, to Bull Run Bridge and removed from its carriage a gun which had been abandoned by some battery because of a broken wheel. We slung the gun under the limber and succeeded in getting away with it before we were noticed by the enemy's pickets, who were but a short distance away.

We next moved to Gainsville and encamped there until December. We then made a force march to Fredericksburg at the time of the battle there, but the battery was not called into action. We remained in camp near Brooke's Station until the movement which ended the battle of Chancellorsville. The battery was actively engaged in the battle of May 2d and had 1 officer, Lieutenant Carlisle and 4 men dangerously wounded and 3 men mortally wounded. One section had to be abandoned as all the horses and most of the men were disabled.

We returned to Brooke's Station and remained there until the opening of the Gettysburg campaign. Captain Dieckmann resigned at this time in order to accept a commission as a major of the Fifteenth New York Heavy Artillery and was succeeded in the command of the battery by Capt. William Wheeler.

After very long and tiresome marches, we arrived at Emmitsburg on the morning of July 1st and at an early hour were ready to move at short notice. When ordered forward it galloped all the way to and through the town of Gettysburg, and out on the Carlisle Road to the left of which it took position. It attacked the advancing enemy and kept fighting until threatened on the flank and rear. Then, with prolonges hitched so as to fire while retiring, the battery fell back to Cemetery Hill. At that place it took part in the battles of July 2d and 3d. On July 3d, when Pickett made his famous charge, the battery was ordered to that part of the field. At the "Bloody Angle" it went into action and continued firing until the enemy retreated from the field.

When moving from this position we hauled off a gun that had been abandoned. This gun replaced one that had been disabled on July 1st. Our loss was 1 man killed, a number wounded and 4 or 5 missing.

The battery marched to Catlett's Station, VA and remained there until the Eleventh and Twelfth Corps were ordered to Chattanooga to reinforce General Rosecrans and open up his line of communication with his base of supplies. It was present at Wauhatchie Valley, when the enemy made a night attack on our position. It took part in the battles of Missionary Ridge, November 25th, Lookout Mountain, November 27th, Ringgold, November 27th

and marched to aid in raising the siege of Knoxville. On November 29th we camped at Bridgeport, AL and in December, when asked to continue in service after our term of enlistment expired, the battery re-enlisted to continue in service to the end of the war.

In May 1864, we left Bridgeport to take part in the campaign which culminated in the capture of Atlanta. The battery took park in the battles of Mill Creek Gap, May 8th, and Resaca, May 15th. After this battle the guns of the battery were exchanged for six twelve-pound brass Napoleons. The object in this change was to keep the battery close to the front of the advancing columns, where it could give the enemy canister at short range as well as shot and shell at longer distance. General Hooker caused this change to be made because the infantry liked to have a battery close at hand when in action. We also were actively engaged at New Hope Church, May 27th. At this battle our battery had 2 men dangerously wounded, and at the battle of Pine Knob, May 28th, we had 1 man killed and 2 wounded. On June 22d, our corps, the Twentieth, marched towards Kennesaw Mountain. The enemy, however, had placed a battery in a position to sweep a clearing a mile long, over which the corps had to march to Mud Creek Gap. General Hooker ordered Captain Wheeler to take the battery to a hill about 300 yards from the enemy's position and silence that battery.

Our command galloped to the position designated, the enemy firing sold shot at us as we advanced; but they only hit the stumps of trees along the road side, and pieces of wood and dirt flew around us as we drove on. When we reached the top of the hill it was necessary to level places for the gun carriages; else they would recoil down its steep incline when firing commenced.

We loaded with case shot and when ready opened fire with the entire battery. This broadside evidently demoralized the enemy's cannoneers as their fire slackened and after a few more broadsides they disappeared. The infantry were advancing in line of battle now and a tremendous cheer for the "Thirteenth" went up along the whole line. Our loss was 2 men dangerously wounded.

On June 22d, the battery was ordered to go with all speed to Kolb's Farm and occupy a position on the right of the line which was unprotected and against which the enemy was advancing. The battery hastened to the place designated, receiving cheers of the infantry as we galloped past them. It quickly opened on the enemy, who were rapidly nearing the position and succeeded in driving them back; not;

however, until our brave and beloved commander, Capt. William Wheeler, was shot through the heart and instantly killed.

Captain Wheeler had been an officer in the battery from the time it was organized and had endeared himself to every man in the company by his gallantry and gentlemanly bearing. His loss was keenly felt by the entire command.

First Lieut. Henry Bundy assumed command, and later he was commissioned as captain. He commanded the battery until it was mustered out of service. The battery took part in the battle of Kennesaw Mountain, June 26th, and in the battle of Noyes' Creek.

On July 20th, we crossed Peach Tree Creek and went into position along the edge of some woods with a large clear field on its front. Shortly after taking position the pickets came running in. We looked for the enemy but seeing none we laughed at the boys for running. A little later, without firing a shot or making a sound of any kind, a heavy force of infantry was in our front and coming on the double-quick for our guns. The command was given, "Load with canister quick!" and the guns poured canister into the advancing so rapidly and accurately that the enemy's line wavered and broke. But it was quickly rallied and again advanced only to be driven back again. But, twice again he came and was repulsed, all except a few bolder than the rest, who reached the right section. But some of our men seized handspikes and the sergeants using revolvers drove them back. A force now came through the woods on our right flank, and gave us a volley, which killed 2 men, mortally wounded 2 and severely wounded 5. The captain, as soon as he saw this new danger, ordered the left section to change front to the right and open on the enemy on our right. This was quickly done and a charge of canister, together with a stocking full of minie balls, of which we had probably thirty or forty stowed in our limber for close works (the men having gathered them at different time from fields of battle)- these were poured into them three times in quick succession. Reenforcements of infantry came to us at this time and drove the enemy from our right when he fell back beaten at all points. The enemy's loss was very heavy, 12,000 all told; and in this were 5 brigadier generals killed and wounded. When General Sherman came to the scene of the battle, Peach Tree Creek, General Hooker took him to our position to show him the New York battery that so courageously and successfully resisted and repulsed the successive and desperate assaults of the enemy.

The company next moved to a position about 800 yards from the enemy's fortifications before Atlanta, remaining there and taking part in the siege, until the enemy evacuated the city.

The battery entered Atlanta on the night of September 2d, and as we saw no other troops while marching through several streets we were about the first to enter the city. In November, we went by rail to Chattanooga, thence to Tullahoma, TN and in December to Murfreesboro. The enemy was discovered a short distance of Murfreesboro, when a section of our guns and a force of infantry went out to reconnoiter. The enemy's artillery opened on us our section replying with shell for shell. A pretty little artillery duel followed during which we blew up one of his caissons. We suffered no serious loss, having one horse killed and one gun carriage shattered. A few days later we occupied the position from which the enemy fired on us. We found there several new-made graves showing that they lost some men. While holding this position four guns and a force of infantry went after the enemy, north of Murfreesboro, and after a sharp artillery fight he fell back. We had 1 man killed and 1 mortally wounded.

A few days later, the enemy was again reported advancing from the south of Murfreesboro and again the battery and infantry went out and met him and drove him back. A week later we went through a similar performance with a like result. He disappeared and was not seen there after.

The battery returned to Tullahoma, TN in the later part of December and remained at that place until July 1865 when it was ordered home. On July 28, 1865, it was mustered out of service in New York City; and thus ended its four years' continuous service in defense of the Union, having fought in Virginia, Maryland, Pennsylvania, Georgia, Tennessee and Alabama.

APPENDIX B
Commands that the Battery was attached to

Attached to Baker's Brigade, Stone's Division, Army of the Potomac (to December 1861); Blenker's Division, Army of the Potomac (to March 1862); Blenker's 2nd Division, 2nd Army Corps, Army of the Potomac (to April 1862); Blenker's Division, Dept. of the Mountains (to June 1862); Reserve Artillery, 1st Corps, Pope's Army of Virginia (to September 1862); Artillery, 1st Division, 11th Army Corps, Army of the Potomac (to May 1863); Artillery Brigade, 11th Army Corps, Army of the Potomac (to October 1863); Artillery Brigade, 11th Army Corps, Dept. of the Cumberland (to January 1864); Artillery, 2nd Division, 20th Army Corps, Army of the Cumberland (to September 1864); Unattached Artillery, Post of Murfreesboro, TN, Dept. of the Cumberland (to December 1864); Defenses Nashville & Chattanooga Railroad, Dept. of the Cumberland (to March 1865); 2nd Brigade, 1st Sub-District, Middle Tennessee, Dept. of the Cumberland (to July 1865)

APPENDIX C
Battery Service

Duty on the Upper Potomac (to December 1861) and in defense of Washington DC (until April 1862); Operations in the Shenandoah Valley until July; Reconnaissance to Rappahannock River and action at Rappahannock Crossing, (April 18); Battle of Cross Keys (June 8); Occupation of Luray (July 22); Pope's Campaign in Northern Virginia (August 16-September 2); Fords of the Rappahannock (August 21-23); Battle of Groveton (August 29); Bull Run (August 30); Duty in defense of Washington DC (until December); March to Fredericksburg, VA (December 10-16); "Mud March" (January 20-24, 1863); At Brooke's Station (until April); Chancellorsville Campaign (April 27-May 6); Battle of Chancellorsville (May 1-5); Battle of Gettysburg (July 1-3); Pursuit of Lee (July 5-24); Near Bristoe Station (until September); Movement to Bridgeport, AL (September 24-October 4); Reopening Tennessee River (October 26-29); Chattanooga-Ringgold Campaign (November 23-27); Orchard Knob (November 23-24); Missionary Ridge (November 24-25); Duty in Lookout Valley (until April 1864); Atlanta Campaign (May 1-September 8); Demonstration on Rocky Faced Ridge, Tunnel Hill and Buzzard's Roost Gap (May 8-11); Dug Gap or Mill Creek (May 9); Battle of Resaca (May 14-15); Near Cassville (May 19); New Hope Church (May 25); Operations on line of Pumpkin Vine Creek and battles about Dallas, New Hope Church and Allatoona Hills (May 26-June 5); Operations about Marietta and against Kennesaw Mountain (June 10-July 2); Pine Hill (June 11-14); Lost Mountain (June 15-17); Gilgal or Golgotha (June 19); Kolb's Farm (June 22); Assault on Kennesaw (June 27); Ruff's Station, Smyrna Camp Ground (July 4); Chattahoochie River (July 5-17); Peach Tree Creek (July 19-20); Siege of Atlanta (June 22-August 25); Occupation of Atlanta (September 2); Ordered to Murfreesboro, TN and duty in that district (until July 1865); Overall's Creek (December 4, 1864); Hood's attack on Murfreesboro (December 5-12); Wilkinson's Pike, Murfreesboro (December 7)

During their service to the Union the battery had one officer and eleven men killed in action; sixteen men died by disease.

APPENDIX D
Battery Officers

CAPTAINS
Emil Sturmfels, October 15, 1861-May 15, 1862
Julius Dieckmann, May 15, 1862-May 26, 1863
William Wheeler, August 12, 1863-June 22, 1864
Henry Bundy, July 26, 1864-July 28, 1865

FIRST LIEUTENANTS
William Wade, October 15, 1861
William Wheeler, October 15, 1861-August 12, 1863
Albert Molitor, December 20, 1861-December 8, 1862
T Delteure, October 16, 1861-March 14, 1862
James Early, March 29, 1862-May 11, 1862
Frank Singer, December 8, 1862-January 16, 1863
James Carlisle, September 1, 1863-July 28, 1865
Henry Miller, June 22, 1864-November 21, 1864
John McGurrin, March 14, 1865-July 28, 1865

SECOND LIEUTENANTS
Peter Boyle, October 14, 1861-December 16, 1861
James Early, October 15, 1861-December 20, 1861
Carl Von Linden, November 5, 1861-May 15, 1862
Frank Singer, December 15, 1861-December 8, 1862
Henry Bundy, May 15, 1862-January 16, 1863
James Carlisle, December 8, 1862-September 1, 1863
Joseph Bohn, January 16, 1863- June 21, 1863
Henry Miller, May 26, 1863-June 22, 1864
Eugene Freeman, February 10, 1864-May 12, 1865
John McGurrin, July 26, 1864-March 14, 1865
Henry Tintenfass, November 22, 1864-July 28, 1865
Edward Baldwin, declined promotion, not mustered in
William Bowes, declined promotion, not mustered in

APPENDIX E
Inscription of the New York State Monument at Orchard Knob, Chickamauga and Chattanooga National Military Park

To the New York troops in Howard's Eleventh Corps of Hooker's command, 11th and 12th Corps, Army of the Potomac at Chattanooga and Missionary Ridge, Nov. 23,24,25, 1863.

Steinwehr's	2nd Division
Bushbeck's	1st Brigade
134th NY Infantry	Lt. Col. A H Jackson
154th NY Infantry	Col. P H Jones
Orland Smith's	2nd Brigade
136th NY Infantry	Col. Jas. Wood, Jr.
Schurz's	3rd Division
Tyndale's	1st Brigade
45th NY Infantry	Maj. Chas. Koch
143rd NY Infantry	Col. Horace Boughton
Krzyzanowski's	2nd Brigade
58th NY Infantry	Capt. M Essembaux
119th NY Infantry	Col J T Lockman
141st NY Infantry	Col W K Logie
Hecker's	3rd Brigade
68th NY Infantry	Lt. Col A von Steinhausen
Osborn's	Artillery
13th NY Battery	Capt WM Wheeler
Headquarters Guard	
Co "A" 8th NY Infantry	Capt A Bruhm

On the morning of November 25, Hecker's Brigade drove the enemy out of his rifle pits in front of Schurz's Division and Krzyanowski's Brigade rejoined that command. The Corps then marched beyond the northern termination of Missionary Ridge to Sherman's support, a part of the column reaching Sherman's pontoon bridge at 10:45 AM, and took position about 2 PM. The right connection with Sherman's left, high up on the ridge to the south the left resting on Chickamauga Creek near Boyce's station (of that day). Here the troops covered themselves with breastworks and remained until the following morning. Schurz's Division occupied the right of the line and Steinwehr's the left.

Three regiments of Bushbeck's Brigade attached to Ewing's Division, 15th Corps, supported Loomis' Brigade of that division in the attack on Tunnel Hill. The 73rd Penna., temporarily commanded by Lieut. Col. JB Taft of the 143rd New York, drove the enemy from the glass building and followed him nearly to the summit of the hill. In this action Lieut Col. Taft was killed.

The infantry and three batteries of the Eleventh Corps, Major General O O Howard, commanding, left Lookout Valley at one PM November 22, 1863, crossing the river at Brown's Ferry. Battery I, First New York Light Artillery, Captain Wiedrich, commanding, remained in Lookout Valley and participated November 24, 1863, in the battle of Lookout Mountain.

Wheeler's 13th NY Battery was sent to a knoll on the north side of the river, overlooking the low ground traversed by the corps, during the following days of the battle. The remaining force of the corps, about 6000 strong, moved over the bridge to Chattanooga and bivouacked that night south of Fort Wood.

About noon November 23rd the corps formed north of Fort Wood in close column, with Steinwehr's Division on the right and Schurz's Division on the left, in support of Wood's Division, Fourth Corps, and assisted in capturing Orchard Knob. After the Fourth Corps was in position on Orchard Knob, the Eleventh Corps extended the line from Orchard Knob to the Tennessee River, driving the enemy beyond Citico Creek. In this movement Schurz's Division formed the right and Steinwehr's the left of the corps.

Sherman's army having crossed the Tennessee River near Chickamauga Creek during the night on the 23rd.; General Howard was directed to open communication with it.

November 24. The enemy was driven from his works immediately in front of the corps, from near the mouth of Citico Creek to the East Tennessee RR.

Three regiments of Bushbeck's Brigade accompanied by General Howard crossed Citico Creek and march along the Tennessee River to Sherman's crossing. Wheeler's Battery fired shots in advance of column to drive away enemy's skirmishers. Krzyzanowski's Brigade supported and was left of Wheeler's Battery to keep open communications.

The 134th New York Infantry and 154th New York Infantry of Bushbeck's Brigade were temporarily assigned to Orland Smith's Brigade.

APPENDIX F
Inscription and Dedication of Battery Monument
Gettysburg, PA

[front]
13th NEW YORK
INDPT. LIGHT BATTERY
(Wheeler's)
ARTILLERY BRIGADE
11th CORPS
JULY 1, 1863, ENGAGED HERE. JULY 2, ON CEMETERY HILL
JULY 3, AT REPULSE OF PICKETT'S CHARGE

Address of 1st Lt. John McGurrin, July 4, 1893

Veterans of the Thirteenth New York Independent Battery:
The great importance of the Union victory won at Gettysburg by the Army of the Potomac, after three days' desperate fighting, has caused the government to purchase and lay out as a National Military Park, the ground on which the Union troops fought and won that victory. The national government has also erected here a grand monument to honor and commemorate the heroism and patriotism of the men who on this battlefield gave their lives for their country.

The loyal states that were represented in the battle of Gettysburg by volunteer military organizations have shown their appreciation of the sacrifices made by their sons on this and other battlefields by erecting here a separate monument to the deceased members of each organization. The State of New York had, in the battle of Gettysburg, a much larger number of volunteer soldiers than any of the other loyal states, and the number of killed and wounded of New York State volunteers was much larger than the number of killed and wounded from the volunteers of any of the other states at Gettysburg.

The people of the State of New York did not rest content with erecting a monument to the deceased members of each volunteer organization from that state, but they also erected here a grand State monument to commemorate the very important part that the sons of New York had in winning the greatest and most important of all the battles fought for the restoration of the Union.

The battle of Gettysburg was not only the greatest of the battles for the preservation of the Union; it was more than that. It was the pivotal battle of the war- the battle upon the results of which depended, to a great extent, the fate of the nation.

The Confederate army at Gettysburg was the best army of the Southern Confederacy, composed as it was of veterans of many hard-fought fields, led by the ablest generals of the Confederacy. They hoped and expected to win on the soil of the loyal State of Pennsylvania a great victory, and thus impress the people of the loyal states with the futility of a further prosecution of the war. But they met here their old antagonist, the great Army of the Potomac; and after three days of most desperate fighting the Confederates were compelled to acknowledge defeat and to retreat from the battlefield after suffering great losses in killed, wounded and prisoners.

This finest army of the Confederacy never won a battle of any importance after its defeat at Gettysburg. It retreated to its strongholds in Virginia only to be driven from one to another until it reached its last ditch at Appomattox and surrendered unconditionally to the general who had hammered it unceasingly until it surrendered. So we see that the tide of victory which was strongly turned in our favor at Gettysburg was never turned back but irresistibly rolled on until it washed out every vestige of opposition to the complete restoration of the Union. This is why the national government and the loyal states that were represented by volunteer soldiers in this battle have joined in doing honor to the men who fought and won the victory at Gettysburg, and saved the Union which now extends from the Great Lakes to the Gulf of Mexico, from the Atlantic to the Pacific, with all its citizens, North and South, East and West, ready and willing to defend it with their lives if necessary.

This visit to the battlefield of Gettysburg vividly recalls some of the thrilling incidents of the engagement in which we, as members of the Thirteenth New York Independent Battery, we took part. It recalls the rapid march of the battery from Emmitsburg to Gettysburg, when on July 1st, it galloped all that distant to take part in the fight which was being fiercely contested by the First Corps of the Army of the Potomac and the Confederate forces. It recalls the part taken in that battle by the battery until the enemy, who then greatly outnumbered the part of the Army of the Potomac which had reached here up to that time, threatened to surround and capture our guns, when with prolonges hitched so as to fire retiring we moved back to Cemetery Hill. It also recalls that part taken by this command in the battle of July 2d, on Cemetery Hill. It recalls to us that when the Confederates under General Pickett, on July 3d, made their desperate attempt to overwhelm the Union lines, the battery was ordered to the point know as the "Bloody Angle" and there it poured canister at close range into the ranks of the advancing Confederates until beaten and baffled at every point they retreated from the field suffering a defeat which proved a death blow to the Southern Confederacy.

Comrades, our visit to this battlefield today is mainly for the purpose of dedicating to our fallen comrades this monument erected to their memory by the people of the State of New York. Of the members of the battery who took part in the battle of Gettysburg only a very few are living. Many of them gave their lives for their country on the battlefields of Georgia and Tennessee in 1863 and 1864 and many others died of wounds received in those campaigns. Of the number who returned to their homes at the close of the war many have died of diseases contracted because of the many hardships and privations they had to suffer in the many campaigns in which they took part during their four years of service from 1861 to 1865.

We sadly miss them today but we miss more than all the gallant and brave Captain Wheeler who commanded the battery at Gettysburg and on many subsequent fields until he gave his life for his country at the battle of Kolb's Farm, in Georgia, on June 22, 1864.

The inscription on this monument is most appropriate. "The Thirteenth New York Independent Battery –Wheeler's!" It was Wheeler's Battery; because to him, as an officer of the command from its enlistment, was due the efficiency which made it such a valuable military organization. This efficiency was continued under his successor in command, Capt. Henry Bundy. He also was a brave and capable officer as was shown on many occasions, notably at Peach Tree Creek, GA, July, 20, 1864, when the battery repulsed several determined charges of the enemy on its front and also drove him from its right flank by changing front with a section, bringing to the Thirteenth the thanks of General Hooker, the commander of the Twentieth Corps, for bravery and efficiency thus displayed under most trying circumstances.

To go into detailed account of the battles and campaigns in which you took part during your four years' service would make this address too long. We will, therefore, conclude by dedicating to our dead comrades of the Thirteenth New York Independent Battery this monument erected to their memory by the people of the State of New York. Comrades, we who shared with them the dangers and perils of many battles the hardships and privations of many campaigns know how truly worthy our deceased comrades are of this tribute of respect to their memory. We know how unflinchingly and courageously they bore every sacrifice demanded of them because they were willing to do and to suffer all things in their power for the restoration of the Union, which they all so dearly loved, and for they were willing to suffer even death.

APPENDIX G
Eulogy of Capt. Wheeler by Rev. Timothy Dwight, Third Congregational Church,
July 17, 1864
New Haven, CT

  The hour that we spend together this evening, my friends, may well be an hour of interest to us all. A soldier has fallen in the service of his country, and a friend has been taken from our society and fellowship. If those who loved him, therefore, are assembled here, the simple story, which I have to tell, may come as the sweet memories of the by-gone years, and they cannot fail to think pleasantly of the one who was just now rejoicing with them. If others are present who never knew him, and who now think of him as one of the many who have passed away in this great conflict, the fact that he has died in the holy cause, and for the hope of the nation, will render it fitting to their thought, I trust, that they should give him the passing tribute of their honor. These sorrows move so rapidly now from family to family, that we are no longer separated as we once were, and you may consent to mingle your grief with ours today, for when tomorrow comes, our sympathy may be needed, as the same sad tidings shall have darkened your life also.

  As I appear before you, then, in accordance with the desire of some of his younger associates, to say a few words in regard to one whom I have long known and loved, I may ask indulgence of every hearer, if I speak to you only as one of a friendly company, where death has entered, might speak to the rest, from the fullness and joy of his own recollection.

  My acquaintance with Captain William Wheeler began soon after he entered College-January, 1852- when he was about fifteen years of age. I was then just beginning my work as an instructor, and by one of those accidents which so often determine the position of the younger College officers, I was assigned to the Greek department in the Freshman Class;- a thing which, as I well remember, I regretted deeply at the time, but which as it has since proved, was the means of deciding my whole future course in life, and of opening to me some of the most valued friendships that I have ever known;- and his among the number. As he came before me in the recitation-room, from day to day, I soon perceived the brightness of his mind, and the ease which- though younger than any of his Classmates- he took a prominent position among them as a scholar. He had received his earlier education, in considerable measure, under one of the most enthusiastic and inspiring of all American teachers[77], and, doubtless, to his influence he owed much of his success. But it was manifest, even then, that the inspiration had been breathed into a thoroughly receptive soul, which must make most rapid progress in every field of learning, that should open to it, as the years should pass. He was a boy, indeed,- with all the incompleteness that that belongs, of necessity, to the boyish age,- but the promise of the future shone forth in everything; and those who have traced his course from that early day even to the end, have never been surprised to see how beautiful was the later development, because the prospect at the beginning seemed so full of hope. His character, also, displayed to his friends, in due measure, the same truthfulness and purity, the same trustfulness and warm affection towards those whom he loved, the same regard for worth and exalted virtue, which were so conspicuous when manhood had brought its maturing and strengthening influence, and the physical life and energy, which made him so easily superior to all around him, in all the playful or athletic sports, was then, as always, the visible manifestation of the same energy and life within. Nor can I ever forget the peculiar beauty of his face, in those College days,- formed, as some one has expressed it, as if of the finest of the clay,- which at once awakened interest in all who looked upon it, and made them feel that a beautiful spirit was mirrored there.

  His kindly feeling toward me, as I recall the past, began soon after we met in the relation of pupil and instructor;- and yet my remembrance of him as an intimate friend does not go father back than his Senior year, when some especially favoring circumstances brought us near together. He was then only in his nineteenth year, but he had already gained for himself high honors in his Class, and was acknowledged by all to be a young man of brilliant gifts. With unusual quickness, he had mastered the various studies of the course, but yet he had not limited himself, like most others, to these alone. He had gone beyond the regular curriculum, and, following up the advantages of his earlier life, he had been, in no ordinary degree, a reader of English literature, as well as a student in one, at least of the Modern Languages. The results of his College life, indeed, were somewhat extraordinary. While few accomplish more than the mere opening of the gateway to the ancient classics,- and thus are compelled to make their future study of them a work, rather than an enjoyment, or even are impelled to lay them aside altogether,- to him they had become already, in no small degree, a source of pleasure. He had entered into the spirit of the authors and the richness of their thoughts,- not, indeed, so fully as he did afterward, but yet far enough to make him appreciate their writings, somewhat after the same manner as those in his native language;- and, had he lived even to old age, I cannot doubt, that he would ever had stood forth as a noble example, to show that the man in professional life need not, because of his many and pressing labors, give up the humanizing studies of his youth, and that there is an inward joy for the widely-cultivated mind, which no amount of wealth or outward success can equal by their gifts.

After his graduation, in July, 1855, he continued in New Haven for nearly two years- first, as a resident graduate on the Clark foundation, and subsequently, as a member of the Law Department of the College;- and then, in the summer of 1857[78], he sailed for Europe. Being abroad at that time myself, I met him soon after his arrival, and, in common with another friend of his, was the means of inducing him to spend the following winter in Berlin. While there, we were very closely connected together, almost as members of the same family, so that I had abundant and most pleasant opportunity to see what had been the growth of his character and mind during the season of opening manhood. I am sure that little circle, who met together every evening, through those winter months, in that foreign city, will never forget how much he added to the comfort and joy of their life,- how appreciative he was of everything that was peculiar among the people around him there, and with what striking power he set it forth,- how gladly and readily his soul received the knowledge offered to in every line,- how wonderfully his enthusiasm urged him forward, and his quickness gave him full possession of all things to which he directed his thoughts. Yet still, there was the same lightness and buoyancy and overflowing humor, as one of his friends has said, which made us feel that he was, and always would be, the loving, joyous spirit that we had know years before- and no one thought that he was growing older, though we saw, indeed, that he was gaining most rapidly in all that the years bring with them.

It was my great good fortune, also, to go with him to Athens[79], and to spend a little while in his society in that land to which his thoughts had turned so often with deepest interest. Would that we might have remained longer and wandered more widely over that land, for everything there,- from the glory of the sunsets and the beauty of the seas and skies, so far beyond the dreams of this western world, to the thousand voices that seemed to be continually whispering to the soul of the bygone centuries,- everything came to him only to fill him with delight, only to find in him that answering sympathy, which made it a joy to every one to follow him and watch his life. But, alas! It could not be so,- and, having caught the sight of the eternal hills and the magnificent ruins for a brief season, we hastened away, with a thankfulness for the remembrance that should not fade from us.

A few weeks later we met again, at the end of our European life, and we stood upon the shores of England, looking off upon the wide ocean, which separated us from the home we loved. I know not how it may be with others, but as I crossed the ocean, once again, and seemed to be separated from all things that I had ever known before, with the great waste of waters on every side, and nothing, as it were, to guide us- it was to me as the emblem of that mysterious passing of the soul from time to eternity, which we call death. At first, the scenes beyond the ocean were strange to me,- the life was new,- the future was all uncertainty,- as the unseen world must always be to the human mind. But, at last, when I crossed again, the land at the end of the voyage, whose existence we believed in, and the sight of which we hoped for, was the land where the friends were living, and where the desires of the soul were to be satisfied. And so it is with the unseen world,- it is not?- as we grow older and come nearer to it.

This day of which we stood thus together- I have called it to mind so many times within these passing weeks- was the 22d of June, six years ago. And now those years have rapidly gone;- and as the day has returned again, I find that he has entered upon that voyage of death, of which the one before us then was but the emblem, and even now I seem to myself to be standing alone upon the shore, and looking off over the waters after him. But he has gone from my sight, and I have the faith only that the land beyond is the home land, and that the friends there are welcoming him to their glorious life.

I have spoken thus far of that portion of our friend's brief career, through the whole of which I met him almost daily, and during the closing months of which I was in those relations of intimacy that always spring up between warm friends, when they travel together in foreign countries. From the time of our landing on the American shores,- though I saw him often, and found more to admire and love in him whenever I saw him,- the separation occasioned by his absence from New Haven seems, so far as I was concerned, to make a new division of his life;- and therefore, as I speak mainly with reference to my own recollections, I ask you to turn aside with me, at this point, from the course of his history, to contemplate, for a few moments, what he was in himself.

His intellect, as it seems to me, was not of the creative order, so much as it was of that class, which appreciates and enjoys everything that is worth enjoying in the world of matter or of mind. He would scarcely have worked out a system of theology or of law, had he lived for years to come, now would he have been regarded as one of the great thinkers of the age. To be sure, he was yet so youthful, that we could not forecast the future with absolute certainty, but, with all the vigor of his mental power, I should not have expected ever to see him leading the way into the recesses of metaphysical science, and I question whether would have given years of laborious thought to the development of any theory in any department of knowledge. We should not have loved him half so well as we did, perchance, if it had been so. The world was too full of attractions, on every side, for him to shut himself up to abstract thought,- too full even, for him to limit himself exclusively to one thing. God had given him another work than this to do. Nor, when we say this, do we depreciate at all his powers. The foundation of his mind, as of his character, was a certain native *strength*, which none who long associated with him, could fail to see displaying itself beneath all the graces that shone so conspicuously. He was patient, also, if need were- industrious- persevering till the end before him was accomplished. Nothing was further removed from his life than indolence. No. A ceaseless activity was even the very resting of his powers; and he was not always at work himself, but always inspiring those around him by his example and enthusiasm. He had, in a word, all that he need, to make a mind of a high order, but it was one of its own order, not of another- appreciative, rather than constructive. If the latter, as men are, perchance, to often prone to regard it, is, of course, the highest rank, then his was not the highest;- nor do we wish to claim such a place for him, as we speak together of what he was. There are not many,- the number diminishes even, most rapidly, as we search for them,- there are not many, to whom such honor can be given, and so long as we know how beautiful his mind was, we willingly leave it in its own class, with no care to measure it by those with which it could be not compared.

He was a scholar, I should say, rather a profound thinker,- and, I may add, a scholar of what might perhaps be called the higher English order, rather than the German. His powers of acquisition, as I have already had occasion to intimate, were quite remarkable. His mind acted with the utmost rapidity, and, as he had the retentiveness of memory which held fast everything that it had once received, he moved on in any branch of learning, where his ardor was awakened, with the greatest success. All his friends, I believe, who have ever studied with him,- especially in some new language,- will remember, as I do myself, the facility with which he made his way forward, and how very soon he surprised them wit his command of words, and his power of entering into the peculiar modes of thought of the strange author. He had such appreciation of the Greek and Latin Classics as is not found in one man among a dozen classes of our College graduates, and so completely did he have at command what he had read, that, when in the camp, far from all books, we would as readily quote from Sophocles or Æschylus as from an English poet. One of the last letters even, that he sent to New Haven,-written at a resting time in the rapid marchings and frequent fightings of General Sherman's army,- was largely occupied, I believe, with a discussion in regard to one of the Greek tragedies. And there was no affectation or ostentation in all this,- nothing was farther from his nature than these things. But it was as natural to him, as our conversation together upon any of the topics in which we are interested is to us. It was the simple outflowing of his own thoughts on these subjects, when he found one who could appreciate them. How many in our army, or even in our country, are there of whom this could be said with truth? He had made unusual progress, also, in at least three of the languages of Modern Europe, the resources of all of which, so far as he had ever known them, were ready for his immediate use at any moment. And having, a few years since, some months of comparative leisure, he joined the theological class who were just commencing the study of Hebrew with the late Professor Gibbs. He was only able to remain with them for a portion of their year, but so much had he accomplished even in that brief period, that he won the high esteem of that distinguished scholar, and at a subsequent time, when he had occasion to instruct a Bible class, in New York, in the Old Testament, he regularly prepared himself for his work by the examination of the Hebrew text[80]. It must be remembered, too, that he was not now a professional scholar lingering within the shades of the University, but a man who had given himself to the Law and was entering upon its practice, or a soldier in all the excitements and turmoil of this terrible war. These studies were not the work of his life,- they were the things which his ardent soul seized upon or bore along with it, as he was hastening forward in his course.

His scholarship, however, was not of the German order. He could never have passed his life-time in making annotations upon a single author, or have lectured for twenty years on the same subject. He could not even have been content to dwell always in the region of grammar, and the drier parts of language. It was the elegances and refinements of scholarship, for which his mind and taste fitted him, and the more varied the fields, the more delightful to his thought. He did not, indeed, neglect or despise thoroughness,- he was not driven back in disgust or despair, by the hard work at the beginning, for he knew that the man who will not patiently make his way through the rules and idioms, can never know anything as he ought to know it. But he used these things only as a means to something that charmed him more; and he soared away from them and above them, as far as he could.

His powers of expression were fully equal to those of acquisition. It was a never-ceasing wonder to me, as I read his letters, or listened to his conversation, how he could set forth his thoughts in such striking language. His facility in this regard made him one of the most delightful of companions or of correspondents, for whether in the description of scenery or in the utterance of his feelings,- whether he was speaking of the sadness and sorrows of life, or giving play to his irrepressible humor, it was all the same. I was led along from point to point, as by a resistless charm, and could not but feel a sense of joy in the contemplation of a mind, which could open itself as he did,- a greater joy for the very reason that his powers were so far beyond my own.

His humor was one of the most striking peculiarities of his mental character. With a sense of the ludicrous beyond that of almost any person I have ever known, and with a power of calling up innumerable things from his recollections of books or of the past, and applying them in the most amusing, yet the most admirably fitting way, he perfectly overflowed with all bright sayings, which seemed to flash upon his own mind as suddenly and unexpectedly, as upon the minds of his hearers. And as the fountain leaped forth so joyously and beautifully, he seemed to enjoy it with as much heartiness and with as perfect freedom from self-praise, as if it has been the word of another, to which he had been a chance listener. The memory of every friend of his will recall what he was in this respect, far more clearly than I can set it forth in words; and the multitude of examples, which might illustrate his power, cannot be referred to here. His mind sparkled and scintillated on every side and at every moment. It was a source of endless delight to all who loved him. We met him always with the kindliest feeling. We left him with a kindlier one, if possible, for he never suffered a word of sarcasm to fall from his lips; he hardly knew how to say anything in which others who were with him would not take pleasure, as he did himself.

He was mad, then, we should say, when we view his mind, for the university and for the society of polished men. And yet he died away from all such scenes, and in the army. But here was one of the remarkable things in his life-,- a thing belonging to his character. He had an unusual earnestness in everything to which he turned his thoughts. I never supposed that he regarded himself as wholly adapted for the legal profession, yet when he determined to enter it, he gave his energy to the work before him, and he had already shown great promise of success, when he was summoned by the call of his country to her defense. We all know, also, that he did not join the army for any love of the military life or military glory. We all know that he would have gladly left the service, at the first moment after the great work had been accomplished. But so long as he continued a solider, he felt it his duty to be a true soldier. He devoted his powers, enthusiastically and earnestly, to the thing before him, and he became a really scientific artillerist.- a most valuable officer, as has been testified from many quarters, both before and since his death Whatever he did, he did with his whole soul, and therefore he did well; equally when engaged in athletic sports,- when he studied the ancient or modern languages,- when he prepared himself for the duties of life, or when he fought the battles of liberty. His was a whole-hearted, earnest, enthusiastic spirit; as earnest today as it was yesterday, as faithful in the new work, as it had been in the old one; and so successful was he in every new work, that we almost wondered how we could have ever thought him fitted for any other.

As closely connected with his earnestness, we may mention his warmth of affection. There was nothing of coldness or sluggishness in his nature, but his whole soul was glowing with strong emotion. His attachment to his own family circle, and his admiration for those who composed it, were such as are rarely seen in a young man; and though he never made a show of his feeling, no one, who knew him well, could fail to remark how very strikingly it displayed itself in all his life. So it was, in fitting measure, towards his other friends,- they never had reason to doubt his affection for them; and even when he disliked those about him, as he sometimes did, it was a warm and hearty dislike, not a cold one. They knew it as plainly as his friends did the opposite sentiment. There is something noble about such a soul, even if it had many prejudices and strong antipathies, as if often has, for we feel sure that these things will pass away more and more, as the years go on; and whatever of them he had in his earlier life, were already passing away. That he was a man of decided, and, at times, perhaps, almost unreasoning partialities, cannot be denied. But so are most men whom we most deeply love. The generous spirit moves often by impulse, and gives itself wholly to its chosen friends. How many, today, remember his friendship as one of the great blessings of their lives, and sorrow most of all because they cannot longer know the light of his affection!

Out of the warmth of his nature, doubtless, grew also that quick sensitiveness to injury, which characterized him, in some measure, and an almost equally quick readiness to forgive and forget, so soon as the explanation has been made, or the misunderstanding had passed away.

I would also connect with this peculiarity of his nature the tendency to despondency, which was noticeable in all his mature life. Whatever special causes there may have been for such a feeling at any given moment, it was a part of his character; there was a tinge of sadness in his soul, as there is, perchance, always in the richest and most charming souls.

Nor can I pass beyond this point altogether, without calling to your thought again for a moment, what I have already alluded to in another connection; his ardent love for everything that was beautiful in the world. With all the strength of a mature intellect, he was like a child in the eagerness with which sprang forth to grasp whatever the realm of nature or of learning offered to him. Who, that ever knew him, will forget his enthusiastic fondness for music or his love of flowers? Who, that ever traveled in his company, will fail to recall how charmed he was with the mountains and valleys of Switzerland, or the glories of the Italian landscape. As he says himself, "I feel like Wordsworth:

> 'A heart leaps up when I behold
> A rainbow in the sky,
> So was it when I was a boy,
> So is it now I am a man,
> So shall it be when I am old,
> Or let me die.'"[81]

And so, as we have already seen, it was as truly and as fully in the world of mind. I do not believe he would ever have lost this brightness of the springtime in his soul, even had he lingered on in life until old age had brought its wintery power upon him. And, as he has passed away so early, I think of him now as having most fitly entered upon the entered upon the eternal springtime.

But the great foundation of his character was the vigor and sturdiness and integrity of the old New England life, which he inherited, in such large measure, from his ancestors. By this he was guarded and strengthened at every step of his course, protected against many of the temptations which assail one in the way from childhood onward, and, when youth had gone, made a man of power to contend with and subdue all evil tendencies. Elevated above the baser passions, and with strictest conscientiousness in regard to duty, he was a pure, true man, one of the nobler short, for whose future we have confidence. His inner life answered to his words; it was deeper, even, and richer than he was willing to confess. Abhorring all hypocrisy and sham of every kind, and possessed of the most transparent honesty and sincerity, he walked before us in the light, and we thoroughly trusted him.

Yes, he was no weak, fickle, childish soul, pleased for the moment with some beautiful thought. But he had depth of nature, in which his friends found the highest satisfaction, and out of which, as we believe, would have come blessings for his fellowmen. He knew the seriousness and sternness of this life of ours, and gave the clearest as well as the noblest evidence of his knowledge of life's meaning and his sense of life's duties, by offering himself a sacrifice to a holy cause.

In this brief and imperfect review of his character, I have spoken of him as I knew him in the intercourse of friendship, with undue warmth of praise, as it may seem to a stranger, but not, as I believe, to those who have lived in his society. That he had faults and failings, every one may have known, for he was not the man to conceal them. But who among his friends thinks of these failings now? I never knew a man,- and I think his most intimate associates will agree with me in saying this,- I never knew a man, the picture of whom was more complete, without his faults; and the picture will remain in my forever as a thing of joy.

After his return from Europe in 1858, he completed his course of study in preparation for the legal profession, at Cambridge, and early in 1860, he settled in the city of New York. His prospects there were very hopeful, and the impression he made upon the older men was a most favorable one. We find him there rejoicing still in music and in books, and praying earnestly "to be kept in safety from the inordinate love and worship of money," which, as it appeared on every side about him, was so shocking to his noble and sensitive soul.

But he was suffered to linger there only for a single year. The sudden call to arms in 1861 came to his hearing, and he could not resist the summons. Like so many young men of education and promise, he had been for years a most hearty opponent of slavery. He had the instincts of freedom, and knew that it must be victorious everywhere, or the country could not hope for permanent safety. He appreciated the Southern character, also, most thoroughly,- few men, that I have ever seen, more thoroughly; and saw, what tens of thousands who then did not understand it are now compelled to admit, that the only way to peace with the slaveholding aristocracy, was to make the respect us by conquering them.

It was not this alone, however, that inspired him to be a soldier. He felt that it was one of the great conflicts of human history, and was to be one of the great triumphs of the right. He would be among those to help it forward. He could not let if fail through any want of devotion or self-sacrifice on his part. In a letter, written just as he was leaving to join the Seventh Regiment, on the 7th of May, 1861, he says; "For myself, I cannot see how a life could be more worthily given up, unless it were for God's sake, and is not this God's cause?" Thus he went forth, deliberately, conscientiously, with ardent love of country, with a willingness to suffer anything, if so be that the dear native land might have a glorious future. And when the hard service of war had continued for three long years, and the suffering had come for his household and himself, on receiving the tidings that his only brother, who, like himself, had made the great sacrifice for the cause, had fallen into the enemy's hands as a prisoner, he writes again, on the 6th of May, 1864, to the same best earthly friend, now filled with anxious solicitude for both her sons; "You must not allow yourself, my dearest Mother, to grieve *too* much over this sad disaster. We cannot do our duty in these stormy times without many risks and sacrifices, and when John and I came out into the field, we had no idea of avoiding our fair share of these dangers; and we are eternally grateful to you for your encouragement, and your sympathy in our plans and views of the right course to be pursued, so that we could go onward with everything in our favor, sense of duty, patriotism, and the cheering voice of those that are dearest to us. And so no loss or sacrifice ought to be regretted or unduly sorrowed over, when viewed in the light which Right and the splendid Future throw over this conflict. I shall not cease hoping that we shall meet once under the family roof, and, in the meantime, I shall that strength may be given him to endure privations, and courage and cheerfulness to buoy his mid up in the dreariness of imprisonment." How does our confidence in the cause, and in its final and triumphant success, grow strong within us, as we read such words! And when the heroic friend who wrote them, falls in the conflict, how sure do we feel that God will watch over the results of his labors, and that, in some distant day in this world or in the other, souls that have inherited the blessings of liberty through his struggles and prayers, will repay him for all, as their song of thankfulness rises to the Everlasting Father.

He returned with the Seventh Regiment, after their brief period of service, but only to enlist in the army again, and in Oct., 1861, he left for the seat of war, as a First Lieutenant in the 13th New York Independent Battery. With this battery he continued to the end; and, according to what would have been his own desire beforehand, he had a most stirring military experience. At first, in the service under Generals Sigel and Fremont, in Western Virginia and the Shenandoah Valley; then in the successive conflicts in the retreat of Gen. Pope from the Rappahannock toward Washington; at the battles of Chancellorsville and Gettysburg; in the supporting body at the celebrated struggle at Lookout Mountain, and in the expedition to relieve Gen. Burnside at Knoxville; and finally, in the campaign of Sherman in Georgia, which is still going forward, he had a most honorable share, and was often, as at the most critical point of the battle of Gettysburg, in the thickest part of the conflict. The story of his life in the army, if it could be told here, would be but one continued record of his faithfulness, his intelligent comprehension of the work before him, his care fore the physical and moral well-being of the men under his command, his fearlessness in danger, and his brave devotion to the cause. The fact that, after three years of service, when his powers had been tested in every line, his entire battery re-enlisted only on condition of his continuing with them, is the best proof of what he was and did; and the sword which they presented to him, as their new term was commencing, will be to his family always a memento of their affection and esteem. His promotion in the service, on the other hand, until he became Chief of Artillery in his division, shows the estimate placed upon his powers and qualifications by his superiors; and I have it from high military authority, that had he been in the infantry service, where the possibilities of promotion are greater, he would have risen to a much more elevated rank. But it is interesting to notice in this connection, his feeling with regard to the artillery. He says to a friend, in 1863, "I enjoy it very much; it is the only arm in which intelligence is needed in every rank, and an officer of artillery has really a fine, wide field for study." How like himself! While his patriotic feeling was satisfied with aiding the country anywhere, his mental activity turned most gladly to that department where intelligence was most demanded, and a sphere for study was most widely opened.

But he was, as we have said, no lover of military glory, for its own sake. Rather did he look forward, with earnest desire, to the time when the conflict should be over, and he could return again to the society of friends and to the joy of his former life. Home had gained in its power over him through his long absence from it. Peace, and the quiet studies and pursuits which peace allows, were more delightful than ever, because he had know, in his own experience, the terrible service of war. God, however, had ordered it otherwise. He was to enter into peace, indeed, but not here;- he was to find his mind opening once more to all beautiful things, but it was in the all-beautiful world.

On Wednesday, the 22d of June, at the battle of Culp's Farm, near Marietta, in Georgia, he was sent forward with his battery to hold a position against the enemy. He secured it and held it for a while, when Gen. Geary, the commander of his division, finding himself unable to support him with infantry, communicated to him the fact of this inability, and at once he answered,- in accordance with is own brave spirit,- "then I will support myself." Just afterwards he fell, shot through the heart by one of the enemy's sharpshooters.

It was the work of a moment. From the fullness of life and activity here to the fullness of life and activity beyond; from the midst of the warfare to the realization of a higher victory; without a sorrow for the loss of the earthly life, until that sorrow was swallowed up on the joys of the future;- can we not bless God that it was thus that the end came, and that the bright spirit we had known so long saw no darkness, for heaven's light beginning was meeting earth's light as it faded.

And we feel sure that it was heaven's light. We have, today, the precious evidences from his letters and his remembered conversations, that he had been, for a long period, a man of constant private prayer; that he was a most earnest seeker for the Divine forgiveness and the light of Christ; that he had come most thoroughly to feel his own want of strength, and deep need of the assistance of a higher power; and that he had given such expression respecting his feelings and purposes, to a friend and pastor in New York, as to indicate his design of uniting with the visible Church, on his return from the army. We have, with this, the evidence of his life; the zeal with which he instructed the Bible class already referred to, and the interest he felt in their religious welfare,- leading them even before the Throne of Grace in prayer; the energy with which, from the beginning of his military career, he labored for his men,- at the very outset, when in the Seventh Regiment, having been the active mover in instituting a prayer meeting, and in opposing the tendency among the men around him to profanity, and in later days, when in the camp in Georgia, helping the men under his command to spend their Sabbaths properly; and finally, and best of all, the growing purity and solid worth of character, so manifest to his friends during the past few years, which was most clear to them when he was last with us, and seemed to be the work of the Holy Spirit in his soul, and of which the growing beauty of his face, as we saw it then, seems to me now almost an emblem.

Such is our ground of confidence. It becomes stronger to me every day, as I think of him, and remember how, in everything good, his honest, truthful spirit was more than he was willing to acknowledge. In the language of his most intimate youthful Christian friend, who had watched his life for years, and seen his progress, I believe, I cannot doubt, "that he has entered upon the higher and holier service of heaven, and that he was prepared for it, for the sudden change which summoned him to it, by the love of Christ and the presence of his Holy Spirit."

We laid him in the grave, therefore, with the hope that we have for Christ's own people,- with the blessed hope of a glorious resurrection. We laid him there, believing that, if the little friendly circle is ever gathered again, in that upper world, he will be with us, the same delightful friend that we loved on earth, and, until that day, rejoicing, that we may bear a part of his life with us, through all the years, and that he may be bearing, also, a part of ours with him.

"This consolation we have," he said some eighteen months ago, "that, if our soldier life is hard, it is also short, and our death is honorable, and we ask of the passer-by, not like Archytas the 'pulvis ter injectus,'" (the three handfuls of dust as a sign of burial,) "but rather three simple words of praise and kindness." These words of kindness and of praise I have spoken tonight, as I could. If they have called his life pleasantly to your memory, or to your thought, my highest desire is satisfied.

"He sleeps now- bright, ever young, in the memory of others that must grow old,- honorably released from his toils, before the hottest of the day."

And now, as I go forth into the life before me, it is with the prayer to the Divine Father,-

"Forgive my grief for one removed,
Thy creature whom I found so fair,-
I trust he lives in Thee, and there
I find him worthier to be loved."

NOTES

[1] John Wheeler, William's brother
[2] Emil Sturmfels who received authorization from the War Department to recruit a battalion of artillery for Col. Baker's Brigade
[3] William Wade; served only 1 day in the Battery
[4] Officially called the 71st Pennsylvania Infantry; commanded by Col. Edward Baker
[5] Col. Charles Devens commanding 15th Massachusetts Infantry; Col. William Lee commanding 20th Massachusetts Infantry; Col. Milton Cogswell commanding 42nd NY (Tammany) Infantry
[6] Lt. Robert Edwards, Co. C, 48th NY Infantry commanded by Col. James Perry
[7] Commanded by Col. Thomas Parker
[8] Capt. Louis Schirmer
[9] Commanding the 28th Pennsylvania Infantry
[10] Sturmfels was later appointed as US Consul in Maracaibo, Venezuela. His wife died while he was there. He died while returning to the US and was buried at sea during November 1868
[11] Dieckmann had served with Co. H, 29th NY Infantry and the 2nd NY Light Battery before joining the 13th NY Light Battery
[12] Wheeler served as a sergeant with Company I, 7th NY Infantry for a 90 day enlistment period
[13] John Wheeler was mustered in as a Captain, commanding Co. G, 15th Connecticut Infantry on August 1, 1862
[14] Anna Davenport
[15] Capt. Frank Buell commanding Battery C, West Virginia Light Artillery
[16] Capt. Robert Hampton commanding Independent Battery F, Pennsylvania Light Artillery
[17] Capt. William De Beck, Battery K, 1st Ohio Light Artillery
[18] Commanded by Col. John Ziegler
[19] Capt. Jacob Roemer commanding Battery L (Hamilton's) NY Light Artillery
[20] Col. Fredrick D'Utassy commanding 39th New York Infantry
[21] Theodisa Wheeler; William's sister
[22] 1st Lt. William Goodrich, Jr, Co. G, 15th Connecticut Infantry and 2nd Lt. Herman French, Co. I, 15th Connecticut Infantry
[23] This name was not mentioned upon the publication of Wheeler's letters
[24] Capt. Aaron Johnson, 12th Ohio Battery
[25] Col. Wilhelm Jacobs commanding 26th Wisconsin Infantry; Col. Adin Underwood commanding 33rd Massachusetts Infantry
[26] The first general engagement of the regiment was the battle of Fredericksburg, VA, December 13, 1862

[27] Col. William Noble commanding 17th Connecticut Infantry
[28] Capt. William Lusk commanding Co. K, 79th New York Infantry
[29] Wheeler is referring to Brig. Gen. Julius Stahel commanding 1st Division, 11th Army Corps, Army of the Potomac
[30] Wheeler is referring to Col. Leopold von Gilsa commanding 41st New York Infantry
[31] Col. Stephen McGroarty commanding
[32] Col. Elias Peissner commanding 119th New York Infantry; Co. Gotthilf Bourry commanding 68th New York Infantry
[33] Maj. Detleo von Einsiedel commanding 41st New York Infantry, Col. George von Amsberg commanding 45th New York Infantry; Lt. Col. Charles Ashby commanding 54th New York Infantry; Col. Charles Glanz commanding 153rd Pennsylvania Infantry
[34] Commanded by Col. William Jacobs
[35] Commanded by Col. Francis Mahler
[36] Commanded by Col. James Robinson
[37] Most likely this is referring to Maj. Gen. Hiram Berry who was killed at Chancellorsville
[38] Brig. Gen. Nathaniel McLean commanding 2nd Brigade, 1st Division, 11th Army Corps
[39] Col. William Noble commanding 17th Connecticut Infantry; Col. John Lee commanding 55th Ohio Infantry; Col. William Richardson commanding 25th Ohio Infantry; Col. Robert Reily commanding 75th Ohio Infantry; Col. Seraphim Meyer commanding 107th Ohio Infantry
[40] This section was commanded by Lt. Joseph Bohn
[41] 1st Brigade, 1st Division, 11th Army Corps
[42] Wheeler is referring to Maj. John Freuauff, inspector-general, 153rd Pennsylvania Infantry
[43] Battery I, 1st Ohio Light Artillery
[44] 2nd New York Light Artillery
[45] Person or item not mentioned upon the publications of Wheeler's letters
[46] Maj. Gen. John Peck commanding Division at Suffolk, 7th Corps, Department of Virginia
[47] It is not know what was urgent that demanded his presence but it must not have been that serious. Within 3 days of handing in his resignation he was a major with the 15th New York Heavy Artillery Regiment. He died in October 1883.
[48] This description is most likely to be the attack of the 21st Georgia Infantry against the positions of the 68th New York Infantry.
[49] Capt. James Hill commanding 2nd Maine Artillery; Capt. Michael Wiedrich commanding Battery I, 1st New York Light Artillery

[50] Originally commanded by Lt. Bayard Wilkeson who was mortally wounded on the first day of battle. Command of the battery was then under Lt. Eugene Bancroft.
[51] Brig. Gen. Robert Tyler, Artillery Reserve, Army of the Potomac.
[52] Also known as Quakers
[53] Killed in action, July 18, 1863
[54] Col. Orland Smith commanding 2nd Brigade, 1st Division, 11th Army Corps
[55] Lt. Frank Crosby, Battery F, 4th US Regulars was shot through the heart and was instantly killed during the battle of Chancellorsville
[56] Records indicate the Lt. Carlisle was promoted to 1st Lt. on September 1, 1863; Wheeler was promoted to captain on August 12, 1863
[57] Named after Gen. Howard's aide Capt. Francis Dessauer who was killed at Chancellorsville
[58] Capt. Charles Aleshire commanding 18th Ohio Light Battery
[59] Capt. Mark Prescott commanding Battery C, 1st Illinois Light Artillery; Capt. George Spencer commanding Battery M, 1st Regiment Illinois Light Artillery; Capt. Frederick Shultz commanding Battery M, 1st Ohio Regiment Artillery; Lt. Giles Cockerill commanding Battery F, 1st Ohio Volunteer Artillery; Capt. Alexander Marshall commanding Battery G, 1st Ohio Volunteer Artillery; Capt. Cullen Bradley commanding 6th Ohio Battery; Capt. George Swallow commanding 7th Indiana Battery
[60] This name was not given upon publication of Wheeler's letters
[61] Lt. Col. Daniel Allen
[62] This request was approved and forwarded to all concerned parties
[63] Wheeler commanded the 13th New York Light Artillery and Battery I, 1st Michigan Artillery
[64] Lt. Crosby was shot, by a sharpshooter, through the heart
[65] Battery E, Pennsylvania Light Artillery commanded by Capt. James McGill
[66] John Wheeler was captured while stationed at Plymouth, NC by Confederate forces under Maj. Gen. Robert Hoke
[67] Brig. Gen. Henry Wessells commanding forces at Plymouth, NC and was also taken prisoner. He was exchanged in August 1864
[68] Wheeler never succeeded in communicating with his brother. John heard about his brother's death when he was at Macon from prisoners who were brought in; Wheeler's death was confirmed in a letter while he was at Savannah. John Wheeler also was interned at Andersonville prison
[69] The passage from Tennyson is:
"For what are men better than sheep or goat
That nourish a blind life within the brain,
If, knowing God, they lift not the hands of prayer
Both for themselves, and those who call them friend?

For so the whole round earth is every way
Bound by gold chains about the feet of God."

[70] This was the battle of New Hope Church on May 25, 1864. Geary's Division ran into troops of Maj. Gen. Alexander Stewart's Division, Maj. John Eldridge's Artillery Battalion and Maj. John Austin's battalion, 14th Louisiana Sharpshooters

[71] Wheeler's body was sent home and was buried on July 7, 1864 following a funeral in New York City. He was buried in the family plot as his father, Russell Canfield Wheeler, at Greenwood Cemetery in Brooklyn, NY. Subsequently, his mother, Theodosia Davenport, is also buried in the same plot.

[72] Assaults were made by units of Maj. Gen. Thomas Hindman's Division, Hood's Army Corps

[73] A spelling variation of Kolb's Farm

[74] Brig. Gen. William Harrow commanding 4th Division, 15th Army Corps

[75] Brig. Gen. Richard Johnson commanding 1st Division, 14th Army Corps

[76] Col. Minor Thomas commanding 8th Minnesota Infantry; Lt. Col. Daniel Grass commanding 61st Illinois Infantry; Col. John Jones commanding 164th Ohio Infantry

[77] Wheeler went to school under the direction of a Rev. B.W. Dwight. It is not know if Rev. B.W. and Rev. Timothy Dwight are related.

[78] May 9, 1857 was the date of departure and they arrived in Europe on June 24

[79] Wheeler and company were in Athens during May, 1858

[80] Wheeler mentions him teaching Bible classes in which he consults Hebrew translation; letter dated April 2, 1861, New York City

[81] From a Wheeler letter dated September 11, 1857, Baths of Leuk, Canton Valais, Swizterland

BIBLIOGRAPHY

Dwight, Timothy. *A Discourse on the life and character of Captain William Wheeler, delivered in the Third Congregational Church, July 17th, 1864.* New Haven, CT: Tuttle, Morehouse & Taylor, 1864.

Dyer, Frederick H. *A Compendium of the War of the Rebellion.* 2 vols. Dayton, OH: Morningside, 1979.

Lord, Francis A. *They fought for the Union.* Harrisburg, PA: The Stackpole Co., 1962.

Macdonald, John. *Great Battles of the Civil War.* New York: Collier Books, 1992.

Military service records of Dieckman, Julius 13 Batty, NY. L. Arty. National Archives Building, Washington, DC.

Military service records of Carlisle, James. 13 Batty, NY. L. Arty.; National Archives Building, Washington, DC.

Military service records of Early, James. 13 Batty, NY. L. Arty.; National Archives Building, Washington, DC.

Military service records of McGurrin, John. 13 Batty, NY. L. Arty.; National Archives Building, Washington, DC.

Military service records of Molitor, Albert. 13 Batty, NY. L. Arty.; National Archives Building, Washington, DC.

Military service records of Singer, Frank. 13 Batty, NY. L. Arty.; National Archives Building, Washington, DC

Military service records of Sturmfels, Emil 13 Batty, NY. L. Arty.; National Archives Building, Washington, DC.

Military service records of Wheeler, William 13 Batty, NY. L. Arty.; National Archives Building, Washington, DC.

New York Monuments Commission for the Battlefields of Gettysburg and Chattanooga. *Final Report on the Battlefield of Gettysburg.* Albany: J.B. Lyon Company, 1900.

-----. *Report on the New York Monuments at Chattanooga and Proceeding of Dedication of the Central Historical Memorial or Peace Monument on Lookout Mountain.* Albany: J.B. Lyon Company, 1928.

Order Book of the 13th New York Independent Light Artillery Battery; General Records of the War Department, Records Group 94; National Archives Building, Washington, DC.

Phisterer, Frederick. *New York in the War of the Rebellion, 1861-1865.* 2 vols. Albany: Weed and Parsons, 1890.

United States War Department. *The War of the Rebellion: Official Records of the Union and Confederate Armies.* 70 vols. in 128 serials. Washington: Government Printing Office, 1880-1901.

Wheeler, William. *Letters of William Wheeler of the Class of 1855, Y.C.* Cambridge: H.O. Houghton and Company, 1875.

INDEX

When ranks are given it signifies that either the first name of the person is unknown or the identity of that person is not certain. Confederate troops and units are not listed. Union armies, corps, divisions and brigades are also not listed.

A

Abell, Capt., 59
Abercrombie, John, 44, 102
Adams, Joseph, 287
Aleshire, Charles, 336, 397
Allen, Daniel, 298, 365
Ames, Adelbert, 215, 216, 217, 224, 239, 240, 244
Anderson, Edward, 411, 414, 417, 418, 419
Armor, Lt., 406
Arnold, William, 241, 244, 246
Asmussen, C H, 285, 297
Atterbury, William, 38, 40
Ayres, Oliver, 358

B

Baird, Absalom, 271
Baird, Capt., 81
Baker, Edward, 2, 3, 8
Baldwin, Edward, 35, 109, 122, 176, 178, 182, 183, 286, 421, 423, 427, 437
Baldwin, H H, 247
Baldwin, Norman, 266, 267, 269
Ballman, Alexander, 58
Bancroft, Eugene, 193, 194, 232, 235, 237, 244

Banks, Nathaniel, 3, 34, 53, 62, 71, 86, 87, 88, 97
Barber, Capt., 59
Barlow, Francis, 147, 158, 159, 193, 210, 215, 218, 232
Barnes, Almont, 242
Barnett, James, 266, 268, 269, 292
Barry, Lt., 40, 44
Barry, William, 6, 15, 16
Bartlett, H C, 365
Baumgardner, Gottlieb, 331
Beardsley, John, 87
Beebe, Yates, 358
Bender, Henry, 142
Berry, Nathaniel, 155
Bigelow, John, 239, 242, 247
Birney, David, 158
Birney, Maj., 410
Bissell, C E, 249
Blair, Francis, 277, 282, 283
Blake, Edward, 63, 170
Blau, John, 82
Blenker, Louis, 17, 23, 24, 25, 33, 34, 53, 427
Blume, Lt., 91
Bock, Jacob, 82
Boe, William, 221, 287, 337
Bohlen, Henry, 72
Bohn, Joseph, 14, 56, 113, 129, 164, 165, 437
Bonner, Charles, 133, 287, 301, 331

Boughton, Horace, 283, 439
Bowes, William, 437
Boyle, Peter, 437
Brady, Allen, 143, 144, 205
Brannan, John, 266, 268, 272, 287, 357, 358, 359
Braun, Frederick, 151
Breck, Lt., 233
Brinton, D G, 285
Brockway, Lt., 39, 40, 41, 44
Brown, John, 287
Brown, T. Fred, 241, 242, 244
Bruhm, A, 439
Bryan, Timothy, 38, 44
Bucklyn, J K, 242
Buell, Frank, 67, 72, 83
Buford, John, 86, 87, 181, 211, 212, 213, 215, 222, 223, 226, 230
Bundy, Charles, 338, 423, 424
Bundy, Henry, 129, 177, 178, 191, 294, 295, 296, 297, 298, 300, 314, 331, 334, 337, 338, 342, 343, 345, 350, 354, 355, 384, 385, 397, 401, 402, 404, 407, 408, 411, 414, 415, 416, 419, 420, 421, 422, 423, 424, 431, 437, 443
Burbank, Elisha, 38, 40
Burns, William, 6, 8, 9, 27
Burnside, Ambrose, 62, 80, 120, 121, 123, 124, 127, 280, 281, 283, 285, 456
Burton, Josiah, 266, 267, 269
Buschbeck, Adolphus, 145, 147, 154, 157, 158, 159, 276, 277, 279, 293, 359, 361, 362, 363, 366, 367, 368, 372, 439, 440

Butterfield, Daniel, 288, 311, 332, 351, 353, 366, 367, 368, 371, 372, 373, 374, 376, 377, 378, 380, 381, 382, 383, 385, 386, 387, 391

C

Calef, John, 231
Caluherty, Maj., 314
Canby, Samuel, 242
Candy, Charles, 338, 343, 359, 362, 363, 365, 367, 368, 370, 373, 374, 375, 376, 379, 381, 382, 383, 385, 386, 393, 394, 395
Canfine, J J, 406
Cantwell, J Y, 66
Cantwell, John, 76, 77, 81
Carlisle, James, 85, 118, 136, 165, 168, 227, 228, 229, 303, 347, 357, 407, 419, 421, 422, 429, 437
Carpenter, John, 335
Carr, James, 92
Carroll, Samuel, 216
Carson, Capt., 410
Chapman, Lt., 406
Chatfield, Harvey, 367, 383
Cheney, John, 266, 267, 268, 269
Chicago Board of Trade Light, 272, 358
Chittenden, Henry, 304
Clark, A Judson, 239
Clarke, James, 14, 20, 58, 62
Clauherty, Maj., 294
Clavin, Joseph, 308, 338, 407, 408, 411, 423
Clift, William, 412, 414

Cobham, George, 368, 369, 370, 374, 375, 376, 382, 387, 397
Coburn, John, 404
Cogswell, William, 266, 267, 269, 405
Comstock, Capt., 157
Cooper, John, 231, 233, 234, 237, 243, 244
Coster, Charles, 213, 218
Cotter, Charles, 268, 288, 292
Cowan, Andrew, 245
Cox, Jacob, 383, 390
Craft, Henry, 308
Craig, J N, 249
Cravens, James, 410
Cravens, Lt., 81
Cresson, Charles, 365, 382
Crosby, Frank, 307
Cushing, Alonzo, 241, 242, 244, 246, 247

D

D' Utassy, Fredrick, 103
Davis, Capt., 405
Davis, Gen., 267
Davis, Henry, 203
Davis, Jefferson, 271, 278, 279, 284, 285, 392
Davis, L R, 376, 391
Davis, Lt., 206
Davis, William, 365
Davison, J, 233, 234
De Gress, Francis, 266, 267, 269
DeBeck, William, 72, 82
Delteure, T, 437
Dessauer, Francis, 160

Devens, Charles, 143, 145, 146, 148, 149, 151, 158, 164, 166, 172, 201, 206
Dickinson, Col., 159
Dieckmann, Julius, 48, 49, 55, 56, 58, 59, 62, 65, 74, 83, 85, 96, 98, 110, 113, 115, 118, 119, 122, 125, 126, 129, 130, 133, 134, 135, 139, 140, 141, 143, 146, 158, 175, 176, 205, 209, 427, 429, 437
Dietr, Gustavus, 183
Dilger, Hubert, 83, 92, 96, 97, 99, 145, 147, 148, 150, 152, 153, 154, 158, 159, 166, 185, 186, 187, 192, 193, 194, 198, 199, 201, 208, 232, 235, 237, 244, 254, 255, 275, 276, 279, 287, 288, 289
Dix, John, 335
Dodge, Grenville, 424
Doubleday, Abner, 211, 213, 233
Douglas, Archibald, 12
Driscoll, David, 308, 338, 423
Duffy, Peter, 14, 55, 122, 346
Dwight, Timothy, 36, 124, 445

E

Eakin, Chandler, 194, 195, 236, 237, 238, 244
Earl, William, 135
Early, James, 15, 437
Edgarton, W P, 310
Edgell, Frederick, 194, 237
Edwards, Capt., 360
Edwards, Robert, 6, 8, 207, 219

Eighteenth Indiana Light, 358
Eighteenth Kentucky Infantry, 302
Eighteenth Ohio Infantry, 302
Eighteenth Ohio Light, 269, 336
Eighth Kansas Infantry, 302
Eighth Minnesota Infantry, 409, 410, 414, 415, 416
Eighth New York Infantry, 53, 439
Eighty-second Illinois Infantry, 147, 150, 153, 154, 155, 315
Eighty-second Ohio Infantry, 66, 76, 77, 81, 145, 147, 149, 150, 153, 154, 302, 306
Ekert, George, 142
Eleventh Indiana Light, 357
Elliott, Thomas, 397, 405
Enoch, Florida, 82
Erickson, C, 242
Eskdale, James, 287, 420, 421
Essembaux, M, 439
Esté, Lt., 79, 81
Ewing, Hugh, 440

F

Faes, Louis, 343
Falk, Jacob, 135
Feisel, Conrad, 411
Fennessy, Thomas, 56, 113
Fessenden, Francis, 380
Fifteenth Connecticut Infantry, 107, 108, 109, 119
Fifteenth Indiana Infantry, 302
Fifteenth Massachusetts Infantry, 3
Fifteenth Missouri Infantry, 302
Fifteenth New York Heavy, 429
Fifteenth New York Light, 239, 240, 242, 244
Fifteenth Ohio Infantry, 302
Fifteenth US Infantry, 405
Fifth Connecticut Infantry, 62, 302
Fifth Indiana Light, 358
Fifth Iowa Cavalry, 302
Fifth Maine Light, 233, 234, 235, 243
Fifth Maine Light, Battery E, 238
Fifth Massachusetts Light, 239, 244
Fifth New York Infantry, 100
Fifth New York Light, 194, 236, 244
Fifth Ohio Infantry, 302, 338, 339, 340, 341, 342, 359, 362, 364, 368, 372, 376, 383, 389
Fifth Tennessee Cavalry, 411, 412, 414, 415, 416
Fifth U.S. Artillery, Battery K, 302
Fifth US Artillery, 242, 247
Fifth US Artillery, Battery C, 240, 245
Fifth US Artillery, Battery D, 241, 242, 244
Fifth US Artillery, Battery I, 240, 242
Fifth US Artillery, Battery K, 236, 238, 243
Fifth Virginia Infantry, 73, 76, 81
Fifth Wisconsin Light, 267, 302

Fifty-eighth Indiana Infantry, 302
Fifty-eighth New York Infantry, 147, 149, 150, 151, 301, 306, 439
Fifty-fifth Ohio Infantry, 146, 163, 302
Fifty-first Illinois Infantry, 302
Fifty-first Indiana Infantry, 302
Fifty-first Ohio Infantry, 302
Fifty-fourth New York Infantry, 146
Fifty-ninth Illinois Infantry, 302
Fifty-seventh Indiana Infantry, 302
Fineauff, John, 166
First California Infantry, 3
First Connecticut Light, 17
First Illinois Light, 269
First Illinois Light, Battery B, 266, 267, 269
First Illinois Light, Battery C, 267, 302
First Illinois Light, Battery F, 266, 267, 269
First Illinois Light, Battery H, 266, 267, 269
First Illinois Light, Battery I, 266, 269
First Illinois Light, Battery M, 425
First Maryland Cavalry, 87
First Massachusetts Cavalry, 206
First Michigan Engineers, 302
First Michigan Light, Battery I, 351, 356
First Michigan Light, Battery L, 310
First Michigan, Battery E, 302
First Michigan, Battery K, 306
First Missouri Engineers, 302
First Missouri Light, Battery G, 425
First New Hampshire Light, 194, 237
First New Jersey Light, Battery B, 239
First New York Light, 84, 187, 243, 244, 245, 247, 249, 250, 336, 358
First New York Light, Battery B, 241, 244, 246, 247
First New York Light, Battery C, 242
First New York Light, Battery D, 239, 240
First New York Light, Battery G, 239, 240, 244
First New York Light, Battery I, 82, 192, 197, 232, 234, 238, 243, 273, 287, 292, 298, 302, 310, 350, 355, 356, 440
First New York Light, Battery K, 245
First New York Light, Battery L, 233, 234, 243
First New York Light, Battery M, 236, 243, 302, 310, 350, 356
First Ohio Cavalry, 302
First Ohio Light, 97, 99, 269, 292, 310
First Ohio Light, Battery B, 266, 267, 268, 269, 302, 310, 425
First Ohio Light, Battery C, 266, 267, 269, 302, 310, 351, 356

First Ohio Light, Battery F,
  269, 302
First Ohio Light, Battery G,
  269, 302
First Ohio Light, Battery H,
  194, 237
First Ohio Light, Battery I,
  192, 197, 199, 201, 232,
  235, 237, 244, 275, 287, 425
First Ohio Light, Battery K,
  192, 197, 232, 234, 273,
  287, 292, 310
First Ohio Light, Battery L,
  242, 244
First Ohio Light, Battery M,
  269
First Pennsylvania Light, 241
First Pennsylvania Light,
  Battery B, 231, 233, 234,
  237, 243, 244
First Pennsylvania Light,
  Battery C, 39, 242
First Pennsylvania Light,
  Battery F, 39, 238, 243
First Pennsylvania Light,
  Battery G, 238
First Rhode Island Light, 241,
  242, 247, 249
First Rhode Island Light,
  Battery A, 241, 244, 246
First Rhode Island Light,
  Battery B, 241, 244
First Rhode Island Light,
  Battery E, 239
First U.S. Artillery, Battery H,
  194
First US Artillery, 247
First US Artillery, Battery H,
  236, 238, 244
First US Artillery, Battery I,
  241, 244

First Virginia Cavalry, 81, 87
First West Virginia Light,
  Battery C, 236, 244
First West Virginia Light,
  Battery O, 194
Fitch, William, 365
Fitzhugh, Robert, 245
Fitzpatrick, James, 365
Flesher, Capt., 81
Flynn, John, 365, 403
Foote, Andrew, 24, 28, 173
Forbes, William, 367, 405, 406
Fortieth Indiana Infantry, 302
Fortieth Ohio Infantry, 302
Forty-eighth New York
  Infantry, 6, 8
Forty-fifth New York Infantry,
  125, 301, 439
Forty-fifth NewYork Infantry,
  146, 301
Forty-first New York Infantry,
  91, 146
Forty-first Ohio Infantry, 302
Forty-fourth Illinois Infantry,
  302
Forty-fourth Indiana Infantry,
  302
Forty-ninth Ohio Infantry, 302
Forty-second Illinois Infantry,
  302
Forty-second Indiana Infantry,
  302
Forty-second New York
  Infantry, 3
Forty-sixth Pennsylvania
  Infantry, 302
Fourat, Enos, 365, 370
Fourteenth Michigan Cavalry,
  302
Fourteenth New York Infantry,
  100

Fourth Connecticut Infantry, 28
Fourth Kentucky Cavalry, 302
Fourth Kentucky Infantry, 302
Fourth New York Cavalry, 94
Fourth New York Light, 239, 241
Fourth New York Mounted Rifles, 59, 60
Fourth Ohio Cavalry, 302
Fourth Pennsylvania Light, 247
Fourth Tennessee Cavalry, 411, 412
Fourth US Artillery, 242, 247, 249
Fourth US Artillery, Battery A, 241, 244, 246, 247
Fourth US Artillery, Battery B, 231, 233, 234, 244
Fourth US Artillery, Battery C, 240, 244
Fourth US Artillery, Battery F, 236, 243, 302, 307
Fourth US Artillery, Battery G, 187, 192, 197, 200, 215, 232, 235, 237, 244, 274, 287
Fourth US Artillery, Battery K, 239, 242
Franklin, William, 23, 28
Freeman, Eugene, 345, 348, 437
Freeman, George, 197
Fremont, Charles, 48, 49, 51, 127, 427
Fremont, John, 456
French, Herman, 107
Freuauff, John, 206
Frey, Joseph, 142
Fridrichs, John, 134
Frowe, Lt., 410

Funk, Deidrich, 287, 308, 338, 407

G

Gardner, George, 267
Garrard, Kenner, 317, 402
Garrett, William, 14, 35, 55, 58, 113, 183, 286, 423
Gary, Marco, 266, 267, 269, 351, 353, 354, 355
Geary, John, 47, 271, 311, 312, 315, 316, 319, 320, 321, 324, 332, 347, 351, 353, 354, 359, 406, 457
Geary, Lt., 238
Geiger, William, 135, 407, 408
Gibbs, Frank, 242, 244
Gilbreth, Lt., 286
Gillette, Capt., 406
Godard, Abel, 367, 400
Godbold, Lt., 39, 40, 44
Goodman, H E, 406
Goodrich, William, 107
Gordon, George, 43, 226, 315
Gould, Capt., 39, 44
Graef, George, 424
Granger, Gordon, 274, 283
Grant, Ulysses, 266, 275, 277, 279, 283
Greasel, Henry, 411
Greene, George, 216
Greenfield, Adam, 15
Griffiths, J J, 218
Grover, Cuvier, 77, 78
Guerts, Theodore, 58, 133
Gutbrad, Christian, 20, 122, 286

H

Hall, Capt., 294, 315
Hall, James, 187, 194, 231, 234, 236, 237
Hampton, Robert, 97
Hampton's Pittsburgh Battery, 69
Hancock, Winfield, 189, 199, 214, 215, 236
Harris, Ellen, 256
Hart, Patrick, 239, 240, 242, 244
Hartman, Charles, 423
Hayes, Edward, 293, 365
Hazard, John, 241, 242, 244, 249
Hazen, William, 256
Hazlett, Charles, 241, 242, 244
Hazlett, R C, 247
Hecker, Frederick, 153, 279, 282, 284, 439
Heckman, Lewis, 192, 193, 194, 232, 234, 235, 273, 310
Heintzelman, Samuel, 103, 112
Hempe, Charles, 20, 85, 118, 122, 182, 259
Henchen, Lt., 355, 358
Hicks, George, 10
Higgins, Capt., 294, 315
Hill, Wallace, 194, 236, 237, 244
Himmel, George, 82
Hitt, Joseph, 339, 376
Hoffmann, Ernest, 146, 202, 285
Holden, L H, 11
Hooker, Joseph, 92, 93, 142, 144, 146, 149, 158, 159, 163, 164, 166, 168, 172, 205, 222, 260, 265, 269, 273, 276, 278, 279, 287, 288, 289, 309, 315, 317, 324, 328, 329, 332, 336, 337, 351, 360, 361, 366, 368, 370, 371, 372, 373, 379, 380, 387, 392, 393, 394, 399, 430, 431, 439, 443
Hopper, Lt., 81
Howard, Charles, 202, 211, 213, 279, 285
Howard, Oliver, 141, 142, 144, 156, 160, 163, 164, 168, 172, 173, 175, 176, 181, 182, 185, 187, 192, 203, 206, 209, 218, 220, 222, 227, 228, 230, 235, 253, 266, 268, 270, 273, 286, 287, 288, 293, 300, 313, 315, 316, 317, 322, 323, 324, 325, 330, 332, 379, 439, 440
Hubbard, Robert, 285
Humphrey, William, 38, 40, 41
Humphreys, Andrew, 155, 240
Hunt, C O, 234
Hunt, Henry, 189, 194, 229, 230, 250
Hunten, Charles, 183
Huntington, James, 194, 196, 237

I

Ireland, David, 312, 360, 364, 366, 367, 368, 369, 370, 379, 380, 381, 382, 383, 384, 385, 386, 393, 394, 395, 397, 405
Irish Philadelphia Infantry, 3
Irish, Nathaniel, 242

J

Jackson, Allan, 365, 381, 382, 439
Jewett, Capt., 294, 315
Johnson, Aaron, 71, 110
Johnson, Gilbert, 377, 409, 412
Johnson, Richard, 271
Johnson, W H, 247
Jones, John, 409
Jones, Patrick, 378, 379, 382, 383, 385, 393, 394, 395, 439

K

Kane, Thomas, 96
Keane, Charles, 35
Kearny, Philip, 90, 91, 92, 93, 94, 96
Keefer, Benjamin, 97
Kellogg, Josiah, 157
Kennedy, L W, 421
Kilpatrick, Hugh, 224, 225, 317, 358, 361, 364
Kilpatrick, Lt. Col., 370
King, Lt., 351
King, Rufus, 71, 92, 93, 428
Kinzie, David, 236, 238, 243
Kirlin, E H, 286
Knapp's Battery, 236, 238, 243, 310, 311, 320, 335, 351, 354, 356, 360, 403
Knox, E M, 242
Koch, Charles, 439
Koltes, John, 92, 95, 97
Krauss, Charles, 308, 337, 343, 419, 420
Krepps, Maj., 74
Kruger, W, 142

Krzyzanowski, Wladimir, 98, 145, 150, 152, 153, 158, 159, 218, 276, 279, 439, 440

L

Lackner, Francis, 314
Lambert, Capt., 365
Lambert, Louis, 272
Lambert, William, 403, 406
Lee, Frank, 334
Lerz, Henry, 407
Lewens, John, 176, 222
Lewis, John, 287
Link, Charles, 20
Livingston, M, 242
Lloyd, Edward, 294, 314, 325, 370
Lloyd, William, 59, 60
Lockman, John, 368, 370, 372, 376, 439
Logan, John, 321, 333
Logie, William, 439
Long, Col., 256
Long, Eli, 281, 285
Long, Richard, 286
Loomis, John, 277, 278, 440
Losh, Sebastian, 24
Lother, George, 82
Lusk, William, 123
Lynch, James, 122, 287, 338

M

Mabies, William, 58
Mahoney, John, 331, 408, 419
Martin, A P, 249
Maryland Light, Battery A, 243
Mason, Philip, 238

Massachusetts Light, Battery E, 247
Matthews, Bob, 257
Matzdorff, Alvin, 152
McAloon, Peter, 277
McClellan, George, 2, 10, 15, 24, 28, 32, 62, 89, 99, 105, 114, 124
McClelland, Samuel, 378
McCook, Edward, 265, 316, 317, 358, 366, 367
McDonald, Capt., 81
McDowell, Irvin, 71, 80, 83, 84, 87, 88, 89, 93, 94, 96
McDowell, Samuel, 266, 267, 269, 358
McGill, James, 320, 321, 351, 352, 353, 362, 363, 364, 379, 384, 385, 389, 390
McGilvery, Freeman, 239, 244, 246, 249
McGilvray, J, 247
McGowan, James, 109
McGurrin, John, 303, 331, 337, 409, 420, 437, 441
McLean, Nathaniel, 72, 83, 84, 90, 95, 143, 145, 146, 150, 163, 165, 166, 168, 170, 172, 205, 206
McMahon, Michael, 14, 28, 29
McPherson, James, 316, 317, 321, 322, 324, 328, 364
Meade, George, 129, 160, 161, 188, 189, 190, 191, 212, 214, 215, 216, 222, 223, 265
Meeker, Daniel, 81
Mendenhall, J, 272
Merkle, C F, 275, 287, 288, 289
Meysenburg, T A, 116, 277, 285

Mickle, William, 220, 221, 257, 312, 336
Miller, Albert, 15
Miller, Henry, 20, 29, 133, 176, 191, 199, 229, 242, 257, 294, 304, 305, 337, 347, 348, 349, 421, 437
Miller, W C, 234
Milley, Christopher, 411
Millspangh, T, 58
Milne, J S, 247
Milroy, Robert, 49, 53, 67, 68, 70, 82, 86, 87, 88, 89, 90, 91, 92, 93, 95, 96, 100, 103, 105, 128, 409, 411, 413, 415, 418, 419, 428
Minor, Oscar, 206
Minty, Robert, 402
Mohler, J G, 410
Molitor, Albert, 22, 39, 40, 45, 56, 66, 85, 101, 113, 115, 116, 118, 437
Moller, William, 83
Moritz, Thielman, 14, 35, 58, 59, 129, 133
Muhleck, Gustavus, 59, 60
Muhlenberg, E D, 236, 243, 249

N

Naylor, W A, 269
Nazer, Ferries, 59, 60, 94
Newton, John, 217, 236, 246, 315, 354
Niles, Lt., 79, 81
Nineteenth Ohio Infantry, 302
Ninth Massachusetts Light, 239, 247
Ninth New York Cavalry, 87

Ninth New York State Militia, 38
Ninth Ohio Light, 302, 310, 425
Nissel, George, 142
Noble, William, 120, 143
Nort, Frederick, 58, 286

O

O'Connor, John, 20, 28, 133, 183, 199, 259, 286, 337
One hundred eighty-first Ohio Infantry, 414, 415, 416
One hundred eleventh Pennsylvania Infantry, 359, 368, 370, 371, 380, 386, 397, 399, 403, 404, 405
One hundred fifteenth Ohio Infantry, 410
One hundred fifty-fourth New York Infantry, 359, 364, 365, 378, 439
One hundred fifty-seventh New York Infantry, 147, 150, 154, 155
One hundred fifty-third Pennsylvania Infantry, 146
One Hundred Fifty-third Pennsylvania Infantry, 166
One hundred forty-first New York Infantry, 314, 439
One hundred forty-ninth New York Infantry, 312, 360, 398, 400
One hundred forty-seventh Pennsylvania Infantry, 339, 340, 341, 342, 359, 360, 362, 379, 395, 397

One hundred forty-third New York Infantry, 283, 315, 439, 440
One hundred nineteenth New York Infantry, 142, 147, 150, 152, 153, 154, 314, 315, 325, 359, 362, 370, 372, 395
One hundred ninteeth New York Infantry, 439
One hundred ninth Pennsylvania Infantry, 302, 359, 362, 382, 395
One hundred second New York Infantry, 360, 382, 403
One hundred seventh Ohio Infantry, 146, 163
One hundred seventy eighth Ohio Infantry, 411, 414
One hundred seventy-eighth Ohio Infantry, 412, 413, 415, 416, 417
One hundred seventy-fourth Ohio Infantry, 409, 410, 414, 415, 416, 418
One hundred seventy-seventh Ohio Infantry, 411, 412, 413, 415, 416, 419
One hundred sixth Pennsylvania Infantry, 217
One hundred sixty-ninth Pennsylvania Infantry, 226
One hundred thirty-fourth New York Infantry, 183, 325, 336, 359, 364, 365, 380, 381, 385, 439
One hundred thirty-seventh New York Infantry, 360, 386, 405
One hundred thirty-sixth New York Infantry, 439

One hundred twenty-third New York Infantry, 421
Osborn, Thomas, 187, 189, 190, 191, 192, 197, 210, 215, 218, 229, 232, 235, 236, 244, 249, 250, 255, 265, 287, 290, 295, 296, 297, 298, 300, 314, 439
Osterhaus, Peter, 288
Otto, August, 216
Ouh, John, 29
Owen, Joshua, 3, 4

P

Palmer, Adam, 408
Palmer, John, 276, 279, 317, 330
Palmer, Lt., 286
Pardee, Ario, 342, 360, 382, 397, 404
Parker, Capt., 406
Patrick, John, 339, 376
Patrick, Marsena, 71
Pearson, Edward, 213, 285
Peck, John, 175
Peissner, Elias, 152
Pennsylvania Light, Battery B, 358
Pennsylvania Light, Battery C, 242
Pennsylvania Light, Battery D, 242
Perkins, Capt., 314
Perkins, H W, 380, 422
Philadelphia Zouaves, 3, 7
Phillips, Charles, 239, 240, 244
Pleasonton, Alfred, 158

Pope, John, 63, 64, 70, 71, 84, 86, 87, 88, 90, 92, 93, 94, 95, 96, 101, 127, 427, 456
Porter, Fitz John, 92, 93, 94, 95, 96

R

Randall, Lt. Col., 370, 397
Randolph, George, 239, 249
Ransom, Thomas, 240
Ranson, Dunbar, 242
Reed, Alfred, 412
Reed, Benjamin, 418
Regan, Thomas, 20, 24
Reichhartz, William, 424
Reily, Robert, 204
Reinhard, John, 59, 62
Reno, Jesse, 86, 87, 91, 93, 94, 96, 101, 184
Reynolds, G H, 234
Reynolds, John, 92, 93, 94, 95, 167, 181, 185, 187, 208, 209, 210, 211, 215, 222, 230, 231, 233, 234, 243, 312, 336, 349, 350, 356, 357, 391, 407
Richardson, Israel, 33
Richart, Capt., 60
Rickards, William, 369, 382
Ricketts, R. Bruce, 237, 238, 242, 243
Riddle, William, 210
Rigby, James, 243
Rippetoe, William, 358
Roache, Francis, 58, 182
Roberts, Benjamin, 87
Robertson, James, 250
Robinson, George, 358
Robinson, John, 212, 231, 381, 382

Rockwell, Alfred, 17
Roemer, Jacob, 97
Roller, John, 287
Rolshausen, Ferdinand, 153
Rorty, James, 241, 244, 246, 247
Rosecrans, William, 265, 429
Rousseau, Lovell, 269, 311, 317
Rowe, Capt., 285
Rowley, Thomas, 231
Rumsey, Israel, 266, 267, 269
Rush, John, 14, 65, 199, 287, 407

S

Sackmann, Adolph, 407
Sahm, N, 287, 288, 289
Schaedler, Pvt., 182
Schenck, Robert, 49, 53, 75, 76, 77, 79, 83, 89, 90, 91, 92, 94, 95, 97
Schenkelberger, Lt., 83
Schilling, Lt., 403, 406
Schimmelfennig, Alexander, 145, 146, 147, 149, 150, 154, 158, 159, 200, 217, 225
Schirmer, Louis, 31, 34, 53, 67, 68, 82, 91, 96, 113, 115, 139, 167
Schmidt, Capt., 294, 315
Schmier, Louis, 135
Schoenleber, Emil, 331
Schofield, John, 321, 330
Schurz, Carl, 76, 77, 82, 89, 90, 91, 92, 93, 95, 96, 144, 156, 158, 159, 166, 192, 200, 204, 205, 206, 210, 211, 213, 215, 216, 217,
218, 223, 226, 232, 275, 276, 279, 314, 439, 440
Scofield, Capt., 286
Scott, H D, 247
Scripture, Clark, 200
Second Connecticut Light, 240, 244
Second Illinois Light, Battery H, 302
Second Illinois Light, Battery I, 302
Second Kentucky Light, 310
Second Maine Light, 187, 194, 231, 236
Second Massachusetts Infantry, 302
Second Minnesota Infantry, 301
Second Missouri Light, Battery A, 424
Second Missouri Light, Battery F, 424
Second Missouri Light, Battery I, 424
Second US Artillery, Battery A, 231
Second Virginia Infantry, 76, 77
Sedgwick, John, 33, 224, 225
Seeley, Aaron, 240
Seeley, Francis, 239, 242
Seventeenth Connecticut Infantry, 120, 143, 144, 146, 163, 205
Seventeenth Indiana Cavalry, 302
Seventeenth Ohio Infantry, 302
Seventeenth Pennsylvania Cavalry, 157

Seventeenth Pennsylvania Infantry, 157
Seventh Indiana Light, 269
Seventh New York Infantry, 3, 455, 456, 458
Seventh Ohio Infantry, 302, 338, 359, 364, 373, 374, 376, 378
Seventh Pennsylvania Cavalry, 302, 402, 403
Seventy-eighth New York Infantry, 360, 367, 383
Seventy-fifth Ohio Infantry, 146, 163, 203, 204
Seventy-fifth Pennsylvania Infantry, 147, 149, 152
Seventy-first Ohio Infantry, 302
Seventy-fourth Ohio Infantry, 302
Seventy-fourth Pennsylvania Infantry, 141, 142, 146, 151, 154
Seventy-ninth New York Infantry, 123
Seventy-seventh Pennsylvania Infantry, 302
Seventy-third Ohio Infantry, 275, 286
Seventy-third Pennsylvania Infantry, 59, 277, 302, 359, 365, 382, 395, 440
Seymour, Ira, 406
Sheldon, A S, 247
Sheridan, Philip, 271, 315
Sherman, William, 266, 267, 268, 269, 270, 273, 274, 275, 276, 277, 278, 279, 281, 282, 283, 284, 287, 288, 292, 293, 324, 325, 326, 330, 335, 351, 379,
399, 400, 405, 431, 439, 440, 450, 456
Sherwood, Capt., 413
Sherwood, Lt., 406
Sickles, Daniel, 149, 159, 212, 213, 214, 236, 239, 240, 242
Sigel, Franz, 34, 54, 56, 65, 66, 68, 70, 80, 82, 83, 85, 86, 94, 97, 98, 99, 101, 103, 104, 105, 112, 113, 124, 127, 128, 167, 172, 173, 429, 456
Simonson, Peter, 357
Singer, Frank, 22, 37, 118, 125, 126, 128, 129, 177, 178, 437
Sixth Kentucky Cavalry, 302
Sixth Maine Light, 244
Sixth Ohio Calvary, 59
Sixth Ohio Cavalry, 59
Sixth Ohio Infantry, 59
Sixth Ohio Light, 269, 358
Sixtieth New York Infantry, 360, 367, 371, 395, 400, 403, 404
Sixty-eighth New York Infantry, 142, 147, 150, 301, 306, 439
Sixty-eighth Pennsylvania Infantry, 59
Sixty-fifth Ohio Infantry, 302
Sixty-first Illinois Infantry, 409, 410, 414, 415, 416, 417
Sixty-first Ohio Infantry, 141, 147, 151, 154, 306, 315
Sixty-fourth New York Infantry, 34
Sixty-fourth Ohio Infantry, 302
Sixty-ninth Ohio Infantry, 302

Sixty-sixth Ohio Infantry, 339, 340, 341, 342, 343, 359, 362, 364
Sliney, Lt., 268
Sloan, Thomas, 320, 354, 355
Sloan, Thomas., 354
Slocum, Henry, 157, 161, 194, 212, 213, 214, 216, 236, 243, 402, 403
Smith, James, 239, 241
Smith, Luther, 351, 353, 354, 355
Smith, Orland, 217, 279, 280, 439, 440
Speed, John, 314
Spence, E., 242
Stafford, Joab, 412
Stahel, Julius, 48, 77, 90, 95, 96, 124
Stanley, David, 378, 379
Stedman, Maj., 59
Stegman, Lewis, 382
Stephenson, J, 247
Sterling, John, 240, 244
Stevens, Greenleaf, 233, 234, 235, 238, 243
Stevens, Issac, 91
Stewart, James, 231, 233, 234, 243
Stinson, Capt., 285
Stock, Christian, 82
Stokes, James, 272
Stone, Charles, 10
Stoneman, George, 157, 371
Sturges, Lt., 268
Sturmfels, Emil, 3, 4, 5, 6, 8, 10, 11, 12, 14, 15, 16, 17, 19, 20, 21, 24, 29, 37, 39, 44, 49, 427, 437
Suckendick, William, 133, 287, 308, 331

Sumner, Edwin, 30, 33, 36, 111
Sutermeister, Arnold, 357
Symmes, Henry, 383, 389

T

Taft, Elijah, 194, 196, 236, 237, 244, 277
Taft, Joseph, 440
Taylor, Col., 269
Tenth Connecticut Infantry, 12, 13
Tenth Illinois Infantry, 301
Tenth Indiana Infantry, 302
Tenth Indiana Light, 269
Tenth Maine Infantry, 302
Tenth Wisconsin Light, 358
Third Kentucky Cavalry, 302
Third Maryland Infantry, 302
Third Massachusetts Light, 249
Third Ohio Cavalry, 302
Third US Artillery, 240, 242
Third Virginia Infantry, 76, 77
Thirteenth Indiana Cavalry, 409, 410, 411, 412
Thirteenth Indiana Light, 302
Thirteenth Michigan Infantry, 302
Thirteenth New York Light, 20, 35, 49, 56, 58, 62, 65, 85, 86, 110, 113, 118, 119, 122, 125, 126, 128, 129, 130, 133, 134, 135, 139, 140, 175, 176, 177, 178, 179, 180, 182, 183, 192, 197, 198, 199, 209, 221, 222, 227, 228, 232, 235, 237, 244, 253, 258, 259, 266, 267, 268, 269, 273,

274, 286, 287, 292, 294,
295, 296, 297, 298, 299,
300, 302, 303, 306, 308,
310, 320, 321, 324, 330,
331, 334, 335, 337, 342,
345, 350, 354, 355, 356,
357, 358, 360, 361, 384,
387, 388, 389, 408, 409,
411, 412, 414, 415, 419,
420, 421, 422, 423, 425,
427, 439, 440, 441, 442,
443, 456
Thirteenth Ohio Infantry, 302
Thirteenth Wisconsin Infantry, 302
Thirtieth Indiana Infantry, 302
Thirty-first Indiana Infantry, 302
Thirty-first Ohio Infantry, 302
Thirty-seventh Indiana Infantry, 302
Thirty-sixth Illinois Infantry, 302
Thirty-third Indiana Infantry, 302
Thirty-third Massachusetts Infantry, 111
Thirty-third New Jersey Infantry, 275, 359, 362, 363, 365, 366, 394, 395
Thirty-third Ohio Infantry, 302
Thomas, Evan, 240, 244
Thomas, George, 265, 273, 274, 276, 278, 301, 303, 306, 310, 313, 315, 318, 337, 354, 360, 376, 379, 420, 426
Thomas, Lorenzo, 419
Thomas, Minor, 414, 415, 416, 417, 418
Thompson, J H, 14

Thompson, James, 240, 241, 242, 244
Tidball, John, 250
Tintenfass, Henry, 20, 56, 178, 183, 286, 301, 421, 437
Tompkins, C H, 249
Trafford, Edward, 65, 199, 286
Trebur, Henry, 423
Tucker, Lt., 39, 44
Turnbull, John, 240
Twelfth Indiana Cavalry, 411, 412, 413, 415, 416
Twelfth Indiana Infantry, 38, 40, 41, 413
Twelfth Massachusetts Infantry, 38, 39, 40, 44, 256
Twelfth Ohio Light, 302
Twelfth Wisconsin Light, 266, 267, 269
Twentieth Indiana Light, 310
Twentieth Massachusetts Infantry, 3
Twenty-eighth Pennsylvania Infantry, 3, 338, 339, 340, 341, 342, 364, 365, 373, 403
Twenty-fifth Ohio Infantry, 146, 163, 203, 204
Twenty-first Illinois Infantry, 302
Twenty-first Kentucky Infantry, 302
Twenty-first Ohio Infantry, 302
Twenty-fourth Ohio Infantry, 302
Twenty-ninth New York Infantry, 100
Twenty-ninth Ohio Infantry, 339, 340, 341, 342, 359, 364, 365

Twenty-ninth Pennsylvania
  Infantry, 359, 369, 382
Twenty-ninth Pennsylvania
  Infantry Infantry, 403
Twenty-second Illinois
  Infantry, 302
Twenty-second Indiana
  Infantry, 302
Twenty-seventh Illinois
  Infantry, 302
Twenty-seventh Indiana
  Infantry, 302
Twenty-seventh Pennsylvania
  Infantry, 253, 277, 359, 372
Twenty-sixth Ohio Infantry,
  302
Twenty-sixth Pennsylvania
  Light, 266, 267, 269
Twenty-sixth Pennsylvania
  Light, Battery B, 268
Twenty-sixth Wisconsin
  Infantry, 111, 147, 149, 150,
  151, 152, 153, 154, 315
Twenty-sixth Wisconsion
  Infantry, 314
Twenty-third Kentucky
  Infantry, 302
Tyler, Robert, 190, 239, 240,
  242, 249
Tyndale, Hector, 226, 279,
  306, 439

V

Van Derveer, Ferdinand, 317
Van Reed, Lt., 238
Van Sciver, Issac, 338, 419
Veale, Capt., 365, 382, 405,
  406
Volmer, Ernest, 129, 183, 286,
  407

von Gilsa, Leopold, 125, 146,
  148, 149, 151, 158, 160,
  164, 202, 203, 204, 205,
  206, 218
von Hartung, Adolph, 141, 142
von Linden, Carl, 22, 23, 49,
  178, 437
von Mensel, Capt., 170, 206
von Steinhausen, Albert, 439
von Steinwehr, Adolph, 58, 89,
  92, 111, 145, 158, 162, 166,
  185, 198, 205, 206, 210,
  211, 213, 214, 215, 216,
  217, 275, 276, 277, 279,
  439, 440

W

Wade, William, 437
Wadsworth, James, 167, 210,
  212, 213, 214, 216, 231, 233
Wainwright, Charles, 193, 194,
  195, 197, 215, 216, 231,
  233, 234, 235, 236, 237,
  243, 249, 250
Wainwright, William, 100
Walker, John, 14
Walker, Thomas, 399, 403,
  404
Walter, Charles, 101, 143, 144
Ward, William, 376, 391, 393,
  394, 399
Warner, Edward, 249
Watson, Malbone, 240, 242
Webb, Alexander, 189
Webb, T V, 272
Weir, Gulian, 240, 245
Weis, George, 110
Weisheimer, John, 287
Wessells, Henry, 319

Wheeler, John, 1, 10, 29, 37,
    51, 52, 61, 63, 70, 85, 101,
    103, 108, 115, 116, 117,
    119, 123, 126, 175, 177,
    220, 299, 318, 319, 320,
    323, 455
Wheeler, Theodosia, 34, 103
Wheeler, William, 1, 2, 4, 5, 6,
    7, 8, 9, 10, 11, 12, 13, 14,
    15, 16, 17, 18, 19, 21, 23,
    24, 26, 27, 28, 29, 30, 32,
    34, 35, 37, 44, 47, 49, 51,
    52, 55, 56, 59, 61, 62, 63,
    65, 66, 84, 99, 102, 104,
    107, 108, 110, 111, 114,
    116, 119, 121, 122, 123,
    126, 128, 130, 134, 135,
    137, 139, 140, 160, 169,
    171, 172, 176, 177, 179,
    180, 181, 182, 183, 192,
    194, 198, 199, 200, 201,
    206, 207, 208, 209, 219,
    221, 222, 227, 228, 232,
    235, 237, 244, 253, 254,
    255, 258, 259, 260, 262,
    266, 267, 269, 273, 274,
    276, 280, 281, 286, 287,
    288, 289, 290, 292, 294,
    299, 301, 303, 304, 306,
    308, 310, 311, 313, 318,
    320, 321, 323, 326, 329,
    331, 334, 335, 347, 350,
    351, 352, 353, 358, 360,
    365, 369, 370, 379, 384,
    388, 405, 429, 430, 431,
    437, 439, 440, 441, 443, 445
When, James, 14, 133, 176,
    286, 423
Whipple, William, 303, 420,
    422
Whitaker, A H, 247

White, John, 407, 423
Wickham, Lt., 286
Wiedrich, Michael, 82, 84, 98,
    147, 150, 153, 158, 192,
    193, 195, 212, 214, 216,
    232, 233, 234, 235, 238,
    243, 257, 273, 287, 288,
    298, 440
Wilber, Lt., 233, 234
Wilber, R H, 405
Wilbur, Capt., 405
Wilcox, Arthur, 412
Wilkeson, Bayard, 192, 193,
    215, 232
Wilkinson, Capt., 312, 410
Williams, Alpheus, 311, 332,
    337, 351, 353, 354, 366,
    368, 369, 371, 372, 373,
    374, 377, 378, 381, 382,
    383, 386, 387, 388, 389,
    391, 393, 394, 395, 398,
    399, 401, 402
Williams, Seth, 11, 12, 13, 14
Wilmot, Pvt., 135
Wilson, Capt., 406
Wilson, Cpl., 81
Winegar, Charles, 236, 243,
    350, 351, 352, 353, 354, 355
Winslow, George, 239, 240
Woeltge, Charles, 371
Wood, James, 439
Wood, Thomas, 271, 386, 440
Woodbury, John, 350, 351,
    353, 354, 355
Woodruff, George, 241, 244,
    247
Worthington, Lt., 410
Wright, W P, 247
Wyman. Lt., 39, 42, 44

Z

Zeigler, John, 76, 81
Zickerick, William, 266, 267, 269

www.ingramcontent.com/pod-product-compliance
Lightning Source LLC
Chambersburg PA
CBHW051334230426
43668CB00010B/1257